The Author

Louis A. Dow (Ph.D., Indiana University) is Professor of Economics at the University of Houston. He has previously taught at the University of Oklahoma and at North Carolina State University. Dr. Dow is a frequent contributor to professional journals.

Business Fluctuations

in a

Dynamic Economy

Louis A. Dow
University of Houston

Charles E. Merrill Publishing Company

Columbus, Ohio   *A Bell & Howell Company*

Library of Congress Catalog Card Number: 68-10432

Printed in the United States of America
1 2 3 4 5 6 7 8 9 10 11 12 13 14 15/76 75 74 73 72 71 70 69 68 67

**THIS BOOK IS FONDLY DEDICATED TO
CHRIS, SCOTT, AND SHANNON**

I would like to take this opportunity to acknowledge those who have helped me in writing this book. I am most grateful to Professor James M. Murphy of the University of Oklahoma for his help in writing Part 5. Many of the ideas embodied in these chapters are traceable directly to him. I would like to thank him also for the encouragement he gave me in writing the earlier chapters of the manuscript.

Special thanks are due also to my former colleague, Professor Jack W. Wilson of North Carolina State University, who read the entire manuscript and made numerous helpful suggestions.

My warmest thanks go to Rodney Cook, who typed the entire manuscript.

Further, I appreciate the aid and advice of those who read portions of the manuscript.

Although it goes without saying that the author alone is responsible for any errors, I am tempted not to let Professors Murphy and Wilson off the hook so easily. Still, any errors are mine, not theirs.

Preface

There is perhaps little need to justify this book. It deals with matters that are vital to the economic well-being of everyone in our society and, insofar as chaotic cyclical economic conditions in this country are transmitted abroad, it pertains also to the economic status of vast numbers of people in the world. The rate of economic growth is also of great concern, not only for the material gains that it yields, but also for the impact that it may have on our social, political, economic, and cultural values and institutions. Since so much is involved it behooves us to understand not only the sources and patterns of the business cycle *and* economic growth, but also the manner *in which they interact.* The chronic unemployment experienced in the United States from 1957 to about 1966, the persistent inflation during the same period, and some continued fears of economic stagnation are matters worthy of careful, intensive study.

This volume is designed to give a fairly rigorous introduction to the analysis of business cycles, economic growth, and the interaction of the two. In many respects it is more than a mere introduction, although it does not presume anything more than an advanced standing on the part of the student. The numerous references to the literature will serve as a guide to further, more detailed reseach and analysis.

The student interested in business cycle analysis will learn in Chapter 1 that the cycle is far from *passé.* And even if, for all practical purposes, we abolish it by means of economic policy, it is still potentially there, lurking behind every change in aggregate private demand. More than that! If we are able to control the cycle adequately, without interfering with economic growth, such an accomplishment will be due in very large part to our analysis of the cycle-growth process.

Another point may be in order. The book has been written on the sup-
position that the curricular dichotomy of "business cycle analysis" and
"intermediate macroeconomic theory" is misleading, if not entirely false.
Business cycle theory and macroeconomic analysis deal with the same
set of variables and problems. The only difference is one of approach.
The latter stresses the determinants of an *equilibrium* level of national
income and employment and the reestablishment of another equilibrium
level when the first one is disturbed. Business cycle analysis, on the
other hand, is more concerned with the continuing process of economic
disequilibrium, with the ebb and flow of aggregate economic activity;
it considers equilibrium as a rather unique conditon. As shown in Part
4, these two approaches complement each other in a particularly fruitful way. One of the main objectives of this book is to reveal this complementarity to the student and to show that equilibrium analysis serves as
an excellent point of departure for disequilibrium analysis.

Finally, institutional, analytical, and policy matters have been
blended wherever possible in an effort to make the discussion as prag-
matic as possible. As shown in Chapter 9 and the Chapters in Part 5,
especially Chapter 20, economic theory is useful and meaningful only
if it aids in problem-solving, and a great deal of modern macroeconomic
analysis performs quite well in this respect. The impact that J. M.
Keynes' *The General Theory of Employment, Interest, and Money*
(1936), not to mention considerable post-Keynesian analysis, has had on
economic policy and actual economic performance can hardly be minimized. But policy is decided upon and implemented in the real world,
and it is necessary for the student to realize that the theories are basically approximations that must be adapted to real situations. While this
interaction between fact and theory is emphasized throughout, it is
stressed particularly in Parts 4 and 5.

The organization of the book is basically an historical one, beginning
with the classical economists. Most of this school concluded that the
capitalist economy would experience smooth, uninterrupted economic
growth until the emergence of the stationary state. Thus they tended to
ignore cyclical disturbances and to concentrate on the full-employment
growth process. Although the classical view is not discussed in detail
until Chapter 15, it can be read following the brief review given in
Chapter 5 without any difficulty. This has the advantage of placing the
cycle theories reviewed in Part 2 into historical perspective. (At this
juncture, however, the section on the Pigou Effect should probably be
omitted.)

Some later pre-Kenesian economics developed theories of the business cycle (Part 2), but for the most part cycle theory remained outside the mainstream of economic thought. The interesting thing to note, however, is that, with some exceptions, these theorists either ignored the problem of growth or simply took for granted that growth would automatically take place over the long haul. Even more important is the fact that none of these theories adequately explained the Great Depression of the 1930's (Chapter 9) and accordingly could not explain how to move the economy from very low to high levels of employment and output.

At this point the Keynesian analysis entered the economic scene (Part 3). But please note that the Keynesian analysis was concerned neither with cyclical fluctuations *per se,* nor with the problem of economic growth. Rather, it was strictly a short-run, static equilibrium analysis. Be that as it may, the Keynesian analysis presented to economists an array of analytical tools and concepts that have been especially fruitful for further understanding of the growth-cycle process.

Consequently, macroeconomics in the post-Keynesian period has made use of these (and other) tools in forging new theories of the business cycle *and* economic growth (Part 4). More than that, it has stressed interaction of economic growth and cyclical disturbances, showing the feedback relationship between these two phenomena. Especially important here are the models developed by Harrod (Chapter 17), Domar (Chapter 17), Fellner (Chapter 16), and Duesenberry (Chapter 17), although the early works of Schumpeter (Chapter 7) should certainly not be overlooked. In all respects, these new theories emphasize the interactive relationships of the cycle and growth. Also in recent years there has been some revival of interest in the possibility of economic stagnation; the stagnation theory is reviewed in Chapter 18.

Thus the history of thought in economics progressed from a disregard of the cycle and a tremendous stress upon growth (the classicists) through a period of disregard of growth and an emphasis upon cyclical disturbances (business cycle theorists) into the Keynesian period of static, short-run equilibrium analysis which tended to minimize both growth and the cycle. In recent years, however, attention has been focused upon both the cycle and economic growth, with neither being emphasized to the neglect of the other.

This development of thought in macroeconomics terminates with Part 5, in which the problems of economic policy are considered. A word of advice to the student! Once you discover that there are no fast and concerete answers to policy questions, do not be disturbed. Consider the tremendous accomplishments in this area during the past three decades, and remember that economic analysis is in a constant state of flux that has led to equally significant accomplishments during the past few years. Questions unanswered today will be answered soon.

Louis A. Dow
Houston, Texas

Contents

part 1

Economic Growth and the Ebb and Flow
of Business Activity

1

Growth and Instability: Changing Economic Patterns

The economic history of the United States has been characterized by two striking facts, both of which provide the major theme of this book. First of all, there has been the tremendous economic growth and expansion of the American economy with total output rising from less than $10 billion in the late 1870's to over $675 billion at the present.[1] At the same time per capita income has risen from about $171 in the early 1870's to about $2,400 today. Surely the economic system has been dynamic and viable, reaping greater and greater material benefits for more and more people.

But the process of economic growth has not been smooth and uninterrupted. To the contrary! There have been numerous (and often severe) ups and downs, booms and busts, accompanying the growth trend. This pattern of irregular growth is clearly observable in Figure 1–1, which

---

[1]The figures cited for total and per capita income are in current dollars, that is, they are unadjusted for changes in the price level. The significance of adjustment of data for price-level changes is discussed in the next chapter.

Ratio Scale
1958 = 100

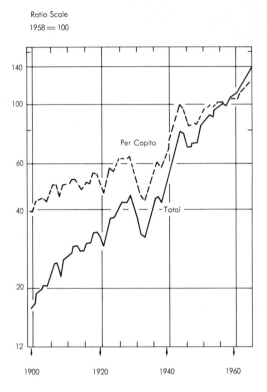

Source: Board of Governors of the Federal Reserve System, *Historical Chart Book, 1966*, p. 68.

FIGURE 1–1

Changes in Total and Per Capita Gross National Product,
United States, 1898-1965, 1958 = 100

traces out the behavior of the total output of the economy over a long time period.[2]

In short, the so-called business cycle has been associated with the growth of the economy, and these cyclical disturbances have often created significant hardships for many people both in periods of depression and periods of inflation. But, of course, the scene shifts drastically and sometimes quickly between depression and inflation. During the

---

[2]These data are given in constant 1958 prices, that is, they have been adjusted for price-level changes so that output for every year is stated in terms of 1958 purchasing power. The recent behavior of GNP is given in the next chapter.

post-World War II period, for example, many people have been concerned with the loss of purchasing power of their incomes because of inflationary rises in the price level. However, during the 1930's the major concern was over unemployment—that is, widespread, involuntary unemployment.[3] As the then Secretary of Agriculture, Henry Wallace, put it, the United States had the ". . . largest wheat surplus and the longest breadlines in its history."[4] There existed at that time the paradox of "poverty midst plenty."

1. The Changing Economic Scene

What gave rise to the economic situation of the 1930's? Why was there so much involuntary unemployment, and why could not the unemployed find jobs? What could be done to cure, or at least to alleviate, the problem? These were some of the crucial questions of that decade, although similar questions had been posed earlier, and they have been raised since. They relate, of course, to those recurring fluctuations in the levels of income, employment, and prices that are called business cycles. These fluctuations are by no means a recent development in the United States (or Western Europe), for, as already implied, the history of the business cycle in this country is quite long and varied. In fact, the economy has experienced these recurring fluctuations ever since it became industrialized.[5]

Although the methods of posing and discussing the problems associated with the cycle have varied considerably from period to period, the essential issues remain the same—involuntary unemploy-

---

[3]The term "involuntary unemployment" is difficult to define precisely, as is the associated term "full employment." For present purposes involuntary unemployment is defined as the unemployment of those persons in the labor force who are ready, able, and willing to work, but are unable to acquire jobs. This does not mean that full employment prevails only when 100 per cent of the labor force is employed, for there are always some workers who are "frictionally" unemployed. These are persons who have voluntarily quit their jobs, or have been discharged, but are actively seeking other employment. Estimates indicate that about 3 to 4 per cent of the labor force is always frictionally unemployed. For a fuller discussion of the concepts of employment and unemployment, see Chapter 20; see also Chapter 13.

[4]A. M. Schlesinger, Jr., *The Coming of the New Deal* (Boston: Houghton Mifflin Company, 1959), pp. 61-62.

[5]For all practical purposes, the origin of the business cycle in the United States may be dated at around the close of the Civil War, although there had been random crises and disturbances before then.

ment and inflation.[6] During the 1930's the major question, as noted above, related to involuntary unemployment. In recent years, however, "creeping" inflation seems to have held the center of attention. Persistent rises in the general price level have eroded the purchasing power of those whose money incomes are fixed or rise less than proportionately to the increases in the level of prices. The average citizen, moreover, has become quite "inflation-conscious" in the post-World War II period, not only because of the continuing rise in the price level that forces him to dip deeper into his pocket just to meet the ordinary expenses of living, but also because of the impact that inflation has on him as a tax payer. As the costs of state and local expenditures rise because of inflationary increases in the prices of the goods and services they must acquire, taxes are raised, and the consumer finds himself more and more hard-pressed to make ends meet. And the pressure is intensified as governments must provide more of their services to an expanding, urbanized population. Under these circumstances, there is little doubt that inflation is one of the major issues of today.[7]

The general attitude towards inflation, however, has changed considerably over time. During the 1930's both the Roosevelt administration and the business community were thoroughly convinced that a rising price level was instrumental in restoring the economy to a position of full employment and growth. As a result, policies such as those in the National Industrial Recovery Act were put into effect to stimulate price increases.[8] Although this act was later declared unconstitutional, it represented fairly well both governmental and business attitudes towards inflation at that time.

During the World War II period, on the other hand, the rising price level interfered substantially with the government's mobilization and military program, and accordingly price controls were put into effect. These served rather well in holding down further price-level increases until 1946, when Congress repealed the legislation.[9] Since then the price level has continued to rise.

---

[6]Like employment and unemployment, "inflation" is also difficult to define precisely. The generally accepted definition of inflation is that it is a rise, no matter how small, in the general price level. This is quite unsatisfactory but will suffice for present purposes. See Chapter 20 for a fuller discussion.

[7]These points, plus several others, are discussed more fully in A. H. Hansen, *Economic Issues of the 1960's* (New York: McGraw-Hill Book Company, 1960), Chapters 1-4. See also G. Haberler, *Inflation: Its Causes and Cures* (Washington, D. C.: American Enterprise Association, 1960).

[8]See any adequate American economic history textbook for a discussion of this and related measures that were taken during the 1930's.

[9]An excellent review of this period is given in L. V. Chandler, *Inflation in the United States, 1940-1948* (New York: Harper & Row, Publishers, 1951), especially Chapter XI.

In recent years, however, the problem of inflation seems to have taken on a new dimension. Prior to the economic setback of 1957-1958, the general pattern had been that a decline in the levels of output and employment was accompanied by a decline in the price level. However, during the recession of 1957-1958 the index of consumer prices rose by 2.7 per cent, paused momentarily in 1958, and has continued to rise since, although at a declining rate. The same phenomenon occurred during the 1960-1961 setback. Because of this coexistence of inflation and unemployment, the period since 1957 has been characterized by some as "inflated recession."[10] As one economist has put it:

> The worry is not so much about the relatively moderate price increases. The worry relates rather to what appears to be a brand-new fact in our economic life; namely, that while prices rise as formerly under the pressure of investment booms, they fail to come down in the recession period and indeed even keep rising, though at a declining rate.[11]

If this "brand-new fact" actually exists, then the outlook for the future is probably one of continued inflation, at least in the absence of any severe and prolonged depression. There has, in fact, been much recent discussion about the possibility and consequences of "creeping" or "secular" inflation.

Obviously, then, the post-World War II period has been characterized by an attitude of fears and doubts towards inflation. This is indeed quite a contrast with the prevailing opinion about inflation during the Great Depression. But the important point to be made here is this— not only is the economy itself quite unstable, but also attitudes are perhaps even more so, and this volatility of views tends to complicate discussion and evaluation of both theory and policy.

There are still other complicating factors to be considered. In recent years, again especially since World War II, another problem has emerged upon the scene—namely, the achievement and maintenance of a "satisfactory" rate of economic growth.[12] This issue has received a considerable amount of attention from economists, politicians, and laymen alike, both here and abroad. In fact, one of the currently popular guessing games is when, if ever, the Soviet economy, with its present high growth rates, will overtake and surpass the economic performance

---

[10]See, for instance, Hans Apel, *"Inflated Recession": A New Economic Paradox* (Westport, Connecticut: Calvin K. Kazanjian Economics Foundation, Inc., 1958). See also Hansen, *Economic Issues of the 1960's,* Chapter 4.

[11]Hansen, *Economic Issues of the 1960's,* p. 22. The problem of inflation is discussed more thoroughly in Part 5.

[12]This term is even more difficult to define than unemployment and inflation. See section 3 for a discussion of some of the problems involved.

of the United States. One eminent student of economic growth and the business cycle, Alvin H. Hansen, has stated that by 1980 the Soviet Union, if it maintains an annual growth rate of around 7 per cent, will catch up with the United States, *provided that the annual growth rate of the United States remains at its historical 3 to 4 per cent per year.* Hansen's estimate for 1980 is a gross national product of approximately $900 billion for each country (in terms of 1960 prices).[13] Whether this is correct remains to be seen, although there is good evidence that in recent years the annual rate of growth of the Soviet economy has declined significantly, so much so in fact that the U. S. S. R. has slipped from second to fifth place among the industrialized nations. The most recent estimates put the growth rate of the total Soviet output at 2.6 per cent in 1963, as compared to 8.5 per cent in 1958.[14]

Be that as it may, it still remains true that there has been much discussion and attention devoted to the problems and potentials of economic growth for the United States, as well as for other countries.[15] However, there may be some danger in this. If too much stress is persistently placed on economic growth, the problem of the business cycle may be pushed to one side. This sort of lopsided emphasis, unfortunately, would result in a deficiency of both analysis and policy, *for it ignores the basic fact that growth and the cycle interact with one another.* Sometimes they interact in opposite directions, while at other

---

[13]Hansen, *Economic Issues of the 1960's*, p. 43. For a good review of some of the studies on the Soviet growth rate, see R. W. Campbell, *Soviet Economic Power: Its Organization, Growth, and Challenge* (Boston: Houghton Mifflin Company, 1959.) See also W. J. Fellner, *Trends and Cycles in Economic Activity* (New York: Holt, Rinehart & Winston, Inc., 1956) pp. 69-74. There is, of course, some dispute over what the Russian growth rate actually is, but most of the studies conclude that it was somewhere around 7 to 8 per cent until 1959.

[14]See Joint Economic Committee, *Current Economic Indicators for the U. S. S. R.*, 89th Cong., 1st sess. (Washington, D. C.: Government Printing Office, 1965).

[15]There are, of course, substantial differences in approach to the problems of economic growth for the so-called underdeveloped countries as compared to the "already advanced" economies. This book is concerned solely with the advanced economy. The underdeveloped countries figure in only indirectly as they have any influence on the growth-cycle pattern and economic policies of the advanced systems. Several good texts have been published in recent years dealing with the social, economic, and political problems associated with the development of the "backward" economies. See, for example, H. Leibenstein, *Economic Backwardness and Economic Growth* (New York: John Wiley & Sons, Inc., 1957); B. Higgins, *Economic Development* (New York: W. W. Norton & Company, Inc., 1959); and W. A. Lewis, *The Theory of Economic Growth* (Homewood, Ill.: Richard D. Irwin, Inc., 1955). See also the interesting studies by P. Baran, *The Political Economy of Growth* (New York: The Monthly Review Press, 1957) and W. W. Rostow, *The Stages of Economic Growth* (New York: Oxford University Press, 1958).

times they reinforce each other. For example, a rapid rate of growth in a short period will often be attended by severe inflationary pressures and indeed may lead to a subsequent decline in the levels of employment and output. On the other hand, a short-period prosperity does much to increase the capital stock of the country and perhaps to stimulate technological advancements, both of which add to the long-run growth potential of the economy. In any event, this feedback nature of economic growth and the business cycle must not be ignored; indeed it is important that it be recognized for both analytical and policy purposes. The danger of concentrating too heavily on growth, or, for that matter, on the cycle, is that sight is lost of their interactive relationships.[16]

2. Some Difficult Policy Issues

One final complicating issue should be discussed here, even though briefly. The interaction of the business cycle and economic growth raises difficult problems of control by economic policy. The reason for this is that usually economic growth is accompanied by important institutional changes. Thus policy matters often range far beyond the traditional scope assigned to monetary and fiscal policy to include evaluation of institutional and structural changes that may, in turn, have significant social and political impacts. For example, much of the recent literature dealing with inflation has been concerned with the role played by labor unions and enterprise monopolies as forces that influence both the level of economic activity and the growth rate.[17]

---

[16]Until recent years, this has been the general tendency among economists (with some few notable exceptions). For instance, the classical economists concentrated almost exclusively on the process of growth in a capitalist economy and thus neglected business cycle theory. The neoclassical economists, on the other hand, concentrated primarily on the analysis of the allocation of relatively scarce resources between alternative, competing ends. They tended to ignore both the cycle and economic growth. However, those economists who developed cycle theories from around the 1870's up to around the 1930's (and this includes J. M. Keynes) were primarily concerned with short-run cyclical disturbances and thus tended to neglect long-term growth. In recent years, finally, the emphasis has been upon the interaction of growth and cycles, so that neither is neglected. A number of these various theories is reviewed in Parts 2, 3, and 4.

[17]See, for example, Haberler, *Inflation: Its Causes and Cures*, and J. M. Clark, *The Wage-Price Problem* (New York: The American Bankers' Association, 1960). See also R. Perlman, ed., *Inflation: Demand-Pull or Cost-Push?* (Boston: D. C. Heath & Company, 1965). The so-called wage-price spiral is discussed at length in Chapter 23.

Now *if* it is concluded that the behavior of these institutions has aggravated economic instability and/or impeded economic growth, does this mean that they should be broken up? If the answer is yes (and several observers have provided this answer), then the further question arises —what will be the social and political repercussions of such a policy?

Consider another example. As subsequent analysis will reveal, a basic requirement for smooth, uninterrupted economic growth is a sufficient degree of resource mobility. Yet many empirical studies indicate that resources may not in fact possess the required degree of mobility. If this is the case, then should policies be devised that would facilitate resource mobility by, say, subsidizing labor and capital in order to stimulate and facilitate their movements between alternative employments?

Consider a further example. As will be seen in Chapters 2-4, investment by private businessmen in plant and equipment turns out to be a dynamic variable in the behavior of the overall economy. Increased investment activity is accompanied (usually) by rising levels of income, output, and employment, while declines in investment activity are associated with economic slumps. Now if private investment activity is so important in the performance of the economy, considerable attention must be devoted to the major determinants of investment. But the point for the present is this—there is a growing body of evidence that indicates that the major determinants of investment have been changing as a result of the process of economic growth. And certainly the determinants of investment behavior are strongly influenced by cyclical disturbances, each of which is different from the others.[18] This means that the behavior of a crucial determinant of cyclical and growth behavior is itself a function (at least in large part) of the cyclical-growth process.

Even at this early stage, therefore, it seems safe to say that the problems of growth, fluctuations, institutional and structural changes are all closely related—so much so, in fact, that they present a many-faceted situation that defies simple solutions and simple remedies. When an adjustment is made in one area, repercussions are felt in others, and these in turn react upon the original data. This is not to

---

[18]R. A. Gordon, "Investment Opportunities in the United States before and after World War II," in *The Business Cycle in the Post-War World*, ed. E. Lundberg (London: The Macmillian Company, 1955), especially p. 310. For further discussion, see E. M. Hoover, "Some Institutional Factors in Business Investment Decisions," *American Economic Review*, May 1954, and H. R. Bowen and G. M. Meier, "Institutional Aspects of Economic Fluctuations," in *Post-Keynesian Economics*, ed. K. K. Kurihara (New Brunswick: Rutgers University Press, 1954).

deny that there is a "remedy" for the business cycle and a program to stimulate full-employment economic growth, but the discussion thus far does clearly illustrate that before the "remedy" and program are to be found a great deal of intellectual spadework is essential. Adequate theories of the growth-cycle process must be developed before policy issues can be discussed in a meaningful way.

But even then the difficulties are not over. The question—and it is a hard one—arises: What does any "remedy" hold in store for us as far as the other dimensions of life are concerned? That is to say, certain ethical and normative problems arise that economic analysis cannot possibly answer or even pretend to answer. For instance, analysis may point out that one way of achieving continued economic stability and full-employment growth is for there to be constant governmental intervention in the areas of spending, and perhaps wage and price controls. But many persons will retaliate by saying, "Economic stability and further growth just aren't worth having if we must bear any more encroachment of government on our private affairs." Others, to the contrary, may argue that given the current international military and ideological tensions, there is need for continued growth at virtually any cost. And still others will argue that if the free enterprise system is left unfettered, it will enter into a period of economic stagnation and so much secular unemployment that direct governmental intervention is essential to preserve even a semblence of free enterprise.

As a final example, consider the observations made by Professor Eduard Heimann, who argues that there is need for continued economic growth in order to provide for continuing full employment, but that the expanding outflow of goods poses the ". . . problem of how to survive sanely and morally in the midst of the orgy of goods."[19] Heimann continues: "The irony . . . of the situation is precisely the turning of the achievement [of past economic growth] itself into a fetter; the miraculously productive technical structure turns into a tyrannical force; the enthusiasm for more goods turns into a moral danger."[20]

These are hard problems that are far beyond the scope of this book, but they are mentioned here to show that once a reasonably satisfactory analysis of the growth-cycle process has been developed, merely the first step has been taken. But it is an essential step, for the ethical questions mentioned in the last two paragraphs can be better dealt

---

[19]E. Heimann, *The Economy of Abundance: An Ethical Problem* (Westport, Conn.: Calvin K. Kazanjian Economics Foundation, Inc., 1957), p. 5. See also the comments by Reinhold Niebuhr, Chester I. Barnard, J. M. Clark, and Noel Sargent in the same publication.

[20]*Ibid.*, pp. 7-8.

with if there is some sound economic analysis to aid us. Thus the first task is to develop some analysis to explain, as best it can, the growth-cycle interaction. As will be seen in Parts 2, 3, and 4, a number of theories have been presented by economists to fulfill this objective. Several of these will be reviewed critically, after which the discussion will turn to evaluation of economic policy as a means of achieving continued economic growth with a minimum of cyclical disturbances.

3. Conceptual Problems in Measuring Economic Growth and the Business Cycle

Any sound discussion of the growth-cycle interaction, of course, should be based on fairly reasonable definitions of the phenomena in question. Yet one problem that plagues the economic theorist—and the problem runs throughout this book—is that many of the relevant magnitudes are quite difficult to measure.[21] This is true of gross national product, capital stock, price and wage levels, capital-output ratio, unemployment, and so on. In fact, it is even true of such general terms as "economic growth" and "business cycle." Yet, interestingly enough, some consensus is usually reached on workable definitions of these variables and terms, at least enough to permit communication and further development of theory and policy. And the efforts to refine the definitions and measurements continue.

This section is concerned with the concepts of growth and cycle, and, as will be seen, the problems of definition are difficult indeed.

A. What is Economic Growth?

Economic growth may be defined in a number of ways, but in each case some criterion is essential. Moreover, the criterion must be susceptible of measurement in some quantifiably acceptable manner. Although several approaches have been devised, only three of the most commonly used are considered here.

First, there is the approach that measures economic growth in terms of the behavior of the total output (gross national product) of the economy over time. As shown in the next chapter, this magnitude can be quantified accurately enough so that meaningful comparisons can

---

[21]See O. Morgenstern, *On the Accuracy of Economic Observations* (Princeton: Princeton University Press, 1963), for an excellent discussion of the problems of definition, data collection, and sources of errors in the use of economic data.

be made from year to year. However, comparisons over long time periods are somewhat tricky, if for no other reason than because of changing types, quantities, and qualities of goods and services produced. The data of total output can then be translated into rates of growth which indicate what would happen to total output over the long run if no disturbing factors were present. Thus in the United States total output has grown at an average rate of 3 to 4 per cent per year.[22] In some years, of course, the growth rate of *actual* output has been above, in other years below, this figure; but the long-run trend appears to be 3 to 4 per cent per year. This is shown in Figure 1–2.

A problem, however, arises. There is a danger that the figure of 3 to 4 per cent may be taken as a normative standard to which the economy must, for some reason, adhere over time, come what may. This is, of course, too much significance to attach to a figure obtained by statistical manipulations.[23] Moreover, the 3 to 4 per cent figure is a matter of historical record, and while history may help to forecast the future, the future may well hold a great number of changes for total production.

Another problem associated with measuring growth by the behavior of total output is that it ignores population. Assume, for example, that total output grows at a rate of 10 per cent from one decade to the next, but that during the same period total population rises by 20 per cent. *Ceteris paribus,* per capita income has been reduced. Thus, this method of measurement overlooks completely the changes in per capita income.

As a result, economic growth is often measured in terms of per capita real income (that is, income per person and adjusted for price-level changes). While this is more revealing than measuring simply the rate of growth of total output, this method tends to overlook the distributional dimensions of economic growth. For example, a rise in per capita income from $1,000 in one decade to $2,000 in the next does not reveal anything about the distribution of total income among the members of the society. Per capita income is obtained simply by dividing total income (output) by the total population; that is, it gives the income figure that would prevail if the total output were equally distributed among all people. Obviously, however, income inequality prevails in the United States, and just as obviously the per capita income figure glosses over and hides the existing inequalities. In fact, the rise in per capita income from $1,000 to $2,000 in the example above may reflect either increasing inequality or more equality in the distribution of total output. If one person alone received an additional $50,000,000 in in-

---

[22]Corrected for price-level changes. See Chapter 2.

[23]See the discussion in sections 5-A and 5-B of this chapter.

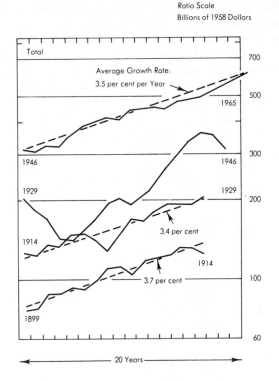

Ratio Scale
Billions of 1958 Dollars

Source: Board of Governors of the Federal Reserve System, *Historical Chart Book*, 1966, p. 68.

FIGURE 1–2

Rates of Growth of Gross National Product,
United States, Selected Time Periods

come, while everyone else received no more than before, the per capita income for the country would rise. But this does not say very much as regards economic growth of the society at large. Indeed, if one or a few persons receive substantial income increases, while the rest experience slight declines, the per capita figure may still rise, but again this does not imply much about economic growth.

The major difficulty in using the per capita figure, in other words, is that it ignores completely the relationship between growth and income distribution. However, since the per capita income figure is relatively easily obtained, there is a tendency on the part of many economists to measure economic growth in terms of this criterion.

Another measure of economic growth is output per man-hour, although over long time periods this is not a very satisfactory measurement. The main reason for this is that there has occurred a significant change in the composition of output. For example, can there be a meaningful comparison between the output of buggies per man-hour and the output of automobiles per man-hour? In short, the number and quality of goods per man-hour in 1967 are so different from the number and quality of goods per man-hour in the "gay 'nineties," and even the "roaring 'twenties," that comparisons of growth begin to lose their significance. However, according to some observers, it is still possible to define progress and growth by this measure in some qualitative sense. As Boulding has put it:

> Whenever one method of doing something displaces another, in the free operation of human choice, we may say after an interval of time long enough that the new method has had a proper trial, that economic growth has taken place.[24]

The behavior of output per man-hour in the United States is shown in Figure 1–3.

About all that can be said is that economic growth is indeed difficult to define in any meaningful quantitative sense. Problems of income distribution, utility weights assigned to different goods and services over long periods of time when the composition of total output changes, and even what constitutes the "good life"[25] complicate the issue considerably. Nevertheless there is some such thing as economic growth, despite the problem of measurement and in this sense the following quotation is quite relevant:

> . . . most of us, in spite of the terrors of modern warfare, would not readily change places with the past; we look from our day of electric light and automobiles to the days even a century ago of candles and coaches with a sense of great technical superiority, touched only with a twinge of sentimental regret. . . . In spite of an uneasy feeling that spiritually and intellectually we may not cut a remarkably good figure

---

[24]Kenneth E. Boulding, *Principles of Economic Policy*, © 1958. Reprinted by permission of Prentice-Hall, Inc., Englewood Cliffs, New Jersey. See also J. W. Kendrick, *Productivity Trends in the United States* (Princeton: Princeton University Press, 1961), and E. F. Denison, *Economic Growth in the United States and the Alternatives before Us* (New York: Committee for Economic Development, 1962), Supplementary Paper No. 13, for evidence of rises in output per man-hour.

[25]Boulding, *Principles of Economic Policy*, Chapter 2.

beside our ancestors, we have a certain confidence that we excel them in economic matters; that economic progress is not a vague and unreal thing, but a real experience of humankind which can be experienced even within the lifetime of a single individual.[26]

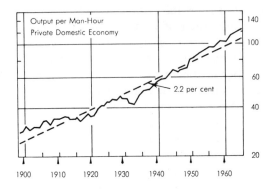

Source: Board of Governors of the Federal Reserve System, *Historical Chart Book, 1966,* p. 69.

FIGURE 1–3

Output Per Man-Hour, Private Domestic Economy
1957-59 = 100

For purposes of most of the theoretical discussion given in the subsequent chapters, nearly any of these measurements of economic growth will suffice. When any specific measure is better than another, it will be used.

B.   The Business Cycle

The discussion in sections 1 and 2 so far has emphasized that there is an interaction between economic growth and the business cycle. Accordingly, some definition of the cycle must be given.[27] For present purposes, the cycle is defined as follows—*the business cycle is the recurring, but not periodic, fluctuations in the levels of income, output, employment, and prices, the aggregates mentioned moving at about*

---

[26]*Ibid.,* p. 22.

[27]This definition is quite preliminary. See Chapter 4, section 3, for more detailed and complete discussion.

the same time and in the same direction and resulting in consequences that pervade the rest of the economy.[28]

There are several things to note about this definition. In the first place, there are many more variables than the aggregates mentioned (output, employment, etc.), and while these all tend to move in the same direction over the course of the cycle, they do not do so at precisely the same time. There are some variables that lead changes in general economic activity, especially at the turning points from expansion to contraction and from contraction to expansion. For example, employment is a lagger, tending to move in the same direction as national income, but only after the latter has begun its expansion or contraction. A safer way of stating this point is as follows: during the expansion the majority of variables rise, although some may actually be declining; on the other hand, during the contraction the majority of variables decline, although some may actually be rising. In the cases of both expansion and contraction, the variables tend to move with a lead-lag relationship. However, the important variables given in the definition—that is, income, employment, prices, and output—tend to move together.

Another point is that the movements in all of the variables tend to become cumulative and self-reinforcing. For instance, when employment begins to decline, generally personal income and consumption also decline, and this in turn leads to a further decline in output. This self-reinforcing aspect of cyclical fluctuations is all-important and will demand a considerable amount of attention in later chapters. About all that can be done here is to point out that during a contraction these variables reinforce each other in a downward direction and that during an expansion they reinforce each other in an upward direction.

However, this cumulative reinforcement does not go on forever. Obviously some end, or turning point, must occur. And indeed this is the case. Once a contraction is underway it will continue until a sufficient number of expansionary forces accumulate and reverse it. Similarly, during the expansionary phase, the variables feed on one another until finally enough contractional forces build up and reverse the expansion. In short, each expansion and contraction contains the seeds of its own destruction, or turning point, and a reversal occurs.

---

[28]Perhaps a word of apology is in order since there is some redundancy in the definition. If we designate money income as Y, real output of goods and services as O, and the general price level as P, then $Y = PO$. This means that prices are mentioned twice in the definition—once explicitly and once implicitly (in "income")—and output is also mentioned twice—once explicitly and once implicitly (in "income").

For this reason most business cycle theorists have attempted to develop theories that would explain how, during a contraction, the very
forces generated during the contractionary stage itself give rise to a
sufficient number of expansionary forces to reverse the economy into
a boom, and how, during the boom, enough contractionary forces
emerge to bring on a turning point and the subsequent contraction.[29]

Finally, as already noted, only a few of the relevant economic variables are included in the definition. Discussion in the next three chapters will reveal that a very large number of variables are at play in an
economy as dynamic and complex as ours. In fact the National Bureau
of Economic Research, which has done so much to enrich our knowledge of the business cycle, collects data for at least 800 time series in
order to measure the business cycle. Not all of these are equally important in cyclical fluctuations, but they are all related to each other in
some manner or other. Thus when a cyclical disturbance gets underway
there is a decided tendency for it to become dispersed and diffused
throughout the rest of the economy. While not all variables will be
moving in the same direction during an expansion or contraction, the
great majority of them will; and once the movement gets underway,
it tends to spread.[30] A decline in the output of the automobile industry, for example, will have adverse repercussions on the steel industry,
the rubber industry, and so on.[31] More than that! Not only does an expansion or contraction spread from industry to industry within an

---

[29]Consider the statement by W. C. Mitchell, *Business Cycles and Their Causes*
(Berkeley and Los Angeles: University of California Press, 1960), p. ix:

> Now the recurrent phases presented by economic activity, wherever it is
> dominated by the quest for profits, grow out of and grow into each other. An
> incipient revival of activity, for example, develops into full prosperity, pros-
> perity gradually breeds a crisis, the crisis merges into depression, depression
> becomes deeper for a while, but ultimately engenders a fresh revival of activ-
> ity, which is the beginning of another cycle. A theory of business cycles must
> therefore be a descriptive analysis of the cumulative changes by which one set
> of business conditions transforms itself into another set.

Mitchell's theory is reviewed in some detail in Chapter 8.

[30]Once started, a revival of activity rapidly spreads over a large part, if not
all, of the field of business. . . . In part this diffusion of activity proceeds along
the lines of interconnection among business enterprises. . . . One line leads
back from the industries first stimulated to industries that provide raw materials
and supplementary supplies. Another line leads forward to the chain of enterprises that handle the increased output of commodities. Still other lines, of
less importance for the transmission of the stimulus, radiate to the industries
that deal in complementary goods or substitutes (*Ibid.*, p. 3).

[31]See the interesting analysis by C. Yan and E. Ames, "Economic Interrelated-
ness," *Review of Economic Studies*, October 1965.

economy, it also tends to spread internationally. Thus the definition given above emphasizes only those variables that tend to be very important in most cycles. However, the number of relevant variables will change from one business cycle to another, and thus each cycle is rather unique unto itself.

4. The Stages of the Cycle

The definition of the business cycle given in the preceding section, while sufficient for present purposes, needs one final bit of elaboration, for all cycle theorists divide cyclical fluctuations into "stages." Inasmuch as there is little agreement on the use of terms here, a brief review of the terminology may be in order.

The National Bureau argues that there are four stages to the cycle.[32] Under this classification the stages are "expansion," "recession," "contraction," and "revival." Now most students of the cycle agree that there are four stages that require analysis, but many of them reject the use of such terms as "recession" and "revival". One reason is that in much of the literature the term "recession" may be used by some to designate either a major important contraction or a mild setback. There is, in other words, no uniformity in the use of this particular term. Another reason is that these terms are rather loaded with political values. A contraction, no matter how severe, nearly always tends to be called a "recession" by the political party in office, and a "depression" by the party that has failed at the polls. If for no other reason, this terminology should be rejected.

G. Haberler, on the other hand, has made use of the following terminology—"expansion," "upper-turning point," "contraction," and "lower-turning point."[33] These terms are preferable to the National Bureau's because they are clearer and more concrete. Still, it should be recognized that there is in actuality no sharp transition from expansion to contraction, as implied by the term "upper-turning point"; nor is there a sharp movement from contraction to expansion as the term "lower-turning point" implies. For this reason, R. A. Gordon has substituted the phrases "upper-turning zone" and "lower-turning zone" to describe

---

[32]A. F. Burns and W. C. Mitchell, *Measuring Business Cycles* (New York: National Bureau of Economic Research, 1946).

[33]G. Haberler, *Prosperity and Depression* 3rd ed. (Cambridge: Harvard University Press, 1958), Chapter 1.

the reversals in economic activity.[34] He argues that instead of a sharp, abrupt change from expansion to contraction and from contraction to expansion, there is a critical zone in which the reversing forces build up enough strength to change the general economic picture.

Haberler's terminology will be adhered to throughout this volume, although Gordon's is also relevant. That is, the four stages of the business cycle are classified as expansion, upper-turning point, contraction, and lower-turning point. To be sure, while the reversals from expansion to contraction and from contraction to expansion are not perhaps as sharp as the term "point" implies, they are still fairly abrupt. At any rate, the terms possess less ambiguity than the others discussed in this section.

5.   Alternative Methods of Measuring the Cycle

As already noted, the dissimilarities between and complexities inherent in business cycles create problems of measurement. But at the same time, measurement is obviously necessary for both analytical and policy purposes. Three alternative methods of measurement are considered in this section.

A.   Deviations Around a Norm: The Residual Method

The most commonly used method of measurement is to eliminate, by statistical methods, as many of the noncyclical movements as possible from the variable being measured, say, gross national product (GNP), employment, or industrial production. This is the so-called "residual" approach.

When the raw data for the time series are collected they include the influences of these noncyclical movements, and once they are removed the residual data illustrate cyclical movement in the time series.[35] The usual procedure is to divide the raw data by the seasonal data, thus eliminating seasonal fluctuations, and then to divide the seasonally adjusted data by the trend value, thereby eliminating the trend influence. The adjusted data, therefore, reveal only the cyclical and irregular movements in the data.

---

[34]R. A. Gordon, *Business Fluctuations* 2nd ed. (New York: Harper & Row, Publishers, 1961), pp. 258-59.

[35]Note, however, that there is no acceptable statistical means of eliminating the irregular influences.

This procedure can be stated as follows:

$$\text{Raw Series} = T \cdot S \cdot C \cdot I,$$

where T stands for the trend, S for seasonal variation, C for the cyclical fluctuations, and I for irregular influences. The residual method then expresses the trend and seasonal as a percentage value and eliminates them by division. Thus,

$$\frac{T \cdot S \cdot C \cdot I}{T \cdot S} = C \cdot I.$$

The resulting data therefore reveal the cyclical influences and, since there is no formal means of eliminating them, the irregular influences.

A hypothetical example will prove useful. In Figure 1–4A GNP is plotted on the vertical axis and time is plotted on the horizontal axis.[36] Please note that the curve in Figure 1–4A is a time series of the raw data, that is, it includes seasonal, trend, cyclical, and irregular influences. In this case, then, total output fluctuates quite frequently around the trend line TT′.

The first step is to eliminate the seasonal element, and this is done by dividing the time series itself by the seasonal values. The result is still a series that fluctuates around TT′, but now the fluctuations appear much smoother since the seasonal disturbances have been divided out. This is shown in Figure 1–4B.

The next step then is to eliminate the influence of the trend by dividing the seasonally adjusted data by the separately calculated trend value. The result of this procedure is that the fluctuations in GNP are shown as *percentage deviations of the seasonally adjusted data around the trend line,* represented by the index line of 100 in Figure 1–4C. The major advantage usually given in favor of this approach is that it strips bare (except for the irregular fluctuations) the cyclical movements in the time series, thus providing a rather clear picture of the business cycle.

There are, however, certain dangers in the residual method of measurement. For one thing, and this is important, it implies the presence of a "norm" from which deviations take place. In other words, the trend value assumes a normative significance that extends far beyond its statistical significance.

The trend is usually measured by fitting a line (linear or curvi-

---

[36]Gross national product is discussed in detail in the next two chapters. For the present it may be defined as the market value of all the final goods and services produced in the economy during a given time period. Thus, it serves as the most comprehensive measurement of aggregate economic activity available.

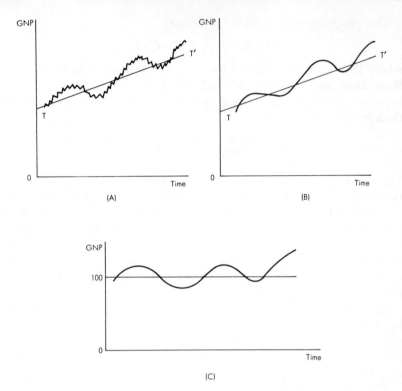

FIGURE 1–4

linear) to the raw data in the time series by some statistically acceptable method, usually by the least-squares method. This provides a
formula from which, in turn, a value for the pure trend can be obtained. The trend value shows what the series would be from period
to period if all other influences were absent. However, since the other
elements are present, the actual observed values will lie at times above
the trend value and at times below it. Generally the observed values
lie above the trend value about as much as they lie below it.

However, interpretation of these deviations from the trend value
must be carried out very judiciously. For instance, do the values above
the trend imply "too much" and do the values lying below it imply
"too little" GNP? In short, there is the danger of the trend value being
accepted as a "normative" value, when in reality it is merely a statistical construction.

This danger points to another problem in this method of measuring
the business cycle. Consider Figure 1–5, where another hypothetical

come distribution. However, since the per capita income figure is relatively easily obtained, there is a tendency on the part of many economists to measure economic growth in terms of this criterion.

Another measure of economic growth is output per man-hour, although over long time periods this is not a very satisfactory measurement. The main reason for this is that there has occurred a significant change in the composition of output. For example, can there be a meaningful comparison between the output of buggies per man-hour and the output of automobiles per man-hour? In short, the number and quality of goods per man-hour in 1967 are so different from the number and quality of goods per man-hour in the "gay 'nineties," and even the "roaring 'twenties," that comparisons of growth begin to lose their significance. However, according to some observers, it is still possible to define progress and growth by this measure in some qualitative sense. As Boulding has put it:

> Whenever one method of doing something displaces another, in the free operation of human choice, we may say after an interval of time long enough that the new method has had a proper trial, that economic growth has taken place.[24]

The behavior of output per man-hour in the United States is shown in Figure 1-3.

About all that can be said is that economic growth is indeed difficult to define in any meaningful quantitative sense. Problems of income distribution, utility weights assigned to different goods and services over long periods of time when the composition of total output changes, and even what constitutes the "good life"[25] complicate the issue considerably. Nevertheless there is some such thing as economic growth, despite the problem of measurement and in this sense the following quotation is quite relevant:

> . . . most of us, in spite of the terrors of modern warfare, would not readily change places with the past; we look from our day of electric light and automobiles to the days even a century ago of candles and coaches with a sense of great technical superiority, touched only with a twinge of sentimental regret. . . . In spite of an uneasy feeling that spiritually and intellectually we may not cut a remarkably good figure

---

[24]Kenneth E. Boulding, *Principles of Economic Policy*, © 1958. Reprinted by permission of Prentice-Hall, Inc., Englewood Cliffs, New Jersey. See also J. W. Kendrick, *Productivity Trends in the United States* (Princeton: Princeton University Press, 1961), and E. F. Denison, *Economic Growth in the United States and the Alternatives before Us* (New York: Committee for Economic Development, 1962), Supplementary Paper No. 13, for evidence of rises in output per man-hour.

[25]Boulding, *Principles of Economic Policy*, Chapter 2.

beside our ancestors, we have a certain confidence that we excel them in economic matters; that economic progress is not a vague and unreal thing, but a real experience of humankind which can be experienced even within the lifetime of a single individual.[26]

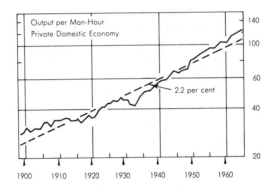

Source: Board of Governors of the Federal Reserve System, *Historical Chart Book, 1966*, p. 69.

FIGURE 1–3

Output Per Man-Hour, Private Domestic Economy
1957-59 = 100

For purposes of most of the theoretical discussion given in the subsequent chapters, nearly any of these measurements of economic growth will suffice. When any specific measure is better than another, it will be used.

B.   The Business Cycle

The discussion in sections 1 and 2 so far has emphasized that there is an interaction between economic growth and the business cycle. Accordingly, some definition of the cycle must be given.[27] For present purposes, the cycle is defined as follows—*the business cycle is the recurring, but not periodic, fluctuations in the levels of income, output, employment, and prices, the aggregates mentioned moving at about*

---

[26]*Ibid.*, p. 22.

[27]This definition is quite preliminary. See Chapter 4, section 3, for more detailed and complete discussion.

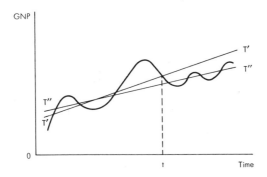

FIGURE 1–5

example is presented. The trend line T'T' is plotted so that one-half of the observed values lie above it and one-half below it. But note that from time period t on, all of the actual values lie below T'T'. This can be settled simply by recalculating the trend value so that now the relevant trend line is T"T". Again, one-half of the actual values lie above the trend and one-half lie below it.

But, and this is the important point, what if the old trend line T'T' reflects pretty accurately the GNP needed for continuing full employment? If this is so, then the trend line T"T" given in Figure 1–5 can be quite misleading. Things do not appear to be as bad as they actually are. After all, only one-half of the deviations from T"T" lie below the trend line. In reality, however, *all* of the actual deviations lie below the full-employment potential of the economy as reflected by the trend line T'T'. It is for this reason that Boulding has stated: "The picture of the cycle which is given . . . as a series of fluctuations alternating between 'too much' or 'too little' . . . may be quite misleading, if in fact all deviations, or what is even worse, *most* deviations are really below the norm."[37]

B. Deviations Below a Norm: Potential GNP

An alternative method of measuring the business cycle is to view cyclical disturbances below the *potential* movement of the seasonally

---

[37]K. E. Boulding, *Economic Analysis* (New York: Harper & Row, Publishers, 1966), II, *Macroeconomics*, 211.

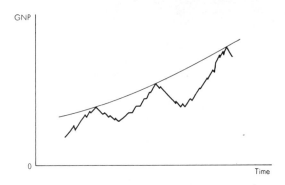

FIGURE 1—6

adjusted variable in question. This is shown in Figure 1–6, where deviations in actual GNP are shown occurring below potential GNP. Potential GNP may be defined as what the total output of the economy would be if all of the growth factors were fully utilized so that there would be continuing full employment.

This procedure, in fact, has been adopted by the Council of Economic Advisers in recent years. The Council has assumed that an unemployment rate of 4 per cent is acceptable, and then it calculates the GNP necessary to provide for continuing full employment at 96 per cent of the labor force. Arthur M. Okun, who was quite instrumental in devising the concept and measure of potential GNP, has stated:

> In estimating potential GNP, most of the facts about the economic system are taken as they exist: technological knowledge, the capital stock, natural resources, the skill and education of the labor force are all data, rather than variables. Potential differs from actual only because the potential concept depends on the assumption—normally contrary to fact—that aggregate demand is exactly at the level that yields a rate of unemployment equal to 4 percent of the civilian labor force. If, in fact, aggregate demand is lower, part of potential GNP is not produced; there is unrealized potential or a "gap" between actual and potential output.[38]

The actual performance of the U. S. economy in recent years, following this method of measurement, is shown in Figure 1–7.

There are, of course, difficult problems involved in determining the

[38]A. M. Okun, "The Gap Between Actual and Potential Output," in *The Battle Against Unemployment*, ed. A. M. Okun (New York: W. W. Norton & Company, Inc., 1965), p. 15.

Billions of Dollars* (Ratio Scale)

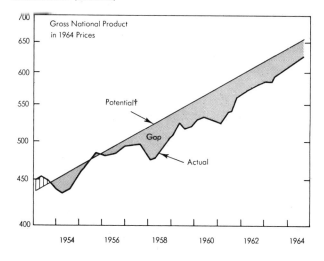

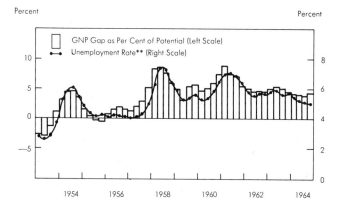

* Seasonally adjusted annual rates.

† 3½% trend line through middle of 1955 to 1962 IV; 3¼% trend line thereafter.

** Unemployment as percent of civilian labor force; seasonally adjusted.

Sources: Department of Commerce, Department of Labor, and Council of Economic Advisers. *Annual Report of the Council of Economic Advisers, 1965*, p. 82.

FIGURE 1—7

Gross National Product, Actual and Potential,
and Unemployment Rate, 1953-1964

23

potential GNP. Obviously the concept of potential GNP can assume a normative tinge,[39] but it is no more nor less normative than the trend in the residual method. However, this method of measurement focuses attention upon *absolute* deviations below the full-employment potential GNP. The problem is to develop an acceptable concept and measurement of potential full-employment GNP, and of course the " . . . quantification of potential output—and the accompanying measure of the 'gap' between actual and potential—is at best an uncertain estimate and not a firm, precise measure."[40] Still, it has proved to be a meaningful and important measurement and can thus be used to measure cyclical fluctuations.

The procedure used by the Council of Economic Advisers is roughly as follows. First, it is assumed that changes in manpower productivity, average hours worked, and labor-force participation are directly related to the rate of unemployment.[41] Second, the procedure assumes that real GNP must rise at about 3½ per cent per year simply to keep the unemployment rate constant over time. Third, at any given time, a *rise* of real GNP by 1 per cent means that the unemployment rate *declines* by one-third of 1 per cent.

Now, on the basis of these assumptions, there are two fundamental ways to calculate potential GNP and thus the gap between potential and actual GNP. The first of these is to use a 3½ per cent trend to represent potential GNP and then to anchor this to a period when the unemployment rate is approximately 4 per cent. The potential GNP in Figure 1–7 is calculated in this manner, with mid-1955 being selected as the base point. Then actual GNP is plotted, and the difference between the actual and the potential curves measures the gap. Moreover, the cyclical fluctuations in actual GNP can be interpreted as deviations below the norm of potential GNP.

The other method of calculation is to subtract 4 per cent from the actual prevailing unemployment rate (U), then triple the remainder

---

[39]This is one of the major points made by A. F. Burns in his criticism of this particular method of measurement. See his "Examining the New 'Stagnation Theory' ", *The Morgan Guaranty Survey* (New York, May 1961), and his "A Second Look at the Council's Economic Theory," *The Morgan Guaranty Survey* (New York, August 1961). Burns' original remarks drew a response from the Council in the August 1961 *Survey*. For a later statement by Burns on the same point, see "Economics and Our Public Policy of Full Employment," in *The Nation's Economic Objectives: Roots and Problems of Achievement*, ed. E. O. Edwards (Houston: Rice University Press, 1963), also reprinted in the July 1963 issue of *The Morgan Guaranty Survey*.

[40]Okun, *The Battle Against Unemployment*, p. 13.

[41]See *The Battle Against Unemployment* for a discussion of these points.

(U — .04), and multiply the result by actual GNP in billions of dollars. That is:

Gap = 3 • (U — .04) • Actual GNP in billions of dollars.

This then is added to the actual GNP since potential GNP is the sum of the gap and actual GNP. Of the two procedures, the Council of Economic Advisers has selected the first (see Figure 1–7).

C. Reference Cycles and the Business Cycle

There is still another method of measuring the business cycle—the procedure that has been developed by the National Bureau of Economic Research. The National Bureau's technique makes use of two important devices—the *reference cycle* and the *specific cycle*.[42] However, the beginning point for a discussion of the Bureau's method must be with the dating of the business cycle. The turning points, and hence the lengths of expansions and contractions, are identified by an examination of a large number of time series and a large number of observations of published comments in various sources. Once the turning points are identified they are shown graphically, with the letter T designating troughs or lower-turning points and the letter P designating peaks or upper-turning points. On the basis of its examination of time series, business annals, and other sources, the National Bureau has identified peaks and troughs all the way back into the nineteenth century. The number of business cycles measured in this way is shown in Table 4–4.

After having dated the peaks and troughs of the successive fluctuations in general economic activity, the National Bureau then constructs "reference" cycles for each of a large number of time series. The first step in the procedure is to convert the actual data into a "standard" form in order to permit consistent comparisons of the behavior of this series over time. This is done by dividing the original data by the average of the data in the series. The result is what is called "reference-cycle relatives," which express the data as percentages of the cycle's average.

Then the "relatives" are divided into nine chronological stages. Stage I is the first trough in the cycle and is arbitrarily defined to be three months long. The timing of Stage I is determined by *the time at which the lower-turning point in general economic activity actually*

---

[42]Of course the National Bureau is engaged in much more work than simply measuring the business cycle.

occurs. Stage V is the peak of the "relatives," and it also is arbitrarily defined as three months long. Similarly, its timing is determined by the *actual peak* or upper-turning point of the *business cycle.* Stage IX, also assigned a length of three months, is the last trough in the cycle. Its timing is likewise determined by the next lower-turning point in the business cycle. Note that the timing of these three stages is given by the turning points of the business cycle, *not* by the turning points in the actual behavior of the data in the series.

The intervening stages are treated slightly differently. Stages II, III, and IV are divided equally, that is, each is assigned one-third of the time between Stages I and V. By the same token, Stages VI, VII, and VIII are each assigned one-third of the time between Stages V and IX.

The next step is to compute reference cycle *patterns* that correspond to the reference cycle itself. To do this, the National Bureau takes the average of the monthly data for the three months of Stage I and plots this at the midpoint of the stage. The same procedure is followed for Stages V and IX. However, for the other stages, more or less than three months may be involved. But once the average for each stage is obtained and plotted, the result is the reference cycle pattern. A hypothetical reference cycle is plotted in Figure 1–8. The reference cycle pattern provides a "standardized" picture for studying the series over successive business cyles. The final operation is to take an average of all of the Stage I's over a number of business cycles, then an average of all the Stage II's, and so on, and to plot the results.

The reference cycle for a given series may now be used for an important type of comparison—namely, with the "specific" cycle.

The specific cycle of the series is computed in the same way as the reference cycle, but with this important difference—the actual dates are used for timing the turning points. (Recall that the turning-point dates used in computing the reference cycle are the dates assigned to the turning points in general economic activity.)

Moreover, the specific cycle is divided into nine stages, just like the reference cycle, although again the actual dates are used. The specific cycle is also averaged, for both each business cycle and a number of business cycles, in the same way as the reference cycle. A hypothetical specific cycle averaged over a number of business cycles is shown in Figure 1–8.

Now comparisons between the reference cycle and the specific cycle for any one series can be made (as in Figure 1–8). Recall that the turning points of the reference cycle (that is, the T's and P's) are given

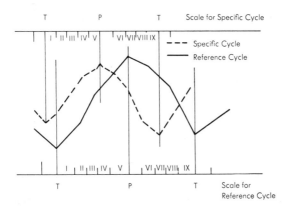

FIGURE 1-8

by the turning points of the business cycle. The turning points of the
specific cycle, on the other hand, are given by the actual behavior of
the series. Note that in Figure 1–8 the turning points of the specific
cycle tend to lead the turning points of the reference cycle. The interesting point about this is that this particular series may be a useful
indicator of the turning points of the business cycle. Other series, however, tend to follow the turning points of the reference cycle, while still
others are roughly coincidental. These leaders, laggers, and coincidents
are discussed in Chapter 4, where their forecasting usefulness is considered.

The National Bureau's method of measurement may be summarized
as follows. First, after extensive study of a large number of developments, dates of the turning points in the business cycle are identified.
Second, reference cycles are constructed for each of a large number
of time series. The turning points of each reference cycle (that is,
Stages I, V, and IX) are identified with the turning points of the business cycle, regardless of the actual behavior of the data in the series.
This procedure thus links the reference cycle chronologically to the
business cycle. Then by an averaging process the Bureau calculates a
reference cycle pattern for each series. Finally, the reference cycle patterns are averaged step by step over a number of business cycles.

Computation of the specific cycle for any particular time series is
identical in procedure to the methods used in obtaining a reference
cycle. The only major difference is that the dating of the turning points
is determined by the actual behavior of the data, not by the timing of
the turning points in general economic activity. As shown in Figure

1–8, lead-lag relationships between the reference cycle and the specific cycle can be ascertained, and this may prove useful in forecasting.[43]

6.   Why Study the Cycle?

Sometimes the question is raised: "Why study the business cycle? After all, the United States has not suffered a serious economic setback in the post World War II period. There is really no need to study the cycle, for it is now obsolete." The adherents to this position point to the relatively short postwar "recessions" of 1947-1948, 1953-1954, 1957-1958, and 1960-1961 as evidence in support of their hypothesis.

This is indeed an important question for a book that is as much concerned with cyclical fluctuations as this one is. So much so, in fact, that apparently the question must be dealt with.

To begin with, is it true that the business cycle is no longer with us? Two of the leading students of cyclical disturbances—Arthur F. Burns and Alvin H. Hansen—have provided an answer. Although these two economists disagree in many theoretical respects (and certainly over policy matters), they do hold to the fundamental position that the cycle is still very much alive. As Burns has put it:

> For well over a century business cycles have run an unceasing round. They have persisted through vast economic and social changes; they have withstood countless experiments in industry, agriculture, banking, industrial relations, and public policy: they have confounded forecasters without number, belied repeated forebodings about "chronic depression." Men who wish to serve democracy faithfully must recognize that the roots of the business cycle go deep in our economic organization, that the ability of government to control depressions adequately is not yet assured, that our power of forecasting is limited, and that true foresight requires policies for coping with numerous contingencies.[44]

Thus, in Burns' view the business cycle is inherent in our type of economic system, and so long as that system continues, so will the cycle.

---

[43]As might be expected, the National Bureau's work has not gone unchallenged. For a very interesting interchange of views, see T. C. Koopmans, "Measurement Without Theory," *Review of Economic Statistics*, August 1947; R. Vining, "Koopmans on the Choice of Variables to be Studied and of Methods of Measurement," *Review of Economics and Statistics*, May 1949; and Koopmans' "A Reply" and Vining's "A Rejoinder," both in *Review of Economics and Statistics*, May 1949. This controversy is reprinted in *Readings in Business Cycles*, eds. R. A. Gordon and L. R. Klein (Homewood, Ill.: Richard D. Irwin, Inc., 1965), readings 9-13.

[44]A. F. Burns, *Stepping Stones Toward the Future* (Twenty-Seventh Annual Report of the National Bureau of Economic Research, March 1947), reprinted in A. F. Burns, *The Frontiers of Economic Knowledge* (Princeton: Princeton University Press, 1954). The statement cited in the text is on p. 45 of the reprinted version.

To be sure, policy makers may possess a number of anticyclical tools, but thus far these tools have served merely to mitigate somewhat the cyclical disturbances, not to eliminate them.

But "ancient history" need not be relied upon in order to observe that the cycle is still very much present. In order to avoid the "optimists' spirit," recall the recent setbacks of 1948-1949, 1953-1954, 1957-1958, and 1960-1961. These serve as strong reminders that the cycle is far from obsolete and that it still requires concentrated study. As Hansen has stated, the postwar contractions

> . . . underscore the fact that the cycle is still with us. . . . All these recessions can be fitted without difficulty into the pattern of business cycle theory. They were not sporadic or accidental. They were the result of well-known forces operating in a price economy which employs a large amount of fixed and working capital.[45]

Similar views have been expressed by a substantial number of other economists.[46] Thus, the argument of the "optimists" may be dismissed.

However, there is still the question posed as the heading of this section—Why study the cycle? There are several answers. In the first place, the Employment Act of 1946 makes it a responsibility to do so. The act states:

> The Congress hereby declares that it is the continuing policy and responsibility of the Federal Goverment to use all practicable means con-

---

[45]Hansen, *Economic Issues of the 1960's*, pp. 137, 138. See also Part V of his *Business Cycles and National Income*, expanded edition (New York: W. W. Norton & Company, Inc., 1964).

[46]See, for example, the various contributions in *Business Cycle Indicators: Contributions to the Analysis of Business Conditions*, ed. G. H. Moore (Princeton: Princeton University Press, 1961), Vol. I. For a detailed exposition of the performance of the American economy since World War II, see B. G. Hickman, *Growth and Stability of the Postwar Economy* (Washington, D. C.: The Brookings Institution, 1960) and *Investment Demand and U. S. Economic Growth* (Washington, D. C.: The Brookings Institution, 1965).

In contrast to the view that the cycle is an intrinsic part of the growth process of the advanced capitalist economy, consider the following:

> There is a widespread belief that a competitive organization of economic life is inherently unstable. It is contended that either periodic or continuous unemployment at an intolerably high level is unavoidable in an economy of free markets. This attitude assumes to be true a point of view which is, at the least debatable. So far as the evidence goes, the alternative conclusion—that the shortcomings of the system in the past have been due to a failure to provide the necessary rules and conditions for the effective functioning of a competitive economy—is equally plausible.

L. W. Mints, *Monetary Policy for a Competitive Society* (New York: McGraw-Hill Book Company, 1950), p. 1.

sistent with its needs and obligations and other essential considerations of national policy, with the assistance and cooperation of industry, agriculture, labor, and State and local governments to coordinate and utilize all its plans, functions, and resources for the purposes of creating and maintaining, in a manner calculated to foster and promote free competitive enterprise and the general welfare, conditions under which there will be afforded useful employment opportunities, including self-employment, for those able, willing, and seeking to work, and to promote maximum employment, production, and purchasing power.[47]

Now this statement of goals is complicated, if for no other reason than that it is couched in the style of legislative writing. But there is more to it than this. The major complications stem from the fact that the act does nothing in the way of providing definitions of the key terms. What, for example, is meant by "maximum employment, production, and purchasing power"? What is meant by the phrase "those able, willing, and seeking to work"? And what is meant by "free competitive enterprise and the general welfare"? Not only does the act fail to provide definitions of these important terms and goals, it also proposes, according to many economists, the achievement of goals that are mutually exclusive—namely, continuing full employment and price-level stability. Perhaps these deficiencies, however, are desirable; the strong point can be made that no general policy statement should be couched in such rigid and binding terms that the flexibility of the policy makers would be greatly reduced.

Second, the full-employment commitment extends beyond the Employment Act of 1946. Under the United Nations Charter each subscribing nation has pledged to take action to promote ". . . higher standards of living, full employment, and conditions of economic and social progress and development."[48] Thus the economic commitments and responsibilities of the United States extend far beyond its own political boundaries to encompass the rest of the "free world."

Finally, note the statement by Neil H. Jacoby, a former member of the Council of Economic Advisers to the President. This statement is similar in spirit to the Burns statement cited earlier to the effect that "men who wish to serve democracy faithfully" must have an adequate

---

[47]*U. S. Statutes at Large*, 79th Cong. 2nd sess., 1946 (Washington, D. C.: Government Printing Office, 1947), Vol. 60, Part I, p. 25. The act has been amended on several occasions (1956, 1959, 1961, and 1964), but Sec. 2, the "Declaration of Policy" cited above, has remained unchanged. See Joint Economic Committee *Employment Act of 1946, as Amended, with Related Laws*, 89th Cong., 2nd sess. (Washington, D. C.: Government Printing Office, 1966). (Both Canada and Great Britain have similar legislation.)

[48]Articles 55-56.

knowledge of the causes and characteristics of business cycles. However, Jacoby's statement obviously goes beyond Burns'.

> The issue between totalitarian Communism and democratic Capitalism, as national ways of life, turns on which kind of system people believe will best advance their welfare. Great nations, like India, which remain neutral in this ideological struggle, are watching closely the performance of the American economy. The Marxist theorists never tire of telling them that Capitalism is an ineffectual way of organizing production because it generates deepening crises and depressions.
>
> The United States can refute this fallacy by showing the world an impressive record of full production and full employment, with a stable dollar, and with benefits widely shared among our people. This, more than atomic weapons and supersonic bombers, can assure our security. This will help the United States win and hold allies who share our belief in the desirability of the "open society" of democracy, civil rights, private property, and free, competitive enterprise.[49]

One need not agree with Jacoby's statement in its entirety in order to subscribe to its central thesis—namely, that the rest of the world is viewing the performance of the American economy, particularly with respect to its continued growth and cyclical instability.

There are, therefore, several important reasons for studying the business cycle, as well as the process of economic growth and the interaction of growth and the cycle. Both domestic and international forces strongly indicate this, and internal socioeconomic factors indicate also the necessity of studying the growth-cycle process. This is not, of course, as simple as it may sound. There is significant disagreement among economists as to the nature and causes of the cycle and growth, and even if there were agreement in this respect, some controversy would still exist over the means of controlling the cycle and growth process. Nevertheless, the challenge is there and it must be accepted.

7. Summary

In this introductory chapter the interaction of the business cycle and economic growth has been stressed. But this interactive process is complicated by the conflict of different economic goals, as well as by the fact that growth brings with it significant institutional changes that in turn affect the growth-cycle process itself. All told, this prelimi-

---

[49]N. H. Jacoby, *Can Prosperity Be Sustained?* (New York: Holt, Rinehart & Winston, Inc., 1956), p. 3.

nary discussion reveals that the subject matter of this volume is complicated. But it also points out that, if for no other reason than the Employment Act of 1946, analysis of the growth-cycle process is essential and important. However, there are no simple remedies for problems of economic instability and retarded growth. The major difficulty with panaceas is that they oversimplify tremendously complex situations. The continuing interaction of the cycle and growth, as well as the policy issues that the interaction poses, then, will be the subject matter of the subsequent chapters in this book.

QUESTIONS

1-1. Discuss some of the pitfalls and dangers involved in measuring the business cycle as "deviations around a norm." Are there any similar dangers involved in the method of measurement used by the Council of Economic Advisers?

1-2. What are some of the difficulties involved in measuring economic growth? Discuss in detail.

1-3. Discuss the tentative definition of the business cycle presented in this chapter. How do you think it can be improved upon? (Be sure to consider the statements in footnotes 29-30 in answering this question.)

1-4. Present and discuss as many reasons as you can as to why the study of the business cycle is a worthwhile effort. Have the recent cyclical disturbances in the American economy directly affected you or your family? How?

1-5. What is meant by "reference" cycles and "specific" cycles? How may a comparison of these two types of cycles be useful?

Bibliography

Apel, H., *"Inflated Recession": A New Economic Paradox.* Westport, Conn.: The Calvin K. Kazanjian Economics Foundation, Inc., 1958.

Burns, A. F., *Prosperity Without Inflation.* New York: Fordham University Press, 1957.

Hansen, A. H., *Economic Issues of the 1960's.* New York: McGraw-Hill Book Company, 1960.

Heimann, E., *The Economy of Abundance.* Westport, Conn.: The Calvin K. Kazanjian Economics Foundation, Inc., 1957.

Hickman, B. G., *Growth and Stability of the Postwar Economy.* Washington, D. C.: The Brookings Institution, 1960.

Nourse, E. G., "Some Questions Emerging under the Employment Act," *American Economic Review,* May, 1960.

Schumpeter, J. A., "The Analysis of Economic Change," reprinted in *Readings in Business Cycle Theory,* ed. G. Haberler. Philadelphia: The Blakiston Company, 1944.

2

The Aggregate
Performance of the
American Economy

How well (or poorly) has the economic system performed over time with respect to growth and cyclical fluctuations? What measurements of total economic activity and its major components are available, and how may these be used to evaluate past and present performance? How can the measurements be used to forecast future performance? These and similar questions are dealt with in this chapter.

As seen in Chapter 1, the American economy has experienced substantial, although irregular and uneven, economic growth. The basic measurement used in arriving at this conclusion is the gross national product (GNP), a concept that is rather widely used (and abused) today. Indeed, of the various national income and production accounts reviewed in this chapter, gross national product is probably the one most commonly mentioned.[1] Congressmen, editorialists, the lay public, and governmental officials, not to mention economists and businessmen, quite often refer to GNP in their discussions of the total performance of the economy and in their decision-making functions.

---

[1]The other accounts are net national product, national income at factor cost, personal income, and disposable income. All of these, not simply GNP, are important. As seen below, the "income" and "product" accounts are merely different ways of viewing the same activity.

Yet gross national product is very often misunderstood and even misused. This is quite unfortunate, for it is a powerful educational tool for understanding and evaluating economic activity. Therefore, every effort must be made to know its meaning, scope, and limitations. In this way the national income and product accounts may be correctly used.[2]

1. The Gross National Product (GNP)

Gross national product is defined as the *market value* of *all final* goods and services *produced* in the economy during a given time period.[3] Accordingly GNP serves as the most comprehensive measure of the total performance of the economy. It includes, for example, the market value of newly grown apples, newly produced automobiles, chairs, plants, haircuts, apartment buildings, LP records, maid services, light bulbs, hair nets, police services, books, educational services, jet fighters, and so on. Truly GNP is a hodgepodge of quite dissimilar things.

The various items counted in the gross national product, however, have one important common characteristic that allows them to be added together into a meaningful total—namely, prices or market values. In fact, some goods have no explicit market prices, but the Department of Commerce "imputes" market values and adds them in GNP.[4] This, of course, helps to account for the comprehensiveness of

---

[2] A great deal of attention has been devoted to the limitations of the accounts, but only because of their extreme significance in aggregative economic theory and policy. See especially G. Jaszi, "The Conceptual Basis of the Accounts," in *A Critique of the U. S. Income and Product Accounts* (Princeton: Princeton University Press, 1958). See also O. Morgenstern, *On The Accuracy of Economic Observations* (Princeton: Princeton University Press, 1963), Chapters XIV-XV.

Moreover, the Department of Commerce subjects itself to a great deal of internal criticism with respect to the accounts. In view of all this, the accounts are continually being revised, and the latest revision is discussed in *Survey of Current Business*, August 1965. For a history of the accounts, see P. Studenski, *The Income of Nations, Theory, Measurement, and Analysis: Past and Present* (New York: New York University Press, 1959).

[3] The data in the United States are reported on an annual basis and, wherever possible, on a quarterly basis. Only personal income is reported on a monthly basis.

[4] A classical illustration is that of persons living in houses they own themselves. If these same houses were owned by others, rent would have to be paid (in money, goods, or services), thereby swelling the national product. To avoid this, a value has to be imputed to owner-occupancy.... Other items have to be treated similarly, *e.g.*, unmarketed food consumed on farms.

Morgenstern, *On the Accuracy of Economic Observations*, p. 246.

GNP. At the same time, however, it is important to note that GNP is not so inclusive that it contains everything that has a market price. Certain items are excluded for a variety of reasons.[5] These complications mean that the definition of GNP given above must be examined in some detail.

A preliminary observation, however, is in order. There is more than one way of viewing GNP, since the total value of currently produced goods and services is exactly equal to the total expenditures by buyers for these goods and services. Moreover, factors of production are employed to produce total current output, and they are paid in the form of wages, salaries, rents, interest, and profits. The sum of these payments to the factors of production constitutes the income that is used to purchase the goods and services being produced. In short, the value of total output (GNP) equals total income equals total expenditures. National product, national expenditures, and national income are, therefore, merely different sides of the aggregate flow of the economy.

This may be stated as follows: Since GNP equals the total expenditures by consumers on consumers' goods (C), businesses for total investment in capital goods (I),[6] and *all levels of government* for various goods and services (G),[7] then

$$GNP = C + I + G.$$

The expenditures on C, I, and G in turn constitute the total revenues of all producing units, whether business, household, or government, who pay out wages and salaries, rents, interest, and profits. These in turn, as noted above, constitute the national income from which the C, I, and G expenditures are made. Thus, aggregate economic activity may be viewed as the market value of the total currently produced output, as the total of expenditures on the currently produced output, or as the total income received by the various factors of production used in producing current output. All three of these approaches are simply different ways of viewing the same general activity.

---

[5]Many of these complications are discussed in the next chapter.

[6]The term "investment" here includes expenditures by businesses on all newly produced capital goods. Even those goods used to replace the capital that was worn out in producing the GNP are included. This is referred to as "replacement" investment. The term also includes expenditures on new capital goods, over and above replacement investment, that are used to add to the capital stock. This is referred to as "net" investment. Finally, investment in inventories is also included. Thus, total or gross investment, as used above, equals replacement plus net investment plus inventory investment. See Chapter 4 (section 1) for a fuller discussion of these types of investment.

[7]Please note that the G in the equation refers to *all levels* of government, including state and local governments. As will be seen later, the expenditures by state and local governments are acquiring more and more economic significance.

For the moment, GNP in terms of the total value of currently produced output is being considered. The relevant definition was given at the very beginning of this section. There are, however, certain terms in the definition that require further discussion.

First, consider the word *final*—that is, GNP is a measure of the *final* total output of goods and services produced during the accounting period. The market values of all the *intermediate* goods and services that enter into the final output are excluded; otherwise there would be double counting and GNP would overstate the performance of the economy. The reason for this is simply that the market values of the intermediate goods and services are already included in the market value of the final product.

For example, there would be a gross exaggeration of the market value of a chair if the separate market values of all the items and services entering into it are also counted. The lumber itself may have cost $10 at the first stage of production. In the next stage it was cut, trimmed, and finished so that its market value rose to $15—that is, the second stage added a *net* value of $5 to the lumber. But to say that the total market value is now $25 (that is, $10 at the first stage plus $15 at the second) would be to count the original $10 twice. Actually the calculation of GNP is concerned only with *value added,* which is the increment to the market value at *each successive stage of production.* (In the above example, then, the market value at the end of the second stage was $15.) The market value of the *final* good is nothing more than a summation of the individual values added at each successive stage. The final prices of the goods and services are then totaled up to give GNP, and hence gross national product excludes the market values of all of the intermediate goods and services that are already included in the final prices.

Of course, those intermediate goods that have not yet entered into any final product, but rather are held in the form of inventories at the time GNP is estimated, are included in GNP at their market prices. In this case they are not intermediate goods at all, but rather are final goods held in the form of inventories. And in the case where intermediate goods are sold directly to the final buyer—*e.g.,* lumber to a "do-it-yourself" addict—they are counted as final goods and thus are included in GNP at their market prices.[8]

---

[8]One category that is particularly bothersome in this respect is government services. As Morgenstern, *On the Accuracy of Economic Observations,* p. 247, has put it: "It is sometimes argued that part of the government output should not be treated as final, since it has utility only insofar as it affects the private sector—*e.g.,* government highway building derives much of its value from the use that business makes of roads, say in the distribution of goods."

Certain other market values are also excluded from GNP. For instance, the values of illegal activities are not counted in, nor are business and governmental transfer payments. A transfer payment is merely an exchange of income between individuals and/or organizations without a corresponding exchange of productive services. A "win-a-trip-to-Paris" prize sponsored by a corporation, therefore, is a transfer payment. Also, such governmental payments as social security benefits are transfer payments, as is the interest on the national debt.[9] In its latest revision of the accounts, the Department of Commerce has excluded interest paid by consumers on the grounds that it is no longer ". . . regarded as reflecting production."[10]

Finally, the market values of *existing* goods that are exchanged during the accounting period are excluded from GNP insofar as they represent past, not current, production. Thus the value of a rare painting or an antique that is sold during the accounting period is not counted in, although if the item is altered or restored the net value added is included.

The important point is that *not all* goods are included in GNP, but only the market values of *final* goods and services that have been produced during the accounting period.[11] Even then, as shown in the next chapter, some items are excluded on various grounds, usually because of conceptual problems and the difficulty of compiling accurate data.[12]

There is another term in the GNP definition that needs to be considered, namely, "market value." The solid curve in Figure 2–1 gives GNP in *current* dollars, that is, GNP for each year is calculated in terms of the prevailing prices of that year. This, however, can be quite misleading, for it is possible that the change in reported GNP from one

---

[9]Some countries include interest on the national debt in their gross national product on the grounds that the debt represents productive activity. In the United States, however, interest payments have consistently been excluded from GNP. For the position of the Department of Commerce on this, see "The National Income and Product Accounts of the United States: Revised Estimates, 1929-64," *Survey of Current Business*, August 1965, p. 10, n. 6.

[10]*Ibid.*

[11]There is one major exception to this point. In the 1965 revision, the Department of Commerce now includes in GNP the market value of existing fixed assets that are exchanged between the major sectors of the economy (households, government, and business). For example, if the government sells fixed assets to the business sector (*e.g.*, old Liberty ships), or if businesses sell their own used cars to their employees, the amount involved is entered in GNP. *Ibid.*, p. 13.

[12]Perhaps the most serious omission in this respect is the value of the housewife's services. If the market value of these were imputed for each housewife and added to GNP the total GNP would be increased tremendously. See Chapter 3 for further discussion.

Billions of Dollars

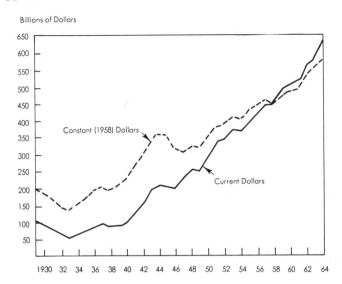

FIGURE 2—1

Gross National Product in Current
and Constant (1958) Dollars, 1929-1964

year to the next reflects merely a change in prices and not changes in the physical amount of goods and services produced, and of course the major concern is to measure changes in real production. Current-dollar estimates of GNP, therefore, do not reveal the desired picture since they include the effects of price changes along with real output changes.

Consider a hypothetical example. Assume that the real output of goods and services in Year 1 is 100 units and that the average price per unit is $1.00. Thus, GNP is $100 (that is, output, O, times price, P). Now assume that O rises by 50 units to 150 in Year 2, but that P rises to $2.00. The question now is how much of the increase in GNP from $100 to $300 is a rise in real output and how much is due to rising prices? In this simple illustration the answer is obvious. But in the real world, where all production is stated in terms of prices, the changes in output cannot be separated from the changes in prices *before* the GNP is calculated. In other words, GNP is always estimated in current-dollar terms and thus tends to conceal the distinct changes in output from the changes in prices. In the above illustration, the increase in current-dollar GNP from \$100 to \$300 implies a much greater gain in economic activity than has actually occurred. For this reason, then, GNP data, when given in current dollars, can be quite misleading.

In order to minimize this problem, GNP is calculated in *"real"* or *"constant-dollar"* terms, that is, GNP in current dollars is "deflated" by some appropriate price index in order to single out the changes in real output. One way of doing this is to divide the current-dollar GNP of each year by the ratio of the prices of that year to the prices of some base year. (In the 1965 revision of the accounts, the Department of Commerce selected 1958 as the base year. Prior to that the base year was 1954.) In terms of the preceding example, real GNP for Year 2 can be calculated as follows:

$$\text{Real GNP}_2 = \frac{\text{Current-dollar GNP}_2}{\dfrac{P_2}{P_1}} = \frac{\$300}{\dfrac{\$2}{\$1}} = \frac{\$300}{\$2} = \$150,$$

where the subscripts 1 and 2 stand for Years 1 and 2, respectively. The real GNP in Year 2, therefore, is \$150, which reflects the rise in real output from Year 1 to Year 2 of 50 units. In short, real or constant-dollar GNP measures change in real output since the production of each year is measured in terms of the prices of the base year.

The Department of Commerce however, uses a more refined technique, making use of what is called an "implicit price deflator." A price index is computed for each component of GNP, say, C, I, and G, and then each component is adjusted in order to state its value in constant dollars. When all the components are added up, the result is GNP in constant dollars. Then, when current-dollar GNP is divided by the constant-dollar GNP, the department obtains a price index (the implicit price deflator).

Consider the following illustration. In 1958, the base year selected by the Department of Commerce, current-dollar GNP was \$447.3 billion. The index value assigned to each of the major components of GNP was 100.0. In 1959, current-dollar GNP had risen to \$483.6 billion, and the implicit price deflator for that year had risen to 101.6. Now dividing the current-dollar GNP of \$483.6 by the implicit deflator of 101.6 gives a constant-dollar GNP of \$475.9 billion. In short, the \$36.3 billion increase in current-dollar terms from 1958 to 1959 overstated the actual rise in physical production of \$28.6 billion by \$7.7 billion. Put otherwise, \$7.7 billion of the current-dollar increase was attributable solely to price rises.

The method used by the Department of Commerce is preferable to using a general price index, as in the hypothetical example above. The reason for this is that the relative importance of each major component of GNP is changing, and some components may experience greater or lesser price changes than others. A general price index would not reflect this and hence is somewhat misleading.

The difference between current-dollar GNP and constant-dollar GNP (with 1958 as the base year) is shown in Figure 2–1.

Despite all the limitations and qualifications involved in the measurement of gross national product, it remains the most accurate and comprehensive statement of the total performance of the economy available. However, caution must be exercised in making international comparisons of the GNP's of different countries, and even of the GNP of the same country over a long time period. These and other problems, both conceptual and statistical, are discussed in the next chapter.

2. Net National Product (NNP)

The major difference between gross national product and net national product (NNP) is that one further element of double counting must be eliminated—namely, the consumption of capital goods (that is, depreciation) that occurs as GNP is produced. Other than this, what was said about GNP earlier applies equally well to NNP.

The difference between these two product accounts can be illustrated very easily by reference to the data given in Table 2–1 and Figure 2–2. Note that in 1964 GNP was $628.7 billion (in current dollars). Note also that during 1964, $55.7 billion of capital goods was "consumed," that is, was worn out in the production of the GNP. Thus, out of the total GNP, $55.7 billion had to be used to replace the worn-out capital, and accordingly this was not a *net* addition to the total output of the economy. (In fact, this $55.7 billion is what is referred to as "replacement" investment in footnote 6.) Net national product, in other words, measures the *net addition to total output*. The difference between GNP and NNP then is that the former includes *all* the new capital goods produced during the accounting period, whereas the latter includes only the *net increments* to the stock of capital goods.[13] Other than this, the two accounts are identical.

As seen in Figure 2–2, NNP and GNP follow each other rather

---

[13]The significance of the distinction between replacement and net investment is discussed in Chapter 4.

closely, although the gap between the two appears to be widening
somewhat, particularly since World War II. This, perhaps, is what is

TABLE 2—1

Gross National Product, Net National Product, and Capital
Consumption as a Percentage of Gross National Product,
1929-1965, United States, in Billions of Current Dollars

Year	Gross National Product	Capital Consumption Allowances	Net National Product	Capital Consumption Allowances as a Per Cent of GNP
1929	103.1	7.9	95.2	7.7
1930	90.4	8.0	82.4	5.8
1931	75.8	7.9	68.0	10.4
1932	58.0	7.4	50.7	12.8
1933	55.6	7.0	48.0	12.6
1934	65.1	6.8	58.2	10.4
1935	72.2	6.9	65.4	9.6
1936	82.5	7.0	75.4	8.5
1937	90.4	7.2	83.3	8.0
1938	84.7	7.3	77.4	8.6
1939	90.5	7.3	83.2	8.1
1940	99.7	7.5	92.2	7.5
1941	124.5	8.2	116.3	6.6†
1942	157.9	9.8	148.1	6.2†
1943	191.6	10.2	181.3	5.3
1944	210.1	11.0	199.1	5.2
1945	212.0	11.3	200.7	5.3
1946	208.5	9.9	198.6	4.7
1947	231.3	12.3	219.1	5.3
1948	257.6	14.5	243.0	5.6
1949	256.5	16.6	239.9	6.5
1950	284.8	18.3	266.4	6.4
1951	328.4	21.2	307.2	6.5†
1952	345.5	23.2	322.3	6.7
1953	364.6	25.7	338.9	7.0
1954	364.8	28.1	336.5	7.7†
1955	398.0	31.5	366.5	7.9
1956	419.2	34.1	385.2	8.1
1957	441.1	37.1	404.0	8.4
1958	447.3	38.9	408.4	8.7
1959	483.6	41.4	442.3	8.6

† Years in which accelerated depreciation allowances were made available
to businesses

Source: *The Annual Report of the Council of Economic Advisers, 1966,*
pp. 222–23, 226.

TABLE 2–1 (continued)

Year	Gross National Product	Capital Consumption Allowances	Net National Product	Capital Consumption Allowances as a Per Cent of GNP
1960	503.8	43.4	460.3	8.6
1961	560.3	45.2	474.9	8.7
1962	560.3	50.0	510.4	8.9
1963	589.2	52.8	536.5	9.0
1964	628.7	55.7	573.0	8.9
1965*	675.6	58.7	616.8	8.7

* Preliminary

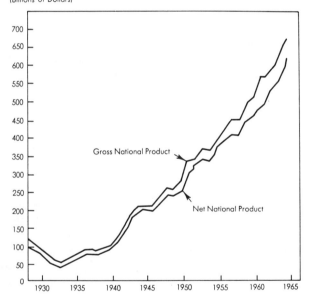

Gross and Net
National Product
(Billions of Dollars)

Source: *Annual Report of the Council of Economic Advisers, 1966,* pp. 222-23, 226.

FIGURE 2–2

to be expected, for as the economy grows and expands, the stock of capital used to produce GNP also expands. As a result, the absolute magnitude of capital consumption allowances will rise. But note also, as seen in Table 2–1, that capital consumption allowances, as percentage of GNP, are growing. The theoretical significance of this will be examined later, although the main implication is that replacement investment is becoming much more important in the American economy.

3.   National Income at Factor Cost

Both gross national product and net national product are measures of production and thus are very important in macroeconomic analysis. But the analysis is equally concerned with measures of income, and one of these—national income at factor cost—is considered in this section. The national *income* accounts, in effect, view the same total economic activity as the national *production* accounts, but from a different perspective.

In order for GNP and NNP to be produced in the first place, the various factors of production must be employed, whether by businesses, governments, or household units. And the payments to these factors of production, while considered as costs for the employers, are treated as income by the factor owners. In short, what is a cost when viewed from one perspective is income when viewed from another, and it is for this reason that the measure considered in this section is termed national *income* at factor *cost*.

National income at factor cost in reality is the sum of the total wage and salary payments, rental payments, profits, and interest payments made during the accounting period.[14] Presumably the total of all payments to the factors of production (national income at factor cost) would be equal to gross national product, as noted early in section 1, above. And once adjustments are made for capital consumption allowances, the total payments would be equal to the net national product, since NNP is the market value of the net production in the economy. This, however, is not the case in modern economic societies, and therefore certain further adjustments must be made in order to make NNP equal to national income at factor cost.

The major difference between net national product and national income at factor cost is due to the presence of indirect business taxes, such as sales taxes, excise taxes, and so on. These taxes are included in the final selling prices of the products involved, and the businesses who

---

[14]Note that profits are viewed as a cost when the economy as a whole is being analyzed. Note also that not all payments to the owners of the factors of production are necessarily received by them. Often some portion of income is withheld, in some form or other, so that it does not reach the factor owner.

collect the tax payments in turn pass them on to the taxing governmental unit. The government then uses the revenues to finance, at least
in part, its activities, and these governmental activities are also counted
in NNP. Note that the problem of transfer payments is not being considered here; they have already been excluded. Rather what is being
considered are the revenues that are used to finance current productive
activity in the form of highway construction, post office construction,
police and fire services, educational services, and so on. Inasmuch as
these activities represent current production, they are included in the
national product accounts. Thus, if the indirect business taxes are not
deducted from NNP, they would be counted twice—once in the prices
of the final products and once in the market value of governmentally
produced goods and services.

A hypothetical example will be helpful. Assume that NNP is $500
billion, but that the sum of wages and salaries, interest, rent, and profits
is $450 billion. In other words, employers in the economy paid out $450
billion to the factors of production (including profits), but in turn received $500 billion in proceeds. How can the $50 billion differential be
accounted for? Assume further that during the accounting period the
government has provided $50 billion of goods and services and has
financed these from the revenues raised through the indirect business
taxes. In short, the $50 billion of indirect taxes has been counted twice
in NNP—once in product prices and once in the final value of government goods and services. Hence, NNP overstates the income received
by the factors of production by that amount, and accordingly the total
amount of revenue received from indirect business taxes must be deducted in order to obtain national income at factor cost. The actual
amount of indirect business taxes in 1964 was $64 billion.

Similarly, business transfer payments must be deducted, for they
involve simply a redistribution of income between individuals and organizations. In 1964 these amounted to $2.3 billion. However, govern-
ment subsidies, less the current surplus of government enterprises,
must be added in to obtain the final national income at factor cost.
This amounted to $1.2 billion in 1964.

Once these adjustments are made, net national product will be equal
to national income at factor cost, and the two figures merely represent
alternative ways of viewing the same productive activity. The movement from NNP to national income at factor cost is summarized in
Table 2–2, and the relationship of GNP and national income at factor
cost is shown in Figure 2–3. Note that these two magnitudes follow
each other rather closely over time but that the distance between the
two curves is widening.

TABLE 2–2

From Gross National Product to National Income at Factor Cost,
United States, 1964
in Billions of Current Dollars

Gross National Product		$628.7
Less: Capital Consumption Allowances	$ 55.7	
Net National Product		573.0
Less: Indirect Business Taxes	58.0	
Business Transfer Payments	2.3	
Statistical Discrepancy	— .8	
Plus: Subsidies, Less Current Surplus of Government Enterprises	1.2	
National Income at Factor Cost		514.4

Source: *The Annual Report of Economic Advisers, 1966*, p. 222.

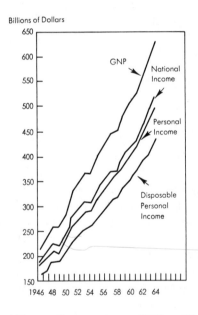

Source: *Survey of Current Business*, August 1965, p. 15.

FIGURE 2–3

4. Personal Income

The next income account to consider is personal income, and this figure is obtained by making certain adjustments in national income at factor cost. The reason for these adjustments is that not always do the factors of production receive all of the income they have earned, and at times some factors receive income that they have not earned in the production process.

Consider, for example, corporate profits. In the first place, these are subject to taxes, and hence a part of them is not received by the owners of the corporation. Then, after the taxes are paid, the board of directors will decide what portion, if any, of the remaining profits will be declared as dividends to the stockholders. The share that is not distributed as dividends—that is, undistributed profits or retained earnings—does not reach the owners of the corporation, and hence it, along with corporate taxes, must be deducted from national income at factor cost.[15] In 1964 these two items amounted to $47.5 billion (profits tax liability of $27.6 billion and undistributed profits of $19.9 billion).

A further deduction has to be made for social security contributions by both employers and employees when these are paid before wage payments are made. These amounted to $27.8 billion in 1964.

However, certain additions have also to be made, for often the owners of the factors of production receive income that they have not earned. The most important of these is government transfer payments ($34.2 billion in 1964). Recall that government transfer payments are deducted from both GNP and NNP on the grounds that they do not reflect productive activity. Similarly, since national income measures the income side of *productive* activity, these transfer payments are not included in it. But now, insofar as they represent income actually received by some people and organizations, they must be added back in. By the same token, business transfer payments, net interest paid on the national debt, and interest paid by consumers must be figured back into the accounts.

---

[15]Undistributed profits, as will be seen later, serve as a very important source of financial funds for businesses. They, along with depreciation reserves, have accounted for about two-thirds of the funds, on an average annual basis, used for financing net investment by corporations. Perhaps it should be noted that the Department of Commerce makes this adjustment in a somewhat different way. They deduct all of corporate profits and then add dividend payments back in. The residual, of course, is the sum of the corporate profits tax liability and undistributed profits.

TABLE 2–3

From National Income at Factor Cost to Personal Income,
United States, 1964
in Billions of Current Dollars

National Income at Factor Cost		$514.4
Less: Corporate Profits Tax Liability and Inventory Valuation Adjustment	$ 25.6	
Contributions to Social Security	27.8	
Undistributed Profits	21.7	
Plus: Government Transfer Payments	34.2	
Net Interest Paid by Government	19.1	
Business Transfer Payments	2.3	
Personal Income		495.0

Source: *The Annual Report of the Council of Economic Advisers, 1966,* p. 223.

Once these adjustments have been made, the resulting figure is personal income. The movement from national income at factor cost to personal income is summarized in Table 2–3, and the relationship of this account to the others is shown in Figure 2–3. Note that over time it has risen along with both GNP and national income at factor cost, but that it does not fluctuate nearly as much as the other two accounts. In fact, since 1954 personal income has shown a remarkable stability with respect to GNP and national income.

5. Disposable Personal Income

The remaining concept is disposable personal income, and it is of extreme importance in what follows. Disposable income may be defined as personal income less all direct personal taxes, such as personal income taxes, gift taxes, personal property taxes, and so on.[16]

After all of the direct personal taxes have been deducted from personal income, the residual (disposable income) is what the income receivers have to dispose of as they see fit. Actually, they have but two basic alternatives—namely, to spend it on consumers' goods or to save it.

The behavior of disposable income is shown in Figure 2–3. As will be

---

[16]Note that personal direct taxes do not include sales and excise taxes and the other indirect taxes. The indirect taxes are accounted for in the calculation of national income at factor cost.

TABLE 2–4

The National Income and Product Accounts, United States, 1964
in Billions of Current Dollars

Gross National Product		$628.7
Less: Capital Consumption Allowances	$ 55.7	
Net National Product		573.0
Less: Indirect Business Taxes	58.0	
Business Transfer Payments	2.3	
Statistical Discrepancy	— .8	
Plus: Subsidies, Less Current Surplus of Government Enterprises	1.2	
National Income at Factor Cost		514.4
Less: Corporate Profits Tax Liability and Inventory Valuation Adjustment	25.6	
Contributions to Social Security	27.8	
Undistributed Profits	21.7	
Plus: Government Transfer Payments	34.2	
Net Interest Paid by Government and Interest Paid by Consumers	19.1	
Business Transfer Payments	2.3	
Personal Income		495.0
Less: Direct Personal Taxes		59.2
Disposable Personal Income		435.8

Source: *The Annual Report of the Council of Economic Advisers, 1966*, pp. 222–23, 226.

seen later, consumption and disposable income are rather closely linked together, implying that consumption is determined primarily by disposable income.[17] But note also, in Figure 2–3, the behavior of disposable income in the period following World War II. At times, when GNP has fallen, disposable income has continued to rise (as in 1953-1954). As will be seen later, this is due primarily to the growing importance of government transfer payments. Note also that insofar as consumption is predominately a function of disposable income, consumption expenditures will fluctuate less than both GNP and NNP.

6. A Summary Statement of the Product and Income Accounts, 1964

Table 2–4 presents a summary statement of the five accounts discussed thus far. The accounts will be discussed in far more detail in the next chapter, and a firm grasp of the relationships between them is essential to an understanding of macroeconomic theory and policy.

---

[17]This relationship is discussed at length in Chapter 10.

7.   The Index of Industrial Production

Another very widely used measurement of economic activity is the Federal Reserve index of industrial production. Not only is the index presented regularly in many important publications,[18] it is also used extensively by businessmen and economists in evaluating and predicting economic activity.

Just what does the index measure? It contains production data for 207 time series, including gas and electricity. These series are classified in two ways—by industrial groupings and by market groupings. The relative weights by groupings are shown in Table 2–5. Note that in the market groupings the output of *final* goods is assigned a weight of 47.35, that is, less than one-half of the total index represents final output. The remainder represents intermediate goods, which, as already observed, do not enter into GNP (except perhaps as inventory

TABLE 2—5

Market and Industrial Groupings In the Index of Industrial
Production, by Relative Weights

Market Groupings			Industry Groupings		
Classification	Relative Weight		Classification	Relative Weight	
Final Products		47.35	Manufacturing		86.45
Materials		52.65	Mining		8.23
			Utilities		5.32
Total Index		100.00			100.00
Final Products		47.35	Manufacturing		86.45
Consumer Goods	32.31		Durable Manufac-		
Equipment, In-			turing	48.07	
cluding Defense	15.04		Nondurable		
			Manufacturing	38.38	
Materials		52.65			
Durable Goods			Mining		8.23
Materials	26.73				
Nondurable			Utilities		5.32
Materials	25.92		Electricity	4.04	
			Gas	1.28	

Source: *Industrial Production, 1957-59 Base* (Washington, D. C.: Federal Reserve System, n.d.), pp. S1-S19.

---

[18]For instance, *Survey of Current Business, Federal Reserve Bulletin, Economic Indicators,* and *Business Week.*

valuations). Further, the index is seasonally adjusted, and adjusted even more for the number of working days in the month. In fact, it ". . . assumes that output per manhour displays a smooth pattern of change."[19]

A very important thing to keep in mind about the index of industrial production is that, as the title implies, it is a measurement of the behavior of industrial production only, and not of general economic activity. Thus the index is not nearly as comprehensive as the national income accounts, since it does not measure performance in the retail, wholesale, financial, and agricultural sectors of the economy.[20] The major exclusion, at least for present purposes, is construction.

Yet, the index is, despite its 'limited coverage, extremely important for a number of reasons. First, ". . . activities covered by the revised index of industrial production account for about 35 per cent of the total national income and product."[21] The major sectors that are excluded— agriculture and construction—account for only about 10 per cent of national income.[22]

Second, ". . . all other sectors of the economy are affected in some way by developments in the industrial sector."[23] One reason is that most of the other areas of economic activity supply goods and services to the industrial production sector, and thus changes in the manufacturing sector obviously will influence activity in the other sectors. Another reason is that changes in employment in the manufacturing sector will influence the demand by consumers for goods and services in the aggregate. Finally, as shown in Figure 2-4 the index is a useful, though limited, measure of both economic growth and the business cycle. However, the cyclical swings in the index are of much greater magnitude than the swings in GNP because of its limited coverage and because one of its components—manufacturing equipment—is extremely sensitive cyclically.

Another widely used index of industrial production is the one prepared by the Cleveland Trust Company. Although it is referred to as the index of business activity, like the Federal Reserve index it measures only the behavior of production. In the next section we shall see

[19]*Industrial Production, 1959 Revision* (Washington, D. C.: Federal Reserve System, July 1960), p. 22. See also *Industrial Production, 1957-59 Base* (Washington, D. C.: Federal Reserve System, n.d.), for discussion of later revisions.

[20]However, much of food processing is included.

[21]*Industrial Production, 1959 Revision,* p. 18.

[22]This, however, does not minimize the importance of construction's being excluded.

[23]*Industrial Production, 1959 Revision,* p. 18.

Ratio Scale
Billions of 1958 Dollars

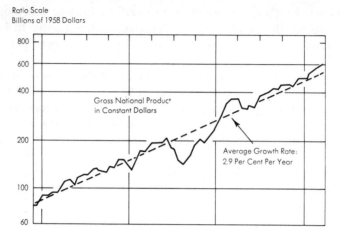

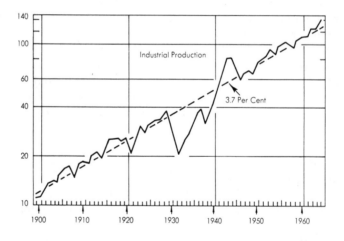

Source: Board of Governors of the Federal Reserve System, *Historical Chart Book, 1966*, p. 69.

FIGURE 2—4

how swings in the index of business activity can be forecast by means of a tool developed by the National Bureau of Economic Research (NBER), namely, the "diffusion" index.

8. The Cross-Current of Forces in the Economy

The cyclical fluctuations that take place in GNP and the other major income and product accounts are made up of a large number of changes in individual magnitudes. These range all the way from investment in plant and equipment, to net gold movements, to boxcar loadings, to wholesale inventories, and to the average workweek of unskilled workers. Only a moment's thought is required to realize that there are literally hundreds upon hundreds of these specific movements, and perhaps only a moment's more thought is required to suspect that these specific movements follow cyclical patterns of their own.[24] And of course they do. There are "specific" cycles in the production of consumers' durables, in business failures, corporate profits, business inventories, stock prices, interest rates, wage rates, and so on. It is the aggregate of these specific cycles that makes up the general wave-like fluctuations in gross and net national product that is termed the business cycle, just as their aggregate behavior over time determines the long-run trend in economic activity.

Fortunately, a good deal of information on these specific cycles is available, most of which is provided by the National Bureau of Economic Research.[25] The National Bureau began its collection of data on these specific cycles some thirty years ago, and it has expanded its research until it now has an array of more than 800 specific time series.[26] Not all of these, of course, are equally relevant. Some behave very erratically (such as net gold movements), and some cover such a short period of time that they are not very useful. Also, new series are continually being added and old ones revised or eliminated from the total collection. All told, the National Bureau works with a collection of time series that amounts to something less than 404.[27] Once the series that are not very relevant are excluded, the remainder can be plotted graphically in a very revealing manner.

This is done in Figure 2–5, where the percentage of time series that

---

[24]The time series in question are seasonally adjusted.

[25]The work of the National Bureau on business cycles and economic growth began during the 1930's. The first significant publication was W. C. Mitchell's *Statistical Indicators of Cyclical Revivals* (New York: National Bureau of Economic Research, 1938). The most important recent publication is Geoffrey H. Moore, *Business Cycle Indicators* (Princeton: Princeton University Press, 1961), two volumes.

[26]G. H. Moore, "Statistical Indicators of Cyclical Revivals and Recessions," Chapter 7 in *Business Cycle Indicators*, Vol. I, pp. 195-96.

[27]*Ibid.,* p. 196.

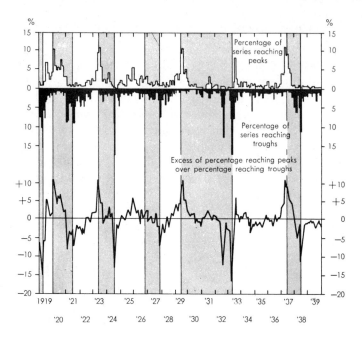

Shaded areas represent business contractions.

Source: G. H. Moore, *Business Cycle Indicators*, Vol. I, p. 15. Reprinted by permission of Princeton University Press, copyright 1961, Princeton University Press.

FIGURE 2–5

Distribution of Turning Points of Specific Cycles in a Sample
of over 600 Economic Time Series, 1919-39

are expanding each month is plotted above the zero line, and the percentage of those contracting is plotted below the line. The resulting picture reveals quite clearly that all magnitudes do not move at the same time in the same direction—while some series are expanding, others are contracting. This cross-current of forces goes on continually. Truly the business cycle is a very complicated creature. As A. F. Burns, who was instrumental in developing this method of measurement, has put it: "If anyone is so naive as to believe that most economic activities reach like turns on the same or almost the same month, this chart should disabuse him. What it shows is a wide dispersion of cyclical peaks and troughs [of specific cycles]."[28]

---

[28]A. F. Burns, "New Facts on Business Cycles," Chapter 2 in *ibid.*, p. 15.

This complex picture can be clarified a great deal by making use of another National Bureau measurement, the "diffusion index." The index measures the percentage of the times series (specific cycles) that are *expanding* each month. So long as the percentage expanding is greater than the percentage contracting, the diffusion index is greater than fifty; but it drops below fifty when the percentage contracting exceeds the percentage expanding. The diffusion index, shown in the bottom panel of Figure 2–5, gives a much clearer picture of the data plotted in the top panel.

A rather complete coverage of the time series and the diffusion index, running from 1885 to 1940, is given in Figure 2–6.[29] Note that at no time does the index ever reach zero (where none of the series is expanding), nor does it ever reach 100 per cent (where all of the series are expanding). Rather it fluctuates consistently between these two extremes.

There are two things about the diffusion index that should be noted. The first of these is far from startling—namely, that during periods of general economic contraction the index tends to fall, and during periods of general economic expansion it tends to rise. This, of course, is pretty much what is to be expected. A general expansion implies that most economic activity, although not all, is expanding, while in periods of general contraction most, although again not all, series are declining. So far, so good.

The second observation, however, is of a different sort—not only is it very important, it is also quite striking. Refer to Figure 2–7, where the diffusion indexes for the periods 1921-1939 and 1948-1958 are plotted on the same graph with the index of business activity.[30] The important thing to note is the lead-lag relationship that exists between the two indexes. Both tend to decline during the same period, but the diffusion index begins to rise before the index of production does. In fact, *in every case* the diffusion index leads the lower-turning point of the index of business activity. Moreover, the diffusion index leads the upper-turning point of the index of general business activity *in every case* also. This implies that the diffusion index might have a great deal of pre-

---

[29]Current data on the diffusion index are found in *Business Cycle Developments,* a monthly publication of the United States Department of Commerce. This publication also describes the procedures used in constructing the diffusion index, not only in the aggregate, but for specific series. Also it contains current data on the leading, lagging, and roughly coincidental indicators developed by the National Bureau and discussed in the next section.

[30]The index of general business activity, as noted above, is compiled by the Cleveland Trust Company and is not to be confused with the Federal Reserve index of industrial production. However, the Cleveland Trust index, like the Federal Reserve index, measures only changes in industrial production.

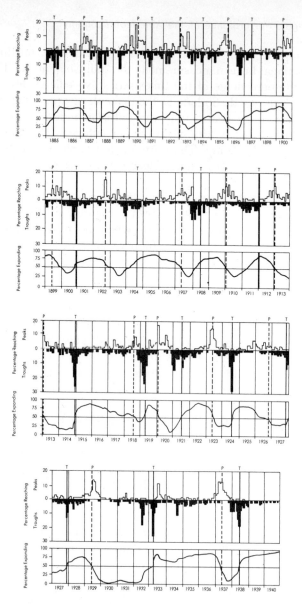

Source: G. H. Moore, *Business Cycle Indicators*, pp. 198-201. Reprinted by permission of Princeton University Press, copyright 1961, Princeton University Press. Solid vertical lines indicate troughs, and broken vertical lines indicate peaks, of the cycle as measured by the National Bureau.

FIGURE 2–6

Percentage of Series Reaching Specific Cycle Peaks and Troughs and the Diffusion Index, 1885-1940

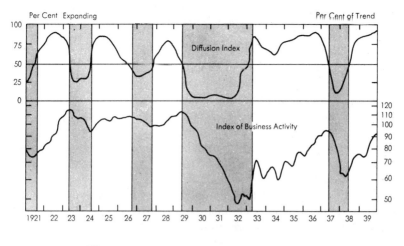

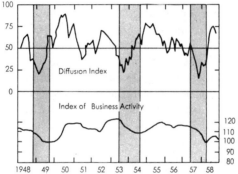

Shaded areas represent contractions of business cycles and white areas expansions, according to NBER chronology.

Diffusion index plotted on arithmetic scale; index of business activity plotted on ratio scale.

Source: B. G. Hickman, "Postwar Cyclical Experience and Economic Stability," *American Economic Review*, May 1958.

Diffusion index, 1885-1939, based on 404 economic series, is from G. H. Moore, *Statistical Indicators of Cyclical Revivals and Recessions* (NBER, 1950), pages 14-17. Diffusion index, 1948-58, based on 213-279 economic series, is from Julius Shiskin, "An Experiment with New Measures of Recession and Recovery" (Bureau of the Census, mimeographed, November, 1958), pages 37-39. The 1885-1939 index is not only based on a different sample of series than the later index, but is constructed in such a way that more of the minor fluctuations are ironed out. Index of business activity is published by the Cleveland Trust Company and is adjusted for long-run trend.

FIGURE 2—7

A Comprehensive Diffusion Index and
an Index of Business Activity, 1921-1958

dictive value, and some observers have contended that the index has chalked up quite a good record in forecasting the turning points.[31]

Perhaps, however, there really is nothing particularly new or startling about this lead-lag relationship. Business cycle analysts have always argued that as an expansion continues it begins to accumulate contractionary forces, and that as the contraction goes on it also begins to develop expansionary forces.[32] Eventually, as these forces become strong enough, the cumulative upward or downward movement is reversed. Thus the data pictured in Figures 2-5 to 2-7 do not necessarily provide any new hypothesis. But they do reveal clearly and strikingly how the reversing forces actually accumulate towards the end of expansions and contractions. If nothing more, they have at least validated the suspicions and somewhat unsystematic observations of many economists about this particular aspect of cyclical fluctuations in economic activity.

But there may be something more. As indicated above, the diffusion index may serve as a rather powerful forecasting weapon. In fact, A. F. Burns has stated that such findings (as depicted in Figure 2-7) ". . . add to the understanding of business cycles, and may even prove helpful in predicting reversals in the direction of total economic activity—or at least identifying them promptly."[33] Moreover, G. H. Moore, also of the National Bureau, has even argued that the diffusion index will be of some value in predicting the severity of contractions.[34]

A word of caution, however, is in order. For one thing, there is a good deal of irregularity in the number of months by which the diffusion index leads the turning points of the business cycle. Thus, while the index may be of some aid in predicting a future turning point, it may be off by as much as six months to a year in timing.[35]

---

[31]Burns, "New Facts on Business Cycles," p. 34. See also G. H. Moore, "Diffusion Indexes, Rates of Change, and Forecasting," Chapter 9 in *Business Cycle Indicators*, Vol. 1.

[32]See the discussion of the cycle in Chapter 1.

[33]"New Facts on Business Cycles," p. 34.

[34]"Statistical Indicators of Cyclical Revivals and Recessions," and "Diffusion Indexes, Rates of Change, and Forecasting." For a critical evaluation of Moore's position, see A. L. Broida, "Diffusion Indexes," *American Statistician*, June 1955. For further critical discussion, see S. S. Alexander, "Rate of Change Approaches to Forecasting—Diffusion Indexes and First Differences," *Economic Journal*, June 1958; B. G. Hickman, "Diffusion, Acceleration, and Business Cycles," *American Economic Review*, September 1959; and S. Valavanis, *Econometrics: An Introduction to Maximum Likelihood Methods* (New York: McGraw-Hill Book Company, 1959), pp. 181-92. All of these contain further references.

[35]This point is stressed by F. E. Morris, "The Predictive Value of the National Bureau's Leading Indicators," Chapter 4 in *Business Cycle Indicators*, Vol. I. See also S. Valavanis, "Must the Diffusion Index Lead?" *American Statistician*, October 1957, and Moore's reply to Valavanis in the same issue.

For another thing, the index is continually being revised. Actually, the National Bureau makes use of about 404 specific time series out of the total of over 800, but since some are always being added and others dropped, the number actually used never reaches 404 at any one time. Of course, a good deal of personal judgment must be exercised in determining which series are to be included and which omitted. Also judgment must be used in interpreting the significance and weight of each of the series. Despite these problems, however, the National Bureau has obviously developed what may turn out to be a powerful forecasting tool; but until further work is done, the index had best be used very carefully in forecasting the behavior of aggregate economic activity. Economic policy, if it is to be effective, usually calls for rather precise timing and hence forecasting.

9. Leaders and Laggers

Work with the diffusion index and forecasting has been refined in recent years. Actually, this work had begun as early as 1937 when Mitchell and Burns selected twenty-one specific series out of the few hundred available and classified them into three groups—those that lead the turning points, those that lag, and those that are roughly coincidental. A diffusion index was then constructed for each of these series. G. H. Moore has subsequently revised the list so that it now includes twenty-six series.[36] The same threefold classification is shown in Table 2–6.

Since Moore constructed the revised list on the basis of pre-World War II data, there was need to test it against the postwar behavior of the economy. If each of the series still showed itself as a leader, or lagger, or coincident, it was retained. The major emphasis, of course, is on the leaders as indicators of what will happen to the general level of business activity. Moore's major conclusion? "On the whole, the indicators did as well in the postwar period as could have been expected. . . ."[37] Their performance for the period 1948 through 1963 is given in Figure 2–8. Although nearly always some leaders lagged and some laggers led, the important thing to note is that on the whole they performed quite well—that is, as a group the leaders led and the laggers lagged.

---

[36]See especially his "Leading and Confirming Indicators of General Business Changes," in *Business Cycle Indicators*, Vol. I.

[37]*Ibid.*, p. 55.

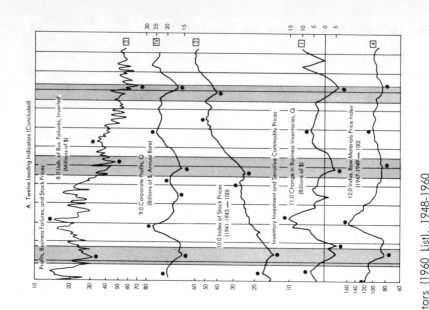

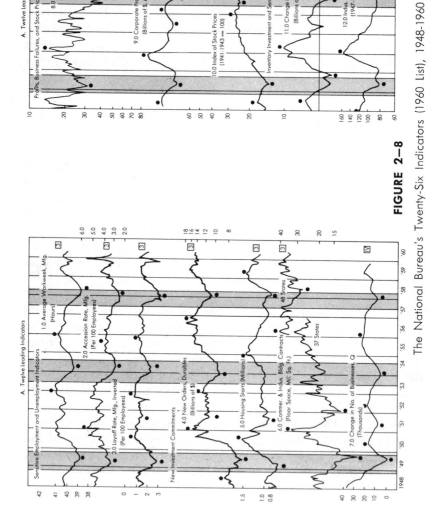

FIGURE 2-8

The National Bureau's Twenty-Six Indicators (1960 List), 1948-1960

60

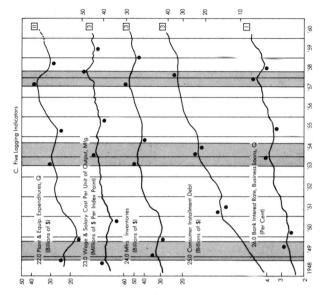

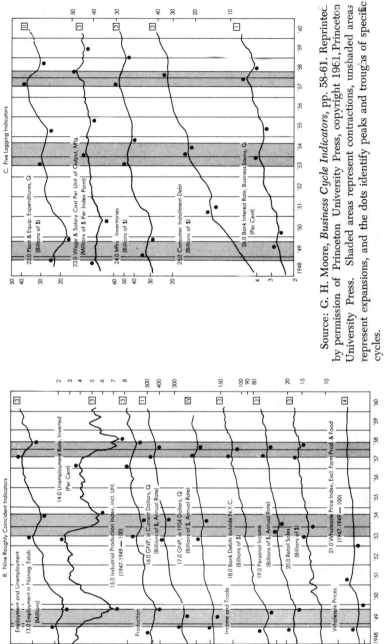

Source: G. H. Moore, *Business Cycle Indicators*, pp. 58-61. Reprinted by permission of Princeton University Press, copyright 1961, Princeton University Press. Shaded areas represent contractions, unshaded areas represent expansions, and the dots identify peaks and troughs of specific cycles.

FIGURE 2-8 (continued)

61

TABLE 2-6

Twenty-Six Statistical Indicators, National
Bureau of Economic Research, 1960 List

A. *Twelve Leading Indicators*

Average workweek in manufacturing, measured in hours
Accession rate of new employees in manufacturing
Layoff rate in manufacturing
New orders by manufacturers for durable producers' goods, measured
   in dollars
Housing starts
Commercial and industrial building contracts, measured in square feet
Change in number of businesses
Liability of business failures, measured in dollars
Corporate profits, measured in dollars
Index of stock prices, 1941-1943 = 100
Change in business inventories, measured in dollars
Price index of industrial raw materials, 1947-1949 = 100

B. *Nine Roughly Coincident Indicators*

Employment in nonagricultural establishments
Unemployment rate, measured as a percentage
Industrial production index, 1947-1949 = 100
Gross National Product, in current dollars
Gross National Product, in 1954 dollars
Bank debits outside New York City, measured in dollars
Personal income, measured in dollars
Retail sales, measured in dollars
Wholesale price index, excluding farm products and food, 1947-
   1949 = 100

C. *Five Lagging Indicators*

Plant and equipment expenditures, measured in dollars
Wage and salary cost per unit of output
Manufacturers' inventories, measured in dollars
Consumer installment debt, measured in dollars
Bank interest rate on business loans

Source: *Business Cycle Indicators,* Vol. I, pp. 56-57.

Two of these series—*new orders* by businesses for durable producers'
goods and *actual business expenditures* on plant and equipment—are
worth examining briefly. The first of these is a leader, while the second
is a lagger. As will be seen in Chapter 4, investment by businessmen in
plant and equipment is a key variable in the business cycle and a major
determinant of economic growth. Nearly always the expansionary stage
of the cycle is characterized by an investment boom, while the contractionary stage exhibits a decline in investment activity. Yet the data reveal that spending by businesses on plant and equipment appears to
lag slightly behind changes in the economy's overall performance. But
on the other hand, the new orders for plant and equipment goods reach

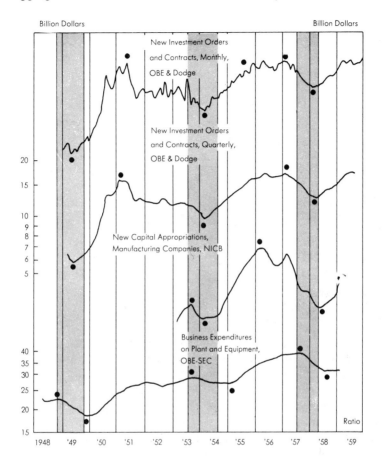

Billion Dollars   Billion Dollars

New Investment Orders
and Contracts, Monthly,
OBE & Dodge

New Investment Orders
and Contracts, Quarterly,
OBE & Dodge

New Capital Appropriations,
Manufacturing Companies, NICB

Business Expenditures
on Plant and Equipment,
OBE-SEC

Ratio

1948   '49   '50   '51   '52   '53   '54   '55   '56   '57   '58   '59

Source: G. H. Moore, *Business Cycle Indicators*, p. 474. Reprinted by permission of Princeton University Press, copyright 1961, Princeton University Press. Shaded areas represent contractions, unshaded areas represent expansions, and dots identify peaks and troughs of specific cycles.

FIGURE 2–9

New Investment Orders and Contracts,
New Capital Appropriations, and Plant and
Equipment Expenditures, 1948-59

their peaks and troughs several months before the turning points in general activity. The behavior of these two series in the post World War II period is shown in Figure 2–9. Manufacturers' new orders thus may ". . . have considerable merit as indicators of revivals and recessions in general business. Their record for leading business cycle turns in the past stands out for consistency in any collection of the available early indicators. . . . there is no reason why their future behavior in regard to business cycles should not be essentially similar to their past behavior."[38]

Similar claims have been made for most of the other indicators, as well as for the leaders as a group. But again there is need for a word of caution. Some specific series have led by as much as two years, while others have led by only a short period or have even lagged. The same pattern of irregularity holds true for the laggers. Thus extreme care must be exercised in using the indicators for purposes of prediction, and the forecaster himself must exercise a good deal of sophisticated judgment. As one observer has put it:

> I think that a competent analyst, using the indicators, might have made some mistakes in trying to forecast the precise timing of cyclical turning points in the economy and he might have made mistakes in judging, very far in advance, the amplitude of swings in the economy. He should not, however, have made any mistakes with regard to the direction of the economy; and, in general, I think that his record in forecasting the recessions of 1948-49 and 1953-54 should have been reasonably good.[39]

The important conclusions to be drawn from this discussion of the National Bureau work are, (1) the data shown in Figures 2–5 and 2–6 reveal clearly the tremendous complexity of the forces at play in cyclical disturbances; (2) the lead of the diffusion index at the turning points of the cycle (Figure 2–7) validates the argument that the later stages of both the expansion and contraction contain the emergent and sufficient forces of reversal; and (3) the indicators, developed by Burns and Mitchell and revised by Moore, serve tolerably well in forecasting the turning points, but they, along with the general diffusion index, must be used very carefully and judiciously.

10. Summary

This chapter has presented the various national income and product accounts, pointing out the limitations and shortcomings of each. However, despite the limitations, they serve as the most accurate and comprehensive measurements of aggregate economic behavior available.

---

[38]V. Zarnowitz, "The Timing of Manufacturers' Orders During Business Cycles," Chapter 14 in *Business Cycle Indicators*, Vol. I.

[39]F. E. Morris, "The Predictive Value of the National Bureau's Leading Indicators," p. 116.

Also there was some discussion of the Federal Reserve index of industrial production, as well as the National Bureau's diffusion index and leaders and laggers. Although the National Bureau's measurements are quite important and show tremendous potential as forecasting devices, they must be used carefully in predicting cyclical swings in general economic activity.

QUESTIONS

2-1. Gross national product may be viewed either from the expenditures side, the income side, or the product side. Yet all three views reduce to the same thing. Comment.

2-2. In calculating GNP, why is only "value added" used? Does this eliminate all double counting?

2-3. Discuss some of the market values that are not included in GNP. Do you think that they should be included? Why?

2-4. What is the major purpose of calculating GNP in terms of "constant dollars?"

2-5. Explain *why* capital consumption has to be deducted from GNP in order to obtain NNP. What has been happening recently to depreciation allowances as a percentage of GNP? Of what significance is this?

2-6. Why should "national income," as it is usually called, really be termed "national income at factor cost"? Discuss the significance of indirect business taxes in calculating national income at factor cost (and refer back to question 2–2).

2-7. Discuss in detail the movement from national income at factor cost to personal income. Of what significance is this latter account?

2-8. What is meant by disposable personal income? Of what significance is this account?

2-9. What is the National Bureau's "diffusion index," and how can it be used for forecasting cyclical turns in aggregate economic activity? Is it a reliable forecaster? Explain.

2-10. How do you account for *new orders by businesses for durable goods'* being a "leader," while *actual business expenditures for durable goods* are a "lagger"?

3

The Sources and Uses of Gross National Product: The Sector Accounts

The discussion of the national product and income accounts in the preceding chapter was rather brief and avoided many of the problems involved in the construction of the accounts. Gross national product was defined as the market value of all the final goods and services produced during the economy during the accounting period, but no mention was made of the contributions that each major sector of the economy—business, household, government, and foreign—makes to GNP. Also national income was defined as the total income received by the owners of the factors of production, but there was discussion of how much income originates in each major sector. Nor was there any analysis of how the income received in each sector is used. This chapter deals with these issues.[1]

---

[1]The following Department of Commerce publications are relevant for this chapter: *U. S. Income and Output* (published November 1958); *National Income Supplement, 1954;* and "The National Income and Product Accounts of the United States: Revised Estimates, 1929-64," *Survey of Current Business,* April 1965.

1.   The Business Sector

In an economy that is strongly oriented towards private enterprise, a large share of the total output, and hence income, logically originates in the business sector. In order to measure this share of GNP the profit and loss (or income) statements of the various business firms must be examined, adjusted, and consolidated. There are, as might be expected, numerous and difficult problems involved in this procedure, but the Department of Commerce carries on.

To begin with, the definition of the term "business," as used by the department, is fairly broad. It includes domestic business corporations, individual proprietorships, partnerships, governmental enterprises,[2] and owner-occupants of houses.[3] The last two types of "firms" require special treatment since their operations and record-keeping procedures differ substantially from those of ordinary business firms. Thus the ordinary business firm will be considered first; owner-occupants and governmental enterprises are discussed below.

The typical business firm periodically constructs a profit and loss, or income, statement.[4] A rather standardized statement is shown in Table 3–1. Note that this statement equates the sales and other income of the period with the costs of production *attributable* to the sales of the period, plus the profit or loss of the period. The profit and loss entry assures the equality between the two sides of the statement.

Some comments about a couple of the cost entries are in order. First, consider depreciation. This is the cost of the fixed assets *assignable* to the goods sold during the period. Depreciation is indeed a cost of doing business because the entire cost of the fixed assets is not assigned to the accounting period in which they were acquired. Rather the total costs are spread out over a number of periods by some method of depreciation accounting. Thus, only the cost of wear and tear of the fixed assets that can be attributed or assigned to the goods sold in the ac-

---

[2]Not all government organizations are counted as "enterprises." Only those whose total revenues are approximately equal to or greater than total costs are included. Where there is no intent to make revenues cover costs, as in the case of schools, the organization is excluded.

[3]The Department of Commerce treats the homeowner as a person in the rental business, and thus a rental income is *imputed* to him. See below for further discussion.

[4]The usual accounting period for the national income and product accounts is the calendar year.

TABLE 3—1

A Standardized Profit and Loss (Income) Statement
of a Business Enterprise

COST OF GOODS SOLD	SALES
Purchased Goods and Services:	Sales to Persons
From Other Domestic Businesses	Sales to Other Domes-
From Abroad	tic businesses
Wages and Salaries	Sales to Government
Supplements to Wages and Salaries	Sales Abroad
Depreciation	
Taxes (Other than Profits Taxes)	OTHER INCOME
Interest Paid	Interest Received
Bad Debts and Contributions	Dividends Received
(Business Transfer Payments)	Subsidies
PROFIT	
Corporate Profits*	
Corporate Profits Taxes	
Dividends	
Undistributed Profits	

* For proprietorships and partnerships this would read "Proprietors' Income," and for income that comes from the rental of real estate it would read "Rental Income of Persons."

count period in question is included in the profit and loss statement of the period.[5]

Another adjustment relates to inventories. Perhaps some of the actual current money outlays during the accounting period were used to accumulate inventories of goods that were not sold. It would be misleading, therefore, to assign these costs to the goods sold during the period. Thus, any increase in the value of inventories must be deducted from the cost side. Alternatively it may be added to the right-hand side of the statement as a separate entry—"Net Change in Inventories." The latter procedure is followed here, for reasons noted below. However, once the net increase in inventory is added to the right-hand side, a similar amount must be entered on the cost side in order to maintain the equality of the statement. The amount added to the left-hand, or cost, side will be allocated between labor costs, material costs, and so on, according to how these inputs contributed to the increase in inventory.

[5] Of the four sector accounts—business, personal, government, and foreign—only the business account is compiled on an accrual basis—that is, the costs, no matter when incurred, are assigned to the sales only when the sales take place. All the other accounts are on a current basis.

TABLE 3–2

Consolidated Income-Product Statement
of Private Domestic Business

CONSOLIDATED COST OF GOODS SOLD	CONSOLIDATED NET SALES
Compensation of Employees	Sales to Persons
Wages and Salaries	Sales to Government
Supplements to Wages and Salaries	Sales to Business on
Net Interest	Capital Account
Net Dividends	Sales Abroad
Taxes (Other than Profits Taxes)	
Business Transfer Payments	NET CHANGE IN
	INVENTORIES
PROFITS	
Corporate Profits	
Corporate Profits Taxes	
Dividends	
Undistributed Profits	
Or: Proprietors' Income	
Or: Rental Income of Persons	

If, on the other hand, there has been a net reduction in inventories accumulated from the preceding accounting period, the sales revenue resulting from this cannot be assigned to the costs of the current accounting period. Accordingly, the reduction in inventories must be deducted from the right-hand side in "Net Change in Inventories," and a similar amount deducted from the cost side of the statement.

The inventory adjustment is very important, for once it is made the profit and loss statement is fundamentally altered. Now it is no longer simply an *income* statement, because the inventory adjustment has also made it a *product* statement. The right-hand side now tells how much output was sold during the period, plus any changes in the inventory position of the firm. In other words, the total sales plus the net change in inventories reveal the total production of the firm during the accounting period.

Once the inventory adjustment has been made in the statement of each firm in the economy, the statements can be consolidated so that there is only one *income-product* statement for all of the ordinary firms. This is shown in Table 3–2. Please note the new entry on the right-hand side, namely, "Net Change in Inventories."

However, do not be misled by assuming that the sum of the figures on the right-hand side of the consolidated statement is the share of gross national product originating in the business sector. It is not! For the value of all intermediate goods is included, and thus the right-hand side substantially overstates the business sector's contribution to GNP.[6] This double counting, however, can be eliminated by a simple adjustment. From the left-hand side of the statement deduct purchases of materials and services from other domestic businesses, and from the right-hand side deduct an equivalent amount from sales to other domestic businesses. But note that there will still be a positive amount left in the entry on the right-hand side. The reason for this is that some of the sales by businesses to other businesses are sales of capital goods or fixed assets that will be used for production in later accounting periods. Thus they are not considered as a part of the materials purchased but rather are treated as a part of the final materials sold. This residual amount is given in the entry "Sales to Business on Capital Account."

The important thing about this adjustment is that it eliminates a great deal of double counting since it deducts completely all intermediate goods and services but still retains the value of the final capital goods sold during the period. As a result the sum on the right-hand side of the statement now approaches a more accurate statement of the share of GNP originating in the business sector.

Still other adjustments have to be made in order to obtain an accurate picture. So far as interest is concerned, it is both a cost to business and a source of revenue. In the *consolidated* statement, however, interest payments by businesses to businesses cancel each other out, leaving the *net* amount of interest paid by business to the personal sector of the economy. Thus, interest received by business is deducted from interest paid by business, leaving the entry "Net Interest" on the left-hand side of the statement.

A similar adjustment is made with respect to dividends—that is, the dividends received from businesses are deducted from the dividends paid by businesses. The net amount, therefore, represents income payments to the personal sector, as shown in the "Net Dividends" entry on the left-hand side of the consolidated statement.

Next an adjustment must be made in the foreign entries. In this case, the purchases from abroad are deducted from the sales abroad, leaving the figure of "Net Sales Abroad." This entry, of course, may be negative if purchases from abroad exceed sales abroad; in any event, it is recorded on the *right-hand side* of the consolidated statement since it directly represents production.[7]

---

[6] See Chapter 2 for a discussion of double-counting and the need to eliminate it.

[7] In the case of subsidies, an equal deduction is made from both sides of the statement. The reason for deducting subsidies is that, in their absence, selling prices would be lower or factor prices would be higher.

Thus far all of the major cost entries on the left-hand side of the consolidated income-product statement have been discussed except for one—indeed, the largest single entry. "Wages and Salaries" and "Supplements to Wages and Salaries" clearly constitute a major cost of doing business. However, it is important to realize that the total figure listed by the Department of Commerce overstates the actual payments to employees made by business enterprises, for it includes compensation made to employees by households and government.[8] The Department, in its accounts for the other sectors, does not provide a separate entry for wage and salary disbursements but rather simply assumes that all such payments made by households to other households and by government to governmental employees pass through the business sector. As a consequence, the total compensation to employees figure reported in the income-product statement of the business sector is indeed the total compensation received by its employees in the economy at large.

At the same time, the total sales figure given in the right-hand side of the statement includes the contributions made by government and households to GNP. These contributions are, as noted below, measured simply by the wage and salary payments to employees. Thus the figure given as the share of GNP originating in the business sector overstates businesses' contribution to total output by the amount that can be attributed to both the government and the personal sectors. We shall return to this matter below.

Once the income-product statements of typical business firms have been consolidated, the next step is to consolidate the income-production statements of the owner-occupants of houses and of government enterprises. So far as owner-occupants are concerned, the only source of revenue is the estimated total revenue of the occupants, which is *imputed* from the rents paid by tenants in comparable dwellings. On the cost side, there are the actual expenditures for upkeep and maintenance (these are included in the wages and salaries account and the purchased materials and services account) and for property taxes and interest on the mortgage. The other expenditure is depreciation, based on the original cost of the dwelling and its estimated life. The consolidated statement for owner-occupied houses is shown in Table 3–3. Note that the net rental income to the owner-occupants is the difference between gross rental income and the total direct and indirect outlays, and insofar as gross rental income is imputed, so also is the net rental income imputed.

Finally, consider government enterprises. As noted above, only those enterprises that are engaged in productive activities and that charge

---

[8]This is discussed in the next two sections.

TABLE 3–3

Consolidated Income-Product Statement of Owner-Occupants

COSTS	SALES
Wages and Salaries	Sales to Persons
Supplements to Wages and Salaries	
Purchased Materials and Services	
Interest	
Taxes	
NET RENTAL INCOME	

prices that at least roughly cover costs of production are included in this category. Some enterprises that logically would be included are the Federal Post Office, T. V. A., municipal water systems, and so on. The consolidated income-product statement of government enterprises is shown in Table 3–4. Note that the "Surplus" entry is quite broad, including a number of items that are specified as costs for business— e.g., depreciation, interest, and taxes, as well as profits. However, until more refined accounting techniques are developed, the Department of Commerce must remain content with this crude measurement.

The last step is to consolidate the income-product statements of all businesses, owner-occupants of houses, and government enterprises. This is done in Table 3–5 for the year 1964. This consolidated statement differs from the one shown in Table 3–2 in several respects, primarily because it is designed to give both GNP and national income at factor cost. In the first place, observe that the depreciation entry is not included in the table. The reason for this is that the depreciation expense is not a direct outlay by businesses and thus does not constitute income for the owners of the factors of production. Second, contributions and prizes by businesses are business transfer payments and thus do not contribute to productive activity. Accordingly, they are also eliminated from the table. And finally, taxes paid by businesses, other than corporate profits taxes, do not reflect productive activity and thus are excluded from the statement. In short, the total figure of the left-hand side of Table 3–5 is the total payments to the factors of production engaged in producing current national output and hence equals national income at factor cost.

The total figure on the right-hand side, however, is the GNP of the period. Of course, GNP exceeds national income at factor cost because it is valued at prices high enough to cover indirect business taxes, business transfer payments, and depreciation. Once these are taken into account, the total on the left-hand side equals GNP, the total on the right-hand side.

TABLE 3—4

Consolidated Income-Product Statement of Government Enterprises

COSTS	SALES
Wages and Salaries	Sales to Persons
Supplements to Wages and Salaries	Sales to Domestic Businesses
Purchased Materials and Services	Sales to Government
	Sales Abroad
CURRENT SURPLUS OF GOVERNMENT ENTERPRISES	

Another way of viewing Table 3–5 is to consider the right-hand side as the total revenues of businesses or, alternatively, total expenditures of the buyers of the output of businesses. The total expenditures *to* businesses are made *by* consumers (C), other businesses for fixed assets (I), government (G), and, on net balance, foreigners (F). Thus,

$$GNP = C + I + G + F.$$

By the same token, the total value of GNP must be large enough to pay all the factors of production (national income at factor cost), plus enough to cover indirect business taxes (T_i), business transfer payments (T_{rb}), and depreciation (D). Thus GNP may also be written as

$$GNP = D + T_i + T_{rb} + \text{National Income at Factor Cost.}$$

By definition, therefore, the two sides of the consolidated statement must be equal.

The left-hand side of the statement, however, yields some further information. First, as already seen, it shows what national income at fartor cost is. Second, the savings of the business sector (S_b) can be derived from it by deducting total costs to the factors of production from total revenue. This gives total business profits before taxes (P). From this, in turn, deduct corporate profits taxes (T_c) and dividends paid (D_v) to stockholders. Thus,

$$S_b = P - T_c - D_v.$$

For 1964 the relevant figures are

$20.0 billion $=$64.8 billion $-$ $27.6 billion $-$ $17.2 billion.

As shown below, however, this formulation understates business savings by a substantial amount because it ignores depreciation, which is

TABLE 3–5

Consolidated Income-Product Statement of All Businesses, United States, 1964
in Billions of Current Dollars

Compensation of Employees		$365.3	Sales to Persons		$398.9
Wages and Salaries		333.5	Sales to Business		
Supplements to Wages and Salaries		31.8	on Capital Account		88.1
Employer Contributions for			Net Sales Abroad		8.6
Social Insurance	$15.4		Sales to Government		128.4
Other Labor Income	16.5				
Proprietors' Income		51.1	Net Change in		
Rental Income of Persons		18.2	Inventories		4.8
Corporate Profits and Inventory					
Valuation Adjustment		64.8			
Profits Tax Liability	27.6				
Profits after Taxes	37.2				
Dividends	17.2				
Undistributed Profits	19.9				
Inventory Valuation Adjustment		– .3			
Net Interest		15.2			
TOTALS: Income Originating in Business Sector		$514.4	Product Originating in Business Sector		$628.8

75

also a source of savings to corporations. Once this is included, total business savings in 1964 amounted to $75.7 billion.[9] In other words, this formulation gives us only undistributed profits, not total business savings. In an important sense, however, Table 3–5 is a statement of the sources of income of businesses and the uses of income (*including a part of total business savings*) by businesses.

2. The Personal Sector

The first thing to note is that the Department of Commerce does not construct a consolidated income-product statement for the personal sector in the same way that it does for the business sector. In one respect this is somewhat unfortunate, for "households"[10] do employ owners of the factors of production (e.g., maids, yardmen, repairmen, etc.) who make a direct contribution to GNP. Actually the contribution made by these factor owners is measured by the wages and salaries paid to them because it is otherwise quite difficult to quantify the productive activities of these persons. However, no separate entry is made for this payment, and as a result there is no explicit statement of households' contribution to GNP. The procedure of the department in this respect is very simple—it merely assumes that household payments to factors are included in the wages and salaries payments made by the business sector. In other words, the statement of wage and salary payments in the business sector overstates the actual amount of these disbursements by the amount paid by households. This, however, is not a significant disadvantage because of the way in which the account for the personal sector is constructed.

The statement for the personal sector is labeled the "Personal Income and Outlay Account." As noted in Chapter 2, the personal owners of the factors of production receive payments for their services, and while these payments are income for them, they are costs to the employees. The *total* amount of the income received by the factor owners is personal income and, as shown in the bottom part of Table 3–6, amounted to $495.0 billion in 1964.

There are, however, several things to observe about the personal in-

---

[9]See the discussion in section 5.

[10]The department used to include many organizations in the "household" or personal sector. In its latest revision, however, it has narrowed the term "household" considerably. Still, some nonhousehold units, such as nonprofit, private educational institutions and voluntary associations (Red Cross), are included in this category.

TABLE 3–6

Personal Income and Outlay Account, United States, 1964
Current Prices

Item	Revised
1. Personal tax and nontax payments (III-10)	59.2
2. Personal outlays	409.5
3. Personal consumption expenditures (I-24)	398.9
4. Interest paid by consumers (II-15)	10.0
5. Personal transfer payments to foreigners (net) (IV-4)	.6
6. Personal saving (V-3)	26.3
PERSONAL TAXES, OUTLAYS, AND SAVING	495.0
7. Wage and salary disbursements (I-3)	333.5
8. Other labor income (I-7)	16.5
9. Proprietors' income (I–8)	51.1
10. Rental income of persons (I-9)	18.2
11. Dividends (I-14)	17.2
12. Personal interest income	34.3
13. Net interest (I-17)	15.2
14. Net interest paid by government (III-5)	9.1
15. Interest paid by consumers (II-4)	10.0
16. Transfer payments to persons	36.6
17. From business (I-19)	2.3
18. From government (III-3)	34.2
19. Less: Personal contributions for social insurance (III-15)	12.4
PERSONAL INCOME	495.0

come and outlay account and its relationship to the account of the business sector presented in Table 3–5. First, as already noted, the wage and salary payments made to persons by other households are included in the business sector account. Thus the statement of GNP originating in the business sector actually overstates businesses' contribution to GNP.

Second, note that the interest received by the personal sector is larger ($34.3 billion) than the interest paid by the business sector ($15.2 billion). The reason that the interest received in the personal sector is larger is because households receive interest income both from government and from other households. However, interest payments by government and households are transfer payments and are not included in GNP. Thus the only interest figure recorded in the business sector account ($15.2 billion) is the amount paid by business to households. In other words, the only contribution to GNP represented by interest payments is recorded in the businesses sector account as "Net Interest Paid" and in the personal sector account it is recorded as "Interest Received from Business."

Third, since business transfer payments constitute income for persons, they are included in the personal income and outlay account. However, they do not represent productive activity and hence are excluded from the national income at factor cost figure given in Table 3–5.

What now of the allocation of personal income (Y_p)? This is shown in the top part of the personal income and outlay account. Note that there are three major types of outlays—personal taxes (T_p), personal "outlay" (O_p), and personal savings (S_p). Thus,

$$Y_p = T_p + O_p + S_p,$$

where the subscript p stands for the personal sector. Further,

$$Y_p - T_p - O_p = S_p,$$

and

$$Y_p - T_p = Y_d - O_p = S_p,$$

where Y_d stands for disposable income.

Personal outlays (O_p), however, are not the same thing as the receipts from sales to consumers in the business sector account. The reason for this is that O_p includes household interest payments and transfer payments to foreigners. In 1964 these amounted to $10.0 billion and $0.6 billion, respectively. Once this $10.6 billion is deducted from O_p of $409.5 billion, the remainder is $398.9 billion of personal consumption expenditures (C). Thus, the personal consumption expenditures (C) equals the total receipts of sales to consumers by businesses (C) in the equation on page 74 and in Table 3–5.

3.   The Government Sector

As in the case of the personal sector, the consolidated statement of the government is not really an income-product statement. Rather it is referred to as the "Government Receipts and Expenditure Account," as shown in Table 3–7. Thus it must be kept in mind that the government's statement does not reveal government's contribution to GNP.

The receipts of the government in 1964 are shown in the bottom part of the account. There is little that needs to be said about the receipts side, except to note that the difference between the total re-

TABLE 3–7

Government Receipts and Expenditures Account, United States,
1964, Current Prices

Item	Revised
1. Purchase of goods and services (I-38)	128.4
2. Transfer payments	38.6
3. To persons (II-18)	36.4
4. To foreigners (net) (IV-3)	2.2
5. Net interest paid (II-14)	9.1
6. Subsidies less current surplus of government enterprises (I-21)	1.2
7. Surplus or deficit (—) on income and product account (V-8)	— 2.4
8. Federal	— 3.8
9. State and local	1.4
GOVERNMENT EXPENDITURES AND SURPLUS	172.7
10. Personal tax and nontax payments (II-1)	59.2
11. Corporate profits tax liability (I-12)	27.6
12. Indirect business tax and nontax liability (I-20)	58.0
13. Contributions for social insurance	27.8
14. Employer (I-6)	15.4
15. Personal (II-19)	12.4
GOVERNMENT RECEIPTS	172.7

ceipts (T) and expenditures (G_x) and government transfer payments (G_t), measures governmental saving (or dissaving). Thus,

$$T - G_x - G_t = S_g.$$

The S_g may, of course, be negative if government is operating with a deficit. For example, in 1964 T = \$172.7 billion, while G_x = \$136.5 billion, and G_t = \$38.6 billion. Thus S_g = —\$2.4 billion.

In practice, the only way to calculate government's contribution to total product is to measure wages and salaries paid to governmental employees. But note that, as in the case of the personal sector, it is assumed that these payments are made in the business sector. All other entries in the government account are already taken care of. The purchases of materials and services are considered as purchases of intermediate goods and thus are already accounted for in the business sector statement. Interest payments are also not included, primarily on the grounds that interest payments on the national debt in the United States are associated with war. All other entries are accounted for in the business sector and personal sector accounts. Thus, government transfer payments are taken care of in the personal sector account ($34.2 billion) and in the foreign account ($2.2 billion). Moreover, these payments are not counted in GNP and thus do not appear in Table 3–5. So far as the surplus or deficit of government enterprises is concerned, this is accounted for in the business sector account in Table 3–5.

4. The Foreign Account

The final account to be considered is the foreign account. The treatment given here is very brief for two reasons: first, the international sector is very small with respect to total United States economic activity; second, most of the subsequent discussion in Parts 2-5 is based on the simplifying assumption of a "closed economy," that is, international elements are abstracted from it.

The "Foreign Transactions Account" is given in Table 3–8. The major reason for having the account in the first place is that some wages and salaries, interest, and profits are received from abroad but still are counted as part of the current earnings of United States citizens. These are incorporated in exports figure on the left-hand side of the account.

By the same token, some incomes are paid by United States firms to persons and firms abroad, and these payments are counted in the imports figure on the right-hand side of the column. Also private citi-

TABLE 3—8

Foreign Transactions Account, United States, 1964, Current Prices

Item	Revised
1. Export of goods and services (I-36)	37.0
RECEIPTS FROM FOREIGNERS	37.0
2. Imports of goods and services (I-37)	28.5
3. Transfer payments from U. S. government to foreigners (net) (III-4)	2.2
4. Personal transfer payments to foreigners (net) (II-5)	.6
5. Net foreign investment (V-2)	5.8
PAYMENTS TO FOREIGNERS	37.0

zens and the United States government make transfer payments
abroad, and these must be accounted for. Table 3–8 gives the foreign
transactions account for 1964. Please note that the residual between the
two sides is labeled "Net Foreign Investment," and this figure may be
negative if transfer payments abroad and imports exceed the total exports.

5. Savings and Investment: Another Look at the Accounts

The preceding sections of this chapter have described the sources
of income and the uses of income for each sector. Of course, one important use of income is savings, that is, the portion of current income
in each sector that is not used directly to purchase goods and services.
In this section the relationship between total savings and investment
in the economy is considered.

Look first at the personal sector. The total income of the personal
sector is personal income (Y_p). But from this individuals and households have to pay direct taxes (T_p), and they make their personal outlays on goods and services, including interest payments and transfer
payments to foreigners (O_p). Any residual, of course, is personal savings
(S_p). Thus,

$$S_p = Y_p - T_p - O_p.$$

For 1964 these magnitudes were $26.3 billion = $495 billion — $59.2
billion — $409.5 billion.

In the government sector, savings (S_g) are calculated differently.
The total receipts of government are comprised of indirect business
taxes (T_i), direct personal taxes (T_p), business taxes (T_b) and social
security contributions (T_s). Thus,

$$T = T_i + T_p + T_b + T_s.$$

For 1964 T amounted to $172.7 billion. That is, T_i was $58.0 billion, T_p
was $59.2 billion, T_c was $27.6 billion, and T_s equaled $27.8 billion.

Government savings are easily determined by deducting government
expenditures (G_x) and government transfer payments (G_t) from government tax revenues (T). Thus,

$$S_g = T - G_x - G_t.$$

In 1964 G_x was $136.5 billion, G_t was $38.6 billion, and T was $172.7
billion. Therefore S_g was —$2.4 billion.

Finally, there is the business sector of the economy. In this case the total cost of doing business is deducted from the total sales revenue, leaving the profit residual (P). Then both corporate profits taxes (T_c) and dividends paid (D_v) must be deducted from profits in order to determine business savings (S_b). Accordingly,

$$S_b = P - T_c - D_v.$$

When viewing aggregate economic activity, however, this procedure underestimates the total savings of the business sector. Depreciation reserves (D) constitute an important source of funds for business enterprises, and thus they must be added on to the formula given above. Total business savings, therefore, are

$$S_b = P - T_c - D_v + D.$$

In 1964 the magnitudes to plug into this formula are as follows:

$75.7 billion = $64.8 billion — $27.6 billion — $17.2 billion
+ $55.7 billion.

However, two further adjustments must be made before the final figure of total savings can be obtained. First, account must be taken of the inventory valuation adjustment (that is, changes in the value of inventories due to changes in price levels), and second, the ever-present statistical discrepancy. In 1964 these amounted to —$0.3 billion and —$0.5 billion, respectively.

Total savings in the economy, therefore, in 1964 were:

$$S_p = \$26.3 \text{ billion}$$
$$S_g = -\$2.4 \text{ billion}$$
$$S_b = \$75.7 \text{ billion}$$
$$\overline{\$99.6 \text{ billion}}$$

Less:
Inventory valuation adjustment $0.3 billion
Statistical discrepancy $0.5 billion

$$S = \$98.7 \text{ billion}.$$

The question now arises: How were these savings used? And the ready answer is, they were used for investment purposes, that is, they were used to purchase plant and equipment, inventories, residential dwellings, and so on, by businesses and individuals. As will be seen, the relationship between savings and investment is of crucial importance in determining the course of aggregate economic activity. Thus the concept of investment must be examined in detail; this is the task of the next chapter.

6. Summary

In this chapter the sources of GNP originating in each major sector of the economy—business, household, government, and foreign—have been examined in some detail. The account for each major sector states its income and outlay, and the difference between income and outlay is savings (which may be negative). The total savings of the economy are then used for investment purposes, which are examined in the following chapter.

QUESTIONS

3-1. Why is the inventory valuation adjustment in the account of the business sector so important?

3-2. In Table 3–5 the income "originating" in the business sector is equal to the product "originating" in the same sector. What are the several adjustments that must be made in order to acquire this equality?

3-3. In Table 3–5 the figures given for the income and product originating in the business sector really overstate that sector's contribution to the economy. Why and by how much is it overstated?

3-4. The consolidated statements of both the personal sector and the government sector are not really income-product statements. Why is this so? What problems can you conceive of in attempting to construct reasonably accurate income-product statements for these two sectors?

3-5. Trace through the various entries that might logically appear in the government and household accounts but actually appear (in one form or another) in the consolidated statement of the business sector. Be sure to show how each entry appears in the business sector's account.

3-6. Calculate the personal, governmental, and business savings for any recent year (other than 1964). Be sure to explain the significance of the "inventory valuation adjustment" when calculating the total savings of the economy.

Bibliography

Barger, H., *Outlay and Income in the United States*. New York: National Bureau of Economic Research, 1942.

Jaszi, G., "The Conceptual Basis of the Accounts," in *A Critique of the the U. S. Income and Product Accounts*. Princeton: Princeton University Press, 1958.

Kuznets, S., *National Income, A Summary of Findings*. New York: National Bureau of Economic Research, 1946.

Morgenstern, O., *On the Accuracy of Economic Observations*. Princeton: Princeton University Press, 1965.

"The National Income and Product Accounts of the United States: Revised Estimates, 1929-64," *Survey of Current Business,* April 1965.

U. S. Income and Output, a supplement to the *Survey of Current Business.* Washington, D. C.: United States Department of Commerce, 1958.

4

Investment and Capital in a Dynamic Economy

Several references have been made in the preceding chapters to the important role that investment plays in the process of economic growth and in triggering cyclical fluctuations. At first glance, however, the importance assigned to investment appears to be somewhat exaggerated, for investment is the smallest component of both domestic gross national product and domestic net national product.[1] Yet, it is the most volatile of the three basic components of GNP and NNP—that is, consumption, investment, and government expenditures—and it is this volatility that makes investment so important in aggregate economic activity.

Because of the significant role played by investment in both the business cycle and economic growth, this particular economic variable warrants closer examination. The present chapter is concerned primarily with basic definitions and relationships which are fundamental to understanding the analytical models developed in Parts 2, 3, and 4, as well as for understanding the effectiveness and implications of the various economic policies discussed in Part 5.

---

[1] Refer back to Chapters 2-3 for a review of the magnitude and volatility of private domestic business investment. Note the use of the word domestic, above, means that the discussion abstracts from the international economy.

1. The Role of Investment

As already noted, nearly all cycle theories have stressed the investment variable as a key factor in cyclical disturbances. In fact, some have emphasized investment so much that they have tended to neglect other important variables, such as changes in expenditures on consumers' durables, changes in monetary conditions, fluctuations in governmental spending, changes in expectations, and so on. Nevertheless, investment is such an important key variable in all cyclical fluctuations that it must be analyzed further.

A. The Meaning of Investment

Quite a number of diverse items figure into the investment category. There are, for example, expenditures by businessmen on plant and equipment and inventories, residential construction expenditures, and governmental expenditures on such things as stockpiles, T.V.A., the Hoover Dam, school buildings, military barracks, highways, and so on. Moreover, it is conceivable, and in some cases useful, to include consumer spending on durable consumers' goods in the investment category,[2] and in recent years there has been some discussion of investment in "human capital" and investment in education.[3] Investment is, in fact, such a variety of things that there is need to simplify.

By investment is meant *expenditures by businessmen on plant, equipment, and inventories.* There is some merit and justification for placing such narrow restrictions on the term. In the first place, although there appears to be a building cycle, it is something different from the business cycle, and thus residential housing investment should be distinguished from investment as defined above. Obviously the determinants underlying investment in housing are substantially different from those that underly investment by businessmen in plant and equipment and inventories.

---

[2]See Chapter 10 for a discussion of aggregate consumer behavior.

[3]See, for example, T. W. Schultz, "Investment in Human Capital," *American Economic Review,* March 1961, "Capital Formation by Education," *Journal of Political Economy,* December 1960, and "Investment in Man: An Economist's View," *Social Service Review,* June 1959. See also J. Mincer, "Investment in Human Capital and Personal Distribution of Income," *Journal of Political Economy,* August 1958; and B. A. Weisbrod, "The Valuation of Human Capital," *Journal of Political Economy,* October 1961. For a critical treatment of man as capital, see H. G. Shaffer, "Investment in Human Capital: Comment," *American Economic Review,* December 1961 (but see also Schultz's reply in the same issue).

In the second place, the determinants of governmental investment are drastically different from the determinants of private business investment. Changing concepts of the general welfare and unstable international conditions determine in large part what governmental investment will be. Although governmental investment is examined in much detail later on (Chapters 24-25), especially as it might be used to mitigate cyclical fluctuations and to stimulate economic growth, for the moment only the behavior of the private business sector of the economy is being considered.

Finally, as far as investment in consumers' durables is concerned, this is best introduced as a complicating factor in the discussion of consumer behavior (Chapter 10). There are two reasons why it is not included at the moment. First, the determinants of investment by consumers are radically different from those that influence businessmen (with the possible exception of the interest rate); and second, thus far adequate data on this type of investment are lacking. Similar observations point toward excluding investment in "human capital" from the present discussion.

Another distinction between uses of the word investment is necessary. In what follows, the word investment is used to mean the expenditures by businessmen on plant, equipment, and inventories; *it does not mean financial investment* by individuals or groups in such things as insurance policies, stocks, bonds, government securities, or any other asset representing ownership or debt. *Economic (or real) investment means capital formation,* that is, contributions to the economy's total stock of real capital (plants, machines, and inventories), whereas financial investment means the transfer of claims of real assets—stocks, bonds, annuities, and so on. The difference is fundamental, and unless otherwise noted the word investment is reserved to mean economic or real investment. Even within these rather narrow restrictions, investment is still something of a hodgepodge category; included in it are store buildings, steel plants, trucks, retail inventories, openhearth furnaces, lathes, and so on. There is, as might be expected a problem in measuring this conglomeration of items, and although no completely satisfactory method has yet been devised, it can be measured in terms of dollars. More specifically, capital is measured in terms of the dollar value of the real assets that enter into the classification. These dollar values are based either on the adjusted historical cost of the capital goods, the estimated replacement costs, or the estimated capitalized earning power they possess. And, of course, depreciation must be deducted in the calculation.

However, no matter which of these bases is used, the data on the capital stock and changes in the stock are nothing more than educated

TABLE 4–1

Increase in Net Capital Stock, United States,
by Decades, 1869-1955 (in 1929 prices)

| Year | Net Capital Stock* | | |
	Total (Billion Dollars)	Increase from Decade to Decade	Per Member of Labor Force ($ Thousands)
1869	27	—	2.11
1879	42	15	2.49
1889	68	26	3.06
1899	108	40	3.79
1909	165	57	4.41
1919	227	62	5.46
1929	306	79	6.33
1939	319	13	6.04
1949	374	55	6.45
1955†	442	68	6.74

* Net after deduction of capital consumption.
† The last figure is for 1949-1955.
Source: S. Kuznets, *Capital in the American Economy: Its Formation and Financing* (Princeton: Princeton University Press, 1961), Table 3.

guesses. But as long as the data can be carried far enough back so that the initial capital stock is small relative to the size of the present stock, and as long as the same measurement is used consistently, the estimates should not be too far off. For present purposes, the capital stock is defined and measured as follows: The capital stock is an accumulation of investment in capital goods (as defined above) over successive periods. The *net* addition to the capital stock from one period to the next (net capital formation) is valued at the cost of acquisition (for the buyer) of the new capital goods acquired. This dollar measure is corrected for price changes, so that the capital items are evaluated in terms of the prices of the same base year.[4]

The data in Table 4-1 reveal how the capital stock has increased in the United States over a rather considerable time period. A word of

[4]See W. J. Fellner, *Trends and Cycles in Economic Activity* (New York: Holt, Rinehart & Winston, Inc., 1956), pp. 196-99, for elaboration of this definition. Fellner, after pointing out the inadequacies of measurement, goes on to say:

In all cases we must require that the general results of the statistical computations should accord with intelligent judgment or common observation. . . . In the present case we may derive quite a bit of consolation from the fact that the general conclusions to which the capital stock estimates lead are in harmony with intelligent informal judgment (*Ibid.*, p. 197).

See also Vernon L. Smith, "The Measurement of Capital," in *Measuring the Nation's Wealth.*

caution, however. As pointed out in the preceding paragraph, measurement of the capital stock is tricky and can often yield misleading results. In his recent study, B. G. Hickman has presented estimates of the stock of capital calculated by several different methods. The results are shown in Table 4–2. The important thing to note is the significant influence that the method of depreciation used has on the final outcome. About the only sure thing that can be said is that any measurement must be net of depreciation; but as Hickman's study reveals, the method of netting depreciation out can be very important. However, each of the estimates presented in Table 4–2 reveals the impor-

TABLE 4—2

Six Estimates of the Capital Stock, as Estimated by
the Department of Commerce, 1948-1961
(in Billions of 1954 Dollars)

Year	I	II	III	IV	V	VI
1948	444.4	371.0	235.0	191.4	189.9	154.2
1949	459.2	386.5	246.3	200.6	199.6	161.7
1950	476.8	402.3	258.8	210.9	210.4	170.2
1951	498.6	417.6	272.2	221.8	222.0	179.5
1952	517.6	434.7	283.9	231.2	231.9	187.2
1953	536.6	452.4	296.2	241.2	241.9	195.4
1954	555.1	467.5	306.2	249.0	249.3	201.1
1955	581.4	483.6	318.5	259.2	258.8	209.2
1956	609.7	498.3	331.9	270.7	269.9	218.7
1957	635.5	508.9	343.9	280.7	280.1	227.2
1958	650.2	511.3	348.1	283.2	283.3	228.7
1959	662.8	516.6	353.4	287.1	288.1	232.1
1960	672.0	524.2	360.6	293.0	295.1	237.7
1961	678.8	532.1	366.4	297.4	300.7	241.9

Notes on variants:
  I.   Gross stock, useful lines according to *Bulletin F* of the U. S. Treasury Department.
  II. Gross stock, useful lines 20 per cent shorter than in *Bulletin F*.
  III. Net stock, straight-line depreciation, *Bulletin F lines*.
  IV. Net stock, double-rate, declining-balance depreciation, *Bulletin F*.
  V.   Net stock, straight-line depreciation, lines 20 per cent shorter than *Bulletin F*.
  VI. Net stock, double-rate declining-balance depreciation, lines 20 per cent shorter than *Bulletin F*.
  Source: B. G. Hickman, *Investment Demand and U. S. Economic Growth* (Washington, D. C.: The Brookings Institution, 1965), p. 208.

tant fact that the stock of capital in the United States has continued to rise.[5]

B.   Gross, Net, and Replacement Investment

The division of private investment that was made earlier—that is, between the two components of plant and equipment, on the one hand, and inventories, on the other—is quite important. While both are extremely volatile, inventory investment changes far more often and quickly than investment in plant and equipment. *However, it is investment in plant and equipment that turns out to be so crucial in major cyclical fluctuations.* Thus more time and attention must be devoted to this key variable.[6]

In the first place it is essential to differentiate between *gross* (or *total*) investment and its two components of *replacement* and *net* investment. At any point in time, as already noted, the economy has so much capital equipment, which is used to create an output of goods and services (GNP). Generally several dollars of capital are required to produce one dollar's worth of output per time period. But as this capital *stock* is used to produce a *flow* of output, part of it is depreciated, that is, worn out. In all likelihood, part or all of the capital that is consumed in the production process will be replaced, and the investment that is devoted to this purpose is called *replacement investment.*

Note that replacement investment does not add anything to the size of the total capital stock; rather this type of investment simply replaces that portion of the stock that was used up in the production process. As long as replacement investment is equal to the capital consumption, and assuming no net, new investment, it simply maintains the size of the capital stock. At times, however, replacement investment has been insufficient to replace completely the capital consumed in the prior period, such as during certain years of the 1930's. This is most apt to occur during a severe contractionary period when businessmen are reluctant to replace completely the plant and equipment that has worn out.

---

[5]The rate at which the capital stock is increasing is also quite important, as is shown in all of the theories reviewed in Part 4. Hickman's study is very important in this respect, and should be consulted by anyone interested in recent growth-cycle developments.

[6]Recall, however, the warning given earlier that there are many other important variables, and that to neglect them is dangerous. The present discussion of investment, therefore, should be considered only as a means of emphasizing this one important variable, but not to the exclusion of others. The role of inventory investment in cyclical fluctuations is considered in section 3-B below.

Gross, or total, investment is merely the sum of the replacement and net investment. Of course, the size of the capital stock can increase only if there is net investment. At times, however, there may be net, new investment in some industries, but not enough replacement investment in other industries to replace the capital consumed in them. If the net plus replacement investment is less than the capital consumption, the size of the capital stock will diminish. But the essential point remains— there must be net investment if the stock of capital is to expand, for replacement investment at best can only maintain the existing size of the capital stock.

This expansion of the capital stock has, of course, been a very important factor in the overall growth of the economy.[7] At the same time, it has introduced new elements into the cyclical process and perhaps into the very process of growth itself. Recall the discussion in Chapter 1 that the pattern and rate of economic growth may often result in institutional and behavorial changes that in turn influence the growth process. Here is an excellent example of this interactive process, for the growth of the capital stock has increased the relative significance of replacement investment. This and other repercussions are discussed in the next section.

2.   Some Recent Developments

As the size of capital stock has expanded over time, so also has the economic significance of replacement investment. This was mentioned earlier in Chapter 2, but it is revealed quite clearly in Table 4–3. Note that as a percentage of GNP, replacement investment has increased substantially, and net investment has dwindled significantly. The same results are obtained when net national product is substituted for GNP. Actually, the decline in net capital formation has been rather large, falling from about 14 per cent in the decade of the 1870's to about 5 per cent in the period from 1946 to 1955. Equally striking is the behavior of replacement investment, which in recent years accounts for about two-thirds of gross investment. In fact, this development introduces an important new dimension into the business cycle, for now

---

[7]Other elements of course have also played an important role in the economic growth of the United States. Among these are population expansion, technological advance, and so on. These are examined at various stages later on, particularly in Chapter 7 and Part 4.

TABLE 4—3

Percentage Shares of Capital Formation in National Product,
by Decades, 1869-1955

Decades	Per Cent of Gross National Product		
	Capital Consumption	Net Capital Formation	Gross Capital Formation
1869-1878	9.5	13.9	23.4
1879-1888	9.8	13.1	22.9
1889-1898	12.1	14.0	26.0
1899-1908	11.3	12.9	24.2
1909-1918	12.3	11.2	23.4
1919-1928	12.3	9.9	22.3
1929-1938	13.0	1.8	14.8
1939-1948	14.2	6.1	20.3
1946-1955	15.5	4.9	20.4

Source: Kuznets, *Capital in the American Economy*, Table 8.

there is the possibility of rather wide fluctuations in replacement expenditures by businesses.[8] No doubt these fluctuations aggravate the business cycle, but they may also come to play a rather important causal role at the upper-turning point.

During a contraction, businesses are apt to hold back on replacement investment since there is a good deal of uncertainty as to future profit prospects. They tend to defer replacement expenditures also because of the desire to hold on to financial funds as a means of weathering the "bad times." However, once the lower-turning point occurs and the expansion begins, these businesses become more prone to carry out the postponed replacement investment. In fact, as the expansion continues, replacement investment expenditures become larger and larger and could well become quantitatively more important than net, new investment. However, the replacement investment eventually peters out, and thus there is a tendency for gross investment to decline. If net investment is not strong enough to compensate for the drop in replacement investment, this is exactly what will take place. The consequence,

[8]S. Kuznets, "Long-Term Changes in the National Product of the United States of America Since 1870," in *Income and Wealth of the United States: Trends and Structure*, ed. S. Kuznets, Income and Wealth Series II (Cambridge, England: Bowles & Bowles, 1952). See also R. A. Gordon, "Investment Opportunities in the United States," in *The Business Cycle in the Postwar World*, ed. E. Lundberg (London: The Macmillan Company, 1955) for an extended discussion of many of these points.

as will be seen, could well be the emergence of the upper-turning point, although certainly many other factors would be at play also. Nevertheless, replacement investment appears to be acquiring more and more significance in cyclical fluctuations in the United States.[9]

Another development that should be pointed out is that there can be continued growth in the total output of the economy without there being any net, new investment. This again is associated with the growing importance of replacement investment. To be sure, replacement investment simply replaces *quantitatively* the capital that has been worn out in the production process. But there is also the *qualitative* aspect that must be considered, especially in light of dynamic technological changes. The result is that when a business replaces a worn-out machine or a depreciated plant, it does not replace them with identical machines or buildings. The new assets that replace the old contain the fruits of technological advance, and no doubt they will be more efficient than the items that have been fully depreciated. Thus even though the capital stock may be constant, it can produce more units of output per unit of input than before. As Kuznets has observed, replacement investment currently signifies additions to the productive capacity of the economy.

These recent developments in the qualitative, as well as in the quantitative, dimensions of private business investment are very important. Their significance and implications cannot be pursued at this juncture, although they will be developed in later chapters.

3.   Investment in the Business Cycle

According to the National Bureau's method of measuring the business cycle,[10] the United States has experienced a considerable number of cyclical fluctuations (see Table 4–4). Some of these have been as short as thirty-some months, while others have been as long as seventy and eighty months. In fact, according to Table 4–4, the shortest cycle was that of 1920-1921 (although this was a rather severe fluctuation), and the longest cycles were those of 1873-1879 and 1929-1937. Obvi-

---

[9]On this, see Gordon in *The Business Cycle in the Postwar World,* and B. C. Hickman, *Growth and Stability of the Postwar Economy* (Washington, D. C.: The Brookings Institution, 1960), Chapter 11.

[10]See Chapter 1 for a review of the National Bureau's technique of measuring the cycle.

TABLE 4-4

National Bureau Chronology of Business
Cycles, United States, 1854-1958

Trough	Peak	Trough	Duration in Months
Dec. 1854	Jun. 1857	Dec. 1858	48
Dec. 1858	Oct. 1860	Jun. 1861	30
June 1861	Apr. 1865	Dec. 1867	78
Dec. 1867	Jun. 1869	Dec. 1870	36
Dec. 1870	Oct. 1873	Mar. 1879	99
Mar. 1879	Mar. 1882	May 1885	74
May 1885	Mar. 1887	Apr. 1888	35
Apr. 1888	Jul. 1890	May 1891	37
May 1891	Jan. 1893	Jun. 1894	37
Jun. 1894	Dec. 1895	Jun. 1897	36
Jun. 1897	Jun. 1899	Dec. 1900	42
Dec. 1900	Sep. 1902	Aug. 1904	44
Aug. 1904	May 1907	Jun. 1908	46
Jun. 1908	Jan. 1910	Jan. 1912	43
Jan. 1912	Jan. 1913	Dec. 1914	35
Dec. 1914	Aug. 1918	Apr. 1919	52
Apr. 1919	Jan. 1920	Jul. 1921	27
Jul. 1921	May 1923	Jul. 1924	36
Jul. 1924	Oct. 1926	Nov. 1927	40
Nov. 1927	Aug. 1929	Mar. 1933	64
Mar. 1933	May 1937	Jun. 1938	63
Jun. 1938	Feb. 1945	Oct. 1945	88
Oct. 1945	Nov. 1948	Oct. 1949	48
Oct. 1949	Jul. 1953	Aug. 1954	58
Aug. 1954	Jul. 1957	Apr. 1958	44
Apr. 1958 Feb. 1961	May 1960	Feb. 1961	34

Source: A. F. Burns and W. C. Mitchell, *Measuring Business Cycles* (New York: National Bureau of Economic Research, 1946), pp. 78–79; G. H. Moore, *Business Cycle Indicators* (Princeton: Princeton University Press, 1961), p. 671.

ously cycles differ considerably in length, and this has led to the distinction between major (longer) and minor (shorter) cycles.[11]

---

[11]This distinction is stressed by A. H. Hansen, *Business Cycles and National Income* (New York: W. W. Norton & Company, Inc., 1964), Chapter 2, and by R. A. Gordon, "Investment Behavior and Business Cycles," *Review of Economics and Statistics*, February 1955. See also Gordon's *Business Fluctuations* (New York: Harper & Row Publishers, 1961), pp. 252, 261-63.

TABLE 4—5

Chronology of Major Cycles, United States,
1865 to Present

Lower-Turning Point	Upper-Turning Point	Lower-Turning Point
1865	1872-73	1876
1876	1882	1885
1885	1892	1896
1896	1907	1908
1908	1913	1921
1921	1929	1932
1932	1937	1938

Source: A. H. Hansen, *Business Cycles and National Income* (New York: W. W. Norton & Company, Inc., 1964), p. 24.

A. The Major Cycle

Generally the longer cycles have had a life of from six to eleven years, while the shorter ones have varied in length from two to four years. Alvin H. Hansen lists seven major cycles from the Civil War to the present.[12] These are shown in Table 4–5.

However, much more than duration is involved in this distinction between major and minor cycles. Another important criterion relates to the behavior of investment during the cyclical process. The important thing about the major cycles is that they have all been associated with rather significant changes in expenditures by businessmen on *plant and equipment.* To be sure, changes in inventory investment also take place during the major cycle, but these are swamped by the changes in plant and equipment expenditures. The statistical evidence shows rather clearly that changes in plant and equipment investment nearly always accompany changes in the level of general business activity. And recall from Chapter 2, section 9, that business orders for plant and equipment generally lead the turning points of the cycle by a few months.

A sketch of the behavior of this type of investment during the course of the major cycle will prove helpful. Assume that, for some reason or other, the expansionary stage of the cycle has gotten underway. As the expansion continues businessmen find themselves facing a situation where they either voluntarily or involuntarily have to cut back on their investment expenditures for plant and equipment. They may cut back

---

[12]*Business Cycles and National Income,* Chapter 2.

for a number of reasons—for instance, their replacement demands have been met, or they become pessimistic and reduce their net, new investment, or the cost of raising capital funds has risen substantially, and so on. In any event, investment spending will decline, and once this happens the upper-turning point occurs and the contraction follows. This is the reason that the majority of economists argue that the investment variable is particularly important in accounting for and explaining the major cycle.

Once the contraction gets underway it may be quite protracted if the business community feels that there is excess capacity due to the "over-investment" in the preceding expansion. Thus pessimism will become deepened, particularly if nothing occurs to stimulate the total demand for the output of the economy. Moreover, replacement demand will be deferred, at least to some extent, and hence total investment spending may decline even more. In fact, the contraction continues until something occurs to bring about an increase in the total amount of investment spending on plant and equipment. This could happen for a number of reasons. Perhaps new technological advances will stimulate innovations. Perhaps the investment activity of young growth industries will become stronger. Or perhaps there is a spurt of replacement investment which managers feel can no longer be deferred. However, once there is an increase in plant and equipment investment spending, the lower-turning occurs and the expansion gets underway. The expansion will continue as long as investment opportunities are strong and buoyant, and it will become intensified by the rising replacement demand that had been deferred during the contraction. However, replacement investment will finally begin to dwindle, and other forces also will develop and tend to reduce total investment expenditures on plant and equipment. As a result the upper-turning point and the ensuing contraction take place. And so the major cycle runs its course.

It must be repeated that this survey is extremely skeletal—many complications have been ignored. Changes in price levels, monetary conditions, consumer behavior, wage levels, costs of production, expectations by businessmen (whether well founded or not)—all of these and many other variables are important in any one particular cyclical disturbance. The major purpose of this discussion is simply to stress that changes in investment spending on plant and equipment turn out to be the primary factor in major cycles; thus the important problem is to determine what are the causes of changes in this type of investment activity. There are, however, certain qualifications to the major cycle-minor cycle distinction that will be considered below.

TABLE 4—6

Chronology of Minor Cycles, United States,
1865 to Present

Peak Year	
Minor Setbacks	Minor Recoveries
1869	
1887	
1890	
	1895
1899	
1902	
1910	
1913	
1923	
1926	
1948	
1953	
1957	
1960	

Source: Hansen, *Business Cycles and National Income*, Chapter 2.

B.   The Minor Cycle

Note that there have been few uninterrupted major cycles. Nearly always they have been characterized by temporary setbacks during the expansionary stage. Thus in the major cycle of 1921-1932 (measured from trough to trough) the expansionary stage was interrupted twice— in 1923 and 1926—by minor setbacks. These are referred to as minor cycles.

All told, in the period from the Civil War to the present, there have been fourteen minor cycles. These are listed in Table 4-6. In the period from the Civil War to the present, only two of the major cycles escaped without at least one minor cycle. All the rest were characterized by one to three minor recessions during the expansion, and only one contraction (during the major cycle of 1885-1896) was halted briefly by a minor recovery.[13]

What is the key variable in the minor cycle? Although every minor cycle surely has more than one factor responsible for it, the one variable that seems to stand out as being the most important is inventory

---

[13]See *Business Cycles and National Income* for a further discussion of the minor cycles.

investment.[14] As the expansion continues, businessmen begin to feel, after some point is reached, that perhaps they have produced too much and will be caught with excessive inventories. Thus they cut back on their orders and attempt to work down their existing stocks. This of course results in a decline in production and some increase in unemployment.

However, if the expansionary forces of the major cycle are strong enough, and this will be the case if investment opportunities have not diminished, the doubts and fears of the businessmen will be overcome. Investment in plant and equipment reverses the minor setback, and the major expansion continues. This seems to be the general explanation of minor (or inventory) recessions, which prove to be only a faltering step in the upward pace of the economy at large.

Changes in inventory investment, however, are not the sole responsible factor in minor cycles. Other elements figure in. For instance, changes in the financial market, as well as changes in particular industries and in consumer tastes, may be responsible for minor reversals. Nevertheless, it seems that changes in inventory investment stand out as the most important variable in these mild contractions and revivals.

C. Some Qualifications

There are two or three further points on the major-minor distinction that are relevant. Some economists have accepted the position that the business cycle in the post-World War II period differs significantly from the prewar cycle. This argument, indeed, concludes that the major-minor distinction is no longer relevant to the postwar period and that there is no need to worry about the major cycle. The adherents of this thesis point to the "minor recessions" of 1948-1949, 1953-1954, 1957-1958, and 1960-1961 as evidence supporting their position.

There is little doubt that the postwar cycles have been relatively short in length. But until a longer time period has elapsed, it is much too premature to lay the major cycle to rest.[15] The continued heavy

---

[14]There is a major qualification to be made. The post World War II cycles have been relatively short, but also some of them have been caused primarily by changes in plant and equipment investment. Thus it is necessary to think in terms of a third category, a "hybrid" cycle, that is made up of elements of both major and minor cycles. The "hybrid" cycles are discussed below.

[15]See especially A. Achinstein, "The Money Economy and Business Contractions," and B. G. Hickman, "Postwar Cyclical Experience and Economic Stability," both in *American Economic Review*, May 1958.

expenditures by government for defense, along with the operations of certain governmental policies that are "built into" the economy have served to reduce the length and amplitude of the postwar cycles. However, more than a quarter of a century of experience is needed in order to take a definite stand on this issue, particularly since that quarter of a century has been so heavily dominated by continued military expenditures. In the absence of high and growing governmental expenditures, any one of the so-called minor cycles in the postwar period could well have turned into a major cycle.

In any event, knowledge of the major cycle is essential in order to combat it as effectively as possible by means of governmental policies. In fact, this is the important reason for making the major-minor distinction in the first place. The causal forces underlying each type of cycle are quite different, and thus the policies used to combat each must be different. Any attempt to control a major contraction by means of policies designed to control a minor reversal is bound to be punitive. On the other hand, attempts to control a minor reversal by policies designed to combat a major contraction may well lead to quite undesirable results. Because of these implications for economic policy, the major-minor distinction will be followed in this book.

Still there are some economists who argue that the distinction is not very useful.[16] Their thesis is that all cyclical fluctuations should be called simply business cycles, and they go on to point out that those who use the major-minor dichotomy must often refer to certain cycles as "hybrids" of major and minor forces.[17] Be that as it may, it is misleading and erroneous to place phenomena like the 1948-1949 and 1953-1954 contractions in the same category as the Great Depression of the 1930's. Cycles *are* different, primarily because different causal forces are at play in different environmental settings. To lump them all together in the same pot is to ignore these changing forces and environments.

But it still remains true that some cycles appear to be "hybrids." This is particularly true of the 1957-1958 and 1960-1961 contractions, when sharp changes in private business investment spending were so very important. However, those who reject the major-minor distinction

---

[16]R. C. O. Matthews in his *The Business Cycle* (Chicago: University of Chicago Press, 1959) p. 212, has rejected the distinction between major and minor cycles, arguing that only the building cycle and the minor cycle should be considered. Fellner, in his *Trends and Cycles in Economic Activity* also rejects the dichotomy; yet he ends up distinguishing between less and more severe cycles.

[17]Gordon, in his "Investment Behavior and Business Cycles," uses this terminology.

and claim that it is best to think only in terms of *the* business cycle end up by admitting ". . . that some of the contractions . . . were generally regarded as minor *recessions* while others were typically recorded as major *depressions.* . . ."[18]

About all that the controversy boils down to is this: some contractions are far more serious than others, some are less serious, and a few seem to contain many of the basic characteristics of both the more and the less serious. But the mere fact that there are "hybrids" does not vitiate the usefulness of the distinction between major and minor cycles, especially for analytical and policy purposes. These two categories can be used productively in constructing theories of the business cycle and in discussing policy measures. And surely the fact must be kept in mind that each cycle is a unique historical episode and thus must be examined on its own grounds. In this respect, then, there are certain cyclical disturbances—the so-called "hybrids"—that call for special analytical effort.

4. The Capital-Output Ratio

Thus far this chapter has been concerned with definitions of investment, capital stock, and major and minor cycles. One important point that has been made is that spurts in investment in plant and equipment are associated with major cyclical fluctuations. Also, as noted above, this investment has added to the size of the capital stock, so that from 1869 to 1955 the net capital stock in the United States grew from $27 billion to $442 billion.[19] During the same time period, of course, both gross and net national product grew substantially. Now the important question is this: What has happened to the relationship between the net capital stock and net national product? The answer to this question is provided by tracing out the behavior of one of the most important ratios in aggregative analysis—the *capital-output ratio.*[20]

In the aggregate several dollars of capital formation are required to produce an increment to the flow of output. Assume, for sake of

[18]Fellner, *Trends and Cycles in Economic Activity,* pp. 41-42.

[19]These figures are taken from S. Kuznets, *Capital in the American Economy: Its Formation and Financing,* p. 65, and refer to the capital stock net of capital consumption. For more recent estimates, see Hickman, *Investment Demand and U. S. Economic Growth,* especially Appendices A and B.

[20]L. R. Klein has referred to the capital-output ratio as one of the five "great ratios" in economic analysis. See his *An Introduction to Econometrics* (Englewood Cliffs, N. J.: Prentice-Hall, Inc., 1962), Chapter 5.

TABLE 4–7

Capital-Output Ratio, 1869-1955, 1929 Prices*

Year	Net Capital-Output Ratio†
1869	—
1879	3.5
1889	2.9
1899	3.4
1909	3.4
1919	3.6
1929	3.5
1939	3.9
1946	2.5
1955	2.5

* The capital stock figure is net of capital consumption; see Table 4–2.
† Ratio of net capital stock to net national product. The net national product figure is based on Department of Commerce data. Kuznets presents an alternative measure.
Source: Kuznets, *Capital in the American Economy*, Table 6.

illustration, that every $1 of additional output *per year* requires a $3 addition to the capital stock. In this case, then, the capital-output ratio is 3 to 1. As will be seen later, especially in Chapters 16-19, the capital-output ratio plays a significant role in modern growth-cycle theories. Accordingly, this concept must be examined in some detail, particularly with respect to the behavior of the ratio over the long run and more importantly in the post-World War II period.

Data on the (net) capital-output ratio are given in Table 4–7. Note that for quite some time, in fact up to the late 1920's, the ratio rose, after which it began to decline (omitting the distorting decade of the 1930's). More recent estimates show that the ratio has continued declining in the postwar period. Thus it now takes fewer dollars, on the average, to produce an extra dollar's worth of goods and services than it took earlier. Why is this so? Why has the capital-output ratio fallen in the last few decades? And of what economic significance is this decline?

Consider first why the ratio rose until the latter part of the 1920's. When the economy began to industrialize, large amounts of investment in both the private and the public sectors of the economy were required. The heavy investment in such industries as the railroad, textile, and chemical industries, along with "social overhead" investment by government in roads, harbors, bridges, and so on, tended to increase the capital stock faster than total output. The reason for this was that the expansionary impact of the spurts of investment on output was spread over a number of years, so that output began to increase rapidly only after a rather long lag. In discussing "technological and related social inventions," Kuznets has this to say:

> The technological innovations are perhaps the most important and, certainly, the most conspicuous. If a small machine costing $100,000 can, because of a new invention, be replaced by one costing $1 million, with somewhat larger capacity but much longer life and much lower cost per unit of product, the replacement will be made. However, unless output can be immediately increased tenfold (which is rarely the case), the capital-output ratio will rise, and may remain at a higher level for a long time. Much of modern technical change inherently involves larger volumes of power, more costly construction materials, and more elaborate functions (mechanical or chemical). Thus, it requires more plant and machinery of ever increasing size, and the rise in the volume of capital thus tied up exceeds, for a long period, the possible rise in the volume of output.[21]

This appears to have been the situation generally in the American economy up to the 1920's—that is, the rise in the capital stock exceeded the rise in output for quite some time. However, after a certain point was reached (sometime during the latter twenties), stimulants came into play to start reducing the capital output ratio. Perhaps the most important of these is the desire by businessmen to reduce costs and to increase profits. Thus economic incentives themselves tend to lower the capital-output ratio as businessmen look for ways and means to lower their costs. In their view, a capital-output ratio of 2 to 1 is preferable to a ratio of 3 to 1, for it ties up only $2 of capital investment per $1 flow of output. Further, improvements in technology and divsion of labor may be oriented towards reducing the ratio.

Presumably, in the American economy, the ratio-reducing forces began, in the aggregate, to outweigh the ratio-rising forces after the 1920's. And this trend has been reinforced by the relative rise in the importance of replacement investment, since replacement capital may have incorporated into it technical improvements that tend to lower the capital-output ratio.

This is not the place to examine the causes of the decline in the capital-output ratio. However, a good deal of subsequent discussion, especially in Chapters 17-18, will be devoted to this issue.

---

[21]S. Kuznets, "Introduction," in D. Creamer, S. P. Dobrovolsky, and I. Borenstein, *Capital in Manufacturing and Mining: Its Formation and Financing* (Princeton: Princeton University Press, 1960), pp. xxv-xxxvi.

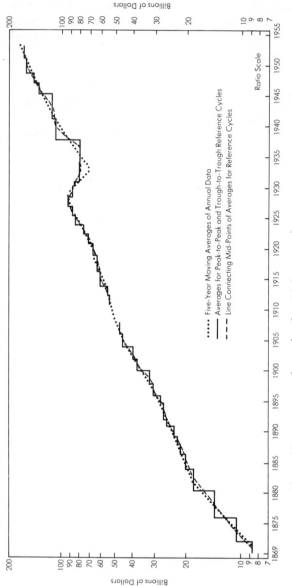

NOTE: No entries are shown for the 1907-1910 and 1908-1911 reference cycles because of the difference in procedure underlying the estimates for 1908 and preceding years and that underlying the estimates for 1909 and following years.

Source: Kuznets, *Capital in the American Economy*, p. 51.

FIGURE 4–1

Averages for Successive Peak-to-Peak and Trough-to-Trough Reference Cycles and Five-Year Moving Averages of Annual Data, Gross National Product, 1929 Prices, 1869-1955

5. Long Waves in Economic Activity

There is one final observation about economic growth that needs to be made. To be sure, the American economy has experienced substantial growth, and to be sure, this growth has been characterized by cyclical disturbances. However, if the total output data are subjected to a five-year or ten-year moving average, so that the influence of the business cycle is removed, a rather clear pattern in the growth rate of output is revealed. This is shown in Figure 4–1. Note that the data deal with *changes in the rate of growth* of output, not with absolute magnitudes.[22]

An examination of the data yields certain important conclusions. First, there have been certain periods of rapid growth in national income (product), followed by periods of retarded growth. These swings in the growth rate have averaged around twenty years in length. Second, the periods of rapid and retarded growth stand out rather clearly. The periods of rapid expansion were from about the middle of the 1870's to around 1907, from around 1915 to about the late 1920's, and finally from the late 1930's to around 1948. The periods of retarded growth were from 1882 to 1895, from 1907 to about 1915, from the late 1920's to the latter part of the 1930's, and possibly from 1948 on.

The long waves seem to be determined by underlying long waves in changes in the rate of growth of resources, particularly labor and capital, changes in the rate of productivity, and changes in the intensity of resource use.[23] This is not the place to examine these long waves. Nor is it the place to examine another important observation—namely the fact that the rates of change in output have become smaller over time. Does this mean that the overall rate of economic growth of the United States is petering out? Can the historical growth rate be maintained in the future? Or are the smaller rates of change an intrinsic part of the growth process itself? These questions are dealt with at length in the chapters of Parts 4 and 5.

One final observation. Numerous empirical studies show quite conclusively that there has been a long cycle in residential construction for quite some time. The pattern and chronology of this long cycle are quite different from the major cycle, although they do follow the long waves in total output rather closely. More recent studies indicate

---

[22]See M. Abramovitz, *Evidences of Long Swings in Aggregate Construction Since the Civil War* for a discussion of this.

[23]*Ibid.*, Chapter 1.

TABLE 4–8

Chronology of the Long Cycle in Aggregate Construction Activity,
United States, 1874 to Present

Peak	Trough	Peak
	1874	1889
1889	1893	1900
1900	1913	1921
1921	1930	1938
1938	1943	1948

Source: M. Abramovitz, *Evidences of Long Swings in Aggregate Construction Since the Civil War* (New York: National Bureau of Economic Research, 1964), p. 101.

strongly that there is also a long cycle in *aggregate construction* activity, not just simply in residential construction, and that this too follows the long waves closely. This is shown in Table 4–8. As Abramovitz, who has done so much constructive research in this area, has put it:

> Since the Civil War, the weight of the evidence suggests that there has indeed been a series of long swings in aggregate construction activity and in the construction work of all the important sectors, not in residential ad railroad construction alone. These waves generally had durations of between fifteen and twenty-five years.[24]

Abramovitz's major conclusion is that the construction cycle reflects changes in the rate of growth of resources, in the rate of change of productivity, and in the intensity of resource use, that is, the same major determinants underlying the long waves in total output.

There is some doubt as to the presence of the long cycle in building activity in recent years, particularly since World War II. There have indeed been changes in the level of construction activity, but they have not followed the rather clear-cut pattern of the prewar cycle. No doubt one of the major reasons for this changed picture has been the increased governmental activity in the housing market. In recent years the federal government has engaged in slum clearance and similar projects, and it has also intervened significantly in the financial markets relating to construction. It may well be that this intervention has tended to mitigate at least the cycle of residential construction, although available evidence does not warrant a final position on this matter.

---

[24]*Ibid.*, p. 7.

6. Summary

In this chapter the meaning of investment, in the economic sense of the term, has been examined in some detail. Moreover, the distinctions between net, gross, and replacement investment were stressed, and it was pointed out that the stock of capital in the economy can grow and expand only if there is net investment. Finally, a distinction was made between investment in plant and equipment, on the one hand, and investment in inventories, on the other.

Certain recent developments pertaining to the structure and composition of the capital stock were also considered. Three of these are very important in aggregate economic activity in an economy that already has a substantial stock of capital. First, replacement investment is growing as a percentage of gross investment, setting up the possibility of there being replacement cycles. Second, when depreciated capital is replaced, the replacement investment may contain the fruits of technological advance, and therefore even if there is no net investment, output per unit of capital input may rise. Third, the behavior of the capital-output ratio is very important. This ratio rose steadily up to the 1920's, after which it has declined. The behavior of this ratio is very important in aggregate economic activity in an economy that

A substantial portion of the chapter was devoted to the distinction between the major business cycle and the minor business cycle. The former is largely attributable to changes in net investment in plant and equipment and has a longer average life than the minor cycle, which is usually due to changes in inventory investment. The distinction is important, although it must be qualified for the post-World War II period, during which some cycles appear to be "hybrids."

QUESTIONS

4-1. Define what is meant by economic investment. How is economic investment different from financial investment?

4-2. Net investment means the same thing as net capital formation. Comment.

4-3. Differentiate clearly between gross investment, net investment, replacement investment, inventory investment, and investment in plant and equipment.

4-4. It is possible for gross investment to equal only replacement investment and there still be economic growth. Comment.

4-5. Discuss in as much detail as possible the differences between the "major" cycle and the "minor" cycle. Of what significance is the so-called "hybrid" cycle?

4-6. Do you feel that the distinction between the major and minor cycle is useful? Elaborate.

4-7. Define what is meant by the capital-output ratio, and trace out the behavior of this important ratio in the economic history of the United States. How do you account for its rise and its subsequent fall?

Bibliography

Abramovitz, M., *Evidences of Long Swings in Aggregate Construction Since the Civil War*. New York: National Bureau of Economic Research, 1964.

Fellner, W. J., *Trends and Cycles in Economic Activity*. New York: Holt, Rinehart & Winston, Inc. 1956.

Hansen, A. H., *Business Cycles and National Income*. New York: W. W. Norton & Company, Inc., 1964.

Hickman, B. G., *Investment and Stability of the Postwar Economy*. Washington, D. C.: The Brookings Institution, 1960.

———, *Investment Demand and U. S. Economic Growth*. Washington, D. C.: The Brookings Institution, 1965.

Kuznets, S., *Capital in the American Economy: Its Formation and Financing*. Princeton: Princeton University Press, 1961.

part 2

The Emergence and Development
of Business Cycle Theory

5

The Methodology of Business Cycle Theory

The historical-statistical inquiry of the last four chapters points the way to the next step—namely, the development of a theoretical explanation of economic growth and cyclical fluctuations. The theme, then, of the next three parts of the book is the critical review and evaluation of the theoretical efforts of a large number of economists who have undertaken the task of constructing analytical explanations of the cycle and growth.

1. The Need for Theory

The preceding review of cyclical fluctuations and economic growth has revealed in some detail the tremendous complexity of the forces at play in a dynamic capitalist economy. In fact there are so many crosscurrents and interactions of variables that the need for some simplified approach to the problems of the cycle and growth is obvious. Without the simplification and manageability provided by theory we should become lost in the rich variety of facts that characterizes the American economic system.

The major methodological position underlying the development of cycle-growth theory has been well stated by Joseph A. Schumpeter. After reviewing a large body of economic data relating to growth and the business cycle, he continues:

> But we have also seen that in any such discussion of economic fact we run up against a wall which blocks the road toward precise answers to many of our questions, and which is not likely to crumble before any amount of fact, however complete, or any statistical method, however refined. *The reason for this is that raw facts, as such, are a jumble.* Even that amount of data which we have been able to derive so far was as much due to the application of our commonsense understanding of the *modus operandi* of our facts as it was to the facts themselves. The consequence of this is that we must now try, with a view to acquiring a more powerful apparatus of analysis, to refine upon our commonsense methods exactly as we must try to increase our stock of facts and to improve upon our statistical methods.[1]

In other words, the analytical approach relies upon both theory and empirical fact. The theory must have a firm foundation in fact; it must not be so abstruse that it can be assigned to the kingdoms of "dreamland of equilibrium" or "cuckoo cloud land."[2] Yet, at the same time, if it is to have any predictive relevance it must abstract from a large number of variables—otherwise we are easily led astray in the maze of interacting and reinforcing variables.

Thus the development of cycle and growth theory rests on these two seemingly contradictory cornerstones—an empirical foundation and an abstraction from much of empirical reality. The contradiction, however, is more illusory than real. The approach used in business cycle and growth theory, as well as in economics and even in science in general, revolves around the *interaction of empiricism and abstraction.* The empiricism is necessary to point out what data are available; and the abstraction is essential to allow the formulation of workable hypotheses which will provide some conclusions. And these conclusions, in turn, must be subjected to empirical test. This symbiotic relationship between "fact"and "theory" has been very well put by the Danish economist F. Zeuthen:

> These conditions of [complex interaction] necessitate partly a continuous collection and arrangement of empirical data and partly, owing to the many simultaneously relevant conditions, the formation of a great

---

[1]Joseph A. Schumpeter, *Business Cycles* (New York: McGraw-Hill Book Company, 1939), Vol. I, p. 30, italics added.

[2]These two phrases are taken from A. F. Burns and W. C. Mitchell, *Measuring Business Cycles* (New York: National Bureau of Economic Research, 1946), and P. J. D. Wiles, *Price, Cost, and Output* (Oxford: Basil Blackwell, 1956).

number of theories. The latter may be simple abstractions which alternatively take small groups of phenomena into consideration or they may be more complicated theories aimed at finding the connection between a greater number of phenomena.

The theories, on the one hand, are final results, the usefulness of which depends on the help they render in predicting and controlling the economic conditions. On the other hand, they serve as orientation . . . for further empirical investigations. In other scientific spheres we are also forced to use deduction, in spite of the general preference for facts . . . . in order to take an illustration from a sphere which we all understand, let us repeat the following conversation from an English detective story:

"Don't you make Theories as you go along, Pointer?" "I like finding facts better," Pointer thought. "Of course, if you cannot find a fact lying around, you have to fish for it with a theory." Both men were silent on that; both lost in thought.[3]

This is the way it has been with the development of business cycle theory—there has been a continual interaction between empirical fact and abstraction, with the result that the body of thought dealing with these economic phenomena has undergone substantial modification over the years. Always new facts are being discovered which result in both the modification of existing theories and the construction of new ones; but on the other hand the new theories are always pointing the way toward the acquisition and interpretation of new data. One major result of this is that modern cycle and growth theories are significantly different from those of some sixty or seventy years ago. This is what is to be expected from the interaction of empiricism and abstraction, and there is no apparent reason to suspect that the interactive process will soon be stopped.

2. An Uneven Balance of Development

A rather clear-cut pattern exists in the chronological development of cycle-growth thought. To begin with, business cycle theory obviously did not begin to emerge until there were actually cyclical fluctuations. This places, for all practical purposes, the birthdate of business cycle theory at around the 1870's. Prior to that time a large enough capital stock did not exist in most western economies (England excepted) for

---

[3]F. Zeuthen, *Economic Theory and Method* (Cambridge: Harvard University Press, 1955), p. 14. This book contains an excellent review of the methodology of economics. See also T. C. Koopmans, *Three Essays on the State of Economic Science* (New York: McGraw-Hill Book Company, 1958), especially essays II-III.

fluctuations in investment to give rise to the major cycle. To be sure, there were earlier "crises" but these were sporadic and random. Many persons, of course, were concerned with this or that particular crisis; but they were not essentially concerned about the business cycle for the simple fact that the cycle as we now know it did not exist. As one eminent student of the cycle, Gustav Cassel, has put it, any study of the cycle which ". . . is to be valid for the whole of Europe cannot, in general, go back farther than the beginning of the 'seventies."[4]

The earlier steps in the development of cycle theory were somewhat unsophisticated and faltering, but in the last sixty years or so more complete and realistic theories have been constructed. Even so, most cycle theories remained outside the main tradition of western economic thought until the 1930's. The chronology of the development of business cycle and growth thought can be roughly divided into the following scheme.

Up until the 1930's the classical economic theory was dominant. The classical view is typically referred to as Say's Law, after the French economist J. B. Say who did so much to popularize it. The basic argument of Say's Law is that a capitalistic, free enterprise economy will continually experience economic growth, though most of the classicists felt that eventually there would emerge the "stationary state." Beyond this there would be no further growth. But in the interim, when growth was still unfolding, the economic system would not experience protracted periods of unemployment or inflation.[5] Indeed the advocates of Say's Law argued that there are certain "natural laws" that will, once they are stimulated by unemployment, operate to eliminate it. Thus the economy continues to grow with a full-employment equilibrium.

The chief equilibrating mechanism in the classical doctrine is the flexible interest rate. If, for example, people in the community increase their savings, the immediate result will be a decline in consumption and hence in income and employment. But with a flexible interest rate,

---

[4]G. Cassel, *The Theory of Social Economy* (New York: Harcourt, Brace & World, Inc., 1932); (London: Ernest Benn, Ltd., 1932), p. 535. For a good review of cycle theories that were developed before the turn of the century, see A. H. Hansen, *Business Cycles and National Income* (New York: W. W. Norton & Company, Inc., 1964), Chapter 13. Our review of the classical doctrine in this chapter is extremely abbreviated; for a fuller discussion, see Chapter 15.

[5]There are major exceptions. Such outstanding classical and neoclassical economists as T. R. Malthus, R. G. Hawtrey, F. A. Hayek, Knut Wicksell, Alfred Marshall, and A. C. Pigou developed explanations of cyclical disturbances. However, it is safe to say that most of them accepted Say's Law in its long-run version but questioned its short-run validity. The theories of several of these "dissenters" are discussed in subsequent chapters.

the increased savings will lower the cost of borrowing capital funds. But note that the reduced rate of interest will also make it less desirable for savers to hold their funds as savings, and thus they will tend to increase their consumption. Still the interest rate remains below its former level. Accordingly, businessmen will respond by borrowing the extra savings at the lower rate and increase their investment spending. This reaction, coupled with the behavior of consumers, will not only restore the economy to full employment, but will also bring about economic growth. In short, savings will always reenter the spending stream, and full employment and growth are guaranteed. True, there may be minor disturbances as the readjusting forces come into play; but the classicists held that they would indeed be temporary. The flexibility of the interest rate insures continuing full employment, so far as Say's Law is concerned.

However, while the advocates of Say's Law were writing and theorizing about smooth, uninterrupted economic growth, cyclical disturbances were actually occurring. Sometimes these were severe, sometimes mild; but in every instance there were complicated changes that required theoretical explanation.

Thus beginning around the turn of the century a more determined effort was made by a growing number of economists to construct theories that would explain the cycle and allow some prediction for policy purposes.[6] Moreover, there was also an increased emphasis on empirical research. The stage was therefore set for later, more refined and useful work. Still it remains true that these more sophisticated and meaningful analyses were considered to be outside the main flow of economic thought, despite the fact that some of the major cycle theorists of the period were among the leading economists of the time and later. Notable here are Knut Wicksell, Ralph G. Hawtrey, F. A. Hayek, Joseph A. Schumpeter, Dennis H. Robertson, and others. But while these economists were developing their cycle theories, the majority of western economists continued in the tradition of classical thought, at least until the Great Depression of the 1930's.

Then during the 'thirties it became generally recognized that there was no substantial body of thought that could possibly explain the behavior of the relevant variables during the Great Depression, let alone point the way toward the creation of a policy program that would restore the economy to full employment of its resources. This decade, however, marked another turning point in the development of cycle

---

[6]We shall review several of these theories in the next three chapters. For a more extensive review of most cycle theories developed during this period, see Hansen, *Business Cycles and National Income*, Part III; see also G. Haberler, *Prosperity and Depression* (Cambridge: Harvard University Press, 1958).

theory. At this time a new body of thought—the so-called Keynesian analysis—was presented to the western world.[7] The Keynesian analysis, so called after its author John Maynard Keynes, provided a frontal attack on the classical view that was still widely accepted. As a consequence the Keynesian analysis, coupled with the pressing conditions of the Great Depression, led to a widescale rejection of the classical analysis.[8] While not all economists became "Keynesians," the majority of them began to make effective use of the various theoretical concepts and tools presented by Keynes in *The General Theory of Employment, Interest, and Money.*

It should be noted, however, that *The General Theory* does not contain, in the strict sense, a theory of the business cycle. Nor does it deal at all with the problems and aspects of long-run growth. In other words, the analysis of *The General Theory* is designed to explain short-run, noncyclical disturbances in the levels of income and employment.[9] More specifically, it is best classified as *short-run equilibrium analysis.* Its procedure is something as follows: first, the necessary conditions for an equilibrium level of income are spelled out in some detail; then a disturbing "shock" is introduced into the equilibrium situation; and the result is the emergence of a new (higher or lower) level of income. Now any theory that explains why income moves from one to another equilibrium level can hardly be called a business cycle theory. A cycle theory deals with *dis*equilibrium, that is, the continuing ebb and flow of general economic activity. Yet as will be seen, the Keynesian analysis contains the groundwork for many of the modern cycle and growth theories that stress the recurring ups and downs of economic activity.

---

[7]J. M. Keynes, *The General Theory of Employment, Interest, and Money* (New York: Harcourt, Brace & World, Inc., 1936). Keynes had provided a preliminary statement of his analysis in a pamphlet, *The Means to Prosperity* (London: The Macmillan Company, 1933), now available as an Economica Books paperback. Several summary statements of his theory are found in *The New Economics: Keynes' Influence on Theory and Public Policy,* ed. Seymour E. Harris (New York: Alfred A. Knopf, Inc., 1947). See also D. Dillard, *The Economics of John Maynard Keynes* (New York: Prentice-Hall, Inc., 1948); L. R. Klein, *The Keynesian Revolution* (New York: The Macmillan Company, 1947), now available as a Macmillan Paperback; and D. M. Wright, *The Keynesian System* (New York: Fordham University Press, 1962). For a recent critical review of the Keynesian analysis, see H. G. Johnson, "The *General Theory* after Twenty-five Years," *American Economic Review,* May 1961, and the comments by D. M. Wright, A. P. Lerner, and L. R. Klein.

[8]But see the discussion in Chapter 15, below, where some "classical" reaction to the Keynesian analysis is reviewed.

[9]However, there are strong hints of both cycle and growth analysis in *The General Theory;* see especially Chapters 22 and 24. The statement in the text, above, is somewhat oversimplified, as we shall see in Part 3.

But for a while the short-run equilibrium analysis presented by Keynes had its heyday.

However, times, conditions, and attitudes change, and today there has developed a body of thought that is usually referred to as "post-Keynesian" analysis.[10] Unlike the Keynesian theory, which ignores the long-run or growth aspects of economic activity, the post-Keynesian analysis concentrates on the *interaction of economic growth and the business cycle*. This is what we shall term "modern cycle theory." It often becomes rather complicated since it takes into account that the business cycle influences economic growth and that the growth process itself influences the business cycle in turn.[11]

In sum, then, there has been an uneven balance in the historical development of business cycle theory. Throughout the nineteenth century and up to the 1930's, the classical (and neoclassical) view held sway. However, from the 1870's on, several cycle theories were developed, though these were considered to be outside traditional economic thought. With the advent of the Great Depression there emerged the Keynesian analysis, which was so widely discussed and had such a broad and deep impact that there has been some reference to the "Keynesian Revolution." However, with the Keynesian analysis the pendulum seems to have swung full arc. With its exclusive concentration on short-run disturbances, the Keynesian approach presents the opposite extreme of the classical view, which was exclusively preoccupied with long-run growth. Now the pendulum is swinging back, for modern cycle theory attempts to integrate the cycle and growth and thus differs from its antecedents in economic thought.

3.   The Variety of Approaches to Business Cycle Theory

With so much attention devoted to business cycle theory we might expect a variety of approaches to it, and this is indeed the case. In fact there are so many alternative approaches to the study of the cycle that to review each is an almost impossible, if not fruitless, task. As Professor Haberler has observed:

> To comment on the state of business cycle theory is more difficult today than ever before; for it is scarcely an exaggeration to say that never be-

---

[10]See, for example, K. K. Kurihara, ed. *Post-Keynesian Economics* (New Brunswick, N. J.: Rutgers University Press, 1954). Many specific references to the post-Keynesian analysis will be made in the chapters that follow.

[11]Several of these theories are discussed in Part 4.

fore in the history of the science of economics has there been a time when the business cycle problem . . . has been so intensively treated; never before has the method of treatment (theoretical, logical, mathematical, econometrical, statistical, historical, psychological, etc.) varied so much, or the subject approached from so many different points of view.[12]

However, a semblence of order (though it is bound to be arbitrary in some respects) can be introduced into this variety of approaches. While several classificatory schemes are available, we shall make use of the simple distinction between "exogenous" theories, "endogenous" theories, and "mixtures" of the two.

Note that this classificatory scheme ignores completely the distinction between the "statistical" and "theoretical" approaches. The discussion of section 1 of this chapter showed that the critical issue is not "facts" versus "theory," but rather the fruitful interaction between facts and theory. Often we go fishing for facts with theories and then use the facts to test the theories.

Note also that this approach avoids the often-used classification of theories according to the prime causal factor assumed to be *the key variable* in the cycle (the "prima donna" theories, as Hansen calls them). A typical classification along these lines would include: psychological theories; pure monetary theories; monetary-overinvestment theories; underconsumption theories; agricultural theories; profit theories; and so on. The major difficulty with this classificatory approach is that it does not reveal very much. Obviously each of the variables referred to in the list plays an important role in the cycle; and in fact the advocates of each type of theory readily concede the significance of the key variables stressed by the other theorists.[13] The difference between the theories revolves around the relative weights assigned to the different variables. Thus while the purely monetary theorists recognize the significance of changing psychological conditions, they assign to them the status of a handmaiden role. The result is, as D. H. Robertson has so aptly put it, that ". . . in the deathless words of the Dodo, everybody has won and all must have prizes, in the sense that almost all writers who have made any serious contribution to the study of the matter appear to have had a considerable measure of right on their

---

[12]"Notes on the Present State of Business Cycle Theory," first published in *Wirtschaftstheorie und Wirtschaftspolitik, Fetschrift fur Alfred Amonn* (Berne, 1953), and reprinted as Appendix I to *Prosperity and Depression*, p. 483.

[13]See G. Haberler, *Prosperity and Depression*, and Hansen, *Business Cycles and National Income*, for views according to this sort of classification.

side."[14] This is hardly a satisfactory state of affairs; and it is for this reason that the endogenous-exogenous-mixture classification is proposed here.

A. Endogenous and Exogenous Variables[15]

It is best to begin with definitions before discussing some exogenous and endogenous theories. The major emphasis in this classification is on *endogenous variables* and *exogenous variables*. All theories contain a number of variables, some of which are exogenous and some of which are endogenous; indeed, rarely is a theory "purely" endogenous or "purely" exogenous. The major concern is with the relative importance assigned to each type of variable.

· Thus, the exogenous theory relies *primarily*, though not exclusively, upon exogenous variables *to explain the cyclical turning points*. This does not mean that there are no endogenous variables in the exogenous theory. All theories are, as noted above, mixtures of the two types of variables. It means simply that greater emphasis is given to the exogenous variables in the explanation of the turning points. On the other hand, an endogenous theory explains the cyclical process with less reliance on the exogenous variables and places a greater emphasis on the interaction of the endogenous variables in explaining the turning points. Finally, there are the *"mixed" models*, where changes in exogenous variables are used to account for one of the turning points and the interplay of the endogenous variables to explain the other. Of the three types of models, the "mixed" ones have dominated cycle thought.

But what specifically are exogenous and endogenous variables? Consider a group or "set" of variables that make up a theory. If any one of these is strongly influenced by the lagged or current values of one or more of the other variables in the group, or perhaps its own lagged value, and if it in turn influences one or more of the other variables, it is referred to as an *endogenous variable*. Take a rather simple, but

---

[14]D. H. Robertson, *A Study of Industrial Fluctuation* (London: London School of Economics and Political Science, University of London, 1948).

[15]For further discussion of the points made in this and the next section, see J. S. Duesenberry, *Business Cycles and Economic Growth* (New York: McGraw-Hill Book Company, 1958), Chapter 9, and Hansen, *Business Cycles and National Income,* Chapters 21-24. See also the essay by L. A. Metzler, "Business Cycles and the Modern Theory of Employment," *American Economic Review,* June 1946, reprinted as Chapter 21 in *Readings in Business Cycles and National Income,* eds. A. H. Hansen and R. V. Clemence (New York: W. W. Norton & Company, Inc., 1953).

important, example from modern theory. It is argued that income is defined as the total of consumption expenditures and expenditures by businessmen on investment. This can be written as $Y_t = C_t + I_t$, where Y stands for income, C for consumption, I for investment, and the subscript t stands for the present time period. Now assume that consumers' expenditures are determined primarily by their current income, given their tastes and the relative prices of the goods and services they purchase. Thus current consumption (C_t) is a function of current income (Y_t). This functional relationship may be written as

$$C_t = f(Y_t).$$

In other words, there is a mutual dependence here—income depends upon consumption in part, and consumption depends upon income. Alternatively, the consumption function may be written with a time lag, where consumption of the present period (C_t) is a function of the income of the preceding period (Y_{t-1}). Thus

$$C_t = f(Y_{t-1}).$$

In this case, since $Y_t = C_t + I_t$, the current level of income (Y_t) is influenced by the income of the previous period (Y_{t-1}), or, in other words, the previous level of income determines the present level of income, through a lagged consumption function.

Consider another important example. Businessmen are influenced by many important factors in making their investment decisions. Many modern cycle theories, however, tend to stress the relationship between current planned investment and the change in total output from an earlier time period (t—1) to the present time period (t). This can be written as

$$I_t = f(Y_t - Y_{t-1}).$$

In other words, since $Y_t = C_t + I_t$, income depends upon investment, but since investment depends upon the past behavior of income, there again is a mutual dependence between the two variables: investment determines, in part, income, and income determines, in part, investment.

The set of relationships between endogenous variables such as these is referred to as an "endogenous system," and any theory that relies exclusively on the interplay of the endogenous variables as a means of explaining the turning points of the cycle is an endogenous theory. However, an endogenous model must also include exogenous variables. To repeat, the distinction between the two types of theories—endogenous and exogenous—revolves around the explanation of the turning points.[16] Thus, the exogenous model relies upon exogenous variables to explain the turning points of the cycle, and the endogenous model relies upon endogenous variables to perform the same task.

As for the *exogenous variables,* these can be defined somewhat negatively. They are those variables which are not influenced very much by the endogenous variables, though they themselves exert an influence on the latter. Some clear-cut and obvious examples are easily thought of. An earthquake is hardly influenced, even in the slightest, by residential construction, though it in turn can have a decisive impact on housing investment. By the same token it is difficult to conceive of consumption influencing the weather, though certainly the weather has an influence on consumption. In short, exogenous variables are those whose influence is excluded from the endogenous system because of this one-way street of cause and effect. Any theory that explains the cyclical turning points solely by reference to the behavior of exogenous varia bles is an exogenous theory.

B. Simple Exogenous, Endogenous, and Mixed Models

Let us examine briefly an example of each of these three types of models in order to see their basic characteristics.

Exogenous models have been present in cycle thought for quite some time. However, since *no* model is *strictly* exogenous, all those theories that we label as "exogenous" contain endogenous variables. Again, the major emphasis is upon which sort of variable is used to explain the turning points of the cycle. In the exogenous models the exogenous variables play this important role.

For example, assume that the economy is at a given level of income and employment and that there is no internal stimulant that will change this level. In other words, there is an equilibrium situation which will persist unless disturbed by some "outside shock." Assume now that such an exogenous shock occurs (it may be caused by a spurt in investment due to war or to technological advances, or it may occur because businessmen lay in more inventories because the monetary authorities have lowered the interest rate, or it may even be due to something like increased sunspot activity) and that this shock starts the economy in an upward direction.

Now the exogenous theories argue that the expansion becomes cumulative—that it feeds on itself because of the interplay of the

---

[16]Metzler, "Business Cycles and the Modern Theory of Employment", stresses this distinction, as do Hansen and others.

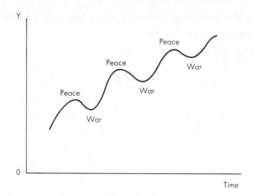

FIGURE 5—1

endogenous variables—and that it will continue to do so unless further changes occur in the exogenous variables. Without these changes in exogenous forces, the expansion would continue. However, once the limiting exogenous changes are introduced and exercise their effects, the upper-turning point occurs and the cumulative contraction gets underway. Now the interplay of the endogenous variables propels the economy downwards without limit, until once again the exogenous forces exercise their limiting effect and reverse the contraction. Thus the play of exogenous variables accounts for both the upper- and lower-turning points.

An example of a purely exogenous model is given in Figure 5–1. Here time is plotted on the horizontal axis, and income (Y) is plotted on the vertical axis. This might be called a "war" cycle, with the outbreak of war causing the lower-turning point, and the emergence of peace causing the upper-turning point. But unless we subscribe to a sweeping philosophy of complete economic determinism, this may be labeled as a purely exogenous theory.[17]

While exogenous theories have always been present in business cycle thought, there were some early efforts at constructing *endogenous theories*. One of the most important of these earlier efforts was the analysis developed by the French economist Albert Aftalion, who published his *Les Crises periodiques de surproduction* in 1913. Endogenous models, traced back to Aftalion and to some other origins, are more popular today, though they have far from replaced the exogenous and "mixed" theories.

---

[17]See Chapter 19 for a brief discussion of an exogenous theory of the cycle that is referred to as a "political theory" of the business cycle.

An endogenous model, as pointed out above, is one that explains the cyclical turning points without any specific reference to exogenous variables. To be sure, exogenous variables figure into the model, but only as "givens" or "constants." For instance, any business cycle theory that purports to explain cyclical fluctuations in a money economy must consider changes in the money supply as a variable of some importance. However, the endogenous model may hold the money supply constant (by assumption) in order to trace out the pattern of interaction among the endogenous variables. On the other hand, changes in the money supply can be made an endogenous variable, as is shown in the next chapter where R. G. Hawtrey's so-called "purely monetary theory" of the cycle is discussed. The exogenous variables are usually referred to as *parameters,* and they are allowed to change only because the theorist wants to see what the effect of a "once-and-for-all" change would be in his endogenous system.

An economic illustration of endogenous theories is a bit difficult to provide at this early stage, though several such models are reviewed in later chapters. However, perhaps a couple of noneconomic examples will illustrate what is meant by such a theory.[18]

Consider a clock pendulum hanging at rest. Now assume that this equilibrium position is disturbed by an outside "shock" and that the pendulum begins its swinging motion. The swinging of the pendulum will gradually die away until it returns to its equilibrium position of rest once more. In this case an "exogenous shock" disturbed the equilibrium and set off a series of swinging (cyclical) movements, the magnitude of which depends upon the severity of the shock, the length and weight of the pendulum, and so on. However, unless another external shock is applied, the swinging movements will die away, and the gradual decline of the "cycle" is determined by the intrinsic qualities of the pendulum itself. This is what is called a "linear" endogenous model.[19]

Consider another example of a linear endogenous model, a rather classical one, that has been provided by Aftalion.

If one rekindles the fire in the hearth in order to warm up a room, one has to wait a while before one has the desired temperature. As the cold continues, and the thermometer continues to record it, one might be

---

[18]For an excellent discussion of these types of models, see R. M. Goodwin, "Econometrics in Business Cycle Analysis," Chapter 22 in Hansen, *Business Cycles and National Income.*

[19]Linearity here means that the variables are proportional to the other variables (or their own lagged values) in the endogenous system. The nonlinear models are those which recognize real-life phenomena that prevent actual linear relationships, such as full employment of resources, technological barriers to full employment, and so on. See Goodwin, *op. cit.,* for a fuller discussion.

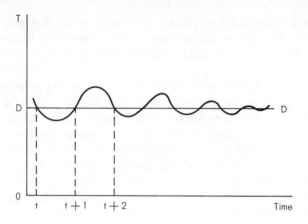

FIGURE 5–2

led, if one had not the lessons of experience, to throw more coal on the fire. One would continue to throw coal, even though the quantity already in the grate is such as will give off an intolerable heat, when once it is all alight. To allow oneself to be guided by the present sense of cold and the indications of the thermometer to that effect is fatally to overheat the room.[20]

In this case, if there were no "lags" involved, there would be no "cyclical" movements in the temperature of the room. That is, if the thermometer recorded that the temperature in the room had reached the minimum desired level, and if the fire were restocked immediately, and if the coal ignited immediately and fully, then the temperature would remain in the desired range. But this would be so only if the person tending the fire knew precisely how much coal to add. However, as it turns out so often, there is a lag between the time the coal is added and the time it ignites, so the temperature continues to decline for a while. And if the tender of the fire is inexperienced, he may be swayed by the thermometer to add even more coal. The result of this of course would be a rise in the temperature above the desired level. Thus there is a constant oscillation of the room's temperature, though the oscillatory swings become less and less as the tender of the fire becomes more and more experienced.

This can be shown in Figure 5–2, where time is plotted on the horizontal axis and temperature on the vertical. The line DD′ shows the desired level of temperature, and the oscillating line around DD′ shows the actual temperature. As the actual temperature drops below DD′

---

[20]Cited in Haberler, *Prosperity and Depression*, pp. 135-36.

at time t, the inexperienced fire tender will add too much coal, and consequently the actual temperature will rise above the desired level at t+1. He then will wait too long, watching the thermometer, to add coal, with the result that the actual level drops below DD'. Thus following t+2 he will again add too much fuel, driving the actual above the desired level once more. But note that the oscillations around DD' tend to become smaller and smaller. It is as if the wavy line were "hunting" the DD' line and coming closer and closer in its search. Finally the two lines merge when the oscillations become zero. This is due to the increased experience of the coal tender.

Actually, the linear endogenous theories deal with three types of oscillatory patterns.[21] The first, already described, is where the amplitude of the cyclical fluctuations becomes less and less until it finally becomes stable. The second is just the opposite, where the amplitude becomes greater and greater as time elapses. And the third is where the amplitude remains constant, neither growing nor declining as time passes. Generally the third is rejected as improbable, and since the second does not accord with our experience, the advocates of the endogenous models tend to rely (though not exclusively) on the ever-diminishing fluctuations. This of course raises the question: If the "typical" pattern is one of gradually declining fluctuations, then how can we account for the continuation of the business cycle? The answer usually given to this is that outside shocks occur often enough that the cycle is revived and starts its course over again. If nothing further happened, it would diminish to a position of rest; but in all probability another external shock will occur. This type of linear model thus really takes the form of a "mixed" theory. In terms of the pendulum example, another tap against the pendulum will prevent its coming to rest, and so long as taps are given often enough, the pendulum will continue its "cyclical swings." In terms of Aftalion's analogy, just as the fire tender becomes accustomed to his duty and the wavy line approaches the DD' line, a new man will replace him and the entire "hunting" process will begin over again.

There is another type of endogenous model, however, that remains purely endogenous—that which is termed a *"nonlinear"* model. An illustration of this is the "billiard table" model. Assume that there is a smooth, frictionless billard table, upon which there is a perfectly round billiard ball. Once the ball is hit it moves in one direction until it hits a cushion, only to bounce off and move in another direction until it en-

---

[21]See Goodwin, "Econometrics in Business Cycle Analysis," pp. 420-22, for a fuller discussion.

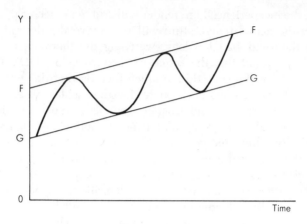

FIGURE 5–3

counters another cushion, from which it bounces off, and so on. In this
case the limiting forces—*the parameters*—are cushions. But this is a
purely endogenous model inasmuch as the exogenous forces (the parameters) are assumed to be constant and unchanging.

For illustration, assume that the growth factors in the economy (population, natural resources, technology, and so on) expand over time so
that total ouput at full employment can increase only at a certain rate.
This is what might be called the "full-employment ceiling," and when
the economy is at full employment, actual output cannot expand at a
rate faster than that permitted by the ceiling, which is shown as the FF
line in Figure 5–3. However, the growth factors (e.g., discovery of
resources, technological advances, etc.) continue to expand at a given
rate, as shown by the GG curve. Now, if actual output expands from
a position of less than full employment up to the ceiling at a much
higher rate, then it will "bounce off" the full-employment ceiling, and
the contraction sets in. The contraction continues until the growth
factors stimulate an expansion in investment and the expansion gets
underway. In this sort of model the parameters set limits to the turning
points and condition the values of the endogenous variables. Several of
these models are examined later on in detail, but Figure 5–3 provides
an illustration where income fluctuates between the FF line and the
GG line, which reflects the growth factors.

Finally, there is the *"mixed"* model. This is the type of business cycle
theory that represents a mixture of exogenous and endogenous models,
and it relies upon changes in exogenous variables to explain one of the
turning points and upon the interplay of the endogenous variables to

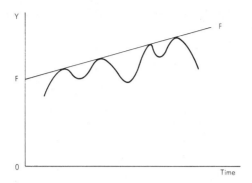

FIGURE 5-4

explain the other. For example, a theory may explain the reversal from expansion to contraction by reference to the interaction of the endogenous variables, and then explain the lower-turning point by use of the behavior of exogenous variables. Conversely, a model may rely upon the exogenous variables to explain the upper-turning point and upon the endogenous variables to account for the lower. It is safe to say that the bulk of business cycle theories developed up to the present represent this "mixed" type of model. In Figure 5-4 the upper-turning point is determined by the full-employment ceiling (the FF line), while changes in exogenous variables determine the lower-turning point. Several "mixed" models are examined in later chapters.

This then is the classification that we shall use. Some models are best described as exogenous, others are best classified as endogenous, and still others as "mixtures." The first accounts for the turning points by reference to exogenous variables, the second by reference to the interplay of the endogenous variables, while the last relies upon both types of variables in explaining the turning points.

C. Selection of Variables

The logical question that arises at this point is, what criteria are available to determine whether a variable should be classified as endogenous or exogenous. That is, why does a theorist select certain variables as endogenous and confine the remaining ones to the category of exogenous? What criteria does he rely upon in choosing between variables?

There are no hard and fast rules that can be followed in selecting between variables as exogenous and endogenous. However, examination of the wealth of available data, along with a little "common sense," indicates that some variables interact strongly with others and that some of these are obviously more important than others. These are the ones that are to be included in an endogenous model, and since there are no clear and hard guidelines, observation and accumulated knowledge must be relied upon to designate which particular variables these are. Of course, arbitrary judgment enters into this selection process, but this seems unavoidable. As Duesenberry, whose theory of the cycle and growth interaction is examined later, has put it:

> In general, we ought to try to include in our endogenous system any variable which interacts strongly and systematically with other variables already in the system. There are, therefore, certain *general* criteria for deciding whether to treat a variable as endogenous or exogenous, *but there is also an arbitrary element of judgment and convenience in the choice.*[22]

Surely a business cycle theory cannot assign private business investment in plant and equipment to the limbo of exogenous—such a procedure would clearly be in error. But what about including in the model investment in residential dwellings? This is a different matter, and here arbitrary judgment and convenience figure in. Some theorists will want to include it, while others will reject it. Similar problems relate to other variables, such as consumption, when they are broken down into their component parts.

Nevertheless, there is a list of rather obvious variables that should be treated as endogenous in an endogenous model—these include investment in plant and equipment (and also in inventories), consumption, the capital stock, employment, and in some cases capital consumption allowances. This is far from a complete list—some models include consumer and/or business debt, dividend payments by corporations, profits, and so on. However, the longer the list of endogenous variables, the more unmanageable the model becomes. Some theorists actually want to work with a minimum of endogenous variables in order to reduce the degree of complications. The theorist, in other words, can always exercise his freedom in the selection of variables according to the type of model that he wants to construct.

When it comes to allocating variables to the category of exogenous, the matter is somewhat simpler. There are several reasons for desig-

---

[22]Duesenberry, *Business Cycles and Economic Growth* (New York: McGraw-Hill Book Company, 1958) p. 185, italics added.

nating certain variables as outside the endogenous system, though this is not always a simple, clear-cut thing.[23]

First, some events are obviously unique and will in all likelihood never occur again. For example, wars may come and go, but there was only one World War II. It is extremely unlikely that the American economy will enter into another mobilization program exactly, or even nearly, like that of the second world war. The development of new military techniques, if nothing else, assures this. When some events are obviously unique, they are easily and readily assignable to the exogenous category.

In the second place, there is need to preserve some degree of manageability in the model. This is particularly relevant with respect to "hybrid" variables, that is, those variables that may be assigned as either exogenous or endogenous. A good illustration of this hybrid-type variable is population. For instance, if population is influenced by the real income of the bread-winner of the family, so that the family is enlarged as real income rises, and if the population increase in turn influences total consumption and hence real income, then population might well be considered as an endogenous variable. Some theories of economic growth have treated population in this way. Notable here is the classical theory of growth, in which (following Malthus) it was argued that as the real market wage rises above the subsistence wage, the propensity to propagate arises. The resulting increase in population will enlarge the labor force, and this in turn will drive the market wage back towards the subsistence level. But inasmuch as this lowers costs of production, businesses will expand their operations, increase their demand for labor, and the process begins over again. Though this is indeed an oversimplification, it does show how population can be treated as an endogenous variable.

However, there are many determinants of population size other than real income; for example, cultural patterns, level of intelligence, the state of technology, and so on will have an influence. With respect to these factors, population is considered as an exogenous variable, for several of them are not directly related to the major economic variables of growth and cycle theory. Still there is some ambiguity here, for such determinants of population as level of intelligence and the state of technology may be, in the long run, determined in large part by the rate of economic growth. This being the case, population once again begins to assume the role and form of an endogenous variable. (It is

---

[23]See Duesenberry, *Business Cycles and Economic Growth*, pp. 184-86, for additional discussion of these points.

probably safe, however, to state that population is *nearly always* treated as an exogenous variable in short-run cycle theory, and *may* be treated as an endogenous variable in long-run growth theory.)

If population is included in an endogenous system, however, certain problems arise. In order to treat it fully as an endogenous variable we would be led on a merry chase in uncovering all of the significant relationships between it and the other endogenous variables in the model. By the time the quarry is tracked down, the model may have become so complex that it is unmanageable. At this point the theorist must exercise his own discretion and make the difficult choice between simplification and manageability, on the one hand, and greater realism, on the other. In fact, many hybrid-type variables are classified as exogenous simply for the sake of preserving some degree of manageability in the model.

Third, there is the problem of ignorance. A variable exists, and we know that it is important, but we find ourselves at a loss to explain it. Changes in expectations of businessmen and consumers are not unique experiences; yet they are extremely difficult to explain. The usual procedure, therefore, is to classify them as exogenous—to take them as "given"—and thus arbitrarily prevent changes in expectations from disturbing the model. While we may be forced to operate in this manner, it is far from satisfactory. As Professor Erik Lundberg has said:

> In most of the "closed" models price changes are excluded; and so often are changes in credit availability and changes in expectations. But it is certainly *not* sufficient to show that we can get an elementary model yielding a nice cycle with a minimum number of variables by excluding these factors.[24]

And finally, some variables are classified as exogenous simply because the theorist wants to see how things work out without their presence. Important here are the "policy variables," that is, decisions on the part of governmental authorities to change the money supply, government expenditures, tax revenues, and so on. In most cases these must be treated as exogenous anyhow, but even if they could be pushed into the endogenous category they would often be excluded for the reason mentioned above. A good illustration of this choice is that most endogenous models hold governmental intervention constant in order to see how the private sector of the economy would function without any attempt on the part of the government to stabilize it. Once some answers are formulated, then further discussion

---

[24]E. Lundberg, ed., *The Business Cycle in the Post-War World* (London: The Macmillan Company, 1955), p. 352.

can be carried out as to what policies government should and could put into effect. But recall the discussion of Chapter 1 in this connection—there is no such thing as a "simple" remedy for the cycle and growth problems.

About all that can be concluded from this discussion of the choice of endogenous and exogenous variables for a particular model is that (1) some variables by necessity must be considered exogenous, (2) some obviously should be considered as endogenous, and (3) there must be some judgment exercised over the remainder as to how they are to be classified. The choice is never easy, and it must somehow or other resolve the conflict between simplification and realism.

4. Summary

The complexity of the cyclical and growth processes requires that some fairly simplified theory be developed in order to explain the activities involved. The alternative is to attempt to deal with all the variables simultaneously, which would hardly yield any answers to the causes of the cycle and growth. However, theory must be founded on empirical fact, and its conclusions must be subjected to empirical testing. At the same time, the development of new theories points the way toward the accumulation of more data. There is thus an active symbiosis—a constructive interaction—between "fact" and "theory."

As cycle theory in the western world has developed, it has gone through several stages. From the time of the early classical economists up to the 1930's, Say's Law dominated western economic thought. This analysis concluded that there would be smooth growth up to the "stationary state" and thus excluded study of the business cycle. This of course was reasonable up to around the 1870's, for that was roughly the time at which the cyclical pattern began to emerge in most western economies. Nevertheless, Say's Law still dominated thought, and as a result the cycle theories that were developed after the 'seventies remained outside the main flow of economic thought.

A growing number of economists, however, devoted more time to analytical explanations of the cycle, and by the 1930's a rather large variety of cycle theories existed. None of these, however, could satisfactorily explain the Great Depression, nor could they point the way to policy programs that would bring us out of the depression. But at that time the so-called Keynesian analysis was developed. Though strictly speaking the Keynesian analysis ignored growth and the cycle, it did provide an analytical foundation for the development of further theories. Accordingly, in the "post-Keynesian" period many new theories evolved that make use of several of the analytical tools presented in *The General Theory*. The outstanding feature of these new theories is that they deal with the interaction of the business cycle and economic growth. While the classicists ignored the cycle, and while Keynes and his disciples ignored growth, the modern emphasis is upon both.

An increasing emphasis upon endogenous theories has accompanied this emphasis on the interaction of growth and the cycle. Theories dealing with the cycle and growth may be classified as endogenous, exogenous, or "mixed." The former attempt to explain the turning points of the cycle with reference to the endogenous variables and the interaction of these variables; exogenous variables figure into such models only as fixed parameters. On the other hand, exogenous models explain the turning points strictly with reference to changing exogenous variables. Endogenous variables figure into these theories only as a means of explaining the cumulative processes of expansion and contraction. The "mixed" theories rely upon both types of variables to explain the turning points, and they are the typical form of cycle theories.

Since many of the modern theories make use of endogenous variables, there arises the problem of how to select between different variables and classify them as endogenous or exogenous. Nearly always some arbitrary, discretionary judgment must be exercised by the theorist, though some variables are obviously best treated as endogenous and others as exogenous.

QUESTIONS

5-1. Business cycle theory has its roots in both empirical fact and abstract reasoning. These two cornerstones of cycle theory, however, are only superficially contradictory. Discuss.

5-2. An "endogenous" model always contains "exogenous" variables and an "exogenous" model always contains "endogenous" variables. If this is so, how can models be termed "exogenous" and "endogenous"?

5-3. A. "Population is, without question, always an endogenous variable." B. "Nonsense! Population is always an exogenous variable." Consider and discuss these two contrasting points of view.

5-4. Give an example of: (a) a "purely exogenous" model of the business cycle; (b) a "purely endogenous" model; and (c) a "mixed" model.

5-5. At times a particular variable may be considered as endogenous, and at other times the same variable may be considered as exogenous. What are some of the major considerations involved in determining whether the variable should be endogenous or exogenous?

Bibliography

Duesenberry, J. S., *Business Cycles and Economic Growth*. New York: McGraw-Hill Book Company, 1958, Chapters 1, 9.

Haberler, G., *Prosperity and Depression*. Cambridge: Harvard University Press, 1958, Appendix I.

Hansen, A. H., *Business Cycles and National Income*. New York: W. W. Norton & Company, Inc., 1951, Chapters 21-24.

Koopmans, T. C., "The Econometric Approach to Business Fluctuations," *American Economic Review*, May 1949.

Leontieff, W., "Econometrics," in *A Survey of Contemporary Economics*, ed. H. S. Ellis. Philadelphia: The Blakiston Company, 1949, Vol. I.

Metzler, L. A., "Business Cycles and the Modern Theory of Employment," *American Economic Review*, June 1946, reprinted as Chapter 21 in *Readings in Business Cycles and National Income*, eds. A. H. Hansen and R. V. Clemence. New York: W. W. Norton & Company, Inc., 1953.

————, review of A. F. Burns and W. C. Mitchell's *Measuring Business Cycles*, *Social Research*, September 1947, reprinted as Chapter 27 in *Readings in Business Cycles and National Income*, eds. A. H. Hansen and R. V. Clemence.

6

Monetary Theories
of the Cycle:
Two ''Mixed'' Models

During the period from the 1870's until the 1930's most business cycle theorists considered monetary factors the prime movers in the cycle. While there were certainly other than just "monetary theories" up to the 'thirties, the major emphasis was on changes in the monetary environment as *the* causal force in the cycle.[1] The money supply, the interest rate, gold reserves, and commercial bank reserves were some of the prima donnas of the period. Nowadays, however, the role of money has been pushed somewhat into the background, though there are some indications of its being revived and placed once more in the center of

---

[1] In this part only a few of the major theories that had been developed prior to the 1930's are considered. For an excellent review of business cycle theory, see A. H. Hansen, *Business Cycles and National Income* (New York: W. W. Norton & Company, Inc., 1964), Chapters 13-24. See also G. Haberler, *Prosperity and Depression* (Cambridge: Harvard University Press, 1958), Chapters 2-3.

cycle theory.[2] Whether this will happen remains to be seen, but the "monetary theories" once had their heyday.

In this chapter two of the more important versions of the monetary theories—R. G. Hawtrey's "purely monetary" theory and F. A. Hayek's "monetary-overinvestment" theory are examined in some detail. In terms of the classification set forth in the preceding chapter, both of these theories may be considered as "mixtures." Both rely upon the interplay of endogenous variables to explain the upper-turning point and upon changes in exogenous variables to explain the lower-turning point.

Although these two theories differ in some respects, there is a fundamental affinity between them—namely, that changing monetary conditions are responsible for getting the cycle off the ground and into its cumulative four-stage flow. This, in turn, indicates another basic affinity between the two theories: since both stress monetary causal forces, both of course stress monetary policy as the prime means of mitigating cyclical fluctuations. These similarities, however, should not mislead one into believing that Hawtrey and Hayek present substantially identical theories. As subsequent discussion will reveal, the differences between the two analyses are often wide and deep. Let us now turn to a review of these theories and see what shape and form some of the earlier cycle analysis took.

1.   The Purely Monetary Theory: A "Mixed" Model

Hawtrey's theory of the business cycle, one of the most widely discussed and criticized explanations of the cycle, is often referred to as a "purely monetary" theory because of the extreme emphasis it places on changes in the money supply as a causative factor. As Hawtrey has put it:

> The general result up to which I hope to work is that the fluctuations are due to disturbances in the available stock of "money"—the term "money" being taken to cover every species of purchasing power avail-

---

[2]See, for example, the essays in section 3 of *Money, Trade, and Economic Growth* (New York: The Macmillan Company, 1951); D. Patinkin, *Money, Interest, and Prices* (Evanston, Illinois: Harper & Row, Publishers, 1956); T. Mayer, "The Empirical Significance of the Real Balance Effect," *Quarterly Journal of Economics*, May 1959; M. Friedman, "The Demand for Money: Some Theoretical and Empirical Results," *Journal of Political Economy*, August 1959; M. Friedman, ed., *Studies in the Quantity Theory of Money* (Chicago: University of Chicago Press, 1956); J. Gurley and E. S. Shaw, *Money in a Theory of Finance* (Washington, D. C.: The Brookings Institution, 1960).

able for immediate use, both legal tender money and credit money, whether in the form of coin, notes, or deposits at banks.[3]

However, before turning to a review and evaluation of Hawtrey's theory, certain prefatory comments are in order. First, Hawtrey developed his theory initially to apply to countries on the pure gold standard. This limitation, however, is not important, for the theory applies equally well to any country that operates on the basis of a fractional required reserve commercial banking system. Thus it applies to those economies where the gold standard, at least in its pure form, is lacking, without any significant modifications in analysis and results.

Hawtrey also uses somewhat confusing terminology, though it may easily be translated into more acceptable modern terms.[4] For Hawtrey, *"effective demand"* is the total demand for goods and services *in terms of money*, and is divided into two parts—expenditures by persons on consumers' goods *and* expenditures by persons on producers' goods. The total of these two types of outlay or expenditures is called *consumers' outlay* (C). In terms of current national income accounting, consumers' outlay is equivalent to national income at factor cost. As Hawtrey defines it: "Consumers' outlay is the total expenditure out of income, including expenditure on investment."[5] Thus in what follows it must be remembered that C *includes expenditures by businessmen on capital goods, including inventories,* as well as expenditures on ordinary consumers' goods and services.

Cash balances are equal to the stock of money (M), as defined above, while *velocity* (V) in Hawtrey's theory is *income velocity,* that is, the average number of times that M is spent or "turned over" in a designated time period. Obviously, the product of MV is equal to the total money expenditures during the designated time period, just as this total amount is also equal to the total money income of the period. Moreover, it is true by definition that the ". . . total effective demand [C] for all finished commodities in any community is simply the aggregate of all money incomes. . . . incomes and expenditures are simply

[3]R. G. Hawtrey, *Good and Bad Trade* (London: Constable & Co. Ltd., 1913), p. 3. See also his *Capital and Employment* (London: Longmans, Green and Co., 1952), p. 115, where he states: "The trade cycle is a monetary phenomenon because general demand is itself a monetary phenomenon."

[4]We say "somewhat confusing" only because Hawtrey developed his concepts and terms prior to the currently used national income accounts. His terms, however, are perfectly respectable.

[5]R. G. Hawtrey, *Capital and Employment,* p. 132. That Hawtrey's C is the same as national income at factor cost is easily seen once it is recalled that government is assumed out of the model. Thus there are no indirect business taxes and no government enterprises to consider.

the same quantity appearing on different sides of the account."[6] Since Hawtrey defines velocity as $V = C/M$, then by definition $MV = C$; that is, the product of the stock of money times its income velocity equals effective demand (C).[7] Therefore, if the product of MV changes, effective demand changes in the same direction and by the same amount. $MV = C$ is truly a tautology.

Hawtrey moreover is convinced that the community holds a fairly constant ratio of cash balances to money income (C).[8] His views on velocity may be put as follows: the proportion of C held in cash balances (k) is some constant, the value of which is determined solely by the preferences of the community. The constancy of k means of course that V is also constant.[9] Thus we may rewrite the tautology $MV = C$ as $M = kC$, where k is a constant. For example, if the community prefers to hold 10 per cent of C in the form of cash balances, and if C is $500, then M must be $50. The significance of this assumption for Hawtrey's analysis is that "autonomous" or unpredictable and volatile changes in V are eliminated as a monetary factor in the cycle. In short, if there is any change in C it must stem from changes in the quantity of M.[10]

A.   The Expansionary Stage

Now let us turn to Hawtrey's explanation of the business cycle. Note that it is necessary to break into the recurring cyclical pattern at some arbitrary point. The procedure followed here is to begin with the expansionary stage, but without explaining how the expansion has gotten

---

[6]Hawtrey, *Good and Bad Trade*, pp. 6, 14.

[7]This is merely a restatement of the Quantity Equation $MV = PO$, where M and V are the same as Hawtrey defines them, P is the average price level, and O is the annual rate of *current* output. This version of the Quantity Equation should not be confused with the $MV = PT$ version, in which T stands for *total transactions;* nor should it be confused with the "crude version" of $MV = PO$, where both V and O are assumed to be constant. See Chapter 8 for a fuller discussion of the Quantity Equation.

[8]See his *Good and Bad Trade*, pp. 11-12, 18. It should perhaps be noted that Hawtrey usually refers to these as "working balances."

[9]Although Hawtrey's concept of velocity has some resemblance to the so-called Cambridge cash-balances theory (and indeed this is why the symbol k is used), there is a basic difference. Hawtrey assumes that as C rises, so also will the absolute demand for cash balances, but that k is constant. Thus as C increases there is a rise in the total demand for money for transactions purposes. In the Cambridge version, on the other hand, k is not constant; rather it is subject to volatile change. See Chapter 8 for a discussion of the Cambridge version of the theory.

[10]It may be simpler to put Hawtrey's theory in terms of the Quantity Equation, but we shall stay within his own framework.

under way. After carrying the discussion through the expansion, upper-turning point, and the contraction, then the causes and origins of the expansion can be dealt with.

According to Hawtrey, the expansion may start for any one of three reasons, although actually he stresses only one.

1. *"Autonomous" forces* (e.g., war, drought, changes in consumer demand, innovation, and so on). While Hawtrey mentions the possibility of such forces, he argues that they are not sufficient to cause the cycle unless monetary conditions are permissive. Thus the emphasis is still on the monetary forces. Hawtrey in fact considers the autonomous factors as stimulants of irregular, not cyclical, fluctuations.

2. *Changes in V.* As already observed, Hawtrey tends to discount changes in velocity as a primary cause of cyclical fluctuations. So long as he assumes a constancy of k (which is merely the reciprocal of V), this position is unavoidable. Note, however, that he does not eliminate completely such a possibility—conceivably the community could have a large legacy of cash balances from the preceding contraction which it can use to increase C. While this would get the expansion underway, Hawtrey assumes that it is not very likely.[11]

3. *Changes in M.* Finally, and most important for Hawtrey, there is the expansion of M, attributable to the behavior of commercial bankers and certain businessmen. It is assumed that the fractional reserve commercial banking system possesses excess reserves, and in the process of lending these out the interest rate is lowered. The reduction in the interest rate, even if by only 1 or 2 per cent, is, in Hawtrey's view, sufficient to stimulate expansion. Thus monetary forces, acting through the commercial banking system and the interest rate, are responsible as the initiator of the expansion.

But is it true that businessmen are so responsive to changes in the rate of interest? Numerous studies have revealed that businessmen do not alter their investment spending plans as a result of changes in the interest rate unless the changes are quite substantial.[12] Hawtrey, on the other hand, insists that there is one class of businessmen that *does*

---

[11]R. G. Hawtrey, *The Art of Central Banking* (London: Longmans, Green and Co., 1933), p. 171. See also his "The Trade Cycle," reprinted in G. Haberler, ed., *Readings in Business Cycle Theory* (Philadelphia: The Blakiston Company, 1944), pp. 346-47.

[12]See section 1-E for a discussion of these studies. See also Chapters 7 and 11.

respond quickly to changes in the interest rate, even to such small changes as 1 per cent—namely, the *merchant class*. As he has put it:

> One of the special functions of a dealer is to keep a stock or "working balance" of the goods in which he deals. This is necessary to enable him to meet the varied demands of his customers without delay. Now a dealer borrows money to buy goods, and repays the money as the goods are sold. . . . When the rate of interest goes up, he will be anxious to reduce his indebtedness if he can reduce his stocks of goods by merely delaying replenishment when they are sold. . . . *In the case of a reduction of the short-term rate of interest an inducement will be afforded traders to hold larger stocks than before and to accelerate their purchases.*[13]

Thus as the result of even a slight reduction in the interest rate, there will be a rise in M and C. This is because the merchants respond to the lowered rate of interest by borrowing for inventory purposes, and in the mere process of borrowing from the commercial banks they increase M. This in turn tends to stimulate production, for as the merchants increase their orders, producers respond by increasing output and employment. As output rises, producers must also borrow and thus increase M (and C) even more. As C continues to rise, the merchants must borrow still more as their stocks are depleted, and (as Hawtrey puts it) "a vicious circle is set up" which is fed and propelled by a continuous expansion of bank credit.

Recall, however, the assumption that the community strives to hold a constant ratio of cash balances to C for transactions purposes, that is, k is constant. Note that, even though the proportion k is constant during the expansion, *the total demand for cash balances rises* simply because the total volume of C increases. For example, assume M = \$100, k = .5, and hence C = \$200. That is M = kC = .5 (\$200). Now if C rises during the expansionary stage to, say, \$400, and k remains constant at .5, the *total demand* for cash balances rises to \$200. Thus even though the *ratio k remains constant*, the *total demand for transactions balances rises during the expansionary stage*. This, as will be seen, plays an extremely important role in ending the expansion.

B.   The Upper-Turning Point and the Cash Lag Thesis

As the expansion continues, both prices and wages rise, but with wages lagging behind.[14] This of course creates rising profit anticipa-

---

[13]Hawtrey, *Good and Bad Trade*, p. 62. The italicized sentence is from *Capital and Employment*, p. 2.

[14]Hawtrey, *Good and Bad Trade*, p. 211. This implies that real wages move inversely to the business cycle—falling in periods of expansion and rising in periods of contraction. Recent evidence, however, shows that this is not necessarily

tions, which in turn induce both merchants and manufacturers to acquire larger stocks of goods. Thus there is more production, more borrowing by businessmen from commercial banks, and a further rise in M and hence C. During the cumulative expansion, however, commercial banks begin to experience a reduction in their excess reserves as they meet the rising demand for loans. The commercial banks may be able to prevent this depletion of excess reserves for a time by acquiring additional reserves from the Central Bank, but as noted below this is not sufficient to prevent the upper-turning point.[15] Eventually the expansion comes to an end. But what is Hawtrey's explanation for this?

At this point the so-called "cash lag thesis" must be introduced into the analysis. Recall that the total demand for cash balances has risen during the expansionary stage, and recall further that as the expansion continues the commercial banks have continued to reduce their excess reserves. Thus just as the total demand for cash balances is rising, the commercial banks discover that they are in an inadequate position to satisfy the demand out of their present reserves. In short, the commercial banks run into a reserve deficiency.

Now a reserve deficiency can be met in either (or both) of two ways: first, the commercial banks may "call in" loans, which would of course reduce both M and C; second, they may borrow from the Central Bank, provided that the latter is both willing and able to lend. Each of these alternatives must be examined.

The first possibility means a reduction in the stock of money and thus consumers' outlay. This may be illustrated as follows. Assume that the commercial banks in Table 6–1 have loaned out all of their excess reserves so that the stock of money stands at $500, loans and investments at $400, required reserves at $100, and excess reserves at zero.[16] To be sure, this is an extreme example, but it illustrates the cash lag

---

the case. While wage rates may lag at the turning points, a very important relationship in which this lag does not always show is between wholesale prices and wage rates. This, of course, is the relationship with which manufacturers are concerned, not with the relationship between wage rates and retail prices. If the "war cycles" are excluded, the data show that during periods of expansion manufacturing wages have risen more than (or as much as) wholesale prices of manufactured goods, and during contractions they have not always fallen as much. For two excellent studies, see D. Creamer, *Behavior of Wage Rates During Business Cycles* (New York: National Bureau of Economic Research, 1950), and Sho-Chieh Tsiang, *The Variations of Real Wages and Profit Margins in Relation to the Trade Cycle* (London: Pitman Publishing Corporation, 1947). See also Chapters 13 and 23 for a further discussion of wage-price relationships.

[15]This is obvious if the economy is on the pure gold standard, but recall that we have abstracted from this financial institution.

[16]This illustration assumes a required reserve ratio of 20 per cent.

TABLE 6–1

Required Reserves°	$100	Demand Deposits	$500
Excess Reserves	0		
Loans and Investments	400		
	$500		$500

° The required reserve ratio is assumed to be .20.

thesis well enough. Since the community's demand for cash balances is rising, it will turn to the commercial banks for the additional needed cash. Assume that the additional demand amounts to $50. The commercial banks must meet this higher demand out of their present reserves if the Central Bank is unable or unwilling to provide any assistance to them; and accordingly their reserve deposits are reduced from $100 to $50, leaving them with a reserve deficiency. This is shown in Table 6–2, where demand deposits now equal $450, and the required reserves *must* equal $90 (that is, 20 per cent of the $450 liabilities), but where the commercial banks are actually holding only $50 in their reserve deposits.

In this event the commercial banks must reduce their liabilities (since it has been assumed that they have no recourse to the Central Bank), and they do this by "calling in" loans, that is, as loans are paid off liabilities are reduced by an equal amount. *But this also means that M is reduced.* The end result is shown in Table 6–3, which shows that there has been a multiple contraction of the money supply. Thus as the commercial banks strive to meet the rising demand for cash balances, the stock of money (and hence C) is reduced by $250. In other words, the upper-turning point materializes because of the inability of the commercial banks to satisfy the community's rising demand for cash balances and still maintain the money supply.

This may all be put in terms of the classification established in Chapter 5. Once the expansion gets underway, the endogenous variables interact in a cumulative manner. That is, M rises, which in turn increases C, and the rise in C stimulates a further rise in M, and so on. There are, however, significant constraints (fixed parameters) in the form of the fractional reserve commercial banking system and the community's psychological motivation to hold a constant k. Accordingly, as the expansion continues, the absolute demand for cash balances rises just as the excess reserve position of the commercial banks declines. This results in a reduction of M, and hence C, so that the contraction gets underway. In short, the cumulative interactive expan-

TABLE 6—2

Legal Required Reserves	$ 90	Demand Deposits	$450
Reserves Actually Held*	50		
Reserve Deficiency	$ 40		
Loans and Investments	$400		
	$450†		$450

    * "Reserves actually held" are the total reserves after payment of $50 to depositors. With a required reserve ratio of .20, the system must hold $90 in required reserves; but since it is actually holding only $50 it is running a reserve deficiency of $40.

    † This $450 is the sum of the $400 of loans and investments and $50 of reserves actually held.

sion of the endogenous variables is reversed because of constraints established by the fixed parameters. The upper-turning point, therefore, is accounted for endogenously.

But may not the Central Bank shift the fixed parameters? That is, may not the Central Bank provide the commercial banks with the necessary funds to meet the rising demand for cash balances and in this way prevent the upper-turning point?

Hawtrey feels that this second alternative will be unsuccessful, except perhaps for a short period of time. If the commercial banks borrow additional reserves from the Central Bank, and if the Central Bank is both willing and able to satisfy their demand, the overall result will be hyperinflation. This, when carried far enough will, in Hawtrey's view, lead to a total breakdown of the monetary and banking system, as well as of the economic system. And the upper-turning point still occurs.[17]

Again, the upper-turning point may be accounted for endogenously, but in this case the fixed parameters are different. They relate to the community's inability to make rational economic decisions under conditions of highly uncertain expectations, and when this is the case, the upper-turning point sets in. This endogenous explanation of the reversal from expansion to contraction, however, is on a much different level than the one given above.

Let us sum up to this point. The commercial banks have two alternatives in meeting the rising demand for cash balances when their excess

---

    [17]Moreover, so long as the monetary system is tied to the pure gold standard, the upper-turning point is bound to occur. Due to rising prices, gold will flow out of the country, thus reducing the Central Bank's ability to provide the necessary reserves to the commercial banks.

TABLE 6—3

Required Reserves	$ 50	Demand Deposits	$250
Loans and Investments	200		
	$250		$250

reserves have been depleted. (1) If they do not borrow from the Central Bank, they must call in loans. In this event, both M and C will decline and the contraction sets in. (2) If they are willing to borrow from the Central Bank, and if the latter is able and willing to lend, the upper-turning point will occur anyhow. In this case the decisive factor is hyperinflation.

C.   The Contraction and Lower-Turning Point

Once the upper-turning point occurs, the contraction logically follows. Since most of the details of the contraction are the same as those of the expansion, except in reverse, there is little need to elaborate on them. Incomes fall, the stock of money falls, unemployment rises, output is restricted, and so on in a downward cumulative fashion. However, certain of these contractionary forces must be considered, particularly those that contribute to the end of the contraction and the lower-turning point.

As incomes continue to fall, the amount of cash that people want to hold for transactions purposes also falls. Thus there occurs an inflow of cash into the commercial banks, resulting in the accumulation of excess reserves. At first the commercial banks may be quite unwilling to lend out their newly acquired excess reserves because of the general contraction. In fact, not many businessmen may be willing to borrow, since wages lag behind prices, and thus profit expectations are quite low. However, the cash inflow continues until excess reserves accumulate to a high enough level that some commercial bankers adopt a willingness to make loans. When they do this the rate of interest, which had risen during the expansion and begun to fall during the contraction, is reduced even more, and indeed it is lowered enough that it stimulates some merchants into borrowing for inventory investment. Once this occurs, the lower-turning point sets in, and both M and C rise. The expansion follows.

Note that this is an exogenous explanation of the lower-turning point, for the reversal from contraction to expansion depends upon the changing psychological expectations of the commercial bankers and the merchants. As long as a sufficient amount of pessimism prevails, the contraction will continue, no matter how many excess reserves there may be. To be sure, the interplay of the endogenous variables increases the amount of excess reserves; but in this theory only a change in exogenous variables (expectations) will bring on the lower-turning point.

What however of the extreme case where the commercial bankers, despite their high excess reserves, are so pessimistic that they simply refuse to lend out their reserves? In this event it is possible for the merchants to use the cash balances accumulated during the prior expansion in order to acquire net additions to their now depleted stocks. But for the most part Hawtrey does not attach much significance to a rise in V to account for the lower-turning point, and he believes that some commercial bankers are always *eventually* willing to lend and some merchants always *eventually* willing to borrow.

There is still the possibility of an even more extreme case, where the commercial bankers are unwilling to lend and the merchants are unwilling to borrow or to use their cash balances. In this event, Hawtrey admits that the lower-turning point can occur only through the monetary policy of the Central Bank, which must buy securities in the open market, particularly from the commercial banks. This will increase the reserves of the commercial banks to the point that, if the open-market operations of the Central Bank are carried far enough, the commercial banks are so strongly induced to lend out their excess reserves that the expansion is started. This, of course, is an exogenous explanation of the lower-turning point.

Nevertheless, Hawtrey feels that the cash inflow into the commercial banks during the contraction will be sufficient to bring about the lower-turning point. Any recourse to Central Bank action must be made only after the commercial bankers and the merchants themselves have failed to bring on the expansion. In any event, Hawtrey rejects almost completely any resort to the more "drastic" measures of fiscal policy.[18]

The preceding discussion reveals clearly that Hawtrey's theory of the trade cycle is a "mixed" one. That is, the upper-turning point is accounted for by the interplay of the endogenous variables reversing

---

[18]Hawtrey, *Capital and Employment*, pp. 3-4, 115-19.

The intervention of the Government with its public works, or other capital outlay, is a device for injecting money into the economic system. It is only called for at all on the assumption that the banking system cannot perform the necessary service. Under modern conditions it is the function of the banks to irrigate the economic system (p. 118).

itself as the constraints established by fixed parameters are encountered. During the contraction the endogenous variables again interact cumulatively, but the process will continue until there is an exogenous change in the expectations of the commercial bankers and merchants. Thus, insofar as the upper-turning point is accounted for by the interplay of the endogenous variables, and the lower-turning point by changes in exogenous variables, Hawtrey's model is neither endogenous nor exogenous, but rather a *mixture*.

D.   Policy Implications

What policy proposals does Hawtrey advance as a means of "controlling" the cycle? In the first place, since the cause of the cycle is monetary, the control of it must obviously also be monetary. As noted above, in the absence of timely self-adjustment by commercial bankers and merchants, the responsibility of bringing on the lower-turning point and the ensuing expansion rests with the Central Bank.

There is however the more important policy of *prevention,* that is, taking action so as to prevent the upper-turning point from occurring in the first place. Instead of allowing the commercial banks to get into the position that they cannot meet the cash demands of their customers, the Central Bank should operate to maintain a constant flow of effective demand. At first glance the relevant policy would seem to be one where the Central Bank tightens up on commercial bank lending policies before the banks run into a reserve deficiency. Yet Hawtrey rejects this possible preventative policy in favor of another. For him the appropriate policy that the Central Bank should pursue is preservation of a constancy of consumers' outlay (C) at full employment. In order to do this effectively, the Central Bank must adhere to some criterion that yields clues as to when monetary action should or should not be taken. Only in this manner, he argues, can cyclical fluctuations be eliminated.

Hawtrey's views on the appropriate criterion have changed somewhat over the years, but the basic principle remains the same. In his *Monetary Reconstruction* he stated:

> So long as credit is regulated with reference to reserve proportions, the trade cycle is bound to recur. The flow of legal tender into circulation and back is one of the very tardiest consequences of credit expansion or contraction. If the Central Bank awaits for the flow to affect its reserves, and sits passively looking on at expansion or contraction gather-

ing impetus for years before it takes any decisive action, we cannot escape from the alternations of feverish activity with depression and un-employment. If the Central Bank watches, not the reserve proportion, but the aberrations of the flow of purchasing power (as measured by prices subject to the necessary allowances) from a perfectly even course, early action will be checked in time and the contraction will be avoided.[19]

However, in later writings he has stressed stabilization, not of the price level, but rather of the wage level. His major reason for advocating this criterion is that he believes account must be taken of changes in the factors of production (both labor and capital). Thus the aim of monetary policy is to stabilize effective demand by changing the money supply inversely to changes in the full-employment price level of the factors of production.[20]

E.   Critical Evaluation

An evaluation of Hawtrey's theory of the cycle is now in order. In the first place, he seems to have over-emphasized the significance of the interest rate, even as it affects merchants. Several important em-pirical studies have revealed that businessmen (including merchants) are not very responsive to changes in the interest rate, particularly small changes.[21] Besides, much more than simply the rate of interest is

---

[19]R. G. Hawtrey, *Monetary Reconstruction* (London: Longmans, Green and Co., 1923), pp. 144-45. A similar proposal has been advanced by some contem-porary American economists. See H. C. Simons, *Economic Policy for a Free Society* (Chicago: University of Chicago Press, 1948), Chapter 7; and for a more extended discussion, see L. W. Mints, *Monetary Policy for a Competitive Society* (New York: The McGraw-Hill Book Company, 1950).

[20]"Money and Index Numbers," *Journal of the Royal Statistical Society*, 1930, reprinted in *The Art of Central Banking*, pp. 303-32.

[21]The classic studies here are H. D. Henderson, "The Significance of the Rate of Interest," *Oxford Economic Papers*, October 1938; J. E. Meade and P. W. S. Andrews, "Summary of Replies to Questions on Effects of Interest Rates," *Oxford Economic Papers*, October 1938; P. W. S. Andrews, "A Further Inquiry into the Effects of Rates of Interest," *Oxford Economic Papers*, February 1940. For a good bibliography of the several studies that have been made, see J. R. Meyer and E. Kuh, *The Investment Decision: An Empirical Study* (Cambridge: Harvard Uni-versity Press, 1957). In two recent articles W. H. White has taken issue with the general conclusions of the earlier studies; see his "Interest Inelasticity of Invest-ment Demand: The Case from Business Attitude Surveys Reconsidered," *American Economic Review*, September 1956; and "The Rate of Interest in the Marginal Efficiency of Capital and Investment Programming," *Economic Journal*, March 1958. For a discussion that argues that changes in the interest rate have become less and less important in recent years, see A. F. Burns, *Prosperity Without In-flation* (New York: Fordham University Press, 1957), Chapter 3.

involved. Merchants, like most other businessmen, are not guided in their decision-making by reference to only one variable. Rather they keep an eye out on several, attempting to weight them as they see fit at the appropriate time.

But *if* one variable does stand out as important in the inventory investment plans of merchants, it is not the interest rate. Rather it is sales or the rate of change in sales. Retailing and wholesaling are complex, multi-product business activities that call for careful planning, especially with respect to inventories. There is little likelihood that merchants will increase their borrowing and lay in extra stocks, even at a relatively low interest rate, if the prospects for future sales look bleak. Thus it seems that sales expectations, which in turn are tied to consumer behavior, are far more important than variations in the interest rate.

The analysis that has been developed to explain the relationship between changes in anticipated sales volume and inventory investment usually goes under the title of the *acceleration principle*. The acceleration principle actually has many applications—it can be applied to the short-run or the long-run; it is relevant for investment in plant and equipment, as well as in inventories; it can even be applied to residential construction; and it plays an important role in modern cycle and growth theory. Thus the accelerator has many applications beyond the one given here.

What does the principle say? It states that there is a definite functional relationship between the rate of change in the total sales volume of consumers' goods and the volume of investment by merchants in inventories. This relationship may be stated as follows:

$$I_t = f(C_t - C_{t-1}).$$

In this equation the subscript t stands for the present time period, and therefore t—1 stands for the preceding time period. The symbol I designates *inventory* investment, and C stands for *consumption* or *sales* (not C as Hawtrey uses the symbol). The equation thus states in a general form that the investment in inventories in the present period is a "function of" (i.e., is determined by) the amount of the change in consumption between the present and the preceding periods.

Note that this is a general formulation and does not specify what the functional relationship is. However, the equation can be rewritten as

$$I_t = a(C_t - C_{t-1}),$$

where *a* stands for a given and unique functional relationship. The coefficient *a* is referred to as the *acceleration coefficient*. For example, assume that *a* has a value of 2; this means that every $1 increment in consumption expenditures between periods t and t—1 will induce extra inventory investment expenditures of $2 in period t. Thus if $C_t = \$150$ and $C_{t-1} = \$100$, then $I_t = \$100$. The $50 change in consumption induces a $100 change in investment expenditures on inventories.

At this point the logical question arises: Just what determines the value of *a*, the acceleration coefficient? For present purposes the value of *a* is assumed to be determined primarily by what the merchants consider to be the "desirable" ratio of inventories to sales. If $a = 2$, then this means that merchants desire to hold $2 of goods in current inventories for every $1 of sales. The actual ratio of course will be determined by a large number of forces, such as recent historical events, trial and error adjustments, and rules of thumb. And although it will differ between industries, and even between firms within an industry, there is some aggregate ratio for all merchants. Also the value of *a* will be subject to wide swings as merchants' expectations change from pessimism to optimism and back again, though for the moment let us abstract from this possibility.

Now under these assumptions it is obvious that when a change in consumption is positive, inventory investment will also be positive. But note that with *a* constant, the *change* in inventory investment may be *negative*, even though the change in consumption is positive. This is because with *a* constant, the behavior of inventory investment depends upon the *rate of change* of consumption. The acceleration principle states that *if consumption is increasing at an increasing rate, the total volume of investment will rise; and if consumption is increasing at a decreasing rate, the total volume of investment will decline.* The reverse of this generalization, dealing with decreases in consumption, also holds true. In other words, according to the acceleration principle, changes in the total volume of inventory investment are a function of changes in the *rate* of sales volume of consumers' goods.

A hypothetical illustration will be helpful. In this illustration assume that the acceleration coefficient is 2 (that is, merchants desire to maintain a ratio of inventory to sales of 2 to 1). Moreover assume that the coefficient is constant throughout the process. Assume further that the merchants believe that every change in sales from one period to the next is a permanent change, and that they adjust their inventory in period t according to the change in sales between periods t and t—1. Finally, for sake of completeness, assume that the prices of goods sold

TABLE 6–4

Hypothetical Illustration of the Acceleration Principle
Applied to Inventories

Period	Sales	Desired Inventory	Replacement Orders	Net, New Orders to Adjust Inventories	Total Orders
1	$100	$200	$100	$ 0	$100
2	100	200	100	0	100
3	112	224	112	24	136
4	130	260	130	36	166
5	145	290	145	30	175
6	150	300	150	10	160
7	150	300	150	0	150
8	145	290	145	—10	135
9	130	260	130	—30	100
8	145	290	145	—10	135
9	130	260	130	—30	100
10	112	224	112	—36	76
11	100	200	100	—24	76
12	100	200	100	0	100
13	112	224	112	24	136

and ordered for inventory do not change, and that inventories are valued by merchants at their sales prices.[22]

To begin with, in period 1 (Table 6–4) sales are $100, and thus at the end of the period actual inventories have been reduced by $100. Since this lowers actual inventories below the desired level of $200, replacement orders of $100 are given at the end of period 1, and these bring the actual inventory level back to the desired level of $200. The same observations apply to period 2. In short, so long as sales continue at the same rate, the only inventory investment is replacement investment—there is no net investment.

But note that in period 3 sales rise to $112. Now the merchants must order $136 of goods for inventory, of which $112 is for replacement and $24 is for net, additional stocks. Thus at the end of period 3 actual inventory was worked down to $98 since sales were $112. In order simply to replace and get actual inventories back to the former level of $200, $112 of goods must be ordered. However sales have increased by $12 between periods 2 and 3, so that now merchants respond by increasing their orders over and above replacement investment. The net, new orders are $24, that is, the acceleration coefficient (2) times $12. Thus the total orders at the end of period 3 are replacement ($112) plus net, new orders ($24)—a total of $136. And in period 4

---

[22]These assumptions are examined below.

the total orders are $166, of which $130 are for replacement and $36 are net, new orders.

Now it is important to observe that even though sales continue to rise beyond period 4, they do not rise as rapidly as before—that is, sales begin to increase at *a decreasing rate*. When this occurs the net, new orders to adjust inventories to the desired level *fall off*, even though total sales and total orders continue to rise. The increase in sales between periods 4 and 5 is only $15, resulting in net, new orders of $30, as compared to the net, new orders of $36 in the previous period. This is the logical result of a fixed ratio of inventory to sales— that is, of a fixed acceleration coefficient.

The same sort of relationship holds at the "lower-turning point." Following period 10 inventory decumulation tapers off even though sales continue to decline. This is because sales are now decreasing at a decreasing rate.

While the application of the accelerator to inventory investment has been widely discussed, there are certain qualifications that must be taken into account. First, consider the role of the economic expectations of the merchants. If, for example, they desire to hold a constant ratio of inventory to sales, and then consumer demand rises, the principle asserts that the demand for inventories will rise by a magnified amount. However, if business expectations are adverse, and there is a general feeling that this is simply a transitory rise in consumer demand, the inventory orders will rise only by the amount needed for replacement and not by the magnified amount. In fact, if expectations are adverse enough, perhaps the replacement demand will not be sufficient to maintain the size of total inventories. Thus a more realistic treatment of the accelerator must take into account the state of expectations of the merchants. The acceleration coefficient, after all, is a subjectively determined thing.

Consider another qualification—where there are surplus inventories held by the merchants. In this case the rise in sales may easily be satisfied out of existing stocks, and there will be no acceleration effect until the excess inventories are depleted. If the rise in sales continues, however, eventually the principle will come into play, once the excess stocks are liquidated. In fact, after this, if the rise in sales continues the merchants may feel the need to revise upwards the value of *a*. Again, if we want to be realistic, the acceleration coefficient must not be assumed to be fixed and unchanging.

Note finally the implicit assumption that the merchants have access to the financial funds required for the additional inventories. If the supply of funds is not elastic, the acceleration principle will not operate as it does in the above illustration. Hawtrey, of course, assumes that some of the commercial banks will be willing to lend some of their excess reserves.

Despite these qualifications, the acceleration principle seems to suffice quite well in explaining the behavior of inventory investment, especially by retailers. Further studies indicate that it also has a good deal of relevance in explaining inventory investment by manufacturers. In fact, this seems to be the consensus of most economists: the acceleration principle explains quite well the pattern of investment in inventories by businesses.[23] (However, as will be seen later, it does not do such a good job in explaining short-run investment in plant and equipment.) This is not to say that the proponents of the acceleration principle argue that it is the only determinant influencing inventory investment, but it is to say that the principle goes rather far in explaining this type of investment behavior.

But to bring this back to Hawtrey. In his theory of the business cycle Hawtrey has over-emphasized the significance of changes in the interest rate by stating that these changes are the primary cause of the cycle. A slight reduction in the rate of interest, working through inventory investment, is supposed to bring on the expansion. However, the discussion of the acceleration principle has shown that inventory investment is far more complicated than Hawtrey assumes. Hawtrey's over-emphasis on the importance of only one causative factor results in a rather restrictive theory that does not do full justice to the rich complexity and changing nature of the business cycle. Other variables

---

[23]See especially the following studies: M. Abramovitz, *Inventories and Business Cycles* (New York: National Bureau of Economic Research, 1950); R. Mack and V. Zarnowitz, "Causes and Consequences of Changes in Retailers' Buying," *American Economic Review*, March 1958; P. G. Darling, "Manufacturers' Inventory Investment, 1947-1958," *American Economic Review*, December 1959; G. M. Cobren and M. Liebenberg, "Inventories in Postwar Business Cycles," *Survey of Current Business*, April 1959; and Joint Economic Committee, *Inventory Fluctuations and Economic Stabilization*, 87th Cong., 1st sess. (Washington, D. C.: Government Printing Office, 1961), Parts II-IV.

For theoretical treatments of inventory cycles, see L. Metzler, "The Nature and Stability of Inventory Cycles," *Review of Economic Statistics*, August 1941, "Business Cycles and the Modern Theory of Employment," *American Economic Review*, June 1946, reprinted as Chapter 21 in A. H. Hansen and R. V. Clemence, eds., *Readings in Business Cycles and National Income* (New York: W. W. Norton & Company, Inc., 1953), and "Factors Governing the Length of Inventory Cycles," *Review of Economic Statistics*, February 1947. R. Nurkse, "The Cyclical Pattern of Inventory Investment," *Quarterly Journal of Economics*, August 1952, summarizes and expands Metzler's theory.

must be introduced, even if only inventory investment is singled out for emphasis, and once these other variables enter the scene more than just changes in the interest rate must be considered.

Finally, to repeat, Hawtrey has developed a "mixed" model of the cycle, in which the interplay of endogenous variables is used to explain the upper-turning point, and changes in exogenous variables (especially bankers' willingness to lend) are used to account for the lower-turning point. Once the expansion gets under way it becomes cumulative, but it cannot continue because of the "automatic" restrictive forces exercised by the fractional reserve commercial banking system and the constancy of k. The depletion of excess reserves, the constancy of k, and the emergence of a reserve deficiency are what bring on the upper-turning point. On the other hand, once the contraction gets under way it could continue indefinitely, except that commercial bankers, finding themselves with accumulated reserves, decide to lower the interest rate, which in turn stimulates merchants to add to their inventories. But a reduction of the interest rate is not "automatically" assured; it all depends upon the psychological status of the commercial bankers. This should be considered as a change in an exogenous variable.

The fact that Hawtrey's analysis fits into the category of "mixed" models, however, should not be considered a criticism. While those who prefer purely endogenous models have criticized it on these grounds,[24] there are others who accept the "mixed" model as desirable and useful. Be that as it may, Hawtrey's purely monetary theory stands as an example of an earlier "mixed" model.

2. The Monetary-Overinvestment Theory: Another "Mixed" Model

While Hawtrey tends to concentrate on changes in the interest rate as the prima donna of the cycle, the theory discussed in this section has combined the monetary element with investment changes as the relevant forces. Because of this combination of forces, this theory has acquired the title of the inventory-overinvestment theory, and though

---

[24]See especially Metzler, "Business Cycles and the Modern Theory of Employment."

a number of economists have advocated it, only the version advocated by its best-known supporter, F. A. Hayek,[25] is discussed here.

Briefly the monetary-overinvestment theory argues that though monetary forces are necessary to get the cycle off the ground, the upper-turning point occurs because of the emergence of a "maladjustment" in the vertical stages of production.[26] Thus, in contrast to Hawtrey's analysis, the upper-turning point occurs, not because of restrictive monetary conditions but because of this maladjustment. The maladjustment is what Hayek often refers to as a "shortage of capital." This terminology has led to some confusion in discussion of this theory, since actually two important words—"savings" and "capital"—are used synomomously by the advocates of the analysis. That is, whatever is saved is assumed to enter automatically into capital investment. Thus when the monetary-overinvestment theorists conclude that the expansion comes to an end because of a "shortage of capital," they are in effect saying that the upper-turning point occurs because of a "shortage of savings." The implications of this assumption will be made clear as we proceed, but the terminology must be kept clearly in mind.

A.   Some Important Concepts and Conditions

The usual exposition of the monetary-overinvestment theory makes use of the concept of general equilibrium as the point of departure, although this is not absolutely essential. There are two important conditions of this general equilibrium that must be understood. First, it assumes that there is full employment of all the productive resources in the economy. This follows in large part from the further assumption that purely competitive conditions prevail everywhere.[27]

---

[25]F. A. Hayek, *Prices and Production* (London: George Routledge & Sons, Ltd., 1935); *Monetary Theory and the Trade Cycle* (London: Jonathan Cape, 1933); and "Price Expectations, Monetary Disturbances, and Malinvestments," in G. Haberler, ed., *Readings in Business Cycle Theory*. For other statements, see L. Robbins, *The Great Depression* (New York: The Macmillan Company, 1934), and especially H. S. Ellis, *German Monetary Theory* (Cambridge: Harvard University Press, 1934), for a review of the theory.

[26]"Vertical stages" of production are the related subsequent stages from raw materials to the finished product. The monetary-overinvestment theorists often refer to the stages farther away from the final consumer, and thus closer to the raw materials, as the "higher stages," while those closer to the final consumer are termed the "lower stages."

[27]The analysis that leads to this conclusion is rather complicated and thus for the moment we brush it aside. It is discussed, however, at some length in Chapter 15.

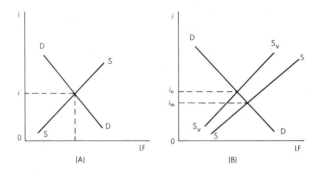

FIGURE 6—1

Second, it is assumed that the prevailing *money rate* of interest is equal to the *"natural"* rate. Following Knut Wicksell,[28] Hayek differentiates between two rates of interest—the natural rate and the prevailing market rate. The significance of these two rates can best be described graphically. In Figure 6–1A the "interest rate" (i) is plotted on the vertical axis, and "loanable funds" (LF) are plotted on the horizontal axis. The demand curve (DD) of businesses for loanable funds for investment purposes is negatively sloped, showing an inverse relationship between the quantity of loanable funds demanded and the interest rate. The demand curve is really an expression of the expected net return from the use of loanable funds in investment projects, and it has a negative slope because of the "law of diminishing returns." Thus at the equilibrium rate of O_i (Figure 6–1A), the expected net return of the last investment project OX is just equal to the interest cost of acquiring the funds to finance that project. Diminishing returns means that further investment projects beyond OX will yield an expected net rate of return below the rate O_i, and hence will not be carried out unless the interest rate is reduced.[29]

The supply curve, on the other hand, is a bit more complex, for it is a sum of *two supply curves of loanable funds*—the curve of *volun-*

<hr>

[28]The most relevant of Wicksell's works for present purposes are *Interest and Prices* (London: The Macmillan Company, 1936); *Lectures on Political Economy,* Vol. I, *General Theory,* and Vol. II, *Money* (London: The Macmillan Company, 1934, 1935).

[29]For a complete modern statement of the analysis involved, see F. A. and V. C. Lutz, *The Theory of Investment of the Firm* (Princeton: Princeton University Press, 1951).

tary savings and the curve of *commercial bank credit.* The equilibrium rate of interest O_i is at the height of the intersection of the two curves (that is, where quantity demanded equals quantity supplied). But, in Figure 6–1A, which rate of interest is O_i—the natural or the market?

To answer this, break down the total supply curve SS into its two component parts. The curve of voluntary savings, which is shown as S_vS_v in Figure 6–1B, indicates the amounts that the members of the community are willing to save *voluntarily* out of their current incomes at different rates of interest. The intersection of the demand curve with the voluntary savings curve indicates the so-called natural rate O_{in}. In other words, *the natural rate is that rate which equates the quantity demanded of loanable funds and the quantity supplied of voluntary savings.*

The other part of the total supply curve SS is made up of commercial bank credit. In Figure 6–1B this is shown as the difference between S_vS_v aned SS. Thus, the intersection of the *total* supply curve with the demand curve yields the *market* or prevailing rate of interest O_{im}. In the situation depicted in Figure 6–1B the market rate lies below the natural rate; this discrepancy, as will be seen, is of crucial importance in the monetary-overinvestment theory.[30]

Note that the natural and the market rates will be identical if there is no supply of bank credit. Thus if the total supply curve is made up solely of the supply of voluntary savings, then the interest rate is both the natural and the market rate. The discrepancy in Figure 6–1B occurs only because the supply of commercial bank credit has been included so that the total supply of loanable funds exceeds the supply of voluntary savings.

Since the analysis begins from a general equilbrium position, the natural rate is equal to the prevailing market rate. To get the expansion started, the monetary-overinvestment theorists must introduce a discrepancy between the two rates so that the market rate lies below the natural. They do this by introducing commercial bank credit into the picture. But they also assume that investment opportunities are unlimited, that new capital formation is, as it were, always lurking around the corner, held back from becoming a reality only by the prevailing market rate of interest. Those investment projects with an expected rate of return in excess of the market rate will of course come into

---

[30]A discrepancy, however, can be caused by a shift of DD to the right because of innovations, population growth, discovery of new sources of raw materials, and so on. These are the forces stressed by Wicksell, who influenced Hayek very much. See also the discussion of Schumpeter's and Hansen's theories in the next chapter.

being, but those with an expected rate of return less than the prevailing market rate are held in abeyance. Thus a reduction in the prevailing market rate below the natural rate will lead to an increase in the quantity demanded of loanable funds merely because investment projects that were not sound at the former, higher market rate now become economically sound.

B. The Expansionary Process

As noted above, the expansionary process can get under way only if the market rate falls below the natural rate. There are three possible changes in the interest rate that should be distinguished here, though only two of these result in the discrepancy necessary to set off the expansion.

1. Assume that the situation is as shown in Figure 6–2A, where the prevailing market rate and the natural rate are equal at O_i. Now assume that there is a rise in voluntary savings, so that the supply curve shifts from SS to S′S′. In this case the rate of interest will fall from O_i to O_i', but there will be no expansionary stage.[31] The reason for this is that the lower rate is still the natural rate. To be sure, there will be some net, new capital formation, but this comes from resources voluntarily released from the consumers' goods industries as a result of the rise in voluntary savings. Thus savings and investment will be equal, and per capita income will be higher.

2. A second possibility is that autonomous forces, such as population increases, the discovery of new markets, and so on, will shift the demand curve to the right from DD to D′D′, as in Figure 6–2B. Though at first glance this does not seem sufficient to get the expansion started, the monetary-overinvestment theorists do in fact rely on this explanation once the cycle has gotten started.

3. The third possibility, and the relevant one here, is shown in Figure 6–2C. In this case begin with the prevailing market rate equal to the natural rate at O_{in}, that is, assume that the supply curve is made up solely of voluntary savings. Now assume that commercial bank credit becomes available so that the total supply curve

---

31There could, however, possibly be an expansion if rigidities and lags of adjustment to changing employment opportunities exist. On this see G. Haberler, *Prosperity and Depression.* p. 41, n. 1.

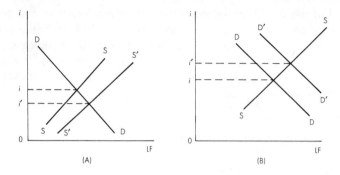

(A)   (B)

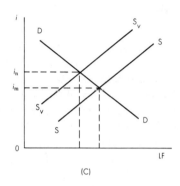

(C)

FIGURE 6–2

shifts to the right SS, and the market rate O_{im} now lies below the natural rate. At this lower market rate businessmen borrow additional funds (EX amount in Figure 6–2C) to finance their new investment projects.

However, there is a fly in the ointment—and according to Hayek it is rather a large fly at that—for a conflict develops between the businessmen and the consumers. Since the economy is initially experiencing *full employment of resources*, the only way that the new investment plans of businessmen in the producers' goods sector can be realized is for some resources to be bid away from the consumers' goods sector. But, and this is the relevant point, *consumers have not increased their voluntary savings*—that is, they have not expressed any desire to cut back on their consumption and hence allow resources to be reallocated towards the producers' goods industries. In short, the plans of the consumers and the plans of the investing businesses are in basic conflict.

In this conflict the businessmen in the producers' goods industries will win out at first, primarily because they possess the extra purchasing power created by the commercial banking system. They use this to bid productive services away from the consumers' goods industries by offering higher rates of remuneration to the resource owners. As the services are transferred over to the producers' goods sector, the output of consumers' goods is reduced and hence their prices rise. The result of this is *"forced" savings*—that is, consumers, because of the cutback in the supply of, and the consequent rise in the price of, consumers' goods, are forced to reduce their consumption. These forced savings are merely the medium by which the resources are released from the consumers' goods sector and made available to the producers' goods sector of the economy.

However, the forced savings are not—indeed, cannot be, according to Hayek—permanent since permanancy characterizes only voluntary savings. Nevertheless the increase in investment must be accompanied by an increase in *real* savings, and at the outset of the expansion this means "forced" savings by consumers. The businessmen will win out in the conflict at this stage of the analysis simply because they have the necessary monetary funds extended to them by the commercial banks.

There is an important qualification to the preceding analysis. The monetary-overinvestment theorists introduce a *time lag* into their analysis to help explain the occurrence of forced savings. Since this time lag is so important in Hayek's theory, it must be elaborated on. The first point to note is that the productive resources that have shifted employments do not receive their higher remuneration until after a certain time period (say, a month) has elapsed. This time lag is the period between the shift of the resources from the consumers' goods industries to the producers' goods industries and the receipt of their higher money incomes. During this period, of course, the supply of consumers' goods is falling off, while at the same time the prices of consumers' goods are rising; and it is this that forces consumers who have not experienced any rise in money incomes to cut back on their quantity demanded of goods and services, thus releasing the resources for the producers' goods industries necessary to carry out the new investment.

But still these forced savings are temporary. The rising price level of consumers' goods enhances the profit expectations of the firms in the consumers' goods industries. Moreover, the monetary receipts of the consumers' goods producers have risen substantially, and thus they can bid the productive resources back away from the capital goods sector. They can do this simply because the conflict between the businessmen and the consumers will, in the final analysis, be won by the latter. By attempting to restore their real consumption position, the consumers transfer relatively more command over resources (that is, money purchasing power) to the consumers' goods industries so that the latter can rebid resources away from the producers' goods sector. This results in a decline in activity in the producers' goods industries, and hence unemployment sets in. The upper-turning point thus occurs and the contraction gets under way.

However, there appears really to be no reason for the upper-turning point to occur, for as the consumers' goods industries experience more profitability, they will increase their demand for the output of the producers' goods industries. This would shift purchasing power back to the producers' goods sector which could then presumably reacquire the resources that they need but have lost to the consumers' goods industries. There thus could be a continual shifting and reshifting of resources between these two sectors at full employment, without any contraction.

The monetary-overinvestment theorists argue nevertheless that the upper-turning point will occur, but to demonstrate this they have to make certain additional assumptions. In the first place, they must assume that the rise in demand for consumers' goods is *relatively greater* than the logically subsequent rise in demand for producers' goods. Since this means higher profit expectations and also higher prices in the consumers' goods sector the productive resources can be kept there.

Accordingly, the only way in which the producers' goods sector can continue its expansion is by turning to the commercial banks for more credit. They are forced to do this since they cannot acquire the necessary resources otherwise. However, the increased demand for bank credit raises the market rate of interest above the natural rate, and this increases *the money costs of the producers' goods sector.* These theorists must argue that the rise in money costs is greater than *the rise in demand for the output of the producers' goods industries.* This of course makes many investment projects unprofitable, with the result that the activity in this important sector declines. It certainly will slow down the rate of investment. The unemployment that results reduces aggregate demand, with the consequence of a decline in prices, output, and employment in general. The contraction thus sets in.

Before turning to the contraction and the lower-turning point, two things need to be cleared up. So far as the notion of a "shortage of capital" is concerned, what the monetary-overinvestment theorists mean is that there is too much consumption and "too little savings" for the expansion to continue. Paradoxically, if only consumers would cut back on their consumption and increase their voluntary savings, the expansion would continue. Since they have no desire to do so, and since the process of expansion has contributed money income in their favor, the businessmen in the producers' goods sector must turn to the commercial banks. During the expansion, however, banks have exhausted their reserves so that there is a general "shortage of loanable funds" so far as the producers' goods industries are concerned. It is this shortage of loanable funds (shortage of capital) which is responsible for the upper-turning point. The monetary-overinvestment theorists point out that this "shortage of capital" is the same thing as a "shortage of investment," by which they mean an insufficiency of the amount of capital formation needed to prevent the upper-turning point. If only the producers' goods industries could acquire the necessary funds to continue their activity, the reversal would not take place.

So far as the notion of "vertical maladjustment" in the structure of production is concerned, what is meant here is that there has been "too much" investment in the producers' goods industries relative to consumers' desires. The initial monetary advantages of these industries facilitated an expansion that did not fit with consumers' needs. Thus there occurred an imbalance which can be corrected only if consumers increase their voluntary savings or if the economy passes through the contractionary stage, during which the activity in the producers' goods sector is brought into balance with consumers' desires.

Note that the upper-turning point in Hayek's theory is accounted for by the endogenous variables. Once the expansion gets underway, the endogenous variables interact cumulatively but eventually are reversed because of the constraints set by the fixed parameters. In this case the most important parameters are the fixed savings habits of consumers and the reserve position of the commercial banks. These are sufficient to create a "shortage of capital" so that the upper-turning point occurs.

C. The Contraction and the Lower-Turning Point

Once the contraction sets in the process becomes cumulative. However the monetary-overinvestment theorists are not very clear about the major characteristics of the contractionary process. But they do agree on three major points.

First, there is a contraction of the money supply as the commercial banks "call in loans." This of course intensifies the contraction. At the same time many businesses strive to increase their cash reserves as a protection against bankruptcy. Still, these theorists agree that as the contraction proceeds the reserve position of the commercial banks is improved.

Second, the preceding expansion created an "excess" of productive capacity in the producers' goods industries, and thus there must be a process of readjustment until a proper balance is restored between the different stages of production. That is to say, the "maladjustment" that was created in the expansionary period must now be eliminated. And since this requires some time, unemployment and low output will prevail until the imbalance is redressed.

Finally, even though the market rate has fallen, these theorists argue that it remains above the natural rate. This discrepancy (of the market above the natural rate) first emerged during the later phases of the expansionary stage, and it continues during the contractionary stage. Even though the commercial banks are acquiring excess reserves—either because of a cash inflow into the banks or because of Central Bank action, or both—the general decline in prices and the widespread pessimism combine to keep the market rate above the natural. Thus as the contraction continues into its later phases, the market rate continues to fall, but according to these theorists its lowest level is still above the natural rate.

The monetary-overinvestment theorists are, however, none too clear as to why the lower-turning point takes place. The major reason given is that as the price level stops falling, and as optimism replaces pessimism, the market rate for some reason lies above the natural rate. But at this point their reasoning takes somewhat of a different approach. The discrepancy occurs, not because the market rate falls below the natural rate (for commercial bankers' pessimism insures that no bank credit will be extended), but because *the natural rate rises above the market rate.* That is, once the readjustment period, during which the maladjustment is eliminated, is finished, businessmen in the producers' goods industries become more optimistic about profits outlooks and thus increase their demand for loanable funds.[32] This shifts the demand curve for loanable funds to the right, with the result that the natural rate is pushed above the market rate. This has been put quite succinctly by Hayek:

---

[32]See Hayek, *Monetary Theory and the Trade Cycle*, pp. 146-47, 151-52, 168-73.

The situation in which the money rate of interest is below the natural rate need not, by any means, originate in a *deliberate lowering* of the rate of interest by the banks. The same effect can be obviously produced by an improvement in the expectations of profit or by a diminution in the rate of saving, which may drive the "natural rate" (at which the demand for and the supply of savings are equal) above its previous level; while the banks refrain from raising their rate of interest to a proportionate extent, but continue to lend at the previous rate, and thus enable a greater demand for loans to be satisfied than would be possible by the exclusive use of the available supply of savings. The decisive significance of the case quoted is not, in my view, due to the fact that it is probably the commonest in practice, but to the fact that it *must inevitably recur* under the existing credit organization.[33]

Once this occurs, the commercial bankers tend to become more optimistic and begin to extend loans, so that the supply curve shifts to the right, lowering the market rate relative to the natural rate even more. And the expansion gets under way.

The interesting thing to note here is that the monetary-overinvestment theorists rely upon exogenous shocks to account for the lower-turning point. The preceding quotation from Hayek clearly illustrates this. Thus, insofar as there has been a recurrence of economic fluctuations, there has been, according to this model, a recurrent clustering of technological advancements and innovations that drive the natural above the market rate of interest. Hayek's theory, therefore, like Hawtrey's, is a "mixed" model.

D. Policy Implications

Are there any means by which the Central Bank can prevent the upper-turning point? The answer of the monetary-overinvestment theorists is an emphatic *No!* The reason they advance is simply that the voluntary choices of consumers and producers do not agree. And it is not the function of the Central Bank to force consumers to change their voluntary decisions so that they would cut back on their consumption and increase their savings. In a free enterprise, capitalist system, this is impossible.[34]

There is, however, the possibility of preventing the expansion from getting off the ground (if it is deemed desirable to do so). In this event the responsibility of the Central Bank is to prevent the commercial

---

[33]*Ibid.*, pp. 147-48.

[34]For a statement of the ideological views of these theorists, see L. Robbins, *Economic Planning and International Order* (London: The Macmillan Company, 1938). For a more recent statement, see F. A. Hayek, *The Road to Serfdom* (Chicago: University of Chicago Press, 1944).

banks from lowering the market rate below the natural rate. But, again, in a free enterprise system, if the discrepancy between the two rates occurs because of buoyant expectations which raise the natural above the market rate, there is little that the Central Bank can do. If it were to force the market rate up to an equality with the natural, then economic growth would be impeded, and again, it is not the function of the Central Bank to make such momentous decisions regarding the well-being of all.

Once the depression has set in, the Central Bank can and should pursue a monetary policy designed to lower the market rate below the natural rate. Institutional limitations and rigidities, however, often make this a slow process. Certainly the Central Bank must operate to prevent consumers from acquiring bank credit and to provide commercial banks with reserves to lend to businesses.

E.   Critical Evaluation

So far as critical observations are concerned, only two will be mentioned. First, the criticism of Hawtrey's theory—that too great an emphasis is placed on the significance of changes in the interest rate— is equally, if not more, relevant here. While Hawtrey confines his impact of the interest rate to inventory investment, Hayek stresses its impact on all types of investment. Again we refer to the studies that indicate that the interest rate does not loom large in investment decisions.[35]

Second, the monetary-overinvestment theorists start from a position of full employment in the economy, and they also begin by having the supply curve of loanable funds rise relative to the demand curve. This lowers the market rate below the natural rate. But in discussing the lower-turning point after the cyclical process has gotten underway, they have the demand curve rise relative to the supply curve as a result of technological advances and improved expectations on the part of businessmen. Moreover, they have to introduce some upward rigidity in the market rate so that the necessary discrepancy emerges, with the natural above the market rate. To be sure, these improved expectations, reflecting an awareness of the development of underlying growth factors in the economy, must operate through the monetary system, but even so perhaps this theory is better classified as an "innovational" theory, with substantial and important psychological elements figuring in.

---

[35]See references in footnote 21 of this chapter; see also Chapter 11.

Finally, to repeat, Hayek relies heavily upon exogenous forces at the lower-turning point—namely, improved expectations of businessmen and awareness of the underlying growth factors. These are changes in exogenous variables. At the upper-turning point he introduces the restrictiveness of commercial bank credit and a constancy of consumers' desires to save, both of which are constant parameters. Thus producers cannot receive enough capital funds to carry their investment projects through to completion. But at the lower-turning point he introduces improved psychological expectations reflecting an awareness of the growth factors in the economy. Endogenous variables play the major role in the expansion, upper-turning point, and contraction; but they are not sufficient to bring on the lower-turning point. Hayek, like Hawtrey, has to call upon external changes to halt the cumulative downward processes once they get underway. Thus he too presents a "mixed" theory of the business cycle.

3. Summary

There is little need to summarize any further the preceding discussion. The critical evaluations of the theories of Hawtrey and Hayek that induce us to reject them as adequate explanations of the business sary. While each of the foregoing theories possess certain limitations provide a sufficient summary. Perhaps only one final word is necessary. While each of the foregoing theories possess certain limitations cycle, certainly each possesses a grain of truth. Changes in the money supply and in the interest rate are important variables in the business cycle, as are changes in the structure of production. Nevertheless, there are also many other important variables that are either neglected or minimized by these theories. In short, a satisfactory theory must be more inclusive than the "purely monetary" and "monetary-overinvestment" theories.

QUESTIONS

6-1. "The acceleration principle, without doubt, nullifies Hawtrey's theory of the trade cycle." Critically evaluate this statement.

6-2. What is meant by a "shortage of capital" and a "shortage of savings" in Hayek's theory of the business cycle? Of what significance are these "shortages"?

6-3. Explain how an increase in commercial bank excess reserves will, *ceteris paribus*, lower the market rate of interest relative to the natural rate of interest.

6-4. What is meant by the "cash lag" thesis? Is the assumed constancy of *k* essential to this particular hypothesis? Explain.

6-5. Explain how both Hayek's and Hawtrey's theories of the business cycle are "mixed" models.

6-6. In Hayek's theory of the business cycle the lower-turning point occurs as a result of the natural rate of interest rising relative to the market rate. What explanation does Hayek provide in order to account for the natural rate rising relative to the market rate?

Bibliography

Abramovitz, M., *Inventories and Business Cycles*. New York: National Bureau of Economic Research, 1950.

Haberler, G., *Prosperity and Depression*. Cambridge: Harvard University Press, 1958, Chapters 2-3.

Hansen, A. H., *Business Cycles and National Income*. W. W. Norton & Company, Inc., 1964, Chapters 18-19.

Hawtrey, R. G., *Good and Bad Trade*. London: Constable & Co., Ltd., 1913.

———, *Capital and Employment*. London: Longmans, Green and Co., 1952.

———, "The Trade Cycle," reprinted in *Readings in Business Cycle Theory*, ed. G. Haberler. Philadelphia: The Blakiston Company, 1944.

Hayek, F. A., *Prices and Production*. London: George Routledge & Sons, Ltd., 1935.

———, *Monetary Theory and the Trade Cycle*. London: Jonathan Cape, 1933.

———, "Price Expectations, Monetary Disturbances, and Malinvestments," reprinted in *Readings in Business Cycle Theory*, ed. G. Haberler.

Mack, R. and V. Zarnowitz, "Cause and Consequence of Changes in Retailers' Buying," *American Economic Review*, March 1958.

Metzler, L., "Business Cycles and the Modern Theory of Employment," reprinted as Chapter 21 in *Readings in Business Cycles and National Income*, eds. A. H. Hansen and R. V. Clemence. New York: W. W. Norton & Company, Inc., 1953.

7

The Innovational Theorists

In this chapter the cycle and growth theories of two important modern economists—Joseph A. Schumpeter and Alvin H. Hansen—are discussed in some detail. The basic affinity between these two theories is that both stress the important role played by "innovational investment." Both Hansen and Schumpeter agree that changes in investment spending on plant and equipment are the cause of the major cycle, and they also agree that changes in investment are related to businessmen's behavior in a capitalist system. Further, both emphasize the distinction between "induced investment" and "autonomous investment," with the latter receiving much more attention in their theories than the former. Roughly, the argument is that changes in autonomous investment are responsible for cyclical fluctuations, while changes in induced investment serve to aggravate the fluctuations once they are underway.

Although there is no completely acceptable definition of "autonomous" and "induced" investment, a rough distinction will serve well enough for purposes of this chapter. "Induced" investment means the net capital formation which is called forth in response to *recent changes* in some important economic variable or set of variables, such as output, sales, income, profits, market value of the enterprise, or what have you. This concept of induced investment is not new, for it was

discussed in the last chapter in the form of the acceleration principle—
that is, changes in the rate of sales volume induce changes in net, new
investment in inventory. Aside from this, however, there is a substantial amount of controversy as to which of the variables mentioned is
most instrumental in inducing new investment in plant and equipment.[1] This is not the place to discuss and evaluate these different
hypotheses; for the moment suffice it to say that induced investment
is that investment which is brought forth in response to recent changes
in any one or more of the variables mentioned above.

"Autonomous investment," on the other hand, is the net capital formation which is called forth in response to anticipated or realized
changes in the *long-run growth factors,* such as technological advance,
population growth, resource discovery, and even changes in the institutional structure of the economic system. Quite often this type of investment is referred to as "innovational investment." An innovation is
any response to long-run changes (or anticipated long-run changes)
that call for a new way of doing things, whether in production or
marketing or organization. Thus innovations "disrupt" the prevailing
methods of production, marketing, and organization, as well as the
prevailing complex of products available to consumers. They require
not only short-run response by businessmen, consumers, and the
owners of productive services, but also long-run adjustments since the
impacts of innovations are often lasting as well as disruptive.

The innovational theorists have, of course, one major task confronting them: they must provide an explanation of the process by which
innovations occur. This often requires some excursions into the psychology and sociology of businessmen, as well as careful scrutiny of
the nebulous future and prognostication of the effects of changing conditions. Let us turn to the analyses of Schumpeter and Hansen to see
how they have met this task.

1.   The Schumpeterian System

The analysis of Joseph A. Schumpeter is difficult to discuss and assess because of its breadth and comprehensiveness.[2] Any thorough ex-

---

[1]These disagreements are discussed in Chapters 11 and 16-19.

[2]The major works are: *Business Cycles* (New York: McGraw-Hill Book Company,
1939), Vols. I-II; *Capitalism, Socialism and Democracy* (New York: Harper & Row,
Publishers, 1947); and *The Theory of Economic Development* (Cambridge: Harvard University Press, 1951). *The Theory of Economic Development* was the first
of these to be published (1911), and the analysis presented in the subsequent
books is largely a variation on the theme developed in this first major work.

position and evaluation of this brilliant work must proceed along economic, historical, philosophical, sociological, and political lines, for the "Schumpeterian System" is so broad as to include all these disciplines.[3] Accordingly, the discussion in this chapter must be relatively brief and will for the most part be restricted to his cycle and growth theory.

Actually the Schumpeterian analysis of the business cycle is only a part, though an integral one, of his more general theory of the economic growth, evolution, and decay of capitalist society. Schumpeter argues that a capitalist society is bound to be successful in achieving substantial economic growth because of the very nature of its institutional arrangements.[4] This growth is possible, however, only because of innovations,[5] but in his framework innovations are also the primary cause of the cyclical disturbances that characterize capitalism. Thus, both economic growth and the business cycle result from innovational activity. Indeed, as will be seen shortly, growth and fluctuations are so inextricably tied together that if policies are introduced to eliminate the cycle, economic growth will also be eliminated. Innovations, in the Schumpeterian system, are the well-spring of both growth and the cycle.

It is with respect to economic growth that Schumpeter enlarges his analysis into a broader theory of "capitalist evolution." According to him, capitalism carries the seeds of its own decay because it is so successful in creating rising per capita real income.[6] Increasing real per capita income will in turn create social, economic, and political changes that carry with them the demise of capitalism. What then does Schumpeter expect to replace capitalism in the future? Socialism! As he puts it:

> Can capitalism survive? No. I do not think it can. . . . The thesis I shall endeavor to establish is that the actual and prospective performance of the capitalist system is such as to negative the ideal of its breaking down under the weight of economic failure, but that its very success undermines the social institutions which protect it, and "inevitably" creates

---

[3]For a survey of the various dimensions of his work, see S. E. Harris, ed., *Schumpeter: Social Scientist* (Cambridge: Harvard University Press, 1951).

[4]Schumpeter's latest statement on this is found in *Capitalism, Socialism, and Democracy*, Part II.

[5]As opposed to inventions; see below for the distinction.

[6]"One way of expressing our result is that, if capitalism repeated its past performance for another half century starting with 1928, this would do away with anything that according to present standards could be called poverty, even in the lowest strata of the population, psychological cases alone excepted." Schumpeter, *Capitalism, Socialism, and Democracy*, p. 66.

conditions in which it will not be able to live and which strongly point to socialism as the heir apparent.[7]

In one important respect, then, Schumpeter is much in debt to Karl Marx, not only because both have used the changing historical pattern of the system to explain its downfall, but also because both have arrived at the same conclusion. Indeed, Schumpeter himself acknowledges his methodological debt to Marx.[8] But this debt must be clearly understood, else we are apt to commit the error of lumping Marx and Schumpeter together into one school of thought. To be sure, Schumpeter did borrow heavily from Marx so far as the analysis of general historical change is concerned. In terms of their predictions of change, however, these two men are far apart. Marx predicted the decline of capitalism as a result of its failure to provide "sufficient" real income for the masses of workers; Schumpeter, on the other hand, predicts the demise of capitalism as the consequence of its success in raising per capita real income and levels of living. Marx was a hostile critic of capitalism, while Schumpeter not only greatly admired the system, he also disliked intensely the "inevitable" emergence of socialism. As he put it: "Prognosis does not imply anything about the desirability of the course of events that one predicts. If a doctor predicts that his patient will die presently, this does not mean that he desires it. One may hate socialism or at least look upon it with cool criticism, and yet foresee its advent."[9] This is indeed a far cry from Marx's position. Although Schumpeter may have had an intellectual debt to Marx, he was certainly not a Marxist.

A. The Circular Flow and the Innovator

Schumpeter's theory of growth and capitalist "devolution" will be discussed later. The first order of business, however, is to set forth his theory of the business cycle. Schumpeter begins his analysis of the cycle with a statement of a general competitive equilibrium or, as he calls it, the "circular flow." The term "circular flow" is chosen to stress the idea that, unless disturbed by some exogenous force, the economic processes and arrangements of the equilibrium will repeat themselves through time.[10] In this circular flow price equals long-run average costs

---

[7]*Ibid.*, p. 61.

[8]*Ibid.*, Part I.

[9]*Ibid.*, p. 61.

[10]Schumpeter does not preclude the possibility of small "internal" changes, for so long as they are small and are connected with the preceding state of affairs, the circular flow will not be disturbed. "This may be called Weiser's principle of continuity." Schumpeter, *The Theory of Economic Development*, p. 9. For another statement of some of the conditions of the circular flow, see W. Vickery, *Microstatics* (New York: Harcourt, Brace & World, Inc., 1965), Ch. 2.

(including normal returns) for every firm; that is, each firm is just covering its costs at its most efficient rate of operation and size and thus has no tendency to increase or decrease its output.

Other features of the circular flow are (1) consumers are also in an equilibrium position, so that their consumption pattern is unchanging; (2) consumers do not have any savings, that is, their total receipts equal their total expenditures on consumers' goods; (3) the interest rate is zero;[11] and (4) there is full employment of all productive resources, with each being in its most productive and efficient employment. Also in the circular flow there is *no net investment*. To be sure, there is some investment by businessmen in capital goods, but it is *only replacement investment*, that is, all the investment that occurs is carried out merely to replace the plant and equipment that is used up in the current production of other goods. All replacement investment is financed out of depreciation reserves, the only type of savings in the circular flow. Finally, the money supply, as well as its velocity, is assumed to be unchanging.

Obviously, the circular flow is simply a refined statement of the stationary state envisioned by the classical economists; also obvious is the fact that it does not now exist, nor has it ever existed.[12] The hypothetical and unrealistic nature of the circular flow, however, is unimportant, for Schumpeter merely uses it as a point of departure. Once the circular flow is disturbed, so that the cycle follows, it will never be restored. Moreover, the disturbance of the circular flow must be "discontinuous"—that is, must be substantially large enough to disrupt the flow—and it must be a part of the capitalist process itself. Such exogenous forces as war and drought could disturb the flow, but are not sufficient to set the cycle into motion—the economy would, after a length of time, adjust to them and restore the equilibrium condition. But the important thing is that these exogenous forces are not intrinsic to capitalism.

The discontinuous force that Schumpeter stresses is *innovation*. In this connection innovation must be distinguished from invention, for while the former cannot come into being without the latter, it is innovation that is the dynamic, moving force in Schumpeter's theory. Inventions by themselves have little economic impact, but when they are put into effect (that is, when there is an innovation) the economic

---

[11]There has been much debate over this point, but we shall ignore it here.

[12]As Schumpeter himself has pointed out. See his "The March into Socialism," *American Economic Review,* May 1950, pp. 449-50. Recall that Hayek begins his analysis from the same set of conditions.

consequences may be substantial. While "great" discoveries are gathering dust in blueprint form, "minor" discoveries, when innovated, can lead to widespread economic repercussions. An innovation is thus an invention that is put into economic reality.

Schumpeter distinguishes between several types of innovations:

> This concept covers the following five cases: (1) The introduction of a new good—that is, one with which consumers are not yet familiar—or a new quality of a good. (2) The introduction of a new method of production, that is, one not yet tested by experience in the branch of manufacture concerned, which need by no means be founded upon a discovery scientifically new, and can also exist in a new way of handling a commodity commercially. (3) The opening of a new market, that is, a market into which the particular branch of manufacturer of the country in question has not previously entered, whether or not this market existed before. (4) The conquest of a new source of supply of raw materials or half-manufactured goods, again irrespective of whether this source already exists or whether it has first to be created. (5) The carrying out of a new organization of any industry, like the creation of a monopoly position (for example through trustification) or the breaking up of a monopoly position.[13]

In the following discussion only one type of innovation—the introduction of a new method of production—is used to illustrate Schumpeter's analysis, though the same general reasoning applies to the other types.

Innovations do not spring full-armed from the brow of any businessman; rather they emerge only under quite special circumstances. Perhaps the most important of these is the presence of the innovating entrepreneur, that is, a special and unique brand of businessman who possesses the vision, courage, and ability to make invention an economic reality. The psychological make-up of the innovator is not possessed by all businessmen. Indeed for Schumpeter only a few businessmen or entrepreneurs can be innovators; the remainder are those who possess only a few of the traits required to introduce an innovation, and these are the "mere managers."[14] As he puts it:

> In the first place it is a question of a type of conduct and a type of person in so far as this conduct is accessible in very unequal measure and to relatively few people, so that it constitutes their outstanding characteristics. . . . The conduct in question is peculiar in two ways. First, because it is directed towards something different and signifies doing something different from other conduct. . . . Secondly, the type of conduct in question not only differs from others in its object, "innovation" being peculiar to it, but also in that it presupposes aptitudes differing

---

[13]Schumpeter, *The Theory of Economic Development*, p. 66.
[14]*Ibid.*, p. 82.

in kind and not only in degree from those of mere rational economic behavior.[15]

Now this must not be interpreted to mean that only a limited percentage of the population possesses some or even several of these characteristics and traits; the relevant point is that only a few persons possess them to the extent required to be an innovator. Schumpeter illustrates this with reference to a noneconomic area of human activity—singing.

> Now these aptitudes are presumably distributed in an ethnically homogeneous population just like others, that is, the curve of their distribution has a maximum ordinate, deviations on either side of which become rarer the greater they are. Similarly we can assume that every healthy man can sing if he will. Perhaps half the individuals in an ethnically homogeneous group have the capacity for it to an average degree, a quarter in progressively diminishing measure, and, let us say, a quarter above in a measure above the average; and within this quarter, through a series of continually increasing singing ability and continually diminishing number of people who possess it, we come finally to the Carusoes. Only in this quarter are we struck in general by the singing ability, and only in the supreme instances can it become the characterizing mark of the person.[16]

Thus at the extreme end of the spectrum there are only a very few persons who possess all of the traits of the innovator—courage, intelligence, persuasiveness, ambition, and so on—that are required to break away from the status quo. Below these are others who can still be classified as entrepreneurs, but who do not possess all of the traits, or at least do not possess them to the same degree, as the "supreme instances." And so on down the line until finally the "mere managers" are left. Schumpeter concentrates his analysis initially on the extreme type of entrepreneur, the innovator, and introduces the other types of businessmen at a later stage.

The chief problem of the innovator in the circular flow is that he has no financial funds with which to carry out his innovational project. Recall that personal savings are nil in the circular flow. Thus the innovator must turn to the commercial bank in order to acquire the funds necessary to finance his innovation. At this point he exercises one of his psychological traits—persuasiveness—and convinces the

---

[15]*Ibid.*, p. 81, n. 2. Indeed, on pp. 86-87, Schumpeter argues that the innovator is a social deviant who reacts against the *status quo* and wishes to do something new and difficult. See also pp. 92-94, where other psychological traits of the innovator are discussed.

[16]*Ibid.*, pp. 81-82, n. 2.

banker of the economic justification and "logic" of his proposed project. Once the banker responds and increases the money supply at the
disposal of the entrepreneur, the circular flow is disrupted; but note
that it is disrupted by a "discontinuous" force that is intrinsic to the
capitalist system. [17]

B.   The Expansion and the Upper-Turning Point

The only way in which the innovator can get his project underway
is, of course, by entering into the resource markets and bidding resources away from their present employments. The results of this activity are already familiar: the prices of productive services rise since
the entrepreneur must offer higher rates of remuneration to attract
them from their present uses; these resources are transferred to the
capital goods industries, thus reducing output and employment in the
consumers' goods industries; consequently there are rising prices and
profit anticipations in the consumers' goods sector of the economy, for
just as the supply of consumers' goods is falling off, the money demand
for them is rising. One of the essential results of this is that forced
savings come into being.[18]

The businessmen in the consumers' goods industries, however, cannot acquire the necessary resources to meet the rising demand. The
reason for this is not because of the additional purchasing power of
the innovator, because this would be insufficient to keep the resources
in the capital goods sector. To account for the inability of the consumers' goods industries in hiring back the resources that they would
like to acquire, Schumpeter introduces a complicating factor—the
"swarmlike appearance of new enterprises." There occurs, he argues,
not just one or a few new enterprises, but rather a "clustering" of them.
He advances several reasons for this, but one will suffice for present
purposes. The Schumpeterian analysis stresses that:

> . . . every normal boom starts in one or a few branches of industry (rail-
> way building, electrical, and chemical industries, and so forth), and it
> derives its character from the innovations in the industry in which it
> appears. But the pioneers remove the obstacles for the others not only in
> the branch of production in which they first appear, but, owing to the
> nature of these obstacles, *ipso facto*, in other branches too. Many things
> may be copied by the latter; the example as such also acts upon them;

---

[17]The question of why an equilibrium position is favorable to innovational activity is discussed below.

[18]The similarities of the analysis thus far to that of Hayek are obvious.

and many achievements directly serve other branches too, as for example the opening up of a foreign market, quite apart from the circumstances of secondary importance which soon appear—rising prices and so on. Hence the first leaders are effective beyond their immediate sphere of action and so the group of entrepreneurs increases still further and the economic system is drawn more rapidly and more completely than would otherwise be the case into the process of technological and commercial reorganization which constitutes the meaning of periods of boom.[19]

Once this swarm-like movement develops, *and this is precisely what Schumpeter means by induced investment,* the period called "prosperity" is under way. The expansion, however, cannot go on indefinitely; it must come to an end because, as Schumpeter argues, it contains the "seeds of its own destruction." But how and why does the upper-turning point take place?

To begin with, it is necessary to introduce a concept that is crucial to the Schumpeterian analysis—the "period of gestation."[20] This is the period that elapses between the beginning of an investment project and its termination, at which time it begins producing the product for which it is designed. Of course, because of the "clustering" of new enterprises, there is a group of gestation periods, but we may easily think in terms of one period for the entire group. Once the gestation period (for the group) ends, three important results take place.

First, there is a reduction in net investment—the rate of investment drops virtually to replacement levels. A decline of this sort, of course, leads to a reduction in aggregate spending unless somehow or other it is offset. It is possible that there might be new investment projects or a rise in consumption that could fill the gap, but Schumpeter considers this to be quite unlikely for the other two reasons.

Second, when the gestation period comes to an end, there is an increase in output of consumers' goods—the objective for which the investment was created in the first place. Note, however, that the increase in the supply of consumers' goods is very large because of the improved methods of production and because of the increased total stock of capital. Thus the prices of consumers' goods tend to drop (while wages and other costs of production remain temporarily high because of lags). Accordingly profits are reduced, and indeed some of the less efficient firms are forced into bankruptcy. A further consequence of this is that expectations become adverse and hence further new investment proj-

---

[19]Schumpeter, *The Theory of Economic Development*, p. 229.

[20]*Ibid.*, pp. 232-33. The notion of the "gestation period" was emphasized earlier by the French economist, Aftalion; see his "The Theory of Economic Cycles Based on the Capitalistic Technique of Production," *Review of Economic Statistics,* October 1927.

ects are postponed. However, in order for this to be a crucial reason
for the upper-turning point, Schumpeter must also assume that the increase in the supply of consumers' goods is, in the end analysis, larger
than the increased money demand for them. During the period of expansion money demand for consumers' goods was rising, while the output of these goods was cut back. At the end of the gestation period,
however, supply rises relative to demand, and while this is sufficient
to lower prices, it is not by itself enough to bring them back to their
former equilibrium level. Nevertheless the fall in prices below their
highest expansionary peak may be sufficient to force bankruptcy upon
a lot of inefficient firms that have ridden the coattails of the expansion.
If, on the other hand, the improvement in productivity (because of
the innovations) is so great as to lower prices below their former
equilibrium level, the impact of the falling price level will be greater.
Of course, the rising unemployment in the investment goods' sector
will contribute to the slump originating in the consumers' goods sector,
and this will aggravate the situation.

These possibilities are illustrated in Figure 7–1. The equilibrium
level of prices of consumer goods is represented by OP, at which the
quantity demanded is equal to the quantity supplied. The initial demand and supply curves are DD and SS, respectively. Now as the expansion gets under way, the supply curve of consumers' goods falls to,
say S'S', while the demand curve shifts to the right to D'D'. Hence the
price level rises to P'. When the gestation period is over, the supply
curve begins shifting to the right until finally it rises to S"S". This pulls
the price level down to P", though the fall in prices from P' to P" is
gradual and persistent, forcing firms out of existence all along the line.
Of course this graphical representation is only a part of the picture—
further repercussions will set in as demand begins to fall (due to rising
unemployment), and the supply curve's shift to the right is intensified
as more firms go bankrupt.

But there is a third reason for the upper-turning point, which Schumpeter refers to as "autodeflation." As the successful entrepreneurs who
led the expansion process complete their projects, they improve their
profits to the point of being able to pay back the bank loans which en-
abled them to get started. That is to say, their very success leads to a
reduction in the money supply "automatically"—hence the term "autodeflation." Note that this reduction in the stock of money occurs just
at the time that many firms are experiencing bankruptcy; and because
of this the commercial banks not only are not willing to extend new
loans, but also will insist upon calling in loans, leading to a further reduction in the money supply. Also the banks find that in the later
phases of the expansion their reserves have become depleted. The

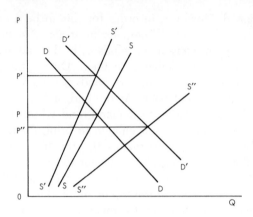

FIGURE 7–1

major result is that now the demand curve (in Figure 7–1) will begin
shifting to the left, intensifying the fall in the price level.

For these reasons, then, the expansion comes to an end. New investment will not be forthcoming to offset the decline in investment
spending at the end of the gestation period because of both the
drop in the prices of consumers' goods and the autodeflation. Under
such conditions pessimism tends to become prevalent, not only among
businessmen, but also among the commercial bankers. Result? The
onset of the contraction or, as Schumpeter calls it, the "recession." For
Schumpeter the period of recession is one of readjustment as forces
tend to move the economy back to the neighborhood of equilibrium.
But in this analysis the downward influence of the forces generated
in the period of recession is so great as to cause the economy to over-
shoot the neighborhood of equilibrium and to pass into the period of
"depression." The combination of these "recession" and "depression"
periods makes up what we have termed the contraction.

C.   The Contraction and the Lower-Turning Point

Schumpeter's explanation of the contraction and lower-turning point
is not entirely satisfactory, and though this may be considered a shortcoming, it is a shortcoming common to most theories of the cycle. For
him the contraction is a period of readjustment in which the firms face
always the imminent threat of destruction. They must somehow either
adjust to the declining position or experience bankruptcy. This adjust-

ment for those firms that survive the initial onslaught of the contraction involves three possibilities: ". . . to decay if they are unadaptable for personal or objective reasons; to rake in sail and try to survive in a more modest position, with their own resources; or with outside help either to change to another industry or to adopt technical or commercial methods which amount to extending production at lower cost per unit."[21] As the necessary adjustments are made by the firms, there is a tendency on the part of the economy to move back toward an equilibrium situation. Indeed, for Schumpeter the "depression" is present until the adjustments have taken place so that the surviving firms have reached peak efficiency and avoid losses.[22]

However, as the economy approaches the equilibrium situation the time becomes ripe for further innovational activity. An essential point in this theory is that "clusters" of innovations occur near the points of equilibria, and for this reason the term "neighborhood of equilibrium" is more descriptive than the complete general equilibrium characterized by the circular flow. But why should innovations tend to occur in a neighborhood of equilibrium rather than at some other stage of the cycle? The reason given is that it is during this phase of the cycle that the innovator is best able to calculate the potential profitability of his proposed project. As two of Schumpeter's students have put it:

Why is innovating activity most favored by equilibrium? A comparison of the difficulties and risks of innovation at different stages of the . . . cycle shows a heavy balance in favor of this situation. The stability of business conditions, as well as the complete absence of profits, is more conducive to innovation than any other stage of the cycle could be. Since the risk of failure is at a minimum, and the pressure to innovate at a maximum, we should expect that innovating activity, under capitalist arrangements would be extraordinarily great.[23]

And once the innovations cluster, the expansion once more gets under way and the cyclical process repeats itself.

D. A "Mixed" Model

In terms of the classification provided in Chapter 5, Schumpeter's theory of the business cycle is a "mixed" model. That is, it does not rely exclusively upon the interplay of the endogenous variables nor exclusively upon changes in the exogenous variables to explain both

[21]Schumpeter, *The Theory of Economic Development*, p. 242.
[22]*Ibid.*, p. 243.
[23]R. V. Clemence and F. S. Doody, *The Schumpeterian System* (Reading, Mass.: Addison-Wesley Publishing Co., Inc., 1950), p. 54. See also O. Lange, review of Schumpeter's *Business Cycles*, *Review of Economic Statistics*, November 1941, p. 192.

turning points. Rather, the upper-turning point is explained by the endogenous variables and the lower-turning point by exogenous changes. Thus, it is a "mixed" model.

With respect to the upper-turning point, the interaction of the endogenous variables comes to an end because of the petering out of investment as the gestation period comes to a close. The rate of investment cannot be maintained because of the drop in the price level and "autodeflation," both of which are the result of the intrinsic operations of the expansionary stage itself. Thus, the interaction of the endogenous variables results unavoidably in the upper-turning point.

The lower-turning point, on the other hand, is a consequence of the "clustering of innovations." The appearance of this autonomous investment depends upon such factors as the rate of technological advance, the changing expectations of innovators and commercial bankers, and the rate at which the contraction has proceeded. These are best considered as exogenous variables, and changes in them are responsible for the lower-turning point.

E.   Trends and Cycles in the Schumpeterian System

As observed earlier, Schumpeter's analysis presents a theory of growth as well as a theory of the business cycle. Further examination reveals that his analysis contains a multi-cycle scheme. Not only does he introduce long waves into the picture, but also both major and minor cycles. In this sense his analysis is quite complex.[24] In this section however, only Schumpeter's analysis of the interaction of economic growth and the cyclical process is considered.

Discussion of this interaction can best proceed graphically. In Figure 7–2 income is plotted on the vertical axis and time on the horizontal axis. The analysis begins at point A, which represents the circular flow equilibrium that is disturbed by innovation. Income rises up to point P, and the stage from A to P is what Schumpeter refers to as "prosperity." Note however that this "prosperity" is characterized by inflation, a decline in the output and consumption of consumers' goods, and "forced" savings. Yet there is still full employment of resources. In other words, Schumpeter's upper-turning point does not coincide with what is usually meant by that term.

The upper-turning point P is brought on by a decline in investment, falling price and profit levels, and autodeflation. The stage from P to B

---

[24]See Clemence and Doody, *The Schumpeterian System*, Chapters 4, 9-10, for a discussion of the three-cycle scheme.

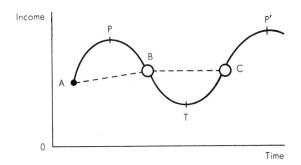

FIGURE 7–2

is termed "recession." Recall that the forces in the "recession" become cumulative so that the *neighborhood* of equilibrium (represented by the circle at B) is overshot, and the economy enters into a period of "depression," that is, the stage from B to T. Finally the painful process of readjustment by the surviving firms represents the "recovery" stage from T to C; and once the neighborhood of equilibrium C is reached, the economy is ripe for innovations, so that the four stages of the cycle follow once more.

There are certain important things to note about Schumpeter's analysis. First, the cycle is measured from neighborhood of equilibrium to neighborhood of equilibrium, not from peak to peak or from trough to trough, as is usually the case. Second, and more important, observe that the neighborhoods of equilibria B and C lie above A, though they themselves are on the same level. The reason for this is that the fruition of the innovations that occurred at A are reflected in the higher neighborhood of equilibrium B. The innovations increased productivity and output and thus stimulated economic growth. However, the decline and subsequent recovery from B merely restore the economy to the same level at C. There is economic growth between A and B but not between B and C. But the growth from A to B (and hence to C) and the four-stage cycle from A to C are the consequence of the innovations that occur at A.

The longer-range picture is shown in Figure 7–3, in which it is easy to see that Schumpeter ". . . treated the trend as a statistical concept— a line drawn through the inflection points of a curve showing the pattern of business cycles."[25] These points of inflection occur, of course, at the neighborhoods of equilibria on the upswing.

[25]*Economic Development* by Benjamin Higgins. Copyright © 1959 by W. W. Norton & Company, Inc., New York, p. 137.

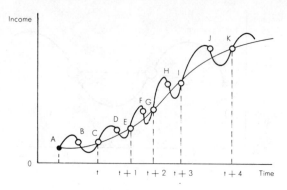

FIGURE 7–3

The important conclusion is that Schumpeter never lost sight of—and indeed emphasized—the interaction of growth and the cycle. To him growth and fluctuations are part and parcel of one of the major elements of capitalist society—innovations; and innovations give rise to induced investment which, while it contributes to growth, is largely responsible for aggravating the cyclical fluctuations.

One final observation is in order. Schumpeter believed that each cycle differs from every other and thus must be treated as a unique historical event, even though all cycles are caused by innovations. One distinguishing feature of each cycle is that its length or duration differs from that of any other cycle, except perhaps by sheer coincidence. This unique characteristic is shown in Figure 7–3, where the length of each cycle is measured on the time axis. The reason advanced by Schumpeter for this characteristic is that ". . . the periods of gestation . . . will not, in general, be equal for all the innovations that are undertaken at any time."[26]

F.   The Declining Entrepreneurial Function and the Close of Capitalism

No explanation was offered above as to why the trend line TT (in Figure 7–3) tapers off towards the right, and this section may well be-

---

[26]Schumpeter, *Business Cycles*, Vol. I, pp. 166-67.

gin with the query: Did Schumpeter believe that the capitalist growth *rate* would decline as the system becomes more successful? His answer is—Yes! He believed that the very process of growth, and also the impact of the business cycle, would create institutional changes that would tend to reduce severely the economic importance of the innovator. In his terms, he believed that capitalism will become less competitive and more *trustified* as time elapses and that *trustified capitalism* deadens the impact and economic significance of the innovator.

Thus Schumpeter's business cycle analysis applies to capitalist economies only before the setting in of trustification, for after the emergence of trustification the innovator—the well-spring of fluctuations—recedes in importance. Perhaps the most important criticism of Schumpeter's theory is this very point—that it is relevant only for a particular historical epoch and that it has declined in predictive and explanatory significance since the emergence of trustified capitalism.[27]

But what precisely is meant by trustified capitalism, and what impact does it have on the innovator and innovational activity? By trustified capitalism Schumpeter means the development of large-scale business organizations that are characterized by bureaucracy and also by depersonalization of the individual. The individual who may have been an innovator is now a member of a team, in which he does not have the freedom to display his entrepreneurial and innovational abilities. In this sense, large-scale, routinized organization is eliminating the important economic and social function that the innovator performed in the competitive epoch of capitalism. Schumpeter's views on this are best revealed by means of a fairly lengthy quotation:

> This social function is already losing importance and is bound to lose it at an accelerating pace in the future even if the economic process itself of which entrepreneurship was the prime mover went on unabated. For, on the one hand, it is much easier now than it has been in the past to do things that lie outside familiar routine—innovation itself being reduced to routine. Technological progress is increasingly becoming the business of teams of trained specialists who turn out what is required and make it work in predictable ways. The romance of earlier commercial adventure is rapidly wearing away, because so many more things can be strictly calculated that had of old to be visualized in a flash of genius.
>
> On the other hand, personality and will power must count for less in environments which have become accustomed to economic change. . . . Thus, economic progress tends to become depersonalized and auto-

[27]As he himself was aware: see *Business Cycles,* Vol. I, p. 145; see also "The Instability of Capitalism," *Economic Journal,* September 1928, pp. 384-86; and "Science and Ideology," *American Economic Review,* March 1949, p. 449.

matized. Bureau and committee work tends to replace individual action.[28]

Nor does Schumpeter concentrate solely on the decline of the entrepreneurial function in his account of the decline of capitalism. Also there are the "destruction of the protecting strata," the decline of the family, and indeed even a deemphasis on the institutions of private property and free contracting.[29]

All of these forces combine to retard the growth rate of the capitalist society, but the one that Schumpeter stresses is the decline in the entrepreneurial function. Large-scale capitalist enterprises tend to automatize progress with emphasis on the regularization of net, new investment and avoidance of disturbing innovations. For these reasons, then, the TT curve in Figure 7–3 tapers off to the right.

One final point: Schumpeter believes that these forces not only operate to slow down the growth rate, but that they also combine to bring about the destruction of capitalism. Let us end this section on Schumpeter with the following paradoxical note:

> The perfectly bureaucratized giant industrial unit not only ousts the small or medium-sized firm and "expropriates" its owners, but in the end it also ousts the entrepreneur and expropriates the bourgeoisie as a class which in the process stands to lose not only its income but also what is infinitely more important, its function. The true pacemakers of socialism were not the intellectuals or agitators who preached it but the Vanderbilts, Carnegies, and Rockefellers.[30]

2.   Hansen on Autonomous Investment and Growth

In this section we shall discuss briefly the cycle analysis of another contemporary American economist, Alvin H. Hansen.[31] There are many similarities between Hansen's and Schumpeter's theories, but there are

---

[28]Schumpeter, *Capitalism, Socialism, and Democracy,* pp. 132, 133.

[29]*Ibid.,* p. 134, and Chapters 12-13 for fuller discussion.

[30]*Ibid.,* p. 134.

[31]Hansen's contributions to the literature of business cycle theory are numerous. Important selective works are *Full Recovery or Stagnation* (New York: W. W. Norton & Company, Inc., 1938); *Fiscal Policy and Business Cycles* (New York: W. W. Norton & Company, Inc., 1941); *Economic Policy and Full Employment* (New York: McGraw-Hill Book Company, 1947) *Monetary Theory and Fiscal Policy* (New York: McGraw-Hill Book Company, 1949); and *Business Cycles and National Income* (New York: W. W. Norton & Company, Inc., 1964). This section relies heavily on Chapter 9 of the last book cited.

also some substantial differences. One of the major differences is that Hansen's analysis is couched in strong Keynesian terms, and this alone means that the discussion in this chapter must be brief.[32]

Perhaps the most significant difference between the theories of the two men relates to the "causes" of autonomous investment. For Schumpeter autonomous investment results from resource discovery and technological advances in which the performance of the innovator figures strongly. For Hansen, on the other hand, autonomous investment, while a function of resource discovery and technological advance (as with Schumpeter), is also a function of *population growth*. The two theorists differ considerably on this point, for Schumpeter tends to treat population growth as exogenous.[33]

A.   The Investment Demand Function

Hansen's theory can best be approached by making use of an important economic concept, the investment demand function.[34] This function may be written as

$$I_a = f(P,T,R,r,i),$$

where I_a stands for autonomous investment, P for population change, and T for technological advancement. The symbol R stands for resource discovery, and the symbols r and i stand respectively for the *marginal efficiency of investment* and the interest rate. For the moment P, R, and T are held constant in order to examine more closely the significance of the marginal efficiency of investment (r) and the interest rate (i). The importance of changes in population, technology, and resources will be discussed in the next subsection, but for the moment the foundations of Hansen's cycle theory must be developed.

The marginal efficiency of investment, r, is the *net* rate of return on the capital outlay that takes the form of investment, and it is calculated as a percentage. Let us examine the concept first from the standpoint of the individual firm; following this we shall aggregate from the single firm to the economy at large.

---

[32]See especially Chapter 18.

[33]Higgins, *Economic Development*, p. 183.

[34]This analytical concept, which is closely associated with the Keynesian analysis, can legitimately be introduced here because of Hansen's extensive use of the Keynesian analytical tools. It will be discussed more thoroughly however in Chapter 11; merely a skeleton treatment is provided here.

Two things must be known in order to obtain the marginal efficiency of investment for the individual firm: first, the series of *expected* annual returns which an investment will yield *after costs of operation have been deducted;* second, the cost of the capital goods in question. Now as long as the sum of the *expected* annual returns exceeds the cost of the capital goods, obviously some positive rate of return will be earned by the firm. Assume that, for a particular investment project for this firm, there is an excess of the sum of expected annual returns over cost. What is the marginal efficiency of investment? In this case, r can be calculated by equating the cost with the expected annual returns (R_1, R_2, R_3, ... R_n) by the use of *some* discount rate, r:

$$C = \frac{R_1}{(1+r)} + \frac{R_2}{(1+r)^2} + \frac{R_3}{(1+r)^3} + \cdots + \frac{R_n}{(1+r)^n}.$$

In this equation the discount rate, r, when applied to the series of expected annual returns, equates the present value of the discounted returns to the cost of the capital equipment. The symbol r then is the marginal efficiency of investment or, in other words, the *net percentage rate earned on the capital investment.*[35]

In order to decide whether to undertake the investment project, the firm's management will compare r with i, which is either the interest rate that it can obtain by lending the firm's funds in the market rather than investing them,[36] or the interest cost that the firm must incur if it borrows the funds from some source external to the firm. So long as $r>i$, then it is worthwhile for the firm to invest rather than to lend, or it will be worthwhile for the firm to obtain funds at the interest rate of i in order to finance the investment.

An excess of r over i means, in effect, that the value, V, of the capital goods is larger than their cost, C. To obtain the value V, all that needs to be done is to discount the sum of the expected returns back to the present at the prevailing rate of interest at which the firm can lend or borrow. Thus,

$$V = \frac{R_1}{(1+i)} + \frac{R_2}{(1+i)^2} + \frac{R_3}{(1+i)^3} + \cdots + \frac{R_n}{(1+i)^n}$$

Now if $r>i$, then by definition $V>C$, for the two approaches are merely different ways of looking at the same thing. So long as $r>i$ (that

---

[35]Risk differentials are ignored in this simplified treatment; see Chapter 11, for a discussion of their significance.

[36]See E. Solomon, ed., *The Management of Corporate Capital* (New York: The Free Press, 1959), for various discussions of the basic issues involved.

is, V>C), then there is an inducement to invest and the more r exceeds i, of course, the stronger is the inducement to invest.

One final property of the investment demand function needs to be discussed here. Recall that P, T, and R are being held constant by assumption. In this case the "law of diminishing returns" will be operative, so that successive increments of investment will yield successively smaller rates of return; in other words, r diminishes. This will occur under the assumed circumstances, but if in a period of expansion the cost of capital goods rises, r will fall more rapidly. Thus there are two major determinants of the declining marginal efficiency of investment—diminishing returns and rising costs.

A hypothetical schedule of the marginal efficiency of investment pertaining to an individual firm is shown in Table 7–1. Note that as the volume of investment in the illustration becomes larger, the marginal efficiency falls off, a fact which is demonstrated more strikingly in Figure 7–4. However, more than the investment demand curve must be known in order to find out how much investment the firm will undertake. The rate of interest is also needed. Assume that the prevailing rate of interest is 6 per cent. In this case $r>i$ for the first increment of $100 of investment and also for the second $100 increment. However, with the third increment, where the total volume of investment is $300, $r = i$. Put otherwise, so long as the value of the additional investment exceeds its cost (that is, where $r>i$), the new investment will be forthcoming. Net, new investment will stop at the point where $i = r$, (that is, where $V = C$). To repeat, this equality will emerge under the assumption of a constant P, T, and R because of diminishing returns and rising costs of capital.

However, in reality P, T, and R are not constant but are shifting. As long as population and technology are expanding, and as long as new resources are being discovered, there exists a potential tendency for the investment demand curve to shift to the right. What this means, of

TABLE 7–1

A Hypothetical Marginal Efficiency Schedule

Increment of Investment	Total Volume of Investment	Marginal Efficiency of Investment (r) (Per cent)
$100	$100	13%
100	200	10
100	300	6
100	400	2

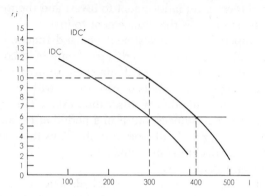

FIGURE 7–4

course, is that as markets expand and as technological advances lower costs or create new products (or both), r rises. Diagrammatically this is shown by a shift to the right of the investment demand curve to IDC′ in Figure 7–4. Note that after the shift the marginal efficiency of investment at the $300 level is greater than the interest rate, which we still provisionally take as given at the prevailing rate of 6 per cent. Specifically, at an interest rate of 6 per cent the new marginal efficiency on the third $100 increment in investment is now 10 per cent. Consequently new investment projects will materialize, but in the short run, when the growth factors change only very slowly, this results in a movement down the IDC′ curve until again $r = i$. At this point the investment of the firm will be approximately $425. Thus even though the long-run forces have the cumulative effect of *shifting the curve to the right*, the shorter-run forces result in a *movement down the new curve*. This is a crucial part of Hansen's theory and will be expanded in the next subsection.

Since the major concern is with *aggregate investment* behavior, it is necessary to summate all the IDC curves of the individual firms in the economy. This is done merely by adding them together horizontally so that now the *aggregate IDC curve* reveals what will be the total investment in the economy at the prevailing rate of interest. In what follows, therefore, only the aggregate demand for investment is considered, not investment demand of any single firm.

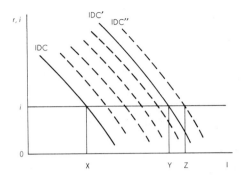

FIGURE 7-5

B.   The Cyclical Process

Let us begin the discussion of Hansen's analysis by considering the investment demand curve IDC (in Figure 7-5), which is a summation of all individual firms' demand curves. Now as long as investment is less than OX, the marginal efficiency of investment is greater than the interest rate, and new investment will be forthcoming until finally $r = i$ (at OX). Recall that for any one investment demand curve, the growth factors are assumed to be constant. Thus the IDC curve has a negative slope and is stable.

At OX the point of investment saturation is reached, and there occurs a sharp reduction in investment spending. This of course results in a sharp drop in income and employment so that the contraction sets in.

However, even during the contraction, the growth factors actually continue to work, creating *new potential* investment opportunities. As Hansen puts it:

> Advances in technology, cost-reducing machinery, the development of new products and new industries, the discovery of new natural resources, the growth of population, will soon open the way for further new investment. These developments are going on all the while, even in the midst of a great depression. But for many months, and often for some years, relatively little investment may be made despite the potential backlog of new investment opportunities which is accumulating.[37]

---

[37]Hansen, *Business Cycles and National Income,* p. 131.

There are two reasons for this lag of *actual* investment behind investment *potentials*. First, investment in the preceding expansion may have created an excess which has to become utilized again before any new investment is forthcoming. Second, expectations of the economic community during this phase of the cycle are characterized by pessimism. Indeed, as Hansen metaphorically puts it: "It may require a large accumulation of 'combustible material' (investment outlets) before the pile catches fire: in other words, it may take a long time before the entrepreneurs acquire sufficient confidence in the future and that new spirit of enterprise which is required to undertake large new ventures."[38]

Thus, in Hansen's theory businessmen's expectations play an important role. Even though the growth factors are at play, the investment demand curve will not shift to the right until businessmen's expectations are permissive. Remember that in the formulas for both V and C, the annual returns (expressed in dollars) are *expected* annual returns. Thus a specific investment opportunity may be valued differently according to the degree of optimism or pessimism of the business community. Certainty in a period of contraction, where investment in untried markets, new products, new methods of production, and so on are concerned, the speculation and risk may appear to be quite large. In these cases the ordinary businessman will not form the expectations necessary to allow his investment demand curve to rise. If the pessimism is general, the aggregate investment demand curve will not shift to the right, even though the growth factors are continually at play.

At this point Hansen introduces the *promoter*, who is not to be confused with Schumpeter's innovator. As regards the promoter, Hansen states:

> It is his task to initiate the [investment] project, to arouse interest in it, and to induce people to raise investment of large or small sums in the hope of unusually large gains. Often thousands of people are induced to participate. The promoter may himself risk very little. Often he comes out with a handsome return for his enterprising organizational work, even though the investors lose all or nearly all of the funds poured into the venture.[39]

In Hansen's analysis, the promoter is responsible to some degree for recognizing the expansive changes in the growth factors and aiding in their translation into actual investment projects. However, the promoter does not assume all of the functions of the ordinary businessman, as does

---

[38]*Ibid.*
[39]*Ibid.*, p. 139.

Schumpeter's innovator. In the period of contraction his major function is to offset, as much as is possible, the pessimism of the businessmen.

Even though pessimism prevails in the contraction so that the investment demand curve does not reflect changes in the growth factors, the growth factors are still at work, and thus new potential investment opportunities are being created. That is, when the assumption of a constant population and technology is relaxed, the investment demand curve shifts gradually to the right, as shown by the dashed curves in Figure 7–5. For some time these shifts may not be recognized, but eventually the increased profitability resulting from the expansionary growth factors will be calculated by some businessmen, so that now the relevant demand curve becomes IDC'. This sets off another investment boom. The volume of investment "warranted" by the growth factors is XY, *at the prevailing rate of interest i,* but once it is achieved the expansion is over and the contraction sets in. "Thus the boom 'dies a natural death'."[40]

Hansen argues further that the upper-turning point is aggravated by the fact that during the expansion investment is carried on at a rate more rapid than is warranted. During the expansion, especially in its later stages, expectations become very buoyant and businessmen tend to overestimate the marginal efficiency of investment. As shown in Figure 7–5, they may think in terms of IDC" rather than IDC', the curve warranted by the growth factors. Thus while the warranted net investment is XY, businessmen may actually invest the amount XZ. Once this happens the contraction will be sharper and longer. Pessimism sets in, and as a result, the investment demand curve shifts to the left. Investment spending is contracted not only because of a fulfillment of the investment opportunities created by the growth factors, but also because of a rapid leftward shift of the curve.

Once the contraction sets in, pessimism develops and investments inherited from the preceding investment boom are not used. As observed earlier, it may take some years for these impediments to be overcome, but all the while the "solid facts underneath" of population growth, resource discovery, and technological advances are at work.[41] These serve to shift the potential investment opportunities to the right, though the new opportunities may go unrecognized. The promoter figures in very importantly at this juncture, though Hansen does not attach as much

[40]*Ibid.,* p. 132. Actually the interest rate will fluctuate during the expansionary period, but this is not important for the analysis now.

[41]*Ibid.,* p. 141.

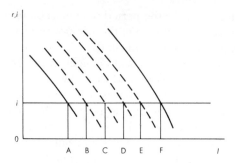

FIGURE 7-6

significance to him as Schumpeter does to the innovator. In Hansen's theory the promoter is a financial and organizational specialist who is instrumental in initiating the more speculative projects. In Schumpeter's analysis, on the other hand, the innovator possesses a much wider range of economic understanding and performs more important functions than mere financial and organizational wizardry. For Hansen, many business-men are capable of recognizing the potential investment opportunities once they overcome their pessimism; only on the more speculative projects is the promoter needed.

Once the growth factors build up sufficiently so that new investment projects materialize (with or without the promoter), the lower-turning point occurs and the expansion sets in. As the expansion continues, with rising investment, employment, and consumption, the adverse expectations carried over from the contraction are erased and the investment capacity also inherited from the preceding period becomes fully used. Optimism prevails and the investment demand curve shifts to the right; investment rises and the cycle continues its course.

Hansen clearly argues that the upper-turning point can be avoided if investment actually proceeds at the rate warranted by the growth factors. During the investment boom the growth factors are still at work, shifting the demand farther to the right. If investment were to continue at the same rate indicated by the growth factors, then there would occur no upper-turning point. This is illustrated in Figure 7-6, in which the rate of interest is held constant at i. Now if the potential investment opportunities created by the growth factors were recognized as they occur, then the new investment would occur continuously over time by the increments of AB, BC, CD, and so on. In this case the rate of investment would proceed at the same rate as the growth requirements.

An integral part of Hansen's analysis, however, is that (as noted earlier) buoyant expectations take hold during the expansion and

> . . . the rate of investment proceeds feverishly, so that investment outstrips the rate of expansion of the growth factors. Accordingly, despite the continued upward shift of the schedule, the movement down it to the minimum, below which further investment is not profitable, assures the end of the expansion. Thus the boom "dies a natural death." The accumulated outlets for investment have been exhausted.[42]

Given the manner in which investment plans are carried out in a capitalist system, the upper-turning point is bound to occur.

C. Some Policy Implications

May not, however, monetary policy, with its potential for lowering the rate of interest, be sufficient to prevent the upper-turning point from setting in? Hansen argues no.[43] In the first place, he contends that in its lower stretches the investment demand curve is quite interest inelastic. Consider the IDC curve in Figure 7–7. When the interest rate is reduced from i to i', the resulting additional investment (XY) is quite small. Note, however, that the curve is assumed to be more elastic in its upper ranges; thus a rise in the rate from i to i'' will choke off investment by a relatively large amount (XZ). Monetary policy may be effective in stimulating net investment down to a certain level of the interest rate, but below this it will have relatively little impact.

Thus if the prevailing rate of interest is i and investment is X, a reduction in the rate of i' will not be sufficient to avert the upper-turning point, nor will it be sufficient to reverse the contraction once it is under way. To be sure, there is still some net investment (XY) as a result of the reduction in the rate, but it is not enough to prevent the contraction in the investment goods sector. The investment goods industries will still contract, though perhaps not as rapidly as if the interest rate had not been reduced.

Hansen argues further that once the contraction has set in, the investment demand curve shifts to the left, further softening the impact of any interest rate reduction. Thus in the absence of governmental activ-

---

[42]*Ibid.*, p. 132.
[43]*Ibid.*, pp. 133-38.

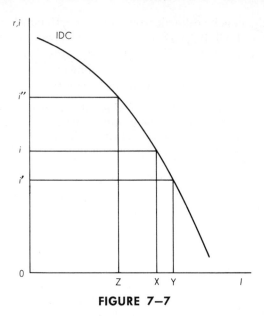

FIGURE 7–7

ity to bring the economy out of the low level of performance, the only alternative is to await a shift of the investment demand curve to the right, and this depends primarily on the growth forces.[44]

Hansen, however, does place heavy reliance upon fiscal policy. As he puts it:

> . . . much can . . . be accomplished by deliberate investment in public projects—regional resource development, urban redevelopment, etc. Public resource developments such as those in the Tennessee Valley, the Columbia River Basin, and elsewhere, have opened the way for much private investment which otherwise could not have been profitable.[45]

Thus fiscal policy can be used to further the long-run growth of the economy, and it can also be used during periods of contraction, or even at the upper-turning point, to stimulate the emergence of private investment spending—just when it is needed.

This discussion of Hansen's theory of the interaction of growth and the cycle has been very sketchy. Further and more elaborate discussion, however, must await the development of analytical concepts that are introduced at a later stage. We shall return to Hansen's analysis in Chapter 18.

---

[44]*Ibid.*, p. 136.

[45]*Ibid.* See also the discussion of Hansen's growth theory in Chapter 18 of this text, where his later views on fiscal policy are considered.

3. Summary

Both Schumpeter and Hansen account for the lower-turning point of the cycle by reference to exogenous variables that are associated with the development of such growth factors as population, technology, and so on. This results in a spurt of autonomous investment which, in turn, increases output and employment and also stimulates induced investment. Once the expansion gets under way, it will die a natural death, and the contraction follows. However, the interplay of endogenous forces accounts for the upper-turning point. With Schumpeter these are output increases relative to demand, price-level reduction, and autodeflation—all of which follow logically from the conditions of the expansion. With Hansen investment proceeds so rapidly that the movement down the investment demand curve occurs faster than the curve shifts to the right. And though both theorists introduce induced investment, it is not sufficient to prevent the upper-turning point.

In short, both of these theories are "mixed" models—that is, they rely upon the interplay of endogenous variables to account for the upper-turning point and on changes in exogenous variables to account for the lower. In this sense they resemble many other cycle theories.

However, Schumpeter and Hansen differ from most of the other theorists covered in this part in one important respect—namely, they stress the interaction of the cycle and growth. Indeed for Schumpeter the two processes are so bound together that to eliminate one is to remove the other. It is for this reason that he makes no specific contracyclical policy recommendations, for control of the cycle means control of innovations, and this in turn would retard the rate of growth. Moreover, Schumpeter argues that the growth process not only generates cycles, it also breeds the replacement of capitalism by socialism. This will happen, Schumpeter concludes, not as a result of the Marxian tenet that increasing misery will come, but because of the very success of the capitalist system. This success leads to institutional and attitudinal changes that result in the decay of capitalism, and one of the most important of these changes is the gradual elimination of the innovator.

Hansen, on the other hand, argues that policy, especially fiscal policy, is necessary to enhance the continued growth of the economy. To be sure, growth generates the cycle, but there are also "cushioning" policies that can be put into effect to mitigate the effects of cyclical disturbance. In a free enterprise economy, the cycle is unavoidable—there will always be investment booms which outrun the investment warranted by the growth factors—and a major danger is that after the economy enters into a slump, it will be a long time before expectations become bright enough to stimulate enough investment to start the economy on its expansionary path. In this event, fiscal policy will be quite important in stimulating private investment, especially since, as Hansen feels, monetary policy is not very effective.

QUESTIONS

7-1. What is meant by the marginal efficiency of investment, and why is the marginal efficiency schedule not stable?

7-2. Compare and contrast Schumpeter's "innovator" and Hansen's "promoter." Be sure to evaluate the relative significance assigned to each of these character-types in these two theories of the business cycle.

7-3. "Hansen's theory and Schumpeter's theory are really the same, for each relies upon autonomous investment to explain the lower-turning point, and each relies upon a dwindling away of investment in order to explain the upper-turning point. There is no fundamental difference between the two theories." Critically evaluate this statement.

7-4. Discuss in detail the similarities between Schumpeter's theory of the business cycle and Hayek's theory.

7-5. "According to Hansen's theory, if investment proceeded at the same rate as the change in the growth factors, there would be no such thing as the business cycle." Critically evaluate.

7-6. Discuss as well as possible the difference between a movement down the investment demand curve and a shift of the curve to the right. Relate both of these movements to Hansen's theory of the cycle.

Bibliography

Clemence, R. V. and F. S. Doody, *The Schumpeterian System.* Cambridge: Addison-Wesley Publishing Co., Inc., 1950.

Fellner, W J., "Employment Theory and Business Cycles," Chapter 2 in *A Survey of Contemporary Economics,* ed. H. S. Ellis. Philadelphia: The Blakiston Company, 1949, Vol. I.

Hansen, A. H., *Business Cycles and National Income.* New York: W. W. Norton & Company, Inc., 1951.

———, *Economic Issues of the 1960's.* New York: McGraw-Hill Book Company, 1960.

———, *Monetary Theory and Fiscal Policy.* New York: McGraw-Hill Book Company, 1949.

Harris, S. E., ed., *Schumpeter: Social Scientist.* Cambridge: Harvard University Press, 1951.

Schumpeter, J. A., *Business Cycles.* New York: McGraw-Hill Book Company, 1939, Vols. I-II.

———, *Capitalism, Socialism, and Democracy.* New York: Harper & Row, Publishers, 1947.

———, *The Theory of Economic Development.* Cambridge: Harvard University Press, 1951.

8

Some Further Theories of Business Fluctuations

The review of the earlier cycle theories is concluded in this chapter, although justice has hardly been done to the rich variety of business cycle theories that had been developed prior to the 1930's. The ones already discussed, however, along with those covered in this chapter, provide an adequate sample. Of the theories reviewed in this chapter—the "psychological," "harvest," and "profit" theories—it is safe to say that they have little acceptance today. Still each stresses an important variable that any satisfactory analysis of the business cycle must take into account.

1. The Psychological Theories

Most theories of the business cycle stress the importance of the "psychological" element in economic affairs. To refer to these as psychological theories of the cycle, however, is somewhat misleading, for it implies that changes in psychological conditions are the major causal factor in the cycle. The theories discussed in the two preceding chapters obviously incorporate changing psychological conditions (e.g., changes from pessimism to optimism during the expansion), but these are generally emphasized only as aggravating elements. In other words, no reasonably accurate account of the major cycle can afford to ignore changing expectations.

However, some analyses of the cycle place so much emphasis on the psychological element that they may well be referred to as "psychological" theories. The major contribution of these theories is that they explain how, under different psychological conditions, changes in important economic variables will produce different results. More specifically they stress the role of uncertainty in economic activity and the impact that uncertainty has on expectations, which, in turn, influence the behavior of other economic variables. But changes in expectations do not spring full-armed from the brow of businessmen (or any other relevant group). They must be associated with some change in the "real" economic environment, such as a rise in the interest rate, a decline in investment, a change in the money supply, and so on. Once one or more of these variables change, businessmen must make plans as to what is going to happen in the future and how these plans are to be implemented.

At this juncture the significance of changing expectations becomes obvious. For example, pessimistic (or optimistic) expectations as to the future may aggravate, soften, or even offset completely the effects of a change in any basic variable. The merit of the so-called psychological theories is that they stress the impact of the psychological environment on changes in the rest of the economic system. But nearly always the psychological elements serve as a *modus operandi* through which the impacts of changing variables are transmitted to the rest of the economy.

But what is a psychological factor? In economic theory it is defined as the interpretation that an individual or group of individuals attaches to an economic phenomenon. Usually the interpretation is put into quantitative terms and becomes an essential part of the plans of the individual or group. For example, a change in the price level may be interpreted variously—expectations may be that the price level may change even more in the same direction or will be reversed, or so on. And of course, one of the major characteristics of expectations is their volatility. However, as argued below, this volatility derives primarily from the ever-changing nature of the basic variables that influence expectations.

In economic theory expectations have been given a concrete quantitative statement. The relationship between the actual percentage change in price and the expected percentage change is called the elasticity of expectations.[1] This is written as:

$$E_x = \frac{\text{percentage change expected}}{\text{actual percentage change}},$$

where E_x stands for the "elasticity of expectations."

Now elasticity of expectations is usually translated into a statement of the *beliefs* of the individual or group as to what will happen in the future. Thus, if E_x is unity, it is believed that the actual percentage price change is a permanent one and is equal to the expected percentage price change. In this case the expectation is that there will be no further changes, that is, there are "stable expectations." On the other hand, if E_x is greater than unity, then the individual or group in question believes that the price change is not permanent but indeed will become greater in the future. For instance, if the price level rises by 2 per cent, but the public believes that it is going to rise by more (say, 5 per cent), then E_x is greater than one. In this event the community will attempt to adjust to the expected future conditions by altering its present position. Third, there is the possibility in which E_x is less than one, that is, it is believed that the price change is not permanent and will subsequently be partially reversed. In the limiting case in which E_x is zero, it is believed that the price change will be reversed completely and come back to its former level.

Of course, the concept of elasticity of expectations can be applied to other economic variables as well as to the price level. In any application, however, there is always reference to a change in some variable. Expectations or states of mind do not exist in a vacuum—they are always associated with some relevant economic variable, such as the price level, employment, inventories, and so on.

Surely there is a strong likelihood that errors in expectations are made, and therefore the elasticity of expectations is constantly undergoing revision. Several economists have emphasized errors in expectations in the business cycle, but even in the more sophisticated of the so-called psychological theories, changing expectations always (or nearly always) derive from changes in real economic factors.

Alfred Marshall, for instance, who stresses the psychological factors probably more than others, argues that the "beginning of a period of

---

[1]This concept was first developed in its present form by J. R. Hicks, *Value and Capital* (Oxford: Oxford University Press, 1946), p. 205. See also O. Lange, *Price Flexibility and Employment* (Bloomington, Ind.: The Principia Press, 1952), Chapter 5.

good credit is often a series of good harvests."[2] These reduce the total amount of consumer expenditures on food, leaving more expenditures available for other commodities.[3] Rising profits in the nonagricultural industries in turn lead to a rise in the demand for productive services, and hence there occurs a general increase in employment and income. Expectations become buoyant—that is, E_x becomes greater than one— and spread generally.

Marshall stated his theory in terms of the quantity equation,[4] $M = k(PO)$, where M is the stock of money, PO is money income (that is, total output, O, times the price level, P), and k is the fraction of income which the community desires to hold in the form of cash balances.[5] Although Marshall's version of the quantity theory is somewhat similar to the "crude version," $MV = PO$, there is a fundamental difference. In the "crude version" both V and O are assumed to be constant. Also V is determined by dividing PO by the stock of money— $V = PO/M$. In the Marshallian version, on the other hand, k is calculated as $k = M/PO$. It thus follows that arithmetically k is merely the reciprocal of V, that is, $V = 1/k$—1. Despite this arithmetic identity, the Marshallian version of the quantity theory is considerably different from the "crude version" in which V is held constant by assumption.

For Marshall, k is the *modus operandi* through which changing expectations operate. That is, with buoyant expectations emerging during the expansionary stage of the business cycle, the community desires to hold less cash balances and to increase its demand for other assets, whether consumers' goods, producers' goods, or what have you. During this stage, therefore, there is a shift away from money into other assets, and consequently aggregate demand for goods and services rises. In the

---

[2]See A. and M. P. Marshall, *Economics of Industry* (London: The Macmillan Company, 1888), especially pp. 152-54; and A. Marshall, *Principles of Economics* (New York: The Macmillan Company, 1950), especially pp. 709-11. Reprinted by permission of The Macmillan Company of Canada Ltd., and Macmillan & Co. Ltd. In his *Money, Credit, and Commerce* (London: The Macmillan Company, 1923), Marshall merely repeats the position taken in his earlier works.

[3]The argument that the series of good harvests increases consumer demand for nonagricultural commodities assumes, of course, that the price elasticity of demand for agricultural products is less than unity. This assumption is quite realistic. See W. W. Cochrane, *Farm Prices: Myth and Reality* (Minneapolis: University of Minnesota Press, 1958) for a survey of demand studies, nearly all of which conclude that the price elasticity of demand for agricultural products is between -0.15 and -0.2.

[4]See especially his *Money, Credit, and Commerce*.

[5]Recall that the k in Marshall's theory is similar to the k in Hawtrey's "purely monetary theory" of the cycle. The basic difference is that Hawtrey assumes k to be constant, while Marshall assumes it is volatile.

Marshallian version, then, a fall in k is the same thing as a rise in E_x above one, and this signifies an increase in total demand.

Conversely, when pessimism sets in, there is an attempt on the part of the community to shift out of other assets into money; or, put otherwise, in a period of pessimism k rises (that is, E_x is still greater than one, but is now relevant for falling prices). The rise in k means a drop in aggregate demand, and thus output and employment fall off. The important thing in the Marshallian equation is that k is not constant but is volatile, reflecting changes in the expectations of the community. This interpretation of k is, of course, substantially different from Hawtrey's, where k is assumed to remain constant throughout the course of the cycle. In Marshall's version of the quantity theory, k is the focal point of attention, whereas in Hawtrey's version, M commands the greater attention.

Once the expansion gets under way because of the "series of good harvests," expectations generally become optimistic. This means a fall in k as the community (both producers and consumers) attempts to shift out of money into other assets. Thus investment rises, as does the demand for loanable funds. The commercial banks respond by extending loans and thus increasing the stock of money. Note however that in Marshall's explanation the fall in k precedes the rise in M, not conversely.

However, for Marshall the expansion cannot go on forever. The rising demand for loanable funds eventually increases the interest rate which, Marshall asserts, serves as the barometer for the development of distrust and *lack of confidence*. Once confidence is shaken, loans from commercial banks are more difficult to acquire, people begin to increase their cash balances, and pessimism sets in generally. The shift from optimism to pessimism is reflected in a rise in k. Now the community desires to hold more in cash balances, and there is a shift away from other assets to money. This results in a decline in aggregate demand and brings on the upper-turning point, and once this occurs there emerges what Marshall calls a state of "commercial disorganization."[6] As he puts it: "The chief cause of the evil is a want of confidence. The greater part of it could be removed almost in an instant if confidence could return, touch all industries with her magic wand, and make them continue their production, and their demand for the wares of others."[7]

Unfortunately confidence does not return and wave her "magic wand"; and also unfortunately Marshall assumes that the upper-turn-

---

[6]Marshall, *Principles of Economics*, p. 711.
[7]*Ibid.*

ing point is almost a purely psychological phenomenon without any basis in "real" factors, other than the rise in the interest rate. This is somewhat paradoxical, for he begins the expansion with a change in real factors—the series of good harvests which increases the real incomes of consumers. Now interestingly enough he does not consider such phenomena in explaining the upper-turning point, which of course is followed by the contraction as confidence becomes more and more shaken.

It is not difficult, however, to develop some explanation of changes in real factors that would shake confidence. As discussed earlier, the marginal efficiency of investment declines as the expansion continues because of diminishing returns and rising costs. These changing real factors are obviously quite important in creating distrust and "want of confidence." Marshall nevertheless fails to consider the changing real factors that underlie the swing from optimism to pessimism and the concurrent rise in k.

Another approach that emphasizes the role of changing expectations has been advanced by Marshall's great disciple, A. C. Pigou.[8] Although Pigou's analysis of the cycle is far more extensive and complicated than a mere psychological theory, for the moment only the psychological aspects of it are considered.

Pigou argues that changes in expectations are usually rooted in such real factors as "a good harvest, an industrial dispute, an industrial invention, the discovery of new mines, the outbreak of war, an error in business forecasts, an autonomous monetary change, and so forth."[9] Actually he divides the "causes" of the cycle into two categories. First, there are the *impulses*, which are further divided into a "change in the quantity of mobile resources available to businessmen"[10] and the changes in expectations mentioned above. Second, there are the *conditions* upon which the impulses act. These conditions are such things as monetary institutions, market structures, the extent of trade unionism, and so on. Thus the impulses operate through the conditions. "Given the impulse, these will determine the nature of the effect it produces, and are, in this sense, causes of industrial fluctuations. The impulse is the dropping of a match; the consequences are determined by the nature of the material with which it comes into contact."[11]

---

[8]A. C. Pigou, *Industrial Fluctuations* (London: The Macmillan Company, 1927).
[9]*Ibid.*, p. 7.
[10]*Ibid.*
[11]*Ibid.*, p. 8.

In Pigou's analysis there is a further distinction so far as expectations are concerned. On the one hand, there are the *real causes,* which consist in changes that have occurred, or are about to occur, in actual industrial conditions; expectations based on these are "true" or "valid" expectations.[12] On the other hand, there are the *psychological causes,* which are "changes that occur in men's attitudes of mind, so that, on a constant basis of fact, they do not form a constant judgment."[13] Since Pigou's analysis is basically similar to Marshall's, though more refined and more rigorous, we need to concentrate only on the "true psychological causes"—errors in forecasting.

What are the causes of errors in forecasting—that is, errors in optimism and pessimism? Pigou provides several answers to this query. First, there is the fact that most production is carried on *in anticipation of demand.* "Producers in group A may enhance their output on their own initiative because they think there is going to be an increased offer from B, C, and D. . . ."[14] A further factor which breeds such errors is the withholding of relevant information by business secrecy.[15] Second, Pigou argues that the movement of facts themselves is not constant and that this induces errors in forecasts.[16] Finally, there is a long period of time that is necessary to produce durable goods, especially housing and plant and equipment. The longer the time required for the production of these things, the greater is the likelihood of error in forecasting. All of these things, Pigou argues, are conducive to errors that create wide swings in the state of expectations.

Once an error in forecast occurs, so that for example there develops a rise in investment spending, the error tends to propagate. There exists a "certain measure of psychological interdependence"; but more important is the fact that "an error of optimism on the part of one group of businessmen itself creates a justification for improved expectations on the part of other groups."[17] In other words, even though some increased investment is based on false expectations, it will no doubt improve the economic status and expectations of other industries. Thus the optimism tends to spread.

Periods of optimism however are replaced by periods of pessimism,

---

[12]*Ibid.,* p. 30.
[13]*Ibid.*
[14]*Ibid.,* p. 65.
[15]*Ibid.,* pp. 69-71.
[16]*Ibid.,* p. 67.
[17]*Ibid.,* p. 79.

and the movement from one to the other occurs once the errors of optimism are recognized. This takes place at the end of the "gestation period" when the errors are brought to the cold test of fact and review.

> When this test has been applied to a fair number of things and found wanting for a fair number, confidence is shaken. The fact that errors of optimism have been made and prospective profits exaggerated is discovered and recognized widely. By the fact of discovery on a large scale the tendency in errors of optimism is necessarily destroyed. As a consequence the flow of business activities is checked.[18]

Liquidation of businesses and reduction in the money supply aggravate the swing toward pessimism, and the contraction gets under way. Now errors of optimism are replaced by errors of pessimism.

Pigou's analysis of the lower-turning point does not differ much from many of the others discussed so far. The depletion of inventories, the use of new techniques, and the appearance of the "bolder spirits of industry," combine to improve expectations. At first the recovery only makes up for the past errors of the expansion, but once expectations improve, errors of forecast occur again and once more the expansion gets under way.

There is little need to discuss any more of the so-called psychological theories of the business cycle. Their major contribution has been to focus attention on the greater or lesser responses to changes in economic variables as they are transmitted through the medium of expectations. The theories discussed in the preceding chapters certainly do not exclude the psychological forces, but neither do they over-emphasize them. The chief claim to fame of the psychological theories is that they stress in greater detail the avenues and impacts of the psychological factor. Perhaps the most important observation to make is that these theories are purely exogenous, that is, both turning points of the cycle are explained by changes in exogenous variables.

2. Agricultural Theories of the Cycle

The close interdependence of the agricultural and industrial sectors of the economy has led some economists to develop so-called agricultural theories of the cycle. However, as the American economy has undergone continued economic growth, the agricultural sector has declined in relative importance. Accordingly, the agricultural theories are

---

[18]*Ibid*, p. 84.

not much discussed today. In this section two schools of thought on the role of agriculture in the cycle are examined very briefly.

First, there is the view which has been advanced by A. C. Pigou, D. H. Robertson, and J. M. Clark.[19] This view argues that although agricultural fluctuations are present, they are irregular in occurrence and are caused by exogenous forces. Such events as war, population change, drought, and so on cause an agricultural fluctuation; and the effects of these are then transmitted to the industrial sector of the economy. A clear and succinct statement of this view has been given by Clark:

> Agriculture appears to have its own cycles, whose timing has no clear or regular relation to the cycles of general business. This is true whether we consider physical production, prices at the farm, or the product of the two, which may be taken to measure the total purchasing power which agriculture generates and has to offer in the general market. . . . The [agricultural] cycle as we know it is the resultant of the combination of random disturbances and an economic system which transmits their effects cumulatively. . . . The random forces are not to be disregarded merely because there is no discernible correlation between their timing and that of the business cycle itself.[20]

The agricultural cycle, thus, is really a series of irregular and random disturbances, and though an agricultural fluctuation will have its impact on the rest of the economy, in the United States this tends to be relatively small for two reasons—first, the agricultural sector is quite small with respect to the rest of the economy, and second, governmental intervention in the agricultural sector has served to minimize considerably the effects of agricultural disturbances. Note, however, that this is not a theory of the business cycle.

The second view is the so-called *sunspot* or *meteorological* theory of the cycle, advanced especially by W. S. and H. S. Jevons and Henry Moore.[21] This view argues that there are periodic fluctuations in physical phenomena, particularly sunspot activity, and that these influence the economic status of agriculture. The effects on the agricultural sector are then transmitted to the rest of the economy. Although this

---

[19]Pigou, *Industrial Fluctuations*; D. H. Robertson, *A Study of Industrial Fluctuations* (Westminster: P. S. King, 1934); J. M. Clark, *Strategic Factors in Business Cycles* (New York: National Bureau of Economic Research, 1934).

[20]Clark, *Strategic Factors in Business Cycles,* pp. 61, 63.

[21]W. S. Jevons, *Investigations in Currency and Finance* (London: The Macmillan Company, 1884); H. L. Moore, *Economic Cycles: Their Law and Causes* (New York: The Macmillan Company, 1904). For a concise statement of Jevons' position, see Chapter 6 in *Readings in Business Cycles and National Income,* eds. A. H. Hansen and R. V. Clemence (New York: W. W. Norton & Company, Inc., 1953).

theory has often been designated as "crankism," it must be noted that it was originally developed when business cycle theory itself was in a rather unrefined state. Aside from the fact that the sunspot theorists have not provided adequate empirical evidence to substantiate their theory, the analysis is weak on the further grounds that its advocates do not spell out clearly how the effects are transmitted from the agricultural sector to the nonagricultural sectors of the economic system. Obviously the sunspot theory of the business cycle is a purely exogenous theory.

3.   An Eclectic Theory of the Cycle

One of the outstanding figures in the development of business cycle thought is Wesley Clair Mitchell.[22] Sometimes it is argued that Mitchell is one of those thinkers who are concerned primarily with "measurement" and actually "disdain" theory—that is, that he is strictly an empiricist.[23] This is hardly so. Not only has he stressed the fruitful interaction between statistical research, historical perspective, and theoretical analysis, he has also developed a theory of the cycle. However, his theory is so intermeshed with statistical findings that it has gained a wide acceptance among both academicians and businessmen.[24]

One of the outstanding features of Mitchell's theory is the emphasis that he places on the self-perpetuating aspect of the cycle—that one stage automatically feeds into the next as the cycle runs its course. The

----

[22]Mitchell, who was so important in founding and operating the National Bureau of Economic Research, died in 1948. For several statements on his contributions to economic and business cycle analysis and research, see A. F. Burns, ed., *Wesley Clair Mitchell: The Economic Scientist* (Princeton: Princeton University Press, 1952). For a particularly interesting and penetrating essay on Mitchell and his work, see J. A. Schumpeter, *Ten Great Economists* (New York: Oxford University Press, 1951), Chapter 9.

[23]This interpretation, at least in part, is found in L. A. Metzler's review of Burns and Mitchell, *Measuring Business Cycles* (New York: National Bureau of Economic Research, 1946); in *Social Research,* September 1947; and in T. C. Koopman's review of the same book, "Measurement Without Theory," *Review of Economic Statistics,* August 1947.

[24]His first major work, *Business Cycles and Their Causes,* was published in 1913 and for quite some time stood as the definitive work in this area. Part III of the book has been republished in paperback form under the same title by the University of California Press, 1960. All subsequent references will be to the republished work.

other outstanding feature is the emphasis he places on the "quest for profits" as the prime motivating force in the cyclical process. Thus it can be called a "profit theory" of the cycle. Mitchell has stated his position clearly:

> Now the recurrent phases presented by economic activity, wherever it is dominated by the quest for profits, grow out of and grow into each other. An incipient revival of activity, for example, develops into full prosperity, prosperity gradually breeds a crisis, the crisis merges into depression, depression becomes deeper for a while, but ultimately engenders a fresh revival of activity, which is the beginning of another cycle. A theory of the business cycle must therefore be a descriptive analysis of the cumulative changes by which one set of business conditions transforms itself into another set.[25]

If there is any one variable in Mitchell's analysis that holds the key position, it is profits. Whatever affects profits, either favorably or adversely, will have an effect upon the general level of economic activity. Out of the myriad of factors that influence profits, Mitchell stresses only a few as critically important. These are the behavior of costs (especially fixed charges, wage costs, the interest rate, and raw material costs), the behavior of prices, and expectations. It should also be mentioned that he relies on a "scarcity of capital" as a partial explanation of the upper-turning point, that is, changes in the money supply and the availability of bank credit also enter into his discussion.

Let us begin by breaking into the expansionary stage and then later on come around and see why the prevailing conditions are conducive for expansion. To begin with, there is a rise in both producer and consumer demand. This leads to a rise in real, physical output, after which prices begin to increase. At first the rising demand calls for only "gradual and well-balanced" price increases which engender increased optimism.[26] Once the expansion and rise in prices get under way, there is a diffusion of economic activity. ". . . the rise in prices rapidly spreads throughout the system of prices in much the same manner as the activity of trade out of which it grew spreads over the field of business."[27] However, different sectors expand at different rates. For instance, Mitchell argues that retail prices lag behind wholesale prices; and raw material prices, on the other hand, rise more quickly.

Very important is the fact that while the price of labor rises, it does

[25]Mitchell, *Business Cycles and Their Causes*, p. ix.
[26]*Ibid.*, p. 11.
[27]*Ibid.*

so at first with a lag. This is largely due to the attitude of laborers themselves. Mitchell has put this rather vividly:

> Futhermore, the economic pressure that drives the great mass of wage
> earners to sustain their arduous struggles for higher wages relaxes just
> at the moment rapid increases might be wrung from employers. The
> relatively moderate rate at which retail prices rise in the earlier stages of
> revival prevents the cost of living from going up fast. On the other hand,
> the economic position of workingmen is being improved by the greater
> regularity of employment and the abolition of "short time." Even with-
> out any increase in their customary rates of pay, the wage earning class
> is better off. They hesitate to demand an increase in their customary
> wages until the feeling of this relative prosperity is dulled by familiarity,
> and until personal savings or trade-union accumulations have put them
> in position to fight with vigor.[28]

The net result of these developments is a rise in profits, and this stimulates the expansion even more. For Mitchell, "the quest of profits is the
great driving force of the economy,"[29] and now that profits have been
improved, the expansion becomes cumulative. Net, new investment
rises, and this adds further impetus to the expansion.[30]

Mitchell feels, however, that the forces of expansion contain the seeds
of contraction, and once these seeds germinate and sprout, the upper-
turning point is inevitable. "Then the bonds that unite different enterprises will become channels through which injury will spread to other
enterprises, just as they were recently channels for the spread of prosperity."[31]

But what is it that brings on the upper-turning point? Since the quest
for profits is the driving force, the emergence of the contraction must
be traced to profit reductions in the later phases of the expansion. And
for Mitchell, profits are reduced for a number of reasons, all of which
are part of the expansionary process itself.

In the first place, the costs of doing business rise more rapidly as the
expansion continues. Fixed costs rise, and more important, "prime costs"
rise also, especially because as demand presses on existing capacity,
standby equipment is put into use.[32] Further, labor costs begin to rise
as full employment of the labor force is approached. More and more

---

28*Ibid.*, p. 18
29*Ibid.*, p. 20.
30*Ibid.*, pp. 23-25.
31*Ibid.*, p. 27.
32*Ibid.*, pp. 30-31.

rather inefficient workers must be hired. Overtime labor is present, and this "is especially expensive to employers, not only because it often commands extra rates of wages, but also because it is tired labor."[33] And finally trade unions begin to push for higher rates of pay. All these rising costs, along with increasing inefficiency as full plant capacity is encountered, tend to raise average costs and to impinge upon profits.

Second, as the expansion continues, there develops a "scarcity of capital," that is, "the supply of funds forthcoming for long loans is no longer equal to the demand *at the old rate of interest*."[34] Consequently the interest rate rises, and businesses must rely more and more on equity issues, a relatively expensive means of acquiring funds. Moreover, the reserve position of the commercial banks becomes impaired and as a result there occurs a stringency in the extension of short-term loans. All told, in the latter phases of the expansion, "tension in the money market"[35] and in the long-term market occurs, and as the cost of capital funds rises many business are induced to defer their expansion plans.

Finally, in the face of rising costs, businessmen are unable to raise prices proportionately and maintain their profit margins. Some prices are regulated, either by custom or by government,[36] but more important there is an increased supply of commodities because of "errors of optimism." As Mitchell has put it:

> The whole tenor of prosperity . . . is in the direction of augmenting errors. The optimistic temper that prevails disposes men to underrate the risks and to overrate the probable gains. Even active and experienced men of affairs do not escape this infection of overconfidence. . . . The twist given by overconfidence to forecasts of future demand, always difficult to make with accuracy, thus leads to overstocking of certain markets.[37]

In short, errors of optimism result in aggregate supply rising relative to aggregate demand, and thus prices cannot rise in general and may even fall. More than that: there has occurred a large expansion in the productive capacity of the economy, and now that the "gestation period" has ended, a large outflow of goods occurs, tending to depress prices even more.

Once all these things happen, the upper-turning point sets in. Inven-

---

[33]*Ibid.*, p. 32.
[34]*Ibid.*, p. 42.
[35]*Ibid.*, p. 45.
[36]*Ibid.*, pp. 55-56.
[37]*Ibid.*, pp. 57-58.

tory orders are cut back, as are other investment expenditures. As prices fall, profit prospects—the moving force—look more and more bleak, and businesses retrench even further. Output is reduced sharply, unemployment rises, and consumers' expenditures drop. As undesired inventories accumulate, prices are cut even lower, and pessimism tends to become diffused throughout the entire system.[38]

But as the contraction continues, the forces of expansion begin to emerge. Undesired inventories are worked down, and even though costs lag behind prices, they are eventually brought into line. These alone begin to strengthen the profit outlook. Moreover, in the process of survival, businesses introduce new products and new methods of production. The interest rate falls, commercial banks build up both reserves and a willingness to lend, and credit stringency lessens considerably. Optimism now begins to prevail, replacing the pessimism of the contraction.[39]

Although all these developments emerge in the latter part of the contraction, they alone are not sufficient to bring on the expansion. They merely set the stage for the principal actor—the profit motive. As Mitchell states: "In this fashion depression ultimately brings about revival. For of course these changes increase prospective profits, and in the money economy prospective profits are the great incentive to activity."[40]

This in broad outline is Mitchell's theory of the business cycle. Though he places great emphasis on the profit motive as a dynamic variable, he introduces such a large number of variables that the theory does not, and can not, assume the degree of simplicity of most other cycle theories. In fact, his emphasis on the "diffusion process" and on the uniqueness of each cycle leads him to the view that there can really be no simple, straightforward theory of the business cycle. He states this very clearly in his *Business Cycles and Their Causes.*

> . . . the broad changes of economic organization are cumulative, like the lesser changes that cause each phase of every business cycle to evolve into its successor. And, being cumulative, their dominating influence upon the phenomena of business cycles stands out clearly in the lapse of years. *Hence economists of each generation will probably see reason to recast the theory of business cycles they learned in their youth.*[41]

---

[38]*Ibid.,* pp. 131-39.
[39]*Ibid.,* pp. 138-47.
[40]*Ibid.,* p. 146.
[41]*Ibid.,* p. 168, italics added.

4. Summary

With Mitchell we terminate the review of the earlier theories of the business cycle.[42] The outstanding feature of each theory discussed in the last three chapters is that, while it contains more than a half-truth, it certainly falls short of providing a complete explanation of the cyclical process. Obviously the quest for profits, changing expectations, spurts of innovations, changes in the money supply and interest rate, and structural maladjustments all figure into any explanation.

Moreover, each of the theories is a "mixed" theory, in terms of the classification set out in Chapter 5. The psychological and agricultural theories (and perhaps Mitchell's theory) are exceptions to this generalization. But the more important theories discussed in these chapters are certainly "mixtures," relying upon changes in exogenous variables to explain the lower-turning point and using the interplay of endogenous variables to account for the upper-turning point.

Finally, no one theory reviewed thus far has commanded very wide assent; nor did any do an adequate job of explaining the Great Depression of the 1930's.[43] During that decade, therefore, an increasing amount of attention was focused on the cycle, and though several contributions were made, the one that has stood out the most is J. M. Keynes' analysis. The so-called Keynesian analysis of economic disturbances forms the subject matter of Part 3.

---

[42]Of course, Hansen's theory, since it was developed during and after the 1930's, does not fit into this generalization.

[43]With Hansen's theory excluded for historical reasons.

QUESTIONS

8-1. Discuss the similarities and differences between Marshall's and Hawtrey's versions of the quantity theory of money.

8-2. What is meant by "elasticity of expectations"? Relate this concept of elasticity to the business cycle theories covered in this and the two preceding chapters.

8-3. Would the sunspot theory of the trade cycle be classified as purely endogenous, purely exogenous, or mixed? Explain.

8-4. How important do you feel changes in psychological expectations are in cyclical fluctuations? Should they be classified as exogenous or endogenous?

8-5. Explain the significance of profits in Mitchell's theory of the business cycle.

Bibliography

Burns, A. F., ed., *Wesley Clair Mitchell: Economic Scientist*. Princeton: Princeton University Press, 1952.

Haberler, G., *Prosperity and Depression*. Cambridge: Harvard University Press, 1958, Chapters 4, 6-7.

Hansen, A. H., *Business Cycles and National Income*. New York: W. W. Norton & Company, Inc., 1964, Chapters 15, 18, 20.

Hansen, A. H., and R. V. Clemence, eds., *Readings in Business Cycles and National Income*. New York: W. W. Norton & Company, Inc., 1953, Chapters 6-7.

Marshall, A., *Principles of Economics*. New York: The Macmillan Company, 1950, eighth edition.

Mitchell, W. C., *Business Cycles and Their Causes*. Berkeley and Los Angeles: University of California Press, 1960.

Schumpeter, J. A., *Ten Great Economists*. New York: Oxford University Press, 1951, Chapters 4, 9.

part 3

Aggregate Income and Employment Analysis:
Keynesian and Post–Keynesian

9

The Development
of Modern
Employment Theory:
The ''Keynesian
Revolution''

Despite the variety of business cycle theories that existed in the early 1930's, none of them seemed to do an adequate job in explaining the Great Depression. More important, none of them was capable of prescribing satisfactorily how the economy could recover from such low levels of output and employment. Recommendations ranged from reductions in the market rate of interest to cuts in the general level of wages, but all of these proposals seemed to be ineffective in bringing on the lower-turning point. As a result, new lines of inquiry were cast out as economists strove to develop a more complete and adequate theory of fluctuations in the levels of income and employment.

Although intellectual efforts were made in several countries,[1] it was the British economist John Maynard Keynes who paved the way for later developments with his *The General Theory of Employment, Interest, and Money*.[2] Keynes had already given some clues in his earlier *The Means to Prosperity*,[3] but it was the more rigorous and better formulated *The General Theory* that captured the attention of western economists. In this work Keynes set the stage for modern growth and cycle theory, though paradoxically, Keynes himself did not develop either a cycle or a growth theory.

It is a bit difficult to assess the income-employment theory advanced in *The General Theory* because of the varied reactions to it. The analysis has been referred to as the "Keynesian Revolution,"[4] as well as the "dismal New Economics."[5] Some have argued that Keynes really said little that was new,[6] though others contend that he did a masterful job of compiling and restating much more meaningfully what had been said before by others.[7] Still others, however, contend that while this in itself

---

[1]Especially in Sweden, where an independent and important body of analysis, following the contributions of Knut Wicksell, was being developed. For discussions of the Swedish contributions, see especially B. Ohlin, "Some Notes on the Stockholm Theory of Savings and Investment," *Economic Journal*, March, June 1937; and F. A. Lutz, "The Outcome of the Savings-Investment Discussion," *Quarterly Journal of Economics*, August 1938, both reprinted in G. Haberler, ed., *Readings in Business Cycle Theory* (Philadelphia: The Blakiston Company, 1944). See also A. H. Hansen, *Monetary Theory and Fiscal Policy* (New York: McGraw-Hill Book Company, 1949), Appendix B.

[2]From *The General Theory of Employment, Interest, and Money* by John Maynard Keynes. Reprinted by permission of Harcourt, Brace & World, Inc.

[3]J. M. Keynes, *The Means to Prosperity* (London: The Macmillan Company, 1933), available now as Part I in the paperback *The Means to Prosperity, Keynesian Economics: Pro & Con* (Buffalo: Economica Books, 1959).

[4]L. R. Klein, *The Keynesian Revolution* (New York: The Macmillan Company, 1947), now available as a Macmillan Paperback.

[5]H. Hazlitt, *The Failure of the "New Economics": An Analysis of the Keynesian Fallacies* (Princeton: D. Van Nostrand Co., Inc., 1959). "The whole of the *General Theory* might be described as an exercise in obfuscation, and the obfuscation begins at an early point" (p. 44).

[6]*Ibid.*, p. 427: "Though Keynes has been praised as the peer of Adam Smith, Ricardo, and even Darwin, not a single important doctrine in his work is both true and original." See also W. Fellner, "What is Surviving? An Appraisal of Keynesian Economics on Its Twentieth Anniversary," *American Economic Review*, May 1957.

[7]"Keynes co-ordinated already known bits of economic theorizing, supplied some missing links, and created a coherent theory of employment out of it. To call this . . . giving a particularly effective formulation to known doctrine, is in my opinion an understatement." T. Scitovsky, "Discussion," *American Economic Review*, May 1957, p. 93.

was a major contribution, the Keynesian analysis did say something new and different.[8] And over a quarter of a century later, these conflicting views are still present.

Obviously there was some sort of "revolution" that accompanied Keynes' *The General Theory,* though it must be stressed that the "revolution" was one of analytical tools and concepts, not of social policy.[9] Like all other intellectual revolutions it had, of course, a firm foundation in earlier thought. But despite the fact that the Keynesian analysis does not provide a sharp and drastic break with the past, it nevertheless has yielded tools and concepts that go farther in dealing with basic issues than the earlier cycle theories did. In any event, the Keynesian tools of analysis are widely used today. As David McCord Wright has put it: "We are all Keynesians today, in the sense that every competent modern economist uses Keynes' income approach for analysis and forecasting, even though that approach has to be supplemented by a good deal more material."[10]

In this part we shall examine the Keynesian system in some detail, as well as point out some basic criticisms and shortcomings of it. Also we shall be concerned with some recent post-Keynesian developments which, though founded in large part on the Keynesian analysis, have gone far beyond it. More specifically there are, as we shall see, four basic cornerstones or connecting links in the Keynesian system, and each of these will be covered in some detail. These are (1) the *consumption function,* which deals with the major determinants of aggregate consumer behavior (Chapter 10); (2) the *investment demand function,* which is concerned with the determinants of planned and realized investment by private business (Chapter 11); (3) the *liquidity preference function,* which provides an explanation of the determination of the interest rate which, in turn, is a determinant of investment (Chapter 11); and (4) the *multiplier,* which brings together, in a rather consistent manner, the consumption, investment, and liquidity preference functions (Chapter 12). Finally we shall relax several of the rather

---

[8]"At this stage, it is easy to look back and deprecate or belittle the Keynesian contribution. I am tremendously impressed by the extent to which I continuously draw upon the *General Theory* in my daily work. It is truly a great book." L. R. Klein, "Discussion," *American Economic Review,* May 1961, p. 25.

[9]As Klein has put it: "The Keynesian theory is viewed . . . as a revolutionary doctrine in the sense that it produces theoretical results entirely different from the body of economic thought existing at the time of its development. The 'Revolution' discussed here is a revolution in thought, not in the economic policies of government." *The Keynesian Revolution,* p. vii. See also D. M. Wright, *The Keynesian System* (New Jersey: Fordham University Press, 1962), Chapter 1.

[10]Wright, *The Keynesian System,* p. x.

restrictive assumptions underlying the discussion of Chapters 10-12 and introduce the important variables of money wages and prices in Chapter 13.

However, before plunging into the technical analysis of the Keynesian system some general comments about the Keynesian analysis appear to be in order. This is the task of the remainder of this chapter.

1.   Pre-Keynesian Views on the Depression

What were the prevailing views of economists during the earlier years of the 1930's? How did economists diagnose the Great Depression, and what policy proposals did they advance? An answer to these questions will show that most of the cycle theories developed up to that time did not serve as a basis for any significant policy program to alleviate the unemployment of the thirties. Let us examine some of the more important arguments and then turn to the Keynesian analysis to see how different it was and therefore why it came to be referred to as "revolutionary."

A.   A. C. Pigou

From 1929 to 1931 an investigatory committee in Great Britain—known as the Macmillan Committee—held a number of hearings on the causes and potential cures of the depression.[11] One of the expert economic witnesses called before the committee to give testimony was the eminent neoclassical economist, A. C. Pigou.[12] The major line of reasoning advanced by Pigou was that certain institutions create impediments to a downward flexibility of prices, and the most important of these is trade unions. The union, in his view, prevents reductions in the wage level, and this is the major reason why general unemployment continues. If only wages are flexible downwards, he argued, so that profit

---

[11]*Report of the Committee on Finance and Industry* (Macmillan Report), presented to Parliament by the Financial Secretary for the Treasury by the command of His Majesty, June 1931. (This section relies heavily on Klein, *The Keynesian Revolution,* especially pp. 33-35, 43-55).

[12]Pigou, a well-known and brilliant disciple of Alfred Marshall, published during his lifetime several significant works, among which are *The Economics of Welfare, Equilibrium and Employment, Lapses from Full Employment,* and *Keynes's General Theory: A Retrospective View,* plus a large number of important contributions in the journals. We have already reviewed his "psychological theory" of the business cycle; see Chapter 8.

prospects are improved, then output will rise and (given the money supply) full employment will be restored.

This analysis, which is far more detailed and complicated than the preceding discussion implies, has come to be referred to as the "Pigou effect." At the moment the Pigou effect can only be mentioned though it is discussed in considerable detail at a later point.[13] One might note, however, that in an important sense the term "Pigou effect" is misleading, for Pigou was merely stating more clearly and explicitly the prevailing neoclassical doctrine. Nevertheless, Pigou's argument was that widespread unemployment exists primarily because labor is pricing itself out of the market by preventing downward wage adjustments. For him, then, the major problem is the presence of imperfections in the competitive system which prevent the system from automatically eliminating the unemployment. Remove these imperfections and you remove the unemployment.[14]

B.   Edwin Cannan

At about the same time another eminent British economist, Edwin Cannan, presented a similar analysis and policy proposal.[15] Essentially his analysis is as follows: consider the individual firms in an *isolated* labor market[16] in which there is some unemployment. If the unemployed workers offer their services at lower wages, the competitive firms will respond to the lower wages and costs by increasing their output which, in turn, can be sold only at lower prices. The lower product prices in turn lead to an increase in quantity demanded by consumers, and thus simultaneously the firms will increase both output and employment. Therefore, within a particular labor market there will be no unemployment so long as there is competition among the employers and among the workers.

Cannan, however, proceeded to transfer the analysis from the single, isolated labor market to the economy at large, arguing that the best way to overcome general unemployment is for workers in the aggregate to take a general wage cut. At lower wages per unit of labor service

---

[13]Chapter 15, section 1B.

[14]In the later versions of his analysis, Pigou no longer held to this view; see Chapter 15, section 1B.

[15]"The Demand for Labour," *Economic Journal*, September 1932.

[16]By isolated labor market is meant one which is small enough, relative to the rest of the economy, that there exists almost complete independence between the wage incomes of the workers in the market and the demand for the products produced by the firms in the market.

offered, employers would respond by increasing both output and employment, eliminating any unemployment that might exist. Thus, Cannan concluded, persistent general unemployment is due to the fact that laborers are pricing themselves out of the market by keeping wages too high, especially via collective bargaining. This, of course, is quite similar to Pigou's position.

C. R. G. Hawtrey

Another expert witness called before the Macmillan Committee was R. G. Hawtrey, whose monetary theory of the business cycle was reviewed in Chapter 6. Among other things, Hawtrey argued against any increased governmental spending as a means of restoring full employment to the economy. Presumably he was arguing that a rise in governmental spending would be at the expense of private spending, and thus any increase in employment in the governmental sector would be at the expense of employment in the private sector. As might be expected, given his purely monetary theory of the business cycle, Hawtrey advocated a reduction in the interest rate; but more importantly, in line with Pigou and Cannan, he also advocated a general wage cut. His argument was that there was need to increase profits in order to stimulate private investment spending.

D. F. A. Hayek

As far as the monetary-overinvestment theorists were concerned, they felt that there was little constructive action that the government could take. Recall that in Hayek's theory the upper-turning point occurs because of a "shortage of capital" (that is, a shortage of savings), and thus any government fiscal policy would merely aggravate the situation.[17] Moreover, Hayek was opposed to increases in the money supply that would result in inflation. As Klein, in his review of Hayek's position, has put it: "In short, he was an ardent supporter of do-nothing economic policy. The business cycle is an immutable law of nature which cannot be defied, and the system, if left alone, will always recover to full employment."[18]

This brief survey of the prevailing attitudes toward the depression of the 1930's, as well as toward contracyclical policy in general, reveals

---

[17] See Chapter 6 for a review of Hayek's theory.
[18] Klein, *The Keynesian Revolution*, p. 51.

one important thing. The widely accepted theories at that time assumed that there might be full employment if only impediments to competition, especially those that stood in the way of wage reductions, were removed, and if there were no governmental intervention in the form of fiscal policy. Of course, there was general agreement that the interest rate should be lowered.

It was in this atmosphere that Keynes presented his *The General Theory*. But how did this work differ from the generally accepted theories? Why and how was it "revolutionary"? And what was the general reaction to it?

2. A Preliminary Statement of the Keynesian Analysis: The Components of Aggregate Demand

All business cycle theories, as well as economic analysis in general, prior to the 1930's made use of what Keynes called *"effective demand,"* that is, the total demand by all classes of buyers for all types of currently produced goods and services.[19] Cycle theorists, however, argued that at times aggregate demand and aggregate supply could be unequal, thus creating either inflation or unemployment. On the other hand, the neoclassical economists (in general) argued that aggregate demand will always be equal to aggregate supply if prices and wages are flexible enough (aside from exogenous factors). More than that, the neoclassical economists argued that with flexible wages and prices, effective demand would always be high enough to provide for *continuing full employment*. They concluded, as noted above, that if there is continuing unemployment, it must be because of sticky wages and prices, and that once this stickiness is removed, full employment will be restored.

Keynes similarly was concerned with aggregate demand, or, as he termed it, effective demand. However, he divided aggregate demand into its several component parts and then in turn broke these down even further and analyzed the major determinants of each. His general conclusion, contrary to the prevailing neoclassical thought, was that the determinants of aggregate demand did not always operate to insure its equality with aggregate supply at full employment. In fact, he argued, at times aggregate supply may exceed aggregate demand, with the result of continuing unemployment and cutbacks in output and produc-

---

[19]Recall from Chapter 6 that Hawtrey called it "consumer outlay."

tion. Nor even with flexible wages and prices is there anything in the
capitalist system that insures that full employment will be restored
without direct governmental action and policy. Thus his analysis of aggregate supply and demand led him to quite different conclusions than
those advanced in the prevailing body of economic thought.

In his analysis, total demand is made up of expenditures by consumers on consumers' goods and services (C), by businessmen on investment goods and services (I), by government on goods and services
(G), and by foreigners for domestically produced goods and services,
less domestic demand for foreign produced goods and services (F).
Thus, using the symbol Y to designate income, we have the identity[20]

$$Y = C+I+G+F.$$

The behavior of income (Y) therefore depends upon the *net* movement
of the various components on the right-hand side of the identity. We
must not make the mistake of concluding simply that because one component (say, G) rises, Y will also rise. Conceivably, a rise in government spending will stifle or actually reduce I, particularly if businessmen respond negatively to government action. In short, we must look
to the *net movement* of *all* the major components of spending in order
to predict the behavior of Y.

For simplicity (at the outset) Keynes abstracted from both G and
F—that is, he assumed that government is neutral in its operations and
that the economy is a "closed" system with no international trade. Thus
the fundamental identity to begin with is the rather simple $Y = C+I$,
which has the merit of allowing us to focus our attention upon the performance of the *private* sector of the economy.

Keynes then proceeded to inquire into the basic determinants of both
C and I, and though he discussed quite a number of these he abstracted
from most as being rather unimportant in the short run. First, there is
the consumption function, which states that aggregate consumption is
a function of aggregate income. While Keynes and his followers recognized that numerous variables other than income have an influence on
consumption, they nevertheless conclude that income is the *chief* determinant. This functional relationship may be written as a behavioral
equation:

$$C = f(Y),$$

where C designates consumption and Y stands for income. In this formulation C is the dependent variable, and Y is the independent vari-

---

[20]See section 4, below, for a discussion of identity and behavioral equations.
Recall also the discussion of the national income accounts in Chapters 2-3.

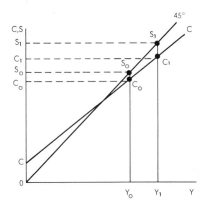

FIGURE 9–1

able; thus consumption will change only as a result of a change in income (although we qualify this below).

But there is more to it than simply this. Keynes advanced what he called a "fundamental psychological law" which states that not only is some portion of consumers' income saved, but also that portions of *net additions* to income are saved. Thus, if consumers experience a rise in their income, they will not spend it all on consumers' goods, but in fact will save a portion of it. Or, in other words, as consumers' income increases, their demand does not increase proportionately. Accordingly a gap between total output and consumer demand emerges which is equal to savings, and unless these savings reenter the spending stream, unemployment will develop.

The relationship between income and consumption can be seen in Figure 9–1, where income (Y) is plotted on the horizontal axis, and consumption (C) and savings (S) are plotted on the vertical axis. Since the axes have equal scales, the forty-five-degree line passing through the point of origin relates the two axes on a one-to-one basis. Thus, $OY_0 = Y_0S_0$, $OY_1 = Y_1S_1$, and so on. Further, out of the income level OY_0, only Y_0C_0 is, given consumer spending behavior, expended on consumers' goods, and the remainder, C_0S_0, is devoted to savings. If income rises to OY_1, then consumption will rise also, but not by the full amount of the income increase. In this case, consumption rises to Y_1C_1, and savings also rise to C_1S_1. Thus, in absolute terms, savings rise as income rises, and this means that larger amounts of investment are necessary to absorb the savings.

This brings us to the investment demand function. Attention here is focused upon the determinants of business expenditures on net investment (net capital formation). The simple formulation of this functional relationship is the behavioral equation

$$I = f(i,r),$$

where I stands for *net* investment and i is the rate of interest. However, we must consider also r, the marginal efficiency of investment, which is provisionally taken as a "given," determined by technological considerations and the prevailing state of businessmen's expectations. Recall from Chapter 7 that the marginal efficiency of investment simply measures the anticipated rate of return on planned investment projects. So long as the rate of return (r) on a project exceeds the interest cost of acquiring funds to finance the project, the investment will be carried out. But because of diminishing returns and rising capital costs, r diminishes as more and more investment is carried out in a relatively short period of time, so that eventually the marginal efficiency falls below i on some investment projects. Just prior to this point (where $r = i$), investment expansion will cease. Recall also from Chapter 7 that changing expectations of businessmen will influence the magnitude of the marginal effciency, and therefore the impact of changing anticipations must be taken into account.

Since the amount of investment spending depends in part upon the rate of interest, this important economic variable must also be examined. Keynes discussed this in terms of the liquidity preference function theory of the interest rate. This is usually written as

$$i = f(M,Y,LP),$$

where i again is the rate of interest, M stands for the money supply, and Y as usual designates income. Actually we must also consider the community's demand for money for various purposes, that is, its preference for liquidity. The magnitude of the demand for money (that is, liquidity preference, LP) is determined by the community's preference to hold money for transactions and precautionary and speculative purposes, and these in turn will be influenced by the interest rate and the level of income. The supply of money (M) we take as given by Central Bank action. We shall return to this rather complex analysis in Chapter 11.

Finally, there is the multiplier, which is an analytical device that relates the three preceding functional relationships in a rather meaningful way. Since it is virtually impossible to explain the multiplier, even in a preliminary manner, at this juncture, we shall postpone discussion of the concept until Chapter 12.

Up to this point we may conclude that there are two major components of private aggregate demand—consumption and investment. The first of these is dependent primarily upon income, while the second is dependent *in part* upon the rate of interest. Changing expectations, however, play a considerable role in determining the volume of investment demand, as do changes in technology and such. Nevertheless, the major conclusion to this point is that aggregate demand for the private sector of the economy is made up of these two major constituents. Now we must inquire into the supply side of the private sector in order to see if aggregate demand will always be sufficient to take off the market the aggregate supply that insures full employment.

3. Aggregate Supply and Income-Employment Equilibria

Total income is defined by Keynes as the payments by businesses to the factors of production employed in producing a given output, *plus* the normal profits of the businesses.[21] Consumption and investment expenditures are made out of this income, and these, of course, become the proceeds (total revenue) of the business community. But under a private enterprise system, especially where there is a good deal of uncertainty as to the future, businessmen can never know ahead of time what their proceeds will be. They must, nevertheless, make some estimate of their future proceeds before they make their production and employment plans and carry them out.[22]

Thus in answering such a question as, "How many workers shall I employ?" businessmen must make some guess as to what their future proceeds will be. If they anticipate, given the present level of output and employment, that the proceeds will be greater than their factor costs of production *plus* normal profits, they will plan to expand output and employment. On the other hand, if they anticipate that the pro-

---

[21]*The General Theory*, Chapter 3. An extremely useful aid in mastering *The General Theory* is A. H. Hansen, *A Guide to Keynes* (New York: McGraw-Hill Book Company, 1953).

[22]See A. G. Hart, "Keynes' Analysis of Expectations and Uncertainty," in *The New Economics: Keynes' Influence on Theory and Public Policy*, ed. S. E. Harris (New York: Alfred A. Knopf, 1950). For more recent studies, see J. W. Angell, "Uncertainty, Likelihoods, and Investment Decisions," *Quarterly Journal of Economics*, February 1960; and M. F. Foss and V. Natrella, "The Structure and Realization of Business Investment Anticipations," in *The Quality and Economic Significance of Anticipations Data* (Princeton: Princeton University Press, 1960). See also R. Ferber, "Measuring the Accuracy and Structure of Businessmen's Expectations," *Journal of the American Statistical Association*, September 1953.

ceeds will be less than their factor costs plus normal profits, they will restrict output and employment. And finally, if the anticipated proceeds just equal factor costs plus normal profits, they will maintain their present output-employment position. Aggregate supply and employment, in other words, depend upon the expectations of businessmen as regards future proceeds in relation to factor costs and normal profits. For this reason Keynes defined "the aggregate supply price of the output of a given amount of employment . . . [as] the expectation of proceeds which will just make it worthwhile of the entrepreneurs to give that employment."[23] To repeat, if businessmen expect aggregate demand (which determines their proceeds) to be greater than their present factor costs plus normal profits, they will expand employment and output in their effort to acquire more profits. Conversely, they may contract output and employment or hold their present position, depending upon their anticipations. The important thing is the relationship between aggregate demand (that is, expected proceeds) and aggregate supply price (that is, factor costs plus normal profits).

Now the neoclassical analysis held that aggregate demand equals aggregate supply, so long as there are flexible wages and prices, at full employment. Keynes, however, objected strongly to this, for he argued that aggregate demand and supply not only could be temporarily unequal, but that in fact *they may be equal at less than full employment.* In short, businessmen may anticipate proceeds just sufficient to cover their factor costs and yield normal profits, but at an output rate that provides for less than full employment. He further argued that this equilibrium situation could, under certain conditions (such as those that characterized the Great Depression), persist for quite some time in the absence of direct governmental policy.

Keynes' positon can be shown in Figure 9–2, where we have the consumption function CC. Begin with the output (income) OY_0 ($= Y_0S_0$). Out of this income consumers will spend Y_0C_0 on consumers' goods and services, leaving the savings gap C_0S_0. The important question now becomes—will businesses demand enough investment goods to fill the gap C_0S_0? If they do, then aggregate demand (Y_0S_0) will be equal to aggregate supply (Y_0S_0), and the income level will be maintained.

What, however, will happen if businesses demand only C_0A_0 amount of investment goods? In this case aggregate demand will be Y_0A_0, which is less than the aggregate supply of Y_0S_0. In short, businesses have over-produced with respect to aggregate demand—they have, in

---

[23]Keynes, *The General Theory*, p. 24.

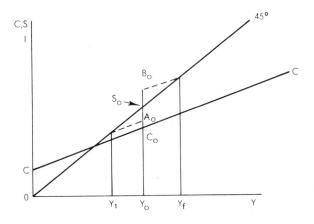

FIGURE 9–2

other words, over-anticipated their proceeds by the amount A_0S_0. Since they cannot now move all their ouptut onto the market and still receive normal profits and cover factor costs, they will cut back on output and employment until, if investment demand remains constant at C_0A_0, aggregate demand equals aggregate supply. This will occur at the income level Y_1, at which businesses are expecting and receiving proceeds that just cover their factor costs and normal profits. Note, however, that if we define full employment to be at the income level of Y_f, there is involuntary unemployment and this will continue unless something happens to increase investment demand.

Let us reverse the case. Again we start at Y_0, but now let us assume that investment demand is C_0B_0. That is, aggregate demand exceeds aggregate supply by S_0B_0 amount. Since businesses now anticipate proceeds greater than their factor costs plus normal profits, they will expand output and employment. In this case, if investment demand remains constant at C_0B_0, the new equilibrium level of income is Y_f, which we have arbitrarily assumed to be the full employment level. Again aggregate demand equals aggregate supply, and this situation will continue until the equality is upset for some reason or other.

For Keynes the major fly in the ointment is that there is no automatic adjustment process that insures that demand will equal supply at full employment. To be sure, consumption is a function of income, but because of the "fundamental psychological law" consumers do not increase their consumption by as much as their income increases. Thus the gap between the consumption function CC and the forty-five-degree line becomes greater and greater as income grows. This, of course, puts pressure upon investment to keep aggregate demand equal to supply at high levels of output and employment. But Keynes argued that there is nothing in the economic system that insures a sufficient amount of investment to absorb the savings of the community; that is, investment demand is not so closely tied to income that the savings gap is continually filled. As Hansen, a leading American Keynesian, has summarized it:

> . . . the demand for investment goods is largely determined by factors (technological developments, etc.) unrelated to current income. Entrepreneurs are likely to base their sales expectations on current demand. They therefore tend to anticipate sales proceeds which will equal the Aggregate Cost of output. But this expectation may prove false in view of the exogenous factors which *autonomously* determine the demand for investment goods. . . . The determinants of consumption and the determinants of investment are not interconnected in a manner which insures an adequate Aggregate Demand so that sales proceeds will necessarily tend to equal the Aggregate Cost of a growing full-employment output.[24]

This, then, is Keynes' major departure from earlier economic analysis—namely, that aggregate demand can equal aggregate supply at less than full employment, even if there are flexible wages and prices. In this sense, along with the analytical tools developed to aid the analysis, there was a "Keynesian revolution." We shall examine the Keynesian analysis in some detail in the next four chapters but some further preliminary comments are in order.

4.   Identity and Behavioral Equations

Most modern macroeconomic theory makes use of mathematical equations, such as $Y = C+I$, $C = f(Y)$, $I = f(i)$, and so on. Therefore at this juncture it might be best to consider, even though briefly, two basic types of equations—*identity* and *behavioral*. Most of the basic conclusions derived from the Keynesian analysis can be stated in terms of either identity or behavioral equations, although subsequent discussion reveals that the latter form of statement is preferable.

An identity equation is a pure tautology—it actually does nothing more than to restate one quantity in terms of another. A classic example of this type of equation is the quantity equation, $MV = PO$, which

[24]Hansen, *A Guide to Keynes*, pp. 28, 29.

merely states that the monetary value of total demand (MV) is equal to (the same as) the monetary value of total supply (PO). Thus far in the discussion of Keynes' analysis we have encountered another popular identity equation, $Y = C+I$. Although identity equations are often useful means of expression, they actually possess little *analytical* usefulness. The major attribute of a simple identity equation is that it provides a framework for associating, albeit loosely, major and usually complex variables which are related to some economic phenomenon or phenomena. While an identity equation is arithmetically precise, it is procedurally vague. Its usefulness is limited by its omission of cause and effect relationships, and indeed it even fails to distinguish between dependent and independent variables. Thus an identity equation does not provide a meaningful approach for systematically accounting for change over time.

A behavioral equation, on the other hand, is analytically far more significant, since it states a functional relationship, such as $C = f(Y)$, and thus implies that a change in one variable (Y) will influence the value of the other (C). Hence a behavioral equation presents a functional relationship that is, potentially at least, subject to verification. If C does not react to changes in Y in the manner indicated by the equation, there is need either to discard or to modify the equation. And as will be seen in the next chapter, this particular behavioral equation has withstood the brunt of empirical investigation quite well.

There are numerous behavorial equations used in economic analysis, but probably one of the best known is the simple $D = f(P)$, that is, the quantity demanded of a commodity is a function of the price of that commodity. But obviously the amount demanded of the commodity is influenced by far more than simply its price. For instance, the income of the consumer (Y) may have an influence, as may the advertising (A) of the producers, the prevailing rate of interest (i), the expectations of changes in the price of the commodity (X), the prices of all other commodities, both complements and substitutes (L), consumer tastes (T), and so on and on. Taking all of these determinants into account, we would have to make the functional relationship far more complex and rewrite it as

$$D = f(P, Y, A, i, X, L, T, \ldots, n).$$

Obviously such a functional relationship is far too difficult to work with and accordingly we usually simplify by using only the two-variable formulation $D = f(P)$. But what does this mean with respect to the other determinants? In effect what we are doing is to hold them constant by means of the *ceteris paribus* assumption—that is, all other things equal. While in reality *ceteris* is never *paribus*, the assumption is used in order to develop a first approximation. Then, after the theory or model is constructed, complications may be introduced by relaxing the *ceteris paribus* assumption.

The use of *ceteris paribus*, of course, means that some of the variables which are considered to be less important are abstracted from, and that the one or few variables that are considered to exercise the major influence are retained. In short, some variables are considered as *parameters*, that is, as "constants" or "givens" which may be abstracted from. Once the theory has been constructed, however, some of these parameters may be allowed to change in order to make the analysis more comprehensive. Nevertheless, we are still limited as to the number of determinants that can usefully be introduced into a behavioral equation. Consider, for example, the behavioral equation $I = f(i,r)$, which was first encountered in Chapter 7. This simple formulation is useful, but some of the modern growth-cycle theories have considered other determinants of investment, such as the capital stock (K) and the level of income (Y). Thus the simple formulation must be expanded to the equation $I = f(Y,K,i,r,)$. But such complications are best postponed.

5.   Wage Units and the Measurement of Income

Economic analysis has long recognized that, while quantities are measured in monetary units, there is need to couch analysis in "real" terms. The reason for this is that significant functional relationships are distorted and give misleading results if the price level changes. Consider, for example, a simple case of a change in Y. In period 1 we assume the output of the economy to be 100 units, with an average price of $1 per unit. Thus in monetary terms Y is $100. Now assume that in period 2 the actual output remains at 100 units, while the price level is doubled. In this case Y equals $200 in monetary terms, though real output has not changed. Thus, in order to ascertain what happens to real output and employment it is necessary to "deflate" monetary Y by some appropriate index. This procedure will reveal what has happened to real output, for the price level changes have been statistically removed.

For purposes of analysis, the behavior of the variables in *real terms* must be known. In the illustration above, the rise in the money value of Y from $100 to $200 might lead the unwary to conclude that obviously aggregate demand has arisen, since $C = f(Y)$, and that therefore both output and employment have also risen. This is not the case, however, for in real terms Y has remained constant. This is the reason for recasting the monetary values in "real" values, though this can never be done with great precision.

Now Keynes could have chosen to measure income in "real" terms by deflating monetary income with some appropriate price index. This is the usual procedure. But instead he elected to measure real income in a different way—namely, by deflating monetary income with an index of money wage rates.[25] The significance of this procedure is that changes in income now measure changes in employment rather than simply output. On the other hand, when deflated by a price index, changes in income measure changes in output. Inasmuch as Keynes was primarily concerned with the employment problem, he chose to deflate by a money wage rate index.

For him the appropriate deflator is the "wage unit," which is the money wage paid for an hour's employment of "ordinary" labor.[26] The concept of "ordinary" labor is, of course, rather vague, but what it means is that labor is being treated as a homogeneous supply. Thus, if one worker is three times more skilled than an "ordinary" laborer, one hour of his work will be counted as three wage units. In this way Keynes attempted to reduce a nonhomogeneous labor supply to homogeneity (for analytical purposes). There is, however, little to recommend this procedure over the more usual one.

Actually it makes little difference whether we follow Keynes' method of deflating with the wage unit or the typical procedure of deflating with an appropriate price index. For the short run, when the stock of capital, technology, population, etc. can be assumed to remain relatively constant, changes in output and employment can be assumed to go hand in hand. Thus in the rest of this volume the typical procedure of measuring income in constant-value dollars, rather than in terms of wage-unit dollars, will be adhered to.

6. Summary

This chapter contains a preliminary sketch of the Keynesian system. Keynes' major conclusion is that aggregate demand may equal aggregate supply at less than full employment for the simple reason that

---

[25]Keynes, *The General Theory*, Chapter 4.
[26]*Ibid.*, pp. 41-42.

there is nothing in the income generating process that insures that investment demand will always be sufficient to absorb the savings of the society. This, of course, runs contrary to the neoclassical argument that aggregate demand will equal supply at full employment, so long as there is perfect flexibility of wages and prices. On the basis of their analysis, the neoclassical economists had recommended a general reduction in wage rates as the major cure for the depression of the 1930's, but the Keynesian analysis obviously leads to other recommendations. Further identity and behavioral equations were considered, and though we will often make use of the identity equations, we shall rely primarily on the behavorial ones. Finally, though Keynes measured income in terms of wage units, we have chosen to follow the usual procedure of deflating money income by an appropriate price index, though we assume a fairly close connection between changes in output and changes in employment.

QUESTIONS

9-1.   In what respect was the "Keynesian revolution" a revolution in economic thought?

9-2.   Discuss what Keynes meant by measuring national income in "wage units." How does this differ from measuring gross or net national product in "constant-dollar" terms?

9-3.   How does Keynes define "total income," and how is total income related to "effective demand"?

9-4.   Discuss the difference between identity and behavioral equations. Elaborate on at least two identity equations that have held a prominent place in economic analysis.

9-5.   Explain the basic reasoning underlying the neoclassical recommendation that the general wage level be reduced when there is widespread unemployment.

Bibliography

Dillard, D., "The Influence of Keynesian Economics on Contemporary Thought," *American Economic Review*, May 1957 (see also the "discussion" by D. M. Wright, W. A. Salant, and T. Scitovsky).

Fellner, W., "What is Surviving? An Appraisal of Keynesian Economics on Its Twentieth Anniversary," *American Economic Review*, May 1957 (see also the discussion by Wright, Salant, and Scitovsky).

Hansen, A. H., *A Guide to Keynes* (New York: McGraw-Hill Book Co., 1953).

Harris, S. E., ed., *The New Economics: Keynes' Influence on Theory and Public Policy* (New York: Alfred A. Knopf, Inc., 1950), Parts I-II.

Hazlitt, H., *The Failure of the "New Economics": An Analysis of the Keynesian Fallacies* (Princeton: D. Van Nostrand Co., Inc., 1959).

Johnson, H. G., "The *General Theory* after Twenty-five Years," *American Economic Review*, May 1961.

Keynes, J. M. *The General Theory of Employment, Interest, and Money* (New York: Harcourt, Brace & World, Inc., 1936).

Klein, L. R., *The Keynesian Revolution* (New York: The Macmillan Company, 1947).

Wright, D. M., *The Keynesian System* (New Jersey: Rutgers University Press, 1962).

10

The Consumption
Function

As shown in the last chapter, changes in the level of aggregate demand are closely bound up with changes in its major components. Each of these components must now be examined in more detail, and in this chapter we begin with the behavior of aggregate consumer demand.

Recall that modern income-employment analysis makes use of the behavioral equation $C = f(Y)$, which is used to express the *consumption function*. Keynes himself held that the consumption function—or as he termed it, the "propensity to consume"—is the basic cornerstone of his general theory.[1] Referring to the propensity to consume as a "fundamental psychological law" of consumer behavior, he stated: "This psychological law was of the utmost importance in the development of my own thought, and it is, I think, absolutely fundamental to the theory of effective demand as set forth in my book. But few critics or commentators so far have paid particular attention to it."[2]

While this contention was perhaps correct when it was made (in

---

[1]Keynes never used the term "consumption function," but rather the terms "propensity to consume" and "fundamental psychological law." The term consumption function was introduced by Alvin H. Hansen, who has stated: "This is an epochmaking contribution to the tools of economic analysis, analogous to, but even more important than, Marshall's discovery of the demand function." "The *General Theory*," in S. E. Harris, ed., *The New Economics: Keynes' Influence on Theory and Public Policy* (New York: Alfred A. Knopf, 1947), p. 135.

[2]Keynes, "The *General Theory*," *ibid.*, p. 190.

1937), empirical and theoretical developments alike have since served to make the consumption function one of the most widely used and discussed concepts in modern aggregative theory. Empirical researchers on both sides of the Atlantic have turned their efforts towards testing and refining the consumption function hypothesis to see if consumers actually behave as the hypothesis contends. The verdict? It seems safe to say that Keynes' basic premise still holds—that is, that the major determinant of consumption is income. However, the studies reveal also that this relationship is not quite as simple as Keynes assumed in *The General Theory.*

Just what is the consumption function hypothesis? And how does it figure into the Keynesian system? In broad outlines the theory states that the major determinant of the level of consumption is the level of income, that is, $C = f(Y)$. It states further that the major determinant of a change in the level of consumption is a change in the level of income, that is, $\triangle C = f(\triangle Y)$. This, in skeletal form, is all that the consumption function hypothesis contends, and yet these two simple behavioral equations turn out to be quite important in modern macroeconomic theory.

However, are they not perhaps *too* simple to explain such a complex thing as consumer behavior? Surely there are determinants other than just income that influence consumption. In fact, even Keynes himself pointed out (in *The General Theory*) that such variables as changes in the interest rate, monetary and fiscal policy, and windfall gains and losses may affect the level of consumer demand. And there are still other variables that may be important—expectations of changes in the price level, the price level itself, advertising, new products, and so on. If these were all taken into account, the consumption function would become far more complicated and would have to be reformulated as

$$C = f(Y,a,b,c,d,e,\ldots,n),$$

where the symbols a through n stand for the variables mentioned above.

However, after examination of several of these other determinants, Keynes concluded that in the short run they are relatively unimportant, especially with respect to the dominant role played by income. As he put it: "... whilst the other factors are capable of varying (and thus must not be forgotten), the aggregate income ... is, as a rule, the principal variable upon which the consumption constituent of the aggregate demand function will depend."[3] In short, by means of the *ceteris*

[3]From *The General Theory of Employment, Interest, and Money* by John Maynard Keynes. Reprinted by permission of Harcourt, Brace & World, Inc.

paribus assumption, Keynes assigned a through n variables to the category of parameters where they are held constant, and thus made C simply a function of Y alone. On the other hand however, empirical studies yield the conclusion that these other determinants are often important in consumer behavior, and accordingly they cannot legitimately be ignored. These are considered later.[4]

The procedure of this chapter is first to find out precisely what Keynes himself had to say about the consumption function. This will entail an examination of some of the technical properties of the consumption function, especially the marginal and average propensities to save and to consume. Second, some of the recent important empirical studies will be reviewed in order to "test" the consumption function hypothesis. Finally we shall examine the *long-run consumption function* and review some of the studies relevant to it.

1. Budget Studies and the Consumption Function

It is necessary at the outset to distinguish between two seemingly similar approaches to the behavior of aggregate consumption. The first of these is the family budget study, the second is the consumption function proper.

A. Family Budget Studies

A family budget study shows the relationship between income and consumption of families ("consumer spending units") in different income brackets *at the same point in time*. It is, as it were, a snapshot

[4]See sections 3-4 of this chapter for a discussion of these other determinants. Some important statistical studies and reviews of studies are D. B. Suits, "The Determinants of Consumer Expenditure: A Review of Present Knowledge," Research Study One in *Impacts of Monetary Policy* (Englewood Cliffs, N. J.: Prentice-Hall, Inc., 1963); D. S. Brady and R. Friedman, "Savings and Income Distribution," in *Studies in Income and Wealth*, Vol. X (New York: National Bureau of Economic Research, 1947); F. Modigliani, "Fluctuations in the Saving-Income Ratio: A Problem in Economic Forecasting," in *Studies in Income and Wealth*, Vol. XI (New York: National Bureau of Economic Research, 1953); J. S. Duesenberry, *Income, Saving, and the Theory of Consumer Behavior* (Cambridge: Harvard University Press, 1949); M. Friedman, *A Theory of the Consumption Function* (Princeton: Princeton University Press, 1957); R. Ferber, *A Study of Aggregate Consumption Functions* (New York: National Bureau of Economic Research, 1953); I. Friend and S. Schor, "Who Saves?" *Review of Economics and Statistics*, May 1959; M. R. Fisher, "Exploration in Savings Behaviour," *Bulletin of the Oxford Institute of Statistics*, August 1956; L. J. Paradiso and M. A. Smith, "Consumer Purchasing and Income Patterns," *Survey of Current Business*, March 1959.

TABLE 10–1

Family Budget Study: Average Income and Consumption
of Urban Families of Two or More, 1944

Disposable Personal Income	Consumption	Savings	C/Y*	S/Y*
$ 313	$ 887	$—574	2.8	—1.8
776	1,053	—277	1.4	—0.4
1,043	1,407	—364	1.3	—0.3
1,779	1,788	— 9	1.0	0.0
1,950	1,877	73	0.96	0.04
2,259	2,051	208	0.91	0.09
2,757	2,410	347	0.87	0.13
3,480	2,838	642	0.81	0.19
4,408	3,439	969	0.78	0.22
7,595	4,305	2,290	0.56	0.43

* Figures in these two columns are rounded off.
Source: *Economic Almanac*, 1956.

that reveals the existing income distribution and the associated pattern of consumption expenditures. Such a study has little to do with the consumption function proper, since the latter is concerned with the *functional* relationship between income *changes* and consumption *changes*. The family budget data, to repeat, simply relate income to consumption at a particular point in time. In other words, the consumption function proper is concerned with the functional changes in the variables, while the budget study gives only a still-life shot of the variables; for this reason the two approaches should not be confused.

An illustration of a family budget study is given in Table 10–1 and in Figure 10–1. The data in the table show how much is consumed and how much is saved out of the income of each income class. There are two important things to note about these data. First, there is a "breakeven point" at approximately $1,750 (see Figure 10–1)—that is, the income recipients in this group "break even" in the sense that their consumption is equal to their income, and thus they have no savings. The breakeven point is indicated by the intersection of the CC line with the forty-five-degree line in Figure 10–1. On the other hand, the consumption of the income recipients in the income brackets above the breakeven point is less than their income, and these families are therefore saving a portion of their incomes. Finally, the income recipients in the brackets below the breakeven point consume more than their income and thus are "dissaving." To repeat, at the breakeven point there are zero savings, to the right of the point there are positive savings, and to the left there are negative savings (dissavings).

240

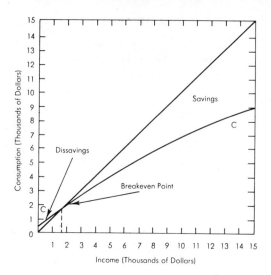

FIGURE 10–1

A Budget Study

Second, the proportion of income saved and spent by the different income classes varies considerably. Note here that the concern is with the proportions, not the absolute amounts, involved. The proportions of income saved and spent (S/Y and C/Y, respectively) are given in the last two columns of Table 10–1. The important thing to observe is that the proportion of income saved (S/Y) is larger for the higher income classes and smaller in the lower brackets. Since the families at the breakeven point save nothing, S/Y = 0 for them. Families in the income group of $2,757 save approximately 13 per cent of their income (S/Y = .13), while families in the highest income class reported ($7,595) save approximately 43 per cent of their incomes. Of course, for those families below the breakeven point S/Y is negative, since these spending units are dissaving.

The important generalization that can be drawn from this particular study, and other similar ones, is that the proportion of income saved is higher in the upper income brackets and lower in the lower income classes. This conclusion—that the bulk of savings is accounted for by the people in the higher income brackets—is, of course, important, though it is hardly startling or novel.

The same observation can be made in a different way. The proportion of income spent on consumption goods (C/Y) is larger in the lower income groups and smaller in the higher brackets. For instance, C/Y is equal to 1 at the breakeven point since all income is devoted to consumption. On the other hand, C/Y = 2.8 for the families in the $313 bracket; and it is approximately .56 in the $7,595 class. Thus the proportion of income saved is higher in the higher income class, and the proportion spent on consumers' goods is lower. The reverse holds true for the families in the lower income classes.

The family budget schedule, as shown in Figure 10–1 and Table 10–1, emphatically is not the consumption function. It is merely a snapshot of the income-consumption relationships of different families at the same time and as such ignores the effects of changes in income on both consumption and savings. The consumption function proper, on the other hand, is designed to show the relationship between income changes and the attendant changes in consumption and savings *for the same group of persons or families.* Let us now turn to a discussion of this important functional relationship.

B.   The Consumption Function: A Hypothetical Case

Figure 10–2 presents a hypothetical consumption function. Consumption and savings are plotted on the vertical axis and disposable income is plotted on the horizontal axis. Recall (from Chapter 9) that the scales on the two axes are identical, so that the forty-five-degree line intersecting the point of origin relates the two axes on a one-to-one basis. The distance, therefore, from any point on the horizontal axis will be equal to the vertical distance from that point to the forty-five-degree line—that is, $OY_0 = OC_0$, $OY_1 = OS_1$, and so on.

It is important to note at the outset that the consumption function *is not chronological*—that is, *it is not a time series* showing the relationship between changing income and changing consumption over time, but rather is a theoretical construction that states what would happen to consumption *if income were changed from its present level.*[5] Some of the time series that have been used to "test" this hypothetical concept are examined in a later section of this chapter; for the present

---

[5]Thus the consumption function curve is analogous to the demand curve used in price theory. There is only one actual point on the demand curve, and that is where the consumers actually are. All other points are statements of what the quantities demanded *would be if* the price were higher or lower than the prevailing price.

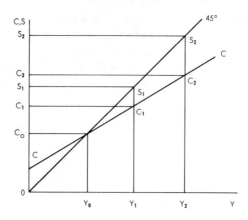

FIGURE 10–2

A Hypothetical Consumption Function

remember that the consumption function proper has *only one actual point on it,* namely, the point at which consumers actually are at the moment. All the rest of the points, both to the left and right of the actual point, are hypothetical—they state what consumption would be *if income were changed from its present level.*

Now it is conceivable, though extremely unrealistic, that the forty-five-degree line itself could be the short-run consumption function. If this were the case, then there would be no savings (nor dissavings) at any level of income! All income would be spent on consumers' goods. While this might possibly be relevant for some societies, such a consumption function does not apply to the already advanced economies (as the United States), where there are actual, realized savings.

A more realistic consumption function is the CC curve in Figure 10–2, which shows what the consumers' expenditures will be at different alternative levels of income. To begin with, assume that consumers in the aggregate have an *actual* income equal to OY_0. Now *if* total income *were* to rise to OY_1, the CC curve tells us that total consumption would rise to OC_1. And *if* income were to rise further to OY_2, consumption would then rise to OC_2. Note that in each case as income rises, consumption also rises, but not by as much as the income increase. Therefore, even though at the breakeven there are no savings, positive savings will begin to emerge if income rises beyond OY_0. These savings are measured, for any given level of income, by the distance between the consumption function CC and the forty-five-degree line. Accordingly, at the income level of OY_1, savings will be C_1S_1.

Now both the height and the slope of the CC curve are important. The height tells us what total consumption will be at any particular income level, and the slope tells us how consumption will change as a result of a change in income. Thus if the incomes of consumers were to rise from OY_0 to OY_1 (in Figure 10–2), total consumption would also rise, in this case from OC_0 to OC_1. However, note that so long as the consumption function CC has a smaller slope than the forty-five-degree line, not all of the increase in income will go into additional consumption expenditures. Rather, only a part will—that is, total consumption will rise from OC_0 to OC_1—and the remainder of the income increase will be devoted to additional savings, by the amount C_1S_1. Thus, at each income level the amount of savings is given by the difference between the forty-five-degree line and the consumption function.

The fact that not all of the income increase will be devoted to extra consumption, but instead will be divided between additional consumption and additional savings, is what Keynes referred to as the "fundamental psychological law . . . that men are disposed, as a rule and on the average, to increase their consumption as their income increases, but not by as much as the increase in their income."[6] Now this incremental income-consumption relationship is not to be taken as a mere untested and untestable hypothesis—like all significant theoretical concepts it must be (and has been) subjected to the cold test of facts. But before turning to these studies, there is need to examine some of the technical aspects or properties of the consumption function.

Three final words of caution at this point. First, recall that the consumption function is not chronological, but rather is a hypothetical construction upon which there is only one actual point. Second, for the moment the analysis assumes that there are no lags in the consumption function. In other words, if income changes from its present, actual level, consumption will be adjusted to the new level *instantaneously*. This assumption is somewhat unrealistic and accordingly must be relaxed at a later point in order to introduce time lags into the analysis.[7] At present, however, lagged relationships are ignored in order to concentrate on certain basic properties of the consumption function.

---

[6]Keynes, *The General Theory*, p. 96.

[7]However, L. A. Metzler, in his essay "Three Lags in the Circular Flow of Income," in *Income, Employment, and Public Policy: Essays in Honor of Alvin H. Hansen* (New York: W. W. Norton & Company, Inc., 1948), argues that such lags are short.

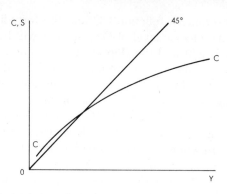

FIGURE 10–3

Finally, the consumption function presented in Figure 10–2 is linear. A number of economists, however, have argued that a more realistic picture of the income-change-consumption-change relationship is that presented in Figure 10–3. In this case, the consumption function is curvilinear. These two types of consumption functions will be contrasted on several occasions in subsequent discussion, but for the moment we shall stick with the linear one.

2. Some Technical Properties of the Consumption Function

So far we have pointed out that, according to Keynes, the major determinant of consumption is income, that is, $C = f(Y)$; and that the major determinant of a change in consumption is a change in income, that is, $\triangle C = f(\triangle Y)$.[8] These two equations must now be examined in more detail. Some hypothetical data for a consumption function are given in Table 10–2 and plotted in Figure 10–4. In this illustration consumption expenditures rise by increments of $80 (in column 2) as the level of income increases by increments of $100 (in column 1). These figures are purely hypothetical and are used simply for illustrative purposes.

---

[8]Actually, since we are speaking in *real* terms, the formulas should be written more accurately as $C_m/p = f(Y_m/p)$ and $\triangle C_m/p = f(\triangle Y_m/p)$, where the subscript m stands for money and p stands for the general price index. Thus both C and $\triangle C$, Y and $\triangle Y$, are to be interpreted as having been deflated.

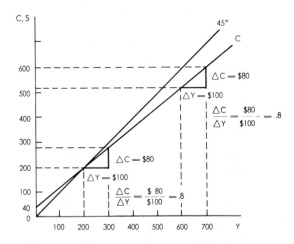

FIGURE 10–4

A. The Average Propensities to Consume and to Save

The first technical propensity property of the consumption function to be examined is the average propensity to consume, which is written as C/Y. The average propensity to consume, obviously, is merely a statement of the proportion of a given level of income that will be devoted to consumption. If, for example, the level of income is $400 and consumers elect to spend on consumers' goods $360 of this, the average propensity to consume is .9. In other words, 90 per cent of this income level will be devoted to consumption. However, in our example, if income were to rise to $600, then 87 per cent of income would be devoted to consumption; and if income were to fall to $200, all of it would be poured into the purchase of consumers' goods and services.

Note that on the sort of consumption function plotted in Figure 10–4 the average propensity to consume declines as income increases. At the breakeven point C/Y is obviously unity, or one, since there are no savings and all income is going into consumption expenditures. At income levels below the breakeven point C/Y exceeds one, for at these income

TABLE 10–2

Hypothetical Consumption Function

Income (Y)	Consumption (C)	Savings (S)	Average Propensity to Consume (C/Y)	Average Propensity to Save (S/Y)
$ 0	$ 40	$—40	—	—
100	120	—20	1.20	—.20
200	200	0	1.00	.00
300	280	20	.94	.06
400	360	40	.90	.10
500	440	60	.88	.12
600	520	80	.87	.13
700	600	100	.85	.15

levels consumers will be spending more than their current income. And for larger income levels, the average propensity to consume is less than one because of the fact that there are some savings out of the current income level. Thus, as income rises toward the breakeven point the average propensity to consume declines in value towards one. At the breakeven point its value is equal to one; and as income rises beyond this point, it drops steadily in value (down to .85 in our illustration). In general, the conclusion is that *as income rises, the absolute amount devoted to consumption also rises, but the percentage amount declines.* However, this generalization does not hold true for all conceivable types of consumption functions; other possibilities are considered shortly.

By the same token, the *average propensity to save,* S/Y, which is the ratio of savings to income, can be calculated. Thus at the income level of $400 the average propensity to save is .1 (that is, S/Y = $40/$400 = .1). On the other hand, at the income level of $600 the average propensity to save is .13; and at the income level of $200 it is zero.

As a matter of simple arithmetic, the sum of the average propensities to save and to consume must always be equal to one, for consumers' incomes must be devoted to either or both consumption and saving. Thus, it follows that the average propensity to save rises as the community moves out along the consumption function to higher income levels, at least on the sort of consumption function given in Figure 10–4, because the average propensity to consume declines as income rises. In short, *as income rises both the absolute and the percentage amounts devoted to savings also rise,* as is shown in Table 10–2.

B.   The Marginal Propensities

An even more important technical property of the consumption function is the *marginal propensity to consume,* which measures the proportion of an *increment* in income that will be devoted to a *change* in consumption, and is written as $\triangle C/\triangle Y$. In our hypothetical case, for every $100 change in income there is an accompanying change of $80 in consumption, and thus the marginal propensity to consume is .8 (that is, $\triangle C/\triangle Y = \$80/\$100 = .8$). In other words, 80 per cent of any $100 increase (decrease) is devoted to an increase (decrease) in consumption.

Actually the marginal propensity to consume measures the slope of the consumption function. On a straight-line consumption function, as in Figure 10–4, where the slope is constant throughout, the propensity to consume obviously remains constant. Consider an example. When the income level changes from $200 to $300, total consumption will rise from $200 to $280, and thus $\triangle C/\triangle Y = \$80/\$100 = .8$. By the same token, when income rises from $600 to $700, total consumption will rise from $520 to $600, and $\triangle C/\triangle Y$ still equals .8. In fact, since it is a common property of a straight line that it has a constant slope throughout, the marginal propensity to consume also remains constant throughout.[9]

The marginal propensity to save, $\triangle S/\triangle Y$, measures the proportion of an income change that is devoted to a change in savings. In the preceding case the marginal propensity to save is .2, since all income changes are accompanied by a 20 per cent change in savings. And the marginal propensity to save, like the marginal propensity to consume, remains constant on a linear consumption function. Finally, since any increment in income must be devoted to either or both an increment in consumption and saving, the marginal propensities to consume and to save must total up to one, just as the average propensities sum up to one.

The values of the average and marginal propensities and their relationship to each other depend upon the shape and position of the consumption function. Thus far only a simple linear consumption function has been considered. Now let us examine some other possibilities. Figure 10–5A presents a consumption function similar to the one discussed above. In this case, the average propensity to consume begins at some value in excess of one, and, as we move out along the income axis, be-

---

[9]On a curvilinear consumption function, such as in Figure 10–3, the marginal propensity to consume as we move out along the consumption function declines, that is, the slope of CC becomes less.

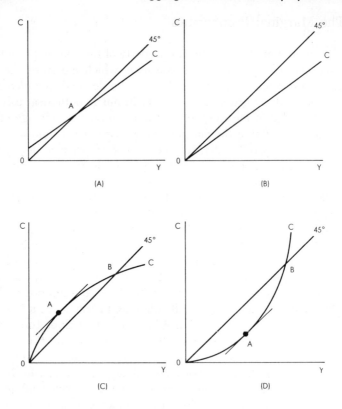

FIGURE 10–5

comes equal to one at point A, and then falls successively below one the farther to the right beyond A income rises. The marginal propensity, on the other hand, remains constant as we move from successively lower to higher levels of income.

In Figure 10–5B the consumption function is still linear but now is drawn through the point of origin. Since this curve has a slope of less than that of the forty-five-degree line, the marginal propensity to consume is less than one. This is also true of the average propensity. But in this instance, the marginal and average propensities to consume are equal and constant, since the consumption function is linear. While this sort of consumption function is unrealistic for the short run, it turns out to be quite significant for long-run analysis.

Consider next Figure 10–5C, where the consumption function is curvilinear downwards. To begin with, the marginal propensity to consume is greater than one at income levels to the left of A. But at A it becomes equal to one, for at that point the consumption function is parallel to the forty-five-degree line. And beyond A the marginal propensity to consume declines as the slope of the consumption function becomes less and less. On the other hand, the average propensity to consume is greater than one all the way up to point B, since the consumption function lies above the forty-five-degree line. At point B it equals one, and beyond that point it is less than one and declines. In this case, then, both the average and marginal propensities to consume begin with values in excess of one, but both eventually begin to decline.

For the final case, consider Figure 10–5D, where the consumption function is curvilinear upwards. Here the average propensity to consume is less than one up to point B and is greater than one beyond that point. The marginal propensity, on the other hand, is less than one up to point A, after which it takes on higher and higher values. This, of course, is a very unrealistic consumption function, for it implies that as income rises, savings after a point decline, and indeed beyond point B, there is dissaving.

An important conclusion to be drawn from the preceding discussion is that the marginal propensity to consume remains constant only on a linear consumption function. On a curvilinear function it is constantly changing, and this, as we shall see, creates analytical difficulties. We might anticipate a further conclusion—namely, that modern employment-income analysis generally assumes, for short-run purposes, a linear consumption function that has a positive intercept on the vertical axis, like the ones in Figures 10–2, 10–4, and 10–5A.

C.   The Consumption Function as an Equation

Before proceeding any farther, one very important point should be made clear. The consumption function is actually an equation and generally must be stated as such. It is not a number or group of numbers, as the preceding discussion may have implied. Even though our illustrations allow us to describe the particular consumption function in Figure 10–4 in this way (that is, at the income level of $400, $C/Y = .9$, $S/Y = .1$, $\triangle C/\triangle Y = .8$, and $\triangle S/\triangle Y = .2$), this is a very clumsy method of expression and is relevant for only a very small segment of the entire function. There is need to be more general. One way of accomplishing this is by referring to the consumption function in the form of the equation $C = a + bY$, where C is total consumption, b is the *marginal* propensity to consume, and a is a constant. Now in the preceding illustration the marginal propensity to consume is .8 and remains constant since the slope of the consumption function is the same throughout.

However, what about the constant a? Note that the consumption function, if extended back to the vertical axis, has a positive intercept. This means that even though the level of income is zero, the total consumption of the community remains positive, at the height indicated by the intercept. In the illustration consumption is assumed to remain at $40, even though income is zero. This sounds reasonable enough, for even at a zero level of income the community needs some food, clothing, housing, and so on. But note, on the other hand, that this formulation does raise a rather ticklish question, for if $Y = C+I$, then Y can never fall to zero so long as there is some positive consumption. Since $a = 40, Y presumably cannot fall below that level, at least in this example.

Aside from this, however, with the formula $C = a+bY$, the total amount of consumption can always be determined once the values of a, b, and Y are known. Thus, if $Y = 600, then $C = a+bY = $40+.8($600) = 520. Other values of C can similarly be determined. This, of course, is a much more general and convenient way of expressing the consumption function.

At this point let us return to the curved consumption functions of Figures 10–3 and 10–5C. Recall that the marginal propensity to consume, b, measures the slope of the consumption function. On a linear consumption function the value of b therefore remains constant, but on a curvilinear function the slope diminishes as income rises. Thus the value of b declines along the consumption function. This is merely another way of saying that the marginal propensity to consume is less at higher levels of income than it is for lower levels. The question naturally arises: Which type of consumption function, the linear or curvilinear, is more relevant with respect to short-run consumer behavior? We turn to this in the next section.

3.   The Historical Consumption Function

The discussion thus far has distinguished between the budget study and the consumption function proper. Recall that the latter has at any one time only one "real" point on it, namely, the point at which consumers are actually consuming from their present income. All other points are hypothetical. For this reason the consumption function cannot be

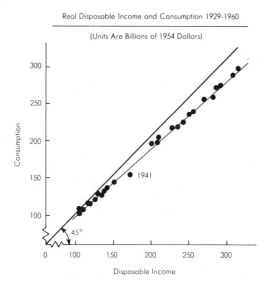

Real Disposable Income and Consumption 1929-1960

(Units Are Billions of 1954 Dollars)

Source: D. B. Suits, "The Determinants of Consumer Expenditure: A Review of Present Knowledge," p. 25.

FIGURE 10–6

measured precisely, although historical data on the consumption-income relationship yield meaningful results. The data for the time period 1929-1960 are presented in Figure 10-6. While these data are not precise measurements of the consumption function proper, they do indicate that this theoretical concept has some empirical significance.[10] Note that a rather close relationship between consumption and disposable income is apparent. There are, however, certain qualifications that must be kept in mind in considering any "historical" consumption function.

In the first place, as Suits has pointed out, the consumption function proper is a statement of cause-effect relationships—that is, changes in income *cause* changes in consumption. The reverse of this, however, may not be true. "The existence of a positive correlation between income and consumption does not validate the causal relationship. The

---

[10]See footnote 4 for reference to important studies. See also B. G. Hickman, *Growth and Stability of the Postwar Economy* (Washington, D. C.: The Brookings Institution, 1960), pp. 224-26, 259-62, 267-69. A. Zellner, "The Short-Run Consumption Function," *Econometrica*, October 1957, contains a good bibliography of empirical studies, as does Suits.

fact is that income, the total of consumption and saving, is necessarily correlated with its parts."[11]

Second, there is the problem of selecting the appropriate time period. In very short-run periods, such as a quarter of a year, consumption is quite independent of income, so much so in fact that the correlation between C and Y disappears. "The movements of consumption in the short run are so nearly independent of income that the usual high correlation between consumption and income is replaced by a substantial negative correlation between consumption and saving."[12]

Over longer time periods, however, such as a year, the usual relationship between consumption and income reappears. Thus, when a given quarter is related, not to its immediate neighboring quarters, but rather to the average of the preceding four quarters, there appears a significant correlation between consumption and income.[13] For longer periods, therefore, the consumption function as discussed in section 1B, above, may be taken as having a substantial enough basis in empirical fact to warrant its use. For shorter periods, on the other hand, the evidence reveals clearly that the consumption function is highly volatile, continually shifting, independent of income changes. This is due to the presence and influence of other determinants of consumer behavior, such as liquid assets, windfall gains and losses, age, occupation, and so on. Apparently these are the forces that underly the short-run volatility of the consumption function, and thus they must be examined in some detail.

4. The "Objective Factors"

In *The General Theory* Keynes discusses several factors that have an influence on consumption, though of all these he considers only income to be the dominant variable. Actually he divides the determinants of consumption into two groups—the *subjective* factors and the *objective* factors. Subsequent research, however, has emphasized that there are even more determinants than those that Keynes considers. These other variables are often very important in accounting for short-run changes in the consumption function. We shall consider them in section 5, below.

---

[11]Suits, "The Determinants of Consumer Expenditure: A Review of Present Knowledge," pp. 23-24.

[12]*Ibid.*, p. 39.

[13]*Ibid.*

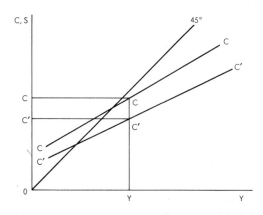

FIGURE 10–7

Keynes refers to the subjective factors as ". . . those psychological characteristics of human nature and those social practices and institutions which, though not unalterable, are unlikely to undergo a material change over a short period of time except in abnormal or revolutionary circumstances."[14] In short, he assumes that the subjective factors are given in the short run and thus do not influence consumer behavior in the aggregate.

The objective factors, on the other hand, he considers to be more important. Yet of the six that he discusses, he attaches significance to only one—changes in real income—arguing that the remaining objective factors are likely to be important only under rather unlikely or occasional circumstances. What are the remaining factors?

First, there are *substantial* changes in the rate of interest. A significant rise in the interest rate may induce people using funds for consumption to shift partially out of these over to loanable funds. Thus the average propensity to consume would decline, for out of a given income people now will consume less and save more because of the attractively high rate. This is shown in Figure 10–7 as a drop in the short-run consumption function from CC to C'C'. Note, however, that C'C' need not be parallel to CC. Whereas before, the community had an average propensity to consume of OC/OY, now with the higher interest rate it is OC'/OY. Thus a substantial rise in the rate of interest will, *ceteris paribus,* cause the consumption function to shift down. Conversely, a signifi-

---

[14]Keynes, *The General Theory,* p. 91.

cant drop in the interest rate would, *ceteris paribus*, induce those holding loanable funds to shift out of these into extra consumption—in this
case the average propensity to consume would rise, and this would be
reflected in an upward shift of the consumption function. However,
Keynes concludes that the ". . . usual type of short-period fluctuation in
the rate of interest is not likely . . . to have much direct influence on
spending either way."[15]

Second, changes in expectations about the difference between present
and future income levels may be important. Though Keynes rather
blithely ignores this determinant—"But, whilst it may affect considerably a particular individual's propensity to consume, it is likely to average out for the community as a whole."[16]—later studies have revealed
that expectations often are quite important as a determinant of consumption. Pessimism and optimism may be so widespread as to be experienced by a large number of persons, in which case there is no bal-
ancing out effect. For instance, L. R. Klein points out:

> Income expectations measured during a personal interview at the begin-
> ning of a period appear to be related to actual savings behavior during
> the subsequent time span. We are especially clear on the finding that
> pessimistic expectations induce high rates of saving, presumably in prep-
> aration for adverse times ahead.[17]

Nevertheless, Keynes himself assumes that this particular factor is relatively unimportant in the short run.

Third, there is the possible determinant of a "change in the difference
between income and net income."[18] In this case Keynes argues that consumption is a function of *net* income. Thus if income changes, but *net*
income remains the same, there will be no effect on consumption; ". . .
and, similarly, a change in net income, not reflected in income, must be
allowed for. Save exceptional circumstances, however, I doubt the practical importance of this factor."[19]

Fourth, windfall capital gains and losses may be important, and

---

[15]*Ibid.*, p. 93. Suits, "The Determinants of Consumer Expenditure: A Review
of Present Knowledge," p. 41, after reviewing the empirical studies, reaches a
similar conclusion.

[16]Keynes, *The General Theory*, p. 95.

[17]L. R. Klein, "Savings and the Propensity to Consume," in *Determining the
Business Outlook*, ed. H. V. Prochnow (New York: Harper & Row, Publishers,
1954), p. 120. Further, see Hickman, *Growth and Stability of the Postwar Economy*, pp. 81-85, 95-96, and 175-76; and F. T. Juster, "Prediction and Consumer
Buying Intentions," *American Economic Review*, May 1960.

[18]Keynes, *The General Theory*, p. 92.

[19]*Ibid.*

Keynes seems to feel that they should be considered as quite instrumental in shifting the consumption function's position. "These are of much more significant importance in modifying the propensity to consume since they bear no stable or regular relationship to the amount of income."[20] Yet he does not devote any further analysis to this determinant.

Last, there are changes in fiscal policy as a determinant of consumption. Income taxes, capital profits taxes, death duties, and the like will clearly have an effect on consumption in that they influence the amount of disposable income. However, in the discussion of fiscal changes, Keynes mentions another factor that influences total consumption. As he puts it: "If fiscal policy is used as a deliberate instrument for the more equal distribution of income, its effect in increasing the propensity to consume is, of course, all the greater."[21] For example, if $100 of *current* income were taxed away from the rich and transferred to the poor (in some manner or other) then *certeris paribus* there is a more equal distribution of income. Note however that the total amount of income, in dollar terms has not been changed; it has merely been redistributed.

However, there seems to be some confusion between the average and marginal propensities to consume at this point, and also Keynes introduces, by implication, a different type of consumption function, one which is actually more like a budget schedule (as in Figure 10–1). Indeed, Keynes' contention rests upon the "consumption function's" being curvilinear, as shown in Figure 10–8. Assume that the present *average* family income is Y_0 and the present average consumption is C_0.[22] Assume further that the wealthy members of the community have a lower marginal propensity to consume (say, .5), while the poorer members of society have a much higher marginal propensity (say, .9). The wealthy persons will be located to the right of the *average* income Y_0, at, say, the income level of Y_w. At this higher level of income, the slope of the "consumption function" is very slight (.5). The poorer members of the community will be located to the left of the average income at Y_p, where the slope of the consumption function is much higher (.9).

Now it is the marginal propensity that is so important in evaluating Keynes' proposition that a redistributive tax policy toward equality will increase the consumption function. In the case illustrated in Figure

---

[20]*Ibid.* Suits, "The Determinants of Consumer Expenditure: A Review of Present Knowledge," points out that the marginal propensity to consume of windfall gains may be as high as .9.

[21]Keynes, *The General Theory*, p. 95.

[22]Note that the curve in Figure 10–8 is not a consumption function in the proper sense of the term. Hansen, in his *A Guide to Keynes,* makes the same point.

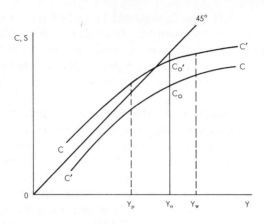

FIGURE 10–8

10–8, total consumption would rise as a result of such a tax program. Assume for instance that the tax policy takes away from the rich man $100 and gives it to the poor person. In this case, the rich man reduces his total consumption by $50, while the poor man increases his by $90— a net increase in total consumption of $40. Thus for the community at large the average propensity has risen, that is, the consumption function will shift up so that at the same average income Y_0, total consumption will be C_0'.

But note that Keynes' conclusion rests on the assumption that the "consumption function" is curvilinear. If, on the other hand, the consumption function were linear, the redistributive tax policy would have no effect at all upon consumption. In this case the marginal propensity to consume would presumably be the same for both the rich man and the poor man, and thus any transfer of income from one to the other would leave total consumption unaffected.

What do the empirical studies reveal as to the shape of the short-run consumption function? It must be admitted that the studies on this are few and that the hypothesis is difficult to test. Yet two important studies —those by Lubell and by Bronfenbrenner *et al.*—yield the tentative conclusion that the short-run consumption function is linear.[23] If this is so, then any redistribution of income toward equality would have only

---

[23]H. Lubell, "Effects of Redistribution of Income on Consumers' Expenditures," *American Economic Review*, March 1947; M. Bronfenbrenner, T. Yamane, and C. H. Lee, "A Study in Redistribution and Consumption," *Review of Economics and Statistics*, May 1955.

a slight effect on the community's total consumption. There are, however, certain things about the statistical studies that need to be kept
in mind.

First, they assume that when a family's income is changed there is
little or no effect on its marginal propensity to consume. But if the
change in income is sufficient to move the family out of the lower class
into that amorphous mass called the middle class, there may be a decided impact on its marginal propensity to consume. Whereas before
the family may have saved something—even a little something—for a
rainy day, cultural pressures may now be such that it spends all of its
income increase. In other words, the cultural pressures may raise its
marginal propensity to consume as high as one. Catching up with and
then keeping up with the Joneses may become an overriding motive for
the family. And if the Joneses feel that they must keep ahead of the "up-
start" Smiths, the net effect may be a rise in the marginal propensity to
consume of the two families. The more generally the redistributive tax
policy may affect families like the Smiths and the Joneses, the greater
the likelihood of the average propensity to consume's being increased,
even when the consumption function is linear. The net result, however,
is difficult to quantify at the moment; far more information about the
cultural impacts on the consumption function is needed before any
meaningful quantitative statement can be made.[24]

On the other hand, if the "self-styled middle income brackets"
($5,000-$10,000 per year), which are not particularly parsimonious,
were to lose income via the tax policy, there is the possibility that the
average propensity to consume would decline. This could occur if the
persons in the lower income brackets, who receive the tax transfers,
were to use a large portion of their new income to pay off debts they
owe to the wealthier members of society.[25] But again the final results
cannot be ascertained with even approximate accuracy until more is
known about the actual determinants of consumption.

Be that as it may, of all the "objective factors" that influence con-

---

[24]Some important work has been done in this area. See Duesenberry, *Income,
Saving, and the Theory of Consumer Behavior*; E. Mueller and G. Katona, *Con-
sumer Attitudes and Demand, 1950-52* (Ann Arbor: Institute for Social Research,
University of Michigan, 1953); E. Mueller, "Consumer Attitudes: Their Significance
and Forecasting Value," in *The Quality and Significance of Anticipations Data*
(Princeton: Princeton University Press, 1960); G. Katona, *The Powerful Consumer*
(New York: McGraw-Hill Book Company, 1960), and *Psychological Analysis of
Economic Behavior* (New York: McGraw-Hill Book Company, 1951).

[25]A similar case is discussed in Chapter 13 though there the emphasis is on
wage cuts.

sumption, Keynes simplified considerably by choosing only one, changes in income. For analytical purposes this is quite permissible; however, when it comes to predicting what will happen to consumption in a particular short-run time period, the other factors may be quite important. These are considered in the next section.

5. Other Determinants of Consumption[26]

Although we shall use the simplified consumption function (that is, consumption is a function of income only), we should be aware of the other factors that influence consumption behavior. In this section some of these other determinants, such as occupation, age, race, family size, liquid assets, and home ownership are considered briefly.

A. Liquid Assets

Some economists have argued that the consumption function should be rewritten to include the impact of the real value of liquid assets on consumption. Thus the consumption function would read $C = f(Y, M/p)$, that is, consumption is influenced by the real value of money.[27] In this case, then, changes in the price level and/or the stock of money will change the level of consumption.

However, a family may possess other assets which, though not money, are highly liquid. Examples are government and private securities. Although there may be variations, it seems safe to say that the more liquid assets a family has, the less need it has for additional ones,[28] and therefore as its income rises, its average propensity to save will tend to decline. Rather than save any more in the form of additional liquid assets, the income increase will be devoted to additional consumption.

---

[26]This section draws heavily from Klein, "Savings and the Propensity to Consume," and Suits, "The Determinants of Consumer Expenditure: A Review of Present Knowledge."

[27]This is often referred to as the "Pigou effect" and is discussed in detail in Chapter 15.

[28]Klein, "Savings and the Propensity to Consume." See also M. Cohen, "Liquid Assets and the Consumption Function," *Review of Economics and Statistics*, May 1954; and J. Crockett, "Income and Asset Effects on Consumption: Aggregate and Cross Section," in *Models of Income Distribution* (Princeton: Princeton University Press, 1964).

The situation, however, is quite complex. Klein has pointed out that "The tendency of liquid-asset holdings to discourage further savings is, in sample-survey data, much less apparent in upper- than in lower-income groups."[29] Apparently therefore income size will influence the impact of liquid assets on the consumption function. The wealthy family with substantial liquid-asset holdings will not lower its average propensity to save when it receives extra income. On the other hand, once a family in the middle- and lower-income brackets acquires what it considers to be sufficient holdings of liquid assets, it will lower its average propensity to save as it experiences further rises in income. Liquid-asset holdings make their full impact on the consumption function only in conjunction with income size.

However, a word of caution is in order, for the empirical evidence is, on the whole, quite inconclusive. After having reviewed a number of studies, Suits concludes:

> The accumulation of conflicting empirical evidence from cross-section studies added to the highly unstable coefficient found for liquid assets in the time series . . . is convincing evidence that the role of liquid assets in the consumption function has not yet been discovered.[30]

B. Family Size

Evidence has indicated that there is an inverse relationship between family size and family savings, all other things being equal. Thus savings tend to be smaller, the larger the family. However, this is not a straight-line relationship, indicating that there may be some economies to scale after the family reaches a size of five members. The obvious reason for such a low propensity to save by the large family is that so much of its income must be spent on food. Indeed, because of this, the large family even spends a smaller fraction of its income on housing than does the smaller family.

C. Occupation

The data also indicate that the farmer and small unincorporated businessman have a higher propensity to save than do others at compar-

---

[29]Klein, "Savings and the Propensity to Consume," p. 116.

[30]Suits, "The Determinants of Consumer Expenditure: A Review of Present Knowledge," p. 43.

able income levels. Probably the major reason for this is that they are very much concerned with "plowing back" their savings into their businesses. This would be particularly true if the businesses are small, have a low rate of profit, and rather poor credit lines. In this case they have to rely on their own savings for business purposes. However, if this type of "investment-savings" is eliminated, the data indicate that the average propensity to save of these business owners is about as high as that of other persons in the same income bracket.[31] On the other hand, there is some evidence that the savings of farmers and businessmen ". . . are much more responsive to the level of liquid assets than is the case with other people."[32]

D.   Home Ownership

One important determinant of consumption and saving is home ownership. Generally young consumers who have just purchased a home are very much concerned with building up their basic household capital. Therefore, they would tend to have a low average propensity to save. However the monthly mortgage payments are often considered as current savings, and the equity in the home is considered as accumulated savings. By the same token, monthly payments on life insurance and into retirement programs are considered as current savings. These factors combine to keep the average propensity to save higher than would first appear.[33]

E.   Age

As mentioned above, young consumers are interested in building up their household capital and thus do not save very much in liquid form. The data indicate that there is a positive relationship between age and savings, that savings increase with age up to a maximum point in the forties or fifties. Beyond that, older people have a declining incentive to

---

[31]See J. N. Morgan, "The Structure of Aggregate Personal Saving," *Journal of Political Economy*, December 1951, and "The Structure of Aggregate Saving: Correction and Addendum," *Journal of Political Economy*, December 1953.

[32]Suits, "The Determinants of Consumer Expenditure: A Review of Present Knowledge," p. 3.

[33]Very little has been done on these important determinants of saving. However, see J. N. Morgan, "Consumer Investment Expenditure," *American Economic Review*, December 1958. See also L. R. Klein and J. N. Morgan, "Decisions to Purchase Durable Goods," *Journal of Marketing*, October 1955.

save any more, for they have already accumulated the bulk of their savings. Actually, many older persons tend to dissave, that, is, to live on their accumulated savings.

F. Race

One interesting point revealed by the data is that Negroes tend to have a higher average propensity to save than do whites at comparable income levels.[34] This, however, is more true for northern urban Negroes than for southern Negroes. In the South the upper-income Negroes save less than whites in the same income class, and perhaps more important, the savings by southern Negroes are not very responsive to income changes.

What is the explanation for the higher average propensity to save by the northern Negro? So far, no completely satisfactory answer has been given to this question, though two rather plausible partial answers have been provided. First, the Negro faces greater economic insecurity and uncertainty than does the white, even though the two may be in the same income bracket. Second, Negroes hold smaller amounts of liquid assets (other than money income) than do whites in the same income class. Thus, even though the two may have equal incomes, the white has accumulated more wealth than the Negro. This allows the white to dissave and to maintain his consumption reasonably well if and when his income declines. The Negro, on the other hand, is less able to dissave as frequently and as much as whites when the need arises. This would account, in part at least, for the larger average propensity to save by the Negro.

This brief review of some other determinants of consumption (and savings) indicates that the actual income-consumption-saving behavior of the community is quite complex. Indeed it seems that the more research that is devoted to it, the more complex it is. However, for purposes of analysis in this part, we shall ignore most of these complexities and concentrate on the simplified relationship $C = a + bY$.

---

[34]See J. S. Duesenberry, *Income, Saving, and the Theory of Consumer Behavior*; and J. Tobin, "Relative Income, Absolute Income, and Saving," in *Money, Trade, and Economic Growth: Essays in Honor of John H. Williams* (New York: The Macmillan Company, 1951); and Klein, "Savings and the Propensity to Consume."

6.   The Secular Rise of the Short-Run Consumption Function

Economists have noted for some time now that there has been a secular upward drift of the short-run consumption function.[35] While this
is not too important for any one particular short-run period, it is of considerable importance for the growth analysis that is discussed in the
next part of this volume. Accordingly we shall examine the major explanation advanced for this phenomenon.

To begin with, the secular rise of the consumption function is an empirical generalization about the propensities to consume and to save
over time. In other words, we are concerned here with the time sequence of the income-consumption-saving relationship. The data reveal
the following: there has been a secular rise in the short-run consumption function, but the resulting long-run consumption function is linear
and virtually intersects the point of origin. This long-run consumption
function is shown in Figure 10-9 as C_L. Any satisfactory explanation of
this behavior must accomplish three things—(1) explain the secular rise
in the short-run function, (2) explain the linearity of the long-run function, and (3) explain the equality of the long-run average and marginal
propensities to consume (that is, explain the intersection of C_L with the
point of origin).

Perhaps the most plausible explanation advanced thus far is the one
that has been provided by James S. Duesenberry.[36] Duesenberry begins
by rewriting the consumption function so that present consumption is a
function of the highest income received in the recent past. Assume that
this income is Y_1 in Figure 10-10B, and assume further that consumers
are actually receiving this income. Out of Y_1 they allocate Y_1C_1 to con-

---

[35]See Duesenberry, *Income, Saving, and the Theory of Consumer Behavior*, and
his earlier statement in *Income, Employment, and Public Policy: Essays in Honor
of Alvin H. Hansen*. For other statements, see W. J. Fellner, *Trends and Cycles in
Economic Activity* (New York: Holt, Rinehart, & Winston, Inc., 1956), pp. 118-23;
and for an earlier statement, his *Monetary Policies and Full Employment* (Berkeley
and Los Angeles: University of California Press, 1946), pp. 55-73. Hansen provided
a similar thesis, though much earlier and less well developed. See his *Economic
Stabilization in an Unbalanced World* (New York: Harcourt, Brace & World, Inc.,
1932), pp. 373-74; and *Fiscal Policy and Business Cycles* (New York: W. W. Norton & Company, 1941), pp. 231-34. For empirical studies, see S. Kuznets, *National
Income: A Summary of Findings* (New York: National Bureau of Economic Research, 1946) and R. Goldsmith, *A Study of Savings in the United States* (Princeton: Princeton University Press, 1955), Vol. I, Chapter 1.

[36]Duesenberry, *Income, Saving, and the Theory of Consumer Behavior;* but see
also the works by Fellner cited in the preceding footnote.

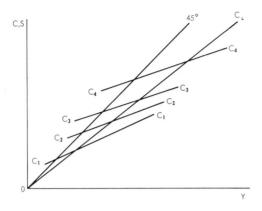

FIGURE 10–9

sumption, and C_1S_1 to savings. We shall assume that this allocation of income between consumption and savings is the *desired* allocation, and thus at Y_1 consumers are in an equilibrium position—that is, they are actually allocating their income in the manner desired.

Note that in Figure 10–10A the highest income level at period 1 is Y_1; this corresponds to Y_1 in Figure 10–10B. In other words, OY_1 on the vertical axis of Figure 10–10A equals OY_1 on the horizontal axis in Figure 10–10B. The reason for using Figure 10–10A is that it allows us to trace out the cyclical and growth pattern of income, while Figure 10–10B allows us to trace out the effects of these income changes on consumption and savings.

Now assume that income falls from Y_1 to Y_0 (in Figure 10–10A). According to the Duesenberry hypothesis, consumption will also fall, but not by as much as income falls. In this time period the relevant short-run consumption function is C_1C_1 (in Figure 10–10B). Since consumption is a function of the highest income previously received (Y_1), consumers will attempt to maintain as best as possible their previous high level of consumption. The fall in income, however, prevents their accomplishing this objective completely, but as they move down C_1C_1, consumers will make an effort to do so. Thus *the movement down C_1C_1 is accompanied by a fall in the average propensity to save and a rise in the average propensity to consume.* At the income level of Y_0 the average propensity to consume is much higher than it is at the Y_1 level of income. Correspondingly, the average propensity to save is less at Y_0

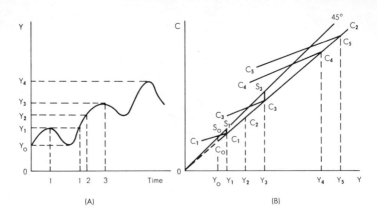

FIGURE 10–10

than at Y_1. In short, consumers dig into their savings in order to maintain as best as possible the consumption level associated with the highest income level previously achieved. Hence, aggregate savings are not
only absolutely less at Y_0 than at Y_1, they are also proportionately less.

Assume now that the lower-turning point of the cycle occurs, so that
income rises back to its former level of Y_1 (see Figure 10–10A). This is
accompanied by a movement back up along C_1C_1 until again at Y_1 consumption is Y_1C_1 and savings is C_1S_1. At this point the realized savings
and consumption of the community once again equal the desired savings and consumption, and consumers are again in an equilibrium position.

If however we assume that there has also been some economic
growth, income will rise beyond Y_1 to a now higher level. Let us assume
that it rises to Y_2. Now once more the highest level of income *is the current level*. But according to the Duesenberry thesis, since consumers desire the distribution of income between consumption and savings at Y_1,
there is no reason for them to alter this pattern. That is to say, the desired average propensity to save established at Y_1 will be maintained at
Y_2, as will the desired average propensity to consume.

If this is the case, then the *proportion* of income saved out of Y_2 will
be the same as the *proportion* saved out of Y_1, and the same generalization applies to the proportions devoted to consumption. Thus
$C_1/Y_1 = C_2/Y_2$, that is, this segment of the long-run consumption
function (C_L) is linear between points C_1 and C_2. The same relationship holds, moreover, for further income increases up to Y_3—that is,
the average propensity to consume is the same at Y_3 as it is at Y_2 and at

Y_1. The entire segment of the long-run consumption function thus is linear between points C_1 and C_3.

However, if income were to fall from the peak of Y_3 back to some lower level, consumers would not move back down along this segment of the long-run function. Rather they are motivated by the consumption level attained at the highest income previously received (Y_3) and thus will reduce their consumption less than proportionately and reduce their savings more than proportionately to the income reduction. They therefore move down along the new and relevant short-run consumption function C_3C_3, and in the process their average propensity to save falls while their average propensity to consume rises. The reason for this is, as noted above, that they desire to maintain as best as possible the consumption level associated with the highest income previously received, which is now Y_3.

It is now time for some important generalizations. First, the entire cycle of income from Y_1 to Y_3 (Figure 10–10A) is accompanied by a movement down the short-run consumption function C_1C_1, then a movement back up along it, and then finally a shift of the short-run function to C_3C_3. The movement down and then back along C_1C_1 is related to the drop in income from Y_1 and the recovery of income back to the Y_1 level. The shift of the consumption function is associated with the growth in income beyond the Y_1 level up to Y_3. There are thus two distinct movements—the *cyclical* (that is, down and back up C_1C_1), and the *growth* (that is, the shift from C_1C_1 to C_3C_3).

It should be noted in this respect that the shift from C_1C_1 to C_3C_3 is not as abrupt as the preceding might imply. Rather the movement of income from Y_1 on the upswing to Y_3 is relatively gradual so that there are successive shifts of the short-run consumption function. We have shown only one of these intermediate points (Y_2), though in reality there are several of them.

A second important generalization is that the movement *up along* the long-run consumption function (C_L) is not reversible. That is, as income rises beyond Y_1 (on the upswing) to Y_3, consumption follows the long-run consumption function. However, as income slumps from Y_3 to some lower level, the consumers *do not move back down the long-run function;* rather, since their consumption is a function of the highest level of income previously received, that is Y_3, they reduce their consumption expenditures less than proportionately. Thus they move back down the now relevant short-run consumption function C_3C_3. In other words, there is a "ratchett effect" that is emphasized by the Duesenberry thesis—the movement up the long-run consumption function is nonreversible. This asserts that, in effect, the upward shift from C_1C_1 to C_3C_3 is permanent.

Third, if we were to extend the long-run consumption function back to the left, we should discover that it intersects the point of origin. It might be repeated here that this is not armchair theorizing, for the available data indicate rather conclusively that this is the case. This is shown in Figure 10–10B by the dashed extension from C_1 to the point of origin. Thus on the long-run consumption function the marginal and average propensities to consume are equal (and therefore the marginal and average propensities to save are equal also). This is simply because if the average propensity to consume at Y_3 is the same as at Y_1, the function is linear and passes through the point of origin.

Two question arise. First, what is the major achievement of the Duesenberry thesis? And second, what are the available data on the secular upward drift? So far as the achievement of the Duesenberry thesis is concerned, it is safe to say that it is twofold. Not only does it explain the secular stability of the marginal propensity to consume (as well as its equality with the average propensity to consume), it also explains that during the course of the cycle the relevant short-run consumption function differs in slope from the long-run function. Thus during the contraction the average propensity to consume rises above the long-run value, the average propensity to save falls below its long-run value, and the marginal propensities remain constant, assuming a linear short-run function. During the expansionary stage up to the point where income reaches its former highest level, the average propensity to consume falls back to its long-run value, and the average propensity to save rises back to its long-run value.

But in terms of secular growth, the average propensity to consume equals the marginal propensity. Thus during the cyclical process, both the absolute amount and proportional amount of savings will vary considerably, but during the secular expansion the proportional amount of savings remains constant, while the absolute amount rises. That is, in Figure 10–10B, $(C_1S_1)/Y_1 = (C_3S_3)/Y_3$. But $C_3S_3 > C_1S_1$.

As for the data pertaining to the secular upward drift of the short-run consumption function, in which the long-run function is linear through the point of origin, about all that we can say is that the statistical evidence is abundant. The shape of the long-run consumption function is given by the empirical data, not by *a priori* and *ad hoc* theorizing.

7. Summary

The short-run consumption function is a very important tool in modern economic analysis. While Keynes set forth the basic relationship involved—namely, that the prime determinant of consumption is income—subsequent research and study have shown that numerous other determinants are often quite important. Among these are expectations, liquid assets, age, and so on. Nevertheless, for simplified short-run analysis we shall assume that $C = f(Y)$.

The *height* of the consumption function indicates the *average* propensity to consume (C/Y) and the *average* propensity to save (S/Y). On the short-run consumption function C/Y falls and S/Y rises as income rises from lower to higher levels. The converse is true for income declines. This implies that the short-run function has a positive intercept on the vertical axis.

The *marginal* propensity to consume states how much of a change in income will be devoted to a change in consumption, and it is given by the *slope* of the consumption function. On a linear function—that is, the type indicated by the few available empirical studies—the marginal propensity to consume remains constant, as does the marginal propensity to save. On a curvilinear function it declines as income rises from lower to higher levels; the marginal propensity to save behaves in the reverse manner. In the postwar period in the United States the historical consumption function has displayed a marginal propensity to consume of about .89.

There has been a secular upward drift of the short-run consumption function, and the resulting long-run consumption function is linear through the point of origin. Thus the average and marginal propensities to consume are equal and constant, and the average and marginal propensities to save are equal and constant. However, during periods of income change the short-run average propensity to consume is not constant. In periods of income contraction, consumers do not move back down the long-run consumption function, but rather down the relevant short-run function. This means that during periods of income decline the average propensity to consume rises. During the following period of income expansion, on the other hand, the average propensity to consume falls back to its former level. If income continues to rise beyond its previous peak, the average propensity to consume remains constant inasmuch as consumers are satisfied with the proportion of income spent on consumers' goods. Thus while there is a constancy of the long-run average propensity to consume, it displays a cyclical sensitivity. These two patterns, however, are not inconsistent; they are reconciled by the explanation offered by Professor Duesenberry.

QUESTIONS

10-1. What is the fundamental difference between a "budget study" and the "consumption function proper"? Explain in detail.

10-2. When there is a cyclical contraction, the average propensity to consume tends to rise (although the marginal propensity remains constant), and during the ensuing expansion the average propensity tends to fall. However, after the expansion continues past the income level from which the contraction took place, the average propensity to consume remains constant. Moreover, the average and marginal propensities are equal as the expansion continues beyond the highest level of income previously achieved. **Explain.**

10-3. What did Keynes mean by his "fundamental psychological law"? Answer in terms of the propensities to consume and to save.

10-4. Explain the behavior of both the average and marginal propensities to consume and to save as consumers move out along:

a. a linear consumption function that begins at the point of origin.
b. a linear consumption function that begins at some point on the vertical axis above the point of origin.
c. a curvilinear consumption function.

10-5. Why are not the data on consumption-income relationships shown in Figure 10-6 a strict measurement of the consumption function?

10-6. Of all the "objective" and "subjective" factors, Keynes considered only one to be an important determinant of short-run consumption behavior. Why did he disregard the others? Do you agree with this procedure? Explain.

Bibliography

Duesenberry, J. S., *Income, Saving, and the Theory of Consumer Behavior.* Cambridge: Harvard University Press, 1949.
Fellner, W. J., *Trends and Cycles in Economic Activity.* New York: Holt, Rinehart & Winston, Inc., 1956.
Ferber, R., *A Study of Aggregate Consumption Functions.* New York: National Bureau of Economic Research, 1953.

Goldsmith, R., *A Study of Savings in the United States.* Princeton: Princeton University Press, 1955, Vol. I.

Hansen, A. H., *A Guide to Keynes.* New York: McGraw-Hill Book Company, 1953.

Keynes, J. M., *The General Theory of Employment, Interest, and Money.* New York: Harcourt, Brace & World, Inc., 1936.

Kuznets, S., *National Income: A Summary of Findings.* New York: National Bureau of Economic Research, 1946.

Suits, D., "The Determinants of Consumer Expenditure: A Review of Present Knowledge," in *Impacts of Monetary Policy.* Englewood Cliffs: Prentice-Hall, Inc., 1963.

Zellner, A., "The Short-Run Consumption Function," *Econometrica,* October 1957.

11

Liquidity Preference, the Interest Rate, and Investment

The importance that private investment plays in cyclical disturbances and economic growth has already been made clear. Further, the various theories reviewed earlier illustrate the important role assigned to the interest rate in business cycle analysis. And, as might be expected, both of these variables hold a significant position in modern cycle-growth theory.

Both the interest rate and private investment are examined in some detail in this chapter. The procedure is to inquire into what Keynes himself had to say about these two variables and then to examine some more recent analysis that pertains to them. It might be noted in passing that the discussion is quite important for the analysis of the next chapter and for the chapters in Parts 4 and 5.

1. The Interest Rate as an Opportunity Cost

Keynes rejected the more or less traditional theory that considers the rate of interest as a payment for "waiting," that is, as a payment for deferring present for future consumption.[1] In his analysis a different set

---

[1] J. M. Keynes, *The General Theory of Employment, Interest, and Money* (New York: Harcourt, Brace & World, Inc., 1936), pp. 166-67. See Chapter 6 and Chapter 16 of this text for a discussion of the more traditional view.

of psychological factors underlies the determination of the interest rate.

Recall (from the preceding chapter) that the community's consumption function determines how much of a given level of income will be devoted to savings. Once the members of the community have decided upon their total amount of savings, they have to make the further decision of the form in which they will hold their savings. The major alternatives available to them are to hold the savings in the form of (1) money,[2] (2) nonmonetary, but financial, assets (e.g., savings deposits, corporate stocks and bonds, government securities, and so on), or (3) some combination of the two. It is obvious that if people or businesses hold their savings in the form of money, they give up the interest income derived from holding bonds.[3] But by holding money rather than bonds they increase their *liquidity*.[4]

---

[2]We must be explicit by what we mean by money, and though we defined the term earlier (Chapter 6), a restatement may not be out of order. By money we mean all hand-to-hand currency and token coins outside of the banking system and the government, *plus* all demand deposits, excluding interbank deposits and governmental deposits. Thus we exclude all time deposits and other "near moneys," interbank deposits (including reserve deposits), and Treasury deposits in the Federal Reserve and commercial banks.

[3]Of course, there are financial assets other than simply bonds, although Keynes limited his analysis to this particular asset. For some critical discussion of this limitation in Keynes' analysis see Joan Robinson, "The Rate of Interest," *Econometrica,* April 1951, reprinted in her *The Rate of Interest and Other Essays* (London: The Macmillan Company, 1952); J. R. Hicks, *Value and Capital* (Oxford: Oxford University Press, 1939); R. F. Kahn, "Some Notes on Liquidity Preference," *Manchester School of Economic and Social Studies,* September 1954; R. Turvey, *Interest Rates and Asset Prices* (Oxford: Oxford University Press, 1960); J. Tobin, "A Dynamic Aggregative Model," *Journal of Political Economy,* April 1955, "Liquidity Preference and Monetary Policy," *Review of Economics and Statistics,* May 1947, and "Money, Capital, and Other Stores of Value," *American Economic Review,* May 1961; R. A. Musgrave, "Money, Liquidity, and the Valuation of Assets," in *Money, Trade, and Economic Growth* (New York: The Macmillan Company, 1951); and W. L. Smith, *Debt Management in the United States* (Washington, D. C.: Study Paper No. 19, Joint Economic Committee, 86th Cong., 2d sess., 1960). See also J. Tobin, "The Theory of Portfolio Selection," Chapter 1 in *The Theory of Interest Rates,* eds. F. H. Hahn and F. P. R. Brechling (London: The Macmillan Company, 1964). Finally, for a critical review of the post-Keynesian literature, see H. G. Johnson, "Monetary Theory and Policy," *American Economic Review,* June 1962.

[4]Money is the only asset with 100 per cent liquidity since it is generally accepted as a medium of exchange. All other assets, even those which are fairly close substitutes for money (that is, the "near moneys," such as government securities, time deposits, and so on), have less than 100 per cent liquidity insofar as they are not generally accepted as media of exchange. The term "liquidity preference" refers to the *preference for money,* although the availability, prices, and other characteristics of other assets, particularly the "near moneys," will influence liquidity preference.

As we shall see shortly, people and businesses demand money for liquidity for several reasons, but the important point here is that the rate of interest is "the reward for parting with liquidity for a specified period."[5] Put otherwise, interest is the cost of holding savings in the form of money. If, for example, the prevailing rate of interest is 6 per cent per annum, and a person decides to hold his savings in the form of money, then he gives up the 6 per cent per year which he could have obtained by lending out his savings. From this point of view, the interest rate is an *opportunity cost,* is "a measure of the unwillingness of those who possess money to part with their liquid control over it,"[6] and thus is a measure of *liquidity preference.*

But why should people and businesses decide to hold even a part of their savings in the form of money and thus pass up an interest income? Why, in other words, do they have a liquidity preference? Of course, people and businesses may decide to hold money for a wide variety of reasons, but Keynes simplified by distinguishing between three psychological reasons or motives for holding cash—the transactions motive, the precautionary motive, and the speculative motive. Each of these is examined in some detail in the first part of this chapter.

2.   The Transactions Motive

To begin with, businesses and individuals must hold cash "to bridge the interval between the receipt of income and its disbursement."[7] In other words, the community must hold cash for the purpose of making its daily, weekly, and monthly transactions. If receipts and disbursements were made simultaneously, there would be no need for cash balances for transactions purposes. In reality, however, there is a time lag between the two, and the longer this lag, the larger the holdings of cash for transactions purposes must be. Thus an individual who receives his income in monthly payments needs to hold more in transactions balances than a person who is paid weekly. In this sense, the institutional pattern of income payments has an impact on the demand for money for transactions balances, although (following Keynes) this pattern may be assumed to be constant over the short run.

If this is the case, what then is the major determinant of the demand

---

[5]Keynes, *The General Theory,* p. 167.

[6]*Ibid.*

[7]*Ibid.,* p. 195. Earlier monetary theorists stressed this lag between receipts and disbursements as an important determinant of velocity.

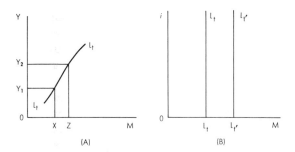

FIGURE 11—1

for transactions balances (L_t)? Keynes simplified and argued that it is the level of income—that is, the higher the level of income, the greater the amount of transactions and hence the greater the demand for money for transactions balances (L_t). On the other hand, a fall in income will lower the demand for L_t balances.[8] Thus:

$$L_t = f(Y).$$

The important thing to note about this formulation is that the demand for L_t balances is not responsive to changes in the interest rate, at least within the typical range over which the rate of interest fluctuates.[9] Of course, if the interest rate were pushed to extreme heights, people and businesses might reduce their transactions balances (*ceteris paribus*) in order to take advantage of the high rate; but this unlikely case may be ruled out.

The demand curve for money for transactions balances may be shown diagrammatically in two ways. In Figure 11–1A income is plotted on the vertical axis and money on the horizontal axis. The positively sloped L_tL_t curve shows that the demand for money for transactions balances is a positive function of the level of income. More important, however, is the L_tL_t curve in Figure 11–1B, where the rate of interest (rather

[8]See the works by Tobin cited in footnote 3, and W. J. Baumol, "The Transactions Demand for Cash: An Inventory Theoretic Approach," *Quarterly Journal of Economics,* November 1952, for a more detailed discussion of the determinants of the demand for L_t balances, especially by business firms. See also D. Patinkin, "An Indirect Utility Approach to the Theory of Money, Assets, and Savings," Chapter 2 in Hahn and Brechling, *The Theory of Interest Rates.*

[9]Tobin and Baumol point out that under certain conditions the demand for L_t balances will display some interest elasticity. See especially J. Tobin, "The Interest Elasticity of the Transactions Demand for Cash," *Review of Economics and Statistics,* August 1956. See E. L. Whalon, "A Cross-Section Study of Business Demand for Cash," *Journal of Finance,* September 1965, for some empirical verification of the Baumol-Tobin thesis.

than income) is plotted on the vertical axis. Figure 11–1B illustrates that the demand for L_t balances is perfectly inelastic with respect to changes in the interest rate.[10] While a rise in income, say, from OY_1 to OY_2 entails a movement along the L_tL_t curve (from OX to OZ) in Figure 11–1A, it results in a shift of the curve to the right (from L_tL_t to $L_t'L_t'$) in Figure 11–1B. A fall in income would cause the curve in Figure 11–1B to shift to the left.

Observe, however, that the demand curve for L_t balances may shift its position because of changes in consumer and business credit. If liberal credit terms are advanced, the L_tL_t curve of Figure 11–1A will shift to the left, showing that at the same income level smaller transactions balances are needed. The same conclusion applies to the curve in Figure 11–1B. Conversely, consumer and business credit restrictions will tend to shift the curve to the right. Note that this does not necessarily mean that the demand for L_t balances is responsive to changes in the interest rate, for there are many terms of credit other than the rate of interest. However, as pointed out in a note above, there is some indication that the demand for L_t balances by businesses tends to be somewhat elastic with respect to the interest rate.

3. The Precautionary Motive

A second reason that people desire to hold cash balances is because of the unforeseen future. Quite often an unexpected event occurs that requires an outlay of cash. Whether the event is an illness, a broken foot, an advantageous commodity purchase, a wedding gift, or what have you, a certain cash reserve must be built up for such expenditures.

In Keynes' analysis the demand for precautionary balances (L_p) is determined in part by the state of expectations of the members of the community as regards "contingencies requiring sudden expenditure and for unforeseen opportunities of advantageous purchases."[11] Similarly, the cheapness and availability of credit for temporary borrowing (including overdrawn checking accounts)[12] will have some influence. Thus the demand curve for L_p balances will display some interest elasticity, though this seems to be rather unimportant in the overall picture.[13] For

---

[10]Again, within the relevant range. At some very high rate of interest the curve would slope off to the left, displaying some interest elasticity.

[11]Keynes, *The General Theory*, p. 196.

[12]*Ibid.*

[13]*Ibid.*

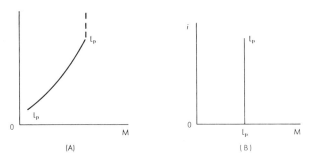

FIGURE 11—2

all practical purposes, therefore, the demand curve for L_p balances is highly inelastic with respect to changes in the rate of interest. This is shown in Figure 11–2B. In fact, in order to lump the L_t and L_p balances together, Keynes assumes that the demand for L_p balances is primarily a function of the level of income, as shown in Figure 11–2A. Thus:

$$L_p = f(Y).$$

However, certain doubts exist as to the shape of the L_pL_p curve in Figure 11–2A. If we follow the argument that $L_p = f(Y)$, does this mean that L_p is always a positive function of Y? That is, will the demand for precautionary balances continue to rise as income continues to rise? And if so, what shape does the curve take? It might be argued that after a certain level of income is attained the "security-mindedness" of the community is pretty well satisfied with existing L_p balances. If this is so, then the L_pL_p curve of Figure 11–2A will become perfectly inelastic in its upper range, and any further increase in money holdings will be allocated to the transactions and speculative balances. Put otherwise, so long as income continues to rise, the L_pL_p curve in Figure 11–2B, which displays the interest inelasticity of the demand for L_p balances, will shift only so far to the right and no farther.[14]

In this connection it is important to note that there has occurred, to a large degree, an "institutionalization" of precautionary balances. Private retirement plans (for both employees and management), as well as private medical and hospital insurance plans, have gone a long way in reducing the necessity of building up adequate precautionary balances out of "take-home" pay. To be sure, payments into retirement and insur-

---

[14]On this, see D. Suits, "The Determinants of Consumer Expenditure: A Review of Present Knowledge," Research Study One in *Impacts of Monetary Policy* (Englewood Cliffs, N. J.: Prentice-Hall, Inc., 1963), pp. 41-43.

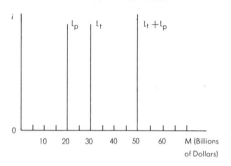

FIGURE 11-3

ance plans are made from current income, though the payments are merely a minute fraction per time period of what would otherwise have to be set aside for adequate L_p balances. By the same token, governmental retirement and insurance plans achieve the same result. Many people are in fact "forced" (under both the public and private plans) to lay aside some precautionary balances. This institutionalization of L_p balances may, as already noted, tend to reduce the responsiveness of the L_p curve in Figure 11–2B to income changes. For example, if employees realize that their company and other health insurance plans provide them with nearly adequate medical attention, then a larger proportion of any increase in their money holdings is available for speculative and transactions purposes. If transactions balances have a stable functional relationship to income, then the increased stability of the L_p balances may add to a greater instability of the speculative balances. Before examining the speculative motive, however, one final point is in order.

Keynes placed the demand for L_t and L_p balances in the same category because of their dependence on the income level and their independence of the rate of interest.[15] Figure 11–3 shows both the L_t and L_p demand curves for the community as a whole, where, given the prevailing level of income, the time lag between receipts and disbursements of income, and psychological expectations, the L_t demand is for $30 billion and the L_p demand is for $20 billion. These two demand curves may now be added together horizontally, so that the resultant $L_t + L_p$ curve shows a demand for $50 billion.

There is still, however, the important speculative motive to be discussed, and since this plays such an important role in the analysis it will require more time and attention.

---

[15]Keynes, *The General Theory*, p. 199.

4. The Speculative Motive

The speculative motive for holding money is quite different from the other two motives. While Keynes argued that the level of income is the major determinant of transactions and precautionary balances, he also argued that the major determinant of speculative balances is the interest rate (i). Thus:

$$L_s = f(i).$$

For this reason Keynes concluded that it is "by playing on the speculative-motive that monetary management (or, in the absence of management, chance changes in the quantity of money) is brought to bear on the economic system."[16]

But just what is the speculative motive, and how does it relate to monetary policy? And why do some persons and businesses hold money for speculative purposes?

If a person (or business) has an accumulation of savings over and above the precautionary and transactions requirements, there is a choice of holding the residual either as money or in the form of bonds.[17] Presumably he would rather hold this residual in the form of an interest-bearing asset, unless his psychology towards liquidity is overwhelming. Probably the typical case involves his holding some of the residual as money and the rest in bonds, although, until more is known about his liquidity preference, little can be said about the actual decision.

---

[16]Ibid., pp. 196-197. On the speculative balances, see also Patinkin, "An Indirect-Utility Approach to the Theory of Money, Assets, and Savings," *Money, Interest, and Prices* (New York: Harper & Row, Publishers, 1965), Chapter VI.

[17]As observed in footnote 3, the Keynesian theory of interest has come under a good deal of criticism because Keynes confined his analysis primarily to bonds and thus ignored other financial assets in which there can also be speculation. See Johnson, "Monetary Theory and Policy," pp. 345-48, for a review of the criticism of Keynes' "aggregation of all assets other than money into bonds implicit in the use of a single (long-term) rate of interest" (p. 345).

Keynes, however, was fully aware of the implications of his simplifying assumption; see *The General Theory,* p. 167, footnote 2. Further, in his discussion of the organized stock exchanges, he tended to lump all securities together as if they were reasonably good substitutes for each other; see *ibid.,* Chapter 12. Yet, paradoxically, he also pointed out (p. 197) that changes in the short-term rate of interest are not transmitted to similar changes in the long-term rate.

Perhaps the major point here is that Keynes was concerned primarily with open-market operations as the main form of monetary policy and thus limited his discussion to bond prices. Still, the process of interest rate adjustments is far more complex than implied by the analysis in *The General Theory;* see especially the discussion in Chapters 21-22 below.

One reason some of the residual will be held as money is because of uncertainty as to the future performance of the bond market. If prices are expected to fall in the future, the individual will attempt to increase his money holdings so that he can reenter the market later on and buy at the lower price. In fact, he may well sell some of his current holdings of bonds in order to avoid a capital loss and at the same time acquire additional speculative balances so that he can purchase later at the expected lower prices. Conversely, if future prices are expected to rise, he will decrease his current money holdings in order to buy more bonds before the price rise proceeds very far. In short, he *speculates* on the market and in so doing continually shifts back and forth between greater money balances and greater bond holdings.

At this point it is necessary to introduce an important feature of the bond market, namely, *the inverse relationship between the market price of a bond and the market rate of interest on the bond*. Actually it is necessary to distinguish between *two rates* of interest—the nominal rate and the market rate—as well as between *two prices*—the face value and the market price of the bond.

First consider the *face value* of a bond. This is merely the dollar amount printed on the face of the bond certificate. Thus if the government issues a security of one-year maturity with the figure $1,000 printed on its face, that amount is the face value of the bond.

Consider secondly the *nominal rate* of interest. Like the face value, this also is printed on the face of the bond instrument. If the one-year government security mentioned above has printed on its face the interest rate of 3 per cent, then this figure is referred to as the nominal rate of interest. These two figures—the face value and the nominal rate—are important for any buyer of the government security, for together they tell him how much he will receive from the issuer at the date of maturity. In the illustration above, he will receive $1,030, of which $1,000 is considered as payment of principal, and $30 is considered as interest income. The interest income on a one-year security, then, is calculated by multiplying the face value times the nominal rate.[18]

On the other hand, the *market price* of the security is the price for which it is actually selling in the market; this, of course, may be above or below the face value, depending upon supply and demand condi-

---

[18]The maturity value which the buyer will receive for the one-year security mentioned above is given by

$$P_t = P_{t-1}(1+i)$$

where P_{t-1} is the face value and i is the nominal rate of interest. More generally,

$$P_t = P_{t-n}(1+i)^n.$$

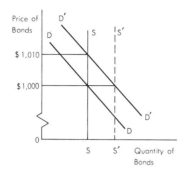

FIGURE 11–4

tions. Assume that the government has already issued a certain amount of these one-year securities and that there is thus an outstanding supply of them (as shown by the SS curve in Figure 11–4).

The *market rate* of interest is the rate that is determined by supply and demand conditions, and therefore it will usually differ from the nominal rate. In fact, the two rates will be equal only when the market price of the security equals the security's face value. To determine what the market rate of interest is, the market purchase price of the security is divided into the interest income received per year.

In order to illustrate these fundamental relationships, let us carry the example farther. Assume that the supply curve of the one-year government security remains constant at SS (in Figure 11–4). Assume further that the original demand curve for this security is DD. The intersection of these two curves is at the market price of $1,000. Thus, at the outset, the face value is equal to the market price, and whoever buys at this price and holds the security to maturity will receive $1,030. In this case, then, the market rate of interest is equal to the nominal rate—that is, the buyer receives $30 of interest income, which turns out to be 3 per cent of his original cash outlay of $1,000. In short, *as long as the market price equals the face value, the market rate equals the nominal rate.*

Assume now that the demand for this particular security rises to D′D′. Since the supply is constant, the price will rise; and we assume it rises to $1,010. Since the face value remains constant at $1,000, the market price exceeds the face value. What now does this imply for the market rate of interest? In reality it means that the market rate has fallen below the nominal rate. The reason for this is simple enough. Whoever buys

one of these securities at the higher market price of $1,010 will still re-
ceive at the maturity date $1,030. However, he will receive only $20
over and above his cash outlay, and this amounts to only (approximately) 2 per cent interest. The arithmetic relation is simple enough:

$$\text{Market price} = \frac{\text{Maturity value}}{(1+\text{Interest rate})} = \frac{\$1,030}{(1+i)} = \frac{\$1,030}{1.019} = \$1,010.$$

Thus, given the maturity value of the security, the market price varies
inversely with the market rate of interest. In this particular case the
market price rose, and thus *the market rate fell below the nominal rate.*

But note that once this occurs, the lower market price may be translated into a lower nominal price. If now some more one-year securities
are to be issued, and if demand stays at D'D', the government will recognize that the market is willing to accept a lower rate of interest than
the 3 per cent nominal rate. If only enough new securities are issued to
pay off the outstanding maturing securities (so that the supply curve
remains at SS), then the government can make use of the new nominal
rate of 2 per cent on each new security of $1,000 face value. However,
if a relatively large *new* issue is offered, the supply curve in Figure
11–4 will shift to the right, lower the market price and hence raise the
market rate. The new supply curve S'S' is drawn far enough to the
right that it intersects D'D' at the earlier price of $1,000. In this event
the market rate will rise back to the 3 per cent nominal rate, that is:

$$\$1,000 = \frac{\$1,030}{(1+.03)}.$$

Let us reverse the case and assume that the market price per security
falls because of, say, a slump in demand. If demand falls enough so
that the market price is now $990, then the market rate rises above the
nominal rate. Whoever buys and holds a security to maturity will still
receive a maturity value of $1,030, but in this case the $40 he receives
over and above his original cash outlay is (approximately) 4 per cent
interest. That is:

$$\$990 = \frac{\$1,030}{(1+.0409)}.$$

Thus the market rate rises above the nominal rate as the market price
falls below the face value. Again, if the government wishes to sell new
securities, it must take this market condition into account. The impor-

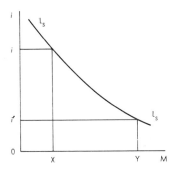

FIGURE 11-5

tant point, however, is that *when the market price falls below the face value, the market rate rises above the nominal rate.*

Let us now return to the speculative motive. As noted earlier, a person has the alternative of holding his money or buying bonds (or some combination of the two). Although he may currently possess money, he may put off buying bonds if he feels that the market price of bonds is going to fall, that is, the market rate of interest is going to rise. On the other hand, he may buy bonds now, and hence reduce his cash balances, if he feels that the market price is going to rise and the market rate fall. In short, he speculates; he tries "to outguess the market." It is in this respect that the demand for speculative balances (L_s) is a function of the market rate of interest.

But what shape does the demand curve for speculative balances take? Keynes argued that the curve is negatively sloped, as in Figure 11-5.[19] When the rate of interest is relatively high, as at Oi, the amount of money demanded for speculative balances is relatively low; for at such a high rate people and businesses would rather part with their speculative balances than to pass up the interest income. The opportunity cost of holding money is considered to be "too high." However, at the relatively low rate of Oi', people are more reluctant to part with their liquidity. Though some will be willing to give up liquidity at such a low market rate of interest, others prefer to hold onto their L_s balances.

In fact, there may be some positive, but low, market rate at which people in general are unwilling to part with their L_s balances for bonds. At such a low rate they feel that the interest income that is foregone by not buying and holding bonds is so small that it is of no concern. This

---

[19]Keynes, *The General Theory*, pp. 171, 201-202.

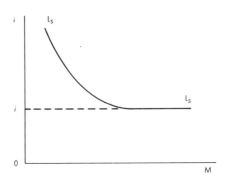

FIGURE 11–6

possibility, to which Keynes gave little credence,[20] is shown in Figure 11–6 where, at a low rate, the L_sL_s curve becomes perfectly elastic. This has come to be referred to as the "liquidity trap," and we shall return to it in section 8 and in Part 5.

It is now possible to add the demand curve for L_s balances to the demand curves for L_t and L_p balances. In Figure 11–7 the L_t+L_p curve (taken from Figure 11–3) is added to the L_s curve, yielding the total demand curve $(L_t+L_p+L_s)$ for money at alternative rates of interest. This total demand curve for money is referred to as the liquidity preference, or LP, curve.

5. Liquidity Preference, the Stock of Money, and Interest Rate Changes

The money supply must now be introduced into the analysis. To begin with, assume that the stock of money at any one time is fixed by a combination of forces emanating from the commercial banking system and the central banking authorities—that is, it is institutionally determined. As such, the money supply is an independent variable in the Keynesian analysis.

In order to see how the money supply enters into the determination

---

[20]*Ibid.*, p. 207: "But whilst this limiting case might become practically important in the future, I know of no example hitherto."

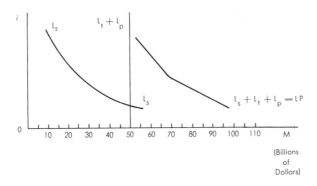

FIGURE 11–7

of the interest rate, let us examine Figure 11–8, which shows the total liquidity preference curve (LP), as well as the perfectly inelastic supply curve of money (MM). Let us arbitrarily begin with the interest rate Oi. At this particular rate of interest, people are willing, given their liquidity preference function LP, to hold only iA amount of money. Yet the money supply is OM, which means that actually AB surplus cash balances are being held. (That is, the LP curve shows that at the interest rate Oi, only the amount iA is demanded as cash balances; but with the stock of money at OM, cash holdings are actually iB, which means an excess of AB in desired cash balances.) What will happen in this case? Since AB represents a surplus amount of money over and above liquidity needs, an effort will be made to acquire bonds. However, the shift from money to bonds results in a rise in the market price of bonds and a decline in the market rate of interest. Suppose that the market rate falls to Oi'. Even at this rate, given the LP curve, some people will feel that they have an excess amount of money balances and still attempt to purchase bonds. Finally the interest rate will be pushed to Oi'', at which the LP and MM curves intersect. This is the new equilibrium rate of interest, for now the amount of money demanded for liquidity purposes is equal to the total supply of money. But for this equilibrium to be established, the market rate of interest has to fall low enough so that actual holdings of cash balances (OM) are equal to the desired amount of cash balances. Please note that since the actual holdings of cash balances (that is, the money supply OM) is given, the equilibrating process takes place through changes in the quantity of desired cash

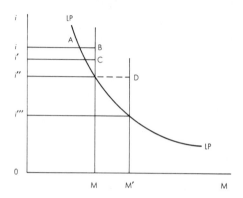

FIGURE 11—8

balances. In this case, as the interest rate falls, the quantity demanded of cash balances rises until it equals the stock of money.

Assume now that the monetary authorities increase the money supply from OM to OM'. No longer is Oi'' the equilibrium rate of interest, for now people feel that they possess CD surplus amount of money at the interest rate of Oi''. Accordingly they shift out of money into bonds, bidding the price of bonds up; but since this lowers the market rate of interest, eventually a new equilibrium will be established at Oi'''.

One point is worth noting. This analysis does not mean, as some have implied, that there will be a wholesale exodus from cash to bonds when the stock of money rises.[21] In fact, not many purchase offers may be necessary in order to raise the market price of bonds sufficiently to lower the rate of interest until a new equilibrium is established. For instance, there may be widespread knowledge of the increase in the money supply from OM to OM', and thus the present bond holders may respond immediately, or rather soon, by asking higher prices. In the extreme case the new equilibrium at Oi''' may be reached without any actual transfer of ownership of bonds. The higher market price may depress the market rate so quickly that no purchases and sales are actually made, though this is extremely unlikely.

Note finally that the interest rate may change even though the stock of money remains constant. The MM and LP curves in Figure 11–9 yield initially the equilibrium market rate of Oi. Now assume that the expectations of bondholders change because they fear a general con-

---

[21]Or from bonds to cash in the case of reductions in the money supply.

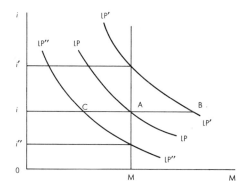

FIGURE 11–9

traction and/or that the prices of bonds in general are going to fall. They will thus want to add to their L_s balances as soon as possible; this is shown by a shift of the LP curve to LP'. Thus at Oi the demand for money exceeds the available supply by AB amount. In order to acquire extra cash balances of AB amount people will sell, or at least attempt to sell, bonds. But since this depresses bond prices, the market rate of interest will rise until a new equilibrium is established at Oi'. Conversely, if expectations change in the opposite direction, the LP curve falls to LP'', and as people attempt to shift out of money into bonds the new equilibrium rate of Oi'' is established. Observe that in both cases the stock of money remains constant and the adjustments are carried out via shifts in the liquidity preference function.

6. The Investment Demand Function

The liquidity preference theory of the interest rate must be put aside for now, and a concept that was discussed much earlier,[22] *the investment demand function,* must be reexamined. In the concluding section of this chapter (as well as in the next chapter) the two concepts— liquidity preference and investment demand—are thrown together into a broader analytical framework. For the moment, however, only the investment demand curve will be considered.

---

[22]See Chapter 7 of this text. For an excellent discussion, review of the literature, and bibliography, see R. Eisner and R. H. Strotz, "Determinants of Business Investment," Research Study Two in *Impacts of Monetary Policy.*

The earlier discussion of this particular cornerstone of the Keynesian analysis pointed out that the rate of investment will be higher or lower according to the relationship between the *cost* of capital goods and their *value*. If the cost is low, relative to the value, there is a strong stimulus to invest. On the other hand, if the cost is high, relative to value, the inducement or propensity to invest is weakened. This version of the investment demand function can be written as:

$$I = f(V, C),$$

where I stands for private net investment,[23] V for the value of the capital goods, and C for their cost.

An alternative way of saying the same thing takes into account *the marginal efficiency of investment and the interest rate.* If the marginal efficiency of investment (r) exceeds the rate of interest (i),[24] the inducement to invest is strong, while if it is less than the interest rate, there is no inducement to invest. Since in this approach the important

---

[23]Recall that investment means only private business investment. Thus, governmental investment, investment in "human capital," and investment in consumers' durables, including housing, are excluded.

[24]The term "marginal cost of acquiring funds" is both more general and accurate than simply the "interest rate." Quite often businesses, especially large-scale corporations, have access to internal sources of capital funds (retained earnings and depreciation reserves) and hence can in some measure avoid the external market (that is, selling securities and/or borrowing). However, a firm that uses its internal sources must pay some sort of interest rate, even though it is not an "explicit" cost. Rather it is an "implicit" or *opportunity cost.* If the firm decides to use its internal funds to finance (either in whole or in part) its own investment project, it thereby foregoes an alternative use of the funds, such as lending them out at a positive rate of interest, retiring debt, or financing some alternative project. In any event, so long as there is an alternative use for the funds (as there will be), the cost of using them for a particular project is what is given up by not using them in the *next best alternative.*

This cost, however, is generally low relative to the cost of raising funds by the sale of stock and bonds (for the typical corporation). We may presume that the opportunity cost of internal funds is around the yield on high grade bonds, or perhaps somewhere between this yield and the still lower yield on government securities. The reason for this is that the usual business is not in business for the purpose of playing the securities market, that is, speculating in other firms' securities. On this see J. S. Duesenberry, *Business Cycles and Economic Growth* (New York: McGraw-Hill Book Company, 1958), especially pp. 93-94. See also J. Meyer and E. Kuh, *The Investment Decision* (Cambridge: Harvard University Press, 1957), and several of the readings in *The Management of Corporate Capital*, ed. E. Solomon (Glencoe: The Free Press, 1959).

relationship is the one between the marginal efficiency of investment and the interest rate, the investment demand function may be written as

$$I = f(r,i).$$

Since the $I = f(V,C)$ approach has already been discussed (in Chapter 7), the alternative approach will be followed here.

The marginal efficiency of investment is really the rate of discount that makes the sum of the series of expected returns from an investment project equal to the replacement cost of the capital goods making up the project.[25] Thus, in the formula

$$C = \frac{R_1}{(1+r)} + \frac{R_2}{(1+r)^2} + \frac{R_3}{(1+r)^3} + \cdots + \frac{R_n}{(1+r)^n}$$

C stands for the *replacement cost* of the capital goods, the R's stand for the estimated series of proceeds expected from the investment, and r is the discount rate which equates the present value of the expected earnings to C. This discount rate, which is termed the *marginal efficiency of investment,* is thus the net percentage rate of return estimated to be earned on the planned investment. As Keynes put it:

> . . . I define the marginal efficiency of capital [investment] as being equal to the rate of discount which would make the present value of the series of annuities given by the returns expected from the capital-asset during its life just equal to its supply price.[26]

Consider, for example, a very simple case in which a business is contemplating an investment project that has an initial cost of $1,000, and the capital goods have an estimated life of only one year. Assume further that the R for this year is anticipated to be $1,200, and that the prevailing rate of interest is 5 per cent. Now the business has the alternative of sinking the $1,000 into the investment project or lending it out at the interest rate of 5 per cent. In this illustration the best alternative is quite obvious.[27] If the $1,000 is loaned out, it will bring in an interest income of $50. But if the $1,000 is invested in the project, it will yield

---

[25]Keynes, *The General Theory,* p. 135. "Over against the prospective yield of the investment we have the *supply price* of the capital asset, meaning by this, not the market price at which the asset . . . can actually be purchased in the market, but the price which would just induce a manufacturer newly to produce an additional unit of such assets, *i.e.,* what is sometimes called its replacement cost."

[26]*Ibid.*

[27]See Solomon, *The Management of Corporate Capital,* for alternative methods of dealing with far more complicated and realistic cases.

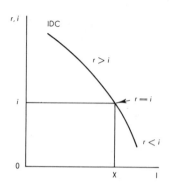

FIGURE 11–10

a net return of $200. In other words, the marginal efficiency of invest-
ment (r) is 20 per cent. That is:

$$C = \frac{R_1}{(1+r)}$$

$$\$1,000 - \frac{\$1,200}{(1+r)}$$

$$\$1,000 = \frac{\$1,200}{(1+.20)} \;.$$

The important thing to note is that so long as $r > i$, the investment
project is worthwhile to the business, for it will yield a net return
greater than the interest return, or alternatively, the cost of borrowing
the $1,000. On the other hand, if $r < i$, the project will be rejected and
the funds will be loaned out (or not borrowed) or held as idle balances
(depending on the firm's liquidity preference). Thus so long as the
marginal efficiency expected from the capital equipment exceeds the interest rate, the purchase of the equipment is worthwhile, but if it is less
than the rate of interest, the capital goods will not be acquired.[28]

Obviously for each firm in the economy there will be a number of
alternative investment projects, some of which will be more profitable
than others, and these projects will be ranked according to the degree
of profitability. The result is a negatively sloped investment demand
curve (that is, marginal efficiency of investment curve), as shown in
Figure 11–10. For this firm, given the interest rate of Oi, the investment projects to the left of X are characterized by $r > i$, and since these

---

[28]Keynes, *The General Theory*, pp. 136–37.

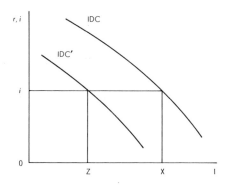

FIGURE 11–11

are profitable to the firm they will, *ceteris paribus*, be carried out. But for the projects to the right of X, $i>r$, and these will be rejected. Thus, given the marginal efficiency of investment curve (that is, the investment demand curve) and the rate of interest, investment by the firm will be carried out to the point where $r = i$.

The marginal efficiency curves of all the firms in the economy can then be summed up, giving an aggregate investment demand curve.[29] The aggregate investment function, however, is very volatile, primarily because of the role of expectations in the investment decisions of businessmen. The series of R's is nothing more than estimates by businessmen as to what the flow of proceeds will be over time, and since the future is uncertain, they are little better than "guesstimates."

Thus, the investment demand curve is subject to sudden shifts as expectations are revised or undergo rapid change. During a period of expansion, for example, when expectations become quite optimistic, the investment demand curve will shift to the right. Rising consumer and business demand makes projects which had formerly been rejected now appear to be profitable. But as the expansion continues, certain forces (whether real or imagined) begin to build up and to depress the psychological expectations of businessmen. Disillusion sets in, and the

> . . . disillusion comes because doubts suddenly arise concerning the reliability of the prospective yield, perhaps because the current yield shows some sign of falling off, as the stock of newly produced durable goods steadily increases. If current costs of production are thought to be higher than they will be later on, that will be a further reason for a

---

[29]*Ibid.*, p. 136.

fall in the marginal efficiency of capital [investment]. Once doubt begins it spreads rapidly.[30]

Consider, for example, Figure 11–11, where adverse expectations shift the investment demand curve as far left as IDC'. Given the rate of interest O*i*, planned investment will slump to OZ. However, is there not monetary policy—especially a reduction in the rate of interest—that will prevent investment from falling so low? Cannot, in fact, the interest rate be reduced enough to stimulate more investment spending and thus reverse the contraction? Keynes' position on this is quite clear. He argues that while later on a "decline in the rate of interest will be a great aid to recovery and, probably, a necessary condition for it," in the early stages of the contraction "the collapse in the marginal efficiency of capital may be so complete that no practicable reduction in the rate of interest will be enough."[31] What would be necessary is some action that would stimulate businessmen's expectations to bring about a "return to confidence," though it is not always clear how to achieve this result. As Keynes put it, ". . . it is not so easy to revive the marginal efficiency of capital, determined, as it is, by the uncontrollable and disobedient psychology of the business world."[32]

7.   Problems in the Calculation of the Marginal Efficiency of Investment

In reality, of course, businessmen find it quite difficult to calculate the expected value of an investment project or, alternatively, its marginal efficiency. Thus, insofar as the curves of individual business firms are based on imperfect calculations, the same limitations are relevant for the aggregate curve. But why is the value or marginal efficiency of an investment project so difficult to calculate?

For one thing, there is the problem of estimating the series of expected returns. When the project is designed to yield earnings beyond one or two years, management finds it more and more difficult to estimate the expected annual returns in the later years.[33] There are many variables that will change future revenue and operating costs, and these

---

[30]*Ibid.*, p. 317.

[31]*Ibid.*, p. 316.

[32]*Ibid.*, p. 317. See also p. 320, where he concludes: "In conditions of *laissez-faire* the avoidance of wide fluctuations in employment may, therefore, prove impossible without far-reaching change in the psychology of investment markets such as there is no reason to expect. I conclude that the duty of ordering the current volume of investment cannot safely be left in private hands."

[33]On this, see G. L. S. Shackle, "The Interest Elasticity of Investment," Chapter 3 in *The Theory of Interest Rates*, eds. Hahn and Brechling. See also M. Shubik, "Approaches to the Study of Decision-Making Relevant to the Firm," *Journal of Business*, April 1961.

cannot possibly be known in advance. Among these are changes in the level and structure of consumer tastes, changes in relative factor-input prices, changes in the level of investment spending itself, the introduction of substitute and complementary products, alterations in the structure and quality of the capital stock, monetary and fiscal policy that will alter the money supply and the rate of interest, and so on. Thus it is that Keynes concludes:

> The outstanding fact is the extreme precariousness of the basis of knowledge on which our estimates of prospective yield have to be made. Our knowledge of the factors which will govern the yield of an investment some years hence is usually slight and often negligable. If we speak frankly, we have to admit that our basis of knowledge for estimating the yield ten years hence of a railway, a copper mine, a textile factory, the goodwill of a patent medicine, an Atlantic liner, a building in the City of London amounts to little and sometimes nothing; or even five years hence.[34]

Still, some sort of estimate must be made, even though it is necessarily rough and subject to later revision. Keynes argues that for the most part such estimates are made primarily on the basis of the recent past and the present, "our usual practice being to take the existing situation and to project it into the future, modified only to the extent that we have more or less definite reasons for expecting a change."[35]

Whatever may be thought of this procedure, obviously it leaves a good deal of room for error. Moreover, once the general economic situation begins moving one way or another, the errors tend to become cumulative,[36] at least for a while. For example, if an expansion begins, then the recent past and the present point to further expansion, and expectations become buoyant. However, this cumulative process cannot and will not go on indefinitely; much depends upon the degree of confidence with which expectations are held—"on how highly we rate the

---

[34]Keynes, *The General Theory*, pp. 149-50. It is for this reason that the majority of firms in the United States seem to rely primarily on the "payback" method of estimating the worth of an investment project. (See W. W. Heller, "The Anatomy of Investment Decisions," *Harvard Business Review*, March 1951, p. 99, where Heller concludes: "Firm capital investment plans are typically limited to a few months. Quick and unpredicted changes in such plans are the order of the day.")

The payback method concludes that if a project recovers its *original* cost by or within an arbitrarily selected time period, it is a worthwhile venture. Two to three years seems to be the commonly accepted period. The major difficulty with this method is that it does not allow the *ranking* of projects according to their profitability, for it ignores completely the time flow of annual proceeds beyond the payback period. For several critical discussions of this method, see Solomon, *The Management of Corporate Capital.*

[35]Keynes, *The General Theory*, p. 148.

[36]Compare this with Marshall's and Pigou's psychological theories of the cycle (Chapter 8).

likelihood of our best forecast turning out quite wrong. If we expect
later changes but are very uncertain as to what precise form these
changes will take, then our confidence will be weak."[37] As pointed out
above, changing expectations cause the marginal efficiency curve to
shift, often widely and unpredictably.

Another problem that arises in connection with the calculation of the
series of expected returns relates to the replacement price of the already
existing capital assets owned by the firm.[38] Recall that capital goods are
not homogeneous, even though for convenience's sake we translate them
into the common denominator of the dollar.[39] In reality, capital goods
are quite heterogeneous; more than that, the new capital equipment
acquired by a firm is worked in conjunction with the firm's already existing capital assets. Most capital goods are indeed complementary.[40]
For example, assume that a firm is contemplating the acquisition of a
certain capital good which will increase output, but which must be
worked in conjunction with certain other capital assets. Obviously the
lower the replacement costs of these existing complementary assets, the
higher the series of expected returns will be.[41] Thus capital prices, as
well as operating costs, must enter into the calculation of the series of
expected earnings when there is capital complementarity. As L. M.
Lachman has put it:

> New capital goods are being used in combination with existing ones.
> This form of complementarity means that the lower the price of existing
> capital goods the greater the profitability of new ones. . . . In the real
> world . . . entrepreneurs have to combine buildings, plants, equipment,
> etc., and the success of the production plans embodying these combina-
> tions determines how long they will be maintained . . . it is surely
> plain that . . . the rate of profit on each capital good depends on the
> cost at which complementary goods can be secured. . . . The lower the
> latter the higher the former.[42]

Another aspect of the complementarity of capital goods relates to the
age structure of the existing capital stock. The prospective yield of a
piece of capital equipment depends, among other things, on the age

[37]Keynes, *The General Theory,* p. 148.

[38]Not the replacement cost of the capital goods to be newly acquired, but the
replacement cost of the capital assets already owned by the firm.

[39]See Chapter 4 for a further discussion of this.

[40]This point has been stressed by L. M. Lachman, *Capital and Its Structure*
(London: G. Bell and Sons, Ltd., 1956). See also E. G. Furubotn, "Investment
Alternatives and the Supply Schedule of the Firm" *Southern Economic Journal,*
July 1964.

[41]See Lachman, *Capital and Its Structure,* pp. 43-48, for a discussion of more
complicated situations.

[42]*Ibid.,* pp. 59-60.

and thus the efficiency of the complementary capital assets with which it will be worked. If these are rather old, their operating costs may be high, and therefore the series of expected returns will be lower. On the other hand, if the age of the existing equipment is less, then, *ceteris paribus*, the series of expected returns will be higher.[43]

Closely related to this is the problem of replacement investment. As noted in Chapter 4, this type of investment constitutes a growing share of total investment. Now if worn-out capital equipment is to be replaced with capital goods that embody technical advancement, then the series of expected returns of new capital assets will be higher. Moreover, even though the new capital good is low-priced, it may not fit well with some of the existing equipment. If nevertheless it is acquired, then some of the existing assets must be either junked or sold, and there is therefore a sort of obsolescence effect that must be taken into account.[44]

All told, the estimation of the series of expected returns is indeed very complicated and hazardous. At best only a sophisticated guess, subject to future revision, can be made. Problems arise with respect to the uncertain future behavior of demand, operating costs, and so on, as well as with respect to the replacement costs of existing assets and the degree of complementarity of capital goods.

But there are still further difficulties, this time on the side of the interest rate. In order to calculate the value of an investment project the series of expected returns must be calculated back to the present at the "prevailing rate of interest." However, just as the series of expected returns is difficult to estimate, so is the rate of interest which should be used. Should the businessman use the rate of interest that actually prevails today, or should he attempt to look into the future to see, as best he can, what the rate of interest will be six months or a year from now? Some judgment as to what will happen to the rate of interest in the future must be made in order to ascertain the value of the project today as compared to the value of the project some months hence. But this entails making estimates of the future behavior of aggregate investment, what will happen to the money supply as a result of monetary and fiscal policies, and changes in individuals' and businesses' desires to hold money for various reasons.[45] It seems that while the "prevailing rate of interest" serves as a link between the present and the future, the link is indeed rather tenuous.

---

[43]*Ibid.*; see also Duesenberry, *Business Cycles and Economic Growth,* pp. 59-60.

[44]See M. Frankl, "Obsolescence and Technological Change in a Maturing Economy," *American Economic Review,* June 1955.

[45]Keynes, *The General Theory,* pp. 202-204.

Perhaps we should note also that the "prevailing rate of interest" is not the same thing for all firms. Consider, for example, two firms, one large and the other small, in the same industry. Assume that each is contemplating precisely identical investment projects; that is, they each estimate the same series of expected returns. Their difference in size, however, creates possibly different values of the project. In this case the value may well be higher for the large firm than for the small one. The reason for this is that the large firm may acquire funds at a lower marginal cost than the small business. This is especially so if the large business can make use of its internal sources of funds. Indeed, if both firms have to turn to the external market for funds, the large firm is probably in a more favorable position since it is better known in the market, has better securities-marketing contacts, and so on, allowing it to raise the funds at a lower cost than the small firm can raise them. This will especially be true if the large firm has a good earnings record and has hitherto built up a policy of using its retained earnings for investment purposes. As W. J. Baumol has observed:

> The magnitude of the firm's own accumulation affects the amount which it can borrow. An increase in its own funds makes it easier to get money elsewhere. Wealth attracts wealth, and so some firms find themselves more richly endowed with money capital than others. . . . this divides them into imperfectly competing groups among which there is occasional migration by merger, or by other means of combining small capital stocks into large ones.[46]

Thus the large firm, with the lower marginal cost of acquiring funds, will calculate a higher value for the capital equipment than the small one, even under otherwise similar circumstances.

8. Monetary Policy, the Interest Rate, and Investment

In this section the liquidity preference analysis and the investment analysis developed in the preceding sections are put together. The discussion, however, is brief and is designed simply to serve as an introduction to the more important analysis of Part 5.

To begin with, assume that there is less than full employment, but that given the prevailing rate of interest the business community is in an equilibrium position with respect to investment. Thus in Figure

---

[46]W. J. Baumol, *Business Behavior, Value, and Growth* (New York: The Macmillan Company, 1959), p. 34. See also D. C. Corner and A. Williams, "The Sensitivity of Business to Initial and Investment Allowances," *Economica*, February 1965.

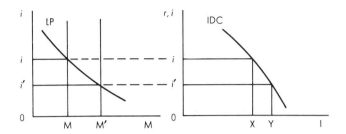

FIGURE 11-12

11-12 investment is at OX and the interest rate is O*i*, given by the stock of money OM, the liquidity preference schedule LP, and the marginal efficiency schedule IDC. Under these circumstances the monetary authorities may decide to lower the rate of interest in order to stimulate more investment spending. To do this, they engage in open-market operations—in this case, purchases of government securities which are designed to increase the money supply. If the stock of money rises to OM′, then the equilibrium rate of interest will fall to O*i*′, resulting in a movement down the investment demand curve so that investment spending rises to OY. In short, monetary policy in periods of less than full employment is designed (in large part) to lower the rate of interest so that investment spending will rise. This is not the end of the story, however, but only the beginning, for the rise in investment increases income, which in turn increases consumption, and so on. The later chapters spell out what the repercussions may be.

Even so, at this stage it is possible to point out certain forces that may reduce the effectiveness of monetary policy. For one thing, business expectations may be so perverse that the cut in the interest rate is accompanied by a fall in the marginal efficiency schedule. This is shown in Figure 11-13, where the schedule shifts to the left to IDC′, in which case the reduction in the rate of interest fails to stimulate any increase in investment spending. Note, however, that if the schedule were to fall anyhow, the reduction in the interest rate keeps investment from falling as much as it otherwise would.

There is a second thing to consider, namely, the "liquidity trap." Assume that the liquidity preference curve has the shape shown in Figure 11-14, and that the stock of money is OM. Now, any further increase in the money supply will fail to lower the rate of interest. The reason for this is that the rate is so low that people would rather hold their extra cash balances than to part with them for such a low interest return. How important the liquidity trap is in reality is a matter of con-

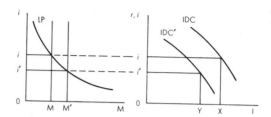

FIGURE 11–13

jecture and prevailing conditions, though its possible existence in a severe contraction should not be ignored.

Finally consider the fact that in its lower stretches the marginal efficiency schedule may be very inelastic with respect to changes in the
rate of interest. This is shown in Figure 11–15, where a reduction in the
rate of interest stimulates precious little net investment spending. Again
it is a matter of empirical conditions and observations as to what the
shape, as well as the changing position, of the curve may be at any particular point in time.[47]

Enough has been said to demonstrate that a reduction in the interest
rate in a period of contraction may not be effective. The reduction may
be accompanied by a leftward shift of the investment demand curve,
which in turn may be very inelastic in its lower stretches. Further, if
there is a liquidity trap, there is the outside possibility of the monetary
authorities' being unable to reduce the rate of interest. In short, "there's

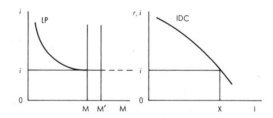

FIGURE 11–14

[47]See Eisner and Strotz, "Determinants of Business Investment," especially pp.
117-92, for a review of empirical studies on the interest rate and other variables as
determinants of investment. For a theoretical discussion of the interest elasticity of
the investment function, see R. Turvey, "Does the Rate of Interest Rule the Roost?"
Chapter 9 in *The Theory of Interest Rates,* eds. Hahn and Brechling.

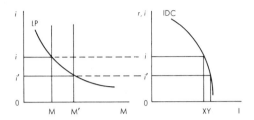

FIGURE 11—15

many a slip twixt cup and lip" when monetary policy is put into effect. But this anticipates later discussion, so let us now move on to the next logical step, namely, the analysis of changes in the level of income and employment.

9. Summary

In this chapter we have examined the liquidity preference theory of the interest rate and the investment demand function. The liquidity preference theory concludes that the rate of interest is determined by the demand for money (the LP curve) and the stock of money. A change in one of these curves, relative to the other, changes the interest rate. The demand for money is based upon the transactions, precautionary, and speculative motives, while the supply of money is institutionally determined.

The demand for transactions and precautionary balances is primarily a positive function of the level of income, and the demand for speculative balances is a function of the interest rate. The aggregate LP curve is negatively sloped, illustrating some interest elasticity. Thus an increase in the money supply will lower the rate of interest as people and businesses strive to shift out of money into bonds; conversely, a reduction in the money supply will raise the rate of interest. This is, for Keynes, the major rationale of monetary policy—namely, to change the rate of interest according to the general economic environment.

The investment demand curve also has a negative slope, showing that a reduction in the rate of interest will, *ceteris paribus,* stimulate some net investment. The *ceteris paribus* assumption, however, is important, for the investment demand curve is subject to sudden, unpredictable shifts as managerial expectations undergo revision. But, given the investment demand curve and the liquidity preference curve, an increase (reduction) in the money supply will decrease (increase) the rate of interest, and this in turn will increase (decrease) investment.

QUESTIONS

11-1. "The marginal cost of capital can always be measured by the prevailing rate of interest." Comment.

11-2. In modern theory the interest rate may be defined as an "opportunity cost." Explain.

11-3. Some economists have concluded that the demand for transactions and precautionary balances displays some interest elasticity. Explain how in a period of "tight" monetary policy the demand for these two types of balances may become rather interest elastic.

11-4. Discuss in detail the inverse relationship between the price of a bond and the interest rate on that bond. Can the analysis be extended to stock prices and dividend rates?

11-5. Show diagrammatically how an increase in the money supply will, given the community's LP curve, result in a lower interest rate. Explain the adjustment on a step by step basis.

11-6. What is meant by the "liquidity trap"? Did Keynes attach much significance to it?

11-7. Discuss in as much detail as possible some of the difficulties involved in the calculation of the marginal efficiency schedule. Do these difficulties vitiate the use of the marginal efficiency schedule as an analytical tool? Explain.

11-8. Explain diagrammatically the potential relationships between the money supply, the interest rate, and investment. Will an increase in the money supply, given the liquidity preference schedule, always result in a rise in investment? Elaborate!

Bibliography

Baumol, W. J., "The Transactions Demand for Cash: An Inventory Theoretic Approach," *Quarterly Journal of Economics,* November 1952.

Eisner, R. and R. H. Strotz, "Determinants of Business Investment," Research Study Two in *Impacts of Monetary Policy.* Englewood Cliffs, N. J.: Prentice-Hall, Inc., 1963.

Hahn, F. H. and F. P. R. Brechling, eds., *The Theory of Interest Rates.* London: The Macmillan Company, 1965.

Hansen, A. H., *A Guide to Keynes.* New York: McGraw-Hill Book Company, 1953.

Johnson, H. G., "Monetary Theory and Policy," *American Economic Review,* June 1962.

Keynes, J. M., *The General Theory of Employment, Interest, and Money.* New York: Harcourt, Brace & World, Inc., 1936.

Lachman, L. M., *Capital and Its Structure.* London: G. Bell and Sons, Ltd., 1956.

Solomon, E., ed., *The Management of Corporate Capital.* Glencoe: The Free Press, 1959.

Tarshis, L., "The Elasticity of the Marginal Efficiency Function," *American Economic Review,* December 1961.

Tobin, J., "The Interest Elasticity of the Transactions Demand for Cash," *Review of Economics and Statistics,* August 1956.

———, "Liquidity Preference and Monetary Policy," *Review of Economics and Statistics,* May 1947.

———, "Money, Capital, and Other Stores of Value," *American Economic Review,* May 1961.

12

The Multiplier,
Accelerator, and
Income Level Changes

In this chapter the multiplier concept is considered in some detail for two important reasons. In the first place, it pulls together and integrates the other components of the Keynesian analysis—the consumption function, the investment demand function, and the liquidity preference function. Thus in an important sense the multiplier represents a culmination of what has been discussed so far in this part. Second, a grasp of the multiplier concept is essential for understanding many modern cycle theories which make use of this important tool.

We shall also consider the acceleration principle in some detail, because several modern theories of the cycle also rely heavily upon the interaction of the multiplier and accelerator in accounting for the cyclical process. Although Keynes himself did not make use of the acceleration principle, the concept has assumed an important role in post-Keynesian discussions of cycle and growth theory. Finally, at the close of the chapter, one of the more popular and widely discussed theories that makes use of the multiplier-accelerator interaction will be examined.

1. The Concept of the Multiplier

In 1931 the British economist R. F. Kahn observed that an increment in investment spending results in a magnified increment in the level of income.[1] Although this was certainly no new discovery, Kahn was the first to state the relationship in fairly rigorous, analytical terms. Obviously most of the cycle theories surveyed earlier (in Part 2) stress this "multiplier effect" of a rise in investment on the level of income, but for the most part the relationship was stated rather loosely. Kahn, however, formalized it and thus set the stage for further development of this concept by Keynes in *The General Theory*. And of course there have been important post-Keynesian modifications in the multiplier analysis.

Like many of the theoretical concepts discussed thus far, the multiplier effect is usually stated in terms of an equation. At this juncture, it is best to recall the distinction between identity and behavior equations, especially since the multiplier can be stated in terms of either.[2] Subsequent discussion, however, will reveal that it is best explained and discussed as a behavioral equation.

A. Identity Equation of the Multiplier

Consider first the identity equation of the multiplier. For the sake of illustration, assume that there is a given investment demand curve and that the rate of interest has been reduced via monetary action. This results in net, new investment of, say $100.[3] The question now is what effect will this net, new investment have on the level of income? Earlier cycle theorists of course recognized that the effect would be expansionary, but the multiplier analysis (*á la* Kahn and Keynes) attempts

---

[1] R. F. Kahn, "The Relation of Home Investment to Unemployment," *Economic Journal*, June 1931, reprinted as Chapter 15 in *Readings in Business Cycles and National Income*, eds. A. H. Hansen and R. V. Clemence (New York: W. W. Norton & Company, Inc., 1953). For a good critical review of the multiplier concept, see H. Hegeland, *The Multiplier Theory* (Gleerup, 1954). See also R. Goodwin, "Secular and Cyclical Aspects of the Multiplier and Accelerator," in *Income, Employment, and Public Policy: Essays in Honor of Alvin H. Hansen* (New York: W. W. Norton & Company, 1948); and R. Turvey, "The Multiplier," *Economic Journal*, November 1948, and "Some Notes on the Multiplier Theory," *American Economic Review*, June 1953.

[2] See Chapter 9 for a discussion of this distinction.

[3] The discussion in the rest of this chapter assumes that all figures are in constant dollar terms—that is, price level changes are "corrected" for.

to provide a precise statement of the effect. Rather than simply concluding that the net, new investment will increase the income level, the multiplier analysis is designed to tell *by how much the income level will rise.*

Let us carry the illustration further. Assume that the *marginal* propensity to consume for the economy as a whole is .75. Assume further that the consumption function is linear in the relevant range and remains constant. Also assume that the increment in investment mentioned above remains constant at $100. Finally, suppose that at the beginning of the example Y is $1000, C is $850, and I is $150. Thus S is also $150.

The rise in investment increases income by $100, since total income equals consumption plus investment, and this in turn raises consumption by $75. Since we have the identity $Y = C+I$, the $75 increase in consumption is the same thing as a $75 increase in income, and this in turn further raises consumption (and hence income) by $56.25 (that is, .75 of the income increment of $75). The process continues, each increase being 75 per cent of the previous income increase. Thus we have

$$\triangle Y = \triangle I + \triangle C_1 + \triangle C_2 + \triangle C_3 + \cdots + \triangle C_n,$$

where each $\triangle C$ signifies a further increase in consumption and income. In our numerical example,

$$\triangle Y = \$100 + \$75 + \$56.25 + \$42.19 + \cdots$$

Note that each income increment is 25 per cent smaller than the preceding increment because of the marginal propensity to save of .25. In other words 25 per cent of each income increase does not reenter the spending stream, but rather is held out in the form of savings.

There is still the question of determining the precise extent of the multiplier effect. The last formula above is for an infinite geometric progression, and may be rewritten more generally as

$$\triangle Y = \triangle I[1+.75+(.75)^2+(.75)^3+ \cdots +(.75)^n] = \triangle I \cdot \frac{1}{1-.75}.$$

That is, the *multiplier effect* (the change in income, $\triangle Y$, resulting from the net investment $\triangle I$) is the change in investment times $\dfrac{1}{1-\frac{\triangle C}{\triangle Y}}$. In the

literature $\dfrac{1}{1-\frac{\triangle C}{\triangle Y}}$ is usually written as k and is called the *multiplier.*

Thus the multiplier *effect* is[4] $\triangle Y = k \cdot \triangle I.$

---

[4]The symbol k is used to refer to the *multiplier.* The *multiplier effect,* on the other hand, is the final change in the income level.

This however, is an identity equation, and though it allows a quick calculation of the final effect on the income level, it does not reveal anything about the *process of adjustment* involved. Indeed the preceding example is nothing more than an illustration of the arithmetic of the multiplier analysis and is certainly not an example of the analysis of the process of economic change. It indicates that a change in investment can cause income to change from a given level to a new and calculable level, but it does not shed much light on *how* the change takes place. A far more relevant and useful approach is to consider the multiplier effect from the behavioral point of view. This is the task of the next subsection.

B. The Behavioral Approach to the Multiplier

Actually several behavioral equtaions are relevant here. First there is the investment function $I = f(r,i)$, that is, investment is a function of the marginal efficiency of investment and the interest rate.[5] Second, there is the liquidity preference function $i = f(M, LP)$, that is, the interest rate is a function of the stock of money and the community's liquidity preference schedule. Third, there is the consumption function $C = f(Y)$. However, in the case of the consumption function there is need for modification. Following D. H. Robertson, we shall introduce a *time lag* into the function and make consumption of the present period a function of the income of the preceding period.[6] Thus the consumption function is written as $C_t = f(Y_{t-1})$, where t stands for the present period and t—1 stands for the preceding period.

The lagged consumption function has a great deal more relevance for consumption behavior since it asserts that consumers do not spend their income increases immediately upon receipt but rather defer their spending decisions for a short time. After this time has elapsed, they adjust their consumption to their new income position. Note that this approach to the consumption function does not assert that consumers wait to determine what their marginal propensity to consume will be—this is already known. The reason for the hesitation is that they need some time, even if only a short period, to determine how they are going to allocate

---

[5]As we shall see shortly, the investment demand function can be expanded to include Y—that is, $I = f(r, i,Y)$. However, for the moment we are concerned only with first approximation. The more general function is discussed in sections 4-5.

[6]D. H. Robertson, "Some Notes on Mr. Keynes' General Theory of Employment," *Quarterly Journal of Economics*, November 1936. See also G. Ackley, "The Multiplier Time Period," *American Economic Review*, June 1951.

their increased income between different goods and services. The problem facing them is not how much more they are going to spend on consumers' goods but rather how the increased expenditures are to be divided between the different goods and services available to them in the market.[7]

The analysis still assumes that the consumption function is linear and nonshifting, at least over the relevant range of time and income. One reason for this is that it is difficult to calculate the multiplier effect when the consumption function is curvilinear and shifting. More important, however, the assumption of the linear function appears to be realistic on both *a priori* and empirical grounds; and the assumption of the function's "staying put" in the short run does not seem strained, barring any significant changes in the other determinants of consumption.

One final point on the consumption function. It is now necessary to distinguish between *desired* consumption and *actual* consumption as well as between *desired* and *actual* savings. So long as actual and desired consumption are equal, so that consumers are realizing their spending plans, and so long as desired and actual savings are equal (that is, consumers are actually saving what they desire to save), then consumers are in an equilibrium position. In this event, they will not alter their existing savings-consumption allocation out of current income unless something occurs to disturb either their current income or their plans. If such a disturbance does occur, consumers will attempt to re-establish their equilibrium position. The major advantage of this behavioral approach is that it focuses attention squarely on the equilibrating process of adjustment.

So much for the assumptions relevant to the consumption function. There is need now to be more explicit about investment, though we may be relatively brief. For sake of illustration assume that, given the marginal efficiency of investment, a drop in the interest rate stimulates net, new investment. The interest rate reduction stems from an increase in the stock of money, given the liquidity preference schedule.[8] Important for present purposes is the further assumption that the net, new investment remains constant over successive time periods. In other words, there is an expenditure of, say, $10 in each successive period. Thus when the new investment project of $10 is completed at the end of period 1, a new project of $10 takes its place at the beginning of period 2. The

---

[7] L. Metzler, in his "Three Lags in the Circular Flow of Income," in *Income, Employment, and Public Policy: Essays in Honor of Alvin H. Hansen*, argues that the lag in the consumption function is quite short.

[8] There may, of course, also be autonomous investment. See Chapter 7, and section 7 below.

reason for this unrealistic assumption is that it permits detailed examination of the complete multiplier effect of the new investment. In subsequent discussion this assumption will be relaxed.[9]

One final point on investment. Just as we distinguished between plans and their realization in the consumption function, we now distinguish between *planned* and *actual* investment. An equilibrium position for the businesses in the economy exists when planned and actual investment are equal, for in this case business will have no incentive to reduce or increase their investment expenditures. If there is, on the other hand, an inequality between the two, businesses will respond by trying to bring them back into an equilibrium relationship.

For the economy as a whole, equilibrium prevails when both consumers and businesses are in their respective equilibrium positions, and when desired and realized savings and investment are equal. This equilibrium condition is shown in Figure 12–1. What it signifies is that con-

$$
\begin{array}{ccc}
\text{Actual Investment} & = & \text{Actual Savings} \\
\parallel & & \parallel \\
\text{Desired Investment} & = & \text{Desired Savings}
\end{array}
$$

The Savings-Investment Equilibrium

FIGURE 12–1

sumers are withholding from the spending stream the amount of savings that businesses desire and actually are putting back into the spending stream via the investment process. So long as both consumers and businesses are realizing their plans, and so long as investment equals savings, then aggregate demand equals aggregate supply, and the level of income will remain constant. An illustration of the multiplier effect, based in part on the assumptions given above, will reveal why this is so.

2.   An Illustration of the Multiplier Effect

A word of caution before we get into the illustration: there is no precise specification of what income concept is used in the example, that is, whether it is gross or net national product, national income, or disposable income. This deficiency is made up in the next section. For the

---

[9]Note the implicit assumption that the length of each time period is determined by the length of time consumers take to make their decisions.

present only a first approximation is developed; qualifications and complications are reserved until later.

This illustration is based on the following further conditions.

1. In period 0 there exists an equilibrium situation where desired and actual savings are equal, where desired and actual investment are equal, and where investment equals savings. The hypothetical figures are Y = \$100, C = \$90, and S and I are each equal to \$10. Thus that part of income which is not devoted to consumption reenters the spending stream via investment. In this equilibrium situation both consumers and businesses are satisfied with their respective positions, given the level of Y.

2. The marginal propensity to consume is .75 and remains constant throughout the adjustment process. The consumption function has a one period lag, so that consumption of any one period is a function of the income of the previous period. Accordingly, any rise in consumption between, say, periods 2 and 3 is a function of the rise in income between periods 1 and 2. Since the marginal propensity to consume is .75, the marginal propensity to save is .25. This is also assumed to remain constant, and just as there is a lag in the consumption function, so is there a lag in the savings function.

3. Finally, in period 1 there occurs net, new investment by the amount of \$10 and this remains constant. Recall the assumption above that the net investment results from an increase in the stock of money, which, given the liquidity preference schedule, lowers the rate of interest, and that this, in turn, increases investment by \$10, given the investment demand curve.

The effect of the net investment is shown in Table 12–1 and Figure 12–2. The net investment of period 1 disturbs the equilibrium inherited from period 0. Whereas before both actual and desired consumption were equal, and thus actual and desired savings were equal (in period 0), a disequilibrium now prevails in period 1. The net, new investment increases income in period 1 by \$10; and this will affect both consumption and savings. But recall that because of the lag in the consumption function, *the income increment goes directly into actual savings.* To be sure, the community's desired propensity to consume is .75 (and hence its desired marginal propensity to save is .25), and thus \$7.50 of the \$10 income increase is earmarked for additional consumption and \$2.50 is earmarked for additional savings. However, consumers will allow some time to elapse before they determine how the \$7.50 earmarked for additional consumption is to be allocated between different commodities and services. Until this decision is made, the \$7.50 is held in actual

TABLE 12–1

A Hypothetical Example of the Multiplier

Period	Y	$\triangle Y$	I	C	$\triangle C$	Savings Desired	Savings Actual	Excess of Actual over Desired
0	100.00	—	10.00	90.00	—	10.00	10.00	0.00
1	110.00	10.00	20.00	90.00	0.00	12.50	20.00	7.50
2	117.50	7.50	20.00	97.50	7.50	14.38	20.00	5.62
3	123.12	5.62	20.00	103.12	5.62	15.78	20.00	4.22
4	127.34	4.22	20.00	107.34	4.22	16.83	20.00	3.17
5	130.51	3.17	20.00	110.51	3.17	17.63	20.00	2.37
n	140.00	0.00	20.00	120.00	0.00	20.00	20.00	0.00

a. I $=$ original investment
b. I_n $=$ net, new investment
c. C $=$ original consumption
d. $\triangle C =$ change in consumption in each period.

savings, though it is really considered by consumers to be "excess" savings. Given their marginal propensity to save of .25, they desire to add only $2.50 to their savings. But until they make their consumption decision, they are actually holding the entire amount of $10 in savings. This means that they have an "excess" of $7.50 over the *desired total* savings of $12.50 (the latter amount being the original savings of $10 plus the additional $2.50 allocated to savings out of the income increment).

During the period in which consumers are deciding on which goods and services to spend their additional savings of $7.50, the actual marginal propensity to consume falls to zero. That is, even though income in period 1 has risen by $10, consumption in the same period remains constant. Thus the marginal propensity to consume is actually zero, while the marginal propensity to save is actually unity. However, there is no basic discrepancy here—the consumers desire to maintain the marginal propensity to consume of .75 and in fact will do so once they make their consumption decision and release the "excess" actual savings of $7.50 into the consumption spending stream. When this is done, the consumers restore their equilibrium position—that is, they increase their consumption by $7.50, leaving the additional $2.50 in their savings. After they have accomplished this, their total savings will be equal to their desired savings at $12.50, and their actual and desired consumption expenditures will be equal at $97.50.

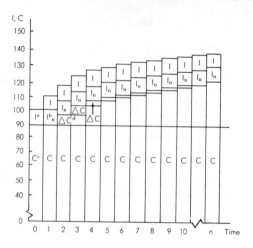

FIGURE 12–2

However, this new equilibrium position is quite temporary (so temporary in fact that it is not even recorded in Table 12–1), for by increasing consumption expenditures the consumers have also increased income by the same amount ($7.50), bringing total income up to $117.50. Once they receive this additional income, consumers discover that their actual savings again exceed their desired savings. And in period 2 the same process is repeated. Consumers desire to allocate the additional $7.50 between additional savings of $1.88 (that is, 25 per cent of the income increment) and additional consumption of $5.62 (that is, 75 per cent of the extra income). The lag in the consumption function, however, means that the additional income will be held in actual savings for a while. But once consumers decide how they are going to spend their $5.62, consumption expenditures will rise in period 3, and again consumers are in a temporary equilibrium—their desired and actual savings are equal at $14.38. Again, however, their effort to restore themselves to an equilibrium position raises the income level, so that once more actual savings exceed desired savings.

The same process will continue through subsequent periods until eventually a new equilibrium is reached. There are a few points about this analysis, however, that should be noted.

First, so long as the marginal propensity to consume remains constant at .75, and the marginal propensity to save at .25, each subsequent income increase is only 75 per cent of the preceding increase. The reason for this is that each time a new income increment is generated, 25 per cent of it is held in the form of savings. Thus the income increment in period 1 was $10, while it was $7.50 in period 2, $5.62 in period 3, and so on. This implies that eventually the income increase will taper off and stabilize at a new equilibrium level of income. We will return to this in a moment.

Second, note that during any one period actual investment equals actual savings (always at $20, in our example). This is sometimes confusing, for it is often stated that a necessary condition for an equilibrium level of income is simply S = I. Recall, however, that even though *actual* savings may (in fact, must) be equal to *actual* investment, there is *no necessary equality between desired and actual savings*. Until consumers are actually saving what they desire to save, consumption (and hence income) will continue to rise—but by successively smaller increments. Since desired savings rise by 25 per cent of the preceding income increase, income will continue to rise until finally desired savings equal actual savings. This should be self-evident, because as long as actual savings are larger than desired savings, consumption will continue to rise. Thus the accounting identity S = I is not analytically meaningful. What is analytically meaningful is the equality between desired and realized savings, on the one hand, and desired and realized investment, on the other. This equality materializes in period n in our example. At this time, consumers are devoting to savings the exact amount of their income that they desire, and this amount reenters the spending stream via investment.

Third, note that the increment in investment (in period 1) sets off a series of income generating responses so that finally income rises by some multiple amount of the net, new investment. Although we are primarily interested in analyzing this process in terms of behavioral equations, we may still use the identity equation $Y = k \cdot \triangle I$ to reveal quickly what the multiplier effect will be. In this case, the multiplier effect is $40. In terms of the equation, we have

$$\triangle Y = k \cdot \triangle I$$

$$\triangle Y = \frac{1}{1-.75} \cdot \$10$$

$$\triangle Y = 4 \cdot \$10$$

$$\triangle Y = \$40.$$

It is significant that the multiplier effect will vary according to both

TABLE 12–2

A Hypothetical Example of the Multiplier

Period	Y	$\triangle Y$	I	C	$\triangle C$	Savings Desired	Savings Actual	Excess of Actual over Desired
0	100.00	—	10.00	90.00	—	10.00	10.00	0.00
1	110.00	10.00	20.00	90.00	0.00	12.50	20.00	7.50
2	107.50	—2.50	10.00	97.50	7.50	11.87	10.00	—1.87
3	105.63	—1.87	10.00	95.63	—1.87	11.40	10.00	—1.40
4	104.23	—1.40	10.00	94.23	—1.40	11.05	10.00	—1.05
5	103.18	—1.05	10.00	93.18	—1.05	10.79	10.00	— .79
n	100.00	0.00	10.00	90.00	0.00	10.00	10.00	0.00

the amount of net, new investment and the magnitude of the marginal propensity to consume. We may generalize as follows: (1) given the marginal propensity to consume, the multiplier effect will be larger the greater the amount of net, new investment; and (2) given the amount of net, new investment, the higher the marginal propensity to consume, the greater the multiplier effect.

The first generalization (1) is obvious, and the second (2) also should be self-evident. Assume that net, new investment is $10 and remains constant. If the marginal propensity to consume is .75, the multiplier effect, as we have seen, will be $40. On the other hand, if the marginal propensity to consume is .90, the multiplier effect will be $100, for in this case $k = 1/(1—.90) = 10$. More specifically, the first round of income generation increases consumption in period 2 by the amount of $90, as opposed to $75 when the marginal propensity to consume is .75. Put otherwise, in each successive round of income increase, only 10 per cent is withheld from the income stream in the form of savings. In fact, in the limiting case, where the marginal propensity to consume equals or exceeds unity, a disequilibrium situation theoretically continues endlessly, though technical and other factors will prevent this from actually occurring.

Before turning to qualifications and complications, another illustration of the multiplier effect may be considered, one in which the increased investment is not permanent. Again begin with the same equilibrium situation in period 0 as before (see Table 12–2), and again assume that a drop in the interest rate increases net investment by $10 in period 1. But this time it is assumed that the net, new investment is present only in period 1 and that there is no investment to replace it when it terminates at the end of the period. Thus in period 2 investment falls back to its former level of $10.

In this case income rises sharply in period 1 but then begins to fall off in subsequent periods until it reaches its former level of $100. Note that each decrease in income is 75 per cent of the decrease in the preceding period (see Table 12–2). Thus in period 2 income drops by $2.50 (that is, $\triangle I = -\$10$, $\triangle C = \$7.50$, and thus $\triangle Y = -\$2.50$), while in period 3 income drops by $1.87. This process of decline continues until eventually the original income level of $100 is restored, at which time desired and actual savings are equal to each other and to investment.

One final important observation. Recall from the discussion of the preceding chapter, as well as Chapter 9, that the equilibrium level of income need not necessarily be a full-employment level. To the contrary, desired and realized savings and investment may all be equal at income levels below full employment. There is nothing in the multiplier analysis that tells us that full employment will automatically and naturally come about; whether there will be full employment depends upon the investment and consumption-savings patterns of the economy.

3.   An Important Qualification

Although the multiplier analysis has served as a powerful economic tool, it nevertheless has come under certain criticisms. Some of these are simply terminological, while some are fundamental. One very important question is: What income concept is used in the analysis? In the preceding illustrations of the multiplier effect, there was no mention of what income was being increased because of the net, new investment. Yet obviously the income concept being used must be specified as precisely as possible.

Usually it is argued that consumption is a function of *disposable income*. But an increase in investment of, say, $10 does not always increase disposable income by $10. The reason for this is that businesses must retain a certain amount of their gross income for depreciation reserves. Moreover, corporations also tend to retain a certain amount of profits rather than distribute them to stockholders in the form of dividends. Thus both depreciation reserves and retained earnings (that is, the "internal" sources of financial funds) must be accounted for in some manner.

Although this is an important issue, it is also quite complicated. Perhaps a simple illustration will help to clear it up. Assume that a certain

group of firms—Group A—increase their investment in plant and equipment by $100. To accomplish this they must expend $100 to the firms
in the capital goods sector of the economy—Group B. Thus the first
round of income generation really ends up in business firms—and these
in turn pay the productive services they use to create the plant and
equipment for Group A. Now the owners of productive services hired
by Group B will use their own incomes for consumption-savings purposes since they are also consumers.

However, as the firms of Group B will retain some of the $100 for
depreciation reserves and for retained earnings, they do not pass on to
consumers all of the $100, but rather, say, only $90, holding the residual
of $10 for the purposes mentioned. In other words, consumers will re-
ceive only $90, out of which they will increase their consumption ex-
penditures by $67.50 (with a marginal propensity to consume of .75),
rather than by $75, as in our earlier example. Further reductions will
occur because of direct taxes.

The significance of depreciation reserves, retained earnings, and direct taxes is that the multiplier effect will not be $40, as was previously
the case, but considerably smaller. All along the line, the process of income generation is lessened as a successive series of firms withhold for
depreciation reserves and undistributed profits a certain share of each
income increase, and governments will tax away part of each increment.
Thus it is impossible to state precisely what the multiplier effect will be
by using the formula $\triangle Y = k - \triangle I$ until this important factor is taken
into account.

While the formula may be used for purposes of first approximation,
keep in mind that it overstates the income increment resulting from
net, new investment. Unfortunately, how much it overstates the actual
multiplier effect is not known, for too little is known about the savings
habits of businesses, especially corporations. The data in Table 12–3
do show, however, that these two sources of financing net, new investment have loomed very importantly in the United States. Indeed they
have averaged about two-thirds annually of the sources of net investment since World War II. Recall the discussion from Chapter 4, where
the growing importance of replacement investment was pointed out.
This implies that the multiplier effect is not actually as large as the typical theoretical formulation makes it out to be.

Perhaps a more serious qualification is that changes in income themselves will induce changes in investment. In short, there is more to
income changes than simply the multiplier effect—there is also the accelerator effect which treats the endogenous relationships between

TABLE 12–3

Percentage Distribution of Sources of Funds,
1947-51, 1952-56, and 1957-61

Source of Funds	Manufacturing and Mining	Railroads	Public Utilities and Communications	All Corpora- tions
Internal Financing				
1947-51	61%	69%	25%	56%
1952-56	72	91	32	62
1957-61	76	114	41	66
External Financing				
1947-51	39	31	75	44
1952-56	28	9	68	38
1957-61	24	—14	59	34

Source: Department of Commerce, *Survey of Current Business*, September 1957, Table 6, p. 12; *ibid.*, October 1959, Table 2, p. 15; *ibid.*, November 1961, Table 1, p. 18, and Table 2, p. 21.

income and investment. This is such an important qualification that it deserves a full section for discussion.

4. The Multiplier-Accelerator Interaction

The acceleration principle was introduced rather briefly much earlier (Chapter 6). At that time it was pointed out that there is such a thing as induced investment, but that there is no basic agreement as to what the major variable is that induces investment changes.[10] Some have argued that the relevant variable is the rate of change in consumers' sales, others contend that the relevant variable is the rate of change of profits, and so on.[11] Probably the most widely held position today is

[10]Of course, in Chapter 6 only inventory investment was considered in explaining the acceleration principle. Now the principle is expanded to include investment in plant and equipment.

[11]Some of the important references are J. Tinbergen, "Statistical Evidence on the Acceleration Principle," *Economica*, May 1938, and *Business Cycles in the United States of America, 1919-1932* (Geneva: League of Nations, 1939); K. Roos, "The Demand for Investment Goods," *American Economic Review*, May 1948; Y. Grunfeld, "The Determinants of Corporate Investment," in *The Demand for Durable Goods*, ed. A. C. Harberger (Chicago: University of Chicago Press, 1960); Taitel, *Profits, Productive Activity, and New Investment* (Washington, D. C.: Temporary

that changes in investment are induced by changes in income. Thus

$$\triangle I_t = f(Y_t - Y_{t-1}),$$

where $\triangle I_t$ stands for net induced investment, Y_t for the income of the current period, and Y_{t-1} for the income of the previous period.

One of the important analytical developments following *The General Theory* has been to bring the multiplier and the accelerator together in the form of the "multiplier-accelerator interaction." Therefore some time and attention must be devoted to this important principle. The major reason for this is that the multiplier-accelerator interaction has been used by some economists as the basis of their cycle theories.[12] One of them is reviewed in section 7.

A.   The Acceleration Coefficient

To begin with, such phrases as the acceleration principle, the acceleration coefficient, the marginal propensity to invest, and the marginal or incremental capital-output ratios are encountered often in the literature. Although all of these mean the same thing, we shall use only the term *acceleration coefficient*.

What is the acceleration coefficient? It is a statement of the value of

---

National Economic Committee, 1941), Monograph 12; J. R. Meyer and E. Kuh, *The Investment Decision* (Cambridge: Harvard University Press, 1957), which contains an excellent bibliography. For a review of recent empirical work, see D. Smyth, "Empirical Evidence on the Acceleration Principle," *Review of Economic Studies,* July 1964. See also A. G. Holt, "Capital Appropriations and the Acceleration," *Review of Economics and Statistics,* May 1965. See also R. Eisner, "Capital Expenditures, Profits, and the Acceleration Principle," in *Models of Income Determination* (Princeton: Princeton University Press, 1964).

[12]Some, such as J. R. Hicks, *A Contribution to the Theory of the Trade Cycle* (Oxford: Oxford University Press, 1950), rely on a strong accelerator, while others, such as A. H. Hansen, *Business Cycles and National Income* (New York: W. W. Norton & Company, Inc., 1951), rely on a weak one. The accelerator has come under a good deal of critical discussion. See A. D. Knox, "The Accelerator Principle and the Theory of Investment," *Economica,* August 1952; J. Meyer and E. Kuh, *The Investment Decision,* and "Acceleration and Related Theories of Investment: An Empirical Inquiry," *Review of Economics and Statistics,* August 1955; S. C. Tsiang, "Acceleration, Theory of the Firm, and the Business Cycle," *Quarterly Journal of Economics,* August 1951; R. S. Eckhaus, "The Acceleration Principle Reconsidered," *Quarterly Journal of Economics,* May 1953; W. J. Baumol, "Acceleration without Magnification," *American Economic Review,* June 1956; and D. Hamberg, "The Accelerator in Income Analysis," *Quarterly Journal of Economics,* November 1952.

the ratio of the change in investment brought forth (induced) by a preceding change in income. This may be written as

$$v = \frac{\triangle I}{\triangle Y}.$$

Here v measures the net, new investment induced by a previous income change. However, because the acceleration coefficient usually relates the effect of a *previous* change in income on *current* net investment, it is logical to introduce a lag of some sort. For simplicity we shall concentrate on only a one-period lag. Thus the formula may be rewritten as

$$v = \frac{\triangle I_t}{(Y_t - Y_{t-1})},$$

where Y_t stands for the income of the current period, Y_{t-1} stands for the income of the preceding period, and $\triangle I_t$ designates the net, new investment of the current period t. This version of the equation may, of course, be alternatively stated as

$$\triangle I_t = v(Y_t - Y_{t-1}).$$

For example, assume that the aggregate of businesses will increase their investment in plant and equipment by \$1 in any particular period when income rises by \$5 from the preceding period to the present. In this case the acceleration coefficient would be

$$v = \frac{\triangle I_t}{(Y_t - Y_{t-1})}$$
$$v = \frac{\$1}{\$5}$$
$$v = .20.$$

Like the multiplier, the accelerator has proved to be a powerful analytical tool. However, it must be used with caution. In the first place, one must distinguish between the short-run and long-run applications of the principle. For the moment, only the short-run accelerator is considered; the long-run versions are discussed later, especially in Part 4.

Second, not too much is known about the actual determinants of the magnitude of value of the acceleration coefficient. Surely technological considerations are important, as are expectations by businessmen. Moreover, institutional factors may play an important role. While these determinants will be discussed later, for the moment the only major determinant is assumed to be technology—that is, the institutional and expectational variables are held constant. This is done strictly for the sake of convenience, for it permits development of the analysis on the basis of a *constant* coefficient.

B.   The Multiplier-Accelerator Interaction

While the accelerator by itself is an important analytical tool (as was seen earlier in Chapter 6), it becomes all the more so when combined with the multiplier. This subsection provides a simple illustration of the multiplier-accelerator interaction, although it is stated in terms of an identity equation which does not reveal much about the actual process of adjustment. Nevertheless, the present illustration lays the groundwork for later and more complicated discussion of the interaction and is thus provided only as a point of departure.

Assume to begin with that there is an equilibrium position in period 0. Thus desired and realized savings and investment are all equal. Suppose now that some businessmen recognize the emergence of the growth factors, so that some autonomous investment occurs in period 1. This autonomous investment is assumed to remain constant for the remainder of the illustration. Suppose finally that the acceleration coefficient is .20 and remains constant, and that the marginal propensities to consume and to save are .75 and .25, respectively, and also remain constant.

Of course, the autonomous investment which occurs in period 1 is sufficient to set off the multiplier effect. However, in this case account must be taken not only of the induced consumption changes (the multiplier effect), but also induced investment changes (the acceleration effect). Thus when autonomous investment rises by, say, $100, both consumption and investment will subsequently rise. The increase in consumption during the first round of income generation will be $75 and the rise in investment will be $20. Note that in the absence of the accelerator the first round of income increase would have been only $75; but with the accelerator now incorporated into the analysis, income rises by $95.

Again we have a geometric progression, which may be stated as

$$\triangle Y = \triangle I \cdot [1+(b+v)+(b+v)^2+(b+v)^3+ \cdots +(b+v)^n],$$

where b stands for the marginal propensity to consume and v stands for the acceleration coefficient. Substituting the assumed figures, we have

$$\triangle Y = \$100 \cdot [1+(.75+.20)+(.75+.20)^2+(.75+.20)^3+ \cdots + (.75+.20)^n]$$

$$\triangle Y = \$100+(\$75+\$20)+(\$71.25+\$19)^2+ \ldots .$$

However, in this case a new equilibrium level of income will emerge, for the marginal propensity to save is significantly larger than the acceleration coefficient.[13] Each successive round of income increase is less than the preceding round since some of the increase is drained off into savings. Nevertheless the new equilibrium level of income will be significantly larger than would be the case if the accelerator were not present. In order to discover the new income level, the instantaneous multiplier equation may be rewritten so that it includes the acceleration coefficient. Thus,

$$\triangle Y = \triangle I \cdot \frac{1}{(1-b-v)}$$

$$\triangle Y = \$100 \cdot \frac{1}{(1-.75-.20)}$$

$$\triangle Y = \$100 \cdot \frac{1}{.05}$$

$$\triangle Y = \$2,000.$$

In this version of the equation, the presence of the acceleration coefficient signifies that part of the savings flows back into the income stream. That is, for every $1 increase in income, $.25 is removed from the spending stream and held in the form of savings; however, $.20 of

---

[13]A word of caution: the emergence of a new equilibrium level is not inevitable; this depends upon the respective values of v and b. Actually, different values of v and b yield different income patterns, sometimes an equilibrium, sometimes an "explosion," and sometimes cycles. Since mathematical reasoning is required to explain the various possibilities, we shall confine ourselves to the simpler cases. However, we may point out here that there are four possible repercussions following a rise in investment—the movement to a new equilibrium, a permanent income explosion, a diverging cycle, and a converging cycle. These are shown in the accompanying diagrams.

The reader who may be interested in the various possibilities should consult the following: P. A. Samuelson, "Interaction Between the Multiplier Analysis and the Principle of Acceleration," *Review of Economic Statistics*, May 1939, reprinted in *Readings in Business Cycle Theory*, ed. G. Haberler (Philadelphia: The Blakiston Company, 1944); J. R. Hicks, *A Contribution to the Theory of the Trade Cycle*, Chapters 5-6; R. G. D. Allen, *Mathematical Economics* (London: The Macmillan Company, 1959), Chapter 7, especially pp. 209-12; K. K. Kurihara, *Introduction to Keynesian Dynamics* (New York: Columbia University Press, 1956), pp. 117-22.

this is borrowed by businesses for the purpose of financing their new induced investment. In short, only 5 per cent of each round of income increase does not reenter the spending stream, though this is sufficient to bring about a new equilibrium level of income.

Since it reveals the *total* income effect of the rise in investment spending, this new equation is referred to as the multiplier-accelerator effect. Recall however that the analysis does not reveal much about the actual process involved in the movement from one income level to another. In order to deal with this it is necessary to use behavioral, not identity, equations.

5. An Illustration of the Interaction

While the instantaneous approach to the multiplier-accelerator interaction is revealing to some extent, it says nothing about the adjustment process. Only the behavioral approach does this. In this section, therefore, the behavioral approach to the interaction is illustrated by means of a numerical example.

A.   The Behavioral Equations

First, the various functional relationships involved in the illustration must be set forth explicitly.

The consumption function is, as before, written with a one-period lag in it. Thus $C_t = f(Y_{t-1})$. The marginal propensity to consume (and hence the marginal propensity to save) is assumed to be .5 and remain constant.

The induced investment function is also lagged. Thus the induced investment of period 2 is a function of the income change between periods 0 and 1. There are several reasons for this lag. For instance, businessmen do not always know immediately what is happening to income since there is always some lag in the reporting of data on income changes (and even sales). Also they may be fairly hesitant about responding immediately to the income change. Finally some time is required to get the induced investment projects off the blueprint table and into the form of brick and metal. For these reasons, then, the acceleration coefficient is characterized by a one-period lag in this illustration, and it is assigned a value of .25, which remains constant.[14]

---

[14]A one-period lag is still quite brief, since the length of the period, recall, is determined by consumer behavior. However, the lag can be made longer and the analysis still holds. Hicks, *A Contribution to the Theory of the Trade Cycle,* discusses several cases where the induced investment is distributed over different time periods.

B.   The Illustration

The relevant data are presented in Table 12–4. In period 0 the economy is in an equilibrium position, with desired and realized savings equal to each other and to desired and realized investment, each at $100. Total income is $1000, and thus consumption is $900. Now in period 1, $100 of autonomous investment is interjected into the system so that income rises initially by this amount. However, because of the lag in both the consumption and induced investment functions, there is no further change in actual spending in period 1.

The important thing to note at this point is that now both consumers and businesses are in a disequilibrium. While consumers desire to save $150, they are actually (in period 1) saving $200—and the "excess" savings will be injected into the consumption spending stream in the next period. Also businessmen desire to increase their investment by an additional $25, given the acceleration coefficient of .25 and the income increase of $100. Because of the lag, however, investment spending will not rise in period 1; rather it will increase in period 2 by $25. Thus the total income increase in period 2 will be $75—that is, $50 additional consumption and $25 additional investment spending.

Because of the increase, however, both consumers and businesses remain in disequilibrium in period 2. Consumers are still actually saving more than they desire to save, though now by a lesser amount ($37.50). They will thus increase their consumption spending in period 3 by the amount of their "excess" savings in the attempt to reattain an equilibrium position. By the same token, businesses still desire to increase their investment beyond their present position by $18.75 (that is, 25 per cent of the income increment of $75). Thus income in period 3 will rise by $56.25. And so on for the subsequent periods.

There are certain points about this analysis that require elaboration. First, when in each period both businesses and consumers find themselves in disequilibrium, they attempt to equate their desired and actual positions. Each effort in this direction, however, breeds a disequilibrium in the next period. The reason for this is obvious. When desired investment exceeds actual investment, a subsequent rise in investment spending may be expected; and when actual savings exceed desired savings, a subsequent increase in consumption spending may also be expected. In other words, the effort to reattain the equilibrium position results in a rise in both investment and consumption spending and hence income in the next period.

Second, each successive round of income increase is less than the preceding round and always by 25 per cent. Why is this so? Simply because the acceleration coefficient (.25) is less than the marginal pro-

TABLE 12–4

The Multiplier-Accelerator Interaction

Period	Y	ΔY*	C	ΔC	ΔI	Investment			Savings		
						Desired	Actual†	Excess	Desired	Actual†	Excess
0	1,000.00	—	900.00	—	—	100.00	100.00	0.00	100.00	100.00	0.00
1	1,100.00	100.00	900.00	0.00	100.00	225.00	200.00	25.00	150.00	200.00	50.00
2	1,175.00	75.00	950.00	50.00	25.00	243.75	225.00	18.75	187.50	225.00	37.50
3	1,231.25	56.25	987.50	37.50	18.75	257.81	243.75	14.00	215.67	243.75	28.17
4	1,273.48	42.23	1,015.67	28.17	14.06	268.37	257.81	10.56	236.78	257.81	21.11
5	1,305.15	31.67	1,036.78	21.11	10.56	276.27	268.37	7.90	257.89	268.37	15.84
n	1,400.00	0.00	1,100.00	0.00	0.00	300.00	300.00	0.00	300.00	300.00	0.00

* Note that the ΔY of any one period is equal to the *sum* of the excess of actual savings over desired savings *and* desired investment over actual investment of the preceding period.

† Note that actual investment and actual savings are always equal. This is the accounting identity mentioned in the text.

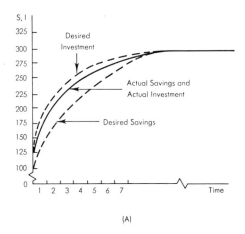

(A)

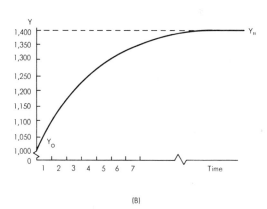

(B)

FIGURE 12–3

pensity to save (.50). Thus 25 per cent of each income increase does not reenter the spending stream but is withheld in the form of savings. As a corollary to this, note that the discrepancy between desired and actual investment diminishes as the income level grows, as does the discrepancy between desired and actual savings. This is shown in Figure 12–3A.

Third, and very important, since the acceleration coefficient is less than the marginal propensity to save, a new stable equilibrium will occur, *ceteris paribus.* The final equilibrium level of income can be ascertained by means of the multiplier-accelerator equation.

$$\triangle Y = \triangle I \cdot \frac{1}{(1-b-v)}$$
$$\triangle Y = \$100 \cdot \frac{1}{(1-.5-.25)}$$
$$\triangle Y = \$400.$$

Note that so long as $1-b$ (the marginal propensity to save) exceeds v (the acceleration coefficient), a determinate equilibrium results.[15] To repeat, this is because 25 per cent (in our illustration) of each income increase does not reenter the spending stream either via investment or consumption but is held back in the form of savings. (As will be seen shortly, the case is quite different when v is larger than $1-b$.) This is shown diagrammatically in Figure 12–3B, where the income line moves over time from Y_0 to Y_n, and where there is a final convergence toward equality of desired and realized savings and desired and realized investment.

6. Another Illustration of the Interaction

What happens to income if the acceleration coefficient exceeds the marginal propensity to save and remains above it? The result of this relationship will be a permanent explosion of income once the multiplier-accelerator interaction gets underway.[16] Each round of income increase is followed by a situation where the businessmen desire to pour more into the investment spending stream than the savings generated by the interaction. Thus for period after period net, new induced investment exceeds the newly created savings of each period. The result? A permanent income expansion.

This, however, appears to be a rather unlikely possibility. Surely

---

[15]This is somewhat inaccurate. Mathematically there are some cases where v could be larger than $1-b$ and there would be no cyclical disturbance. Actually only the more extreme case is considered here where $1-b$ exceeds v substantially. For the mathematics and more difficult cases, see Allen, *Mathematical Economics,* pp. 209-12.

[16]Again, this is not quite accurate. More specifically, any value of the acceleration coefficient substantially greater than unity creates an explosive income situation if the marginal propensity to save is small. Thus, if $v = 2$ and $1-b = .5$, an explosive situation results. For higher values of $1-b$, the value of v must be higher still. See Allen, *Mathematical Economics,* p. 211.

there is some upper limit to income creation (in real terms). Income cannot continue expanding indefinitely. Once full employment is reached, all further income increases are nominal, in the sense that they are purely monetary rather than real. Put otherwise, once full employment is reached, an acceleration coefficient greater than the marginal propensity to save breeds substantial inflation. But note that this is, in effect, what both Hayek and Schumpeter have assumed in their respective theories of the expansionary stage.

Nevertheless, this situation should not be ruled out as a possibility for short periods of time. Indeed it is quite likely to hold for the expansionary stage of the cycle—or, better, for the later phases of the expansionary stage. Recall that the expectations of businessmen have a great deal to do with the determination of the value of the acceleration coefficient, and if expectations during the expansion become buoyant, the acceleration coefficient may well lie substantially above the marginal propensity to save. By the same token, the acceleration coefficient will have a very low value, perhaps zero or even negative, during the contractionary stage of the cycle. In other words, the value of the acceleration coefficient is not constant over the course of the cycle, as our earlier examples have assumed but is subject to volatile changes. Thus, the particular case discussed in this section may be unrealistic over protracted periods of time, but not necessarily for the expansionary stage of the cycle.

7. An Accelerator-Multiplier Model of the Cycle

In recent years several economists have used the multiplier-accelerator interaction as the basis for their theories of the business cycle.[17] Probably the most noted of these theories is the one advanced by J. R. Hicks in his *A Contribution to the Theory of the Trade Cycle*, although

---

[17]Hansen, *Business Cycles and National Income,* has a theory based on the interaction, but in his theory the accelerator is quite weak. For further discussion of the interaction, see R. F. Harrod, *The Trade Cycle* (Oxford: The Clarendon Press, 1936); R. Goodwin, "The Nonlinear Accelerator and the Persistence of Business Cycles," *Econometrica,* January 1951; M. Kalecki, "A Theory of Business Cycles," *Review of Economic Studies,* February 1937; N. Kaldor, "A Model of the Trade Cycle," *Economic Journal,* March 1940, reprinted as Chapter 8 in his *Essays on Economic Stability and Growth* (Glencoe: The Free Press, 1960); and Kaldor, "The Relation of Economic Growth and Cyclical Fluctuations," *Economic Journal,* March 1954, reprinted as Chapter 10 in *Essays on Economic Stability and Growth.* For a recent "nonaccelerator model," see J. S. Duesenberry, *Business Cycles and Economic Growth* (New York: McGraw-Hill Book Company, 1958).

there is far more to Hicks' theory of the cycle than merely the multi-plier-accelerator interaction. It also brings into play the role of autono-mous investment and the "full-employment ceiling." All of these are integrated in a model characterized by economic growth over time. In this section Hicks' model is examined in some detail.

A. Hicks' Model of the Business Cycle

Two or three prefatory comments are in order. First, Hicks provides only a skeleton outline of the cycle, and in so doing he of course omits reference to many complicating factors. As has been pointed out, how-ever, this is not a fundamental weakness of his theory. S. S. Alexander, after his critical review of Hicks' theory, concludes:

> Mr. Hicks' cycle looks different from other theories of the cycle because only the bare bones show. Those who object that Mr. Hicks' presenta-tion is oversimplified and too monistic and rigid will find that the qual-ifications and multiplicities they wish to introduce can easily be fitted into the framework he provides.[18]

Second, Hicks' contribution is really a contribution once removed. There is little that is really original in his theory.[19] Rather it stands as a very able synthesis of much work that has gone before. This of course does not detract from the theory, for it still is an important milestone in the development of business cycle analysis.

Further, the model is presented in real rather than monetary terms. This raises once again the question of what the major determinant of induced investment is. Hicks' model interprets the acceleration coeffi-cient in a rather rigid manner, making current induced investment a function of prior changes in *real* output. Recall, however, that other economists have stressed that such monetary variables as changes in profits play a far more fundamental role in inducing current invest-

---

[18]S. S. Alexander, "Issues of Business Cycle Theory Raised by Mr. Hicks," *American Economic Review,* December 1951, p. 877. For other reviews of Hicks' theory, see W. W. Rostow, "Some Notes on Mr. Hicks and History," *American Economic Review,* June 1951; J. S. Duesenberry, "Hicks on the Trade Cycle," *Quarterly Journal of Economics,* August 1950; A. F. Burns, "Hicks and the Real Cycle," *Journal of Political Economy,* February 1952, reprinted in *The Frontiers of Economic Knowledge* (Princeton: Princeton University Press, 1954); and A. D. Knox, "On a Theory of the Trade Cycle," *Economica,* August 1950, reprinted as Chapter 20 in *Readings in Business Cycles and National Income,* eds. A. H. Han-sen and R. V. Clemence.

[19]As he himself notes. He gives specific credit to his intellectual "antecedents" in Chapter 1 of *A Contribution to the Theory of the Trade Cycle.*

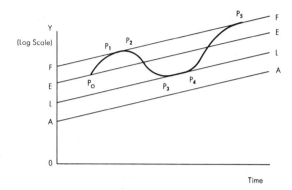

FIGURE 12–4

ment.[20] As will be seen in the next subsection, this may not be a very important issue, but for the moment keep in mind that Hicks presents his analysis in real terms.

So much for prefatory comments. Let us now turn to a discussion of the theory. Consider Figure 12–4, where income is plotted on the vertical axis and time on the horizontal. Note that the scale on the vertical axis is logarithmic, so that a straight line (such as FF) shows that income is increasing at a constant rate.

The FF line is the "full-employment ceiling" which is determined by the scarcity of resources. In other words, given these scarcities, output at any particular time cannot rise beyond the FF line. The EE line is the "equilibrium path of employment," and the AA line shows that autonomous investment increases also at a constant rate. The LL line is considered later on.

Now assume that income has moved along the EE line up to point P_0, at which time some autonomous investment occurs. This sets off the multiplier-accelerator interaction and raises income towards the full-employment ceiling. It is important to note here that Hicks assumes that the acceleration coefficient is considerably larger than the marginal

---

[20]See Meyer and Kuh, *The Investment Decision,* where it is concluded that monetary factors play an important role in investment decisions. Very little has been done in discussion of the accelerator in strictly monetary terms; see H. Minsky, "Monetary Systems and Accelerator Models," *American Economic Review,* December 1957, and J. Tobin, "Dynamic Aggregative Model," *Journal of Political Economy,* April 1955. See also the references in footnotes 11-12 of this chapter for further discussion of the accelerator.

propensity to save. Thus the income expansion set off by the autonomous investment is explosive.[21]

Once the full-employment ceiling is reached, output cannot rise any
faster than the rate at which the ceiling is rising. Thus technological
considerations imply that the acceleration coefficient will drop in
value—that is, the significant drop in the *rate* of output increase has a
depressing effect on induced investment. At this juncture no more induced investment will be generated than is necessary to support output
at the full-employment level, and if the lag in induced investment is
long enough, income will for a while move along the FF line. Nevertheless there will be a decline in *total* investment spending since the induced investment along the FF line is less than that leading up to the
line (from P_0 to P_1). This can be restated as follows: when the full-employment ceiling is reached, technological limits to output reduce the
value of the acceleration coefficient and thus total investment.

Once the decline in total investment spending occurs, the upper-
turning point sets in and the contraction follows. Here we encounter
what appears largely to be a terminological problem. Hicks argues that
there is no reverse or negative accelerator, that is, that there is no induced *dis*investment. As he puts it:

> . . . falls in output (absolute falls, that is) do not induce disinvestment
> in the same way as rises in output induce investment. There is a marked
> lack of symmetry. Disinvestment in fixed capital can only take place by
> a cessation of gross investment; thus the adjustment of fixed capital to a
> decline in the level of output can only take place by a slow process of
> wearing-out, which must take considerable time. Once this condition has
> been reached, further falls in output can induce no further disinvestment
> in fixed capital—at least not immediately.[22]

Hicks' argument here can easily be restated. When output falls absolutely, gross investment will, after a point, also fall. Thus *there will be
negative induced net disinvestment,* since gross investment is not sufficient to maintain the size of the capital stock. Put otherwise, as the capital stock wears out, it is not completely replaced, though this process
may take some time.

This still sounds suspiciously like the accelerator (in reverse), though

[21]See footnote 16, above. Hicks distinguishes between "free" (explosive) and
"constrained" (nonexplosive) cycles. Only the former is discussed here; the latter
is based on such a weak multiplier-accelerator interaction that the upper-turning
point occurs before the FF line is reached. Hicks, moreover, believes that in the
real world the values of both b and v are such that the "free" cycle is far more
relevant.

[22]Hicks, *A Contribution to the Theory of the Trade Cycle,* p. 101.

with a time qualification introduced into it. The major point is that net investment can occur more quickly than can net disinvestment, and thus the accelerator still works in reverse, but far more slowly than in the upswing. With the multiplier working in reverse, the income level will fall below the equilibrium line EE. Indeed, Hicks argues that it will be sufficient to reduce the income level to the "slump equilibrium line LL."[23] Once the LL line is reached, income starts moving along it. However, it cannot stay long on this line, for Hicks assumes that LL is "geared to the autonomous investment line AA, and rises with it."[24] In other words, some autonomous investment occurs, and once more the multiplier-accelerator interaction sets in, raising income towards and then beyond the EE line up to the full-employment ceiling. And the cycle repeats itself.

Note that the lower-turning point is the *combined* result of the induced net disinvestment and the positive autonomous investment. That is, as the contraction continues, induced net disinvestment becomes smaller so that eventually the sum of both it and autonomous investment yields a positive net investment. The autonomous investment at the second lower-turning point (P_4) must be higher than it was during the previous peak level of income. The reason for this is that it must be high enough to more than offset the induced net disinvestment so that the multiplier-accelerator interaction can once more get underway.

B.   Some Criticisms and Qualifications[25]

As might be expected, Hicks' model of the business cycle has aroused a good deal of comment and discussion. In this subsection some of the major topics of this discussion will be considered.

In the first place, there is the problem of the major determinant of induced investment. Some economists, such as Tinbergen, have concluded, on the basis of statistical studies, that there is a rather weak relationship between changes in output and induced investment.[26] Tinbergen in fact argues that there is a much stronger relationship between induced investment and profits. This of course would tend to cast doubt on the economic significance of Hicks' theory, as well as on

---

[23]*Ibid.*, p. 103.

[24]*Ibid.*, p. 105.

[25]This subsection relies heavily on Alexander, "Issues of Business Cycle Theory Raised by Mr. Hicks." See also the references in footnote 18, above.

[26]The major reference here is Tinbergen, "Statistical Evidence on the Acceleration Principle," and *Business Cycles in the United States of America, 1919-1932.*

the general analysis of the multiplier-accelerator interaction. Hicks'
model, since it is in real terms, implies that businessmen think in terms
of some technological relationship between real output changes and
their investment plans.[27]

On the other hand, both Grunfeld and Taitel[28] have found a real relationship between profits and induced investment. Taitel, for example,
concludes that the stronger relationship is between output changes and
investment, while Grunfeld concludes that the relationship between
investment and the "market value" of the business firm is quite strong.

Somewhat in between these positions is the stand taken by Roos to
the effect that investment changes for the economy at large can be reasonably accurately predicted on the basis of both output changes and
the level of profits.[29] If this is so, then we may conclude (tentatively)
that changes in profits depend largely on both the income level and
changes in the income level. In other words, *it matters little whether we
take the primary variable that induces investment as either income
changes or profit changes.*[30]

While it may not matter, for general purposes, whether we take output or profit changes as the major determinant, there are certain advantages to the latter variable. The major reason is that it focuses attention on important wage, price, and credit relationships that the real
approach ignores. For example, if in the later phases of the expansion
money wages rise relative to prices, both profits and expectations may
become adversely affected. This could result in a reduction in the value
of the acceleration coefficient, no matter what the technological conditions imply, and hence a fall in investment activity. This, however, is no
basic criticism of Hicks' model; rather it is a qualification which asserts
that the value of the acceleration coefficient may start falling before the
full-employment ceiling is reached. This possibility is shown in Figure
12–5, where the upper-turning point sets in before the FF line is
reached.

A second criticism is that the FF line in Figure 12–4 is really the aggregate of many *specific* FF lines of different industries and sectors of

[27]Excluding, of course, autonomous investment.

[28]Grunfeld, "The Determinants of Corporate Investment"; Taitel, *Profits, Productive Activity, and New Investment.*

[29]See Roos, "The Demand for Investment Goods." It is interesting to note that
Tinbergen assumes that profits depend largely on the rate of change of income. See
especially his *Statistical Testing of Business Cycle Theories*, Vol. 2 of *Business
Cycles in the United States of America, 1919-1932.*

[30]This is one of the major points made by Alexander, "Issues of Business Cycle
Theory Raised by Mr. Hicks," pp. 867-69.

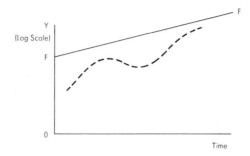

FIGURE 12–5

the economy. Thus there is not a single ceiling curve, but rather a "com-plex of curves, each indicating an optimum course for output and ca-pacity in different sectors of the economy."[31] If the induced investment in the expansion happens to occur in those sectors which have low FF lines, the upper-turning point of the cycle may occur before the aggre-gate FF curve is reached (see Figure 12–5). As Rostow puts it:

> In short, a boom could turn down not only because investment prospects had been dimmed by rising costs or by a falling off of new orders due to the failure of total output to expand at the previous rate, but also be-cause, in the leading lines of new investment, the market had come to appreciate that expansion in certain sectors had proceeded beyond the optimum level, or that decisions already taken would lead to such dis-proportionate expansion.[32]

Although this point is well taken, it stands more as a bit of flesh applied to Hicks' skeletal framework than as a basic criticism.[33] The major merit of Rostow's important point is that it stresses once more that each cycle is unlike every other cycle, except in broad outline; and it points out also the need to disaggregate whenever we examine any particular cycle.

Another, and more important, criticism is that Hicks does not discuss the role of changing expectations so far as the value of the acceleration coefficient is concerned. As the movement from P_0 to P_1 (in Figure

---

[31]Rostow, "Some Notes on Mr. Hicks and History," p. 317.

[32]*Ibid.*, p. 322.

[33]In fact, Hicks himself hints at this point in his *A Contribution to the Theory of the Trade Cycle.*

12–4) proceeds at a rate faster than the FF line is rising, some excess capacity is bound to emerge, at least in those industries that are expanding at a rate faster than the rate from P_0 to P_1. This may tend to reduce the value of the acceleration coefficient for at least two reasons. First, the excess capacity already created can serve as the basis for subsequent output increases in these industries. In any event, the excess capacity may lead to a reduction in investment spending in these specific industries. And second, investment spending may be reduced even more as the excess capacity creates pessimistic expectations. If these adverse expectations set in in the so-called basic industries, their impact may be propagated throughout other industries. Thus again the upper-turning point could occur before the full-employment ceiling is reached.

Finally, and more fundamentally, Hicks may be criticized on his assumption that autonomous investment grows at a constant rate and that businessmen always respond to its change in periods of low economic activity. It may be, to the contrary, that there are fluctuations in autonomous investment[34]—that is, autonomous investment projects are more likely to be undertaken in the expansionary stage of the cycle rather than in the depths of the contractionary stage. If this is the case, then perhaps much of what is called "autonomous investment" had best be grouped with "induced investment."

This, however, is not the major point. The important thing is that "autonomous investment" may depend on the *income* level, not on changes in the income level. Thus autonomous investment may expand at a certain rate once the income level reaches and surpasses a particular point. But even though income continues to grow at the same, or even higher, rate, once the autonomous investment opportunities are exhausted, this type of investment expenditure is reduced. And accordingly the drop in investment spending following this could bring on the reverse multiplier-accelerator. Thus again the upper-turning point can occur before the FF line is reached.

Despite these criticisms and qualifications, Hicks' *A Contribution to the Theory of the Trade Cycle* stands as an important work in the development of cycle thought. It represents, as it were, a modern "general theory" of the cycle, into which many particular qualifications and modifications relevant for any specific cycle may be introduced—but the general framework, spare as it is, still stands. Many other modern

---

[34]This of course is one of Hansen's and Schumpeter's major points, that there is a "clustering" of autonomous investment; see Chapter 7. See also Alexander, "Issues of Business Cycle Theory Raised by Mr. Hicks," p. 873, and the discussion of W. J. Fellner's growth-cycle model in Chapter 16.

cycle theories are truly variants of Hicks' model. And note that in terms of the classification of cycle theories (set forth in Chapter 5), this is a purely endogenous model. The turning points occur because of the interplay of the endogenous variables alone. There are no exogenous forces at play here, for Hicks holds both the FF and AA lines constant—they are fixed parameters, and given the two lines, the interrelationships of the endogenous variables account for the turning points of the cycle once it gets under way.

8. Summary

In this chapter we have examined the concept of the multiplier, and while it has come under a good deal of criticism, it does serve well to tie together the different functions in the Keynesian system. For example, given the liquidity preference function, the consumption function, and the investment demand function, a rise in the stock of money lowers the interest rate. *Ceteris paribus*, this stimulates net investment and this in turn sets off a series of rounds of income generation. However, so long as the marginal propensity to save is positive and constant, a new equilibrium level of income will emerge. The height of the new income level depends upon the amount of net investment and the value of the marginal propensity to consume. The higher the marginal propensity to consume, the greater the multiplier, and hence the multiplier effect, given the net, new investment.

While the multiplier analysis is useful, it becomes even more so when combined with the accelerator. Different values of the marginal propensity to save and the acceleration coefficient yield different income patterns, though in this chapter we concentrated on only two cases. One of these occurs when the marginal propensity to save significantly exceeds the acceleration coefficient. In this instance, a rise in investment yields a new higher equilibrium level of income. The other case occurs when the acceleration coefficient is substantially larger than the marginal propensity to save. In this instance a rise in investment generates an explosive increase in income.

In his theory of the business cycle, Hicks assumes the second case. Thus given a spurt of autonomous investment, income moves explosively upwards. However, given the parameters embodied in the full-employment ceiling, the expansion must come to an end. That is, as full employment is reached, induced investment must decline, and there emerges a negative multiplier-accelerator interaction. The contraction continues (in the absence of governmental intervention) until the rising investment (due to a continually expanding base of autonomous investment) exceeds the disinvestment caused by the contraction. In this case, then, the economy experiences positive net investment and a resulting positive multiplier-accelerator interaction; thus the cycle repeats itself. In terms of our classification of theories, this is a non-linear endogenous model.

QUESTIONS

12-1. Explain in detail how Hicks' theory of the trade cycle is "purely endogenous." What assumption must be made in order to provide a purely endogenous explanation of the lower-turning point?

12-2. What is the basic difference between the identity and behavioral approaches to the multiplier? Which is analytically more useful? Why?

12-3. Why, usually, in the multiplier analysis is the short-run consumption function assumed to be linear and constant? Is this a "realistic" assumption? Explain.

12-4. Discuss the difference between planned and actual savings and between planned and actual investment. What relationship must exist between these four variables if the level of income is to be in equilibrium? Explain in detail.

12-5. Of what influence are depreciation reserves and undistributed profits of businesses in calculating the multiplier effect?

12-6. Define the acceleration coefficient and discuss why it may not remain stable over the course of the business cycle.

12-7. Discuss in as much detail as possible some of the criticisms of Hicks' theory of the trade cycle. What is your position on these criticisms?

Bibliography

Alexander, S. S., "Issues of Business Cycle Theory Raised by Mr. Hicks," *American Economic Review*, December 1951.

Allen, R. G. D., *Mathematical Economics*. London: The Macmillan Company, Ltd., 1959.

Duesenberry, J. S., "Hicks on the Trade Cycle," *Quarterly Journal of Economics*, February 1952.

Hicks, J. R., *A Contribution to the Theory of the Trade Cycle*. Oxford: Oxford University Press, 1950.

Meyer, J. and E. Kuh, *The Investment Decision*. Cambridge: Harvard University Press, 1957.

Rostow, W. W., "Some Notes on Mr. Hicks and History," *American Economic Review*, June 1951.

13

Money Wages and Prices in the Keynesian System

When Keynes elected to measure changes in output and hence employment in terms of "wage units," he chose to speak in real rather than monetary terms.[1] Accordingly, the discussion in the preceding chapters of this part has also been couched in real terms; but now, following Keynes, it is necessary to relax this condition and inquire into the significance of changes in the levels of money wages and prices.[2] This means that the discussion in this chapter is put in monetary, not real, terms.

As far as changes in money wages are concerned, Keynes was primarily interested in what would happen to the level of employment as a result of a *general reduction* in the money-wage level. However, he was also interested in the behavior of money wages as the economy ap-

---

[1]See the discussion in Chapter 9, section 5 on the meaning of "wage units"; also see A. H. Hansen, *A Guide to Keynes* (New York: McGraw-Hill Book Company, 1953), pp. 39-44.

[2]The procedure of beginning an analysis in real terms and then introducing the monetary elements at a later point is typical in economic theory; for an example, see J. R. Hicks, *A Contribution to the Theory of the Trade Cycle* (Oxford: Oxford University Press, 1950), where the monetary elements are not discussed extensively until the last two chapters.

proaches full employment, with its attendent inflationary pressures. As far as the price level is concerned, he was interested in how prices would respond to a rise in the stock of money (and hence the level of aggregate demand). It must be noted that in all three cases the consequences must be traced through changes in the basic functional relationships—the consumption function, the liquidity preference function, and the investment demand function. Thus, if for any reason the level of money wages falls, the repercussions it sets off must be transmitted through changes in these functional relationships; and similarly, the effects of a rise in the money supply must come about through its impact upon aggregate demand, which, in the Keynesian analysis, can be influenced only by changes in these three fundamental relationships.

1.   The Aggregate Supply Curve of Labor

To begin with, any discussion of Keynes' analysis of wage and price levels must be based upon his concept of the aggregate supply curve of labor.[3] While Keynes himself never defined the labor supply curve, both its shape and position can be inferred from his definition of full employment.

> My definition is, therefore, as follows: *Men are involuntarily unemployed if, in the event of a small rise in the price of wage-goods relatively to the money-wage, both the aggregate supply of labour willing to work for the current money-wage and the aggregate demand for it at that wage would be greater than the existing volume of employment.*[4]

The first thing to note about this formulation of the concepts of full employment and involuntary unemployment is that it assumes that the aggregate supply curve is a function of the *money-wage rate*. This, of course, is contrary to what economists prior to Keynes had assumed,

---

[3]For a more extended discussion of the aggregate supply curve of labor in the Keynesian system, see J. Tobin, "Money Wage Rates and Employment," A. Smithies, "Effective Demand and Employment," and S. E. Harris, "Introduction: Keynes' Attack on Laissez Faire and Classical Economics and Wage Theory," all in *The New Economics: Keynes' Influence on Theory and Public Policy*, ed. S. E. Harris (New York: Alfred A. Knopf, 1950). For a critical approach, see R. Perlman, "A Reformulation of Keynesian Wage Theory," *Southern Economic Journal*, January, 1960. Finally, see Yasuma Takata, "An Introduction to Sociological Economics: Implications of Keynesian Theory," *Osaka Economic Papers*, May 1952.

[4]From *The General Theory of Employment, Interest, and Money* by John Maynard Keynes, p. 15; see also p. 26. Reprinted by permission of Harcourt, Brace & World, Inc.

for they had made the supply curve of labor a positive function of the real wage rate.[5] Thus a fundamental difference between the two approaches is that one (Keynes') assumes that workers think and behave in terms of money wages, while the other has workers thinking and acting according to changes in the real wage rate.

The supply curve of labor implied in the Keynesian definition of involuntary unemployment can be shown graphically (Figure 13–1). The money wage (W) is plotted on the vertical axis, while employment (N) is plotted on the horizontal axis. Now, according to this definition, a small rise in the price of "wage goods"[6] will shift the demand curve for labor to the right, say, from DD to D_1D_1.[7] If this rise in demand is followed by an increase in employment *at the prevailing money-wage rate* (Ow), there is less than full employment at the demand DD. In this case employment rises from OX to OY, and according to Keynes the XY amount of workers are involuntarily unemployed. And as long as further rises in the demand for labor are succeeded by increases in employment at the wage rate Ow, there is less than full employment.

However, once demand rises so much that any further increase in employment is possible only with a rising money-wage rate, full employment has been reached and passed. This situation may be de-

---

[5]Graphically this is shown as follows:

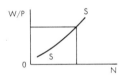

where W/P is the "real" wage, that is, the money wage (W) deflated by an appropriate price index (P), and where N stands for employment.

[6]"Wage goods" are those goods which are consumed by workers, or as Keynes put it (*The General Theory*, p. 7) they are the goods whose prices determine the marginal utility of the money wage.

[7]It should be noted that the aggregate demand curve for labor is the summation of all the various firms' respective values of the marginal product curves, when labor is the variable input factor. It will be recalled from price theory that a purely competitive firm's short-run demand curve for labor is the schedule of labor's marginal physical product (MPP) multiplied by a given product price (P). The demand curve has a negative slope because of short-run diminishing returns. A horizontal summation of the marginal value product curves of each and every firm gives us the aggregate demand curve for labor. Since P × MPP gives us the marginal value product curve of labor (that is, the demand curve for labor), a rise in P will shift the curve to the right. This is presumably what Keynes meant when he referred to a "small rise in the price of wage-goods" increasing the aggregate demand for labor.

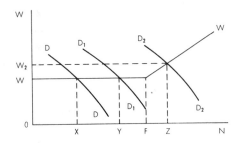

FIGURE 13–1

scribed as "over-full employment," for any additional increment in em
ployment can occur only with a higher money-wage rate in order to
attract into the labor force extra workers who were formerly *voluntarily*
unemployed at the wage Ow. The conditions of over-full employment
are shown in Figure 13–1, where, given the demand curve D_2D_2, a
wage of Ow_2 is necessary to bring out voluntary idleness FZ amount of
extra workers.

The Keynesian supply curve of labor, in other words, is characterized
by a perfectly elastic segment (at the prevailing money-wage rate) up
to full employment and a positively sloped segment beyond full em
ployment. Full employment, therefore, is indicated by the kink in the
supply curve, that is, at OF in Figure 13–1.[8]

This interpretation of the aggregate labor supply curve implies that
workers suffer from a "money illusion," that is, they react asymmet
rically to changes in *real* wages. The perfectly elastic segment of the
curve means that workers will reject reductions in the real wage caused
by cuts in the money wage below the prevailing level of Ow and in fact
prefer unemployment to wage cuts, even though they are willing to
work at Ow. Keynes referred to this as "the actual attitude of workers"
and stated further that "a situation where labour stipulates (within
limits) for a money-wage rather than a real wage, so far from being
merely a possibility, is the normal case."[9] In short, workers resist money-
wage cuts that will reduce their real wages.

---

[8]It is not necessary to be so rigid in interpretation; rather than a kink in the
curve there may be a smooth, though still relatively sharp, turn from the elastic to
the inelastic segment. See section 4 for further discussion indicating that Keynes
actually thought in terms of the supply curves becoming less elastic *before* full em
ployment is reached.

[9]Keynes, *The General Theory*, pp. 8-9.

However, Keynes' definition of full employment tells us that workers voluntarily accept reductions in their real wage as the economy moves towards full employment. This is because the prices of wage goods are rising while the money-wage rate remains constant. In this respect, then, workers do behave asymmetrically—that is, suffer a "money illusion." While they will resist a reduction in their real wage that results from a fall in the money wage, they will accept a reduction resulting from a rise in the price level, with the prevailing money wage constant.[10] Whether this is rational behavior is no matter, so far as Keynes was concerned, for this is the way he believed workers actually behave.

Now from this analysis a conclusion can be drawn which in turn can be subjected to empirical testing. As the economy moves towards full employment, real wages fall, and, conversely, as unemployment deepens, real wages rise. In short, money and real wages move inversely to one another; and Keynes thought that this is nearly always the case: "... in the case of changes in the general level of wages, it will be found, I think, that the change in real wages associated with a change in money-wages, so far from being usually in the same direction, is almost always in the opposite direction."[11]

Keynes was perhaps justified in making this assertion in the absence of adequate empirical data. In fact, until the empirical studies were presented, economists in general held that real wages did move inversely to the business cycle. This premise is certainly found in most of the cycle theories reviewed in earlier chapters. However, Keynes' statement stimulated a number of empirical investigations of the behavior of real wages,[12] and these reveal that the behavior of real wages over

---

[10]See *The General Theory*, pp. 7-15, for a fuller discussion. See also C. D. Long, "Impact of Effective Demand on the Labor Supply," *American Economic Review*, May 1953, where the "money illusion" is rejected as being empirically insignificant.

[11]Keynes, *The General Theory*, p. 10.

[12]J. T. Dunlop, "The Movement of Real and Money Wages," *Economic Journal*, March 1938, and L. Tarshis, "Changes in Real and Money Wages," *Economic Journal*, March 1939, were two of the early empirical studies. These, however, were questioned by R. Ruggles, "Relative Movements of Real and Money Wage Rates," *Quarterly Journal of Economics*, November 1940, as not being statistically conclusive. In fact, J. H. Richardson, "Real Wage Movements," *Economic Journal*, September 1939, concluded that the generally held position is accurate.

Later studies include: Sho-Chieh Tsiang, *The Variations of Real Wages and Profit Margins in Relation to the Trade Cycle* (New York: Pitman Publishing Corp., 1947); Daniel Creamer, *Behavior of Wage Rates During Business Cycles* (New York: National Bureau of Economic Research, 1950), Occasional Paper No. 34, and "Behavior of Wage Rates During Business Cycles," in *The Relationship of Prices to Economic Stability and Growth*, United States Joint Economic Committee, March 21, 1958; and A. Rees, "Patterns of Wages, Prices, and Productivity," Chapter 1 in *Wages, Prices, Profits, and Productivity*, ed. C. A. Myers (New York: The American Assembly, 1959).

the course of the cycle is far from simple. Nonetheless, the evidence indicates that during the later stages of the expansion, real wages tend to rise (that is, money wages rise faster than the prices of consumers' goods), and thus Keynes was not quite correct.[13] Keynes, however, was fully aware of the complexities involved in the behavior of real wages over the cycle and in fact discussed them at later points in his analysis.[14]

Another important aspect of the aggregate supply curve of labor relates to the determinants of the perfectly elastic segment. Keynes argued that the workers' behavior implied by the curve is perfectly logical and sound. In his view each worker or group of workers will obviously resist a cut in the money wage relative to the money wages of others, for a reduction would mean that the worker or group ". . . will suffer a relative reduction in real wages, which is sufficient justification for them to resist it."[15] This means, of course, that workers make invidious comparisons of relative real wages, despite the fact that elsewhere Keynes argues that they think and bargain in terms of money wages. This, however, is not necessarily inconsistent. If the worker takes the price level as given and beyond his control, then a fall in his money wage relative to the money wages of others means that his "real" position has been worsened. Thus each worker makes his real wage comparisons in terms of his relative money-wage position.

But what of worker reaction to a declining real wage as employment rises? Is this not inconsistent and unrealistic behavior? Not so, says Keynes, for ". . . it would be impracticable to resist every reduction of real wages, due to a change in the purchasing power of money which affects all workers alike."[16] Thus, the elasticity of the supply curve of

---

[13]In his "Relative Movements of Real Wages and Output," *Economic Journal*, March 1939, Keynes conceded that his position may have been wrong.

[14]Especially in Book V of *The General Theory;* his more detailed analysis is discussed in sections 3-4 below.

[15]Keynes, *The General Theory*, p. 14.

[16]*Ibid.;* see also p. 15, where he states: "Every trade union will put up some resistance to a cut in money wages, however small. But . . . no trade union would dream of striking on every occasion of a rise in the cost of living. . . ." With respect to this statement, two comments are relevant.

First, there is the possibility of the union's tying its money wages to some cost-of-living index, so that the real wage is maintained. For a discussion of "escalator clauses" in collective bargaining contracts, see Hansen, *A Guide to Keynes*, pp. 193-96.

Second, Keynes did argue that as the expansionary stage of the cycle continues, unions will begin to bargin for and obtain increases in money wages. Thus the behavior of real wages is more complicated than assumed. As he put it (*The General Theory*, p. 301):

"Since each group of workers will gain, *cet. par.*, by a rise in its own wages, there is naturally for all groups a pressure in this direction, which entre-

labor up to full employment is determined by the attitudes and behavior of workers and trade unionists; and these must be taken as "givens," at least for purposes of analysis. The height of the supply curve, or course, is determined by the level of the prevailing money wage, and this is largely a result of past economic experience.

An important point to be stressed, and we shall return to this later, is that the perfectly elastic segment of the supply curve implies a downward rigidity of the money wage at the prevailing level; Keynes attached a great deal of significance to this "stickiness" of the money-wage level. Finally, we must note that, up to this point, the Keynesian wage analysis has been based on rather simplifying assumptions which are relaxed at a later stage in the discussion. But Keynes' purpose so far has been to refute the traditional neoclassical economic view on wage reductions as a means of eliminating unemployment. Let us now examine this traditional view and then turn to a discussion of the effects of reductions in the general wage level so far as Keynes was concerned.

2.　The Traditional View on Wage Cuts

Recall from earlier discussion[17] that the neoclassical economists argued that if there is any persistent involuntary unemployment, it must be due to a downward rigidity of wage rates. The main line of reasoning runs as follows: if there is involuntary unemployment, the unemployed workers can acquire jobs by offering their services at a lower real wage. This they can do, of course, by offering to hire out at a lower money wage; and since they have no control over product prices, a reduction in their money wage lowers their real wage. Further, if there is pure competition in product markets, the lowered wage costs result in lowered product prices, at which consumers can take a larger quantity from the market. By accepting money-wage cuts and thereby a lower real wage, the workers can become employed; and if there is still unemployment, wages and prices can be further reduced until full employment is reached. In short, if there is persistent unem-

---

preneurs will be more ready to meet when they are doing better business. For this reason a proportion of any increase in effective demand is likely to be absorbed in satisfying the upward tendency of the wage unit. . . . In actual experience the wage unit does not change continuously in terms of money in response to every small change in effective demand; but discontinuously. These points of discontinuity are determined by the psychology of the workers and by the policies of employers and trade unions."

[17]See Chapter 9, section 1.

ployment, it must be because unions and institutionalized wage behavior create a downward rigidity in the wage level.[18]

At first glance, Keynes' observations on the aggregate supply curve of labor seem to substantiate this thesis. If the aggregate demand curve for labor is DD in Figure 13–2, and there is involuntary unemployment by the amount XF, it must be due to the fact that the workers will not accept a wage cut. Keynes, however, rejected the traditional view that wage reductions would serve to restore the economy to full employment for two major reasons.

In the first place, as already noted, he argued that the workers simply refuse to accept money-wage cuts (within limits) and thus, even if the policy were theoretically sound, it is not practically feasible. But, in the second place, workers are not in fact able to work for a reduction in the real wage, even if they are willing to do so. Keynes argued that the traditional wage policy overlooks the significance of wage income as a share of total income and hence as a determinant of aggregate demand. Thus not only will a wage reduction lower production costs and product prices, it will also lower the income and demand of workers for consumers' goods. If the reduction in money prices is proportional to the fall in money wages (as Keynes contended it would be), there will be no reduction in the real wage and thus no increase in employment.[19] It must be remembered that throughout *The General Theory* Keynes assumed pure competition in all product markets and thus concluded that the lowered wage costs would be followed by a proportional reduction in prices. For this reason, then, even if workers are willing to offer their services at a lower real wage, they are unable to do so. Keynes' fundamental criticism of the neoclassical analysis and policy, therefore, was that it was based on the assumption that changes in the money wage have no effect upon aggregate demand. For him, on the other hand, the money income of the workers constitutes the lion's share of the total demand for consumers' goods, and there is thus a direct linkage between changes in wages and aggregate demand.[20] This linkage, however, need not always be detrimental to labor, as Keynes assumed; and as we shall see later, this issue is far from closed.

---

[18]For an excellent review of the literature on monetary theory and policy, see H. G. Johnson, "Monetary Theory and Policy," *American Economic Review,* June 1962; this article contains a good bibliography.

[19]Of course, if money prices fall less than money wages, real wages will decline. But Keynes was quite insistent that under conditions of pure competition the fall in money wages and prices would be equi-proportional; see *The General Theory,* p. 12.

[20]*Ibid.,* pp. 11-13.

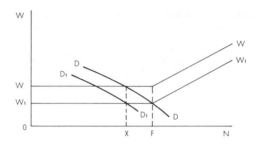

FIGURE 13–2

Keynes' argument is shown in Figure 13–2, where the demand curve (DD) cuts the supply curve (ww) at less than full employment (OX). The neoclassical economists argued that if the workers take a money-wage cut, so that they lower the supply curve to w_1w_1, there will be a movement down the demand curve to the full employment equilibrium at OF.[21] However, the Keynesian argument is that the demand curve will not remain stable, but rather will fall as the workers' incomes fall. Thus the demand curve drops (proportionately, as he argued) to D_1D_1, and employment remains at the OX level.

While there are several qualifications to this conclusion that will be discussed in the next section and in section 5 the two major conclusions drawn thus far may be repeated. First, Keynes rejected the neoclassical recommendation that unemployment can be eliminated by a general cut in money and real wages because workers will not in fact accept reductions in the money wage. Second, he rejected the traditional view because it ignores the interaction and interdependency between money wages, real wages, and aggregate demand; accordingly, even if workers were willing to accept a reduction in real wages in order to improve their employment opportunities, they are in reality unable to do so.[22]

3.   The Keynesian Analysis of Wage Reductions

As noted above, Keynes developed a more thorough analysis of the effects of wage cuts upon the level of employment than the preceding

[21]The neoclassical theory is put in real terms, whereas in Figure 13–2 we place money wages on the vertical axis. However, a drop in the supply curve in Figure 13–2 is the same thing as a movement along the supply curve in neoclassical analysis, where supply is a function of the real wage. See footnote 5.

[22]For an excellent discussion of all this, see Tobin, "Money Wage Rates and Employment."

discussion indicates. Of course, the final effects of money-wage reductions must be traced through the consumption function, investment demand function, and liquidity preference function. While Keynes concluded that there are two conceivable, though "impractical," cases in which a money-wage cut can increase employment, his analysis is far from complete. Let us examine his observations in more detail.

To begin with, what impact will a cut in wages have on the level of consumption? Keynes was rather doubtful that a drop in money wages would have much effect upon aggregate consumption, for he argued that money prices would fall proportionately, and hence total real income would remain constant. With total real income remaining constant, then any rise in total consumption resulting from a fall in money wages must stem from some redistribution of real income. Since the fall in money wages and prices will not affect all equally, there will surely be some redistributive effect. As Keynes put it: real income will be redistributed "(a) from wage-earners to other factors entering into marginal prime cost whose remuneration has not been reduced, and (b) from entrepreneurs to rentiers to whom a certain income fixed in terms of money has been guaranteed."[23]

Keynes felt that the first effect (a) would have an unfavorable impact on consumption since the wage earner has a higher propensity to consume than do the other income recipients. And he was uncertain as to what the second effect (b) would entail. On net balance, therefore, he believed that the wage cut would probably have an unfavorable impact upon aggregate consumer demand.

Note, however, that Keynes was thinking in rather restrictive terms— that is, he was assuming that the other factors of production will not lower their prices when wages are cut. If they do not, then labor will be substituted for them and this would, of course, be favorable for labor. On the other hand, if these other factors cut their prices to prevent such substitution, labor's position will not be adversely affected. It seems therefore that Keynes was assuming, rather inconsistently, that all factors other than labor are either fully employed or that labor cannot be substituted for them. Both of these assumptions seem rather unrealistic for the conditions assumed by Keynes, though perhaps the second is somewhat more plausible than the first for the short run. However, so long as there is some short-run substitutability of labor for other factors, a wage cut will have some favorable impact upon employment, if the prices of the other factors are not cut proportionately.[24]

---

[23]Keynes, *The General Theory*, p. 262.
[24]On this, see Tobin, "Money Wage Rates and Employment," pp. 578, 582-83; see also A. P. Lerner, "The Relation of Wage and Price Policies," *American Economic Review*, May 1939.

A far more fundamental criticism of Keynes' analysis of the impact of a wage cut on consumption revolves around the so-called "Pigou effect" or "real balances effect."[25] Keynes completely overlooked (or ignored) the effect that a cut in wages and prices would have on the real demand for consumers' goods. First, consumers may expect the price cut to be temporary and will increase their propensity to consume in order to buy ahead of the anticipated price increase. This, of course, could have a favorable impact on employment. But second, and far more relevant to the "Pigou effect," if the stock of money remains constant when wage and price levels fall, the real purchasing power of savings will rise. Therefore, a smaller amount of dollars is required to satisfy the propensity to save,[26] and consumers can increase their real demand for goods. This could have a favorable impact on employment, though, as we shall see later, only under certain conditions.

While it is sound to say that Keynes overlooked the importance of changing wage and price levels on the purchasing power of money and the amount of dollars needed to satisfy the propensity to save, it is also true that perhaps the advocates of the Pigou effect have not carried their analysis far enough.[27] Since we shall examine the Pigou effect in detail later on, just one illustration will suffice here. Consider the case where workers in general hold a *net money debtor position* (that is, their monetary debts exceed their monetary assets). This means that they must make fixed money payments to their creditors or relinquish some of their real assets. Now, if the wage and price levels fall, an increasing burden is placed on the workers, for they must continue to make the same fixed money payments out of a lowered money income. It can be argued that, under these conditions, extra members of the family will enter the labor force, swelling the ranks of the unemployed, in order to obtain jobs and aid in meeting the fixed money payments. Thus, a fall in money wages may well raise the aggregate supply curve of labor, making for more, rather than less, unemployment.[28]

---

[25]The "Pigou effect" is discussed in detail in Chapter 15, section 1-B.

[26]Assuming, of course, that the propensity to save does not rise *pari passu* because of the increasing unemployment and declining wage and price levels.

[27]However, it must be noted that Pigou himself did not recommend wage cuts as a means of restoring full employment to the economy, at least in the later versions of his analysis. See his *Lapses from Full Employment* (London: The Macmillan Company, 1952), p. v.

[28]For extended discussion of this possibility, see L. Hough, "An Asset Influence in the Labor Market," *Journal Of Political Economy*, June 1955. See also Long, "Impact of Effective Demand on the Labor Supply," who concludes that over the long period there is a rather stable relationship between the labor force and real or money hourly earnings. However, he also concludes that in the short period, "the labor force seems to vary inversely with real wages and salary earnings of adult male workers" (p. 460).

Note that this criticism is equally relevant for both the Pigou effect and Keynes' analysis of cuts in money wages. We shall refer to the Pigou effect again and in more detail, but it seems rather obvious that Keynes' analysis of the effects of a wage cut on aggregate consumption did not go far enough. Much more can be and has been said in this connection.[29]

On the other hand, what did Keynes have to say about the impact of a wage cut on investment demand and the interest rate? Here he did point out and discuss two cases in which employment could be favorably affected, though he did not attach much practical significance to them.

First, there is the instance in which a general reduction in the level of money wages results in a lower product price level. If the stock of money is held constant, this will lead to a shift of money from transactions to speculative balances, for now consumers and businesses need fewer dollars to finance their current expenditures. Accordingly the liquidity preference curve will fall, which means, with the stock of money held constant, a reduction in the interest rate. This, in turn, will stimulate an increment in investment spending and a positive multiplier effect.[30] Though he conceded this conclusion, Keynes did not recommend it as a policy. To the contrary, he felt that the same result could be achieved more quickly and easily by increasing the money supply. As he put it:

> A change in the quantity of money . . . is already within the power of most governments by open-market policy, or analogous measures. Having regard to human nature and our institutions, it can only be a foolish person who would prefer a flexible wage policy to a flexible money policy. . . .[31]

The second possible expansive effect resulting from a general money-wage reduction occurs when the economy has reached the depths of unemployment. Under these circumstances, the wage cut occurs when the entrepreneurs believe that in the future money wages will rise. Thus a cut is "favourable to an increase in the marginal efficiency of capital" because "money-wages are believed to have touched bottom, so that further changes are expected to be in the upward direction."[32] But again Keynes rejects this proposal, though it is theoretically sound,

---

[29]See Chapter 15, section 1-B.

[30]Assuming, of course, that the investment demand function has not fallen substantially to the left, that it is relatively elastic, and that there is no liquidity trap. For Keynes' discussion, see *The General Theory*, pp. 263-64.

[31]*Ibid.*, pp. 267-68. We should note that Keynes actually discussed seven possibilities but considered only the two covered here as relevant.

[32]*Ibid.*, p. 265.

because it entails a good deal of unemployment, and because, again, interest rate policy will achieve the same result.[33]

What major conclusions can be drawn from Keynes' analysis of money-wage cuts? As noted above, Keynes felt that workers will not only refuse reductions in real wages via cuts in money wages, but also cannot in fact reduce real wages. Thus he rejected the neoclassical policy of general wage cuts. Then he proceeded to show how, *within the framework of his own analysis,* in two cases a general wage reduction could stimulate employment by means of an increase in investment. However, he rejected such a policy program on the grounds that it would seriously impair basic institutions, and, more importantly, because the same results can be achieved more quickly and easily by increases in the stock of money. But even so, if the speculative balances demand curve is very elastic, and if the investment demand curve is very inelastic, neither policy would have much of a positive impact on the economy at large. Finally, it must be noted again that Keynes' analysis of the effects of a money-wage reduction on the propensity to consume was rather inadequate.

4.   The Theory of Inflation in the Keynesian System

Keynes' concern about changes in the money wage and price levels went much farther than the preceding discussion indicates, for he was quite interested in the impact that a rising money supply would have on the level of prices. At the outset he assumed that the most important prime (variable) cost is wage cost and thus concentrated almost exclusively on the behavior of money wages and prices as aggregate demand rises. If the supply curve of labor is perfectly elastic (at least up to near full employment), then an increase in aggregate demand may not influence the price level much. In other words, an increase in the stock of money that lowers the interest rate and increases investment and consumer spending will for the most part increase output, with wages and prices remaining relatively constant. However, as full employment is approached, the wage level begins to rise (as do other costs of production), and as the short-run supply curves of products become less and less elastic, the price level begins to rise. In fact, if the supply curve of products becomes perfectly inelastic, prices will rise proportionately with increases in the money supply, and the Quan-

---

[33]*Ibid.*

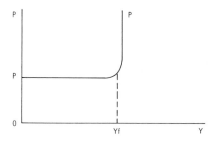

FIGURE 13–3

tity Theory comes into its own.[34] The behavior of the price level is shown in Figure 13–3, where income is plotted on the horizontal axis and the price level on the vertical. In the figure Y_f represents the full employment level of income.

In this rather simplified analysis, the price level begins to rise before full employment is reached; but up to near-full employment, the major result of rise in the money supply (and hence aggregate demand) is primarily an increase in output, with the price level remaining relatively stable. However, as full employment is approached, "bottlenecks," trade-union pressure for higher wages, and rising marginal costs begin to push the price level up. Keynes referred to this sort of situation, in which a further rise in aggregate demand (in terms of money) is shared between both rising output and prices, as "semi-inflation."[35] Finally, when further increases in the money supply simply increase total money demand but do not call forth any increase in output, there is "pure" or "true inflation."[36] This probably occurs somewhere beyond OY_f (in Figure 13–3) because the rising money wage will entice some new people into the labor force and will stimulate overtime work and the use of standby equipment; thus some output increases can be expected, though they will be swamped by the rising price level. When these possibilities are exhausted, "true inflation" sets in.

However, as Keynes argued, the process of inflation is complicated,

---

[34]*Ibid.*, pp. 289, 295-96. For good discussions of Keynes' theory of inflation, see Hansen, *A Guide to Keynes*, Chapter 11, and J. Lintner, "The Theory of Money and Prices," in *The New Economics: Keynes' Influence on Theory and Public Policy*, ed. Harris. For a more critical discussion, see Johnson, "Monetary Theory and Policy."

[35]Keynes, *The General Theory*, p. 301.

[36]*Ibid.*, p. 303.

and no simple analysis and no simple answer or generalization can be made. As he put it:

> Up to this point [of true inflation] the effect of monetary expansion is entirely a question of degree, and there is no previous point at which we can draw a definite line and declare that conditions of inflation have set in. Every previous increase in the quantity of money is likely, in so far as it increases effective demand, to spend itself partly in increasing the cost-unit and partly in increasing output.[37]

The problem, of course, is predicting the degree to which an increase in the money supply will affect both output and prices; and many important factors figure into the analysis, so that it is difficult, if not impossible, to reach a simple, sound conclusion.

For one thing, not all firms and industries will have the same marginal costs, and thus what happens to the price level and to output depends to a large extent upon which firms are affected by the rising aggregate demand.[38] If, for instance, the bulk of the rising demand is for products produced by firms with constant or only slightly rising marginal costs, the output effect will be greater than the price effect. On the other hand, if firms with sharply rising marginal costs benefit primarily from the rise in demand, the price effect will outweigh the output effect. In order to be more specific about inflation, then, we need to disaggregate both the total supply and demand functions; and this is a difficult task.[39]

Keynes also stressed the significance of bottlenecks, that is, inelastic supplies of some commodities and productive services, which emerge before full employment is reached. The prices of these specific products and services will begin to rise, and thus inflation will set in, before full employment is reached. As already noted, Keynes felt that the money-wage level will begin to rise as full employment is neared, particularly through trade union policy and action, and this will have a further inflationary impact.[40]

Because of the large number of variables that figure into the analysis of inflation, Keynes refused to draw any sweeping generalization as to

---

[37]*Ibid.*

[38]The analysis in this paragraph assumes the money-wage rate to be constant; that is, we are concerned with the shape, not the position, of the marginal cost curve. See A. H. Hansen, "Cost Functions and Full Employment," *American Economic Review,* September 1947, reprinted as Chapter 7 in his *Monetary Theory and Fiscal Policy* (New York: McGraw-Hill Book Company, 1949).

[39]For an excellent discussion of the problems of aggregation and disaggregation, see H. Theil, *Linear Aggregation of Economic Relations* (Amsterdam: North-Holland Publishing Company, 1954). See also J. Tinbergen, *Econometrics* (Philadelphia: Blakiston Company, 1952), Chapter 2; and R. G. D. Allen, *Mathematical Economics* (London: The Macmillan Company, 1959), Chapter 20.

[40]See footnote 16, above.

how increases in the money supply will be distributed between output and employment, on the one hand, and prices, on the other. Rather, his approach to the problem of inflation was cautious and tentative, based largely upon methodological considerations.

> The object of our analysis is, not to provide a machine, or method of blind manipulation, which will furnish an infallible answer, but to provide ourselves with an organized and orderly method of thinking out particular problems; and, after we have reached a provisional conclusion of isolating the complicating factors one by one, we then have to go back on ourselves and allow, as well as we can, for the possible interactions of the factors among themselves. This is the nature of economic thinking. Any other way of applying our formal principles of thought (without which, however, we shall be lost in the wood) will lead us into error.[41]

Thus the only concrete conclusion that Keynes was willing to draw was that as full employment is neared, the price level begins to rise and will rise more sharply after full employment is reached and the money supply continues to be increased. While this conclusion is hardly novel or exciting, it does point up a basic conflict between the goals of full employment and price-level stability.[42] The choice is, on the surface, relatively simple: either there is full employment, with some inflation; or there is price-level stability, with some unemployment.

What sort of evidence is there that will allow us to evaluate the argument that wage and price levels rise before full employment is reached? More specifically, what would the unemployment rate have to be if the price level is to remain relatively stable? Unfortunately, there is all too little evidence bearing on this issue, though what there is does *suggest* that, for the United States and the United Kingdom, about 5 to 6 per cent of the labor force must be unemployed if price and wage levels are to be stable.[43] This can be shown by a modified form of the so-called Phillips' curve (Figure 13–4).[44] The average yearly

---

[41]Keynes, *The General Theory*, p. 297.

[42]See discussion of this conflict in Chapter 1, but more particularly the discussion in Chapter 20.

[43]A. W. Phillips, "The Relation between Unemployment and the Rate of Change of Money Wage Rates in the United Kingdom, 1861-1957," *Economica*, November 1958; P. A. Samuelson and R. M. Solow, "Analytical Aspects of Anti-inflation Policy," *American Economic Review*, May 1960; L. R. Klein and R. J. Ball, "Some Econometrics of the Determination of Absolute Prices and Wages," *Economic Journal*, September 1959; and L. G. Reynolds, "Wage-Push and All That," *American Economic Review*, May 1960.

[44]The Phillips' curve, so named after A. W. Phillips, cited in the preceding footnote, relates increases in average hourly earnings to the rate of unemployment. The curve in Figure 13–4, which we label a *modified* Phillips' curve, shows the relationship between increases in the price level and the rate of unemployment. This modification of the Phillips' curve is attributable to Samuelson and Solow, "Analytical Aspects of Anti-inflation Policy."

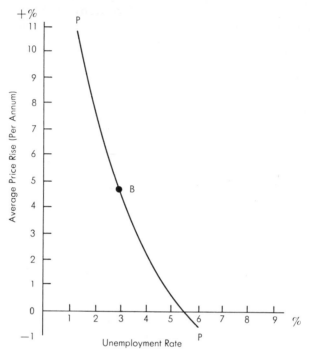

FIGURE 13–4

rise in the price level is plotted on the vertical axis, and the unemployment rate is plotted on the horizontal axis. The curve PP, thus, reveals how much the price level will rise as the rate of unemployment drops towards zero. The curve cuts the horizontal axis at point A, which indicates that price-level stability can be achieved at the cost of unemployment of 5½ per cent of the labor force. On the other hand, if full employment is defined as 97 per cent of the labor force, leaving a residue of 3 per cent as "frictional" unemployment, then full employment can be achieved at the expense of an annual rise in the price level of about 4 to 5 per cent. This is shown at point B on the PP curve. As Professors Samuelson and Solow conclude: "That much price rise would seem to be the necessary cost of high employment and production in the years immediately ahead."[45]

---

[45]*Ibid.*, p. 192. It must be noted that Samuelson and Solow are indeed quite tentative and cautious in advancing their conclusions, primarily because of rather inadequate data.

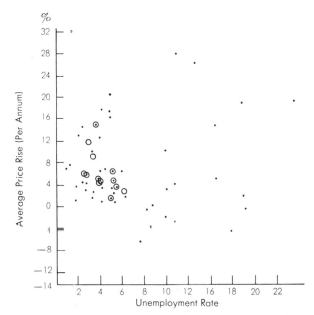

Source: Samuelson and Solow, "Analytical Aspects of Anti-inflation Policy," p. 188.

FIGURE 13–5

But is the modified Phillips' curve in Figure 13–4 based on empirical data, or is it simply a hypothetical conjecture? Figure 13–5 is a scatter diagram that relates increases in *average hourly earnings* to the unemployment rate. While at first glance it seems that the points do not indicate any meaningful relationship between changes in unemployment and the money-wage rate over the span of years from 1861 to 1960, there does appear to be a rather consistent picture with respect to the period from 1946 to 1960. These points are circled, indicating a negatively sloped Phillips' curve; and *if increases in money wages* are translated *into increases in prices,* then a modified Phillips' curve somewhat like that in Figure 13–4 emerges. However, and this point must be stressed, the available data do no more than to *suggest* these findings. They must be interpreted very cautiously and actually treated as "guesstimates" rather than sound, solid conclusions.[46]

We shall return to the problem of inflation particularly in the discussion of economic policy for stabilization and growth. Needless to

---

[46]See Reynolds, "Wage-Push and All That," pp. 197-98, for a critical evaluation of the methods and findings.

say, the analysis of inflation has progressed beyond Keynes' discussion in *The General Theory*, though it still remains in an unsatisfactory state. The basic conclusion for now is that Keynes was very much concerned with inflation, did develop some analysis of it, but did not draw any concrete conclusion, other than that as full employment is neared, the price level begins to rise and will rise more sharply once full employment is reached and the money supply continues to be increased. He also stressed the complexity of the inflationary process and the need to examine each inflationary situation on its own merits.

5. The Significance of "Sticky" Wages

We have already reviewed Keynes' position on the neoclassical policy of wage reductions as a means of eliminating involuntary unemployment. His contention, recall, was that a cut in money wages is followed by a proportionate fall in money prices, and thus employment is not raised. Moreover, if this policy were adhered to, and if the initial wage reduction did not increase employment, then a further wage cut would be called for; then still another; and so on. For this reason (that the wage and price levels would continue to fall, without employment's increasing), Keynes was so critical of this policy. As he put it: "The chief result of this policy would be to cause a great instability of prices, so violent perhaps as to make business calculations futile in an economic society functioning after the manner in which we live."[47] The difficulties of estimating rates of return on investment projects, of adjusting consumption plans to expected changes in the price level, and of making adjustments in investment portfolios are obvious if the price level is continually falling. Further, Keynes felt that if the wage level were to fall without limit, "there would be no resting-place below full employment until either the rate of interest was incapable of falling further or wages were zero."[48]

Accordingly, Keynes advocated that some factor should have a money value which must be, "if not fixed, at least sticky, to give us any stability of values in a monetary system."[49] And for him the preferable "sticky value" was the money wage. A stable money-wage level, he felt, would stabilize prices (in a downward direction), and thus private

[47]Keynes, *The General Theory*, p. 269.
[48]*Ibid.*, p. 304.
[49]*Ibid.*

economic decisions and public policies could be more effectively carried out. We should note, however, if only in passing, that while he
advocated rigid wages in a downward direction, he also advocated a
rising wage level over the long run, with money wages rising *pari passu*
with productivity.[50] Thus the price level would remain relatively
stable over the long haul.

In sum, Keynes recommended sticky wages as a device for stabilizing
expectations (in the short run). And though he was aware that this prevents downward wage adjustments and thus eliminates the neoclassical
wage policy, he argued that the policy would not work anyway. At
best it would leave unemployment where it is; at worst, it would depress expectations, especially those of the entrepreneurs who would
revise their investment demand schedules downward even more.

6. Summary

In this chapter we have examined how Keynes introduced money
wages and prices into his analysis. While at an early stage he defined
the aggregate supply curve of labor as perfectly elastic up to full employment, his discussion of the role of money wages and prices as the
economy approaches full employment led him to revise this interpretation. That is, the supply curve begins to rise as full employment is
approached, reflecting the fact that part of the increases in aggregate
demand are absorbed by rising money wages (and thus prices). But
up to this point, most of the effect of an increase in aggregate demand
is to raise output, leaving money wages and prices relatively constant.
It is only as full employment is reached that the rising aggregate demand is partially absorbed by rising prices and wages. This condition
he referred to as "semi-inflation," while he defined "true inflation" as
the situation in which further rises in aggregate demand will not raise
real output, but only wages and prices. All told, Keynes did not draw
any sweeping conclusions about the inflationary process.

However, he did reject the neoclassical contention that a reduction
in the real wage level would, if carried far enough, restore full employment. His position here was that (1) workers refuse money-wage cuts,
and (2) that the workers cannot, in reality, accept reductions in their
real wages because of the interdependency between wages income and
aggregate demand. He did conclude that money-wage cuts might lower

---

[50]*Ibid.*, pp. 306-09.

the rate of interest and hence stimulate investment spending, though he rejected this as a practical means of combating unemployment. Further, he admitted that a fall in money wages, if they have already fallen substantially, might indicate to entrepreneurs that soon wages would rise, and this might raise their investment demand curve. But again he rejected this on grounds of practicality. Rather than pursue such a policy, he contended, established monetary policy should be used. Finally, Keynes' analysis of the effects of falling wages and prices on aggregate consumption was deficient, because he overlooked the impact of a falling price level on the real purchasing power of assets, especially money.

QUESTIONS

13-1. Discuss in detail the Keynesian distinction between "semi-inflation" and "pure inflation." Do you think that this is a meaningful distinction? Explain.

13-2. What is Keynes' definition of "involuntary unemployment," and how is this definition related to his concept of the aggregate supply curve of labor?

13-3. What is meant by the "money illusion," and is it necessarily inconsistent so far as worker behavior is concerned? Explain.

13-4. Keynes took a strong, definite stand against cuts in money wages as a means of restoring full employment. What were his views on this policy? What were his views on the downward rigidity of the general money-wage level? Do you agree? Explain.

13-5. Discuss the two situations in which Keynes agreed that a reduction in the money-wage level might lead to a rise in employment. What, however, were his major conclusions with respect to these two situations?

Bibliography

Dunlop, J. T., "The Movement of Real and Money Wages," *Economic Journal*, March 1938.

Hansen, A. H., *A Guide to Keynes.* New York: McGraw-Hill Book Company, 1953.

Hough, L., "An Asset Influence in the Labor Market," *Journal of Political Economy*, June 1955.

Johnson, H. G., "Monetary Theory and Policy," *American Economic Review*, June 1952.

Keynes J. M., *The General Theory of Employment, Interest, and Money.* New York: Harcourt, Brace & World, Inc., 1936.

Lintner, J., "The Theory of Money and Prices," in *The New Economics: Keynes' Influence on Theory and Public Policy*, ed. S. E. Harris. New York: Alfred A. Knopf, 1950.

Long, C. D., "Impact of Effective Demand on the Labor Supply," *American Economic Review*, May 1953

Perlman, R., "A Reformulation of Keynesian Wage Theory," *Southern Economic Journal*, January 1960.

Phillips, A. W., "The Relation between Unemployment and the Rate of Change in Money Wage Rates in the United Kingdom, 1861-1957," *Economica*, November 1958.

Rees, A., "Patterns of Wages, Prices, and Productivity," in *Wages, Prices, Profits, and Productivity*, ed. C. A. Myers. New York: The American Assembly, 1959.

Samuelson, P. A. and R. M. Solow, "Analytical Aspects of Anti-inflation Policy," *American Economic Review*, May 1960.

Smithies, A., "Effective Demand and Employment," in *The New Economics: Keynes' Influence on Theory and Public Policy*, ed. Harris.

Tarshis, L., "Changes in Real and Money Wages," *Economic Journal*, March 1939.

Tobin, J., "Money Wage Rates and Employment," in *The New Economics: Keynes' Influence on Theory and Public Policy*, ed. Harris.

part 4

Dynamic Interactions of Economic Growth
and Cyclical Fluctuations

14

The Post-Keynesian
Emphasis on Growth

Although the impact of *The General Theory* was substantial and enduring, its analysis has come under a good deal of criticism. As is usually the case in the development of economic thought, however, many of these criticisms (both positive and negative) have led to important further theoretical advancements. The result of all the debate and controversy has been the emergence of a substantial body of thought on the business cycle and economic growth that is usually referred to as post-Keynesian analysis.[1] We have, in fact, already examined certain post-Keynesian developments in the preceding part, especially Hicks' theory of the business cycle. In this part, however, we shall investigate several other important recent developments.

The title "post-Keynesian" is at once revealing and misleading. It is revealing in the sense that it implies that modern cycle and growth theory is based in large part upon such Keynesian concepts as the consumption function and the multiplier. In fact, it is beyond dispute that

---

[1]For an illustration of "post-Keynesian" economics, see the essays in *Post-Keynesian Economics*, ed. K. K. Kurihara (New Brunswick: Rutgers University Press, 1954). H. J. Bruton, in his "Contemporary Theorizing on Economic Growth," Chapter VII in *Theories of Economic Growth*, ed. B. F. Hoselitz (Glencoe: The Free Press, 1960), gives a good review of recent literature in the field.

modern cycle and growth theory relies heavily upon the analytical concepts developed in *The General Theory*. But there is more to it than simply this.

The title is misleading in that it implies that the theoretical concepts developed in Keynes' work are merely being used in somwhat different ways than they are used in *The Genral Theory*. This is incorrect—modern cycle and growth theory is much more than a variation on a theme. For example, the consumption function has been modified so that it is more useful for growth theory, and the multiplier-accelerator interaction is relied on heavily.[2] Other important concepts, such as the capital-output ratio and the full-employment ceiling, have been extensively used.

All in all, post-Keynesian analysis is best interpreted as an active symbiosis of *General Theory* and post-*General Theory* analysis. But the resulting framework, despite its diversity and lack of systematic coherence, has contributed much to our understanding of the process of economic growth in industrially advanced countries. Moreover, it has opened up policy avenues and raised questions and problems hitherto largely neglected. Indeed, it may be that modern analysis raises more questions than it answers, though this could well be a merit.

In this part we shall examine some of the more important developments in post-Keynesian economics. More specifically, we shall discuss the theories advanced by such economists as Harrod, Domar, Fellner, Duesenberry, and Hansen.[3] The outstanding feature of these theories is that they stress the interdependence of economic growth and the business cycle. In this sense they differ significantly from the analyses presented in Parts 2 and 3, which, with a few notable exceptions,[4] tend to neglect the growth dimensions of cyclical fluctuations. The theories discussed in the present part are specifically oriented toward explaining the requirements for smooth, uninterrupted economic growth and the occurrence of cyclical disturbances when one or more of these requirements is absent. In other words, their basic premise is that the cycle and growth are so interrelated that one cannot be discussed meaningfully without the other. However, they nearly all begin with a consideration of the requirements for a smooth, uninterrupted growth

---

[2]We have already encountered one example of this in Hicks' theory of the cycle (see Chapter 12). In Chapters 16-18 we shall review several other theories that make use of the multiplier-accelerator interaction.

[3]While several other economists (such as Goodwin, Kaldor, Kalecki, Smithies, Matthews, Solow, and others) have developed growth theories, the ones mentioned in the text are representative of modern thought.

[4]Especially Hansen, Schumpeter, and Hicks.

process and then move to an examination of cyclical disturbances when the growth process is upset.

It should be noted that the new concern over growth represents a reemphasis. The classical economists, as already noted,[5] were very much concerned over the requirements, nature, and potential of economic growth, so much so in fact that they tended to neglect the business cycle. Many cycle theories, on the other hand, and certainly the Keynesian analysis, tended to neglect growth almost completely. In the post-Keynesian period, however, we find an emphasis on both growth and the cycle.

1.   The Reemphasis on Growth Theory: Empirical Concern

Why is post-Keynesian analysis so much concerned with growth theory? Although several reasons can be advanced, only two are discussed here. First, there is the empirical concern of many American economists—a concern that stems from empirical observations of the growth rate of the economy of the United States as contrasted with the growth rates of the economies of the Soviet Union and other countries. The growing availability of statistical data and the changing performance of different economies in the world have focused attention more and more upon the processes of economic growth.

Second, there has developed, following *The General Theory,* an intellectual concern that revolves around a certain inconsistency in any aggregative analysis that concentrates simply on the short run. Though this inconsistency is discussed in the next section, we may give a provisional statement of it here. The condition for an equilibrium in the short run is that (actual and desired) savings equal (actual and desired) investment. While this may be an adequate statement so far as the short run is concerned—and when the long-run aspects are neglected—there still remains the basic fact that an increase in investment (until it equals savings) has a two-fold impact. In the first place, it adds to the purchasing power of the economy via the multiplier-accelerator effect; but in the second place, it adds to the productive capacity of the economic system. Consideration of this second point brings the analysis around to its long-run aspects, for if the increase in purchasing power is not sufficient to utilize fully the added productive capacity, the short-run equilibrium will not be maintained. But this anticipates discussion

---

[5]See Chapter 5 for a brief review of this movement, and see the next chapter for a detailed treatment of the classical view.

in the next section; for the present we are concerned with the empirical concern over growth.

There is the cold fact that the so-called military race between the United States and the Soviet Union is more than a military conflict—it is also an economic race. To a large extent, of course, military power derives from economic power, though we must not confuse the quantitative and qualitative aspects of this. A rise in gross national product is no strict assurance that military strength has increased. The rise in gross national product may be devoted entirely to increased consumption of private goods and services. Moreover, even with a constant or declining gross national product, military strength may be increased by the process of reallocating productive services away from the private sector of the economy toward the military sector. When it comes to the relationship between gross national product and military power, it seems that the allocation of GNP is just as important as its total size.[6]

It would be a mistake, therefore, to conclude that the race between the major powers is strictly military. To the contrary, it has its roots deep in ideological and political differences. For our purposes it is much more meaningful to view it, not as a military contest, *but rather as a production race*, where gains are scored as significant "wins" for the various sides. This was made evident in 1956 when Nikita S. Khrushchev addressed the Congress of the Soviet Communist Party as follows:

> In its economic competition with capitalism, our country, owing to the advantages of the Socialist system of economy, is showing immeasurable higher rates of increase in production than the most advanced capitalist countries.
>
> For instance, our average annual rates of increase in industrial output during the past five-year period were more than three times as high as that of the U. S. A. and 3.8 times that of Britain.
>
> The great advantages of the Socialist economic system, the high rate of development of social production, make it possible for us to carry out in an historically brief period the main economic task of the U. S. S. R.—to catch up and surpass the most developed countries in the output per capita of population.
>
> When we say that in the competition between the two systems of capitalism and socialism, socialism will triumph, this by no means implies that the victory will be reached by armed intervention on the part of Socialist countries in the internal affairs of the capitalist countries.
>
> We believe that after seeing for themselves the advantages that Communism holds out, all working men and women on earth will sooner or later take to the road of the struggle to build a Socialist society.[7]

---

[6]This point is stressed by J. K. Galbraith in his *The Affluent Society* (Boston: Houghton Mifflin Company, 1958), Chapter 12.

[7]© 1956 by The New York Times Company. Reprinted by permission.

The Post-Keynesian Emphasis on Growth

TABLE 14–1

Indexes of Soviet Industrial Production

Index	1928	1937	1940	1950	1955
Official Soviet	100	446	646	1,119	2,065
Hodgman	100	371	430	646	—
Jasny	100	287	330-350	411	—
Clark	100	311	340	—	—
National Bureau	100	257	279	421	688
Shimkin	100	274	296	434	715

Source: Campbell, *Soviet Economic Power,* p. 48.

This is obviously a production challenge, with a "winner-take-all" prize being offered. As a consequence, western economists have devoted more time, attention, and analysis to the rate of growth of production in both the Soviet Union and western countries, as well as to the economic problems of the underdeveloped economies.

The Soviet record, even after statistically expansionary biases have been removed,[8] is impressive. Although we need pay little attention to the Soviet claim that Russian industrial output was twenty-one times larger in 1955 than it was in 1928, numerous calculations made by persons and groups disassociated with the Soviet Union reveal a high rate of economic growth. These calculations are summarized in Table 14–1.[9]

The United States record, on the other hand, has also been impressive, and for a much longer period of time, as was shown in Part 1. For example, the growth rate in manufacturing and mining has been quite high for a sustained period.[10] From 1880 to 1953 the value of output in manufacturing and mining rose almost twenty-fold, from $8.83 billion to $173.66 billion (in 1929 prices). During the same period, gross national product rose only ten-fold, from $18 billion to $185 billion. But it is important to keep in mind that the growth rates of manufacturing, mining and gross national product have shown some retardation. Recall the discussion in Chapter 4, section 2, in which this process of retarda-

[8]See R. W. Campbell, *Soviet Economic Power: Its Organization, Growth, and Challenge* (Boston: Houghton Mifflin Company, 1959), for a good discussion of this point.

[9]See also the recent study by A. Tarn and R. W. Campbell, "A Comparison of U. S. and Soviet Industrial Output," *American Economic Review,* September 1962.

[10]These data are taken from D. Creamer, S. P. Dobrovolsky, and I. Borenstein, *Capital in Manufacturing and Mining; Its Formation and Financing* (Princeton: Princeton University Press, 1960). See also the more comprehensive study by S. Kuznets, *Capital in the American Economy: Its Formation and Financing* (Princeton: Princeton University Press, 1961).

tion was examined. Needless to say, this has created some concern among economists as to the possible future performance of the American economy. To be sure, there are disagreements, with some economists arguing that the future will be characterized by continued retardation of the rate of output and others insisting that the possibilities point to continued and sustained growth.[11]

2.   The Reemphasis on Growth: The Intellectual Concern

Economists have become concerned with growth theory also because examination of the Keynesian analysis raises certain intellectual questions. The most important of these relates to the fact that investment in the short run has certain long-run implications. While the short-run Keynesian analysis may be sufficient for certain problems, the longer-run dimensions cannot be overlooked.

Consider the basic requirements for a short-run equilibrium—namely, that desired and actual savings be equal to each other and to desired and actual investment. So long as some inequality prevails between these four magnitudes, disequilibrium exists. In fact, the major task of Chapter 12 was to show how a disequilibrium situation is, under the necessary assumptions, self-corrective so that equilibrium emerges. But we must note and stress that this "equilibrium" is relevant for only a short period of time. The situation becomes quite different when we examine the longer-run characteristics of the economy.

To illustrate this, let us assume that there is a certain amount of savings in the economy. Now if an insufficient amount of investment is forthcoming, so that savings remain larger than investment, the income level will drop until once again savings and investment are equal. On the other hand, when investment exceeds savings, the level of income rises until a higher-level equilibrium is established. Finally if just the correct amount of investment materializes, then the equilibrium is established at that income level. In other words, so long as investment equals savings (as long as all relevant plans are realized), there is no tendency for the income level to change.

However, this short-run analysis overlooks the significant fact that

---

[11]For example, E. F. Denison, *The Sources of Economic Growth in the United States and the Alternatives Before Us* (New York: Committee for Economic Development, 1962), concludes that use of the alternatives facing us will yield, perhaps at best, an extra 0.1 percentage point for the growth rate. For an excellent critical review of this book, see M. Abramovitz, "Economic Growth in the United States," *American Economic Review*, September 1962.

net investment not only absorbs current savings, but that it also creates additions to the productive capacity of the economy. After all, net investment basically is an addition to the productive capital stock of the system, and as such it creates further questions as to the profitable rate of its use in the future. In other words, will the net investment create enough additional demand (in the aggregate) to provide for full use of the extra productive capacity it also creates?

As we shall see, this is a crucial question. For if the net investment creates an insufficient demand to call for the full use of the additional productive capacity, some of the investment will turn out to be unprofitable. In this event, businessmen will (again, in the aggregate) become dissatisfied with their past investment activity and accordingly will reduce their current and future investment plans. The result: obviously a decline in the levels of income and employment.

On the other hand, if the increase in demand generated by the net investment exceeds the increase in productive capacity, inflation will result; and inflation is, *if substantial enough*, incompatible with the short-run equilibrium level of income and may retard the growth process.

Now if it is assumed, and most modern growth theories make the assumption, that the propensity to save is given and constant, then the crucial question becomes this: Will the net investment in the current period induce enough investment in the next period to absorb all the savings of the next period? If an insufficient amount of induced investment is forthcoming, or if on the other hand too much induced investment materializes, then the short-run Keynesian equilibrium is merely a temporary phenomenon. Of course, if just the precise amount of investment is induced, the short-run equilibrium is maintained into the next period, but the problem is then merely postponed to the subsequent period. In sum, the basic analysis now revolves around the requirements necessary for a moving equilibrium from one period to the next.

While this approach to aggregative analysis may sound rather strange at this point, its importance will be made apparent in the next few chapters. The preceding comments are meant merely to set the stage for more detailed discussion and analysis. One final comment is in order. Although we shall be primarily concerned with modern theories of the interaction of growth and the business cycle, most of modern theory has a rich heritage in classical economics. While an understanding of the classical growth theory is not essential to comprehend modern growth-cycle theory, we feel that it is an important part of aggregative economic analysis. Accordingly we shall begin our review of growth theory with a discussion of the classical view; following this we turn our attention to the modern approaches.

15

The Classical View

During the late eighteenth and early nineteenth centuries western Europe, particularly England, experienced a period of dynamic economic change which was characterized by significant technological advances and economic growth. Old ways of doing things were discarded and replaced by new techniques and organizations, and, as might be expected, the resultant economic and social repercussions were far-reaching. The economists of this period were, of course, able to observe the expansionary effects of the "Industrial Revolution," and they devoted a good deal of study to it. They tended to focus their attention upon two important questions: first, the direction that the economic change would continue to take; and second, the final economic structure that would emerge from the growth process.

These economists have since come to be referred to as members of the "Classical School," and they include in their number such outstanding men as Adam Smith, David Ricardo, Thomas Robert Malthus, John Stuart Mill, Nassau Senior, and J. B. Say. Although all of these economists can be conveniently grouped together into a school of thought, this does not mean that they were in complete agreement on all points. To the contrary, there were some important "dissenters" (especially Malthus) from the "classical view." However, despite these few dissenters,[1] the classical economists were sufficiently similar in approach,

---

[1]These classical "dissenters" are discussed briefly in section 3.

method, and conclusions that we are justified in speaking of the "classical view."

Chronologically the period of classical economic thought ran roughly from 1776—the publication date of Adam Smith's *The Wealth of Nations*—to approximately 1850-1875—the time of John Stuart Mill.[2] Classical thought, however, did not go unchallenged, and accordingly it underwent several changes from about the midpoint of the nineteenth century on. The resulting body of thought is what is now referred to as neoclassical economic thought. Although this transition was somewhat gradual, it is safe to say that neoclassicism blossomed forth in the last quarter of the last century. Before examining the neoclassical and later contributions, however, the intellectual foundation laid by the classicists must be examined.

1. Say's Law

As noted above, the classical economists lived in the period of the Industrial Revolution, a period of tremendous economic expansion which they conceived of as the "take-off point" for further economic growth. Yet paradoxically, the classicists paid little attention to the problem of the business cycle, despite the obvious fact that there were "crises" in 1815, 1825, 1836-39, 1847-48, 1857, and 1866. Indeed, with the possible exception of Malthus, they did not bother to develop a theory of business fluctuations but instead concentrated on the growth patterns and potentials of the capitalist economy. In doing this they constructed a body of analysis which concluded that not only could there be no substantial fluctuations around the growth trend, but that the growth trend itself would continue until there eventually emerged the so-called "stationary state."

This does not mean, however, that the classicists argued that there would not be *no* small, temporary disturbances from the growth trend. They pointed out that there may indeed be *temporary* disturbances, but once any disturbance does occur, certain forces built into the capitalist system itself will come into play to correct it.

---

[2]See any adequate textbook on the history of economic thought for a more extensive discussion of the various dimensions of classical economic thought. Two especially good references are O. H. Taylor, *A History of Economic Thought* (New York: McGraw-Hill Book Company, 1960), and L. Rogin, *The Meaning and Validity of Economic Thought* (New York: Harper & Row, Publishers, 1956). For a more thorough and advanced treatment, see J. A. Schumpeter, *A History of Economic Analysis* (New York: Oxford University Press, 1954).

Now why, according to the classical view, do not cyclical disturbances last for any appreciable length of time? The answer is largely to be found in their views on the very nature of the capitalist economic system. That is to say, if either inflation or unemployment occurs, certain adjustments "naturally" and automatically come into play to eliminate it; and these adjustments were viewed by the classicists as being an intrinsic part of the capitalist structure. Indeed this characteristic of the system was viewed as being provided by "natural laws" and would be operative so long as man does not interfere with the behavior of these laws. The logical outcome of this approach is, of course, *laissez faire*—"do not interfere with the natural operations of capitalism, and this holds for aggregate disturbances as well as for particular ones." One major consequence of this view is perhaps obvious—namely, it delayed the development of an adequate analysis of the business cycle for quite some time.

The classical analysis and its major conclusion that the economy would naturally and automatically operate at continuing full employment and price-level stability have traditionally gone under the title of Say's Law, named after the French economist Jean Baptiste Say.[3] Note, however, that the classical economists did not themselves fully develop, at least in rigorous analytical form, the theory implied by such a phrase as Say's *Law*. In fact, the rigorous formulation was not forthcoming until the time of the neoclassical school, which argued that there can be continuing full employment only under conditions of *perfect flexibility of wages and prices*. One specific version of this later analysis is known as the "Pigou effect," after A. C. Pigou, the British economist who did so much to make clear the necessary assumptions and logical reasoning underlying Say's Law.[4]

Closer examination actually reveals that there are *two versions* of Say's Law. While some economists argue that the law is inoperative without perfect adjustability of wages and prices (as stressed by the Pigou effect),[5] there is another, and older, version of the law which posits that all that is needed for continuing full employment at stable

---

[3]Actually this conclusion was common to nearly all the classicists (aside from Adam Smith and the "dissenters" discussed below). The title "Say's Law" has become generally accepted because of J. B. Say's popularization of the classical doctrine.

[4]The Pigou effect is discussed in section 1-B of this chapter; see also the earlier references in Chapters 9 and 13.

[5]See, for example, the statement by W. J. Fellner, *The Emergence and Development of Modern Economic Analysis* (New York: McGraw-Hill Book Company, 1960), p. 82.

price levels is *perfect flexibility* of the interest rate.[6] This latter view, which is closer to the classicist's general view, is discussed immediately below; the Pigou effect is discussed subsequently. It should be emphasized, however, that the classical view and the Pigou effect are not contradictory, but rather arrive at the same conclusions by stressing the significance of different variables.

A. The Classicists' Emphasis on the Interest Rate

Why, according to the classical economists, will the economy operate at continuing full employment without inflation or contraction? Why do not serious cyclical disturbances occur? What are the automatically adjusting procsses that iron out the cycle? These are the major questions to be considered at this point.

Say's Law is based upon a host of assumptions, most of which will emerge as the discussion proceeds; but three of these must be stated explicitly at the outset. First, there is assumed to be no hoarding of monetary funds by anyone (or, if hoarding already exists, it is assumed that there will be no change in the amount hoarded). Second, pure competition is assumed to exist in all markets, and as a corollary to this, all economic units are motivated by pecuniary maximization, whether it be of wages, interest, or any other type of income.[7] Third, it is assumed that as a psychological fact people prefer present satisfaction to future satisfaction, and that if they are induced to forego immediate pleasure in favor of future satisfaction, they must be given additional compensation in the form of interest payments. This last assumption usually goes under the name of the "time-preference theory of the interest rate."[8] Thus if people are to be induced to cut back on their present consumption and increase present savings, they must be offered a sufficiently high interest rate so that future satisfaction will be increased enough to offset the loss of present enjoyment.

Two cases are analyzed here, one of which will indicate why there can be no serious unemployment over time; the second why there can be no significant problem of inflation.

---

[6]The "classical view" also assumes pure competition in all relevant markets. The major difference between it and the Pigou effect version of Say's Law is that it stresses the flexibility of the interest rate as the major equilibrating force, while the latter stresses flexibility of wages and prices as the major equilibrating device.

[7]This, of course, is an assumption common to much of economic theory, whether microeconomics or macroeconomics.

[8]The time-preference theory of the interest rate is usually attributed to Nassau Senior.

(1) Why, in the classical view, can there be no serious contraction? To begin with, assume that, for some unexplained psychological reason, consumers have cut back their consumer demand and increased their present savings; that is, there has occurred an autonomous change in their time-preference calculations. This decline in demand would initially lead to a drop in employment and output in the consumers' goods industries, but according to the classicists this unemployment will not be permanent. The increased savings will be made available in the financial funds market so that the supply of loanable funds increases relative to the demand for them. This of course will lower the interest rate. Two consequences of different sorts and different timing will follow. First, in the short run the lower rate of interest will bring about a reduction in the amount of savings since at the lower rate people are more willing to consume in the present rather than in the future. This fall in the rate of interest will at first be relatively large, though by itself it will not immediately stimulate any net investment. In other words, the short-run demand for loanable funds is perfectly inelastic with respect to changes in the interest rate. Second, however, there will be a stimulation of net investment as time passes. That is, in the long run production techniques can be altered and new investment plans can be drawn up and put into effect so that the demand for loanable funds becomes more elastic with respect to the rate of interest. Thus as a result of the drop in the interest rate, there will be some increase in net investment in the long run.

All of this can be explained more explicitly with reference to Figure 15–1, in which the DD and SS curves designate the community's desires to demand and to supply loanable funds at various rates of interest. The short vertical D'D' curve designates the short-run demand curve for loanable funds; it is perfectly inelastic with respect to the rate of interest because of sunk capital and because of the time required to put new investment projects into operation. In Figure 15–1 we initially assume that the supply curve of loanable funds increases (shifts to the right) so that at the prevailing rate of interest (i) the community is willing to increase its holdings of loanable funds by the amount D'E. At the interest rate of i, however, the quantity supplied in the short run is in excess of the quantity demanded (D'D') by the amount of D'E. As a result, competition in the financial funds market will reduce the interest rate to the level of i', at which the short-run quantity demanded is equal to the quantity supplied. This means that for a large number of individuals, consumption will increase back to its former level, since they are unwilling to hold loanable funds by the extra amount D'E when the interest rate is at such a low level (i'). Thus, in the short run

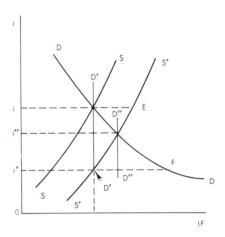

FIGURE 15–1

the attempt to increase the amount of loanable funds is thwarted, and the total amount supplied is equal to the total amount demanded, though now at a lower rate of interest. Total consumption expenditures, in other words, return to their former level and full employment is restored.

The rate of interest is now much lower than before, however, and this will, as time passes, stimulate net investment. Projects which were formerly unprofitable at the higher rate now become profitable, as shown by the long-run DD curve which measures the anticipated net return from net, new investment projects.

At the interest rate of i' the long-run quantity demanded of loanable funds exceeds the long-run quantity supplied by the amount D'F. However, as firms bid for the loanable funds in the effort to put their now profitable investment projects into being, the rate of interest rises, thus cutting off some of the potential investment projects. The rate eventually begins to rise to the level of i'', where the quantity demanded again equals the quantity supplied. At this new equilibrium the short-run demand curve becomes D''D'', and it is again perfectly inelastic with respect to short-run changes in the rate of interest. Actually, the new equilibrium rate of interest, it should be noted, relates to the long-run demand curve for loanable funds (DD) and it is still below the initial equilibrium level of i.

Now in this sort of analysis there are two effects to be considered—the short-run and the long-run. In the short run the increased savings will not cause unemployment because the lowered rate of interest (due to the excess of quantity supplied over quantity demanded) will reduce the quantity supplied until it again equals the short-run quantity demanded. Thus total consumption remains the same, though there is now a lower rate of interest. In the long run, on the other hand, there is economic growth since the lower rate of interest stimulates net investment. Accordingly, even if population is expanding, there will be continuing full employment, both in the short run and the long run. Also in the long run there will be growth.

It must be observed here that the classical economists placed a heavy responsibility on the flexibility of the interest rate. Later economists, as noted above, have seriously questioned that the interest rate does in fact perform the job assigned to it by the classicists, if for no other reason than that the rate is institutionally determined and thus does not always reflect changes in the quantities of loanable funds demanded and supplied. Also studies reveal that businessmen and consumers do not respond as fully to changes in the rate of interest as the classicists assumed.[9] These objections have been met *theoretically* by A. C. Pigou and his now celebrated Pigou effect which assumes that the rate of interest is perfectly rigid and introduces flexibility of wages and prices as the equilibrating mechanism. We return to this in the next subsection; now, however, to the second case mentioned above.

(2) Why did the classicists think there could be no serious problem of inflation? In the event of inflation there is, according to the classical view, little to worry about so long as there is pure competition within each country and free trade between countries. To illustrate this, let us assume that businessmen want to increase their net investment when there is already full employment. To acquire the financial control over productive resources necessary to carry out their plans, they attempt to borrow money. That is, the demand for loanable funds rises relative to supply, and thus the rate of interest rises. This in itself will cut off some of the planned investment, just as the amount of funds supplied will increase and consumption will decline somewhat; and so again the interest rate participates in the self-adjustment process.

But still some inflation results. Since the economy is already at full employment, the new investors cause prices and wages to rise because

---

[9]These studies have been discussed in Chapters 6, 7, and 11.

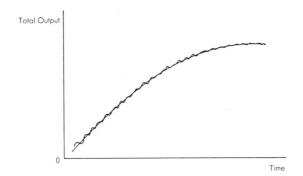

FIGURE 15–2

they borrow "newly created" money from the banking system or acquire it from gold production or gold imports. As prices rise, however, both businessmen and consumers find it to their advantage to buy goods from abroad at relatively lower prices, and thus domestic demand falls. As the demand for domestically produced goods and services declines, the upward pressure on domestic prices is reduced—and this process continues until the inflation is eliminated. Moreover, this shift from domestic to imported goods means a loss of gold so that the money supply is reduced.

Thus the problem of inflation was considered by the classicists to be kept under control by the mechanism of international adjustments and readjustments in the import-export structure and associated changes. A basic presumption here is that political and national boundaries are of no economic significance. On the other hand, assuming appropriate determination of the money supply, via the operation of the gold standard, inflationary pressures in a given country are likely to be transmitted to other countries in the first place.

In conclusion, according to the classicists, the economy experiences only slight fluctuations around the growth trend. There is neither substantial and prolonged unemployment nor inflation, though there is economic growth over time. However, growth in this analysis does not continue forever; to the contrary, the classical economists argued that the economy would level off and culminate in what they called the "stationary state."[10] This is shown in Figure 15–2. The primary reason that the economy tends toward the stationary state is that technological ad-

---

[10]The stationary state is discussed in detail in section 2.

vances will not be sufficient to provide for continued growth. The classicists assumed that technological development is relatively static, so that the emergence of the stationary state is inevitable. The classical view may thus correctly be characterized as (1) being primarily concerned with economic growth that results in the stationary state, and (2) assuming a self-adjusting mechanism that eliminates any substantial short-run deviations from the growth trend. As the economy experiences economic growth and approaches the stationary state, it does so without significant unemployment and inflation.

B. The Pigou Effect

Before turning to a description of the stationary state and of the process by which it is reached, let us look at Pigou's refinement of Say's Law.[11] As the functional role of the interest rate came to be questioned, particularly during and after the 1930's, Pigou attempted to preserve Say's Law from the rubbish heap of intellectual thought. In discussing his analysis, however, we must begin with an important observation. Pigou presented the Pigou effect purely as an intellectual defense against the Keynesian attack; and, since this defense is so abstract and based on such unrealistic assumptions, he did not base any policy recommendations on it. Indeed he enjoined others not to use it as the analytical basis for any policy prescriptions.[12] While some modern economists have not heeded Pigou's warnings and have proceeded to use different versions of the effect as an essential element in their policy pro-

---

[11]A. C. Pigou, *Lapses from Full Employment* (London: The Macmillan Company, 1952). See also Pigou's "The Classical Stationary State," *Economic Journal,* December 1943, and his *Employment and Equilibrium: A Theoretical Discussion* (London: The Macmillan Company, 1952). For further important and revealing discussion of the Pigou effect, see A. H. Hansen, "The Pigovian Effect," *Journal of Political Economy,* December 1951; G. Haberler, "The Pigou Effect Once More," *Journal of Political Economy,* June 1952, reprinted as Appendix II in *Prosperity and Depression* (Cambridge: Harvard University Press, 1958); D. Patinkin, "Price Flexibility and Full Employment," *American Economic Review,* September 1948, reprinted in *Readings in Monetary Theory,* eds. L. W. Mints and F. Lutz (Philadelphia: The Blakiston Company, 1951). Finally, see Thomas Mayer, "The Empirical Significance of the Real Balance Effect," *Quarterly Journal of Economics,* May 1959.

[12]In the Preface to *Lapses from Full Employment,* Pigou states: "Professor Dennis Robertson, who has very kindly read my proofs, has warned me that the form of the book may suggest that I am in favour of attacking the problem of unemployment by manipulating wages rather than manipulating demand. I wish, therefore, to say clearly that this is not so. . . . the subject matter of this book is not policy at all. . . . (p. v.)"

grams, we must nevertheless keep in mind Pigou's own attitudes towards his analysis.

There are four basic assumptions relevant for the following illustration of the Pigou effect. These are as follows.

1. Consumption (and savings) is a function of the real value of money. This relationship may be written as $C = f(M/p)$, where C stands for consumption, M for the stock of money, and p for the price level. The savings function is thus written as $S = f(M/p)$. More accurately, Pigou considered both C and S to be functions of other variables as well as the real value of money. He wrote the two functional relationships as $C = f[(M/p),i,Y]$ and $S = f[(M/p),i,Y]$, where i and Y stand respectively for the interest rate and income. For present purposes, however, we shall ignore i and Y.
2. The stock of money (M) remains constant throughout the analysis, while the price level (p) is allowed to vary in response to changes in aggregate demand.
3. Prices and wages are, because of prevailing competitive conditions, perfectly flexible, both relatively and absolutely.
4. Expectations do not become perverse—no matter what sort of adjustments businessmen and consumers are forced to make throughout the adjustment process.[13]

Let us begin with a situation where all savings are going into investment and where there is full employment. Now assume that people decide to increase their savings and that, for some reason or another, the increased savings do not go directly into increased investment spending—in fact, Pigou holds the interest rate constant (by assumption) so that businesses will not respond to the increased supply of savings. The rise in savings means of course a decline in consumption, so that some unemployment now exists. But, according to the Pigou effect, this unemployment will not persist, but rather will be eliminated.

Because of flexible wages, the wage level will decline; and because of flexible prices (due to competition), the price level also declines. Since the stock of money is constant, its real value rises. That is, since the real value of money equals M/p, and since p has fallen while M has remained constant, the real value of money increases. This will result in a rise in consumption, and this process will continue until the contractionary effects of the increase in savings are eliminated.

---

[13]The important concepts of changing expectations and elasticity of expectations are discussed more fully in Chapter 8.

But why will consumption increase? Inasmuch as $S = f(M/p)$, and since M/p has increased, fewer dollars are now required to satisfy the increased desired savings. Accordingly dollars will be shifted out of savings into consumption, and this shift will continue until full employment is restored. Such a result is virtually inevitable, under the assumed conditions, for so long as there is unemployment the competitive pressures in the labor market will lower wages, and the competitive pressures in the product market will lower prices. In short, the wage and price levels will continue falling until full employment is restored.

A numerical example may be helpful in illustrating this conclusion. Assume that the total stock of money (M) equals $100, of which at the outset $80 is going into consumption (C) and $20 into savings (S). The price level (index) is assumed to be 1.00. Consumers are using the $80 of consumption expenditures to buy eighty physical units of goods at an *average price* of $1.00 per unit. At this output of eighty units of product, full employment prevails. We may also say that the real value of M is $M/p = \$100/1$; the real value of C is $C/p = \$80/1$; and the real value of S is $S/p = \$20/1$. These conditions are shown in row 1 in Table 15–1.

Now let us assume that the community decides to increase its S to $30, that is, it desires to save $30 *in real terms*. With a price index of 1, this means S must rise from $20 to $30 and, therefore, C must fall from $80 to $70. Now unemployment will result, since at a price index of 1, $70 of C will buy only seventy units of goods, and full employment exists only at an output of eighty units of consumer goods. This is shown in row 2 of Table 15–1.

TABLE 15–1

Hypothetical Illustration of the Pigou Effect

Time Periods	Money Income	Price Index	Money Savings	Money Consumption	S/p Desired	S/p Actual	C/p	Total Consumer Demand
1	$100	1.00	$20	$80	$20	$20	$80	$80
2	100	1.00	30	70	30	30	70	70
3	100	.50	30	70	30	60	140	140
4	100	.50	15	85	30	30	170	170
5	100	.90	15	85	30	16.6	94.4	94.4
6	100	.90	27	73	30	30	80	80

The decline in employment and consumer demand will, however, lead to a fall in the price index. Let us, simply for sake of illustration, assume that it falls all the way from 1.00 to .50, as shown in row 3. In this case, the public will be dissatisfied with its level of money savings; it wanted to save $30 of purchasing power (real income) when the price index was 1.00. To do this it saved $30 of money. But now that the price index has fallen to .50 (because of competitive pressures in the labor and product markets), the $30 of money savings is equivalent to $60 in real terms. This follows since real savings equals $S/p =$ $30/.50 = $60 (see row 3). Thus while the public desires to save only $30 in real terms, it ends up with $60 of real savings.

By the same token, the purchasing power of consumption expenditures has also risen. In row 2, the $70 of C expenditures would buy only seventy units of consumers' goods (and it is for this reason, of course, that the price index falls). Now at the lower price level, the same amount of expenditures can, if only it were possible, buy 140 units; that is, $C/p = $70/.50 = $140. Thus with goods priced on the average at $.50 per unit, there is a potential purchasing power of $140. In reality, however, this is impossible, for full capacity output of consumers' goods is only eighty physical units. In other words, the total demand for consumers' goods has risen beyond maximum potential output, and inflation will result. Nevertheless, it must be stressed that the *real purchasing power of consumers' expenditures has risen sufficiently* (because of the fall in the price level) *to restore full employment*. This is also shown in row 3. Note further that since consumers are saving in real terms far more than they desire to save, the stage is set for a shift out of money savings into consumption.

Since consumers are saving twice as much purchasing power as they had intended, they will reduce their money savings in order to end up with $30 of real savings. How much will this be? With the price index at .50, it is simple to ascertain how much money savings will be reduced and money consumption increased. Desired savings are $30; thus since $S/p = $30, and since $p = .50$, then S must equal $15 ($S/p = $30 = $ $S/.50$, and thus $S = $15). Accordingly, consumers will cut their money savings to $15 (from $30) and transfer the "extra" $15 to consumption. This is shown in row 4 of Table 15–1, where total money consumption expenditures rise from $70 to $85.

Now, after this transfer, consumers are holding $30 of purchasing power once again, but now it is in the form of $15 of money savings. So far as savings are concerned, the public is in equilibrium, but this equilibrium cannot persist because the rise in consumption spending will raise the price index.

Let us assume that the price index rises all the way to .90. Once this happens, consumers are saving less purchasing power than they desire to save. Prior to the price rise, they were in equilibrium (see row 4); now they are not. The $15 they are holding in money savings has a purchasing power of only $15/.90 = $16.66, while they still desire to hold $30 in real terms. Accordingly they will transfer some money out of their consumption over to savings so they will again end up with $30 of real savings. The amount necessary to accomplish this end will be $S/p = $30 = $27/.90$. Thus money savings must rise from $15 to $27 in order for the public to maintain real savings of $30. This is shown in row 6.

But this means also that money consumption expenditures must drop by $12, the amount that is transferred to money savings. Further, since total money consumption expenditures are now $73, the total demand for consumers' goods will drop to eighty units (that is, $C/p = $73/.90 = 80). Finally, therefore, consumers are in equilibrium with respect to total demand and total supply at full employment, and they are saving in real terms precisely what they desire to save. There will be no further adjustments in the wage and price levels.

According to the Pigou effect, therefore, full employment will be maintained, even though the interest rate does not participate in the process. But note the assumptions basic to the Pigou effect, for it is only on these that the conclusion that full employment will be restored at a lower price level holds true. These assumptions, however, are not likely to occur in reality, and it is for this reason that Pigou himself stated that the analysis is of little, if any, policy significance. Despite this warning, a small but vocal group of economists have continued to use the Pigou effect, or rather a modified version of it, in their analysis and policy prescriptions. Notable here are the late H. C. Simons, L. W. Mints, M. Friedman, and G. Haberler. It must be noted, however, that this group introduces a modification into the analysis in that they allow the stock of money to vary inversely with the price level.[14] Thus the real value of money changes because of changes in both the price level and the stock of money. The basic argument here is that full employment will be restored much more quickly than would be the case if the stock of money is held constant, as Pigou assumes. Accordingly we may refer to this as a "two-edged Pigou effect," but it is subject to all the criticisms of the Pigou effect proper.

---

[14]See L. W. Mints, *Monetary Policy for a Competitive Society* (New York: McGraw-Hill Book Company, 1950); H. C. Simons, *Economic Policy for a Free Society* (Chicago: University of Chicago Press, 1948), Chapter VII; see also Haberler, "The Pigou Effect Once More." See Chapter 23 for a discussion of Friedman's position.

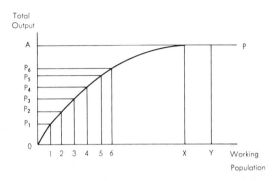

FIGURE 15-3

2. The Stationary State

So far we have seen how Say's Law played an important part in the classical scheme of things, indeed to the extent that (with the exception of a few dissenters) the classicists believed both unemployment and inflation to be unimportant. They strongly felt that the self-adjusting mechanism insured this.

The classical economists, moreover, believed that the economy was dynamic, was growing, and would continue to grow up to some final point.[15] The growth trend itself possessed certain characteristics, which were determined primarily by *historically diminishing returns*. Land (that is, natural resources) was assumed to be fixed in quantity— thus, as population and the capital stock grow, diminishing returns to land set in. This is shown in Figure 15-3, where OP is the growth trend that shows the path of total output as time passes and population expands. Each additional worker contributes a smaller and smaller increment to total output, so that the addition of worker 6 is less than that of worker 5, which in turn is less than that of worker 4, and so on. Eventually, as the working population grows from OX to OY, total output remains constant at OA, that is, zero marginal product. This is the high-

---

[15]W. J. Baumol has referred to the classical growth theory as "the Magnificent Dynamics," magnificent not necessarily because of quality, but in breadth and boldness of generalization. See his *Economic Dynamics* (New York: The Macmillan Company, 1959), Chapter 2. Our Figure 15-4 is adapted from Baumol's Figure 2, p. 19.

est level that total output can reach. Thus when additional capital is forthcoming to supply XY additional workers, and no positive returns materialize for the owners of the capital, net capital formation will cease. The only investment that could possibly occur from here on is replacement investment, that is, the investment necessary to replace that part of the previously existing capital stock that wears out as total output is maintained at OA.[16]

However, this is not necessarily the level of output that the classicists had in mind so far as the stationary state is concerned. They argued that the stationary state could be reached at some output level below OA. In setting forth this part of their argument, the classical economists relied heavily on the so-called "subsistence theory of wages." This theory asserts that there is always a tendency for real market wages to settle at the subsistence level. To explain the role of the subsistence wages theory in the classical scheme, let us refer to Figure 15–4.

The OP curve is, as before, the total product curve, but now it is calculated as total product *less rent and normal returns*.[17] The OS curve is the total subsistence wage curve, and it is assumed to be linear and intersecting the point of origin. Units of "corn" (foodstuffs in general), are measured on the vertical axis, and the quantity of the working population is measured on the horizontal axis. The *slope* of the OS curve measures the subsistence wage rate, while any point on the curve reveals the total wage payments at that point. In Figure 15–4 the subsistence wage remains constant at two units of "corn" per unit of population. Thus the total subsistence wage income necessary to sustain any given population can be found by reading up to the OS curve and across to the vertical axis. For example, the total subsistence wage bill of a population of four is eight units of "corn."

Now for sake of discussion let us begin with a population of four, and the total subsistence wage income of eight units of corn. Note, however, that at this population the total ouput exceeds the total subsistence wage income by the amount AB, and accordingly entrepreneurs are

---

[16]Of course, technological advances could and would shift the curve upwards, pushing the range of zero marginal productivity farther to the right. The classical economists, however, did not place much faith in this possibility of putting off the achievement of the stationary state. J. S. Mill, for example, argued that while new investment opportunities are shifting the investment demand schedule to the right, capital accumulation proceeds over the long haul at a more rapid rate so that profits are driven to a minimum. See his *Principles of Political Economy* (Ashley edition, 1909), pp. 725-45, reprinted as Chapter 5 in *Readings in Business Cycles and National Income*, eds. A. H. Hansen and R. V. Clemence, (New York: W. W. Norton & Company, Inc., 1953).

[17]"Normal returns" are those minimum returns which any factor of production must receive in order for it to stay in its present occupation.

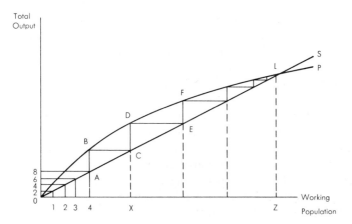

FIGURE 15–4

receiving "excess profits." This induces them to increase their demand for labor, and competition will tend to push the market wage rate above the subsistence wage, thus raising the total wage bill to B. The theory argues however that when the market wage exceeds the subsistence level, as is the case here, population will increase to such an extent that competition among the now "excessive workers" would force the market wage rate back to the subsistence level. Thus population will rise to OX, at which the total wage income will be XC.

However, at XC total wages, "excess profits" are once more being received by the entrepeneurs (in this case, by the amount CD = XD — XC). Accordingly, in the classical theory, the situation will repeat itself until eventually the final equilibrium position is reached at the population of OZ. Note however that this equilibrium occurs before the total product curve becomes parallel with the horizontal axis. In other words, the stationary state will emerge before the potential real rise in output has been fully exhausted.[18] All that is required for the stationary state to be present is that the certain necessary conditions be fulfilled. These are (1) only "normal returns" are being received by the

---

[18]In fact, by necessity this is the case. The reason is simple enough—so long as the subsistence wage is positive, the marginal product of the workers must also be positive. Put otherwise, an intersection of the OS curve with the OP curve in the latter's horizontal segment would imply a subsistence wage of zero.

entrepreneurs; (2) total wages equal total product (less "normal profits" and rent); (3) all new investment equals replacement investment, for no further profitable investment opportunities are available; and (4) population can increase no more, for any additional members of society will receive a wage less than the subsistence wage.

Although most classicists felt that the emergence of this sort of economic structure was (for them, at least) in the very distant future, they nevertheless argued that it would eventually occur. Increasing technology, which would shift the total product curve up, would tend to delay the emergence of the stationary state, but the classicists did not place much faith in this redeeming possibility. On the contrary, they felt that increasing technology would never be sufficient in the very long run to prevent the development and emergence of the stationary state.

For these economists, then, there would be continued economic growth with few and temporary economic fluctuations, and eventually the growth process would result in the stationary state. This theory, to be sure, did not go unchallenged, but despite the criticisms it brought, it had a long life and a tremendous influence on the development of economic thought. Let us now turn to a discussion of some of the earlier criticisms of Say's Law (but remember also the criticisms contained in the Keynesian analysis).

3.   Some Early Dissenters

Despite the fact that Say's Law concluded that there could be no serious and prolonged unemployment, the very presence of economic fluctuations set some men off on different lines of thought. There were crises in 1815, 1825, 1836-39, 1847-48, and 1866, as there had also been fluctuations in the eighteenth century, though only a few persons went deeply in trying to explain them. Most economists tended to attribute these crises to random, exogenous forces; and very few thought in terms of their being inherent in the economic process itself. There were major exceptions, however, and these are discussed briefly in this final section. The important names here are T. R. Malthus, J. S. Mill, Tooke, Overstone, and Mandeville.

A.   Thomas Robert Malthus

Although Malthus did not systematize his theory of cyclical fluctuations, most economists have tended to label it as an underconsumption theory.[19] However, there are several types of underconsumption theories, and thus it is necessary to be more specific. Malthus held that people save to such an extent, and that these savings are invested to such an extent, that both prices and profits fall. Really, the basic point here is that there exist no further outlets for investment, and hence the savings that have been accumulated; accordingly the demand for capital goods falls off. Malthus' theory, in other words, is best classified as an oversaving-underconsumption theory. In modern terminology, we may put it this way: total demand for goods and services is made up of consumption demand and business demand for capital goods. When the community decides to consume less and to save more, consumption demand falls off. While the increase in savings will stimulate business demand, this will occur only up to a point, for diminishing returns will set in. Thus further investment eventually becomes unprofitable and business demand will also decline. When this occurs—that is, when both consumption and business demand fall off, then so will employment; and as employment drops off, consumer demand will decline even more, as will business demand. The result will then be prolonged and severe unemployment—a form of secular economic stagnation.

It must be noted that not only is this a direct refutation of Say's Law, it is also an important antecedent of the Keynesian analysis. Keynes' debt to Malthus is obvious, so much so indeed that one is not surprised to read in Keynes' biographical sketch of Malthus the following: "If only Malthus, instead of Ricardo, had been the parent stem from which nineteenth-century economics proceeded, what a much wiser and richer place the world would be to-day."[20]

Inasmuch as the decline in aggregate demand is the cause of prolonged unemployment, and inasmuch as this decline is due to oversaving, Malthus set forth specific proposals to eliminate the unemployment. He stated them quite explicitly, and it should be remembered that they were being advocated in 1820.

---

[19]The best single reference on Malthus is M. Paglin, *Malthus and Lauderdale: The Anti-Ricardian Tradition* (New York: Augustus M. Kelley, Publishers, 1961), especially Chapters IV-V. B. A. Carry, "Malthus and Keynes—A Reconsideration," *Economic Journal*, December 1959, has argued that Malthus had a rather poorly conceived cycle theory and certainly was not an important percursor of the Keynesian analysis (as Keynes himself contended). R. G. Link, *English Theories of Economic Fluctuations: 1818-1848* (New York: Columbia University Press, 1959), argues that while there are important similarities between Malthus' and Keynes' analyses, there are also important differences (see Chapter 2). Link's book is excellent for its coverage of some other important "dissenters"—such as Thomas Attwood, Thomas Joplin, and James Wilson; it also includes good chapters on Malthus, Mill, and Tooke.

[20]J. M. Keynes, *Essays in Biography* (New York: Horizon Press, 1951), p. 120.

Altogether, I should say, that the employment of the poor in roads and public works, and a tendency among landlords and persons of property to build, to improve and beautify their grounds, and to employ workmen and menial servants, are the means most within our power and most directly calculated to remedy the evils arising from that disturbance in the balance of production and consumption. . . .[21]

Thus Malthus, one of the outstanding classical economists, was definitely a heretic when it came to Say's Law, and he was moreover definitely an early forerunner of much modern thought and policy.

B.   John Stuart Mill[22]

Mill also recognized the crises that were occurring, and though he had no doubts about the long-run validity of Say's Law, he did feel that these disturbances must be explained.[23] For him, the presence of a contraction was merely an indication of either a "glut of commodities or a dearth of money," and he believed that any restorative measures must concentrate on increasing the amount of money demand and on restoring confidence. Mill also felt that the immediate cause of depression is excessive speculation, and this theory, along with his insistence that the restoration of confidence is necessary to bring the economy back to full employment, leads one to place him among the so-called "psychological theorists" of the cycle.

Mill, however, did not feel that the recurrence of depressions warranted casting aside Say's Law. Rather, he considered a depression to be merely a "temporary derangement of markets" which can be corrected by restoring confidence. Moreover, even in the absence of any positive anti-contractionary action, the long-run forces emphasized by Say's Law would, he felt, return the economy to full employment. Mill, therefore, was quite willing to reject Say's Law in the short run, but certainly not for the long run.

C.   Lord Overstone and Thomas Tooke[24]

One of the major contributions of these two men was their recognition that fluctuations assume a "cyclical" pattern. In this respect, they

---

[21]Cited in the above source, p. 122.

[22]These brief quotations are taken from Mill's *Principles of Political Economy,* Ashley edition, (New York: Augustus M. Kelley, Publishers, 1961), p. 561.

[23]*Ibid.*

[24]See J. A. Schumpeter, *A History of Economic Analysis,* for fuller discussion of these two men; and see Link, *English Theories of Economic Fluctuations: 1818-1848,* for an excellent chapter on Tooke.

deviated from the prevailing notion that "crises" were the result of random causes. To them the cycle is a periodic phenomenon—and more than that, each stage naturally follows from the preceding stage; that is, they argued that each stage of the cycle is induced by the conditions of the preceding stage. This was an important observation. Their other important contribution was that both associated expansion with rising investment in fixed capital, and in this respect anticipated much of modern thought. Unfortunately, they did not systematize their views into a conceptual framework, and accordingly, from the point of view of cycle theory, their contributions have been minimized.

D. Bernard Mandeville

Mandeville was certainly one of the most interesting dissenters of this period, or, more accurately, one of the most interesting forerunners of the dissenters of this period. He was born in 1670, or thereabouts, in the Netherlands, and though he thus preceded the classical school, at the same time he had a significant impact upon the development of classical thought. Born in Holland, he received the degree of Doctor of Medicine at the University of Leyden in 1691. Later he moved to England, became a citizen there, and continued the practice of medicine.

Mandeville, however, is best noted for his poem published in 1705, *The Gumbling Hive.* Its publication aroused much discussion and controversy, and in 1714 it was republished together with a commentary and an essay entitled "An Enquiry into the Origin of Moral Virtue." The entire work was called *The Fable of the Bees: or Private Vices, Public Benefits.* It is based on the assumption of individualism, that is, that man is egotistic, self-centered, and self-seeking, an assumption which the classical economists later on turned into the ideal of "the invisible hand." Further, Mandeville felt that man is vicious and is only induced to practice moral virtues through the flattery of politicians. He argued that there must be no state interference except in three major areas: protection of property rights, maintenance of the public peace, *and* provision of continuing full employment of the labor force. Indeed, he felt that full employment is the ideal state of society and that society's activities ought to be directed toward the achievement and maintenance of this end.

In the absence of governmental action, Mandeville argued, society would be characterized by chronic unemployment. Thus not only did he recognize that unemployment is a definite possibility, he also sought the causes and cures of it. He regarded luxury and the spending of money as a very important means of achieving the ideal aim of full employment. Indeed, frugality is the cause of the depression and unemployment; spending, even if on what might be considered luxury, is the cure of it.

Spending stimulates higher employment, production, and levels of living. And included in luxury spending are public works by the state. In his view, any form of pleasure is equated with vice, but that vice, when accompanied by enough spending, will provide for continuing full employment.

Mandeville, moreover, advanced a monetary policy, namely, that "monetary circulation" should follow the rise in employment, and as prices rise due to the increased demand, wages should automatically rise also. If public works are insufficient to provide for full employment, Mandeville argued, then direct subsidies should be given to the workers. He also wanted productivity to rise as employment increases, so that inflationary pressures would be minimized.

Thus Mandeville was quite heretical for his day—arguing that private vices become public benefits since they stimulate aggregate demand, and public works and direct consumer subsidies are also desirable to stimulate full employment. Indeed his views raised quite a hue and cry, and the *Fable* served as the source of controversial discussion for quite some time.[25]

4. Summary

The classical economists developed a rather elaborate theory of economic growth, a theory which concluded that in the short run there would be no significant departures from the full-employment growth equilibrium. The flexibility of the interest rate was set forth by the classicists as the chief equilibrating mechanism that would insure continuing full employment and growth. To be sure, there were some dissenters from the classical doctrine—especially Malthus and J. S. Mill—but the majority of economists held to the basic analysis of Say's Law for quite some time. Later, when the economic significance of the interest rate came to be questioned, A. C. Pigou demonstrated how Say's Law still holds true (theoretically) as long as there is perfect flexibility of wages and prices. This is the so-called Pigou effect, which is based on rather

[25]J. M. Keynes, *The General Theory of Employment, Interest, and Money* (New York: Harcourt, Brace & World, Inc., 1936), pp. 358-62, discusses the place of Mandeville in the history of economic thought.

unrealistic assumptions, but which argues that under these assumptions continuing full employment is assured.

While the classical view was important for a long time, from about the 1870's on a number of economists began to construct cycle theories. In effect, however, these were treated as outside the main flow of economic thought. It took a combination of the Keynesian analysis and the Great Depression to create a widespread rejection of Say's Law, though some few economists still hold to some version of the Pigou effect.

The Keynesian analysis, however, ignores growth, but in recent years there has been a growing reemphasis on the patterns and processes of economic growth. The recent growth models differ substantially from classical theory in that they argue that the growth process is uneven and, in fact, characterized by major cyclical disturbances. Also they do not accept the notion that economic growth will eventually culminate in the stationary state, a view to which most classical economists subscribed. But, as we shall see, some of the recent growth models do argue that economic "stagnation" may occur. We shall examine some of the leading modern growth-cycle models in the next three chapters.

QUESTIONS

15-1. "The advocates of the 'Pigou Effect' usually assume an elasticity of expectations of one." Explain the significance of a unitary elasticity of expectations for the Pigou effect.

15-2. "The Pigou effect is relevant only under conditions of pure competition in all product and input markets." Evaluate this statement.

15-3. Explain the significance of the flexibility of the interest rate in the classical version of Say's Law.

15-4. Explain how T. R. Malthus deviated from the classical point of view on economic growth.

15-5. "In the classical theory of economic growth, the interest rate will eventually dwindle to zero." Critically evaluate this statement.

Bibliography

Adelman, I., *Theories of Economic Growth and Development*. Palo Alto: Stanford University Press, 1961.

Baumol, W. J., *Economic Dynamics*. New York: The Macmillan Company, 1959.

Haberler, G., "The Pigou Effect Once More," *Journal of Political Economy*, June 1952, reprinted as Appendix II in *Prosperity and Depression* (Cambridge: Harvard University Press, 1958).

Hansen, A. H., "The Pigovian Effect," *Journal of Political Economy*, December 1951.

Hoselitz, B. F., ed., *Theories of Economic Growth*. Glencoe: The Free Press, 1960, Chapters III-V.

Link, R. G., *English Theories of Economic Fluctuations: 1815-1848*. New York: Columbia University Press, 1959.

Mayer, T., "The Empirical Significance of the Real Balance Effect," *Quarterly Journal of Economics*, May 1959.

Pigou, A. C., *Lapses from Full Employment*. London: The Macmillan Company, 1952.

16

Dynamic Growth and the Business Cycle

As might be expected, the variations among the post-Keynesian growth theories are quite numerous. However, for all practical purposes these theories may be grouped together under two headings—the "capital-stock adjustment" theories and the looser, less rigorous analyses. The rest of this part is concerned primarily with the capital-stock adjustment theories.

Despite the differences between the various capital-stock adjustment models, they all agree on the basic fundamentals. For instance, all of them set forth the conditions required for smooth, uninterrupted growth—not with the idea of supposing that these conditions actually exist but of determining what they are. The theories agree that when one or several of these requirements is lacking, the economic system is, as it were, derailed from the growth track, and short-run fluctuations follow. Probably the most serious difference between the variants of the capital-stock adjustment theories relates to the pattern that the short-run disturbances take once the growth process is interrupted.

Finally, the theories agree in that they place the burden of smooth uninterrupted growth on the investment process—that is, savings are assumed to play a passive, though still important, role in the growth process. This is the reason that they are referred to as capital-stock adjustment theories—if there is to be smooth, uninterrupted growth, the capital stock of the economy must be adjusted to the growth requirements. All told, the various capital-stock adjustment models are characterized more by similarities than by dissimilarities. The major differences relate primarily to the pattern of the cyclical disturbances that occur once the growth process is interrupted, and often to matters of exposition.

In this chapter one variant of the capital-stock adjustment theories—the model developed by William J. Fellner—is discussed in detail.[1] In the following chapter we shall examine the Harrod-Domar model.[2] This may appear to be somewhat redundant, for in skeletal form these two models are virtually identical. However, there is an advantage in this approach, for Fellner does not make the rigid assumptions that characterize the Harrod-Domar model. Discussing Fellner's analysis first, therefore, has the merit of focusing attention on the detailed economic and institutional requirements for smooth growth. As he puts it:

> The difference between the Harrod-Domar framework and ours is a difference in degree. Possibly it is merely a difference in method of presentation. For Harrod and Domar have presented a first approximation in the form of algebraic formulae which were explained in concise articles. Developing ideas in that form has great merit. But algebraic presentation frequently requires sweeping simplifying assumptions which introduce more rigidity into the system than is truly intended.[3]

Because Fellner's analysis has the advantage of less rigidity, and because it poses rather squarely some of the institutional problems encountered in economic growth, we shall concentrate on it first. At a later stage the Harrod-Domar model can be introduced with better understanding. This procedure has the additional merit of allowing a more realistic approach to the algebraic formulation of the Harrod-Domar model.

As will be seen in the following discussion, Fellner's theory of the business cycle is a "mixed" model, following the classification set forth

---

[1]The major reference is W. J. Fellner, *Trends and Cycles in Economic Activity* (New York: Holt, Rinehart, & Winston, Inc., 1956). See also his "The Capital-Output Ratio in Dynamic Economics," in *Money, Trade, and Economic Growth: In Honor of John Henry Williams* (New York: The Macmillan Company, 1951), and his *Monetary Policies and Full Employment* (Berkeley and Los Angeles: University of California Press, 1946).

[2]A "purely exogenous" theory is also discussed in the next chapter.

[3]Fellner, *Trends and Cycles in Economic Activity*, p. 145. Since Fellner does not rely on the rigid assumptions that Harrod and Domar do, his analysis does not call for a precise equality between planned investment and actual savings. In this case, as in others, approximate equality suffices.

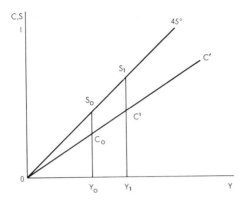

FIGURE 16–1

in Chapter 5. The upper-turning point is accounted for by the interplay of endogenous variables as they encounter the limits set by the fixed parameters. The lower-turning point, on the other hand, is explained by exogenous changes in the variables, more specifically a "clustering of innovations." Thus, the model is neither purely endogenous nor purely exogenous, but rather a "mixture."

1.   The Secular Consumption Function

The capital-stock adjustment theories rely heavily on the statistically observable fact that there has occurred a secular upward drift in the short-run consumption function. Moreover they stress certain important characteristics of the resultant long-run consumption function. In the first place, the data indicate that the long-run consumption function is linear, and therefore both the marginal propensity to consume and the marginal propensity to save are *constant*. Second, and quite important, the data indicate that the long-run consumption function (the C' curve in Figure 16–1) has only a *slight* positive intercept on the vertical axis. In other words, for all practical purposes, the long-run consumption function may be assumed to intersect the point of origin. This is shown in Figure 16–1.

Of what significance is this? For one thing, it means that the average and marginal propensities to consume are *equal*; and given the linearity of the function, they are also constant. By the same token, the average and marginal propensities to save are equal and constant. This means that as income grows, the *absolute* amount of savings also grows, but not the *percentage* amount. As will be seen shortly, this is of extreme importance in assessing the economy's future growth potential and possible future performance.

Consider the income level OY_0 (in Figure 16-1), of which Y_0C_0 is devoted to consumption and C_0S_0 to savings. The propensity to save[4] is thus C_0S_0/OY_0. Now if income rises to OY_1, the total amount of savings will also rise—that is, C_1S_1 is larger than C_0S_0. However, because of the constancy of the propensity to save, the proportion of income saved remains the same at OY_1 as at OY_0—that is $C_0S_0/OY_0 = C_1S_1/OY_1$. In other words, as income rises, savings rise absolutely, but not relatively.

One explanation of this behavior of long-run consumption—the Duesenberry hypothesis[5]—has already been examined, and Fellner's explanation is quite similar. There are two major propositions in Fellner's approach. On the one hand, if an *"average"* family's income is improved relatively to that of other families, the family will act as if it is "better off"; it has improved its "normal" living standard relative to other families. Both its consumption and savings will increase, but the latter will rise as a proportion of the average family's total income. Thus changes in income distribution indicate that there is some economic significance to the curvature of the "consumption lines" revealed by the budget studies.[6]

But on the other hand, if *all* families experience roughly proportional income increases as national income rises, none will act as if it is better off. In this case, each family will tend to save the same proportion of its income as before. As Fellner puts it:

> This seems to be the reason for the failure of the typical family, in advanced economies, to save a higher proportion of its income when national income rises, even though in any period a high-income family

---

[4]It is no longer necessary to distinguish between the average and marginal propensities to save, for on a linear consumption function that passes through the point of origin they are identical. In what follows we shall simply refer to the propensity to save, unless analysis indicates the need to distinguish between the average and the marginal.

[5]See Chapter 10, section 6. See also F. Modigliani, "Fluctuations in the Saving-Income Ratio: A Problem in Economic Forecasting," *Studies in Income and Wealth* (New York: National Bureau of Economic Research, 1949).

[6]See Chapter 10, section 1.

saves a very much higher proportion of its income than a low-income family.[7]

The important thing, however, is that *over time* the *proportion* of the economy's income saved by consumers tends to remain approximately constant as income grows. Still, the *absolute* amount of savings rises. In more formal terms, $S/Y = s$, where s is the propensity to save and is constant. Further, for any income level, total savings are $S = sY$. By the same token, $C/Y = b$, where b, as before, is the propensity to consume and is also constant. For any income level, total consumption is $C = bY$. Of course, $b+s = 1$.[8]

Now Fellner does not argue that b and s are constant during *short-run fluctuations*. His position is that there is a long-run tendency toward a "normal" living standard by the "average" family as income rises, this was discussed above. But he also argues that when the income of the family falls sharply, as in a period of contraction, ". . . both consumption and savings are reduced, but consumption shows greater resistance than savings."[9] In other words, as income drops, the *short-run* average propensity to consume rises, while the *short-run* average propensity to save falls.

This is shown in Figure 16–2, where C_sC_s is the short-run consumption function, and C' the long-run function. If income drops below the OY_0 level, consumers move back along C_sC_s as they try to maintain as well as they can, the consumption level achieved at OY_0. As income rises back to OY_0, consumers move back up C_sC_s until they re-establish their former equilibrium (at OY_0) average propensity to consume. Income growth beyond OY_0 is accompanied by a movement up the C' curve, that is, the average propensity to consume remains constant. All this, of course, is consistent with the Duesenberry thesis, though Fellner also stresses the relative income status of the "average" family.[10] The important thing to keep in mind is that the cyclical behavior and the long-run behavior of the propensities to consume and to save are different—and either Duesenberry's or Fellner's explanation is satisfactory in dealing with this.

---

[7]Fellner, *Trends and Cycles in Economic Activity*, p. 120.

[8]The assumption of a constant b and s is relevant also for the Harrod-Domar model, as we shall see in the next chapter. However, Fellner points out that in his analysis, "the saved proportion of output will not be regarded as rigorously fixed" (*Trends and Cycles in Economic Activity*, p. 145). Yet for all practical purposes he treats it as fixed—or if it varies, it does so within acceptable limits. Like all capital-stock adjustment theories, Fellner's places the burden for smooth continued growth on investment change.

[9]Fellner, *Trends and Cycles in Economic Activity*, p. 300.

[10]For this reason he calls it the "relative income thesis."

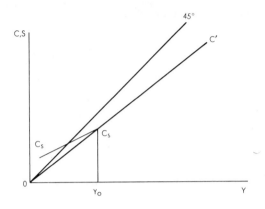

FIGURE 16–2

Finally, in Fellner's analysis (as in the Harrod-Domar model), *planned* savings and *actual* savings are assumed *to be equal always.* Thus if the income level moves from OY_0 to OY_1 (in Figure 16–1), consumers not only plan to save C_1S_1, but actually will save that amount (so long, of course, as the income level remains at OY_1). If for some reason the income level were to fall back to OY_0 consumers would plan to save and actually would save C_0S_0. The implication of this, of course, is that in a free enterprise economy we cannot rely much on consumers to ease the problems of growth. Their decisions to save and to spend are their own to make, and Fellner does not question this premise. This leaves therefore the burden of continued growth on the investment side of the equation—in other words, if there is to be economic growth, there must be capital-stock adjustments of a positive nature (that is, net investment, period after period). As income grows, the amount of savings to be absorbed becomes increasingly larger, and the pressures on investment and technology thus become greater. In this analysis, therefore, since consumers' decisions to save are taken as given data, the focal point is on rising investment. But, as will be seen, when investment expands to match the increasing savings generated by economic growth certain problems arise with respect to the profitability of further investment, as well as with respect to the *capital-output ratio.* We now turn to this last concept—the capital-output ratio—which plays such an important role in modern growth-cycle theory.

2. The Capital-Output Ratio

Another basic ingredient of modern growth analysis is the ratio of capital to output. This is usually written as K/Y, where K stands for the total stock of capital and Y for current income (both calculated in constant dollars).[11] This is the *average* capital-output ratio, or as it is often called, the "average capital coefficient." If, for example, the *stock* of capital is $500 and the current output (income) *flow* is $250, the *average* capital-output ratio is K/Y = $500/$250 = 2.

Some versions of the capital-stock adjustment theory—such as the Harrod-Domar model—assume that the average capital-output ratio is constant over time. This of course means that the average ratio and the incremental (marginal) capital-output ratio are equal, that is K/Y = $\triangle$K/$\triangle$Y. Now the incremental capital-output ratio is merely another dress for an old friend—the acceleration coefficient. Earlier we wrote the acceleration coefficient as $v = \triangle I/\triangle Y$.[12] Of course $\triangle$K and $\triangle$I are simply symbols for the same thing—namely, an addition to the capital stock of the economy or net investment. In what follows the symbol v will be used to stand for the acceleration coefficient.[13]

Of course, the equality of the average and incremental capital-output ratios implies the existence of certain economic conditions[14] that Fellner does not accept for his analysis. "We are opposed to treating the incremental capital-output requirement as a constant because the available statistical materials do not point to the constancy of this ratio."[15]

---

[11]There are difficult problems involved in measuring the stock of capital, especially when qualitative changes in it have taken place. See Fellner, *Trends and Cycles in Economic Activity*, pp. 196-99, and S. Kuznets, *Capital in the American Economy: Its Formation and Financing* (Princeton: Princeton University Press, 1960), for a discussion of the problems involved. We shall follow Fellner's suggestion, *Trends and Cycles*, p. 197: "In the present case we may derive a bit of consolation from the fact that the general conclusions to which the capital stock estimates lead are in harmony with intelligent informal judgment. To take an example, it is obviously reasonable to conclude that the quantity of physical capital per man has shown a substantial rise in the long run." See also Chapter 4, section 2 of this text.

[12]Recall however that the earlier discussion (Chapter 12) assumed a time lag in the accelerator—that is, $v = \triangle I_t/(Y_t - Y_{t-1})$.

[13]Alvin H. Hansen argues, however, that the incremental capital-output ratio is greater than the acceleration coefficient, "because autonomous investment provides part of the additional capital stock which is required. Autonomous investment, when completed, contributes to output no less than induced investment." *Business Cycles and National Income* (New York: W. W. Norton & Company, Inc., 1964), p. 482.

[14]See section 4 below.

[15]Fellner, *Trends and Cycles in Economic Activity*, p. 145.

Recall the earlier discussion in Chapter 4, where the historical behavior of the capital-output ratio in the United States was examined. The data show that the *average* ratio rose until the 1920's and then fell. This means therefore that the average and marginal (incremental) ratios *are not equal.*[16]

One of the major themes in Fellner's analysis is that, in the absence of the necessary technological advancements and improvements, the incremental capital-output ratio will rise; and the major reason for this is that (again, without the technological improvements) there will be diminishing returns to capital. For example, in the United States the stock of capital has been increasing much more rapidly than has the labor force—indeed, approximately twice as fast. Thus, for analytical purposes, the capital stock may be treated as the (relatively) variable factor of production and the labor force as the (relatively) fixed factor. *All things equal,* the increase of capital in relation to labor means that there will be diminishing returns to capital. In this case, therefore, the incremental capital-output ratio will rise, for now it takes a larger increment to the capital stock to produce the same increment to the income flow.

Fellner's contention is that under such circumstances economic growth cannot be expected to proceed at a very rapid pace. Indeed, growth could cease entirely and the economy could conceivably be characterized by stagnation. A continually rising incremental capital-output ratio implies decreasing profitability of net, new investment and thus a declining rate of investment expenditures in the economy.[17] Thus there must be sufficient and adequate offsets to diminishing returns to capital if economic growth is to continue. These offsets, however, must be both quantitatively and qualitatively adequate in order to do the job. But we anticipate. The first task is to develop Fellner's model in some detail.

3.   The Time Sequence of Economic Growth

The capital-stock adjustment theories are based on the recognition that investment in the current period is closely related to the invest-

---

[16]As all students of economics know, when the average magnitude is rising, the marginal magnitude must lie above it, and when the average is falling, the marginal must lie below it.

[17]Fellner, *Trends and Cycles in Economic Activity*, pp. 144-45, 121-22, 141-42, and Chapter 8. This is not meant to imply that Fellner is a "stagnation" theorist, for later discussion (Chapter 18) will show that he is quite opposed to the stagnation theory.

ment in both the preceding and the subsequent periods. Thus *the time sequence of the investment-savings process holds the center of the stage in these theories.* Put in rather rough terms, the argument is that the economic conditions of the subsequent period must justify the private investment of the prior period if the economy is to experience smooth, continued growth, just as the economic conditions of the present period must justify the private investment of the preceding period.

Since the analysis is concerned with the full-employment growth of the *private sector* of the economy, Fellner assumes that the governmental sector is economically neutral. That is, he assumes that governmental budgets are in balance and that there is neither anticyclical nor growth fiscal policy. Second, and this is closely related to one of the "corollaries" discussed below, Fellner assumes that the price level is relatively stable. Finally, as noted earlier, he assumes that consumers' desired and actual savings are always equal.

In conjunction with these assumptions, certain "corollaries" are also set forth. As will be seen shortly, these are of crucial importance in Fellner's theory of the business cycle. The three corollaries are (1) a sufficient degree of mobility of resources; (2) sufficient technological and organization improvements, both quantitatively and qualitatively, to offset diminishing returns to capital, and (3) no basic institutional and legal changes that would interfere with the "proper" regulation of the money supply.

These corollaries are made only for purposes of first approximation, and they are relaxed at a later point in the analysis. We may, however, anticipate Fellner's major conclusions. First, he recognizes that when the corollaries are not present in reality, their absence generates business cycles. The process of economic growth therefore is not always smooth and uninterrupted. But second, he argues that the deviations are not, and have not been, so substantial as to have prevented economic growth over time. "It is an essential characteristic of Western economies that violations of the corollaries of the growth conditions have remained temporary, in the sense of having merely interrupted, but not permanently arrested, the process of growth."[18] It is convenient however to begin with an examination of the model of uninterrupted growth; this points out the essential character and significance of the corollaries. Following this we can better examine Fellner's position on the causes and pattern of cyclical fluctuations.

---

[18]Fellner, *Trends and Cycles in Economic Activity,* p. 294.

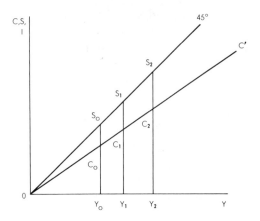

FIGURE 16–3

A.   The Model of Smooth, Uninterrupted Growth

One of the fundamental requirements for smooth, uninterrupted growth is that *planned investment is equal to actual savings.* Consider the *full-employment* level of income Y_0 in Figure 16–3, where savings are C_0S_0 and consumption Y_0C_0. We shall identify the initial full-employment level of income Y_0C_0 with period 0, the income level of OY_1 with period 1, and so on. Since in period 0 the actual and desired savings are equal at C_0S_0, *planned investment* must be equal to C_0S_0 or the income level will drop below full employment—that is, there would be a reverse multiplier-accelerator effect. On the other hand, if planned investment exceeds C_0S_0, inflation will result, and as will be seen shortly, *substantial* inflation is incompatible with smooth, uninterrupted growth. *The first requirement, then, is that planned investment of the period be equal to the actual (that is, desired) savings of the period.*

Note that the entire stress is placed on planned investment, not actual investment. As will be seen in a moment, *actual investment is always equal to actual (and thus desired) savings in any period.*[19] But this is purely definitional—an accounting identity—and has no analytical significance. The really important relationship is the equality (or, as the case may be, the inequality) between planned investment and actual savings.

---

[19]See below, subsection 3-B.

Assume that at the full-employment level of income OY_0 enough planned investment is forthcoming to absorb the savings C_0S_0. The economic system, therefore, is in an aggregative equilibrium where planned investment equals actual savings. Note, however, that this is a dynamic, moving equilibrium, for the emergence of the planned investment at OY_0 will result in a multiplier-accelerator interaction that will lead to a higher income level.

Assume that the new level of income is OY_1, so that *total* savings are larger (at C_1S_1), though they are the same proportion of OY_1 that C_0S_0 is of OY_0. Despite this constancy of the propensity to save, absolute savings are now higher, so that planned investment in period 1 must be greater if the dynamic equilibrium is to be maintained. Now planned investment in period 1 must be larger than the planned investment in period 0, for it must absorb the larger savings of C_1S_1. If this amount of investment materializes in period 1, income will rise to OY_2 in the next period (via the familiar multiplier-accelerator interaction), so that actual savings are even larger. Thus planned investment in period 2 must rise to C_2S_2 if the moving equilibrium is not to be disrupted. This is the basic requirement for smooth, uninterrupted growth, and it may be stated as follows: "Only if the equality of savings with planned investment stays satisfied all along (with positive savings and investment) will the system be in a state of uninterrupted growth or 'dynamic equilibrium'."[20]

However, if this requirement is to be satisfied, certain conditions relating to the *profitability* of the investment in any one period must be met. Unless the planned investment of the next period, say period 1, is sufficient to absorb the actual savings of C_1S_1, not all of the investment undertaken in period 0 will be profitable. This is shown in Figure 16–4. If the planned investment in period 1 does not reach the amount C_1S_1, then the market demand for the income level OY_1, is insufficient to take all of OY_1 off the market. Consumers will, of course, demand Y_1C_1 of consumers' output; but so long as planned investment is less than C_1S_1 there will be some excess output. In other words, aggregate demand is less than aggregate supply.

Assume that the planned investment in period 1 is only C_1T_1. In this case the total market demand for OY_1 is the sum of consumers' demand Y_1C_1 and planned investment C_1T_1, that is, a total of Y_1T_1. Thus the total or aggregate demand is less than the aggregate supply, and in this case some of the investment undertaken in the previous period must be unprofitable. This is reflected in the accumulation of unplanned, excess

---

[20]Fellner, *Trends and Cycles in Economic Activity*, p. 113.

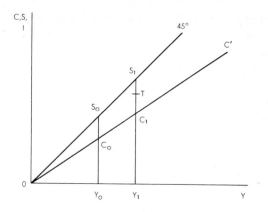

FIGURE 16–4

inventories in period 1 by the amount T_1S_1, which is the difference between aggregate demand and aggregate supply. The income level will
therefore fall until planned investment *(if it does not change)* is once
again equal to actual savings, *and economic growth has been interrupted.*

There is an alternative way of viewing this situation. The investment
of period 0 has two effects—first, it increases output (income) from
OY_0 to OY_1, and second, it increases aggregate demand. In this case,
however, the income increase did not induce enough investment
(which, of course, is a part of aggregate demand) in period 1 to absorb
the savings that resulted from the income increase. Some planned investment was induced, but not enough to preserve the dynamic equilibrium. In other words, the demand increase generated by the investment in period 0 was not sufficient to match the supply increase generated by the same investment. In this event, unplanned inventories
accumulate, reflecting the unprofitability of some of the investment in
period 0.

Now consider the opposite case, where planned investment exceeds
actual savings. Here the results are rather indirect, but again the growth
process is interrupted. Since aggregate demand exceeds aggregate supply, the price level will rise. Also, since the analysis begins with full employment, product and resource scarcities will develop. "Such a process
must be financed either by excessive creation of new money or by the
'dishoarding' of previously idle (inactive) purchasing power. Sooner or

later the inflationary process will have to come to an end, and economic growth will be interrupted."[21]

Thus Fellner concludes that if there is to be continued and uninterrupted growth, the planned investment in any one period must be approximately equal to the actual savings of the period. Otherwise the investment of the preceding period will not pay for itself and an income contraction will ensue, or it will "more than pay" for itself and inflation, which must ultimately be followed by contraction, will ensue. In both cases, the growth process is stifled. In short, the basic requirement for smooth, uninterrupted growth must be revised to read as follows: *the planned investment of any one period must be equal to the actual savings of that period, if the investment that took place in the previous period is to be profitable.*

Restatement of a major conclusion of this subsection will aid the following discussion. A dynamic equilibrium will be maintained only if the aggregate demand in each period is (approximately) equal to the aggregate supply of the period. But for this to happen, the increase in aggregate demand generated by the investment of any period must be sufficient to take off the market the increase in aggregate supply generated by the investment of the same period. Since consumers are assumed always to match their planned and actual savings, this boils down to the fact that the planned investment induced in period 2 (induced, that is, by the income increase between periods 1 and 2) must be large enough to match the actual savings in period 2. And so on for subsequent periods.

B.   The Identity of Investment and Actual Savings

Since Fellner assumes that desired and actual savings are always equal, the burden for smooth growth is placed on the investment process. However, in this analysis investment is, in one sense of the word, always equal to actual and desired savings. The reason for this is that unplanned investment and disinvestment may occur, so as to make savings and investment equal in every period.

More specifically, why are investment and actual savings always equal? Refer back to Figure 16–4, where planned investment in period 0 is sufficient to match the savings C_0S_0 of that period. The result, as already noted, is a rise in the income level to Y_1 and an increase in savings to C_1S_1. Assume now that the planned investment in period 1 is

[21]*Ibid.*, p. 117.

only C_1T_1, so that aggregate demand (Y_1T_1) falls short of aggregate supply (Y_1S_1). In this case, of course, the growth process is interrupted.

Still, even though planned investment is less than actual savings, actual investment and savings are equal. Since aggregate demand falls short of aggregate supply (by T_1S_1), there will be an *unplanned accumulation of inventories*. The amount of this unplanned accumulation is T_1S_1, the excess of aggregate supply over aggregate demand. The sum of the planned investment C_1T_1 and the unplanned investment T_1S_1 equals the actual savings of the period, C_1S_1. However, so long as planned investment is less than actual savings, the dynamic equilibrium is disrupted.

Consider the opposite case, where planned investment exceeds actual savings so that aggregate demand outstrips aggregate supply. In this instance, sellers will experience an *unplanned decumulation of inventories* as they strive to meet the higher demand. Thus the net investment of the period is *planned* investment *minus* the *unplanned* disinvestment, and again the identity is present.

In the identity sense, then, investment always equals actual savings. *But analytically, the important relationship is between actual savings and planned investment.* To repeat, if there is to be a smooth, dynamic equilibrium, the planned investment of each period must be equal to the actual savings of the period. The accounting identity of investment (planned+unplanned) and actual savings has no significance for the dynamic growth process, except where unplanned investment and disinvestment are zero. Put otherwise, uninterrupted growth requires that unplanned investment and disinvestment be zero and that planned investment be equal to actual savings in each successive period. The accounting identity is merely a matter of definition.

4. The Problem of Diminishing Returns

Since continued economic growth requires an ever larger amount of planned investment period after period, eventually tremendous pressures will be placed on the returns to capital. *Unless the necessary improvements are made,* the rising planned investment will eventually result in diminishing returns to net investment. This of course results in a diminishing rate of profitability on the new planned investment so that perhaps in some later period not enough planned investment will be forthcoming to match the savings of that period.

This problem becomes all the more important when, as in the United States, the stock of capital is increasing faster than the labor force. Given the state of technology, the investment in capital will encounter diminishing returns; and the diminishing returns are all the more likely to occur when, as noted above, the capital growth requirements are large and increasing.

If technological and organizational improvements are constant, the diminishing returns to capital can be stated in terms of the behavior of both the average K/Y and incremental $\triangle K / \triangle Y$ capital-output ratios. For instance, assume that the stock of capital in period 0 is $500 and the income of the same period is $250. In this case, K/Y = 2. Assume also that the incremental capital-output ratio in period 0 is 3; that is, between the previous period and period 0 it took an additional $3 of capital stock to produce an additional output flow of $1 ($\triangle K / \triangle Y =$ $3/$1 = 3$). Now in period 1, it may be, in the absence of technological and organizational advancements, that $5 of additional capital are required to produce the extra $1 in output flow—that is, there are diminishing returns to capital.

This is what would be expected as long as there are no technological and organizational improvements and if the capital stock is the (relatively) variable factor of production. If, however, diminishing returns are persistent and appreciable, ultimately some low rate of return to net investment is going to result—a rate which, in fact, is too low to warrant any further net investment. This minimum rate is comprised of "an uncertainty premium ('risk premium') for undertaking the physical investment itself" and the interest rate on business loans.[22] If the rate of return is so low that after deducting the interest cost on the borrowed money not enough remains to cover the "uncertainty premium" (that is, the minimum expected rate of profit), the investment project will not be undertaken.

As long as this condition is fairly general, no new planned investment will be forthcoming, and the output (income) level will drop until there will be no savings in the economic system. This is so because there is no positive planned investment once the minimum rate

---

[22]*Ibid.*, pp. 200, 201. Fellner breaks the interest rate on business loans into two constituent parts—an uncertainty premium "for lending money to business investors rather than to an absolutely safe borrower," and "the pure rate of interest on perfectly safe loans." The sum of these two components is the interest payment that a business must make to the lender of funds or that it must recover if it finances the investment project out of internal sources of funds. In any event, the business must recover, after payment of other costs, an amount equal to the interest constituents plus the "uncertainty premium" for undertaking the investment project in the first place.

of return is encountered.[23] The final result would be substantial unemployment and performance of the economy far below its full-employment potential. As Fellner puts it: "... persistently and appreciable diminishing returns would not merely stop the growth process but would make it exceedingly difficult to maintain output near the capacity level of private enterprise economies."[24]

In order to avoid such a situation, there must be sufficient offsets to diminishing returns to capital—that is, the incremental capital-output ratio must not be allowed to rise "too high." These offsets take the form of technological and organizational improvements which are designed to prevent the incremental ratio from rising appreciably, or at least to prevent the minimum rate of return from being reached.

However, more is needed than simply a sufficient *amount* of improvements, for the *qualitative* as well as the quantitative aspects of the improvement process are important. Since the factors of production are increasing at different rates, "the character of improvements must adjust to the resource scarcities in the system."[25] In the United States, this means that not only must the offsets be quantitatively sufficient, they must also be "labor-saving" since labor is the relatively scarce factor.[26]

Two rather extreme examples can be used to illustrate this. Consider first the case where the improvements raise the marginal productivity of labor but leave unaffected the marginal productivity of capital.[27] This is an extreme example of "capital-saving" improvements. In this instance, the higher productivity of labor results in a rise in the demand for labor and hence a rise in real wage rates. Since the supply of labor cannot be increased appreciably for some time,[28] the rise in real wage rates will tend to be relatively permanent. Such a result of course tends to reduce the rate of return on investment even more, so that eventually net planned investment would cease. In the absence of some subsequent offsetting "labor-saving" improvements, the only alternative to prevent the rate of return from declining to the minimum level

---

[23]Fellner argues that although there is a minimum floor under which the rate of return cannot decline, it does have some downward flexibility until the floor is reached.

[24]Fellner, *Trends and Cycles in Economic Activity*, p. 203.

[25]*Ibid.*, p. 209.

[26]But, as we shall see, not "too labor-saving."

[27]The discussion is simplified by using only the two-factor case, involving the relationship between labor and capital. The basic analysis is not altered if the third factor (land) is included.

[28]Except, perhaps, in times of national emergency, such as war.

is to change the social system so that investors can compensate themselves at the expense of the cooperating factors of production. This, however, is unlikely at the moment, and the major conclusion to be drawn is that an improvement that is "capital-saving" will interrupt the growth process.

For the other extreme example, assume that the improvements are quite "labor-saving," that is, they raise the marginal productivity of the capital substantially but leave labor's marginal productivity unaffected. Fellner argues that ". . . in the long run a flow of such improvements would create unmanageable social friction."[29] To be sure, the marginal productivity of capital has risen, so that apparently sufficient planned investment will be forthcoming to absorb the actual savings; but in this extreme case the planned investment will more than match the savings. If the labor force remains constant, the real wage will also remain constant; but if the labor force expands, as we would expect it to do, the real wage rate must decline.[30] As long as the real wage rate does not fall as the labor force expands, there will be unemployment. Given institutional impediments to a downward flexibility of the real wage rate, the improvements that are too *"labor-saving"* create an overabundance of labor. If, on the other hand, these impediments do not exist, social friction will rise as a result of the fall in the real wage rate.

Another requirement then for smooth growth at full employment (and without declining real wage rates) are improvements that are labor-saving, *but not too much so.* Certainly the improvements must not be capital-saving. The required improvements, therefore, must *at least maintain* the marginal productivity of capital so that a sufficient flow of planned investment is forthcoming to match the growing actual savings. But, to repeat, the improvements must not be too labor-saving, or trouble follows. This is surely a straight-and-narrow path for the economy to tread, and it seems likely that excursions off the path are virtually inevitable. And when such excursions take place, the growth process is interrupted and some sort of cyclical disturbance ensues.

Thus far, then, there are two basic requirements for smooth, uninterrupted growth. First, the planned investment of each period must be sufficient to match the actual savings of each period, or else the investment of the previous period will not prove profitable. Second, there must be sufficient offsets to diminishing returns to capital to

---

[29]Fellner, *Trends and Cycles in Economic Activity*, p. 211.

[30]This follows from the fact that labor's marginal productivity is unaffected by the improvement.

insure that a sufficient amount of planned investment is forthcoming period after period. This second requirement means that the offsets must be labor-saving, though not too much so. As Fellner puts it:

> *Improvements, by raising the marginal productivity of capital for given capital inputs, that is, by not letting the marginal productivity of capital fall too low for rising capital inputs, must achieve the result that the new investment should stay sufficiently profitable in spite of the relative land-labor scarcity. But while a sustained labor-saving effect is implied by this, the labor-saving character of improvements must not overshoot the mark to such an extent as to turn the relative labor scarcity into a chronic overabundance of labor.*[31]

5.   The Two Remaining Corollaries

Discussion of the preceding section revolved around the first corollary for smooth growth—sufficient offsets to diminishing returns to capital. In this section the two remaining corollaries are examined briefly. These are, first, a sufficient mobility of resources and, second, a legal and institutional framework that permits "proper" regulation of the money supply. Like the first corollary, these must be present if the dynamic equilibrium is to be preserved.

A.   Resource Mobility

While the first corollary stresses a particular type of scarcity— namely, the *general scarcity* of labor relative to capital, the second corollary stresses *specific scarcities*. The improvement process is unable to cope with these specific scarcities. At best, it can adjust to general scarcities, but it is not flexible enough to adjust to specific scarcities of types of labor, capital, and natural resources.

Why is this second corollary so important for smooth, continued growth? The reason is that as the capital stock grows period after period, it also undergoes structural changes. The structure of demand is never constant in a dynamic economy, and a changing structure calls for changing use of resources. Consider, for example, two producers' goods industries, A and B. Assume that A is producing a certain type of machinery and that B is producing another type; assume further that A is planning expansion while B is contracting by the same

---

[31]Fellner, *Trends and Cycles in Economic Activity*, p. 216.

amount that A plans to expand. Theoretically, A's expansion and B's contraction will offset each other, leaving the total amount of investment spending unaffected.

If however there are impediments that prevent the movement of resources from B to A, the expansion planned by A will not materialize. In this case, total investment expenditure will be reduced by the amount of contraction in B. And of course, the general improvement process cannot quickly adjust itself to make up for the specific scarcities being experienced by A. The essential problem here is one of specific short-run resource immobility, and its significance is that this immobility may prevent the planned investment of a period from matching the actual savings of the period. Thus the growth process may be interrupted. In other words, not only must *general* scarcities be offset (by the improvement process), but also *specific* scarcities must be prevented from interfering with the growth process.

Resource immobilities may be of different kinds. For instance, there is geographic immobility. A worker finds it difficult to move easily and quickly from one labor market (say, Chicago) to another (say, Philadelphia) in a relatively short time period, even though there may be significant job opportunities at the latter location.[32] Another resource impediment is specialization and past training. It is often difficult for a worker who is trained in one occupation to shift easily to another that requires a considerable amount of new training and schooling. The shift, of course, can often be made, but it may be so expensive and time consuming that the impact of the specific scarcities is still felt. This impediment of specialization is possibly even more important when it comes to the capital stock. A piece of equipment or a building designed for a certain specialized productive activity cannot easily be used for other purposes.[33]

The impediments to resource mobility are especially important when the change in the structure of demand for resources is substantial and abrupt. Slow, predictable changes can often be accommodated; but when the accommodation calls for significant geographic and specialization changes in a very short time period, the necessary adjustments

---

[32]See H. S. Parnes, *Research on Labor Mobility* (New York: Social Science Research Council, 1954), for a discussion of the various impediments to labor mobility.

[33]The time length involved in the immobility of capital is both more expensive and time consuming: more expensive in that obsolescence may be involved, more time consuming in that disinvestment is a lengthy process. See Joan Robinson, "The Impossibility of Perfect Competition," in *Monopoly and Competition and Their Regulation*, ed. E. H. Chamberlin.

will not be forthcoming quickly enough to allow for smooth growth.

Although Fellner believes that this corollary has been lacking for certain periods of time, it has not served to interrupt permanently the growth process. Still, it is almost unavoidably absent at times. When the economy is passing through the expansionary stage of the business cycle, significant and abrupt changes in the structure of demand are bound to occur. This is especially so during the later phases of the expansion, when there is a tendency for the consumers' goods industries to expand relative to the producers' goods industries. In this event, as will be seen in section 6, the growth process is likely to be interrupted.[34] However, the full importance of this cannot be assessed until we have examined Fellner's theory of cyclical disturbances.

B.   Legal and Monetary Institutions

The basic requirement here is that the money supply expand *pari passu* with the growth in output over time. Only if this happens will there be the general price-level stability that is conducive to smooth growth. However, in order for this corollary to be satisfied, there must not be any legal or institutional changes that would interfere with the monetary authorities' "proper" regulation of the money supply over time.

Of course, the price level may be subject to quite wide fluctuations (even though there are no basic legal or institutional changes) because of the absence of either or both of the other two corollaries. On the other hand, this third corollary could be absent while the other two are present, and thus it deserves some discussion.

Fellner believes, however, that like the first two corollaries, this one is not always present, but that also like the first two, deviations from it have not been sufficient to block long-run growth. "No specific disturbance has persisted long enough to cause permanent stoppage. In this sense there has existed a long-run tendency to satisfying all three corollaries."[35] Still occasional absences occur, and these are followed by cyclical disturbances. The full significance of the absences cannot be evaluated until we have reviewed Fellner's theory of the business cycle. This is the task of the next section.

---

[34]See the example of industries A and B, given earlier in this subsection. Although one industry was assumed to be expanding and the other to be contracting, the same analysis applies if one (A) expands relative to the other (B).

[35]Fellner, *Trends and Cycles in Economic Activity*, pp. 232-33.

6.   A "Scarcity" Theory of the Cycle

As noted in the two preceding sections, there are, in Fellner's analysis, three possible types of scarcities. These may be labeled as *general* scarcities, *specific* scarcities, and *monetary* scarcities. A general scarcity exists whenever a general class of productive factors, such as labor, is scarce relative to the other factor classes. In the United States, as we have seen, labor is relatively scarce and capital relatively abundant. A general scarcity can be overcome only by adjustments in the improvement process—that is, improvements must be labor-saving (though not too much so). However, there is no reason to believe that the improvement process occurs smoothly and without interruption. Indeed, Fellner argues that since "clusters" in the improvement process are virtually unavoidable, there may be fairly long periods during which no significant improvements take place.

Specific scarcities arise as a result of abrupt and substantial shifts in the structure of demand for resources. Since in the short run resources are not sufficiently mobile—either geographically or in terms of specialization—to adapt to the demand shifts, the growth process may be interrupted. Finally, a monetary scarcity exists when the monetary authorities do not, or cannot, expand the money supply *pari passu* with the long-run rise in output. In this case, deflation sets in.

If one or more of the growth corollaries is lacking, the growth process is interrupted and a cyclical disturbance follows. For this reason, Fellner's theory may be referred to as the "scarcity theory" of the cycle. However, no matter what sort of scarcity occurs, the immediate impact is that planned investment falls short of actual savings. The scarcities are important only in that they result in this relationship between planned investment and actual savings.

A.   The Expansion and the Upper-Turning Point

Assume that the economy begins its expansionary march from some low level of income and employment. This is set off by net, new investment, the causes of which will be examined later. Once started, the expansion generates its own steam via the multiplier-accelerator interaction, and the economy proceeds rapidly towards full employment.

In such a situation, " ... the rate of expansion must of course be greater than is the possible rate of growth *in* a condition of full utilization."[36] In other words, the *actual* rate of growth of income is greater

---

[36]*Ibid.*, p. 304.

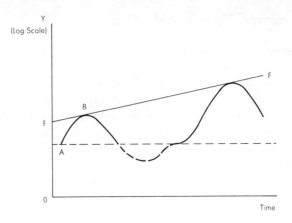

FIGURE 16–5

than the rate of growth permitted by the "full-employment ceiling," as is shown in Figure 16–5, where the rate of income expansion from A to B exceeds the upward tilt of the FF line. Recall from the earlier discussion of Hicks' theory of the cycle that the upper-turning point in this case is unavoidable. However, Fellner's analysis is somewhat more detailed and requires more extensive discussion.

Once the income level of the economy reaches the full-employment ceiling, aggregate output can grow only at the rate permitted by the three corollaries—the improvement process, resource mobility, and monetary expansion.[37] If these corollaries are present, then output will creep along the full-employment ceiling (FF in Figure 16–5), for there will be sufficient planned investment to match each period's actual savings. This, however, is quite unlikely, for surely one or more of the scarcities will emerge at some point; and once this occurs, the upper-turning point sets in. Here Fellner differentiates between two possibilities—a major contraction and a minor contraction.

First, *even if the monetary factor and the improvement process are permissive for smooth growth,* the rapid rate of expansion of income up to the full-employment ceiling will result in specific scarcities. That is, if resources are specialized—both occupationally and geographically—they will not be adaptable (in the short run) to the changing requirements that characterize a rapid expansion. The structure of

---

[37]This of course assumes that planned investment equals actual savings.

demand will be shifting sharply and quickly as between industries and sectors of the economy. In this case, some planned investment, even though conceived of by the business community, cannot match the actual savings of the economy, and a contraction follows. (A specific illustration of this was given in section 5-A.)

Now Fellner argues that in such cases, the resulting contractions are ". . . likely to be either *minor recessions* or *rather sharp but short depressions*."[38] The major thing required is a "breathing spell" long enough for the scarcities and immobilities to be ironed out. Ordinarily this may not take long, though both pessimism and institutional impediments to reducing immobilities may lengthen the period.[39] The major danger is that the decline in output and the rise in pessimism may lead to a further reduction in investment as investment plans are revised downwards. In this event the "minor recession" may become quite prolonged. On this point, however, Fellner is fairly optimistic:

> But there exists a general presumption that contractions caused merely by the need for rearranging the structure of production will usually not be very long. The common characteristic of these disturbances is that there exists a latent demand, at profitable prices, for goods and services the production of which is temporarily blocked by the limited mobility of resources.[40]

In contrast to the minor contractions, there are the *major setbacks,* which are attributed primarily to inadequate technological and organizational improvements and to monetary scarcity. Let us examine these two possibilities in turn.

Even if there are adequate resource mobility and monetary expansion, insufficient offsets to diminishing returns to capital will pull planned investment down below actual savings. Since this was discussed above in some detail (section 4), there is little need to elaborate at this point. When the net return on planned investment falls to the minimum level, not enough investment will be forthcoming to match the actual savings. The result of this, of course, will be an income contraction which may be intensified by pessimism on the part of business investors. As Fellner puts it: "Such insufficiency may last for many years and thus cause a *long and deep* depression."[41]

It is important to note here that Fellner believes that the rate of the

---

[38]Fellner, *Trends and Cycles in Economic Activity,* p. 305, italics added.

[39]*Ibid.,* pp. 376-77. Fellner does not believe that labor unionism provides any significant threat to the growth process.

[40]*Ibid.,* p. 305.

[41]*Ibid.,* p. 306.

improvement process is irregular,[42] though he does not explain this in any detail. "Periodic declines in the rate of overcoming general labor scarcities and natural-resource scarcities by improvements are, of course, inevitable."[43] The significance of this is obvious! If a major contraction occurs during a period in which there is little improvement activity, the contraction may be quite severe and prolonged. In this connection, Fellner's analysis is somewhat similar to Hansen's, in which it is argued that eventually the growth factors will "cluster" sufficiently so as to stimulate investment activity, though pessimism may prolong for some time the emergence of the "cluster." And of course, the similarity to Schumpeter's analysis is also obvious. But note that Fellner's theory differs substantially from Hicks' in that the latter assumes that autonomous investment occurs at a rate equal to the full-employment ceiling.

The final "scarcity cause" of the upper-turning point relates to the situation in which there is an insufficient expansion of the money supply as growth proceeds. Fellner argues that the resulting price deflation will interfere with the growth process. Investment calculations become more and more difficult to make, and unless wages fall *pari passu* with the price level, not enough planned investment will be forthcoming. In this case, the lack of ". . . expandibility of the money supply may also cause long-lasting depressions, and it may cause the recurrence of severe depressions with relatively high frequency in periods extending over several decades."[44] Fellner, however, does not attach much significance to this type of scarcity contraction, at least under our present monetary system.

Although Fellner advances the preceding as the "central proposition" of his analysis of cyclical fluctuations, he provides in addition a "nonscarcity" explanation of the upper-turning point. While this is not completely separate from the "scarcities," it deserves special mention. The major factor here is *uncertainty* in an industrially advanced economy. Fellner observes that uncertainty is far more significant in the producers' goods industries than in consumers' goods industries. Thus as investment activity expands, so does the degree of uncertainty; and it may well be that businessmen become quite reluctant to carry out enough planned investment to match the economy's savings. The reason for this is not because of scarcities, but rather because of the increasing uncertainty—". . . what has *changed* from one period to

---

[42]*Ibid.*, pp. 281, 306.

[43]*Ibid.*, p. 281.

[44]*Ibid.*, p. 306.

the next, when more saving is not matched by more investment, may sometimes be the appraisal of uncertainty rather than the relationship between investment needs and resource scarcities."[45]

However, in Fellner's analysis, the major causes of the upper-turning point are (1) insufficient offsets to diminishing returns to capital, which permit the contractionary impact of general scarcities, and (2) insufficient offsets to shorter-run resource immobilities, which permit the contractionary impact of specific scarcities. In the former case the contraction may be quite long and severe, while in the second case the contraction is apt to be shorter, awaiting only the removal of the immobilities.

B.   The Contraction and the Lower-Turning Point

The contraction is characterized by a fall in income, employment, and savings. Moreover, if the contraction is a major one, there will be some major "disinvestment" as the consumed stock of capital is not entirely replaced. The minor contractions, on the other hand, are characterized primarily by inventory decumulation and adjustments to resource scarcities. This section deals only with the major contraction.

Fellner argues that the contraction will not be "bottomless," but will rather, *at worst*, settle at a new equilibrium level characterized by *zero savings*. Assume, as an extreme example, that there occurs a complete stoppage of the improvement process. In this case, planned investment becomes zero and the contraction sets in. The new equilibrium level of income, since planned investment is now zero, must theoretically be where actual savings are zero. This, however, should not be interpreted to mean that the new equilibrium level will be at, or even near, a zero level of income. To be sure, the long-run consumption function (as shown in Figures 16–1, 16–2, 16–3, and 16–4) reveals that zero savings, and hence zero investment, occur at some income level at or near the point of origin. This possibility, however, is absurd—at least it has never occured in the United States, not even during the bleak 1930's.

How then is Fellner's position that the lower-level equilibrium will occur at some positive level of income compatible with the long-run consumption function that he uses in his growth analysis? The answer is simple enough—the long-run consumption function must be replaced by the short-run function for analysis of cyclical disturbances.

---

[45]*Ibid.*, p. 280.

Thus the relevant consumption function is the C_sC_s curve in Figure 16–2, rather than the C' curve, once the contraction gets under way. Recall that Fellner argues that as income falls consumers strive to maintain the living levels associated with the highest income previously received. Thus the lower-level equilibrium will be at the income level indicated by the intersection of the C_sC_s and forty-five degree lines. At this income level savings are zero and thus match the zero planned investment.

However, even though output will finally settle at this lower equilibrium level, it will first take a "detour."[46] The reason for this is that there will occur some capital consumption. That is, as output falls, consumption exceeds output. Though this may, on the surface, sound paradoxical, the answer is relatively simple—during the contraction there is some dissaving as businessmen do not replace completely the capital stock as it is worn out. Since this "dissaving" does occur, Fellner concludes that ". . . output will at first have to fall below the *zero-saving* level."[47] This is shown by the dashed segment of the curve in Figure 16–5.

Still, output will rise to the zero-saving level, whatever height it may be. But this situation will not persist forever. Ultimately the improvement process reasserts itself[48] and new investment is carried out.

The expansion thus gets underway, but once again it proceeds at too rapid a pace to be maintained. As the income level approaches the full-employment ceiling, specific scarcities, if nothing else, will cause it to be reversed. If specific scarcities do not do the trick, then general scarcities and an inadequate improvement process will ultimately bring on the upper-turning point. In any event, the upper-turning point is bound to occur under normal circumstances, though in the past the interruptions have not been sufficient to block permanently the growth process. Nevertheless, they have occurred often enough that the American economy's growth pattern is and has been far from smooth.

C.   A Mixed Model

According to the classificatory scheme established in Chapter 5, Fellner's theory of the business cycle is a "mixture"—that is, the endoge-

---

46*Ibid.*, pp. 295-98.

47*Ibid.*, p. 296.

48*Ibid.*, p. 304.

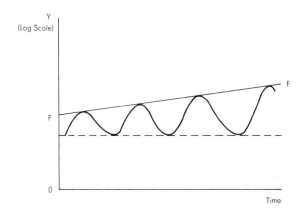

FIGURE 16–6

nous variables explain the upper-turning point, while the exogenous variables explain the lower-turning point.

The upper-turning point occurs as a multiplier-accelerator sets off a rate of expansion that cannot be maintained because of the limitations established by the full-employment ceiling. Given the fixed parameters, scarcities develop and these set off the contraction. The lower-turning point, on the other hand (again ignoring the detour), is explained by changes in the exogenous variables, more specifically a clustering of innovations that gets the expansionary process underway. Thus, Fellner's theory differs from Hicks' in that the latter is purely endogenous, explaining both turning points in terms of the interplay of the endogenous variables.

D.   The Secularly Rising Lower-Level Equilibrium

One important aspect of the analysis is that the lower-level equilibrium discussed above rises secularly because of the secular upward drift of the short-run consumption function. If this were not the case, then the economy would be characterized by ever-deeper fluctuations, as shown in Figure 16–6. A more realistic picture, however, is that in Figure 16–7. The left-hand panel illustrates the secular upward drift of the short-run consumption function (from C_sC_s to $C_s'C_s'$ and so on) and the resultant long-run consumption function C'. The right-

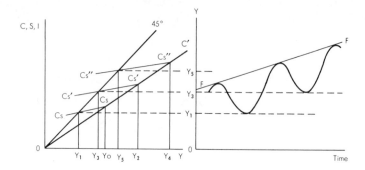

FIGURE 16-7

hand panel is similar to Figures 16-5 and 16-6, showing the rising full-employment ceiling FF.

Begin with the income level of OY_0, at which an insufficient amount of planned investment occurs to match the actual savings of that period. In this event, of course, the income level falls. But recall that consumers do not move back down the long-run consumption function C', but rather strive to maintain their living standards achieved at the income level of OY_0. Thus they move down the short-run consumption function C_sC_s; in other words, they increase their average propensity to consume and lower their average propensity to save. Now if planned investment in period 0 falls to zero, then the resulting lower-level equilibrium will be at the income level of OY_1, at which actual savings are also zero. (Note, we ignore the "detour.")

This lower-level equilibrium is shown on the vertical axis of the right-hand panel as OY_1 and the income of the economy settles at this level. Assume now that, because of a "clustering" of improvements, investment rises, increasing the level of income substantially beyond Y_0, up to Y_2. At first consumers move back up along C_sC_s until their former income level of OY_0 is reestablished. At this point they are satisfied with the allocation of their income between savings and consumption, and as income rises beyond the OY_0 level up to OY_2, they maintain the same propensities to save and to consume. That is, they move up along the C' curve from C_s to C_s'. Assume however that in period 2 insufficient planned investment is forthcoming, so that the level of income falls once again.

The new lower-level equilibrium will not be at the same height as the first contraction, for the simple reason that the short-run consumption has shifted upwards from C_sC_s to $C_s'C_s'$. In other words, the

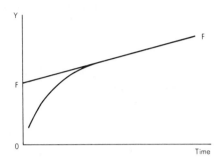

FIGURE 16–8

income level at which zero savings now occur is at Y_3, which lies above the earlier zero-savings level of income at OY_1. (Stated graphically, the intersection of $C_s'C_s'$ with the forty-five-degree line lies above the intersection of C_sC_s with the forty-five-degree line.) Thus the new lower-level equilibrium is now higher. If this were not the case, that is, if the lower-level equilibrium remained at the same height, the cyclical disturbances of the economy would become ever larger (as shown in Figure 16–6). However, the secular rise in the lower-level equilibrium, which is due entirely to the secular rise in the short-run consumption function, prevents this from happening and keeps the cyclical disturbances within the realm of reason.

E. Can the Upper-Turning Point Be Avoided?

In this theory, the upper-turning point cannot be avoided so long as the full-employment ceiling is reached by an expansion rate greater than the rate of growth of the ceiling itself. In other words, as income approaches the ceiling more rapidly than the ceiling is tilted upwards, substantial structural changes are required in order for income to move along the FF line. However, since the economy is characterized by short-run immobilities and an irregular improvement process, the income level is virtually bound to "bounce off" the ceiling.

The only way in which the upper-turning point can be avoided is for there to be a general policy that slows down the rate of income expansion as it approaches the full-employment ceiling. This is shown in Figure 16–8. The objective here is to make the actual rate of income expansion equal to the long-run rate. This policy, of course, would have to be a continuing one, designed to keep the two rates equal through time. It would be oriented toward (1) speeding up the improvement process and enhancing resource mobility, and (2) not allowing the actual rate to exceed or fall short of the full-employment rate.

Such a program, however, would call for tremendous institutional and ideological changes—so much so that the basic nature of the enterprise system would have to be drastically altered. Among other things, direct control over resource allocation and over the investment decisions of private businesses would be required. Indeed only in a completely centralized economy could any such policy be successful, and even then the planners are apt to make mistakes in estimating future actual savings and planned investment, as well as resource allocation needs. In light of such requirements and changes, Fellner's conclusion as regards this sort of policy—"it cannot be expected to accomplish its objectives with full success"[49]—is indeed quite modest.

This should not be interpreted to mean that monetary and fiscal policy cannot be used to slow down the actual rate of income expansion as the full-employment ceiling is approached. This surely can be done. But in a private enterprise type of economy, the upper-turning point is still to be expected. All that monetary and fiscal policy can do is to soften the resulting contraction. Still the upper-turning points will occur so long as the economy misses any or all of the three corollaries. Fellner's policy position is discussed again in Chapter 18, where it is contrasted with Hansen's.

7. Summary

In this chapter one of the modern growth-cycle theories has been examined. The theory first sets forth the necessary requirements for smooth, uninterrupted growth at full employment. Two of these basic requirements are that (1) planned investment of any period must be equal to the realized savings of the period, if the investment of the previous period is to be profitable, and that (2) there must be sufficient offsets to diminishing returns to capital to insure that an adequate amount of planned investment is forthcoming period after period. The second requirement implies that, since capital is increasing faster than the labor force, there must be sufficient improvements of a labor-saving variety (though they must not be too labor-saving). If these improvements do not materialize, the rate of profitability on in-

---

[49]*Ibid.*, p. 305.

vestment declines, and an insufficient amount of planned investment in some period will be forthcoming. In this case, there will be a major contraction. Until improvements in technology and organization are made, the unemployment will continue, though the contraction will not proceed below a lower-level equilibrium at which there are zero savings. Once improvements are made, the expansion gets under way, although it will occur at a rate faster than the rate of the FF line. Hence, another upper-turning point will occur. This is what Fellner designates as the "major" cycle, and while it is bound to occur, so far it has not been sufficient to prevent continued economic growth.

There are two other possible sources of the cycle. One of these is a general scarcity of money, though Fellner does not attach much significance to this. The second is a relative scarcity of specific resources, but in this case the resulting cyclical disturbance is a "minor" cycle. After a short while the specific scarcities are overcome and growth continues.

Thus Fellner has presented a "scarcity" theory of the cycle—a general scarcity of capital relative to labor (and without an adequate improvement process) will cause a major cycle, as will a general scarcity of monetary resources (though this is not likely). Relative scarcities of specific resources can result in the minor cycle, which is fairly easily overcome. However, we can continue to expect the cycle—both major and minor—because it is unlikely that the requirements for smooth growth will be continuously met. We shall continue to refer to Fellner's theory in the next three chapters.

QUESTIONS

16-1. Consider and evaluate the following statement: "One of the chief sources of specific immobilities is labor unionism. Eliminate unionism and you have eliminated one of the more important causes of minor disturbances."

16-2. In order for output to grow without interruption the elasticity of expectations of producers and consumers alike must be equal to unity. Explain.

16-3. Explain in as much detail as possible the differences between general, specific, and monetary scarcities. Which of these is most likely to create a major contraction? Why?

16-4. Why, in Fellner's theory of economic growth and the business cycle, do not the cyclical disturbances grow larger and larger?

16-5. What are the major reasons advanced by Fellner to account for sufficient offsets to diminishing returns to capital? Do you agree?

Bibliography

Alexander, S. S., "The Accelerator as a Generator of Steady Growth," *Quarterly Journal of Economics,* May 1949.

Burton, H. J., "Contemporary Theorizing on Economic Growth," in *Theories of Economic Growth,* ed. B. F. Hoselitz. Glencoe: The Free Press, 1960.

Fellner, W. J., *Trends and Cycles in Economic Activity.* New York: Holt, Rinehart & Winston, Inc., 1956.

———, "The Capital-Output Ratio in Dynamic Economics," in *Money, Trade, and Economic Growth: In Honor of John H. Williams.* New York: The Macmillan Company, 1951.

———, *Monetary Policies and Full Employment.* Los Angeles and Berkeley: University of California Press, 1946.

Hansen, A. H., "Trends and Cycles in Economic Activity," Appendix B in *Economic Issues of the 1960's.* New York: McGraw-Hill Book Company, 1960.

Kuznets, S., *Capital in the American Economy: Its Formation and Financing.* Princeton: Princeton University Press, 1961.

Matthews, R. C. O., "Capital Stock Adjustment Theories of the Trade Cycle, and the Problems of Policy," Chapter 7 in *Post-Keynesian Economics,* ed. K. K. Kurihara. Brunswick, N. J.: Rutgers University Press, 1954.

17

The Warranted Rate of Growth, Economic Fluctuations, and Exogenous Shocks

In this chapter two other variants of the capital-stock adjustment theory are examined—the Harrod-Domar model and Duesenberry's theory of growth and the cycle. These two models are substantially different, especially because Duesenberry presents an "exogenous theory" of the cycle. On the other hand, the Harrod-Domar model is quite similar to Fellner's analysis in that it is a "mixed" model—that is, it accounts for the upper-turning point by means of the interplay of endogenous variables and the lower-turning point by means of exogenous variables. Despite this similarity with the Fellner analysis, the Harrod-Domar model is different for several reasons.

First, the Harrod-Domar model assumes that the average and incremental capital-output ratios are equal and constant; second, it assumes that there are always sufficient offsets to diminishing returns to capital; and third, it provides no analysis of cyclical fluctuations, although it does provide an explanation of economic disturbances.[1] This last point

---

[1]In all these respects, Fellner's analysis goes beyond the Harrod-Domar model.

may seem somewhat confusing, but it means this: the Harrod-Domar model concludes that once smooth growth is interrupted, deviations from the dynamic equilibrium ensue, but these deviations do not reveal a *complete* cyclical pattern. This, of course, might be considered as a basic weakness of the analysis, despite its other merits.

Although these assumptions seem rather rigid, they are made by Harrod and Domar primarily for the purpose of setting forth, at least in one form, the requirements for steady, uninterrupted growth. This obviously does not mean that these economists believe that the assumptions are met in reality. In fact they assert that often they are absent, and consequently departures from the dynamic equilibrium follow. Thus the model should not be evaluated strictly in terms of the assumptions necessary for setting forth a first approximation. We shall return to critical evaluation in a later section of this chapter after the model and its implications have been examined.

1.   The Savings and Capital-Output Assumptions[2]

The first basic assumption of the model is that the savings of the economy are a constant percentage of the income received. Thus the average and marginal propensities to save are equal, as are the average and marginal propensities to consume. In other words, the long-run consumption function is linear and passes through the point of origin. Thus

$$S_t = sY_t,$$

where for period t, total savings are a fixed percentage of the income of the period (Y_t).[3]

Also, in this analysis (as in Fellner's) the desired and actual savings

---

2Although the theories of both R. F. Harrod and E. D. Domar are quite similar and were independently developed, we shall concentrate primarily on Harrod's model. The relevant references are R. F. Harrod, *Towards a Dynamic Economics* (London: The Macmillan Company, 1948), "An Essay in Dynamic Theory," *Economic Journal*, March 1939, reprinted as Chapter 16 in *Readings in Business Cycles and National Income,* eds. A. H. Hansen and R. V. Clemence (New York: W. W. Norton & Company, Inc., 1953) and as Chapter 13 in *Economic Essays* (New York: Harcourt, Brace & World, Inc., 1953), and "Supplement on Dynamic Theory," Chapter 14 in *Economic Essays.* The major contributions of Domar are found in his *Essays in the Theory of Economic Growth* (New York: Oxford University Press, 1957).

3See Chapters 10 and 16 for a discussion of this.

of the community are assumed to be equal. Thus the burden of the growth process is placed on investment (that is, on capital-stock adjustments), and more specifically on *planned* investment. The reason that planned investment holds the center of the stage is that, by definition, actual investment always equals actual savings.[4]

The second basic assumption relates to the capital-output ratio. The model in question assumes that the average and incremental capital-output ratios are equal, that is $K/Y = \triangle K/\triangle Y$. As has already been seen,[5] empirical evidence does not support this assumption, but the premise is made only for purposes of first approximation.

The third assumption also relates to the capital-output ratio, though it is stated in terms of the long-run accelerator. This assumption states that businessmen's desires (or plans) to undertake investment expenditures depend on the *rate of change* in income. More specifically, the model assumes that planned investment for any period is a constant proportion v of the change in income between the two preceding periods. Thus

$$\triangle K_t = v(Y_t - Y_{t-1}),$$

where $\triangle K$ is current planned investment, $(Y_t - Y_{t-1})$ is the difference in income between periods t and t—1, and v is the capital-output ratio.[6]

Finally, keep in mind that Harrod assumes that the ratio v remains constant throughout the growth process. This assumption is made, however, not because he believes that v actually is constant, but rather for the purpose of setting forth the requirements for smooth, uninterrupted growth. At a later point he relaxes this assumption, and the complications of changes in v are introduced.

On the basis of these three assumptions, along with others that are implicit in the analysis, Harrod sets forth his analysis of the requirements for a dynamic equilibrium. The fundamental theory is discussed in the next section, and following this we shall examine what happens to the level of income and employment when the growth requirements are not always present. In fact, major implications of Harrod's analysis may be anticipated here—namely, that Harrod is quite concerned with the end result of economic activity, fearing that it may well end up in chronic economic stagnation and unemployment, a proposition which is examined in more detail in the next chapter.

---

[4]See Chapter 16 for a review of this identity.
[5]As was pointed out in Chapter 4.
[6]The capital-output ratio, recall, is $v = \triangle K_t/(Y_t - Y_{t-1})$; see Chapters 12 and 16.

2.   The Warranted Rate of Growth

According to Harrod there is a warranted rate of growth of income (G_w) which he defines as follows:

> I define G_w as that over-all rate of advance which, if executed, will leave entrepreneurs in a state of mind in which they are prepared to carry on a similar advance. Some may be dissatisfied and have to adjust upwards or downwards, but the ups and downs should balance out and, in the aggregate, progress in the current period should be equal to progress in the last preceding period.[7]

In other words, the warranted rate of growth of income is such that businessmen are (in the aggregate) quite satisfied with the investment that they have carried out in the previous period; and because of this they plan to carry out the amount of investment in the present period indicated by the change in income and the acceleration coefficient.

Note that, in this analysis, businessmen base their current investment plans on the rate of income change, not on the total amount of income change. Also note that since v is assumed to be constant, the burden of the investment decision is placed on the rate of income change itself. Thus if income is actually rising at an "insufficient" rate, businessmen may become dissatisfied with their last period's position and not provide enough current investment to allow for continued growth. On the other hand, if income is rising faster than the warranted rate, they are more than satisfied and attempt to invest currently more than savings permit. If this occurs in a period of full employment then inflation and hence interruption of the growth process will occur. There is, in Harrod's analysis, only one rate of growth that will leave businessmen precisely happy, and that is the warranted rate of growth. *If the actual rate of growth deviates from the warranted, the growth process is disrupted.*

There are two aspects of this that call for further comment. First, the theory can easily be restated in terms of the analysis of the preceding chapter; and second, it yields certain implications about the future growth of income that are worth further study.

A.   A Restatement

One of the important points made in the previous discussion of Fellner's growth theory was that the planned investment of each period

---

[7]Harrod, *Towards a Dynamic Economics*, p. 82. Reprinted by permission of St. Martin's Press and Macmillan & Co. Ltd.

must be equal to the actual savings of the period. If this equality does not occur, the investment in the preceding period will either not "pay off" or will more than "pay off," with the result that the dynamic equilibrium is disrupted.[8] If, for example, the planned investment of period 1 is insufficient to match the actual savings of that period, there is an excess of aggregate supply over aggregate demand. The accumulation of excess unplanned inventories in period 1 is a measure of the unprofitability of some of the investment in period 0. Thus income will contract, and a cyclical disturbance follows.

In Fellner's analysis, then, if the growth process is to be smooth and uninterrupted, the planned investment of each period must be equal to the actual savings of the period. Put otherwise, a dynamic equilibrium requires that aggregate demand and aggregate supply be equal, period after period, so that the investment of each previous period proves to be profitable. Under these circumstances, businessmen will be content with their prior investment activity and will plan to implement their new investment projects.

This is, of course, merely another way of stating the warranted rate of growth. Only if the planned investment in each period equals the actual savings of that period will businessmen be satisfied with the investment (the "advance") that they carried out in the prior period. In other words, so long as the aggregate supply generated by the investment of the preceding period is being demanded in the current period, businessmen are happy with their previous investment. Moreover, they will be willing to undertake the amount of investment in the current period indicated by $v = \triangle K_t / (Y_t - Y_{t-1})$.

But note the significance of this. As long as v is constant, and Harrod's analysis does assume it to be constant, *the burden for smooth growth is placed on the actual rate of growth of income.* If the actual rate is less than the warranted rate (that is, if current aggregate demand is less than current aggregate supply)[9] businessmen will not be satisfied with the profitability of their investment in the prior period, and the growth process will be halted, at least temporarily. On the other hand, if the actual rate exceeds the warranted rate (that is, if current demand outstrips current supply), businessmen are more than happy with their prior investment activity and inflation results. The important conclusion is that the actual and warranted rate must be equal (at full employment) if the dynamic equilibrium is to be main-

---

[8]See Chapter 16.

[9]That is, if planned investment is less than actual savings.

tained. This is the same conclusion that Fellner puts forth, though in somewhat different terms.

B.   Some Implications for Steady Growth

The requirement for steady growth is that the rate of growth of income and the capital-output ratio (the acceleration ratio) must be sufficient to induce enough planned investment in the current period to absorb the savings of the period. Under these conditions businessmen will be left in "a state of mind in which they are prepared to carry on a similar advance." Now, as already observed, if the capital-output ratio and the propensity to save are given, the burden of steady growth rests with the actual rate of income growth—that is, it must equal the warranted rate. For purposes of present discussion these two rates are assumed to be equal; discrepancies between them, will be examined below (sections 3-4).

The requirement for smooth growth may be stated algebraically as follows:

$$(Y_t - Y_{t-1}) Y_t \cdot \frac{\triangle K_t}{(Y_t - Y_{t-1})} = \frac{S_t}{Y_t} .$$

That is, the actual (= warranted) rate of growth of income, $(Y_t - Y_{t-1})/Y_t$, times the capital-output (acceleration) coefficient $\triangle K_t/(Y_t - Y_{t-1})$, must equal the propensity to save, S_t/Y_t. More simply, we can rewrite the left-hand side of the equation as $\triangle K_t/Y_t$, which of course is the same thing as the ratio of net investment to current income, $\triangle I_t/Y_t$. Thus we have

$$\frac{\triangle K_t}{Y_t} = \frac{S_t}{Y_t} .$$

For the economy to remain in a dynamic equilibrium the ratio of planned investment to income must be equal to the propensity to save. This is the *warranted rate of growth equation* and is designed to show that there is a specific and unique rate of growth of income that will keep businessmen satisfied and happy with their previous investment activity.[10] (Recall that for the moment the warranted and actual rates are assumed to be identical; this is not always so, and complications will be introduced later.)

---

[10]Harrod, *Towards a Dynamic Economics,* writes this equation as $G_w C_r = s,$ where G_w is the warranted rate of growth, C_r is the capital-output ratio, and s is the propensity to save.

The warranted rate of growth equation is merely an algebraic formulation of the requirement that planned investment must always equal actual savings, and that planned investment is itself closely related to the rate of change of income. Another way of stating this requirement, and one more amenable to numerical illustration, is

$$\triangle K_t = v(Y_t - Y_{t-1}) = sY_t,$$

that is, the acceleration coefficient times the change in income must yield a current planned investment ($\triangle K_t$) equal to the current savings (sY_t).

A numerical example may aid in understanding this. Assume that $s = .2$. Also assume that $Y_t = \$1100$, and $Y_{t-1} = \$1000$, so that the change in income is \$100. Thus the rate of growth of income is $(Y_t - Y_{t-1})/Y_t = (\$1100 - \$1000)/\$1100 = .09$. Current savings are \$220, that is, $sY_t = .2 \cdot \$1100 = \$220$. In this case, then, the value of v is 2.2. That is:

$$\triangle K_t = v(Y_t - Y_{t-1}) = sY_t$$
$$\triangle K_t = v(\$1100 - \$1000) = .2\,(\$1100)$$
$$\triangle K_t = v(\$100) = \$220$$
$$\triangle K_t = 2.2\,(\$100) = \$220$$
$$\triangle K_t = \$220.$$

In this instance the requirement for smooth growth is satisfied, for the change in income of \$100 induces enough planned investment to absorb the savings of the current period.[11] Only in this case will businessmen be satisfied with the investment of the previous period.

However, if $s = .2$ and is given by consumer preferences which do not change, and $v = 2.2$ and is given by technological forces which do not change, attention is necessarily focused on the rate of change of income. In other words, income must grow by a specified rate in order to keep businessmen satisfied. Using the *warranted rate of growth equation*, we find this required rate to be

$$\frac{(Y_t - Y_{t-1})}{Y_t} \cdot v = s$$
$$\frac{\$1100 - \$1000}{\$1100} \cdot v = .2$$
$$.09 \cdot 2.2 = .2.$$

----

[11]The same answer is given by what we shall call the *warranted rate of growth equation:*
$$\frac{(Y_t - Y_{t-1})}{Y_t} \cdot v = s$$

The warranted rate of growth then, given s and v, is .09. Therefore, the income must grow by this rate between the present period (t) and the next period (t+1) if businessmen are to be satisfied with their present investment of $220 in the current period t.

Given this warranted rate of growth, income must rise between the present period and the next period to the level of $1210, or by the increment of $110. Note again that with this rate of income growth, the basic requirement that induced planned investment in the next time period, t+1, be equal to the actual savings of that period is satisfied. That is,

$$\triangle K_{t+1} = v(Y_{t+1} - Y_t) = sY_{t+1}$$
$$\triangle K_{t+1} = v(\$1210 - \$1100) = s(\$1210)$$
$$\triangle K_{t+1} = 2.2(\$110) = .2(\$1210)$$
$$\triangle K_{t+1} = \$242 = \$242.$$

Thus planned investment in period t+1 equals the actual savings of the same period, but only if income grows at the warranted rate of .09. Table 17-1 shows different levels of income at this warranted rate of growth. To repeat, so long as $s = .2$ and $v = 2.2$, and each remains constant, a warranted rate of .09 (and only .09) will yield enough planned investment for each period. If this does not occur, then (as will be seen in section 3) deviations from dynamic equilibrium result. For example, if income had grown at a slower rate than was warranted, actual savings would exceed planned investment. On the other hand, if income had grown faster than the warranted rate, planned investment would exceed actual savings. In both cases there would *not* be steady growth. *Steady growth occurs only so long as the actual rate of income growth is equal to the warranted rate, given the capital-output ratio and the propensity to consume.*

TABLE 17-1

Income of Previous Period	Warranted Rate of Growth	Income of Current Period	Change in Income	Actual Savings°	Planned Investment†
$1000	.09	$1100	$100	$220	$220
1100	.09	1210	110	242	242
1210	.09	1331	121	266	266
1331	.09	1464	133	293	293
1464	.09	1610	146	322	322
1610	.09	1771	160	352	352

° Actual savings = .2 • income of the current period.
† Planned investment = 2.2 • the change in income.

Before turning to an examination of the consequences of departures of the actual rate from the warranted rate, one important implication of the analysis thus far presented must be stressed. This implication is at once both startling and illusory—startling in that it states that income must grow forever faster and faster in order to keep businessmen happy and content with their previous investment activity, and illusory in the sense that we know that income cannot and does not behave in this manner.

If the data in Table 17–1 are plotted graphically, as in Figure 17–1, the pictured income curve must slope upwards quite steeply after a point. This is indeed a startling conclusion—that in order for planned investment always to equal actual savings (given the capital-output ratio and the propensity to save), income must increase at an ever-increasing rate. Not only does this conclusion jar the imagination, it also raises questions about the actual limits to income growth. Certainly it is illusory to believe that income will behave consistently through time in this fashion.

However, Harrod does not intend that income actually does, or will, grow in this manner. Rather he uses the analysis thus far presented simply to show the consequences and requirements of steady growth. In the next stage of his analysis he raises questions as to what is more likely to happen in reality when the actual rate departs from the warranted rate.

3. Departures from the Warranted Rate

What will be the repercussions on the economy if, for some reason, the actual rate of growth is greater or smaller than the warranted rate? Consider, for example, a situation where the actual rate falls short of the warranted rate. For sake of illustration, assume that the warranted rate is as before, .09, but that the actual rate of income growth is only .05. Thus, instead of income's rising from $1000 to $1100 between periods t—1 and t (as in the earlier example), it rises only to (approximately) $1055.

The consequence of this would be "overproduction" in the sense that the planned investment will be less than the actual savings of the period t. Actual savings would be $s(Y_t) = .2(\$1055) = \$211$, and planned investment would be $v(Y_t—Y_{t-1}) = 2.2(\$55) = \$121$. Thus there is an excess of aggregate supply over aggregate demand for the simple reason that the growth rate of .05 does not induce enough investment to absorb the actual savings of period t.

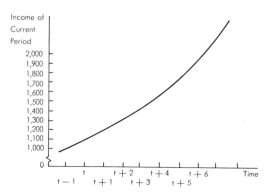

FIGURE 17–1

Earlier, when this possible situation was discussed in terms of Fellner's analysis, it was noted that a contraction would result, which in turn would be followed by a lower-turning point and an expansion. In other words, an insufficiency of planned investment results in the business cycle. In the Harrod analysis, on the other hand, an insufficiency of planned investment is not followed by the business cycle, though a deviation from the dynamic equilibrium certainly occurs. Indeed, Harrod argues that a departure of the actual rate below the warranted rate is self-sustaining—that is, there is no lower-turning point.

In order to arrive at this conclusion, however, a further assumption must be made—an assumption relating to businessmen's behavior. Harrod states this premise quite explicitly, though he provides no empirical evidence in favor of it. Using the symbol G_w for the warranted rate of growth and G for the actual rate of growth, he states:

> G is a quantity determined from time to time by trial and error, by the collective trials and errors of vast numbers of people. It would be great luck if their collective appraisals caused them to hit precisely upon the value of G_w. But if they do not do so, their experience will drive them farther and farther from it. . . . there will not be any tendency to adapt production towards G_w but, on the contrary, a tendency to adapt farther away from it, whether on the higher or lower side.[12]

In other words, when unplanned excess inventories build up, as will be the case when planned investment falls short of actual savings, businessmen become so pessimistic that they keep the actual rate of growth below the warranted rate. This seems, upon examination, a fairly rea-

---

[12]Harrod, *Towards a Dynamic Economics,* p. 82. Reprinted by permission of St. Martin's Press and Macmillan & Co. Ltd.

sonable assumption. If businessmen are experiencing an unplanned accumulation of inventories at the actual rate of increase of production, they may be expected to become pessimistic and reduce their rate of output even more. This, they calculate, is the chief means of reducing their unplanned excess inventories.

But note the consequence. So long as the actual rate is below the warranted rate, and so long as it leads to further reduction in the actual rate, the divergency between the two rates becomes ever greater. As this continues period after period, more and more fuel is added to the flames, and the situation becomes worse and worse. Final result? A very low rate of actual output and the emergence of substantial, perhaps chronic, unemployment.

Conversely, a departure from the warranted rate upwards will result in a further rise in the actual output rate above the warranted rate. Again the divergency increases. However, in this case there must be some upper limit which is set by the availability of productive resources (including the labor supply) and technology.[13] These factors determine what Harrod calls the *natural rate of growth,* which can expand, but only rather slowly over time.[14] Once the actual rate of growth results in an income expansion that hits the ceiling set by the natural rate, the upper-turning point occurs and the contraction is bound to follow.

The conclusion that a contraction is bound to follow is based on the condition that the natural rate of growth is less than the warranted rate. Thus as output hits the full-employment ceiling, the actual rate must (at least temporarily) become equal to the natural rate, for output at full employment cannot grow any more rapidly than the full-employment growth factors permit. When this occurs, the actual rate falls below the warranted rate. This follows from the assumption above that the natural rate is less than the warranted rate, and now, since the actual rate equals the natural, it also must lie below the warranted rate. This downward divergency tends to become larger and larger once it occurs. And as businessmen cut back on their production even more, the actual rate falls even lower and the contraction becomes more severe.

Harrod, however, does not provide (nor does he even attempt to do so) an explanation of the lower-turning point. His major observation here is that eventually ". . . requirements for replacements must become positive, if any output at all is to be maintained. . . . This will

---

[13]*Ibid.,* p. 87.
[14]This is the same thing as the "full-employment ceiling" in Hicks' and Fellner's analyses.

arrest the downward movement and turn it into an upward one."[15]
(By "replacements" Harrod means replacement investment.)

This section may be concluded by stressing that Harrod does not purport to provide a thorough and detailed theory of the business cycle.[16] He does, however, set forth a growth framework into which a fairly complete theory can be incorporated, as has been done by both J. R. Hicks and W. J. Fellner, whose theories were discussed earlier.

4.   A Major Implication

One very important implication of Harrod's analysis relates to the possibility of secular stagnation—that is, a situation of chronic unemployment. Indeed, he states: "The ideal which underlies these lectures is that sooner or later we shall be faced once more with the problem of stagnation, and that it is to this problem that economists should devote their main attention."[17] This important possibility deserves careful study.

Suppose that the actual rate of growth exceeds the warranted rate *and* natural rate. In this case the output expansion would hit the full-employment ceiling, and the actual rate would become equal to the natural rate. Recall that once output hits the full-employment ceiling, the actual rate can rise no faster than resources and technological change permit. Thus, the upper-turning point will occur.

Now suppose further that the natural rate is less than the warranted rate. In other words, the rate of income along the full-employment ceiling is not sufficient to induce enough planned investment in subsequent periods to absorb the actual savings of the economy. (Recall that thus far the Harrodian analysis assumes v to be constant.) Thus a divergency develops between the actual and warranted rates, with the actual falling below the warranted. On the basis of Harrod's assumption as regards businessmen's reactions to this sort of situation, the divergency widens. The result then is further decline in output and a rise in unemployment.

Now under these circumstances, so Harrod argues, there is a tendency for the warranted rate of growth to fall. Since output now increases at a lesser rate, less investment plans are warranted. This result can be stated in terms of the equations developed earlier. Recall that

---

[15]Harrod, *Towards a Dynamic Economics*, p. 91. Reprinted by permission of St. Martin's Press and Macmillan & Co. Ltd.

[16]*Ibid.*, pp. 90-91.

[17]*Ibid.*, p. v.

the propensity to save (s) is constant. Now if the warranted rate of growth, $(Y_t-Y_{t-1})/Y_t$, has fallen, then the capital-output ratio must, *by definition*, rise. Thus more capital per unit of output flow is now required than before.

This rise in the capital-output ratio of course signifies that since more capital per unit of output is being used, investment is "capital-using"; and under such circumstances there would occur a lower rate of investment and chronic unemployment. However, the lower rate of income growth could leave businessmen satisfied with their prior investment activity, and indeed there is the possibility that the warranted rate could fall low enough to become equal with the actual rate at far less than full employment. Thus economic stagnation could set in and be perpetuated.

Recall that this conclusion depends upon a particular sequence of events; (1) the warranted rate's being larger than the natural rate, but less than the actual rate; (2) the actual rate's exceeding and then becoming equal with the natural rate, and hence falling below the warranted rate; (3) the actual rate's falling, so that the discrepancy between it and the warranted rate widens; (4) the warranted rate's falling, which (given the propensity to save) means a rise in the capital-output ratio, until the warranted and actual rates are once again equal, but less than the natural rate.

How long these conditions could persist before social unrest would lead to a change in the social-economic system is unpredictable. Nevertheless, Harrod feels that this future contingency is fully possible and must be avoided if the present type of economic system in most western nations is to be preserved. We shall return to the stagnation issue in the next chapter.

5. Some Critical Observations

Several economists have criticized Harrod's model on the grounds that it is too rigid and depends upon too precise definitions. Other criticisms relate to the *a priori* and empirical plausibility of his assumptions as to businessmen's behavior.[18] However, many of these criticisms appear to be well taken only if Harrod intends his growth model to be

---

[18]See, for example, L. B. Yeager, "Some Questions about Growth Economics," *American Economic Review,* March 1954. See also the excellent reviews of *Towards a Dynamic Economics* by D. M. Wright, Joan Robinson, and J. R. Hicks in *Readings in Business Cycles and National Income,* eds. Hansen and Clemence.

reasonably descriptive of what actually takes place in the economy. It is one thing to assume that the average and incremental ratios are equal as a first approximation; it is quite another to assert that in fact they are equal. By the same token, it is one thing to assume that there is a warranted rate of growth, which leaves businessmen satisfied, for the purpose of providing a point of departure for subsequent and more realistic analysis; and it is quite another to assert that businessmen actually think in terms of such a rate of growth.

The Harrod-Domar model is, of course, intended to be nothing more than a first approximation—a point of departure for subsequent analysis—and in this sense the criticisms that it is too rigid and too austere are not particularly well taken. The model is skeletal in nature, requiring a number of significant additions before it acquires any reasonable semblance of reality.[19] Efforts to do this (such as those by Hicks and Fellner) have proved to be quite worthwhile. Still it is worth bearing in mind that if a model such as Harrod's is to be used, it must always be treated only as a first approximation from which more realistic treatments and theories can be derived. And in the movement towards the construction of more realistic and disaggregated theories, models such as Harrod's will lose their simplicity and elegance.

However, some of the more important criticisms of the model are worth examining. In the first place, the model of uninterrupted growth assumes a rigid capital-output ratio, and this in turn implies a number of further important assumptions. The aggregate production function is assumed to be given by technological considerations alone—that is, input-output ratios are technically determined (in the aggregate). This means that the production of a given increment in capacity always requires the use of an unchanging amount of inputs. But it also means that there are no significant changes in the rate and quality of technology. The simple model, in short, assumes a steady, unchanging rate of technological advance. As Mrs. Robinson has put it, the analysis assumes that ". . . technical progress falls like the gentle dew from heaven and is not susceptible to any economic influence."[20] This, of course, is only one means of maintaining the constancy of the capital-output ratio. Recall that Fellner introduces institutional, technical,

---

[19]This position regarding Harrod's analysis is quite similar to the one taken by S. S. Alexander regarding Hicks' theory. See S. S. Alexander, "Issues of Business Cycle Theory Raised by Mr. Hicks," *American Economic Review*, December 1951. See also G. M. Meier, "Some Questions about Growth Economics: Comment," *American Economic Review*, December 1954.

[20]"Mr. Harrod's Dynamics," in *Readings in Business Cycles and National Income*, eds. Hansen and Clemence, p. 248.

and organizational responses in order to account for offsets to diminishing returns to capital and thus maintain the constancy of the ratio.

Moreover, the technology must be "neutral" in that it must not entail significant capital-saving or capital-using advances. If it does, then the capital-output ratio will no longer remain constant. In this respect also Fellner's analysis goes beyond the simple model, for it considers that there may be diminishing returns that must be offset by labor-saving (though not too much so) innovations in order for the capital-output ratio to be constant.

A further comment with respect to the aggregate production function is that it ignores noncapital inputs. More specifically, if the actual, warranted, and natural rates are all equal, there is still no reason to assume that there will be full employment of the labor force.[21] Full employment of labor will exist only if the rate of growth of the capital stock is equal to the rate of growth of the labor force. The reason for this is that the technically determined capital-output ratio means that once full employment of the capital stock is achieved, any further growth in income must be technically proportional to the growth of capital. But, at the same time, a constant capital-output ratio means that there is also a constant labor-output ratio. In short, the assumption of a constant ratio of capital to output is merely another way of saying that the aggregate production function is linear and homogenous.[22] This type of production function may be written as

$$Y = Y_1 K + Y_2 L,$$

where Y_1 and Y_2 are constants. Thus there is a fixed rigidity between the proportions of the inputs. But, of course, there is no reason to assume that there will be an equality between the rates of growth of both capital and labor; and if this equality is not present, then there may be unemployment of one factor, even though the other is fully employed.

For example, if the capital stock is growing at a rate faster than the labor force, and if savings permit the capital to be invested, then

[21]On this see D. Hamberg, "Underemployment Equilibrium Rates of Growth," *American Economic Review*, June 1953; H. M. Wagner, "Underemployment Equilibrium Rate of Growth," *American Economic Review*, June 1953; R. Eisner, "Underemployment Equilibrium Rates of Growth," *American Economic Review*, March 1952; D. Hamberg, "Full Capacity vs. Full Employment Growth," *Quarterly Journal of Economics*, August 1952; H. Pilvin, "Full Capacity vs. Full Employment Growth," *Quarterly Journal of Economics*, November 1953; and I. Adelman and O. Lobo, "Some Observations on Full Employment vs. Full Capacity," *American Economic Review*, June 1956.

[22]See Adelman and Lobo, "Some Observations on Full Employment vs. Full Capacity," for a good discussion of this.

chronic unemployment would result. Conversely, if the labor force grows at a rate faster than the capital stock that is allowed by savings, again there will be inadequate investment to provide for full employment of the labor force. Examination of problems such as these leads one to question the significance and importance of the purely technical determinants in the aggregate production function. Surely other factors figure in.

Consider, for example, a situation in which all labor and all capital are placed on the market and in which pure competition prevails everywhere. In this case, wages and other costs would adjust rapidly enough so that nearly always the actual capital-output ratio is the desired one. But the important thing is that once flexible wages and other input prices are introduced, there will be continuing full employment of both capital and the labor force. Note, however, under these circumstances the capital-output ratio is flexible, not constant, as it is under the Harrod model, for capital and labor will be substituted for one another. More important, under these conditions the model may not be as unstable as Harrod implies, once an expansion or contraction gets under way.[23]

These conditions, of course, are quite different from the production function assumed in the Harrod analysis. In effect, Harrod's production function prevents response by businesses (in the aggregate) to changing relative prices of inputs; but the other approach allows the substitution of one input for another as their relative prices change. This latter type of production function need not actually be based on the assumption of pure competition in all markets; rather it need only assume that there are in fact mechanisms that permit managerial response to changing relative input prices over the long run. Actually this assumption seems to have some significance for the long haul; as was pointed out earlier, in the United States the capital stock has been increasing more rapidly than the labor force. Over the long run the accumulated capital has been used, though not of course in every year, as there have been cyclical disturbances. But the long-run use of the capital stock implies that businesses have tended to substitute factor inputs for one another, depending in large part on their relative prices. More specifically, it implies that capital has been substituted for labor. Thus in reality, the aggregate production function, and hence the capital-output ratio, is not as rigidly fixed as the simple model assumes, and if

[23]On this see R. Solow, "A Contribution to the Theory of Economic Growth," *Quarterly Journal of Economics,* February 1956; see also Adelman and Lobo, "Some Observations on Full Employment vs. Full Capacity," and Pilvin, "Full Capacity vs. Full Employment Growth."

there has tended to be a long-run constancy of the ratio, it is because inputs in the production function are not rigidly fixed with respect to one another, but rather are variable.

One final point. The cycle theories discussed so far in this and the last chapter represent "mixed" models. The upper-turning point is caused by the actual rate of growth "bumping up" against a full-employment ceiling, while the lower-turning point is brought on by spurts of autonomous investment. Thus the upper-turning point is caused by the interplay of the endogenous variables running up against *fixed parameters* (the full-employment ceiling), while the lower-turning point is caused, if at all, by a clustering of innovations. This clustering, however, may occur rather sporadically—at least, autonomous investment in these theories does not proceed at the smooth, constant rate assumed by Hicks. This, in fact, is the major difference between Hicks' model and the others. While they all agree upon the approximate cause of the upper-turning point, they disagree on the lower. But because Hicks assumes a constant advance of autonomous investment, he builds into his model an endogenous explanation of the lower-turning point and thus has constructed a "purely endogenous" model. Fellner and Harrod, on the other hand, rely heavily upon an endogenous explanation of the upper-turning point but fall back on shifting parameters in order to explain the lower-turning point, and hence theirs are "mixed" models.

6. Exogenous Shocks and Adjustments by the System

In this section we shall examine another growth model, the one advanced by James S. Duesenberry.[24] This model is unique in that it argues that in the United States the conditions necessary for sustained growth have historically been present and, moreover, that cyclical disturbances have been caused by exogenous "shocks," that is, changes in the parameters. Still, these shocks have not been sufficient to drive the values of the parameters outside the "stability range," and the system has therefore been able to adjust to them. In short, the economic system has always been able to recover from contractions, sometimes sooner, sometimes later, but nevertheless it has been able to readjust and to restore the fundamental conditions for growth.

---

[24]J. S. Duesenberry, *Business Cycles and Economic Growth* (New York: McGraw-Hill Book Company, 1958). For an excellent review of this work, see R. C. O. Matthews, "Duesenberry on Growth and Fluctuations," *Economic Journal,* December 1959.

Duesenberry rejects completely all models that rely upon endogenous forces to explain the upper-turning point on the grounds that they do not explain most American business cycles. His major argument in this respect is that these models

> . . . imply that the rate of growth of capital exceeds the rate of growth of income for some time before income actually begins to fall. That must be so because no appreciable change in the ratio of capital to income can occur in a short period (unless we introduce an outside shock). The stock of capital rarely increases by more than 4 per cent per year. If income is still increasing, the ratio of capital to income must increase by less than 4 per cent per year. It follows that the moment of absolute decline must be preceded by a long period during which profits are slowly falling and the rate of growth of income is slowly falling. That does not seem to square with the experience of the period since the Civil War.[25]

Further, in such models the lower-turning point occurs only when the capital-output ratio rises, that is, during the contraction capital must have decumulated faster than income fell. But, as Duesenberry points out, "If endogenous models require capital decumulation to explain the upswing from a depression, they cannot be used to explain any observed upswing except the upswing of the 1930's. . . ."[26] This historical observation, of course, throws serious doubts on the explanatory usefulness of such models as Hicks', Fellner's, and others, in which capital decumulation plays an important role in explaining the lower-turning point.

Since in Duesenberry's view cyclical fluctuations cannot be explained by the other models, there is need to look elsewhere for a theory that will yield better results. In his model the major role is played by a ". . . combination of exogenous factors working on the system, such as spurts in autonomous investment, speculative booms, wage-price spirals, and changes in both foreign balances and monetary conditions."[27] In an important sense this is hardly a novel conclusion, for the real-life parameters of the economic system are always changing. Techniques are altered, institutions change, population rates fluctuate, and so on; and all of these are bound to create some disturbance. As Duesenberry observes: "The problem is not so much to explain the fact that fluctuations occur as to find out what limits their magnitude and why some of them are more violent than others."[28] The changes in the parameters are, as will be seen, the "shocks" in his model.

---

[25]Duesenberry, *Business Cycles and Economic Growth*, p. 244.
[26]*Ibid.*, p. 245.
[27]*Ibid.*, p. 248.
[28]*Ibid.*

At the outset Duesenberry assumes that the parameters of the system change slowly and smoothly, and then under this assumption he proceeds to set forth the conditions for smooth, noncyclical growth. Following this he allows rapid shifts in the parameters (that is, "shocks") to show how cyclical disturbances are created.

A. The Equilibrium of Growth

The basic point of departure in Duesenberry's theory is his "simple, dynamic model," which is based on two behavioral and two identity equations. The first of the identity equations is the familiar

$$Y_t = C_t + I_t,$$

which states that current income is equal to current consumption and investment.

The other identity equation, which is very important in Duesenberry's analysis, deals with the capital stock and is written as

$$K_t = K_{t-1} + I_t - kK_{t-1}.$$

Here K_t is the capital stock of the current period and is equal to the sum of the capital stock of the preceding period (K_{t-1}) *plus* current net investment (I_t) *minus* capital consumption of the preceding period (kK_{t-1}). In this equation capital consumption is assumed to be proportional to the stock of capital. As will be seen in a moment, the behavior of K is quite important since it influences *both* investment and consumption.

As for the behavorial equations, one deals with consumption, the other with investment. Duesenberry writes the consumption function as

$$C_t = cY_{t-1} + bK_{t-1}.$$

In this equation c is the marginal propensity to consume out of gross national product and is assumed to be constant. But note that Duesenberry also introduces the influence of the capital stock on consumption, as shown by b. The reason for this is that changes in the capital stock influence profits, which in turn affect dividend distribution by corporations. Since dividends enter into the income of the economy, changes in dividend payments will influence consumption. Thus the line of influence is from changes in the capital stock to changes in profits, from profits to dividends, and from dividends to consumption.[29]

---

[29]*Ibid.*, p. 196.

Finally there is the investment function, which is written as

$$I_t = vY_{t-1} + \beta K_{t-1}.$$

Here v is not a technically given datum, and it represents a "duel effect"—that is, v signifies that a change in income affects investment through both the marginal efficiency of investment and the marginal cost of funds. The reason for including the additional variable of the marginal cost of funds is because profits are included in the consumption function. Thus a change in income affects profits, which in turn serve as a significant source of funds for modern business. And last, β "reflects the influence of capital stock on investment working through both marginal efficiency and profits."[30]

Given the behavorial equations it is possible to rewrite the identity equations by substituting the former into them. Thus:

$$Y_t = (cY_{t-1} + bK_{t-1}) + (vY_{t-1} + \beta K_{t-1}), \text{ and}$$
$$K_t = K_{t-1} + vY_{t-1} + \beta K_{t-1} + kK_{t-1},$$

or more simply,

$$Y_t = (c+v)Y_{t-1} + (b+\beta)K_{t-1}, \text{ and}$$
$$K_t = vY_{t-1} + [\beta + (1-k)]K_{t-1}.$$

Let us now turn to the rates of growth of both income and the stock of capital. Consider first the rate of growth of income R_y, which can be written as

$$R_y = \frac{Y_t - Y_{t-1}}{Y_{t-1}} = \frac{(v+c-1) + (\beta+b)K_{t-1}}{Y_{t-1}}.$$

The rate of growth of the capital stock, on the other hand, is given by

$$R_k = \frac{K_t - K_{t-1}}{K_{t-1}} = \frac{vY_{t-1} + (\beta-k)K_{t-1}}{K_{t-1}}.$$

Note that in both cases the capital-output ratio figures directly as a major determinant of the rate of growth. Further, if there is to be smooth, uninterrupted growth, *the two growth rates must be equal.* However, they will be equal *only if the capital-output ratio remains constant.* As Duesenberry puts it, ". . . income *can* grow steadily if there is a real, positive ratio of capital to income at which the rate of growth of income equals the rate of growth of capital."[31]

But why should these equilibrium conditions ever be expected to

30*Ibid.*
31*Ibid.,* p. 204.

emerge? The answer to this question points up the significance of changes in the capital-output ratio. Assume, to begin with, that R_y and R_k are equal and that the capital-output ratio remains constant. In this event the equilibrium conditions are the same as in the Harrod-Domar model. Now examine what would happen if, for some reason, the capital-output ratio rises. In the first place, this means that the rate of growth of capital, R_k, is greater than the rate of growth of income R_y. Why the capital-output ratio may rise is dealt with later, but for the moment suppose it is due to a fall in income *relative* to capital, which in turn may be the result of any of a number of shocks that would independently affect income.

In the second place, there are forces built into the system which tend to reduce the rate of growth of income and the rate of growth of capital under these conditions. However, Duesenberry argues that the growth-rate of capital will fall more rapidly than the growth-rate of income until they once more become equal. The rate of growth of capital tends to fall for three reasons: "(a) because the returns on investment are reduced by an increase in the capital-output ratio (with a given state of technology), (b) because profits per unit of capital tend to fall, (c) because a given ratio of investment to income produces a smaller percentage increase in capital stock."[32] And the reason that the rate of growth of capital declines more rapidly than the income growth rate is because "investment is almost certain to fall by more than business saving when the capital-income ratio rises."[33] In short, even though both growth rates fall, R_k falls faster than R_y and will continue to do so until the equality between them is reestablished. And of course, with R_k falling faster than R_y, the capital-output ratio tends to move back to its former position.

Now reverse the argument and assume that the capital-output ratio falls because of some shock. This, of course, will increase returns on investment and raise profits per unit of capital. Business accordingly would respond by carrying out more net, new investment until eventually (given the state of technology) the capital-output ratio would tend to rise back to its equilibrium value. Again, while the rate of growth of income will rise, the growth rate of the capital stock will rise faster until profit possibilities are exhausted. At this juncture, the two growth rates will again be equal.

Thus Duesenberry argues that so long as the growth rates of income and capital are unequal because of changes in the capital-output ratio,

---

[32]*Ibid.*, p. 205.
[33]*Ibid.*

corrective forces will come into play to restore the equality. Note, however, that the interactive process discussed above will yield an equilibrium rate of growth *only if the parameters of the system have values which lie within a certain range*, that is, if there are no substantial shocks. Put otherwise, if there are shocks that raise the capital-output ratio substantially (that is, out of the relevant "stability" range), the economic system will enter into a disequilibrium pattern that may persist for a long time period. Duesenberry argues, however, that for the most part the parametric values have actually been in the relevant range.[34]

B.   The Cyclical Process

Let us now examine the cyclical process in some detail.[35] As Duesenberry points out, the economic system is constantly being disturbed by exogenous shocks, such as changes in the rate of population growth, alterations in financial institutions, changes in technology, and so on. These disturbances can be fitted into the following classification.

First, there are fluctuations in autonomous investment which occur for a number of reasons. Second, there are fluctuations in "speculative investment," which Duesenberry defines as ". . . investment which is based on an unwarranted estimate of the future movement of the variables determining the profitability of the investment."[36] Third, shortages of factors of production may lead to speculative booms. And finally, changes in techniques, tastes, and expectations due to political events, export demand, and monetary-fiscal policy may serve as shocks.[37] The problem now is to see how these shocks cause cyclical disturbances.

Begin with an equilibrium situation in which the capital-output ratio, the rate of growth of income, and the rate of growth of the capital stock are at their equilibrium values. Now assume that there occurs a shock that lowers income *relative* to capital, that is, raises the capital-output

---

[34]Matthews, "Duesenberry on Growth and Fluctuations," pp. 757-58, has plugged figures into the variables in order to discover what set of numbers yields a moderate rate of growth. He concludes that the range is quite narrow, but he also points out that such a test, although unfavorable to Duesenberry's thesis, is not decisive.

[35]Our brief account here can hardly do justice to the rich, detailed analysis given in Duesenberry's book, where many elements such as complicated lags, intersectoral relationships, and so on are worked into the analysis.

[36]Duesenberry, *Business Cycles and Economic Growth*, p. 250.

[37]This classification is discussed in *Business Cycles and Economic Growth*, pp. 248-52.

ratio. It does not matter whether the shock operates directly upon capital or upon income; the important thing is that it raises the ratio of capital to income. For instance, a spurt of autonomous investment will raise the capital-output ratio in the short run. Or, on the other hand, a decline in the demand for export goods will, *ceteris paribus,* lower income relative to the capital stock. In both cases, however, the important repercussion is a rise in the capital-output ratio, and this in turn induces a fall in the investment demand schedule as current investment becomes less profitable. This, of course, leads to a fall in income, which fosters a further decline in investment. Thus a cumulative downward process is generated, with the growth rate of income falling more rapidly than the rate of growth of the capital stock.[38] This means that the capital-output ratio rises even more, and this may be reinforced by adverse expectations, falling security prices, and so on.

According to Duesenberry, however, the original conditions that cause the shock will, in most cases, be eliminated. Consider, for example, a financial crisis which has caused investment demand to fall. As the crisis is eliminated, equity prices begin to rise, as do bond prices, and both business and commercial bank credit become easier to obtain. These phenomena contribute to a rise in investment demand back to its original level, particularly if the population is growing at a constant or higher rate. It must be noted that the shift in investment demand back to its former level is not, in and of itself, sufficient to bring on the lower-turning point, though it is a necessary condition. Other requisites must also be met, the most important of which is that the ratio of savings to income must fall more than than the ratio of investment to income. If this occurs, not only will investment rise, it will be in excess of savings, and the level of income will begin to rise faster than the stock of capital. Thus the capital-output ratio will begin to fall until its equilibrium position is reached. At this point all the equilibrium conditions once more emerge, with the capital-output ratio, the rate of growth of income, and the rate of growth of capital at their respective equilibrium values.

If, however, expectations have deteriorated badly, if income has fallen quite rapidly, and if savings continue to be in excess of investment, the recovery process may be put off for quite some time. Moreover, if these circumstances are present, then the rise in investment (when the conditions that caused the shock have been removed) will cause income to rise at the same time. In this event, ". . . recovery cannot occur until there has been sufficient capital decumulation to reduce

---

[38]*Ibid.,* p. 255.

the ratio of capital to income."[39] Thus a great deal depends upon the extent of the rise in the capital-output ratio during the contraction, the speed with which income falls, and the manner in which both savings and investment respond to the fall in income. Further, the contraction may induce structural changes in the economic system, creating more difficulties.[40]

7. Summary

In this chapter we have reviewed the Harrod-Domar "mixed" model, as well as Duesenberry's "exogenous" model. The first of these is, in its form as a first approximation, based upon a few technical, restrictive assumptions, which if fulfilled guarantee continued full-employment growth. The important point is that steady growth will occur so long as the actual rate of income growth is equal to the warranted rate, given the capital-output ratio and the propensity to consume. This implies, however, that income must increase at an ever-increasing rate, a rather unlikely probability. But Harrod does not mean to imply that his simplified model is descriptive of reality; rather he argues that there will be departures from the warranted rate, with disturbances resulting from this. Still Harrod does not present a complete theory of the cycle; his analysis in this respect accounts only for the upper-turning point and the possibility of secular stagnation. Nevertheless, while Harrod's model may be subjected to a number of significant criticisms, it should be remembered that it has set off further inquiry that has resulted in such theories of the growth-cycle interaction as those presented by Hicks and Fellner.

Duesenberry's theory, on the other hand, sets forth as a first approximation the conditions necessary for continued full-employment growth, and quite importantly he argues that in reality the values of the parameters of his system have more or less kept the system within the range of relative stability. Nevertheless, disturbances occur, though they are not of the same type as those discussed in Hicks', Fellner's, and Harrod's theories. Rather in Duesenberry's analysis the disturbances are caused by changes in the parameters of the system, that is, exogenous shocks. But generally the economic system has responded to these shocks in

---

[39]*Ibid.*

[40]This was, in Duesenberry's view, particularly relevant for the depression of the 1930's.

such a manner that growth has been insured. The shocks initially raise the capital-output ratio, and this leads to repercussions that eventually lower the ratio back to its equilibrium value, though occasionally the rise in the capital-output ratio, the rapidity in the fall in the rate of growth of income, and other complicating factors create periods of long contraction.

QUESTIONS

17-1. Why, in Duesenberry's model, have not the exogenous shocks been strong enough to prohibit continued economic growth?

17-2. In Duesenberry's theory why does the capital stock enter into the consumption function?

17-3. Explain verbally the significance of the "warranted rate of growth equation." Is this equation relevant to Fellner's theory of growth? Explain.

17-4. Discuss why and how a reduction in the warranted rate of growth below the actual rate is of economic significance in Harrod's model.

17-5. Trace through Harrod's analysis as to how chronic economic stagnation may come about.

17-6. Critically evaluate some of the basic assumptions underlying Harrod's model. Are these relevant also for Fellner's model? In fact, what are the basic differences between these two theories? Elaborate.

Bibliography

Adelman, I. and O. Lobo, "Some Observations on Full Employment vs. Full Capacity," *American Economic Review,* June 1956.

Domar, E. D., *Essays in the Theory of Economic Growth.* New York: Oxford University Press, 1957.

Duesenberry, J. S., *Business Cycles and Economic Growth.* New York: McGraw-Hill Book Company, 1958.

Hansen, A. H. and R. V. Clemence, eds., *Readings in Business Cycles and Economic Growth.* New York: W. W. Norton & Company, Inc., 1953, Chapters 16-20.

Harrod, R. F., *Towards a Dynamic Economics.* London: The Macmillan Company, 1948.

Matthews, R. C. O., "Duesenberry on Growth and Fluctuations," *Economic Journal,* December 1959.

Solow, R., "A Contribution to the Theory of Economic Growth," *Quarterly Journal of Economics,* February 1956.

18

Economic Growth and Stagnation

As noted on several occasions in the preceding chapters, modern growth theorists are divided over the prospects of future economic growth for the already advanced economies. Fellner, for example, argues that there have been and will be enough offsets to diminishing returns to capital, provided that we preserve the present type of capitalist society, to insure continued growth (though to be sure this growth will not be smooth and uninterrupted). On the other hand, Harrod has stated explicitly his fears that the mature and advanced economies will deviate downwards from the natural growth path and enter into a period of stagnation where growth, if any, will be slow enough that chronic unemployment will persist.

This issue of continued full-employment growth versus stagnation is by no means new. Economists have been concerned with it, off and on, for quite some time—recall, for instance, the position taken by T. R. Malthus in the early nineteenth century.[1] However, aside from the earlier sporadic attention devoted to the possibility of economic stagnation, the controversy over the "mature economy" did not become widespread until the Great Depression of the 1930's. At the same time, the kit of tools presented by Keynes induced several economists to develop the analysis that mature economies were entering into a prolonged period

---

[1]See Chapter 15 for a discussion of Malthus's views.

of stagnation.[2] They concluded that, *in the absence of positive governmental* action, the mature economies would not realize their full growth
potentials and hence would come to be characterized by chronic unemployment.

Note, however, that the "stagnationists," as they came to be called,
did not predict that economic stagnation is unavoidable, come what
may. Though several of their critics ascribed this position to them, the
fact of the matter is that the stagnationists argued that certain governmental policies could and should be put into effect in order to prevent
stagnation.[3] They felt that in the absence of such policies, but only then,
stagnation was inevitable. Thus Alvin H. Hansen, the leading propo-
nent of the stagnation thesis, proposed that certain monetary-fiscal
policies, which would substantially enlarge the scope of governmental
activity in the economy, be introduced and implemented.[4] These not
only would prevent stagnation but would in fact stimulate full-employment growth. As Hansen put it: "The answer to stagnation is not the
dogma of automatic adjustment. The answer is the vastly enlarged role
of democratic governments—the assumption of the responsibility for
the maintenance of full employment."[5]

[2]Keynes himself hinted at this, although he never developed his views in system-
atic detail; see *The General Theory of Employment, Interest, and Money* (New
York: Harcourt, Brace & World, Inc., 1936), pp. 217-21 and 374-77, and "Some
Economic Consequences of a Declining Population," *Eugenics Review*, April 1937.
See also the references in footnote 4, below.

[3]Among the critics of the stagnation thesis, see E. W. Swanson and E. P.
Schmidt, *Economic Stagnation or Progress* (New York: McGraw-Hill Book Company, 1946); W. I. King, "Are We Suffering Economic Maturity?" *Journal of Political Economy*, October 1939; W. J. Fellner, "The Technological Argument of the
Stagnation Thesis," *Quarterly Journal of Economics*, August 1941, and *Trends and
Cycles in Economic Activity* (New York: Holt, Rinehart & Winston, Inc., 1956),
pp. 387-90; G. Terborgh, *The Bogey of Economic Maturity* (Chicago: Machinery
and Allied Products Institute, 1945).

[4]A. H. Hansen, "Economic Progress and Declining Population Growth," *American
Economic Review*, December 1938, reprinted in *Readings in Business Cycle Theory*,
ed. G. Haberler (Philadelphia: The Blakiston Company, 1944). While the preceding
is the most succinct statement of Hansen's position, see also his *Fiscal Policy and
Business Cycles* (New York: W. W. Norton & Company, Inc., 1941). For other
statements, see B. Higgins, "The Concept of Secular Stagnation," *American Economic Review*, March 1950, "Concepts and Criteria of Secular Stagnation," in
Income, Employment, and Public Policy: Essays in Honor of Alvin H. Hansen
(New York: W. W. Norton & Company, Inc., 1948), and "The Theory of Increasing
Under-Employment," *Economic Journal*, June 1950. Reference should also be made
to Hansen's "Some Notes on Terborgh's *The Bogey of Economic Maturity*," *Review of Economic Statistics*, February 1946.

[5]A. H. Hansen, *The American Economy* (New York: McGraw-Hill Book Com-
pany, 1957), p. 23. This work, along with his *Economic Issues of the 1960's* (New
York: McGraw-Hill Book Company, 1960), and Part V of his *Business Cycles and
National Income* (New York: W. W. Norton & Company, Inc., 1964), contains
Hansen's latest views.

During the period from the 1930's to the 1960's Hansen's basic position has of course been modified, although only slightly. Despite the fact that governmental activity has expanded to prevent substantial stagnation, he feels that it still has not done enough to allow the economy to achieve its full potential rate of growth. Thus there is in his view need for continued expansion of government in the form of a "Dual Economy," that is, ". . . a full partnership of private enterprise and government [which] is necessary to provide the requisite rate of economic growth."[6] More than that, there are now emerging, he contends, the burning issues of values and preferences to be emphasized as growth continues. But more on this later on; the point for now is that in Hansen's view the problem of economic stagnation is still present and calls for continuing action if it is to be avoided.

1. The Stagnation Thesis in Brief

The growth theories reviewed in this part have all made use, at least implicitly, of some sort of aggregate production function which states the dependence of aggregate output upon the rates of inputs of the various factors of production. Hansen similarly makes use of an aggregate production function, which may be written as

$$Y = f(K,P,R,T),$$

where Y, as usual, designates income, K stands for the capital stock, P for population, R for the supply of natural resources, and T for the state of technology. In other words, the level of aggregate output depends on the rates of inputs of labor, natural resources, capital, and technology.

Hansen, however, views the aggregate production function from another perspective—what we may call the *"potential* production function," which relates what output can potentially be if P, K, T, and R are *fully employed.* The "potential production function" may be written as

$$Y_p = f(K_p,P_p,R_p,T_p),$$

where the subscript p stands for the full employment rate of the inputs.

Of course, according to Hansen, there is no reason to assume that automatically $Y = Y_p$. In his view, in fact, this was the basic error of the classical economists. In the classical doctrine, recall, Y always grows at the Y_p rate. Hansen, on the other hand, argues that the major influ-

---

[6]Hansen, *Economic Issues of the 1960's,* p. 44.

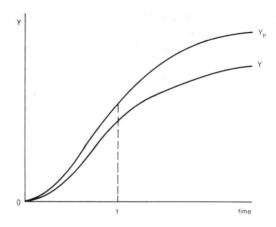

FIGURE 18–1

ence of the determinants of the actual level of income will, in the absence of appropriate policies, operate to hold Y farther and farther below Y_p. This is shown in Figure 18–1, where the potential full-employment curve is labeled Y_p and the actual income curve is shown as Y. Note that up to time period t the two curves are, for all practical purposes, identical, but that beyond this period the Y curve falls more and more below the Y_p curve.

The dynamic variable in Hansen's analysis, as in all the theories discussed so far, is investment. However, he insists upon differentiating between two types of investment—*induced* and *autonomous*—and it is the latter which is really the dynamic keystone.[7] The induced investment, of course, is a function of the rate of change of income, while the autonomous investment, and the level of income will, *ceteris paribus*, ress, population growth, and resource discovery. Since induced investment depends upon the rate of change of income, it enters into the analysis only when something has occurred to change the level of income. In short, induced investment is simply an aggravating force that reinforces change once the change itself has gotten under way.[8] But the

---

[7]See Chapter 7 for an earlier discussion of this distinction.

[8]This, of course, figures strongly in Hansen's theory of the cycle, though he also uses a weak accelerator; see Chapter 7.

initial change, *ceteris paribus,* comes from and through autonomous investment, which in turn is determined by the behavior of population, resource discovery, and technological change. If the combined forces of these are expansive, then there will be autonomous investment (which in turn will induce further investment as the level of income rises). On the other hand, if the combined forces are constant, there will be no autonomous investment, and the level of income will, *ceteris paribus,* remain constant. Finally, if the combined effects are contractionary, autonomous investment will decline, as will the level of income, and the economy will enter a period of stagnation.

When Hansen first developed his stagnation thesis in the late 1930's, he felt that the combined growth forces embodied in population, technology, and resource discovery were declining. At the same time, *given the constancy of the long-run consumption function,* the absolute amount of realized savings was increasing, with the end result that planned investment lagged behind realized savings. The outcome of this, he felt, would be a low-level equilibrium, characterized by extensive unemployment. Thus he concluded that, in the absence of positive governmental action designed to compensate for the declining autonomous investment with public expenditures of various sorts, the outlook for the future was prolonged stagnation.

This set of circumstances was quite different from the situation that had prevailed throughout the nineteenth century, when significant technological advances, a rising population, the development of new markets, and the continuing discovery of new resources were characteristic of the growing economies. In short, during the nineteenth century there was a decided tendency for investment to outstrip savings and for the economy to experience continued, though irregular, growth and expansion. For this reason the Y and Y_p curves in Figure 18–1 were drawn close to one another until time period t, that is, roughly until the close of the nineteenth century. But since then, according to the stagnation school of thought, the combined growth forces have dwindled in importance so that the Y curve has lagged farther and farther below the Y_p curve, though the recent population upsurge and both hot and cold wars have kept it from falling as far below Y_p as it might otherwise have done.

This, in brief, is the stagnation thesis, although it must be noted that the thesis does not conclude that there will be no growth whatsoever. To the contrary, the important conclusion is that the actual level of Y continues to grow, but at a retarded rate. Nor does the stagnation thesis argue that the "stagnating" economy will not experience cyclical disturbances. There will indeed be cyclical fluctuations, though with this important qualification—that in the absence of appropriate monetary-fiscal policies, the contractions will be long and deep, while the expansions will be weak and fall short of full employment. Still, it is quite conceivable, so long as there is some economic growth, that the peaks of the successive cycles will be higher than those that preceded them, even though they still fall short of the full-employment level of income.[9]

At this point a logical question arises: Why does the actual income level, though still growing, fall below the potential level by increasing amounts, as in Figure 18–1? Put otherwise, what has happened to the determinants of autonomous investment so that they yield insufficient private investment for continuing full-employment growth? In dealing with these questions Hansen's explanation of the behavior of the rates of population growth, resource discovery, and technical progress must be evaluated. However, keep in mind for the next three sections that Hansen's views have been somewhat modified over the years; thus at a later point his more recent observations must be examined.

2.   Population and Investment

When Hansen first formulated his stagnation thesis he was able to point out that the *rate* of population growth in the United States had declined during the decades of the 'teens, 'twenties, and 'thirties. As he put it, ". . . the advancing tide has come to a sudden halt and the accretions are dwindling toward zero. Thus, with the prospect of actual contraction confronting us, already we are in the midst of a drastic decline in population growth."[10] That Hansen's position was well taken is shown by the data in Figure 18–2. These data have been statistically constructed so as to eliminate the influence of shorter-term cyclical fluctuations, and hence they indicate the behavior of population over the long run. Note that the curves measure decadal increments to population, not total population, though we can infer the latter from curve a.

From the mid-'twenties to the mid-'thirties, the increments to total population declined substantially, that is, total population was increas-

---

[9]For an interesting discussion of how modern fiscal policy, particularly that which takes the form of "automatic stabilizers," may contribute to this behavior, see D. Hamberg, "Fiscal Policy and Stagnation Since 1957," *Southern Economic Journal*, January 1963.

[10]Hansen, "Economic Progress and Declining Population Growth," pp. 366-67. All references to this essay are to page numbers in *Readings in Business Cycle Theory.*

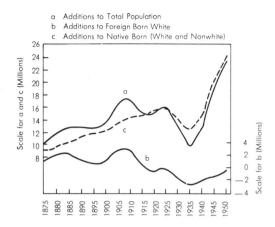

a Additions to Total Population
b Additions to Foreign Born White
c Additions to Native Born (White and Nonwhite)

Source: S. Kuznets, *Capital in the American Economy*, p. 318.

FIGURE 18–2

Decadal Additions to Native Born, Foreign Born White, and
Total Population, 1870-1955

ing at a significantly decreasing rate. This was one of the phenomena that concerned Hansen so much, for a rapidly rising population stimulates more and more investment, both public and private.[11] An increasing number of people requires more houses, roads, highways, school buildings, hospitals, consumers' goods, and so forth, all of which serve as an important stimulant to investment spending and growth. However, once population begins to rise at a decreasing rate, the net investment in these and other ventures begins to drop off, *ceteris paribus*. Moreover, much of the investment that responds to population growth is usually quite durable.

Thus even though total population continues to rise, and even though total consumer demand for goods and services of all sorts continues to rise also, the required net investment becomes less and less. A major

---

[11]Some economists, however, seemingly remain unconvinced that changes in the rate of population growth have a decisive impact on all types of private investment or aggregate output. See, for example, the comments by R. E. Quandt and M. Friedman in *Demographic and Economic Change in Developed Countries* (Princeton: Princeton University Press, 1960); but see also S. Kuznets' essay in the same work.

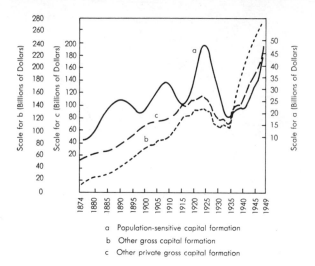

a Population-sensitive capital formation
b Other gross capital formation
c Other private gross capital formation

Source: Kuznets, *Capital in the American Economy*, p. 328.

FIGURE 18–3

Decadal Levels of Population-Sensitive Gross Capital Formation,
1929 Prices, Compared with Decadal Additions to Population,
1869-1955

reason for this is the decreasing rate of population growth itself.[12] This can be seen in the hypothetical data presented in Table 18–1, which assumes a constant capital-population ratio (K/P) of two; that is, an average amount of $2 of capital goods is required to satisfy the demands of each person. Note that in generations 3 through 5, while population is still rising, it does so at a decreasing rate, and accordingly the net increments to the capital stock ($\triangle$K) in these years are declining.

The data in Table 18–1 are, of course, hypothetical and thus do not reveal what has actually happened to net investment and the capital stock as a result of changes in the rate of population growth. The actual picture is presented in Figures 18–3 and 18–4, where investment of var-

---

[12]There have been some questions over whether population must experience a decline in the absolute or percentage rate of growth. For the first view, see Higgins, "Concepts and Criteria of Secular Stagnation," p. 99; Hansen, *Economic Policy and Full Employment* (New York: W. W. Norton & Company, Inc., 1947), p. 300; and H. A. Adler, "Absolute or Relative Rate of Decline in Population Growth," *Quarterly Journal of Economics*, August 1945. For the latter point of view, see C. L. Barber, "Population Growth and the Demand for Capital," *American Economic Review*, March 1953; and Terborgh, "Dr. Hansen on 'The Bogey of Economic Maturity,'" *Review of Economic Statistics*, August 1946.

TABLE 18—1

Generation	Total Population	Additions to Total Population	K/P	Total Capital Stock (K)	ΔK
0	100	—	2	200	—
1	110	10	2	220	20
2	130	20	2	260	40
3	160	30	2	320	60
4	180	20	2	360	40
5	190	10	2	380	20
6	195	5	2	390	10

ious sorts is related to changes in population. In Figure 18–3 the comparison is between investment in railroads and nonfarm residential construction, on the one hand, and additions to population on the other. Note that, with the exception of railroad investment since the 1930's, there is a close relationship between changes in total population and

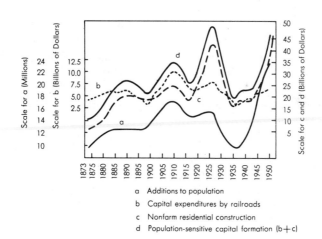

a Additions to population
b Capital expenditures by railroads
c Nonfarm residential construction
d Population-sensitive capital formation (b+c)

Source: Kuznets, *Capital in the American Economy*, p. 332.

FIGURE 18—4

Population-Sensitive Capital Formation Compared with Other Gross Capital Formation and Other Private Gross Capital Formation, Decadal Levels in 1929 Prices. 1870-1954

this kind of investment, especially nonfarm residential investment. In short, this type of investment appears to be very "population-sensitive," and thus a decreasing rate of population growth tends to reduce net investment spending.[13]

But what of other types of investment spending? May they not offset the behavior of railroad and nonfarm residential investment as population grows at a decreasing rate? Turn to Figure 18–4, where the relationship of other types of investment to population-sensitive investment has been plotted. Curve b ("other gross capital formation") is rather a hodgepodge, including changes in inventories, government investment, changes in claims against foreign countries, and "other" producers' durable equipment. Note that in this case there is no close relationship, perhaps even a semblance of a negative association, up to the 1930's. But since the 'twenties there has been a positive relationship. In curve c government expenditures have been eliminated, and the close relationship since the 'twenties still holds.

What does this imply for the stagnation thesis? For one thing, it indicates that the stagnationists were on reasonably solid ground when they posited that changes in the rate of population growth are a basic determinant of both public and private investment. Thus, despite the "population explosion" in the United States since the early 'forties, which was unpredictable, the stagnationists were logically correct in this part of their analysis. The population upsurge itself has at least postponed one element of the stagnation thesis, although what will happen in the future remains to be seen; it is probably too soon to determine if the upsurge is a permanent reversal of the secular decline that prevailed for a number of decades up until World War II. However, in looking towards the future the economic significance of the rate of population growth on investment had best be kept in mind.[14] As Professor Kuznets has put it:

> Increase in population is of obvious bearing upon future trends in national product and capital formation. More people mean additional demand for consumer goods and, during the period of formation of family

---

[13]By "population-sensitive" investment is meant investment that responds directly to additions in population (and its redistribution). On this, see S. Kuznets, *Capital in the American Economy: Its Formation and Financing* (Princeton: Princeton University Press, 1961), pp. 327-28. See further R. A. Gordon, "Population Growth, Housing, and the Capital Coefficient," *American Economic Review,* June 1956.

[14]Gordon, "Population Growth, Housing, and the Capital Coefficient," p. 320. See also H. J. Bruton, "Contemporary Theorizing on Economic Growth," Chapter VII in *Theories of Economic Growth,* ed. B. F. Hoselitz (Glencoe: The Free Press, 1960), p. 270.

units, increased demand for residential construction. Addition to the number of working-age people means a rise in the labor force ready to man the economic system and waiting to be equipped with capital.[15]

There is another aspect of population that has loomed important in the views of some stagnation theorists. These writers have emphasized the limiting factor of a stationary labor force upon net capital formation. Their basic proposition is that since capital and labor are complementary, a stable labor force restricts the amount of investment opportunities that can be exploited.

> Sooner or later . . . the point is reached where all the available labor is absorbed in production. . . . For if "machines" and "labour" are complementary in production, and there is not enough labour to work all the machines, output cannot be augmented by merely adding more machines. Thus excess capacity in equipment will make its appearance, which in turn will lead to a breakdown in the demand for investment.[16]

In short, this analysis stresses that a "shortage of labor" may well be an important variable that must figure into long-run growth analysis. Of course, where there is a shortage of labor, technical improvements of the "labor-saving" variety may be introduced; but this brings us back full round to the question of whether there have been and will be sufficient offsets to diminishing returns to capital.

One final point. Hansen also argues that a population growing at a decreasing rate has a further negative impact on net capital formation and hence growth. It does this via a shift in the composition of aggregate demand. As total population continues to rise, the proportion of people in the older age brackets increases, while the proportion in the younger brackets declines. But the people in the older age groups are those who have already acquired most of their durable goods and houses. Accordingly an increasing share of their demand goes for services and "soft goods." The major result of this is a drop in the capital-output ratio, for housing and consumer durables have a much higher capital-output ratio than do consumer nondurable goods and services. "It is therefore not unlikely that a shift from a rapidly growing population to a stationary or declining one may so alter the composition of the final flow of consumption goods that the ratio of capital to output as a

[15]Kuznets, *Capital in the American Economy*, p. 435.
[16]Reprinted with permission of The Macmillan Company from *Essays on Economic Growth and Stability* by Nicholas Kaldor. © Nicholas Kaldor 1960. See also A. Sweezey, "Declining Investment Opportunity," Chapter XXXII in *The New Economics: Keynes' Influence on Theory and Public Policy*, ed. S. E. Harris (New York: Alfred A. Knopf, Inc., 1950), and A. Murad, "Net Investment and Industrial Progress," Chapter 9 in *Post-Keynesian Economics*, ed. K. K. Kurihara (Brunswick, N. J.: Rutgers University, 1954).

whole will tend to decline."[17] Thus one of the major inducements to capital formation is, in Hansen's earlier views, dwindling away.

Hansen, of course, has recognized the tremendous expansionary effects of the population upsurge in recent decades, and this has led him to alter his views somewhat. His modified position is examined at a later point (section 5).

3.   Resource Discovery

Hansen also stressed the discovery of new resources and new territories as a stimulant to private investment. However, he actually had little to say about this determinant of investment, other than that many territories are fully occupied and that mature economies will find it increasingly difficult to pour capital into the remaining underdeveloped territories. This distinction between the two types of territories forces us to break the discussion into two parts—one pertaining to the expansionary impacts of underdeveloped areas as they undergo change and development, the other relating to the institutional and political barriers that prevent the mature economies from participating in the expansion of the remaining underdeveloped territories.

First, with respect to the development of the underdeveloped areas, the United States was in a rather fortunate position for quite some time with the expanding western frontier. Not only were new lands and deposits of resources being discovered, but also the westward movement tended to keep the "spirit of enterprise" high[18] and to create outlets for capital equipment produced in the East. This, of course, tended to stimulate economic growth, for it seems that an economic and social environment that encourages the entry of new firms and development of new ideas is more apt to provide a higher stream of innovational activity. On the other hand, if the environment is characterized by established firms and ideas, the rate of innovation is apt to be lower. In short, an economic and social environment that fosters the birth of new firms and creates a receptiveness of new ideas is quite important in the innovational process.[19] In this respect it is interesting to note that for a wide range of industries, the cumulative series of patents is S-shaped.

However, an unoccupied (or "underoccupied") territory by itself does not have much economic significance. Much more is required. For

---

[17]Hansen, "Economic Progress and Declining Population Growth," p. 375.

[18]Higgins has stressed this point; see also pp. 464-66 below.

[19]Bruton, "Contemporary Theorizing on Economic Growth," pp. 284-93.

instance, it must provide markets, and it must yield natural resources that are usable, whether because of technical advances or for other reasons. In short, the economic significance of the frontier derives from the fact that the underdeveloped area is present, plus the fact that population in it is increasing, plus the further fact that technological advances make more of its resources economically useful. Thus the frontier is important only in that it is intertwined with both population growth and technological progress.

Nevertheless, difficult analytical problems arise. For instance, does the opening up of a new territory necessarily serve as a stimulus to capital formation? To be sure, the people moving into it require investment for transportation, housing, food and clothing; but does not their migration reduce the demand for similar investment in the areas from which they move? If so, then aggregate capital formation for the economy at large may remain constant.

On the other hand, if the movement into the new territory is made up of *net additions* to total population, then there will be net capital formation. While perhaps there would be net capital formation even if there were no movements between territories (since the increment to total population alone stimulates net investment) the migration does result in the discovery of new agricultural lands and new resources, and it does call for new investment in transportation and housing facilities. Thus the opening up of new territories, coupled with an expanding population, does serve to stimulate net, new capital formation. Similarly, advancing technology creates an economic feasibility of some of the resources in the new territory; and transportation and marketing advances facilitate the growth of markets in the area.

But, in Hansen's view, these stimulating forces were no longer present, for he felt that in the United States the West had, for all practical purposes, been settled by the 1920's and thus another factor making for economic growth and expansion had dwindled away.

However, what of the underdeveloped areas overseas? Here he argued that political barriers operate to prevent private United States investment in some countries (*e.g.*, Russia and India), while "present and prospective turmoil" in others (*e.g.*, China) prevents the flow of capital abroad. Thus, he concluded, ". . . foreign investment will in the next fifty years play an incomparably smaller role than was the case in the nineteenth century."[20] Obviously Hansen could not foresee the in many of these underdeveloped countries, and just as obviously he great expansion that was to take place in the post-World War II years

[20]Hansen, "Economic Progress and Declining Population Growth," p. 378.

has altered his views with respect to this source of investment outlets.

However, with regard to his position of the late 1930's, he concluded that two of the three major stimulants to private investment—population growth and new territories—were dwindling away. This then places an increasing burden upon technology to stimulate enough autonomous investment to fill the savings gap at continuing full employment. As he put it: "We are thus rapidly entering a world in which we must fall back upon a more rapid advance of technology than in the past if we are to find private investment opportunities adequate to maintain full employment."[21] What, then, were his observations and analysis of the role and behavior of technical change?

4. Technology

In approaching this determinant of autonomous investment, it is best to differentiate between two forms that the growth in real investment can take—the "deepening" of capital and the "widening" of capital. By the "deepening" of capital Hansen means more capital *per worker,* the result only of changes in technology. Thus the emphasis is placed upon technical advances. "Widening" of capital, on the other hand, means simply the provision of new capital of the prevailing types, so that the amount of capital per worker remains the same. Thus, widening means simply an increase in the capital stock with no change in techniques and is divided into both replacement and net investment.[22]

Now economic growth requires both deepening and widening of capital, though the major catalytic agent in the stagnation thesis is autonomous investment (deepening of capital). The widening of capital is associated primarily with replacement investment (which has little to do with growth) and population growth. In fact, it is the rate of population growth that is the major determinant of investment of the widening sort; and, as noted above, in the 1930's Hansen felt that net investment of the widening variety was insufficient to provide for continuing full employment.

The deepening process, on the other hand, was in Hansen's view also

---

[21]*Ibid.*

[22]Hansen has changed his views on the meaning of "widening" and "deepening" of capital. For his earlier views, see "Economic Progress and Declining Population Growth," p. 372, where he defines widening and deepening in terms of the amount of capital *per unit of output.* For his later views, as expressed above, see his *Business Cycles and National Income,* p. 477, footnote 10.

insufficient to provide for full employment. Not only were there no new great industries (such as the railroad, electrification, automobile) in the offing, certain impediments to the deepening of capital had emerged in the economic system. Thus he concluded that both the widening and the deepening processes had, in the aggregate, slowed down enough that the net investment required for full-employment growth was not forthcoming.

> In the beginning stages of modern capitalism both the deepening and widening processes were developing side by side. But in its later stages the deepening process, taking the economy as a whole, rapidly diminished. And now with the rapid cessation of population growth, even the widening process may slow down.[23]

The logical problem to be dealt with now is why technical advances were not sufficient, at least in Hansen's opinion, to provide the capital-deepening process necessary for full-employment expansion. Hansen offered several reasons for this. First, he pointed out that product and labor monopolies tend to stifle technological advance. "The growing power of trade unions and trade associations, the development of monopolistic competition, or rivalry for the market through expensive persuasion and advertising, instead of through price competition, are factors . . ." which figure in strongly in this respect.[24]

Further, there is the "monopoly principle of obsolescence"—that is, the idea that new machines will not be introduced until it is certain that the economies they will provide will cover the undepreciated value of the old machines they will replace. This, of course, is quite different (according to Hansen) from what would occur under a competitive price system, in which capital losses cannot be avoided. Hansen's point, however, is that under an economic system that is "more closely integrated by intercorporate association and imperfect competition," these losses are avoidable.[25] And unfortunately, their avoidance slows down the rate of net, new investment of the deepening sort.

Thus Hansen arrives at the conclusion that the closing of the frontier and slowing down of population growth reduced net investment of the widening sort, and that impediments to net investment of the deepening variety have sprung up. With respect to this latter point, he argued that if ". . . we are to save the one remaining outlet for private capital

---

[23]Hansen, "Economic Progress and Declining Population Growth," p. 375.

[24]*Ibid.*, p. 380. See also E. D. Domar, "Investment, Losses, and Monopolies," in *Income, Employment, and Public Policy;* as well as M. Frankel, "Obsolescence and Technological Change in a Maturing Economy," *American Economic Review,* June 1955.

[25]Hansen, "Economic Progress and Declining Population Growth," p. 375.

formation, deliberate action of a far bolder character than hitherto envisaged must be undertaken in order to make the price system and free enterprise sufficiently responsive to permit at least that measure of capital formation to which the rate of technical progress has accustomed us in the past."[26]

However, in the view of the stagnationists, even this was not enough. Even if the historical rate of technological progress were to be reestablished and reflected in the capital-deepening process, the negative impact of population growth and the closing up of new territories would reduce investment of the widening variety. In short, the historical rate of technical progress ". . . would not be sufficient for investment outlets to give us full employment of our resources,"[27] and thus the stagnationists concluded that there was a growing need for increased governmental economic activity, especially in the form of fiscal policy.

Now Hansen's analysis of technological advance raises certain questions that call for further discussion. Two of these stand out as particularly important. First, does rapid technological change stimulate aggregate demand? Second, is it true that "monopoly elements" tend to stifle inventive and innovative activity and thus slow down the rate of capital accumulation? Since both of these questions are important for growth theory in general, as well as for the stagnation thesis in particular, they need to be examined in a bit more detail.

First, does rapid technological advance stimulate aggregate demand? The generally held position with respect to this question is that technical advance may well have two positive effects—it may raise the demand for capital, particularly if the technological advance is "slanted" towards capital-using and labor-saving investment; and it may raise the consumption function, particularly if the technological change results in the creation of many new goods confronting the consumers. However, with respect to the impact of rapid technological change upon the investment demand, there are certain complicating factors that should be considered.[28] For one thing, not all technological advance is oriented toward being capital-using; and given the circumstances of particular firms and industries, the emphasis may well be upon technical change slanted toward capital-saving investment. Accordingly the capital-saving innovations must be deducted from the capital-using ones in order to ascertain the net impact of the technological change on the demand for capital.

---

[26]*Ibid.*

[27]*Ibid.*

[28]The following comments rely heavily on H. R. Bowen, "Technological Change and Aggregate Demand," *American Economic Review,* December 1954.

But there is still another complicating factor, for the presence of rapid technical advance may result in increasing risk. Rapid technological change does hasten the expected rate of obsolescence of existing productive capacity, and thus businessmen are apt to demand higher anticipated rates of return on planned investment projects in order to take the obsolescence of a short number of years into account. In short, the subjective reaction to rapid technical change is to require higher rates of return before the investment projects are considered satisfactory.

Another complicating factor relates to the impact that technological advance may have on the form or structure of the demand for capital goods. For instance, the increased probability of obsolescence may encourage businessmen to acquire assets that are less durable, or perhaps less specific in their uses, and they may be less willing to maintain their assets as well as they otherwise would. Finally, there is the problem of long-term financing of these assets via debt, for the lenders may be unwilling to lend at low interest rates under conditions of rapid obsolescence.

All in all, considering these complicating elements, the impact of rapid technological advance on the total demand for capital goods is a bit difficult to determine.

But there is the other point—does not rapid technological change increase the propensity to consume of the consumers in the economy? If this is so, then the gap between the forty-five-degree line and the long-run consumption function may be narrowed, and thus there would be some lessening of the pressures on planned investment. The major argument here is that consumers will increase their propensity to consume because of (1) the fact that they are confronted with a plethora of new goods, and (2) rapid obsolescence of consumers' goods stimulates aggregate demand.

However, again complicating factors enter into the picture. Consumers have always been confronted with a myriad of goods beyond their reach, and thus the introduction of new goods does not automatically mean that they will spend more of their income than they otherwise would have. Consumers probably substitute new goods for those that they might have purchased in the absence of the new products, though dynamic new goods (such as televisions and automobiles) may have tapped funds that otherwise would have been saved. But the main point is that the mere introduction of new goods may have its major impact in a shift of the composition of total demand rather than in changing the level of demand. Moreover, the rapid technological change may speed up obsolescence of consumers' goods, and consumers may react pretty much as businessmen under the ensuing conditions of increasing risk. Rapid obsolescence could entice consumers to buy goods that are cheaper and less durable; or, alternatively, it may simply shift demand from goods where technological change is slow to those where it is more rapid.

In sum, it appears that rapid technical advance, by itself, provides little assurance that the demand for capital will automatically rise, and thus it ". . . may not prove to be the bulwark of future high-level stability that current literature frequently suggests."[29] Thus, technology itself need not provide the *necessary* deepening of capital to avoid economic stagnation.

As for the second question raised above, little that is definitive can be said. There is a growing body of evidence that indicates that businesses, particularly large-scale enterprises, are beginning to regularize their expenditures on research and development (R & D).[30] However, this in and of itself, does not guarantee that innovations of the findings will automatically be made, for many factors can contribute to delay or slow down the innovational process. As noted above, Hansen stresses one of these, namely, the "monopoly principle of obsolescence," though there is no clear-cut evidence as to how important this "principle" actually is. There are, as might be expected, important considerations on both sides of the issue.[31]

For instance, an innovation may raise profits enough to stimulate entry into the industry, and the entry of new firms could conceivably reduce the market shares of each firm, leaving the innovator perhaps in a less profitable position than prior to the innovation. But, on the contrary, a firm in a fairly competitive industry may carry out the innovation, especially if it has patent protection or secret information, and if the prospective profits warrant it. Some writers have stressed the fact that a competitive firm is much more apt to innovate, under conditions of protection, in the hopes of achieving a monopoly position. There is a growing consensus that most innovations come from the new or younger firms in the more competitive industries, though this does not mean that the older, already established firms do not innovate.

Another aspect is that a monopoly position may enhance the desire for the "easy life," an existence of quiescence, on the part of manage-

[29]*Ibid.*, p. 921.

[30]See the several essays in *The Rate and Direction of Inventive Activity: Economic and Social Factors* (Princeton: Princeton University Press, 1962).

[31]A good review of the conflicting issues is found in P. Hennipman, "Monopoly: Impediment or Stimulus to Economic Progress?" in *Monopoly and Competition and Their Regulation*, ed. E. H. Chamberlin (London: The Macmillan Company, 1954).

ment—that is, it fosters the "why rock the boat" attitude. Also the development of high-level bureaucracy may stifle innovation, a point, it will be recalled, that was stressed by Schumpeter. By the same token, a firm that may want to innovate may find its hands tied and its desires thwarted by the existence of a fairly strong cartel or other collusive agreement between the firms in its industry. But, to the contrary, its management may be farsighted enough to recognize the eventual emergence of a substitute product and thus innovate today to protect its position tomorrow. This, of course, is a response that characterizes Schumpeter's "gale of creative destruction."

However, most evidence indicates that innovations are carried out in market structures characterized by a high degree of entry by new firms, rather than in market structures where existing firms have solidified their position. To be sure, the latter innovate, but usually with respect to the further development of existing products. As noted above, the cumulative time series of patents in many industries tend to take an S-shaped pattern, implying that inventive and, no doubt, innovative activity is high in the early stages of the industry's life cycle as each new firm jockeys for a better position and a higher relative market share. Further, the innovative activity in the early stages of the industry's life cycle may be accompanied by indivisibilities that foster further investment and perhaps innovation.

However, a counteractive argument that is usually advanced is that only the large, monopolistic firms are in a position to acquire the funds necessary to finance the R & D and the subsequent innovation. This does not mean that smaller firms, and even individuals, cannot acquire funds from other sources than retained earnings, but the deterring factor here is that this type of capital expenditure, especially for R & D, is extremely risky in terms of potential rewards. There is no assurance that the funds poured into any one or any set of R & D projects will "pay off" in the long run. This tends to give the large-scale firms an advantage over the smaller-sized businesses.

Out of all this, what can be concluded as regards the impact of monopoly and competition on innovation? Until further evidence is gathered and evaluated, perhaps we had better go along with Professor Hennipman who, after a survey of the problem, cautiously concludes:

> From the preceding considerations no clear-cut answer to the question . . . has emerged. On the contrary, if anything definite can be said, it is that the simple and sweeping generalizations still frequently met with have no foundation in either theory or fact. The effects of monopoly on progress are not universally the same. In some cases, monopoly is a necessary condition of progress; in others, its effects are wholly negative,

while frequently it evokes conflicting tendencies whose relative importance can diverge widely in different circumstances. This diversity is
merely a corollary to the fact that monopoly comprises a variety of situations in many respects very dissimilar, and resulting from different
causes.[32]

While this may not be a very satisfactory conclusion to some, it does
point up the danger of sweeping generalizations in this area. However,
the threat of obsolescence via innovation may often be a significant
factor in slowing down innovative activity by large-scale, established
firms.

5. Recent Views on Stagnation

The American economy has experienced substantial growth and expansion since the 1930's, in large part because of increased and continuing military expenditures by the government. What does this imply
for the stagnation thesis? Does it mean that the fears of stagnation are a
thing of the past and that the outlook for the future is one of continued
growth? What are the views of the stagnation theorists on the recent
economic performance?

Hansen is among the first to point out that the decades of the 'forties
and 'fifties have been characterized by high levels of employment and
output, though not necessarily full employment and full use of productive capacity. But this does not mean that stagnation is, in his view, a
problem to be ignored. The main reason that we need not fear stagnation at the present is because of the increased importance of governmental spending, and so long as government continues in this role, eco-
omic stagnation seems to recede into the background. As Hansen puts
it:

> The forties and fifties witnessed immense forward strides in production
> and employment. The capitalistic system was in no small measure re-
> modeled during these decades in terms of new institutional arrange-
> ments, such as the built-in stabilizers and other ways of coping with
> depression. In a word, these decades introduced an expansion of the
> role of government hitherto undreamed of. Far from weakening the
> capitalistic system, this expansion has given it a new dynamism.[33]

Further, this spending has tended to reduce the degree of cyclical
fluctuations, not only because it itself is relatively stable over the course

---

[32]*Ibid.*, p. 454.
[33]Hansen, *Economic Issues of the 1960's*, p. vii.

of the cycle, but because it tends to stabilize private investment expenditures. Still, as Hansen points out, the cycle is with us and remains a problem. However perhaps a greater problem is the one revolving around the *qualitative* dimensions of future growth—that is, while the means to growth in the strictly economic sense may have been mastered, there are still the issues involving social values. Hansen places great stress on education as a means of resolving, at least in large part, these issues.

> If by 1970 we can have laid a firm foundation for a society in which *education* has become a "major industry," we shall have gone a long way toward building a truly civilized country—one in which the whole citizenry can *actively* participate in cultural, artistic, and recreational programs, not a citizenry which can merely *sit* and passively view a TV show.[34]

As noted above, Hansen argues that the main reason for the continued growth of the economy at high levels of output and employment is continued governmental action. Because of military and welfare spending, government, along with the private sectors of the economy, has been able to sustain an adequate aggregate demand. This is in sharp contrast to the decades of the 'twenties and 'thirties, during which for the western world as a whole there was insufficient total demand. "The lesson to learn is this: Efficiency, adequate plant and equipment, able entrepreneurs, and skilled workmen are not enough. These alone do not give us prosperity or full employment. The one thing missing before the war, the one thing the American economy needed, was adequate *aggregate demand*."[35]

However, World War II, the Korean War, and the continuing cold war have provided a high and rising governmental demand for goods and services produced by the private sectors of the economy. In light of these vast expenditures, it is unlikely that the economy would have suffered from severe unemployment. But there is more to it than simply this. Since the bleak 'thirties significant institutional changes have occurred in the economy. Hansen describes this as "a new partnership between government and private enterprise," in which government has assumed the role of promoting stability. This in itself, he argues, creates an atmosphere of confidence that allows management to make long-term investment plans which in turn contributes to the growth process.

---

[34]*Ibid.*, p. viii. Also: "Education and leadership—that is the answer. Without these the people perish," *Ibid.*, p. 77.

[35]Hansen, *The American Economy*, p. 26.

Further, the "American Economic Revolution" involves the introduction of the "welfare state," a point which Hansen stresses at some length. For him the "welfare state" and the expenditures associated with it have done much to contribute to stability and growth. Not only has the welfare state added to the viability of private enterprise, but its continued expansion may well preserve capitalism. As he has put it:

> Indeed the welfare state constitutes a solid foundation upon which to build a full employment program. It is the welfare state which has furnished most of the so-called "built-in stabilizers"—the progressive income tax social security payments, farm-support programs, etc. It is the welfare state which provides the continuing support of governmentally sponsored housing programs, rural electrification, and lending and guaranteeing operations. The welfare state does not consist of socialistic enterprises. The welfare state, does, however, involve governmental outlays large enough to permit fiscal policy to play a controlling role in the adjustment of aggregate demand to the productive potential of which the private-enterprise economy is capable. It is this that distinguishes the welfare state from socialism.[36]

In fact, Hansen argues that there is further need for expansion of the welfare state if continued full-employment growth is to take place.

In this respect, he feels that there has been too much emphasis on the strictly "economic" aspects of economic growth, especially the capital-output ratio and material capital accumulation, and too little emphasis on the "noneconomic" facets of growth. "It is just not true that one can build more and more plants and more and more equipment and out of this process grow richer and richer. . . . The answer, I believe, is not capital accumulation, though this plays a necessary, albeit restricted role. The answer, I suggest, is rather scientific research and invention."[37] So long as these continue to grow at a rapid rate, more rapid than in the past, then deeper and broader investment outlets will be opened up.[38] And while this will accelerate economic growth, there is no reason to believe that it will necessarily increase the capital-output ratio.[39] Of course, investment in science and invention entails investment in education, a task that is generally carried out by government. But, Hansen argues, this is an essential program for action. "We are concerned

---

[36]*Ibid.*, pp. 38-39.

[37]*Ibid.*, pp. 133, 134.

[38]See, however, the discussion on pp. 462-63.

[39]Hansen, *The American Economy*, p. 134. Kuznets, however, in *Capital in the American Economy*, pp. 445-46, points out that "past records do suggest that revolutionary changes in power production result in rises in capital-output ratios. . . . If the next two or three decades witness a power revolution, it is not unlikely that there will be consequent pressures for raising the capital-output ratios. . . ."

altogether too much about increased investment in brick and mortar, and not enough about investments designed to improve the quality and productivity of our people."[40]

Closely related to this, in Hansen's analysis, is the need for government to provide more of the cultural elements in our society. Not only schools, but also recreational facilities, slum clearance, health and medical facilities, and so forth fall into the category of responsible fiscal policy. As he puts it, social values are not determined in the market place, especially in a mixed public-private economy. If there is to be growth, Hansen asks, then what is the growth for? ". . . the problem of social priorities is hard upon us. It is not enough to achieve maximum employment and production. It is not enough to have quantitative goals. We cannot allow full employment to become merely a device to make our economy an efficient treadmill."[41]

A contrast of the views of Fellner and Hansen is interesting on this point. As noted earlier (in Chapter 16), Fellner argues that the private sector of the economy has provided sufficient offsets to diminishing returns to capital, so that there has been continued economic growth. Moreover, Fellner is fairly optimistic about the "improvement factor" in the future. But, in his view, if there should develop an insufficiency of private capital formation so that fiscal policy of the sort recommended by Hansen would have to be used to provide for continued full-employment growth, then private enterprise would go by the boards. "In an economy in which the bulk of the new investment activity is undertaken all the time by government agencies, the entrepreneurial function loses its essential content."[42] Finally, Fellner feels that the tendency toward equalitarianism and security-mindedness has served to stifle capitalism.[43]

In contrast, Hansen argues that fiscal policy, if correctly designed and implemented, serves to strengthen capitalism. For example, public power projects such as T. V. A. have stimulated a great deal of private economic activity, even though it may have supplanted private power to some extent. For Hansen, however, the basic question is: "Will it

---

[40]Hansen, *The American Economy*, p. 136. One preliminary study, however, concludes that the "direct, economic returns" to students from capital invested in college education is about the same as the return on private manufacturing capital. See G. Becker, "Underinvestment in College Education?" *American Economic Review*, May 1960; but see also the critical remarks by H. H. Villard, in the same issue.

[41]Hansen, *The American Economy*, p. 147.

[42]Fellner, *Trends and Cycles in Economic Activity*, p. 363.

[43]*Ibid.*, pp. 381-87.

be a profitable undertaking *from the standpoint of the economy as a whole?* The gains in cost-reducing *productivity* for the economy as a whole will almost certainly far exceed the net revenues of the enterprises undertaking the project. Such developments should tend to raise the profitability of industry generally."[44] And as for the lethargy and lack of inventiveness created by the tendency towards equalitarianism and security-mindedness, Hansen argues that there has been only at best a modest move towards equality in income distribution.[45] He points out further that the entrepreneurial function seems to be quite viable in both the United States and western Europe. As he puts it:

> . . . sustained full employment offers unparalleled stimulus to entrepreneurial inventiveness and ingenuity. Give a businessman an *adequate market* and you can be fairly sure that he will find his way. . . . Private enterprise has been and is proving itself to be a pretty tough animal—an animal which thrives very well indeed on an adequate food supply, namely adequate aggregate demand.[46]

What conclusions can be reached on these issues? Unfortunately, quantitative accuracy is lacking. It is difficult, if not impossible, to say at what point increased governmental activity begins to destroy capitalism, if it does at all. Nor can it be said with any sense of accuracy if and when security-mindedness and equality-mindedness begin to destroy incentives. Since quantitative propositions cannot be made with any significant degree of scientific accuracy, about all that can be concluded is that the issues involved are difficult, important, and need to be resolved. Perhaps in the future we will be better able to be more concrete in this respect; but for the moment we can only recognize the challenges raised and attempt to deal with them as objectively as possible.

6. Summary

In this chapter we have reviewed the so-called stagnation theory, which, when developed in the later 'thirties, concluded that the growth factors in the mature capitalist systems were yielding insufficient investment opportunities for full-employment growth. A declining rate of population growth, the closing of the frontier, and dwindling technology—that is, the forces making for investment opportunities—were

---

[44]Hansen, *Economic Issues of the 1960's*, p. 204.
[45]*Ibid.*, p. 209.
[46]*Ibid.*, p. 206.

considered, at that time, to stimulate an insufficient demand to absorb the savings of the community. The net result, then, was the prediction of chronic unemployment and stagnation. While it is safe to say that the stagnation theory is not as closely knit and as rigorous as the other growth theories reviewed in this part, it does tend to point to certain important problems of growth. Finally, in recent years the stagnationists, especially Hansen, have argued for further governmental intervention in the economy as the chief means of preserving capitalism and of providing for full-employment growth. At the same time, this intervention, it is argued, will provide cultural and other benefits that are now lacking. Obviously there is no general agreement on points such as these.

QUESTIONS

18-1. Explain what Hansen means by the term "Dual Economy."

18-2. Discuss in detail Hansen's analysis of population, resource discovery, and technology as determinants of economic growth. Do you believe that recent developments have contradicted his earlier analysis? Elaborate.

18-3. Critically compare and evaluate Shumpeter's theory and Hansen's theory of economic growth. How fundamentally different are they?

18-4. Critically compare and evaluate Hansen's and Fellner's views on the "improvement process."

18-5. Do you believe that Hansen's more recent views contradict his earlier analysis of economic stagnation? Elaborate.

Bibliography

Hansen, A. H., "Economic Progress and Declining Population Growth," *American Economic Review*, December 1938, reprinted in *Readings in Business Cycle Theory*, ed. G. Haberler. Philadelphia: The Blakiston Company, 1944.

———, *Fiscal Policy and Business Cycles*. New York: W. W. Norton & Company, Inc., 1941.

———, *The American Economy*. New York: McGraw-Hill Book Company, 1957.

———, *Economic Issues of the 1960's*. New York: McGraw-Hill Book Company, 1960.

Higgins, B., "Concepts and Criteria of Secular Stagnation," in *Income, Employment, and Public Policy: Essays in Honor of Alvin H. Hansen*. New York: W. W. Norton & Company, Inc., 1948.

Terborgh, G., *The Bogey of Economic Maturity*. Chicago: Machinery and Allied Products Institute, 1945.

19

Some Observations on Growth Theorizing

The review of growth-cycle theories presented thus far has ranged over three rather distinct types of models. First, there was Hicks' "purely endogenous" model; then the "mixed" models of Fellner, Harrod, and Domar; and finally the "purely exogenous" model developed by Duesenberry. Since several specific critical comments were made with respect to each of these theories, this chapter will present some critical observations on growth theorizing in general.

Probably the most frequent criticism made of contemporary growth theory is that it is overly simple, that it attempts to explain a highly complex situation with only a few aggregated variables. Thus the critics point to the simplified assumptions of a constant capital-output ratio, a constant long-run savings function, and simple assumptions about business behavior, contending that in reality the behavior of these phenomena is at variance with the assumptions. Moreover, they contend that many of these variables and definitions are lacking in operational significance. As one critic has put it:

> Everything flows from mere definitions and assumptions—the concepts of "warranted" and "natural" rates of growth and the assumed proportionalities between saving and income and between investment and change in income. Now, if the conclusions spun out from such assumptions and definitions strike us as strange and "extraordinarily impres-

sive," we need not necessarily conclude in astonishment that we have learned something new. Instead, we may re-examine our assumptions. . . . it strikes me as wholly illegitimate to suppose that the economic system gets into trouble if it does not satisfy the *precise* conditions implied by one's overly precise assumptions.[1]

Now the merit of this sort of criticism rests entirely with one's methodological position. All science, in fact, is based upon "overly precise" definitions and assumptions; but then all science takes as its point of departure the construction of rather simplified models. Indeed, the necessity for the construction of simplified models requires precise definitions and explicit assumptions. However, in all cases of scientific advance, once the simple, abstract model is shown to be logically consistent and to yield predictions that are not at variance with the behavior of real phenomena, the simple skeletal construction can be added to in various ways to deal with specific situations (whether real or imagined). In short, the simplified model is used only as a point of departure for further work. And while these subsequent models become more "realistic" in their content, they still are quite some distance from the real world. Reality, after all, is extremely complex, so much so in fact that we have to fall back on theoretical reasoning in order to cope with it. But in every case, we need to begin somewhere, and usually the beginning is rather far removed from the real world.

However, a more basic point is that the very simple growth-cycle models do not long stay that way. Consider for example Harrod's use of his own analysis to explain the upper-turning point and the possibility of chronic stagnation. More important, consider how Hicks has added to Harrod's model and how Fellner, in his turn, has embellished it even more, bringing into it such phenomena as specific scarcities and shortages, institutional elements, and resource mobility. There has been a steady movement away from the over-simplified models, but this is what is to be expected. In fact, it might be argued that this is the very process of scientific inquiry, for the simple models do raise questions and arouse curiosity and interest about new methods and relationships. One commentator has put it this way: "We want to be able to look at the old phenomena in a new way, and so need to be given new questions to ask about them and new techniques with which to draw inferences about them. A fundamental merit of the growth models is that they have done just this."[2] In fact, they *have* done just this, even to the

---

[1]L. B. Yeager, "Some Questions about Growth Economics," *American Economic Review*, March 1954, pp. 56-57.

[2]G. M. Meier, "Some Questions about Growth Economics: Comment," *American Economic Review*, December 1954, pp. 932-33.

extent that some economists have developed "exogenous" theories of the cycle. And this is the major point: a simplified, abstruse first approximation is perhaps best judged in terms of the inquiries and new techniques that it stimulates rather than simply as a first approximation *per se*. In the case of the growth models in general, there has been a decided tendency toward movement from the more abstruse to the more concrete and detailed.

Nevertheless, there still remain the criticisms that the models, even in their more concrete forms, are too aggregative and concentrate on too few variables. There is no doubt considerable merit in this position, particularly when problems of forecasting and policy arise. Perhaps new gains will be made in this direction, but the path ahead seems to be particularly rough if we confine ourselves strictly to the "economics of it all." Consider a few of the basic problems.

For one thing, most of the growth-cycle models make use of a rather simple acceleration concept. But it remains true that we do not quite know why businesses accumulate capital stock, nor do we understand yet the major behavioral determinants of autonomous investment. The empirical evidence certainly indicates strongly that the technical acceleration principle fails in explaining investment behavior.[3] In fact there is a growing suspicion that businesses do not invest strictly for purposes of maximizing profits, at least as profits are traditionally conceived of in economic theory. If non-profit, non-technical considerations influence the investment decision, then the sociological and psychological dimensions of business must be examined. As Mrs. Robinson concludes, "To understand the motives for investment, we have to understand human nature and the manner in which it reacts to various kinds of social and economic systems in which it operates. We have not got far enough yet to put it into algebra."[4] Thus the "noneconomic" elements must be considered more thoroughly than they have in the past. While Schumpeter, Keynes, and others have made some contributions in this direction, much more remains to be done, whether it is ever put into algebra or not.

Similar comments can be made with respect to consumer behavior. To be sure, empirically the long-run consumption function is linear through the point of origin, and both Duesenberry and Fellner have provided explanations of this. But as socioeconomic relationships and

---

[3] J. R. Meyer and E. Kuh, *The Investment Decision* (Cambridge: Harvard University Press, 1957) contains a good discussion and review of the literature.

[4] J. Robinson, *Economic Philosophy* (Chicago: Aldine Publishing Company, 1962); (London: C. A. Watts & Co., Ltd., 1962), p. 107.

ideologies change, so may aggregate consumer behavior; thus the "satisfactory" explanations of today may not perform well a few years hence. For instance, what does the increasing proportion of consumer expenditures on services imply? In an era of rising and intense nationalism, with continued high-level employment and growth becoming ideological targets and symbols, will consumers voluntarily restrict their consumption as their income rises, allowing more resources for governmental expenditure? It is not inconceivable that the problems presented by slums, education, juvenile delinquency, conservation, health, and so on may foster changes in social attitudes and hence consumption. Again, it is necessary to probe more deeply into consumer behavior and attitudes, not only to explain better the short-run volatility of the consumption function but also to aid in predicting long-run consumption patterns.[5]

Another problem arises with respect to the political elements of the nation. In this connection consider the so-called "distressed areas" which have received so much political attention in recent years. These areas are characterized by two things—substantial labor immobility and a shortage of capital. In a significant sense they resemble the underdeveloped countries of the world.

To begin with, there is a relatively high degree of unemployment in these areas, and also per capita incomes are rather low.[6] Not only does this latter fact reduce the opportunity of mobility of the people out of the area, but it also tends to keep the total demand of the area low, thus impeding the entry of firms to produce goods and services for the local market. This does not mean that there is no movement out of the areas; indeed most of them experience a loss of population due to net out-migration. But not all can move out, nor can those who do, with their particular skills (or more often, lack of skills) always acquire employment elsewhere.[7] Moreover, agriculture in these areas tends to be characterized by a low marginal productivity of labor and, in many cases, a low marginal productivity of capital, especially where topography militates against large, consolidated landholdings.

What is needed, of course, in these areas is a rise in investment—they are capital poor. Yet the only way that the inhabitants themselves can

---

[5] A good deal of excellent work has been done by the Survey Research Center at the University of Michigan.

[6] There is a vast amount of literature on this problem. For two excellent summary statements of the problems confronting the distressed areas, see H. S. Perloff, "Lagging Sectors and Regions of the American Economy," and F. J. Welch, "The Evolving Low-Income Problems in Agriculture," both in *American Economic Review*, May 1960.

[7] See especially Welch, "The Evolving Low-Income Problem in Agriculture."

do this, with no outside aid, is to reduce their propensity to consume. The hope here would be that less consumption today would, as the savings go into an increase in the capital stock, mean more consumption tomorrow. But the question arises: In what direction and what form will the investment take? Will it be for the production of goods and services to be produced for "home consumption," or will it be for the production of "export goods?" In both cases the returns on the investment will be quite low. Even more important is the question of whether the inhabitants can be enticed to raise their propensity to save when they already suffer low per capita incomes.

Is it not possible, however, for private investment from other areas and regions to flow into the distressed areas? But, with the low employment and per capita income levels, along with a usually unskilled labor force and poor transportation facilities, private investment tends to shun the distressed areas.

There is a final alternative, nonetheless, and that is for the government to direct investable funds into the areas. And here political and ideological arguments are encountered on all sides, ranging from "those people obviously have no initiative" to "those people obviously need substantial public works programs." Economic analysis may be able to explain the economic situation of the capital-poor distressed areas, but it will be political and social decisons that ultimately determine what actions will be taken.

Another facet, and a rather intriguing one at that, of the political dimensions of growth may be mentioned here. Some observers have argued that smooth, uninterrupted growth is impossible because of political attitudes. In fact, Kalecki has advanced what we might call a "political theory" of the cycle or, better, of the deviations from the full-employment equilibrium. As the major political parties and other power groups of an economy come to accept a commitment to "full employment," along with an acceptance of the use of the fiscal policy, then the levels of income and employment will fluctuate according to political attitudes. It may be best to let Kalecki speak for himself.

> In the slump, either under the pressure of the masses or even without it, public investment financed by borrowing will be undertaken to prevent large-scale unemployment. But if attempts are made to apply this method in order to maintain the high level of employment reached in the subsequent boom a strong opposition of "business leaders" is likely to be encountered. As has already been argued lasting full employment is not at all to their liking. The workers would "get out of hand" and the "captains of industry" would be anxious to "teach them a lesson." Moreover, the price increase in the up-swing is to the disadvantage of small and big *rentiers* and makes them "boom tired."
> In this situation a powerful block is likely to be formed between big

business and the *rentier* interests, and they would probably find one economist to declare that the situation was manifestly unsound. The pressure of these forces, and in particular of big business—as a rule influential in Government departments—would most probably induce the Government to return to the orthodox policy of cutting down the budget deficit. A slump would follow in which Government spending would come again into its own. . . .

The regime of the "political business cycle" would be an artificial restoration of the position as it existed in nineteenth-century capitalism. Full employment would be reached only at the top of the boom, but slumps would be relatively mild and short lived.[8]

But Mrs. Robinson has stated that the ". . . reason why Full Employment has become a right-wing slogan is that if employment is an end in itself no questions can be asked about its content. What is work for? Only to keep the workers out of mischief. Any product is as good as any other."[9]

In a somewhat more subdued vein, Professor Davidson has introduced political elements into the growth process. He points out that after unemployment falls below a certain percentage of the labor-force (about 6 per cent), money wages and prices begin to rise, with the latter rising faster than the former.[10] Thus the workers already employed experience a decline in their real income, as do the *rentiers*, though the unemployed workers improve their real income position as they acquire jobs. However, the employed workers and *rentiers* constitute the overwhelming majority of the electorate and thus, in order to protect their real incomes, are politically oriented toward anti-full-employment policies. As Davidson puts it:

It is not surprising, therefore, that the United States tolerated a 7 per cent unemployment rate throughout most of 1961, while politicians and financial writers claimed that 1961 was a year of unprecedented prosperity. The political fears of inflation overshadow the desire to mop up the remnants of unemployment once a relatively high level of employment has been obtained.[11]

Thus a major and overpowering enemy of the unemployed worker is the employed man.

We shall not comment on these passages, but the student would do well to ponder them and their bases, whether founded or not, as well

[8]M. Kalecki, "Political Aspects of Full Employment," *The Political Quarterly*, (London: Thomas Nelson and Sons Limited), October-December, 1943.

[9]J. Robinson, *Economic Philosophy*, p. 95.

[10]P. Davidson, "Income and Employment Multipliers, and the Price Level," *American Economic Review*, September 1962.

[11]*Ibid.*, p. 749.

as their implications. The major point, for present purposes, is that political forces may have a decisive influence on the growth process, though the economic growth models typically ignore them.

In summary, not only have the growth models tended to minimize certain important economic variables, but they have also ignored sociological, psychological, and political variables that may have a substantial impact upon the growth process. If the models are overly simplified for some critics on economic grounds alone, they are decidedly limited for others on noneconomic grounds. But, to repeat again the methodological observations made earlier, they are intended to serve solely as a point of departure for subsequent, more detailed economic (and perhaps noneconomic) analysis. What the future holds in store in this respect remains to be seen.

QUESTIONS

19-1. The theories reviewed in Part 4 have been referred to as "capital stock adjustment" theories. This means that the emphasis for continued growth is placed upon changes in the capital stock of the economy.

   a. What does this imply about the long-run behavior of the consumers?

   b. What significance will depreciation have on the capital stock adjustment process since depreciation investment is increasing as a percentage of the total capital stock?

   c. What implications do the models have for higher education, government financing of research and development, and leisure time?

19-2. Discuss some of the criticisms given in this chapter of the capital stock adjustment models. Do you agree with the criticisms? Why?

19-3. Of what significance do you believe are the political elements discussed by Robinson, Kalecki, and Davidson?

19-4. Present your *general* views of the capital stock adjustment models reviewed in this part.

part 5

Economic Policies for Growth, Full Employment, and Price-Level Stability

20

What Is Economic Policy?

In the preceding chapters, particularly in Parts 2-4, problems of public policy have continually cropped up. Questions have been raised pertaining to monetary policy, fiscal policy, and even wage-price policy. But for the most part these questions, and hence the issues of public policy, were relegated to the background. The major reason for doing this was that we were primarily concerned with developing alternative theories of the business cycle, economic growth, and cycle-growth interaction; and in most of these theories the public sector is assumed to be either neutral or minimal. Now, however, as we turn to a review of economic policy, we must recognize that the public sector is neither minimal nor neutral. Moreover, in many cases there is need to modify the theory so that it includes the actions and effects of government.

Since the major concern of these chapters is economic policy, the term should be defined at the outset. For present purposes policy may be defined as a general plan for using organization—in this case government—to achieve certain preestablished goals. Thus at least one additional complication appears in the transition from theory to policy—for no longer can the establishment of economic goals or objectives for either the economy at large or the various levels of government be ignored. Nor can the goals be unstated, poorly stated, or implicit, as is the case in many of the preceding chapters on theory.

Another complication must be stressed. A theorist may structure his own setting or environment for the analysis of a particular problem. There is nothing unusual about this, for it is an integral part of the scientific procedure. The physicist and chemist, for example, do the same thing, though they are usually in the position of structuring the setting of their problems under controlled laboratory conditions. The economic theorist, on the other hand, does not have laboratory facilities at his disposal; hence he is driven to the use of the *ceteris paribus* method of making assumptions about physically uncontrolled (and perhaps uncontrollable) variables. Essentially the assumptions regarding human behavior are simple; the institutional arrangements are accepted as given and static; the members of society are assumed to have roughly similar sets of social values; and the cause-effect relationships analyzed are relatively simple and direct.

The policy maker, on the other hand, faces a different situation.[1] He must make continuous decisions in which he finds human behavior complex, puzzling, and inconsistent. He finds that the "body politic" disagrees substantially over the definitions and interpretations of goals. Most important, he does not possess an adequate knowledge of the most important, not to mention the minor, economic variables relevant to his decisions. This does not mean, of course, that the policy maker carries out his assignment in complete darkness and ignorance. Econometric and other empirical studies have provided a great deal of data for the policy maker, and at the same time economic analysis in recent years has undergone a substantial degree of refinement. Yet as one eminent economist, who has been very much concerned with this problem, has observed:

> There is still a considerable gap between pure theory and a theory that lends itself to application in the formulation of stabilization policies. No scientific progress is possible without the thinking that can best be done in the contemplative atmosphere of the ivory tower. But the work in the ivory tower can be fruitful only if it is in two-way communication with the decision makers or with those who aid the decision makers. In this respect, what Veblen wrote exactly sixty years ago in his article, "In Dispraise of Economics," is still true: "There is the economic life process still in great measure awaiting theoretical formulation."[2]

The purpose of theory is to explain the past and to predict, as accurately as possible, the future. And the purpose of prediction is to pro-

---

[1] In what follows the term "policy maker" is used to mean the organizational unit that makes the policy decisions; see the definition of policy given in the text.

[2] G. Colm, "Economic Stabilization Policy," Chapter 2 in *Economics and the Policy Maker* (Washington, D. C.: The Brookings Institution, 1959), The Brookings Lectures, 1958-59, p. 44.

vide aid in controlling or modifying the future, again as best as possible, so that our preestablished goals are better realized. The skeptic may suggest, and rightly so, that economic theory is a long way from being developed to the extent that this function can be fully realized— in other words, theory has not progressed to such a point that it can be applied with confidence in the attempt to control the future. The state of development of economic theory, however, is almost irrelevant to the question of whether the attempt should be made to apply theory to the area of public policy. As long as public policy *will* be made and implemented, there is need for guidelines, and economic theory to a very large extent provides us with some of them. To be sure, the guidelines may be crude and "over-aggregated," but the policy maker still thinks and acts in terms of savings, investment, GNP, and so on. He is also forced to take into account variables that nearly all of the models of growth and the cycle exclude for sake of analytical manageability. Thus, the "gap" between theory and policy exists and is real, and we can only hope that more empirical studies and further refinement in theory will lessen it.[3] Beyond this, however, public policy is a necessity, especially in our modern economic society, and it remains a necessity despite the state of development of economic analysis.

1. The Necessity of Policy

As noted above, public policy must be administered irrespective of the state of development of economic theory. There are two basic arguments underlying and supporting this generalization.

First, *some kind* of economic theory, no matter how crude or unsatisfactory, no matter how implicit or explicit, has always been applied in the day-to-day world. As long as a society has an economic organization and carries on economic activities, some sort of theoretical underpinnings are present. These may be part and parcel of the religion or myth of the community, or they may take the form of disorganized utterances by businessmen and others, but nevertheless they are there.[4]

Second, in the United States today, and in fact in most of the capitalistic democracies of the western world, the emergence and rise of big government has forced the questions of public policy upon us; and this has been done regardless of the state of economic analysis. Every

---

[3]See "Economic Stabilization Policy," pp. 43-44.

[4]For an excellent discussion, see J. J. Spengler, "The Problem of Order in Economic Affairs," *Southern Economic Journal*, July 1948.

time government—whether federal, state, or local—taxes a dollar or spends a dollar there is an economic effect. At times, of course, this economic effect can be quite sizeable and important. In the United States the current expenditures for military defense and the continuing cost of previous wars have run in excess of $50 billion annually for most of the last decade. The only purpose for pointing out military expenditure at this stage is to suggest that this single category of expenditures gives a fiscal effect so large that some attempt must be made to control it; in short, fiscal policy in some form or other has become a necessity. When the other expenditure activities of government are added to the picture, along with the massive taxation program that we have, the importance of the fiscal effect and the need for fiscal policy become even greater.

Thus the basic question is not whether the government has a fiscal impact; the only question in the real world of the 1960's is *how* will government affect economic activity? If the question of *how* is ignored, the resulting consequences of government spending and taxing would no doubt be erratic and capricious. There is indeed some necessity to apply what knowledge of economics we possess in order to control as well as possible the consequences of governmental spending and taxing. In other words, we have been forced into the position of adopting fiscal policy.

So far only the fiscal affairs of government have been considered, that is, the effect on the economy of the goverment's taxing, spending, and (by implication) debt management activities. But there are still other ways in which the government must apparently inevitably exert an economic influence. Some of these activities are treated in substantial detail below, while others are simply mentioned or discussed very briefly. However, one more area of governmental activity that has forced policy upon us—the provision of the money supply—may be mentioned here, even though in a preliminary manner.

Money is a man-made institution and has been associated with the wheel, fire, and printing as one of man's greatest discoveries. Moreover, there is no law of nature or deity dictating the proper amount of the money supply at any given time. There is, approximately at least, general agreement among economists that there is no way in which the market system itself can be geared automatically to provide the proper amount of money. It is almost unthinkable that any purely private organization should be in a central position to regulate the money supply. The execution of monetary policy, then, involving most importantly the regulation of the quantity of money, must be left exclusively to the national government. This is a conclusion which the vast majority of economists—regardless of their position on the "left" to "right" political scale—will support.[5]

Thus both monetary and fiscal policy—two of the most important areas of economic policy in the public sector of the economy—are necessary and are almost as inherent in government as the basic police power itself. The remaining chapters of this book, therefore, are based on the assumption that the economic effect of government is major, continuing, and unavoidable. The major concern is with the nature and extent of this economic effect and how it may be regulated over time. "Regulation" and policy, however, imply some sort of set goals for the community at large, and the discussion must revolve around the question of how well policy can be used to achieve these goals. But the limitations of public policy, as well as its potentialities must also be considered, and thus we must make every effort to be as fully aware as possible of our ignorance as well as of our knowledge in the formulation and direction of public policy.

These policy chapters apply only to the American economy as we enter the second half of the twentieth century. American institutional arrangements are sufficiently different from those of other productive capitalist democracies, such as Canada and Great Britain, that we would complicate our subject greatly if these other economies were included in the discussion. Furthermore, the public policy issues confronting the "emerging underdeveloped" economies are vastly different from those that confront us at the present time, and accordingly these are also excluded from discussion.

2. Goals of Public Policy

Actually, before one sets out to consider goals of public policy he probably should join forces with the philosophers and theologians and inquire into the essence and purposes of man, nature, and society. But most American economists concerned with policy tend to resort to a Pontius Pilate type of behavior and thus accept a certain materialistic bias in contemporary American behavior. But note that this procedure

---

[5]Even the majority of economists who classify themselves as "liberalists" (that is, in the eighteenth and nineteenth century tradition) recommend centralized control over the money supply, although they disagree with other economists as to *how* the control should be implemented. We discuss a specific illustation of this in Chapter 23.

avoids basic questions that should logically precede a discussion of the goals of public policy.[6]

Perhaps the appropriate starting place is to review the purposes of an economic system.[7] Advanced students will recall that, probably no later than the second or third day of class in "Principles of Economics," they learned of certain fundamental decisions which must be made in any and every type of economic system. These may be summarized as follows:[8]

  a. How much employment will there be?
  b. What will resources be used for?
  c. How much will the economy save?
  d. What techniques of production will be used?
  e. How will the final product be distributed?

Economic policy, then, is merely a system or set of decisions that are designed to influence the manner in which these decisions are made and carried out. But actions designed to influence how these decisions are made and implemented presuppose some kind of value system— that is, a set of objectives or goals that are considered "desirable" for the community at large. There is a wide range of literature dealing with this matter, but we shall follow Millikan, who suggests six objectives of economic policy, as well as three institutional corollaries:

Objectives of Economic Policy
  a. Minimum unemployment.
  b. Ideal employment.
  c. Maximum technical efficiency.
  d. Consumer-guided allocation.

---

[6]As one eminent philosopher has put it:

The most morally dedicated and socially concerned philosopher cannot avoid passing, if he is both thorough and honest, to an examination of the logic of his social program and moral aspiration and the nature of that world which serves both to nourish and frustrate them. The social critic is driven to be a logician in the interest of his own integrity and circumspection, and a metaphysician in the desire to achieve clarity as to what ideals nature will permit as possibilities. It happens thus that no serious social philosophy can do without a philosophy of nature as its basis.

Charles Frankel, ed., *The Uses of Philosophy: An Irwin Edman Reader* (New York: Simon and Schuster, Inc., 1955), p. 26.

[7]For a brief treatment of some of these issues, see Max F. Millikan, "Objectives for Economic Policy in a Democracy," Chapter 1 in M. F. Millikan, ed., *Income Stabilization for a Developing Democracy* (New Haven: Yale University Press, 1953); and for a fuller treatment, see H. M. Oliver, Jr., *A Critique of Socioeconomic Goals* (Bloomington, Indiana: Indiana University Press, 1958).

[8]Millikan, "Objectives for Economic Policy in a Democracy," pp. 28-54, discusses these at some length.

    e.   Optimum rate of saving.
    f.   Optimum income distribution.
Institutional Corollaries.
    a.   Primary use of the private market.
    b.   Promotion of competition.
    c.   Optimum level of governmental expenditures.

The six objectives of economic policy are largely independent of the type of economic organization, though they are not of course completely independent of the value system of the society. So long as there is general agreement on such terms as "ideal" and "optimum," most individuals and most leaders in western cultures would probably accept these objectives.[9] The three institutional corollaries, however, are obviously applicable only to a society in the capitalistic democratic tradition, a society in which the citizenry wishes to remain in that tradition.

3.   A Reformulation of the Objectives of Economic Policy

These six objectives are worthy of the most serious and deliberate consideration by professional economists, politicians, and the lay public alike. Economists, as a group, are presumably able to formulate fairly precise definitions and interpretations of each objective. From the standpoint of economic policy, however, it is probably much more important for the public at large to devote some thought to the meaning of these objectives, even though there might be a great deal of disagreement as to their meanings once the face-saving qualifications of *minimum, ideal,* and *optimum* have been removed. The first requisite of intelligent formulation of public policy in a democratic social order is that the rank and file citizen have his own rather definite idea of what he thinks should be done through public policy.

There is, we feel, good reason to place a great deal of faith in the democratic processes taking place through representative government *if* the *individuals* in the society have a fairly definite idea of the objectives of public policy. It can even be argued that these processes have a way of giving recognition to the problems of political minorities. But public policy and the problem of "majorities" and "minorities" are likely to be handled unsatisfactorily until individuals give more attention to what they really think the objectives of economic policy should be. Once the individual has determined them to his own satisfaction, his

---

[9]Consider, for example, that in the United States we do have the Employment Act of 1946 and that both Canada and Great Britain have similar legislation.

recommendations for governmental action are likely to be positive and clear cut.

In recent years a good deal of attention has been devoted to three goals of economic policy—reasonably full employment, relative price-level stability, and continued economic growth. The first two of these are usually combined together under the more general heading of the goal of "economic stability." Yet, as will be seen in the following discussion, precise definition of these goals is virtually impossible; and further, any reasonably meaningful statement of them requires an examination of the actual and potential conflicts among the six objectives listed above.

A. The Concept of Reasonably Full Employment

For both economic and noneconomic reasons, it would appear desirable that all those persons—or almost all of them—who make up the work force (which itself is culturally determined) and who desire a job should be able to find one.[10] This is the objective of *minimum unemployment*. Admittedly, the process of resource allocation is dynamic and ever-changing. Old industries die out and new ones are born, leaving some people unemployed. Consumer preferences change over time, reducing the demand for some commodities and increasing the demand for others. And technological changes are always taking place, forcing some people out of jobs as capital is substituted for labor. Often the people who are unemployed as a result of these developments are left stranded in certain geographical areas with certain skills that they spent a lifetime perfecting, but which are now not in demand. Further, these unemployed often do not possess a high degree of geographical mobility, nor can they easily acquire the retraining necessary for the development of the new skills now in demand. As a result, there is always a certain amount of unemployment in an ever-changing, growing economy. This may be referred to as "structural-technological" unemployment, and it is possible that in much of the period since World War II there has been a considerable amount of this type of unemployment in the United States.

There is also another type of unemployment that should be mentioned—what is termed "frictional" unemployment. So long as people voluntarily quit one job before they have another, or are fired from their positions but are actively seeking reemployment, there will be a mini-

---

[10]See Oliver, *A Critique of Socioeconomic Goals*, for a good discussion of the ambiguous definitions involved in defining full employment, labor force, and so on.

mum of unemployment in the economy. These persons, however, will eventually reacquire employment, *ceteris paribus,* and hence we designate them as "frictionally" unemployed. Most estimates put frictional unemployment at about 3-4 percent of the labor force, and most economists place full employment therefore at 96-97 per cent (or less) of the labor force.

While minimum unemployment is concerned with only how many jobs are provided, the objective of *ideal employment* involves the *kinds* of jobs that are provided. Ideal employment implies that the vast number of people in the labor force are employed in positions that require the highest order of their respective skills. This concept further implies, of course, that as young people enter the work force for the first time they possess new skills or are ready and willing to acquire new skills. It assumes also a certain amount of mobility of labor, particularly at the younger end of the age scale, so that workers will be able to move into the positions that demand and require these new skills. But the objective of ideal employment hardly presumes that the sixty-three-year old celluloid collar cutter will follow his employer as he moves his plant from New England to the South, learning the Orlon spinner-spotter trade in the process.

Thus the discussion of *ideal* employment means that the third objective, *maximum technical efficiency,* must be brought into the picture. Maximum technical efficiency simply implies a maximization of an "input-output" ratio, and this requires not only the employment of workers in their highest skills, but also the use of the most efficient and advanced machines and other capital goods. In other words, the whole economic process of men and capital would have to be organized in the most efficient way. Consider, for example, the hypothetical situation during the days of the WPA, in which fifty men of varying degrees of diverse skills were outfitted with picks and shovels to dig a ditch, a job which three men and a ditchdigging machine stored in a nearby warehouse could have done better and quicker. This project, of course, made a contribution to the minimum unemployment objective, but it would not have gone very far in achieving either ideal employment or maximum technical efficiency. In other words, fulfillment of the first three objectives at the same time is quite difficult in the real world.

The three objectives of minimum unemployment, ideal employment, and maximum technical efficiency may be combined into a single objective which is frequently referred to as *"reasonably full employment."* In other words, no one of the three specific objectives discussed so far is particularly satisfied, but all three of them are "reasonably" fulfilled at the same time. Thus in what follows, whenever the term "full employment" is used, it should be understood that it entails a recognition of the difficulties discussed above. "Reasonably full employment" does not mean that the three objectives of minimum unemployment, ideal employment, and maximum technical efficiency are simultaneously fulfilled; but it does mean that they are all three approximately satisfied. Finally, "reasonably full employment" recognizes that there is some "frictional unemployment" and some "structural-technological" unemployment.

B. Price-Level Stability

The goal of price-level stability is as difficult to define as the goal of reasonably full employment. Again, it is a composite of other objectives. Certainly price-level stability does not mean that *all* prices are to be frozen and kept perfectly rigid over time. If this were done, the objective of "consumer-guided allocation" could hardly be achieved since its fulfillment requires the movement of relative prices. Moreover such an interpretation of the goal would mean that the existing income distribution, which may *not* be optimum, would be maintained through time. Presumably, then, in achieving price-level stability we also want the price system to operate, and we want the distribution of income to move closer towards the optimum.

There are, for present purposes, two dimensions of prices—the general price level and the structure of relative prices—and the goal of price-level stability refers only to the price level. Thus, while public policy may be used to maintain stability in the price level, it must not (in general) be used to interfere with the adjustments of relative prices. Insofar as the objectives of consumer-guided allocation, maximum technical efficiency, and optimum income distribution are important, then relative prices must be allowed to change freely over time.

However, does the goal of price-level stability mean that *all* changes in the general price level are to be prevented? As has already been seen, in periods of expansion the price level tends to rise, often quite some time before full employment is reached; and in periods of contraction the price level has, at least until recently, tended to decline. Since 1957, however, it has continued to rise, even though unemployment was at times as high as 5 to 7 per cent of the labor force. If the goal of price-level stability is to be interpreted literally, then there should be no changes in the general level of prices at all. This obviously is a misinterpretation of the goal, and thus the term "price-level stability" must be interpreted to mean *relative* price-level stability. There will be, in other words, some changes in the general level of prices that are "acceptable." The alternative of having complete price-level stability would probably entail direct controls over wages and prices by the central government, and this of course would interfere with the achievement of other fundamental objectives.

Since World War II discussion of the goal of price-level stability has usually revolved around the problems of inflation. In fact, quite a large number of theories have been devised to explain inflation. For example, some writers have talked about "demand-pull" inflation, others about "cost-push" inflation, others about "mixed" inflation, "mark-up" inflation, "demand-shift" inflation, "administered price" inflation, and so on.[11] The economists who use these varying terms all agree that inflation means a rise in the general price level; they disagree as to the major causes of the inflation. Thus those who use the "demand-pull" theory argue that aggregate demand outruns aggregate supply, and hence the price level is pulled up. On the other hand, those who use the "cost-push" theory conclude that monopoly forces (usually labor unions) push up costs (usually wage rates), and that this in turn pushes up the general price level. In light of all these various theories, perhaps some comments on the definition of inflation are in order.

Probably the most popular definition of inflation is that it is a rise in the general price level, no matter how small. The difficulty with this concept is that it is too broad and too vague. Recall the discussion in Chapter 13 in which a distinction is made between *pure* inflation and *semi*-inflation. By pure inflation is meant a rise in the price level with no accompanying increase in output at all. Thus if the economy is at full employment and the stock of money is increased, there would be pure inflation. Semi-inflation, on the other hand, refers to the rise in the price level that occurs as full employment is approached. That is, before full employment is reached bottlenecks and shortages create inflationary pressures and rises in the price level, and hence the rise in aggregate demand is divided between increasing output and employment on the one hand and the rising price level on the other. During the Great Depression of the 'thirties, for example, the price level began rising long before full employment was reached; and according to this definition there was inflation. Does this mean, however, that if the goal of price-level stability were to be fulfilled the monetary authorities should have put into effect restrictive monetary policies? Obviously what is needed is some "desirable" base year or period for the authorities to rely upon. So very much depends upon the year or period of

---

[11]These different theories of inflation are discussed in Chapter 23.

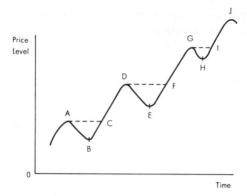

FIGURE 20—1

time that is selected as being characterized by stable prices. If, for example, 1932 is taken as the base year, then there has been considerable inflation in the United States. On the other hand, if 1949 is taken as the base year, is it meaningful to say that the rise in the price level from 1932 to 1949 was inflationary?

It appears necessary, therefore, to recognize that there are *degrees* of inflation, some of which are acceptable, others of which are unacceptable because of the distortions they introduce into income distribution and because of the difficulties they impose upon ordinary economic decision making. In order to elaborate on this, refer to Figure 20–1, which traces out a hypothetical pattern of price-level behavior over a period of time. Note that overall there has been an inflationary trend, though it has been rough and irregular. In fact, at times there has actually been deflation, as in the periods AB, DE, and GH. The inflationary periods have been those leading up to A, BD, EG, and HJ. However, the inflation experienced at point B is not very significant, particularly when it is recognized that at that time there is a good deal of unemployment. As the expansion continues, the inflationary forces and processes begin to build up, and the price level exceeds its previous peak (as shown by the dashed line AC) and rises to higher levels. At this time the monetary authorities become more and more concerned about the problem of inflation—that is, about the problem of relative price-level stability—and put into effect restrictive monetary policies. Also fiscal policy may be used to contain the inflation.

The important question is, of course, at what point does inflation become so significant that restrictive policies have to be put into effect? And there is no clear-cut answer to this. As will be seen in the next chapter, the monetary authorities in the United States exercise a good deal of discretion in determining when they will begin to tighten up in their monetary policies. It is strictly a matter of subjective judgment, implemented with empirical data and historical experience, as to when the authorities decide that further increases in the price level are undesirable and unwarranted. Unfortunately, they do not possess any perfect guideline to assist them in making *the* correct decision.

Two final points on the goal of "reasonable price-level stability" should be made. Please note in Figure 20–1 that there is a tendency towards *secular* inflation. Although the data in the figure are hypothetical, they do point out one of the important economic phenomena that have been experienced since World War II—namely, the problem of "creeping" inflation.[12] The other observation is related to the fact that it seems unlikely that we can achieve reasonably full employment and reasonable price-level stability simultaneously. At least this is the conclusion that has been reached by a large number of economists.[13] There is little need to elaborate on this conflict of goals at this juncture; recall the discussion in Chapter 13 in which the problem was discussed at some length. The really important point is that, so long as there is a conflict, any dogmatic "either-or" position should be avoided. To be sure, price-level stability can be achieved, but only with some unemployment; on the other hand, continuing full employment at, say, 97 per cent of the labor force can be achieved, but only with some inflationary consequences. For this reason, the qualifying terms "reasonably" and "reasonable" must always be kept in mind.

C. The Goal of Economic Growth

With respect to the goal of economic growth, there is little that need be added to the analysis and discussion of the chapters in Part 4. There it was pointed out that growth is two dimensional—that is, it must be viewed from both the supply side and the demand side. From one point of view, growth is defined as an increase in the capacity to produce, and this focuses attention upon the major determinants of production over

---

[12]See, for example, N. H. Jacoby, "The Problem of Creeping Inflation," Chapter 3 in *Economics and the Policy Maker.*

[13]See, for example, A. F. Burns, *Prosperity Without Inflation* (New York: Fordham University Press, 1957); and P. A. Samuelson, "Full Employment versus Progress and Other Economic Goals," Chapter XII in Millikan, *Income Stabilization for a Developing Democracy.*

the long run. Included among these are technological advances, the rate of population growth, the discovery of new markets, and so on.

But from the other perspective the emphasis is on the rate of growth of aggregate demand—that is, if there is to be reasonably smooth growth over time aggregate demand must expand *pari passu* with aggregate supply. But this has been discussed at great length in the chapters of Part 4, and there is no need to cover the same ground again.

There is, however, one important point about the goal of growth that should be made. There is a conflict or dispute among economists as to the relationship between economic growth and secular or creeping in-flation.[14] On the one hand, there are those economists who contend that some gentle, creeping inflation serves as an essential spur to fur-ther growth. On the other hand, there are those who argue that growth and creeping inflation are incompatible, or at least are at odds with one another. This dispute, of course, has a direct policy bearing for the economy at large. If creeping inflation is a stimulant to continued growth and expansion, then monetary-fiscal policies should be oriented toward fostering some, but not too much, inflation. Conversely, if secu-lar inflation is a drag on the growth process, then more attention should be devoted to achieving the price-level stability goal more fully than perhaps has been the case in the recent past.

This is not the place to discuss this controversy, but we shall return to it in subsequent chapters. The important thing to keep in mind is that it is extremely unlikely that we can ever achieve *perfectly* smooth and uninterrupted growth and at the same time fulfill the other two main economic goals.

D.   The Remaining Objectives

The remaining objectives in the list presented earlier may be dis-cussed very briefly. First, the objective of consumer-guided allocation of resources may be stated very rigorously. Or, on the other hand, it may be put less elegantly in terms of simply producing the kinds of goods and services that most people want the most. This "maximum aggregate satisfaction" criterion, however, becomes a bit troublesome when we depart from the traditional model and its underlying assumptions and

---

[14]For alternative points of view, see Jacoby, "The Problem of Creeping Infla-tion," and G. L. Bach, *Inflation—A Study in Economics, Ethics, and Politics* (Provi-dence, R. I.: Brown University Press, 1958), on the one hand, and A. H. Hansen, *The American Economy* (New York: The McGraw-Hill Book Company, 1957), and S. S. Slichter, "On the Side of Inflation," *Harvard Business Review*, September-October, 1957, on the other.

observe that in our economy today by no means are all allocation decisions made through the operation of the price system. That is, in some areas legislative and executive governmental decisions have been substituted for the price system in making allocation decisions. By way of illustration, consider why the Pentagon is not financed in the same way that the production of automobiles or even the construction of churches are financed. The answer would appear that in this case dollars are not accepted as votes in making allocation decisions, but rather only votes are considered simply as votes. Although there are some bothersome aspects in any elaboration of the meaning of consumer-guided allocation, the basic theme is clear enough. There is no point in allocating more resources to the production of horses and buggies if people instead want more automobiles and airplanes. At this point, however, there is still the question of the extent to which people want freeways and expressways, or even turnpikes, to go along with the new automobiles.

The optimum rate of saving, which has been discussed in some of the preceding chapters on theory, involves the extent to which society in the aggregate prefers to have consumption now as opposed to presumably a higher level of consumption in the future. This of course is also intimately related to the structure of current production, that is, the allocation of current output between consumer goods, on the one hand, and producer or capital goods, on the other. It is difficult to suggest guideposts for the determination of the optimum rate of saving. To be sure, we can say that if the community wants smooth, uninterrupted growth at full employment then there must be some optimum rate of savings. But the actual rate of savings in a democratic capitalist society is something that individuals and businesses decide upon voluntarily. About all that can be hoped for is that the operation of the price system, in conjunction with certain activities of government (especially those that fall under the heading of fiscal policy), cause something approximating the optimum level of saving to be achieved. By way of emphasis, note once again that only at full employment levels (as defined above) does a given additional amount of saving have to be matched, *ceteris paribus,* by a reduction in consumption of the same amount.

The last objective of economic policy is optimum income distribution. Only three points will be made with respect to this objective. First, there is some optimum income distribution, though we are not at all sure what it is; certainly, however, this does not mean an equal distribution of income; but just as certainly, it does not mean the status quo in income distribution.

4. Summary

In this chapter we have introduced the difficult and thorny problems of economic policy. Although policy ranges all the way from inspecting the kitchens of restaurants to the larger decisions of a general tax reduction, we have concentrated only on certain areas of policy. Following Millikan, there are six basic objectives of economic policy, and from these we reformulated three goals of policy. These are "reasonably full employment," "relative price-level stability," and continued economic growth. The first two were further combined under the more general heading of "economic stability." In each instance, however, the goal is really a composite of two or more of the six objectives, and thus some sort of compromise is necessary in attaining the goals. It is for this reason that the qualifying terms "relative" and "reasonable" are so important.

We further noted that there is apparently a conflict of sorts between the goals of full employment and price-level stability—and again some sort of compromise is necessary. Indeed there may be a conflict between the goals of continuing full employment and price-level stability. In any event, this preliminary discussion has served one purpose—it has pointed out that the area of economic policy is complex and dynamic, as well as vague and often ambiguous. Still, as noted very early in the chapter, economic policy is necessary—it has been forced upon us by recent events, and thus we must face up to its challenge as best we can. In this respect, economic theory, while often abstruse and "unrealistic," serves to provide us with some very important guidelines and concepts.

QUESTIONS

20-1. Discuss some of the difficult problems that the policy maker faces. Be sure to include both theoretical and practical issues and to provide some historical illustrations.

20-2. In the text of this chapter it is asserted and emphasized that economic policy is necessary and unavoidable. Discuss and elaborate.

20-3. Explain what is meant by "reasonably full employment" and "relative price-level stability." Why must the qualifying words—reasonably and relative—be used?

20-4. Give as many examples as possible of the conflict between the various economic goals discussed in this chapter. Does this mean that we must sacrifice any one goal?

Bibliography

Economics and the Policy Maker, Brookings Lectures, 1958-1959. Washington, D. C.: The Brookings Institution, 1959.

Millikan, M., ed., *Income Stabilization for a Developing Democracy.* New Haven: Yale University Press, 1953.

Oliver, H. M., Jr., *A Critique of Socioeconomic Goals.* Bloomington, Indiana: Indiana University Press, 1958.

Saulnier, R., *The Strategy of Economic Policy.* New York: Fordham University Press, 1962.

21

Monetary Policy: Its Framework and Mechanisms

Prior to the 1930's economists generally considered monetary policy to have one major objective—stabilization of the price level. Changes in the total volume of commercial bank reserves and in the money supply, with attendant changes in the level of interest rates, were used to achieve this goal. Further, the traditional view on monetary policy held that the major impact of policy was supposed to be on borrowers and savers as they respond to changes in the interest rate.[1] Since the 'thirties, however, the economic objective of continuing full employment has entered the picture, and in the years since World War II there has been some discussion of the contribution that monetary policy can make to the goal of economic growth.[2] All told, monetary policy has a rather complicated task cut out for it. •

The first two of these objectives—price-level stability and continuing

---

[1]See Chapters 6, 9, and 15.

[2]In still more recent years, especially in the early 'sixties, there has been a good deal of discussion on the relationship between monetary policy and the "balance of payments" problem. This issue is discussed in the next chapter.

full employment—which make up the goal of "economic stability" will be discussed in this and the next chapter. The possible contribution of monetary policy to economic growth is considered in Chapter 23. While such a sharp separation between the cycle and growth is unrealistic, it is necessary for purposes of discussion. In fact, it is unrealistic to separate monetary policy from fiscal policy, for they also are interacting continually. But again it is essential to do so for purposes of preliminary discussion. The interactive aspects of monetary and fiscal policy will be considered in the closing chapters of this book.

1. A Brief Review of the Changing Attitudes towards Monetary Policy

The prevailing attitude towards monetary policy has followed quite a checkered pattern. Prior to the 1930's monetary policy held the pre-eminent position in nearly any program for economic stability, only to sink to a secondary or handmaiden role during the 'thirties and most of the 'forties. Indeed, fiscal policy had risen in importance and replaced monetary policy in the front ranks of stabilization policy. However, during the early 'fifties there was a "rediscovery" of the importance of money and monetary policy, and accordingly more attention has been devoted to the use of and the effectiveness of this type of public policy.[3] This does not mean that all economists favor monetary over fiscal policy—to the contrary, there is still a good deal of disagreement on this particular issue. Nor does it even mean that the advocates of monetary policy agree on the means and purposes of policy actions. The fundamental twin goals of economic stability are not in question; rather the disagreement revolves around the area of immediate impact of monetary policy. A brief review of these changing attitudes will help to set the stage for this and the next two chapters.

As already noted, monetary policy was, prior to the 1930's, considered to be the major weapon of aggregative policy, and there was

---

[3]H. S. Ellis, "The Rediscovery of Money" and R. V. Roosa, "Interest Rates and the Central Bank," both in *Money, Trade, and Economic Growth* (New York: The Macmillan Company, 1951); H. C. Wallich, "Postwar United States Monetary Policy Appraised," Chapter 4 in *United States Monetary Policy*, ed. N. H. Jacoby (New York: Columbia University Press and the American Assembly, 1958); J. H. Williams, "The Implications of Fiscal Policy for Monetary Policy and the Banking System," *American Economic Review*, March 1942. See also *Monetary Policy and the Management of the Public Debt* (82d Cong., 2nd sess., 1952), Part 1. (We shall refer to this as the *Patman Replies*.)

a general consensus that the major function of the Federal Reserve System was to decide and implement monetary policy by controlling the total amount of reserves in the commercial banking system.

The catastrophic onslaught of the Great Depression of the 'thirties, however, cast increasing doubt over the effectiveness of traditional monetary policy. Despite Federal Reserve action, the contraction continued, so that by 1932 about one-fourth of the labor force was unemployed. And despite expansionary policies put into effect by the Federal Reserve, this large-scale unemployment continued.[4] The widespread failures of commercial banks during the early part of 1933, resulting in the closing of all banks in March, aggravated the situation severely. When, under the efforts of the Roosevelt administration, the banks began to reopen, the Federal Reserve eased its monetary policy further, but with no appreciable results. Finally, as the recovery got underway, the price level (as might be expected) began to rise; and the Federal Reserve authorities, concerned over this, put into effect a tighter monetary policy in 1937. While this alone did not account for the upper-turning point of 1937, it certainly was one of the decisive factors.

By the end of the decade, there was a general adverse reaction to the efficacy of monetary policy. More than that, Keynes' *The General Theory* had provided an explanation for the failure of monetary policy and an analytical support for fiscal policy. This, along with the fact that the Treasury was running larger deficits (see Table 21-1), led to further examination of the effectiveness of fiscal policy as a policy weapon. Though there was still much debate among economists and others, by the end of the decade monetary policy had sunk to such a low position that fiscal policy has virtually eclipsed it.

Then, during World War II direct price-wage rationing controls were put into effect. Also the annual deficits continued mounting until by 1946 the national debt stood at nearly $270 billion (See Table 21-1).[5] In fact, during the war period the monetary and economic environment were altered to a significant extent, leaving a postwar legacy that contributed further to the downgrading of monetary policy.

Early in the war years the economy had regained a position of full employment; in fact, the productive capacity of both the labor force

---

[4] For a brief historical review of Federal Reserve action during these years, see the replies of W. McC. Martin (Chairman of the Board of Governors of the Federal Reserve System) in the *Patman Replies,* pp. 216-21.

[5] For an excellent analysis of the war and immediate postwar years, see L. V. Chandler, *Inflation in the United States, 1940-1948* (New York: Harper & Row, Publishers, 1951).

TABLE 21-1

Federal Administrative Budget Receipts and
Expenditures and the Public Debt, 1929-1965

Fiscal Year	Net Receipts*	Expenditures	Surplus or Deficit (—)	Public Debt at End of Year†
1929	3,861	3,127	734	16,931
1930	4,058	3,320	738	16,185
1931	3,116	3,577	— 462	16,801
1932	1,924	4,659	— 2,735	19,487
1933	1,997	4,598	— 2,602	22,539
1934	3,015	6,645	— 3,630	27,734
1935	3,706	6,497	— 2,791	32,824
1936	3,997	8,422	— 4,425	38,407
1937	4,956	7,733	— 2,777	41,089
1938	5,588	6,765	— 1,177	42,018
1939	4,979	8,841	— 3,862	45,890
1940	5,137	9,055	— 3,918	48,497
1941	7,096	13,255	— 6,159	55,332
1942	12,547	34,037	—21,490	76,991
1943	21,947	79,368	—57,420	140,796
1944	43,563	94,986	—51,423	202,626
1945	44,362	98,303	—53,941	259,115
1946	39,650	60,326	—20,676	269,898
1947	39,677	38,923	754	258,376
1948	41,375	32,955	8,419	252,366
1949	37,663	39,474	— 1,811	252,798
1950	36,422	39,544	— 3,122	257,377
1951	47,480	43,970	3,510	255,251
1952	61,287	65,303	— 4,017	259,151
1953	64,671	74,120	— 9,449	266,123
1954	64,420	67,537	— 3,117	271,341

* Gross receipts less refunds of receipts and transfers of tax receipts to the old-age and survivors insurance trust fund, the disability insurance trust fund, the railroad retirement account, the unemployment trust fund, and the highway trust fund.

† Includes guaranteed issues. The change in the public debt from year to year reflects not only the budget surplus or deficit but also changes in the Government's cash on hand, and the use of corporate debt and investment transactions by certain Government enterprises.

TABLE 21—1 (continued)

Federal Administrative Budget Receipts and
Expenditures and the Public Debt, 1929-1965

Fiscal Year	Net Receipts	Expenditures	Surplus or Deficit (—)	Public Debt at End of Year
1955	60,209	64,389	— 4,180	274,418
1956	67,850	66,224	1,626	272,825
1957	70,562	68,969	1,596	270,634
1958	68,550	71,369	— 2,819	276,444
1959	67,915	80,342	—12,427	284,817
1960	77,763	76,539	1,224	286,471
1961	77,659	81,515	— 3,856	289,211
1962	81,409	87,787	— 6,378	298,645
1963	86,376	92,642	— 6,266	306,466
1964	89,459	97,684	— 8,226	312,526
1965	93,072	96,507	— 3,435	317,864

Source: *The Annual Report of the Council of Economic Advisers,* January 1966 (Washington, D. C.: Government Printing Office, 1966), p. 278.

and the capital stock were being hard pressed. At the same time the federal government increased its expenditures substantially because of the increasing war demands. In fact, government expenditures rose from $8.8 billion in 1939 to nearly $95 billion in 1944 and to slightly over $98 billion in 1945 (see Table 21–1). But governmental tax revenues lagged considerably behind expenditures. Accordingly, the government was forced deeper and deeper into deficit financing; and while the Treasury borrowed from nonbank investors, it was forced to rely heavily on borrowing from the total banking system (that is, from both commercial banks and Federal Reserve banks). This amounted to slightly over $115 billion in 1945 (see Table 21–2). Since this method of financing deficits adds to both the money supply and the reserves of the commercial banking system, the results were quite inflationary.

At the same time, personal income was rising via the multiplier-accelerator interaction, and consumers were striving to fill the "consumption gap" they had inherited from the Great Depression. Their increased demand for consumers' goods and services, however, meant that they were competing directly with the government for the resources necessary for the war effort. Consequently both wholesale and retail prices rose, making it even more difficult for the government to finance its rising expenditures unless borrowing was also increased (see Table 21–2). And so long as the government borrowed from the total banking system, the inflationary pressures were intensified.

The outcome of all this was the imposition of direct controls—price, wage, and rationing—in 1942; and for the rest of the war period both the wage and price levels remained relatively constant.[6] Personal incomes continued to rise however; but now, because of the direct controls, consumers found themselves severely restricted in their spending. In effect, they were "forced" to save and, at the same time, they were forced to "make-do" with the same old consumer durables. Thus their pent-up demand continued to build up, though now the inflationary pressures were repressed by the direct controls.

Then, following the war, the direct controls were lifted (in 1946), and the repressed inflationary pressures that had accumulated during the preceding five years were released. The wage and price levels rose sharply, and the heretofore repressed inflation became manifested in a real inflation of considerable magnitude. Profit expectations became buoyant, and the demand for loanable funds increased. Both commercial banks and nonbank financial intermediaries were able to shift out of their government securities (which they had acquired during the war) and make additional loans to the private sector of the economy. Thus the money supply and velocity continued to rise, adding more fuel to the inflationary flames.

Yet in all this inflation the Federal Reserve did not pursue an anti-inflationary policy (for reasons to be discussed below); moreover, there were strong feelings that it should not pursue such a policy. Before we examine these feelings, one major point should be kept in mind. The economic situation in the immediate postwar years was unique in the experience of policy makers and economists. The large national debt, the widespread distribution of ownership of government securities, pervasive fears that the financial market might collapse unless the Federal Reserve supported it—all these and other factors created great concern and uneasiness. It seems safe to say that for a period (up to the latter part of 1947) the Federal Reserve voluntarily kept its hands tied and thus acquiesced to the inflation.[7]

---

[6]It should be noted that the rise in the wage and price levels up to March 1942, was not very great. The major reason for this was the presence of widespread unemployment of both labor and the existing capital stock. This is an illustration of what Keynes referred to as "semi-inflation"; see the discussion in Chapter 13.

[7]From the end of the war to March 1951, the Federal Reserve "cooperated" with the Treasury in order to support the government securities market. It is possible to view this period as a "contest" between the Federal Reserve and the Treasury, and many have done so. However, as Wallich, "Postwar United States Monetary Policy Appraised," p. 93, has pointed out: "There is no need . . . to view the contest as a battle in which the forces of light gradually overcame the powers of darkness. Most of the time the contestants differed over relatively minor points."

TABLE 21–2

Estimated Ownership of U. S. Government Obligations, 1939-1965 (Par Values, Billions of Dollars)

End of Year	Total	Held by U. S. Government Investment Accounts	Held by Federal Reserve Banks	Held by "The Public"						
				Total	Commercial Banks	Mutual Savings Banks and Insurance Companies	Other Corporations	State and Local Governments	Individuals	Miscellaneous Investors
1939	47.6	6.5	2.5	38.6	15.9	9.4	2.2	0.4	10.1	0.7
1940	50.9	7.6	2.2	41.1	17.3	10.1	2.0	0.5	10.6	0.7
1941	64.3	9.5	2.3	52.5	21.4	11.9	4.0	0.7	13.6	0.9
1942	112.5	12.2	6.2	94.0	41.1	15.8	10.1	1.0	23.7	2.3
1943	170.1	16.9	11.5	141.6	59.9	21.2	16.4	2.1	37.6	4.4
1944	232.1	21.7	18.8	191.6	77.7	28.0	21.4	4.3	53.3	7.0
1945	278.7	27.0	24.3	227.4	90.8	34.7	22.2	6.5	64.1	9.1
1946	259.5	30.9	23.3	205.2	74.5	36.7	15.3	6.3	64.2	8.1
1947	257.0	34.4	22.6	200.1	68.7	35.9	14.1	7.3	65.7	8.4
1948	252.9	37.3	23.3	192.2	62.5	32.7	14.8	7.9	65.5	8.9
1949	257.2	39.4	18.9	198.9	66.8	31.5	16.8	8.1	66.3	9.4
1950	256.7	39.2	20.8	196.8	61.8	29.6	19.7	8.8	66.3	10.5
1951	259.5	42.3	23.8	193.4	61.6	26.3	20.7	9.6	64.6	10.6
1952	267.4	45.9	24.7	196.9	63.4	25.5	19.9	11.1	65.2	11.7
1953	275.2	48.3	25.9	201.0	63.7	25.1	21.5	12.7	64.8	13.2
1954	278.8	49.6	24.9	204.2	69.2	24.1	19.1	14.4	63.5	13.9

TABLE 21-2 (continued)

Estimated Ownership of U. S. Government Obligations, 1939-1965 (Par Values, Billions of Dollars)

End of Year	Total	Held by U. S. Government Investment Accounts	Held by Federal Reserve Banks	Held by "The Public"						
				Total	Commercial Banks	Mutual Savings Banks and Insurance Companies	Other Corporations	State and Local Governments	Individuals	Miscellaneous Investors
1955	280.8	51.7	24.8	204.3	62.0	23.1	23.2	15.4	65.0	15.6
1956	276.7	54.0	24.9	197.8	59.5	21.3	18.7	16.3	65.9	16.1
1957	275.0	55.2	24.2	195.5	59.5	20.2	17.7	16.6	65.9	16.6
1958	283.0	54.4	26.3	202.3	67.5	19.9	18.1	16.5	63.7	16.6
1959	290.0	53.7	26.6	210.6	60.3	19.5	21.4	18.0	69.4	22.1
1960	290.4	55.1	27.4	207.9	62.1	18.1	18.7	18.7	66.1	24.2
1961	296.5	54.5	28.9	213.1	67.2	17.5	18.5	19.0	65.9	25.0
1962	304.0	55.6	30.8	217.6	67.2	17.6	18.6	20.1	66.0	28.0
1963	310.1	58.0	33.6	218.5	64.3	17.1	18.7	21.1	68.2	29.2
1964	318.7	60.6	37.0	221.1	64.0	17.0	17.9	21.2	70.0	31.2
1965	321.4	61.9	40.8	218.7	60.2	16.9	16.0	22.9	72.3	31.4

Source: *The Annual Report of the Council of Economic Advisers*, January 1966, p. 274.

What were the general feelings that served to keep the attitude towards monetary policy at such a low level? There were several. First, many economists and policy makers continued to look upon monetary policy from the perspective of the 'thirties. The attitude seemed to be: "If it did not work then, why should we expect it to work now, especially in a new economic environment?"

Second, and very important, there was a widespread fear among economists that the war would be followed by a severe contraction. There were two reasons underlying this fear. For one, every major war in which the United States had participated up to this time had been succeeded by a contraction; so why not this one? More important, perhaps, was the use of an over-simplified Keynesian model. Using the formula $Y = C+I+G$, a large number of economists pointed out that the cessation of hostilities would mean a sharp and significant drop in G, and this would likely set off a negative multiplier effect. Thus expansive public policies were needed. And if, on the other hand, the Federal Reserve were permitted to, or did, put into effect anti-inflationary policies, the contraction might be triggered off.

We now know, with the aid of hindsight of course, that these predictions were in error.[8] To be sure, government expenditures did drop sharply—from an annual rate of $98.6 billion in the first quarter of 1945 to an annual rate of $35.4 billion in the first quarter of 1946—but this was compensated for in large measure by a rise in the other components of aggregate demand. Actually, consumption expenditures for the same period rose from $119.0 billion to $137.2 billion, investment from $7.7 billion to $24.5 billion, and net foreign investment from $—2.7 billion to $2.6 billion. In fact, by the close of 1946 GNP stood at $220.4 billion as compared with $220.6 billion in the first quarter of 1945. What was overlooked by the forecasters, of course, was the large and sharp rise in consumer and business demand as resources were released from the war effort to private use. Be that as it may, in 1945 and 1946 there still were pervasive fears of a serious postwar contraction.

A third fear related to the large national debt. A vigorous anti-inflationary policy by the Federal Reserve would have resulted in the de-

---

More important, see the *Patman Replies,* in which it is made clear that there was a great deal of cooperation between the two agencies. In fact, the testimony on this point by the Secretary of the Treasury (pp. 74-76) and the testimony of the Chairman of the Board (pp. 349-51) are precisely identical.

[8]For reviews of the forecasts of this time, see E. C. Bratt, "A Reconsideration of Postwar Forecasts," *Journal of Business,* April 1953; and E. E. Hagen, "The Reconversion Period: Reflections of a Forecaster," *Review of Economic Statistics,* May 1947.

pression of government security prices; and many persons felt that this would result in attempts by both bank and nonbank holders to sell heavily, which would have depressed security prices even further. Not only would this have meant a rise in the interest cost on the national debt—a cost that stood at about $10 billion in 1946—but it was also feared that bond prices would collapse completely. As Allen Sproul, president of the Federal Reserve Bank of New York City, put it, security prices might tumble into a "bottomless pit."[9] Further it was felt that the rise in interest rates that would result from a vigorous anti-inflationary policy would stifle investment spending to the point of perhaps creating negative investment. More than that, the entire securities market (so it was feared) would be completely distorted, making for even more economic havoc.

As a result of these fears, the Federal Reserve authorities collaborated with the Treasury and pursued a policy of "pegging" the prices of government securities, a policy that had been started during the war years.[10] This meant that the Federal Reserve stood ready to purchase government securities at fixed prices. Thus as banks and nonbank holders reduced their holdings of government securities, the Federal Reserve was forced to buy and thereby increase its holdings in order to maintain the prices. This of course resulted in a monetization of part of the national debt and hence further inflationary pressures. All in all, the pegging policy contributed significantly to the postwar inflation; and it lasted until March 1951, at which time the growing disagreements between the Federal Reserve and the Treasury were reasonably resolved.

A fourth reason for the rejection of monetary policy in this period was the growing belief that fiscal policy could do an adequate job in containing instability. The "automatic stabilizers" had been "discovered," and a good deal of effort was put into the analysis of discretionary fiscal policy. This is not the place to examine fiscal policy;[11] the only point to be made here is that the growing acceptability of fiscal policy occurred in the face of a growing antipathy towards monetary policy.

Finally, both analytical and empirical effort had gone into an examination of the interest elasticity of the investment demand curve. While the data are not conclusive, many economists strongly felt that the

[9]Cited in Wallich, "Postwar United States Monetary Policy Appraised," p. 93.

[10]*Ibid.*, pp. 91-95; *Patman Replies*, pp. 290-93, 346-63; Chandler, *Inflation in the United States, 1940-1948*, Chapter XIII.

[11]See Chapters 24-25.

aggregate investment demand function is very interest inelastic; this, coupled with a rise in the function under conditions of inflation, prevented the carrying out of an effective anti-inflationary policy unless it was pushed to such an extent that it would bring on a contraction.

In light of these doubts and fears, monetary policy was shunted to one side in the immediate postwar period. However, as the inflation continued and as fears of a contraction diminished, the Federal Reserve began to chafe under the pegging policy. In the late 'forties the Federal Reserve authorities began to express strong disagreement with the policy, pointing out that so long as the inflation continued they could do nothing to control it—and, in fact, they could only add to it by purchasing government securities offered for sale in the open market. Finally, as noted above, in March 1951, an "accord" was reached between the Federal Reserve and the Treasury, under which the Federal Reserve authorities were given far more flexibility in monetary policy. From that time on, the Federal Reserve began to use monetary policy more aggressively. This does not mean that monetary policy has displaced fiscal policy, nor does it mean that there is complete agreement among economists as to the effectiveness of monetary policy. Indeed, as will be seen later on, there are even disagreements within Federal Reserve circles as to what sorts of monetary policies should be carried out and how effective they may be.

Despite these disagreements, however, the position and attitude of the major policy makers in the Federal Reserve System can easily be ascertained. It is perhaps best to let the official spokesmen of the System speak for themselves:

> The primary responsibility of the Federal Reserve System is to determine the volume of member bank reserves. These reserves serve directly as the base for the deposits and asset-acquiring functions of member banks and indirectly for those of non-member banks. Those commercial banks that are members of the Federal Reserve System hold about 85 per cent of the deposits of all commercial banks. By regulating the volume of member bank reserves, the Federal Reserve thus exerts a dominant influence on the size of the money supply and on the flow of commercial bank loans and investments.[12]

The same position has been repeated much more recently:

> Whatever broad influences may flow from their actions, the Board of Governors and the Federal Open Market Committee are fully aware that the particular economic or financial variable over which they have any-

---

[12]*Memorandum of Evidence,* presented by W. W. Reifler to the Radcliff "Committee on the Working of the Monetary System," *Principal Memoranda of Evidence* (London: Her Majesty's Stationery Office, 1960), Vol. I, p. 299.

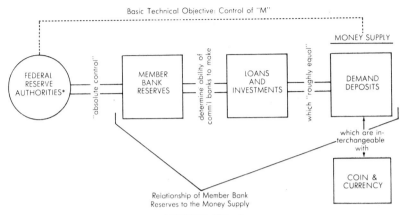

FIGURE 21—1

thing approaching full and direct control is the total of commercial bank reserves. Through this control, they exert a strong influence directly on total loans and investments and total deposits of banks and indirectly some influence on spending, investment, and saving by the public in general. At any given moment, therefore, the choice for Federal Reserve policy lies between various degrees of restraint upon or encouragement to expansion of bank credit through altered reserve availability.[13]

Thus the position of the Federal Reserve authorities on monetary policy is quite straightforward. By controlling commercial bank reserves—especially "excess" reserves—they control commercial bank lending (that is, "money creating") abilities.[14] All this is shown in Figure 21-1.

---

[13]*The Federal Reserve and the Treasury: Answers to Questions from the Commission on Money and Credit* (Englewood Cliffs, N. J.: Prentice-Hall, Inc., 1963), p. 3. For a much earlier statement, see "The Monetary System of the United States," *Federal Reserve Bulletin*, February 1953, p. 98. "It is the function of reserve banking, by regulating the volume of bank reserves, to counteract the tendency for excessive swings in the volume of money." An excellent source of excerpts from Federal Reserve statements is D. P. Eastburn, ed., *The Federal Reserve on Record: Readings on Current Issues from Statements by Federal Reserve Officials* (Philadelphia: Federal Reserve Bank of Philadelphia, 1965).

[14]For definitions of reserves, see the September 1963 *Review* of the Federal Reserve Bank of St. Louis, p. 6. *Required reserves* are defined as follows: "Member banks are required to maintain as reserves an amount equal to a prescribed portion of their deposits. Currently, reserve requirements are 4 per cent of total time deposits plus 16.5 and 12 per cent, respectively, of reserve city and country bank net demand deposits." *Excess reserves* are defined as "Total reserves less required reserves." And total reserves are defined as "Member bank deposits with Federal Reserve Banks plus member bank vault cash." The concept of "free reserves" is discussed in section 3 below.

See any standard money and banking textbook for a discussion of the organization of the Federal Reserve System and for the distinction between member and non-member banks, as well as for the distinction between "reserve city" and "country" banks.

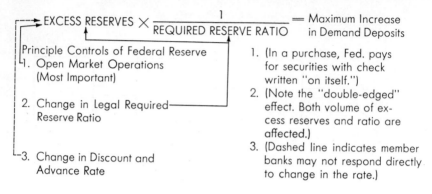

$$\text{EXCESS RESERVES} \times \frac{1}{\text{REQUIRED RESERVE RATIO}} = \begin{array}{l}\text{Maximum Increase}\\\text{in Demand Deposits}\end{array}$$

Principle Controls of Federal Reserve
1. Open Market Operations
   (Most Important)

2. Change in Legal Required
   Reserve Ratio

3. Change in Discount and
   Advance Rate

1. (In a purchase, Fed. pays
   for securities with check
   written "on itself.")
2. (Note the "double-edged"
   effect. Both volume of excess reserves and ratio are
   affected.)
3. (Dashed line indicates member
   banks may not respond directly
   to change in the rate.)

FIGURE 21–2

For the most part the existence of "nonmember" commercial banks will be ignored, although, since the member banks of the System hold about 85 per cent of total demand deposits, this omission is not very important. Thus, in what follows the term "reserves" is used to mean "member bank reserves," that is, the reserve deposits of the member banks in the Federal Reserve banks. As is well known, the Federal Reserve authorities exercise monetary policy to control member bank reserves by use of three principal devices—open market operations, changes in the discount and advance rate, and changes in the required reserve ratio. How these three devices are used to affect reserves and hence the money supply is summarized in Figure 21-2.

2. Federal Reserve Controls

Of these devices by far the most important is open market operations. The Federal Reserve authorities, however, do not always use open market operations as a policy weapon. The major reason is that open market operations are sometimes used in a technical manner to offset changes in the reserve position of the commercial banking system attributable to a number of factors that are beyond the direct control of the Federal Reserve. Such factors as changes in "float," changes in the net gold position of the United States, and changes in the types of money that people desire to hold—all these and other forces influence the reserves of the commercial banks. The Federal Reserve officials may then, by means of open market operations, offset these changes in order to maintain the level of member bank reserves at the level they desire. This sort of open market operation is referred to as a *technical* operation. On the other hand, an open market operation that is designed to change the level of member bank reserves—that is, an operation that is designed to change monetary policy, will be referred to as a *policy* operation. Thus an open market operation designed to keep monetary policy the same is a *technical* one, while one designed to change monetary policy may be called a *policy* operation. The significance of this technical-policy distinction will be seen in section 3, below.

Let us now summarize how the three traditional policy devices used by the Federal Reserve can affect the volume of member bank reserves.

A.   Open Market Operations

As noted above, open market operations constitute the most important weapon in the hands of the Federal Reserve. The term refers simply to the purchase and sale of government securities.[15] The decisions to purchase and sell are made by the Federal Open Market Committee, which manages the government securities portfolios of the twelve Federal Reserve banks.

There is little need to concern ourselves with the intricate organization of the government securities markets through which the Open Market Committee buys and sells securities. Suffice it to say that the Committee places a "buy order" or a "sell order" in a manner quite similar to the way in which private citizens, commercial banks, and nonfinancial corporations place similar orders. In fact, there are only two important differences.

First, the Open Market Committee places its orders directly with one or more of a small number of *dealers* who are the most important intermediary dealers in the government securities market. Second, when the Committee buys securities, it does so by creating "money," that is, it pays for the securities purchased from a dealer by "writing a check on itself." The dealer then deposits the check in its commercial bank, and accordingly the volume of demand deposits in the commercial banking system has been increased. More importantly, the total volume of member bank reserves has also been increased.

Now at this point the secondary market organization for government securities comes into play. From the standpoint of monetary policy, this secondary market has two important functions. (1) to transmit the

---

[15]For a detailed statement of the operations of the Open Market Committee, see R. V. Roosa, *Federal Reserve Operations in the Money and Government Securities Markets* (New York: Federal Reserve Bank of New York, 1956).

effect of the Open Market Committee purchases and sales throughout the rest of the country, since the immediate effect of the operations is centered in New York City; (2) to allow commercial banks that are short on reserves and long on government securities to trade assets with those banks that find themselves in the reverse condition. Thus, if open market operations are to be effective as a device that controls member bank reserves, a highly organized and smoothly functioning secondary market for government securities is quite essential.

The immediate effect, therefore, of an open market purchase operation is twofold—it increases the money supply and it increases member bank reserves. Usually, however, the future or potential effect of the purchase is much more important. The major reason for this is that since the supply of member bank reserves has been increased, the commercial banks can now increase their loans and investments and thus further increase the money supply.[16] If, for example, the purchase creates new excess reserves of $10 million, and if the "average" required reserve ratio is 20 per cent, then the formula in Figure 21–2 states that the money supply can be increased, *ceteris paribus,* by an additional $50 million. The *ceteris paribus* provision, however, is very important in this case for, as will be seen in section 4, the link between member bank reserves and changes in the money supply is sometimes loose and tenuous. Despite this qualification, the Federal Reserve continues to rely very heavily upon the open market operations for two important reasons.

First, there is a much greater degree of flexibility in the use of open market operations than there is in the exercise of the other two traditional controls. That is, open market operations may be conducted on a small scale or on a large scale. Also, action is quickly reversible; the Federal Reserve may buy securities in the morning and sell in the afternoon. Another important element of flexibility is that open market operations may be used in a *technical* manner to offset changes in member bank reserves that result from sources beyond the direct control of the Federal Reserve itself.[17]

Second, and perhaps most important, open market operations take place purely at the initiative of the Federal Reserve authorities themselves. If the Federal Reserve wishes additional bank reserves to be created, it can do so directly by means of a purchase. In this respect, the authorities do not have to wait for action on the part of the commercial banks, as they would, for example, if they were to lower the

---

[16]Refer back to Figure 21–1 of this chapter.

[17]This point will be explained more fully in section 3.

discount and advance rate. In this latter case, they would have to wait and hope that the commercial banks would be induced to borrow additional reserves from the Federal Reserve banks. At any rate, if the discount and advance rate is reduced, much (if not all) of the action taken is initiated by the commercial banks. Not so, however, in the case of an open market purchase.

The other two Federal Reserve controls, as well as their relative importance, are discussed in the next few pages. But it is important to keep in mind that the open market operations are far more important and significant.

B. Control of the Discount and Advance Rate

The control device that has actually received the most attention in the Anglo-American central banking tradition is changes in the rate of interest charged by the Central Bank when it lends to the commercial banks. In the United States this takes the form of changes in what is termed the "discount and advance rate"—that is, the interest rate charged by the individual Federal Reserve banks when they lend to member banks.[18]

The traditional explanation of the significance of the control over the discount and advance rate is that the Federal Reserve raises the rate to discourage the borrowing of reserves by member banks and lowers the rate in order to encourage borrowing on the part of the banks. But a great deal of what has been written on the effectiveness of this traditional control largely misses the mark. In short, commercial banks do not respond in any significant manner to changes in the discount and advance rate.[19] Simply because the rate has been lowered is no sign that the banks will go rushing to the "discount window" and borrow more reserves. In fact, it appears that the commercial banks' demands for discounts and advances is almost totally interest inelastic.

---

[18]Usually these loans are advances secured by United States government securities. Earlier, "eligible commercial paper" was also used—and by eligible commercial paper is meant high-grade, short-term (ninety days) commercial paper. In recent years short-term government securities are generally used.

[19]For two excellent discussions of the discount and advance rate, see W. L. Smith, "The Discount Rate as a Credit-Control Weapon," *Journal of Political Economy*, April 1958; and M. E. Polakoff, "Reluctance Elasticity, Least Cost, and Member-Bank Borrowing: A Suggested Integration," *Journal of Finance*, March 1960. See also W. L. Smith, "The Instruments of General Monetary Control," *The National Banking Review*, September 1963, pp. 49-68; and M. E. Polakoff, "Federal Reserve Discount Policy and Its Critics," Chapter 11 in *Banking and Monetary Studies*, ed. D. Carson (Homewood, Ill.: Richard D. Irwin, Inc., 1963).

The major reason for this is that a member bank borrows from a Federal Reserve bank because it is already short, or expects to be short in the near future, in its reserve position. Thus, borrowing is primarily a matter of operating necessity; and the level of the discount and advance rate (at least within its historical range of fluctuation) has little if anything to do with the member bank's decision to borrow or not. So long as this is the case, then control of the discount and advance rate has very little to do directly with the total volume of member bank reserves or with the volume of money.

A much better explanation of the significance of the discount and advance rate seems to be that once Federal Reserve policies have been decided and carried out by means of open market operations, the discount and advance rate is adjusted to make it consistent with the new policy. In this sense, changes in the discount and advance rate tend to play a definite subsidiary role in monetary policy.

Discounting and advancing does, however, serve one very important function in the process of monetary policy since it acts as a "shock absorber" for the banks that bear the brunt of the effect of open market sales by the Open Market Committee. Such a sale will, of course, reduce the total reserves of the member banks as a whole, although the effect will be unevenly distributed between the banks. Thus some banks will find themselves short on reserves as a result of the open market operations, and these may, as a last resort, borrow from the Federal Reserve in order to avoid a deficiency in their reserve positions.[20] However, it is the open market sale that comes first, rather than any adjustment in the discount and advance rate.

In short, control of the discount rate is a handmaiden of open market operations and thus plays a definite secondary and supplementary role. Oddly enough, however, changes in the discount and advance rate receive widespread publicity, while on the other hand changes in open market operations receive little publicity outside of the purely financial press. Thus changes in the discount and advance rate serve somewhat as a "publicity weapon"—sometimes called a "psychological weapon"—with which basic decisions in monetary policy may be dramatized.[21]

There is one final point that should be made with respect to the discount and advance rate. The suggestion is often made that changes in

---

[20]See Smith, "The Instruments of General Monetary Control," p. 52.

[21]For a critical discussion of changes in the discount rate serving as a "psychological weapon," see Smith, "The Instruments of General Monetary Control," pp. 59-64. For the opposite point of view, see C. E. Walker, "Discount Policy in the Light of Recent Experience," *Journal of Finance,* May 1957, pp. 229-30.

the rate are important because so many other rates of interest are closely linked to it. This position, however, is highly questionable. The general structure of interest rates in the American economy changes as general monetary conditions change—that is, depending on the tightness or looseness of money and credit. The Federal Reserve will, of course, adjust the discount and advance rate accordingly; but remember that the extent and direction of change in monetary conditions are themselves largely a function of Federal Reserve policy in general and open market operations in particular.[22]

Thus far, then, we may conclude that control by the Federal Reserve of the discount and advance rate can hardly be called a direct tool in the management of the quantity of money in the economy. It is rather a device that dramatizes changes in monetary policy to the general public and serves as a "shock absorber" for particular commercial banks that find themselves in a real or potential reserve shortage resulting from an open market sale.

C. Interactions between Open Market Operations and the Discount and Advance Rate

There may be a countervailing, or at least partially offsetting, effect of discounting and advancing on open market operations. This is most likely to occur under tight money conditions when the Open Market Committee is selling government securities. The sales will, of course, reduce the total volume of member banks' reserves; but at the same time the banks may increase their discounts and advances, thereby causing an offsetting increase in reserves.[23]

Consider, for example, a generally tight monetary condition—that is,

---

[22]There is, however, one way in which changes in the discount and advance rate lead rather directly to changes in some other rates of interest. Several of the interest rates that make up the total interest-rate structure are, in effect, "administered prices"—particularly in the case of negotiated loans, as opposed to open market financial investment transactions. Thus the change in the discount rate becomes a signal for the "price administrators" of these particular interest rates to change their own rates on newly negotiated loans. This relationship seems to be particularly true in the case of rises in the discount and advance rate. Thus, although some interest rates are closely linked to the discount rate, one cannot say that a large number of individual interest rates, let alone the entire interest rate structure, are directly tied to the discount and advance rate.

[23]On this, see Smith, "The Instruments of General Monetary Control," pp. 54-55, 64. See also the exchange between C. R. Whittlesey, "Credit Policy at the Discount Window," *Quarterly Journal of Economics*, May 1959, and R. V. Roosa, "Credit Policy at the Discount Window: Comment," *Quarterly Journal of Economics*, May 1959.

the Federal Reserve is very much concerned about inflationary conditions. Assume that excess reserves are exactly zero in the banking system as a whole, and the Federal Reserve, wishing to tighten up even further, sells $100 million of government securities in the open market. This will, *ceteris paribus*, reduce the volume of member bank reserves by $100 million and thus cause a deficiency in required reserves by the same amount. Under these circumstances we may logically expect some member banks throughout the system to apply to their respective Federal Reserve banks for discounts and advances in the amount of approximately $100 million. *If* all of these discounts and advances are granted, the total volume of member bank reserves of course remains unchanged, and the Federal Reserve will have failed in its objectives of reducing reserves and the money supply. If this is the case, then of what significance was the open market sale?

The important thing to note is that, although the total volume of member bank reserves is unchanged, the *source* of these reserves has been altered by the action. On the assets side of the balance sheet of the Federal Reserve banks there is now $100 million less in government securities and $100 million more in discounts and advances. Put otherwise, on the liabilities side of the balance sheets of the commercial banks there is now $100 million more in discounts and advances, and this represents $100 million of debt to the Federal Reserve. This change in the source of member bank reserves is important because of the traditional attitudes of commercial bankers towards "being in debt to the Fed." When reserves are provided to the banking system by an open market purchase, no individual bank feels any pressure to change its method of operation. But when the source of additional reserves is discounting and advancing, the individual commercial banks that are affected feel pressure to repay their indebtedness to the Federal Reserve banks. In fact, there appears to be a tradition among American commercial banks to avoid as much as possible going into debt to the Federal Reserve, and when in debt to get out of it as quickly as possible.[24]

Thus, insofar as member banks are reluctant to get into debt to the Federal Reserve, but have been forced to do so by the open market sale, they will tend to refuse new loans and to refuse to renew outstanding loans as they come due. In this way, then, the Federal Reserve achieves its objective of reducing the total volume of reserves and the money supply. But the availability of the "discount window" to the member banks softens the impact of the open market sale. Note, how-

---

[24]See the references in footnote 19, as well as R. A. Young, "Tools and Processes of Monetary Policy," Chapter 1 in *United States Monetary Policy*, pp. 24-25.

ever, that the entire procedure depends heavily on the reluctance of banks to borrow from the Federal Reserve.

How strong the "reluctance effect" is depends upon many factors— for instance, how much the individual commercial bank has been in debt to the Federal Reserve in the past, how much it is currently in debt, and even perhaps what sort of hints the Federal Reserve officials may have given to the bank at the time of the discount negotiation. In general, the American commercial banking tradition suggests that a bank "does not stay in debt to the Fed very often, very much, or very long," and that thus the "reluctance factor" is quite important. However, as the experience of member banks at the "discount window" grows, their reluctance to borrow from the Federal Reserve may be lessened.[25] The greater the amount and frequency of discounting and advancing on the part of individual banks, the less binding this tradition tends to become. For this reason the Federal Reserve authorities state that discounting and advancing is a *privilege*, not a right, and that as a privilege it should not be abused. Further, the Federal Reserve may, by means of warnings, tend to bolster and continue the tradition. In fact, on occasion a Federal Reserve bank may even inform a member bank in its district that it is expected to borrow no more when it has repaid what it currently owes.

The important point is that the effectiveness of monetary policy is partially dependent upon the "reluctance factor," but at the same time an increase in discounts and advances at the time of an open market sale tends to soften the impact of the restrictive tightening of monetary and credit conditions. Thus the restrictive effects of the open market sale are postponed as member banks acquire reserves at the "discount window," though their reluctance to be in debt to the Federal Reserve means that they will gradually reduce their loans and investments and hence demand deposits. In recent years, however, as member banks have acquired more experience at the "discount window," their reluctance to be in debt to the Federal Reserve seems to be weakening. This means then that the establishment of new, and presumably lower, limits of discounts and advances that the Federal Reserve will tolerate will also have an influence on the effectiveness of monetary policy.

D.   Control of the Required Reserve Ratio

Since the Banking Act of 1935, the Federal Reserve authorities have had the power to change the legally required reserve ratios for member banks, though only within the limits prescribed by Congress. This con-

---

[25]See especially the Polakoff essays cited in footnote 19.

trol device, however, has been used quite sparingly, and only since World War II has it been used to any great extent.

The economic significance of a legally required reserve ratio is obvious. As long as commercial banks are legally required to adhere to a minimum reserve ratio, the deposit-creating abilities of the commercial banking system are limited. Recall the two important variables— the amount of excess reserves and the reciprocal of the required reserve ratio—on the left hand side of the equation given in Figure 21-2. These two variables, *ceteris paribus*, determine the additional amount of demand deposits that the commercial banking system can create. That is, given the required reserve ratio, the amount of new money that can be created depends upon the amount of excess reserves that the commercial banks possess. On the other hand, changes in the required reserve ratio also will determine the banking system's ability to create new money. The record of the Federal Reserve authorities indicates, however, that they have most often concentrated on changing the amount of excess reserves (via open market operations) rather than on changing the required reserved ratio. In this respect, it is perhaps more important to have some given required reserve ratio than it is to determine exactly at what level that ratio should be set. Given any required reserve ratio, the Federal Reserve can exercise its control over the money supply by changing the amount of excess reserves in the commercial banking system.[26]

At any rate, the power to change required reserve ratios is the least frequently used of the major control devices of the Federal Reserve. For that reason alone it may be regarded as among the less important of these powers. But note that this statement is relevant only because of the infrequency with which the Board of Governors has changed the ratios. Potentially, of course, it is a power of extreme influence, because as required reserve ratios are changed, both the volume of ex-

---

[26]We may note parenthetically that the power to impose a legal required reserve ratio on member banks is a power that indirectly affects the level of bank earnings. Funds that must be held in the form of reserve deposits cannot be loaned out or invested and therefore cannot earn interest. Thus legal required reserves impose an "opporunity cost" on member banks, and some economists, as well as the American Bankers Association, have on these grounds recommended abolition of the legal required reserve ratio. See, for example, N. H. Jacoby's article in the *Commercial and Financial Chronicle*, November 21, 1957, as well as the American Bankers Association statement, reprinted as Chapter 41 in *Money and Economic Activity: Readings in Money and Banking*, ed. L. S. Ritter (Boston: Houghton Mifflin Company, 1961). For a critical view, see A. H. Hansen, "Bankers and Subsidies," *Review of Economics and Statistics*, February 1958, reprinted as Chapter 42 in the Ritter readings. See also A. G. Hart, "Making Monetary Policy More Effective," *United States Monetary Policy*, pp. 182-83.

cess reserves and "expansion multiple" (that is, the reciprocal of the required reserve ratio) are changed. Hence there is a double-edged effect upon the maximum amount of credit creating abilities of the commercial banking system.

3. Further Analysis of the Control of Member Bank Reserves

The three monetary control devices discussed in the preceding section interact over time, of course, as the Federal Reserve puts them into effect. This interaction will be examined in some detail in this section, and in the process the distinction made earlier in this chapter— namely, *technical* versus *policy* open market operations—will be used. In a sense, this distinction is somewhat artificial inasmuch as the so-called technical open market operations are used to maintain an already agreed upon policy position. If, for example, the Federal Reserve officials had decided that member bank reserves should be $17 billion, but factors beyond their control cause reserves to rise to $18 billion, they would use the "technical" open market operations to restore the reserve level to $17 billion. The technical open market operations, in this respect, could really be considered as "policy" operations; but as the subsequent discussion shows, the technical-policy distinction is very useful for analytical purposes.

In the remainder of this section Table 21–3, the "Table of Factors of Increase and Decrease," will be heavily relied upon.[27] This table includes twelve so-called "factors," six of which are labeled as "factors of increase," and six of which are referred to as "factors of decrease." Further, two of the "factors of increase" are listed as "policy factors," while the remaining ten factors are listed as "non-policy factors." Obviously some definitions are in order.

The *factors of increase* are those which, when rising, cause member bank reserves to *rise*. For example, if Federal Reserve holdings of United States government securities rise, member bank reserves will also rise. Consider row 1 in the table, in which Federal Reserve holdings of government securities increased by $932 million between June 1960 and October 1960. This was the equivalent of increasing member bank reserves by the same magnitude. On the other hand, if Federal Reserve holdings of government securities decline, then member

---

[27]The data for the "factors of increase and decrease" are found in the table entitled "Member Bank Reserves, Federal Reserve Bank Credit, and Related Items," published monthly in the *Federal Reserve Bulletin*.

TABLE 21–3

Table of the Factors of Increase and Decrease
(Data in Millions of Dollars)

Account	Daily Average June, '60	Daily Average Oct., '60	Changes in Accounts +	Changes in Accounts −	Changes in Member Bank Reserves +	Changes in Member Bank Reserves −
Factors of Increase						
1. U. S. Government Securities at Federal Reserve	26,124	27,056	932		932	
2. Discounts and Advances	425	170		255		255
3. Float	1,159	1,225	66		66	
4. Other Federal Reserve Credit	29	39	10		10	
5. Gold Stock	19,343	18,571		772		772
6. Treasury Currency Outstanding	5,353	5,382	29		29	
Total	52,433	52,443				
7. Sub-Totals			1,037	1,027	1,037	1,027
8. Net Sub-Totals			10		10	
Factors of Decrease						
9. Currency and Coin in Circulation	31,926	32,183	257			257
10. Treasury Cash Holdings	414	406		8	8	
11. Treasury Deposits at Federal Reserve	496	488		8	8	
12. Foreign Deposits at Federal Reserve	221	226	5			5
13. Other Deposits at Federal Reserve	381	405	24			24
14. Other Federal Reserve Accounts	994	891		103	103	
Totals	34,432	34,599				

TABLE 21–3 (continued)

No.	Item						
15.	Sub-Totals			286	119	119	286
16.	Net Sub-Totals			167			167
17.	Member Bank Reserves at Federal Reserve (Derived)						157
18.	Member Bank Reserves at Federal Reserve (Actual)	18,001	17,843				158
19.	Member Bank Reserves and Currency and Coin (Vault Cash Adjustment)	293	390		597		597
20.	Total Member Bank Reserves (Derived)	18,294	18,733		439		439
21.	Total Member Bank Reserves (Actual)	18,294	18,733		439		439
22.	Required Reserves	17,828	18,095				267
23.	Excess Reserves	466	638				172
24.	Change in 10 Nonpolicy Factors plus Vault Cash Adjustment		677				
25.	Change in 2 Policy Factors						238

Source: *Federal Reserve Bulletin*, January 1961.

Basic Equations:

1. (Sum of actual balances of factors of increase) − (Sum of actual balances of factors of decrease) = Member bank reserves at Federal Reserve.

2. (Sum of changes in factors of increase) − (Sum of changes in factors of decrease) = Change in member bank reserves at Federal Reserve.

3. (Change in member bank reserves at Federal Reserve) + (Change in vault cash of member banks) = Change in total member bank reserves at Federal Reserve.

bank reserves will fall. Examine another factor of increase—discounts and advances extended by the Federal Reserve to member banks. So long as these are rising, so also will member bank reserves rise. But if to the contrary, they are declining, as they do in row 2 of the table, then member bank reserves will also decline. For a final example, if there is a net increase in the country's gold stock, reserves in the commercial banking system will rise; and if there is a net decrease (as shown in row 5), then member bank reserves fall.

Note that the factors of increase are either assets of the Federal Reserve banks or are items arithmetically and functionally closely related to Federal Reserve assets. In fact, they represent, for all practical purposes, the asset side of the balance sheet of the Federal Reserve System. As of June 1960, the asset side of the Federal Reserve balance sheet totaled $52,433 million. It is important to note also that the first two factors of increase are designated as the "two policy factors." This is because the Federal Reserve officials have a high degree of control over them. The remaining four factors of increase are designated as "non-policy factors" because the Federal Reserve either does not have *direct* control over them or has chosen not to exercise any direct control.

The *factors of decrease,* on the other hand, are important because when they are *rising,* member bank reserves are simultaneously *falling.* For instance, if the public demands more hand-to-hand currency and coins for transaction balances, then demand deposits and hence member bank reserves will decline. Conversely, if they reduce their demand for currency and coin, then demand deposits and member bank reserves rise. The same relationships hold for the other factors of decrease.

Note that the factors of decrease are either liability or net worth items of the Federal Reserve banks (*other than member bank reserves,* of course), or are items closely related to the liabilities and net worth side of the Federal Reserve's balance sheet. For all practical purposes, then, the total of the factors of decrease at any one time gives us the total liabilities and net worth of the Federal Reserve System (again, except for member bank reserves). As of June 1960, this amounted to $34,432 million. All of the factors of decrease are designated as "non-policy factors" because the Federal Reserve does not have, or does not exercise, any *direct* control over them.

Since the factors of increase represent, for all practical purposes, the asset side of the Federal Reserve System at a particular date, and since the factors of decrease represent the liabilities and net worth side (excluding member bank reserves), then we have the following simple accounting identity:

$$F_i - F_d = MBR,$$

where F_i stands for the sum of the factors of increase at a particular date, F_d stands for the sum of the factors of decrease at the same date, and MBR stands for member bank reserves on deposit at the Federal Reserve. Thus, for June of 1960:

$$\$52,433 \text{ million} - \$34,432 \text{ million} = \$18,001 \text{ million}.$$

By definition, then, the total member bank reserves at any particular date are equal to the difference between the sum of the factors of increase (the asset side of the System's balance sheet) and the sum of the factors of decrease (the liabilities and net worth side of the balance sheet, excluding member bank reserves).

Much more important for present purposes is that the "Table of Factors of Increase and Decrease" can be used to analyze *changes* in member bank reserves over periods of time. It does not matter whether the period of time is short, such as a day, or longer, such as several days or even several years. In Table 21–3 the time period from June 1960 to October 1960 has been selected in order to illustrate how the various powers of the Federal Reserve interact in determining changes in the total volume of member bank reserves. Since the major concern is with changes in the factors of increase and decrease, the two columns at the extreme right-hand side of the table—the "+" and "—" columns must be examined.

Now, as shown in the "+" column, row 21, member bank reserves actually increased by $439 million over this four-month period. *We shall assume that this increase was the policy objective of the Federal Reserve officials*—that is, that by October 1960 they wanted an additional $439 million dollars of reserves in the member banks. Presumably, therefore, they were pursuing a policy of "loosening up" monetary and credit conditions. But note that our assumption implies that they actually did achieve their policy objective. Let us examine how they went about accomplishing their task.

Look first at the behavior of the *"ten non-policy factors of increase and decrease."* On net balance they, along with the vault cash adjustments made by member banks, would have caused member bank reserves to decline by $238 million during this period, so long as the Federal Reserve authorities took no action to offset them. The impact of the "ten non-policy factors" (again, in the absence of Federal Reserve action) are summarized in Table 21–4. Now, if the Federal Reserve

TABLE 21—4

Factor of Increase or Decrease	Row Number in Table 21–3	Net Change during Period +	—
Float	3	$ 66	
Other Federal Reserve Credit	4	10	
Gold Stock	5		$ 772
Treasury Currency Outstanding	6	29	
Currency and Coin in Circulation	9		257
Treasury Cash Holdings	10	8	
Treasury Deposits at Federal Reserve	11	8	
Foreign Deposits at Federal Reserve	12		5
Other Deposits at Federal Reserve	13		24
Other Federal Reserve Accounts	14	103	
Vault Cash Adjustment by Member Banks	19	597	
TOTALS		821	1,058
Net Difference*		237	

* The net difference does not quite equal the figure of $238 used in the text because of errors due to rounding off.

officials were planning ahead over this four-month period, presumably they would have made some estimates or predictions as to what would happen to the "ten non-policy factors" and vault cash adjustments by the member banks. In the example we assume them to have predicted correctly that these factors and adjustments would have, if left alone, caused member bank reserves to decrease by $238 million. And certainly, if the authorities wanted to achieve their policy objective of increasing member bank reserves by $439 million, this meant that they would have had to use their "two policy factors" to increase reserves by more than $439 million. In fact, if the Federal Reserve were to achieve its goal, it would have to increase the total volume of member bank reserves by $677 million, of which $238 million would be designed to offset the estimated decrease caused by the "non-policy factors" and vault cash adjustment, and $439 million to achieve its objective by October.

But note this! In order to create $677 million of member bank reserves ($238 million to offset the decrease and $439 million of additional, new reserves), the Open Market Committee actually had to purchase $932 million in government securities, as shown in row 1 of Table 21–3. The reason for this is that member banks were using $255 million of the additional reserves they were getting to retire discounts and advances at the Federal Reserve (see row 2). Thus, in order to achieve the policy goal of $439 million extra member bank reserves, the Open Market Committee had to buy a total of $932 million in government securities. Of this $932 million, $238 million was used to offset the decrease in reserves due to the non-policy factors and member bank vault cash adjustment, and $255 million was bought to offset the reduction in member bank reserves caused by retirement of discounts and advances.

The preceding discussion can be stated in a manner which emphasizes the distinction between technical and policy open market operations. During this four-month period, the Open Market Committee purchased $932 million in government securities in the open market. Of this, $238 million can be considered to be merely *a technical kind of open market operation* needed to offset the $238 million negative change in the non-policy factors and vault cash adjustment. Another $255 million can be considered, however, to have more than mere technical significance; that is, the purchase of $255 million that was used by member banks to retire discounts and advances is a *policy* operation. The reason that it is designated as policy, rather than technical, is that it represents a change in the *source* of member bank reserves. Recall the earlier discussion about member banks being reluctant to be in debt to the Federal Reserve. Now that they have reduced their indebtedness to the Federal Reserve by $255 million, presumably they will feel less constrained in making loans and investments out of their additional reserves. Thus, since the open market operation did alter the *source* of member banks reserves, it should be thought of as *a policy change*. Finally, the last $439 million of purchases, which was the presumed target of the Federal Reserve authorities for this period, represents a net addition to the total volume of member bank reserves. This, therefore, was also *a policy-type change*.

This distinction between policy open market operations and technical open market operations is important if we are trying to interpret what the Federal Reserve is actually doing day by day or week by week in its open market operations. Generally it is understood that, *ceteris paribus,* the Open Market Committee buys when it wishes to increase the volume of member bank reserves. But as so often happens in the real world, *ceteris* is not always *paribus.* And unless the difference between technical and policy operations is understood, it is difficult to understand what the Federal Reserve is doing. Consider, for example, a situation where there is enough unemployment that the Federal Reserve decides to increase the volume of member bank reserves, makes public pronouncements to that effect, and actually begins buying. Then, very shortly, it "appears" to reverse itself and begins selling government securities in the open market, even though at the same time it continues its pronouncements of combating the unemployment and increasing reserves. Does the selling action mean that the Federal Reserve is inconsistent, or "two-faced," or completely confused? Not at all! The explanation, of course, is that it is using a *technical* operation, probably because the non-policy factors and vault cash adjustment, if not counteracted, are changing the volume of reserves to a level greater than what the Federal Reserve considers desirable. Thus, technical open market sales are used to offset, in part at least, this change.

In other words, in the real world of actual markets and monetary policy, the rationale of open market operations cannot be ascertained by looking simply at changes in the volume of United States government securities being bought and purchased by the Federal Reserve. In order to determine what the rationale really is, the changes in all twelve of the factors of increase and decrease must be analyzed, in order to differentiate between technical and policy operations.

4. The Concept of Free Reserves

Another important concept that should be introduced at this point is *"free reserves,"* primarily because of the significant position they seem to hold in Federal Reserve policy making. By definition, free reserves equal excess reserves minus discounts and advances. It is therefore something of a *net excess reserve* concept, where, for the system as a whole, excess reserves are netted out against the discounts and advances. Assume, for example, that one-half of the member banks have excess reserves of $20 billion and are not in debt at all to the Federal Reserve. Assume further that the remaining banks have $10 billion of excess reserves but also are in debt to the Federal Reserve banks by $5 billion. In this case, the "free reserves" would be $25 billion—that is, $30 billion of excess reserves minus $5 billion of discounts and advances.

Free reserves may be either negative or positive (see Figure 21-3). For example, when inflationary pressures are very strong, the Federal Reserve becomes determined to minimize further increases in the money supply and in member bank reserves—that is, it puts into effect a very tight monetary policy. In this case, free reserves will become negative, and at times this negative balance may be as large as half a

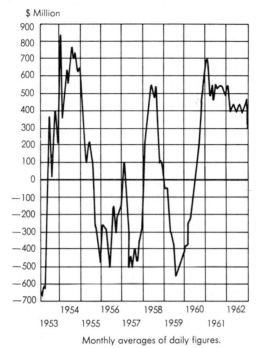

Monthly averages of daily figures.

Source: Board of Governors of the Federal Reserve System, in Smith, "The Instruments of General Monetary Control," p. 55.

FIGURE 21–3

Free Reserves of Member Banks

billion dollars. In other words, some member banks in the system are discounting and advancing by an amount larger than the excess reserves held by the other banks. On the other hand, when the Federal Reserve is willing to allow increases in the money supply—that is, when concern over inflationary pressures is low—free reserves may become positive. In this case, then, the Federal Reserve allows the excess reserves in the commercial banking system to exceed the discounts and advances of the system as a whole. Thus loans and investments, and therefore the money supply, may be increased.

In a very important sense the behavior of free reserves can be used as an index of Federal Reserve policy.[28] This can be seen in Figure 21–3, in which during the periods of ease (1953-1954, 1958, and 1960-

---

[28]For a critique of free reserves as a guide to monetary policy, see Smith, "The Instruments of General Monetary Policy," pp. 55-59.

1963), free reserves were positive. Conversely, during periods of credit restriction, free reserves were negative. In short, in order to analyze monetary policy in general, as well as the open market operations in particular, changes in both member bank reserves and free reserves must be examined. In the four-month period covered in Table 21–3 (this was a period of substantial ease in monetary conditions), total member bank reserves increased by $439 million. During the same period, excess reserves rose by $172 million (see row 23, Table 21–3), while discounts and advances declined by $255 million. Thus, free reserves in the banking system increased by $427. In a period of substantial tightening, however, open market sales by the Federal Reserve would reduce excess reserves while, at the same time, member banks would increase their discounts and advances at the "discount window." Accordingly, free reserves would tend to become, and probably would become, negative.

Thus far the discussion of the factors of increase and decrease has concentrated primarily upon the open market operations. However, what was the Federal Reserve doing with its other control devices during the four-month period we have selected for illustration? Assume that the discount and advance rate charged by the Federal Reserve Bank of New York is representative of all the twelve banks for this period. During this period the rate was lowered from 4 per cent to 3½ per cent, and then subsequently to 3 per cent. Note, however, that while the discount and advance rate was being reduced, the volume of discounts and advances was likewise being reduced, as commercial banks repaid their indebtedness to the Federal Reserve banks.

So far as the required reserve ratio is concerned, one change took place during the period. Although technically speaking the results of this change should have been included in the preceding discussion, it was excluded for purposes of simplicity. This omission, however, is not as serious as it appears and does not significantly alter the results of the analysis of data in Table 21–3.

To what extent does the Federal Reserve have control over the volume of member bank reserves and over the volume of free reserves? The answer to this question can be quite categorical. The degree of control is, for all practical purposes, nearly absolute. It depends upon the ability of the authorities to predict day by day the changes in the ten non-policy factors and the changes in vault cash held by the commercial banks. The Federal Reserve personnel have generally been quite modest when they refer to the effectiveness of their abilities to make such predictions. All in all, however, their record in this respect seems to be quite adequate. And even if their current estimate of tomorrow's movements in the ten non-policy factors and vault cash adjustment is slightly in error, they can correct their policy actions by a slightly different set of open market operations on the following day. It is of course also necessary for them to predict the interaction between open market operations and discounting and advancing, but here again the degree of predictive success which the Federal Reserve has experienced seems to be adequate. After all, if the member banks increase their discounting and advancing in a period of credit restraint by more than the Federal Reserve predicted, the Federal Reserve may, as a last resort, simply refuse to permit any additional discounts and advances if they think it necessary. In general, the control of the Federal Reserve authorities over the reserve positions of the commercial banks seems to be highly effective.

5. The Relation between Bank Reserves and the Money Supply

Although the Federal Reserve's control over the reserve positions of the commercial banks may be virtually complete, a different situation exists with respect to the ability of the Federal Reserve to control the money supply. In other words, the relationship between member bank reserves and excess reserves, on the one hand, and the volume of demand deposits, on the other, is much more uncertain.[29]

First, consider irregular fluctuations in the money supply.[30] Historically, one of the greatest problems in this respect has been recurring bank panics—that is, "runs on the banks." In fact, this country experienced a very major bank crisis as recently as 1933. A banking crisis, by definition, is a situation in which a large number of money holders wish to change the form of their money holdings from demand deposits to currency and coin. Thus as they write checks for cash, the commercial banks find their vault cash quickly depleted and accordingly must find some other source of currency and coin to satisfy the depositors' demands. This means that the commercial banking system must have some means of converting its present loans and investments quickly

---

[29]Control over seasonal fluctuations in the money supply seems to be almost complete. So far as control over secular changes is concerned, we postpone discussion to Chapter 23.

[30]See any good study of the history of money and banking in the United States for a discussion of the impact and significance of these irregular fluctuations in the stock of money.

into currency and cash. In short, they must have some immediate source of "liquidity of the highest degree."

Of course, a run on a single commercial bank is of no great consequence. The single bank can "sell off" its loans and investments to other commercial banks or even perhaps use them as collateral to borrow from other commercial banks until it has satisfied its customers that there is no need to panic. But the situation is quite different for the commercial banking system as a whole. The banks cannot acquire the necessary liquidity from each other, for each bank is in the same situation as every other bank. Thus there is need for some source outside of the commercial banking system that can and will provide the banks with the necessary liquidity. And in the United States this source is the Federal Reserve System.

As of the 1960's, the "liquidity-giving powers of the Fed" appear to be effective enough to prevent another banking crisis. A number of developments permit this generalization to be made with confidence.

First, the Banking Act of 1935, which amended the Federal Reserve Act, broadened the liquidity-giving powers of the Federal Reserve. Not only can a Federal Reserve Bank, through an Open Market Committee purchase of government securities, provide commercial banks with currency, but it can also make loans (discounts and advances) in the form of currency. Generally discounts and advances are made on the basis of eligible commercial paper and/or United States government securities, but the Federal Reserve (through an amendment of the Federal Reserve Act) is permitted to loan to the member banks on the basis of "any sound asset." The asset that is, of course, most commonly used is government securities, primarily because of the rise in the national debt since the 1920's. Commercial banks hold a large amount of the national debt, and the ownership of government securities can easily be transferred to the Federal Reserve for currency.

In fact, if necessary, any or all of the earning assets of the commercial banks can be transferred to the Federal Reserve in order to avoid an old-time banking crisis. The reason for this is that the amended legislation does not stipulate what is a "sound asset," and presumably, if need be, the Federal Reserve could designate the ballpoint pens owned by the member banks as "sound." No doubt a certain amount of legal "mumbo jumbo" might have to be complied with if the Federal Reserve were driven to such an extreme in order to avoid a banking crisis, but legally it can declare virtually any member bank asset as a "sound asset." Such an extreme case may be hard to imagine, but it is somewhat comforting to know that if every single depositor in the United States should wish to withdraw in the form of cash every last dollar of his deposits, it is quite possible for him to do so.

In addition, there is now the Federal Deposit Insurance Corporation. While the F.D.I.C seems to symbolize the safety of bank deposits, at least in the public's mind, its successful operation in the time of crisis depends upon the liquidity-giving powers of the Federal Reserve. The important point really is that if in the future some sort of banking crisis were to occur, it should not result in the closing of any basically sound commercial bank. Further, and also important, since decreases in demand deposits would be matched dollar for dollar by increases in currency and coin, the Federal Reserve would not necessarily lose control over the money supply. Of course, new types of irregular fluctuations might occur in the future; but at least the type that has caused the most trouble in the past is now adequately under control.

This brings us now to the behavior of the money supply, which has always been, and continues to be, a major problem of monetary policy. Cyclical fluctuations in the supply of money have during much of our history been economically devastating in their effects. In fact, they have been so important that some economists, as noted in Part 2, have made them the central theme in their theories of the business cycle. Furthermore, in the past there have been radical changes in the relationship between the volume of commercial bank reserves and the money supply. In other words, an increase in the volume of member bank reserves will not automatically result in an increase in the money supply. Not only is the link or relationship between reserves and the money supply tenuous and often unpredictable, but also at times it has been completely broken (as during the 1930's).

But of course conditions have changed, and what was true for yesteryear is not necessarily true for today. In fact, it appears that much, though not all, of the cyclical variation in the money supply has been removed.

In order to examine this point in more detail, let us abstract momentarily from empirical realism and consider an "extreme case." Assume that the economy is operating on the gold standard and, therefore, the central bank has only a minimal control over the volume of bank reserves. Assume also a negligible national debt, but that the business cycle is a real economic phenomenon. Under these circumstances, changes in demand deposits would be a function of changes in bank loans, which in turn would reflect changing business conditions. Thus changes in demand deposits would reflect the business cycle, acting at least as an important aggravating factor. This is shown in Figure 21–4A. While this case has been labeled "extreme," it is not too inaccurate a description of the American situation during much of the nineteenth century, especially since circulating bank notes were in existence in relatively large volume during roughly two-thirds of that century.

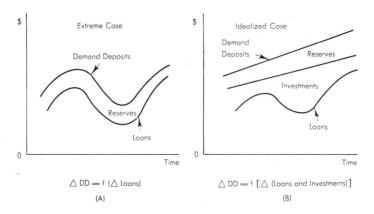

FIGURE 21–4

Now consider the "idealized case," in which the volume of bank reserves is free of the vicissitudes of the gold standard and is, at least potentially, under absolute control of the central banking authority. This situation is shown in Figure 21–4B, where it is assumed that a large volume of high quality, highly marketable investment instruments, the volume of which does not vary up and down with the business cycle, is present. For our purposes, United States government securities fit the bill quite well. Finally, assume that commercial bankers are willing to accept these instruments in times of receding loan demand, primarily because the securities are high grade and easily marketable. Thus bankers could buy securities in complete confidence that, if it becomes necessary and/or desirable, they can liquidate them to pay off depositors in case of a run on the bank or to acquire reserves to make additional loans. The important point is that these securities, because of their high quality and easy marketability, serve as a good substitute for both loans and excess reserves, and this has contributed significantly to reducing the cyclical variability of the money supply.

Consider for example, a situation in which these securities are not present at all, in which the Federal Reserve authorities, responding to strong inflationary pressures in the latter stages of the expansion, have stabilized the volume of member bank reserves. Assume further that the bulk of commercial bankers are aware of this and that each feels that, in order to protect himself, he needs a larger amount of reserves. The outcome, of course, would be that as each scrambled about in order to acquire for himself a larger amount of the fixed volume of reserves, the money supply would be decreased. But, and this is the important point, so long as the commercial bankers feel that government securities are good substitutes for loans and reserves, the cyclical fluctuations in the money supply are reduced.

It is, of course, too optimistic to suggest that this "idealized case," as shown in Figure 21–4B, characterizes the American economy of the 1960's. But certainly a great deal of progress has been made in this direction. The change in demand deposits is now a function of the change in the *combined* total of loans and investments, not just loans themselves (as in Figure 21–4A). Further, since World War II, an inverse cyclical variation between the volume of bank loans and the volume of investment instruments owned by commercial banks can be observed. Thus as loans decline, the banks substitute investments for them, at least in large part.

There is still some cyclical variation in demand deposits and hence in the total money supply, but it has been vastly reduced in the last quarter-century. Some commercial bankers, for years to come no doubt, will continue to accumulate and hold some excess reserves in times of the contractionary phase of the cycle; but the great majority of bank managements—particularly of the larger banks—do not appear to feel compelled to attempt large accumulations of excess reserves once they prognosticate that the upper-turning point has been reached. In general, they are willing to increase their investments as their loans fall off, and insofar as this is the case, one very important contributory factor of the cyclical variation in demand deposits has been largely eliminated.

6. Moral Suasion

No discussion of monetary policy in the United States can be complete without some reference, even though brief, to "moral suasion."[31] Although there is considerable reference to moral suasion as a control device of sorts, a rigorous definition of the term is difficult to find. Perhaps the best way to think of it is simply as "talk" or "open-mouth" policy. It may take the form of scolding bankers, or even life insurance company officials, at a press conference by the chairman of the Board

---

[31]A non-award-winning Hollywood production of several years ago pictured an indiscrete senator whose campaign posters indicated that he was against inflation, against deflation, but most certainly in favor of "flation." While not denying that *suasion* might be a perfectly respectable word, in moments of scepticism we find it interesting that the Federal Reserve authorities have chosen this term instead of *persuasion* or *dissuasion*.

of Governors. On the other end of the hierarchy, moral suasion may take the form of bank examiners scolding commercial bank officers for extending repayments on automobile loans over "too long" a period of years. In any event, moral suasion can be effective only if it causes bankers or other parties in the economy to act differently than they would otherwise have behaved.

The burden of proof that moral suasion is effective would appear to rest with those who maintain that it *is* effective; after all, the Federal Reserve authorities work within the constraints set by the law. Thus the effectiveness of moral suasion depends to a great extent upon the breadth of administrative law and regulations or perhaps upon the degree of economic education of the public. But if moral suasion is to accomplish anything positive, it apparently must be accompanied by the threat of retaliatory action by the Federal Reserve—and once again, the Federal Reserve is limited by the statutory bases of their operations.

Actually, probably the only situation in which any significant results from moral suasion can be expected would be one in which there was the threat of withdrawing the discount and advance privilege from individual commercial banks. All in all, however, talk is probably much overrated as an instrument of monetary policy.

7. Summary

Although the attitude towards monetary policy has followed somewhat of a cyclical pattern, the major objective of the Federal Reserve today is to control the volume of member bank reserves. In doing this, they hope in turn to be able to control the money supply. Of all the control devices at its disposal, the Federal Reserve relies primarily upon open market operations, though sometimes these operations are *technical* rather than *policy-oriented*. All in all, it seems that the Federal Reserve has just about complete control over the volume of commercial bank reserves. This does not mean, on the other hand, that they have control over the money supply. The link between the volume of member bank reserves and the money supply is often loose and tenuous, as well as unpredictable. While irregular fluctuations in the money supply have been eliminated, we have not been able to eliminate completely the cyclical variations in it. Significant improvements, however, have been made in this direction.

QUESTIONS

21-1. Discuss the historical fortunes of monetary policy from the 1920's up to the present.

21-2. Discuss in detail why monetary policy was pushed to one side during the immediate postwar period.

21-3. "The immediate effect of any open market purchase operation is two-fold—it increases the money supply and it increases member bank reserves." Comment.

21-4. Why are open market operations used more frequently than the other controls available to the Federal Reserve authorities?

21-5. What is the so-called "reluctance effect," and how does it influence open market operations?

21-6. Explain how each "factor of increase" and each "factor of decrease" affects the reserve position of the commercial banking system and thus the money supply.

21-7. What is meant by "free reserves," and what role do they play in Federal Reserve policy making? Do you think that they should be given more or less attention?

21-8. "As of the 1960's, the liquidity-giving powers of the Fed appear to be effective enough to prevent another banking crisis." Explain.

21-9. How has the existence of a large number of government securities reduced cyclical fluctuations in the money supply?

21-10. Discuss the significance of "moral suasion" as a tool of monetary policy.

Bibliography

Carson, D., ed., *Banking and Monetary Studies.* Homewood, Illinois: Richard D. Irwin, Inc., 1963.

Eastburn, D. P., ed., *The Federal Reserve on Record: Readings on Current Issues from Statements by the Federal Reserve Authorities.* Philadelphia: Federal Reserve Bank of Philadelphia, 1965.

Money, Trade, and Economic Growth. New York: The Macmillan Company, 1951.

Monetary Policy and the Management of the Public Debt. 82d Cong., 2nd Sess., 1952, Part 1.

Ritter, L. S., ed., *Money and Economic Activity: Readings in Money and Banking*. Boston: Houghton Mifflin Company, 1961.

Roosa, R. V., *Federal Reserve Operations in the Money and Government Securities Markets*. New York: Federal Reserve Bank of New York, 1956.

Smith, W. L., "The Instruments of General Monetary Control," *The National Banking Review*, September 1963.

The Federal Reserve and the Treasury: Answers to Questions from the Commission on Money and Credit. Englewood Cliffs, New Jersey: Prentice-Hall, Inc., 1963.

22

Monetary Policy: Implementation, Potentiality, and Limitations

The discussion of the preceding chapter revolved around two important points: (1) that control over the quantity of money is the basic technical objective of monetary policy; and (2) that the American monetary authorities attempt to achieve this objective by controlling member bank reserves. But, as was also pointed out, sometimes the link between changes in member bank reserves and changes in the money supply is unpredictable and tenuous. Nevertheless, the Federal Reserve officials concentrate on control of the volume of member bank reserves in order to control changes in the money supply.

Some economists, however, prefer to take a broader view of the purposes and objectives of monetary policy,[1] arguing that policy should be

---

[1]See, for example, J. Tobin, "Towards Improving the Efficiency of the Monetary Mechanism," *Review of Economics and Statistics,* August 1960; C. R. Whittlesey, "Reserve Requirements and the Integration of Credit Policies," *Quarterly Journal*

broadened to include not simply control over the money supply, but also control of the total volume of liquid assets. They point out, and rightly so, that "near money" items (such as savings deposits, savings and loan shares, series E bonds, and so on) are very close substitutes so far as individuals are concerned. And they argue further that short-term, highly marketable, high quality debt instruments (such as United States Treasury Bills) are good substitutes for money so far as financial and nonfinancial insitutions and businesses are concerned. These economists therefore conclude that since changes in the quantities of the "near moneys" influence strongly and directly the public's demand for and use of money itself, monetary policy should be broadened enough to include control over these other highly liquid assets.

This broader definition of the objectives of monetary policy, however, would launch us immediately into a consideration of several rather complex issues that had best be postponed to later chapters. These issues would include not only such problems as what are the most appropriate "raw materials" for open market operations, but also such questions as the appropriate "mix" of debt items that make up the national debt, the most appropriate ways of regulating the financial intermediaries that issue near moneys, and the extent to which public policy should be used to encourage additional issues of private debt instruments versus private equity instruments. For the present these far more complicated issues and problems had best be put to one side. Thus, for purposes of this chapter, the narrow definition of the objective of monetary policy will be retained. The other issues will be introduced in the concluding chapters.

---

of Economics, August 1944; "Controversial Issues in Recent Monetary Policy: A Symposium," Review of Economics and Statistics, August 1960; J. G. Gurley and E. S. Shaw, "Financial Aspects of Economic Development," American Economic Review, September 1955, and "Financial Intermediaries and the Savings-Investment Process," Journal of Finance, May 1956; J. M. Culbertson, "Intermediaries and Monetary Theory: A Criticism of the Gurley-Shaw Theory," American Economic Review, March 1958; J. M. Guttentag, "Credit Availability, Interest Rates, and Monetary Policy," Southern Economic Journal, January 1960; P. A. Samuelson, "Reflections on Central Banking," National Banking Review, September 1963, and "Reflections on Monetary Policy," Review of Economics and Statistics, August 1960; R. V. Roosa, "The Revival of Monetary Policy," Review of Economics and Statistics, February 1951; R. V. Roosa, "Interest Rates and the Central Bank," and H. S. Ellis, "The Rediscovery of Money," both in Money, Trade, and Economic Growth (New York: The Macmillan Company, 1951); W. L. Smith, "Financial Intermediaries and Monetary Controls," Quarterly Journal of Economics, November 1959, and "On the Effectiveness of Monetary Policy," American Economic Review, September 1956; and especially D. S. Ahearn, Federal Reserve Policy Reappraised, 1951-1959 (New York: Columbia University Press, 1963), for an excellent review of recent views and controversy.

1.   Intermediate Effects of Monetary Policy

Any discussion of monetary policy must, of course, concentrate on the effects that changes in the stock of money will have on such important aggregate variables as the level of employment, the general price level, and the process of economic growth. Thus, in the following analysis we shall inquire into how changes in the money supply may be expected to bring about certain "intermediate" results and how these, in turn, affect directly or indirectly the basic aggregative variables mentioned above.

A.   The Effect of Changes in M on the Level of Interest Rates

A common theme in monetary thought for almost two centuries has been the relationship between changes in the money supply and changes in the level of interest rates. Two theoretical explanations of this relationship have been developed.

Recall first the liquidity preference approach (discussed in Chapter 11), and assume a liquidity preference function as shown in Figure 22–1A. So long as the liquidity preference function has a negative slope, and so long as the economy is not experiencing a "liquidity trap," an increase in the money supply will, *ceteris paribus,* result in a fall in the rate of interest. The analysis is based, as usual, on the assumption of *ceteris paribus;* but much, if not most, of what is observed in actual market transactions with respect to the "intermediate" effects is completely harmonious with this assumption.

On the other hand, there is the "loanable funds" theory of the interest rate (which was discussed in Chapter 6). This theory predicts a similar result—that is, that an increase in the supply of money will cause the interest rate to fall. So long as the demand curve for loanable funds is negatively sloped, then an increase in the money supply, represented by a shift of the supply curve of loanable funds to the right, will lower the rate of interest.

At this juncture the important thing to stress is that regardless of which theoretical approach is used, an increase in the quantity of money will result in an almost immediate reduction in the market rate of interest. This assumes, of course, that the relevant portion of the liquidity preference function is not perfectly interest elastic (that is, that there is no liquidity trap); and it assumes also, in the case of the loanable funds theory, that the relevant segment of the supply curve is also not perfectly elastic (as shown in Figure 22–1B).

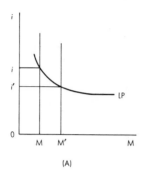 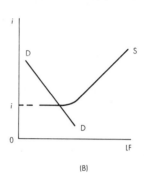

(A)   (B)

FIGURE 22—1

Although the change in the level of market rates of interest resulting from a change in the money supply may be almost immediate, the end results of the change—the effects it will in turn have on investment, saving, income, and employment—may take a longer time period to work out. This topic is discussed in more detail in sections 4-8.

B. Changes in the Shape of the Yield Curve

Monetary policy may do more than affect simply the level of interest rates; it may also be used to alter the structure of interest rates. This can best be shown by making use of a device called the "yield curve." The yield curve is merely a statistical picture that shows the relationship of different rates of interest to different lengths of maturities of debt instruments. Generally speaking, the shorter the maturity, the lower the rate of interest; and the longer the maturity, the higher the rate of interest. Two yield curves—each for a separate date—are shown in Figure 22–2.

Now assume that the Federal Reserve authorities, because of their interpretation of the prevailing domestic economic situation, do *not* wish any change in the volume of member bank reserves. But assume at the same time that the Federal Reserve desires, again because of its interpretation, to alter the structure of interest rates—that is, to change the shape of the yield curve.[2] In this particular case we assume that

---

[2]We discuss a special case of this in section 8.

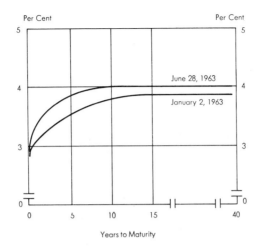

Source: Federal Reserve Bank of St. Louis *Review*, September 1963.

FIGURE 22–2

Yield on U. S. Government Securities

they want to reduce the long-term rates of interest and to raise the short-term rates. In order to accomplish this, and at the same time not change the volume of reserves and money supply, they will simultaneously sell a substantial amount of short-term securities and purchase an equal amount of long-term securities. This action would, *ceteris paribus*, tend to lower the price of short-term securities and raise the price of long-terms. Thus, although the volume of reserves and the money supply have remained unchanged, the short-term interest rates rise and the long-term rates decline.

On the other hand, it is conceivable that the Federal Reserve, again for reasons of its own, would want to rotate the yield curve in the opposite direction. That is, the monetary authorities may consider it desirable to raise the long-term rates and lower the short-term rates (or at least hold the short-term rates approximately constant). This is the situation depicted in Figure 22–2, in which the yield curve was rotated in a counterclockwise direction between the two dates.

The extent to which the yield curve would be rotated and the duration of time for which the new shape of the curve would hold depend upon many factors, and one of the most important of these is the maturity distribution of the Federal Reserve banks' portfolios of government securities. Nevertheless, the possibility of rotating the yield curve in in either direction can be considered as an "intermediate" effect of monetary policy.

C.   The Expectations Effect

Virtually every economist agrees that monetary actions on the part of the Federal Reserve—and particularly the obvious changes in monetary policy—have some bearing on the expectations of individuals and businesses in the economy. However, few agree on exactly what the "expectations effect" really is. Certainly it is there, but just as certainly it is elusive and multi-dimensional.[3] Nevertheless, there is general agreement that changes in monetary policy do result in an "expectational effect" and that at times this is quite important.

Let us consider a few possibilities. Assume, for instance, that the Federal Reserve has been pursuing a rather tight monetary policy, keeping *free* reserves at a negative balance. Then, perhaps because of fears that the upper-turning point is being approached, they reverse their policy and allow free reserves to move from a negative balance of, say, $500 million to a positive balance of $50 million. What will be the predominant reaction to this change in policy? How many firms, if any, will reason that the Federal Reserve has detected weak points in the economy and that the level of economic activity is going to decline in the near future? If a large number of firms interpret the Federal Reserve action in this manner, they may reduce their own plans for expansion and thus, by decreasing their volume of real economic investment, bring on a negative multiplier-accelerator interaction.

But on the other hand, there may be some firms who, within their own spheres of economic activity, are still optimistic and disregard the Federal Reserve action. And there may be still others, especially the security market specialists and financial investment portfolio managers, who think that this change in Federal Reserve policy is already resulting in a slight decline in interest rates and that before long interest rates will fall substantially as the Federal Reserve increases its purchases of government securities. Thus they may react by increasing their current purchases of long-term debt instruments before the Federal Reserve loosens monetary conditions further and bond prices rise considerably.

---

[3] For a good discussion of expectations, see W. L. Smith, "The Instruments of General Monetary Control," *National Banking Review*, September 1963, pp. 61-64. See also A. Lindbeck, *The "New" Theory of Credit Control in the United States* (Stockholm: Almqvist & Wiksell, 1959), pp. 25-29, 38-39.

These are just three examples of hypothetical, but likely, responses to a change in Federal Reserve policy. Obviously the "expectations effect" is quite complicated, and it is further complicated by the fact that the Federal Reserve seldom provides immediate or forthright explanations of its actions.[4] As a result, the "expectations effect" is difficult to evaluate.

Thus far three points have been established. First, a change in the money supply will cause an almost immediate change in the level of interest rates. Second, monetary policy can also be used to alter the structure of interest rates, that is, to change the shape of the yield curve. And finally, a change in monetary policy will almost certainly have an "expectations effect," but it is difficult to say precisely what this will be until the particular economic situation has been examined in considerable detail. The further impact that these "intermediate" results will have on the important variables of savings, investment, income, employment, and the price level are still to be examined. But first, some other important observations are in order.

2. The "Troublesomeness" of Interest Theory

Since much of the final effect of monetary policy, whatever it may be, must be realized through the results of changes in the interest rate, it may be relevant to consider for a moment the general status of interest theory in economics. In fact, this is all the more relevant since several economists have suggested that interest (and capital) theory is perhaps the most troublesome single part of economic theory.[5]

The beginning student in economics is introduced to the subject of interest in two different areas: (1) in distribution theory, where he learns something of marginal productivity, on the one hand, and time preference, on the other; and (2) in aggregative theory, where he learns something of both the loanable funds and the liquidity preference approaches, which he then learns can be reconciled.[6]

But somehow the inquiring student is never quite satisfied if his instructor advances the proposition that the long term tendency (like the

---

[4]An excellent case for requiring the Federal Reserve to be more explicit in explaining its policy changes has been made by C. R. Whittlesey, "Federal Reserve Policy: Disclosure and Nondisclosure," *National Banking Review*, September 1963.

[5]See the various references given in Chapter 11.

[6]See, for example, G. Haberler, *Prosperity and Depression* (Cambridge: Harvard University Press, 1958), pp. 183-87.

waves) is determined by a productivity-time preference interaction, while market rates of interest (like the ripples on the waves) are determined by liquidity preference or loanable funds variables. What the rank and file of professional economists have been unable to do in a satisfactory manner—that is, develop an adequate theoretical explanation that takes into account both the long-run and short-run determinants of interest rates—can hardly be done here. Suffice it to say, however, that interest rate theory in general is in a rather unsatisfactory state.

Unfortunately, the only condition under which all versions and dimensions of interest rate theory seem to be completely consistent is in the "never-never land" of equilibrium at full employment under conditions of perfect competition in all markets—product, factor, and money. Under these conditions, of course, there would be virtually no problems in the policy area, at least no problems of providing for full-employment levels of output at a stable price level. For under these conditions, presumably, the Pigou effect would be fully operable.[7]

But, as was emphasized before, policy must be administered in the real world, a world in which pure (let alone perfect) competition does not exist. It is a world in which cost-price inflexibilities, at least on the downward side, seem more prevalent than cost-price flexibilities; a world in which price administration, price leadership, and mixtures of giant firms, and small firms both on the buying and selling side of product markets, are becoming more common; a world of labor unions, big government, and to an increasing extent, big agriculture.[8] But it is, nevertheless, a world in which the policy maker is compelled to operate, and in which it is increasingly difficult to predict the effects of not only monetary policy actions, but all types of public policy actions. At the same time, however, it is a world in which these same policy actions are that much more imperative.

3. A Preview of the Remainder of the Chapter

The purpose of this chapter is to see how the intermediate effects of monetary policy can influence the important aggregative variables. Unless otherwise indicated, government is assumed to be both neutral and minimal in its economic actions—that is, fiscal policy is abstracted from. The procedure is to pass through the successive stages of a hypothetical business cycle, noting both the potentialities and limitations of

---

[7] Recall the discussion of the Pigou effect given in Chapter 15.

[8] Many of these points are elaborated on in the next chapter.

monetary policy during each of its major stages. Thus, monetary policy is considered with respect to each of the following situations: (1) the expansionary stage, in which the major concern is largely over decreasing the amount of unemployment and increasing the level of output; (2) the later part of the expansionary stage, during which the upper-turning point is being approached, and in which control of the price level becomes the major concern; (3) the upper-turning point itself; (4) the early stages of the contraction; and (5) the area at the lower-turning point.

Before turning to this stage-by-stage examination of monetary policy, however, a few initial observations are in order. First, let us dismiss (though with all due respect) the cynic who is ever ready to point out that any type of policy action requires predictions of the future course of economic activity and then reminds us that economics "as a science" is not sufficiently well developed to allow accurate predictions. This indictment is, of course, quite valid. Economics, as a science, is not at all that well developed. But as noted in Chapters 20 and 21, the money supply is a man-made device and as such must be managed by men. Thus far no "automatic device" has been invented that will manage the supply of money satisfactorily.[9] Thus, despite inadequacies in predictions of the future, there exists a man-made institution of extreme economic significance and importance that must somehow or other be managed—and this is in large part the task of monetary policy.

It is interesting to note that in this respect there is really little difference in monetary policy and fiscal policy; that is, both of them require predictions of future economic events. Yet while the antagonists of fiscal policy are quite vocal in their statement of this indictment when they criticize fiscal policy, they are remarkably silent about it when they advocate principal reliance on monetary policy. The biggest difference is that a small, organized group—that is, the Board of Governors, the Open Market Committee, and their respective staffs—have the responsibility for prediction with respect to monetary policy. Being a small, well-organized group utilizing a line-staff organization, it can "predict fast," regardless of the accuracy of its predictions. In the area of fiscal policy, on the other hand, prediction must be made by a cumbersome combination of the legislative and executive branches of the federal government, the very organization of which is designed, if anything, to necessitate slowness in making decisions, including economic predictions.

The only other difference is that the monetary policy makers, if they do make a mistake in prediction, can act rather quickly to reverse both

---

[9]We discuss one such proposal, however, in the next chapter.

the prediction and the policy based upon it. With these two exceptions, which are essentially organizational, the problem of diagnosis and prediction is no different under the heading of monetary policy than under the heading of any other version of public policy.

Once a prediction is made, the implementation of it through changes in the money supply can be quick and immediate, and the intermediate effects, such as a change in the level of interest rates or a rotation in the yield curve will normally be felt quickly also. The final outcome, however—that is, the effects on the levels of output, employment, and prices—sometimes may require a considerable amount of time.[10]

The following discussion assumes that there will be no changes in the existing institutional framework of the American economy. In fact, this is the same assumption that the monetary policy makers act upon. Perhaps this explains, at least in part, the popularity of monetary policy in conservative political circles and a preference for it over other types of public policy, especially fiscal policy. In other words, monetary policy basically involves making "one big decision" by which the size of the money supply is determined. Once this decision is made and the implementing action taken, the private market system takes over. The monetary policy makers—who are in effect themselves instrumentalities of the central government—thus have few commands or prohibitions to extend directly to individual members of the economy. Except for the charges of a few vocal congressmen, who do not seem to have developed much of a national following, the Federal Reserve authorities can, as it were, hide behind the skirts of several thousand loan officers in commercial banks and other financial institutions who are forced to say "no" to the applicants for new and/or larger loans.

Perhaps there is one other reason for the general acceptability, if not outright popularity, of monetary policy. It has been around for a long time. People are used to it, and they expect it.

4. Monetary Policy During the Expansionary Stage of the Cycle

Let us begin our discussion of monetary policy and its application by assuming that the lower-turning point has occurred and expansion

---

[10]See W. G. Dewald and H. G. Johnson, "An Objective Analysis of American Monetary Policy, 1952-61," Chapter 9 in *Banking and Monetary Studies*, ed. D. Carson (Homewood, Illinois: Richard D. Irwin, Inc., 1963); M. Friedman, "The Lag in Effect of Monetary Policy," *Journal of Political Economy*, October 1961, and the "Reply" by J. M. Culbertson in the same issue.

is now underway. However, even though economic conditions are improving, there are still substantial amounts of idle capacity and unemployment. Thus, even though investment activity is increasing, inflationary forces are at a minimum. Under these conditions the Federal Reserve may be expected to keep free reserves substantially positive and to be relatively unconcerned about any inflation resulting from future increases in the money supply. Further, the Federal Reserve would want to provide every encouragement to additional private investment activity by making financing and credit "easy"—that is, they would not want to restrict the availability of funds that could be used to finance additional investment activity. Finally, for what it is worth, they would presumably prefer a low interest rate structure.

Earlier discussion has revealed that it is debatable as to how interest elastic the investment demand schedule is in this (or any other) stage of the business cycle.[11] Few, however, would argue that the aggregate investment demand curve is *completely* interest inelastic. Thus, to the extent that the schedule shows some degree of interest elasticity, the Federal Reserve would not want to be judged guilty of allowing interest rates to rise rapidly enough to choke off any investment activity in the private sector, particularly in this stage of the cycle. For this reason, the Federal Reserve will follow the policy of keeping free reserves positive and allowing the money supply to rise. If they do not do this, there is every reason to believe that the level of interest rates would begin rising and would tend to stifle the expansion in its early stages.

However, as the expansion continues, pressures that are beyond the direct, and even indirect, control of the Federal Reserve begin to develop. In an economy in which bottlenecks are likely to exist, and in which most product and resource markets are imperfect, some upward pressures on the price level begin to occur long before full employment is reached. (Recall the discussion of the "Phillips curve" in Chapter 13.) In other words, the aggregate supply curve, expressed in monetary terms, begins to curve upward well ahead of the time that full employment is reached. At this point the Federal Reserve authorities, even though they may be still more interested in encouraging higher output and employment than in preventing any increases in the price level, will gradually feel constrained to "put on the brakes" as the upward movement in the price level becomes more obvious. Moreover, the decrease in unemployment makes it politically more feasible for the Federal Reserve to begin exacting tighter monetary conditions. This is a time when the traditional major monetary control devices would be

---

[11]See the discussion and references in Chapters 7 and 11.

exercised in the traditional way, and the Federal Reserve would tend to reduce the level of positive free reserves to zero.

Note that thus far in the expansionary stage, monetary policy has actually been permissive and not causal with respect to the recovery process. That is, some factors (either or both endogenous and exogenous) have caused the lower-turning point and started the expansionary process on its way. Of course, if monetary policy becomes too tight, it could choke off the recovery before it gathers full steam. But during most of this part of the expansionary stage inflationary pressures are no great problem, and there is thus no excuse for a tight monetary policy. All that the Federal Reserve can do under these circumstances is to provide generally easy money market conditions that facilitate the increasing employment, income, and output. However, as the expansion continues, inflationary pressures develop, and these entice the Federal Reserve to tighten up gradually on monetary conditions.

5.   The Approach to the Upper-Turning Point

In the latter stages of the expansion, but before the Federal Reserve authorities feel that the upper-turning point is imminent, the objective of price-level stability tends to become much more important. And in order to accomplish the goal of price-level stability, the Federal Reserve authorities will tend to stabilize the money supply. This policy action occurs at a time when employment and output levels are high, though unemployment may not have been reduced to "acceptable" levels. As a hypothetical example, take 97 per cent employment of the labor force as the "accepted" goal of full employment. Even if unemployment may actually be running at the rate of 5 to 6 per cent of the labor force, the Federal Reserve may begin acting to stabilize the volume of money.

In this sort of situation, which appears to have characterized the American economy in the post-World War II period, the pressures of "creeping inflation" are apt to be forceful and real. Moreover, it is the sort of situation in which the two objectives of continuing full employment and reasonable price-level stability do not seem to be harmonious.[12] In other words, the Federal Reserve begins to combat the inflation before "full employment" is reached, but the dilemma confronting the Federal Reserve is both real and important. It bears repeating: ac-

---

[12]See the references in Chapter 20. For an excellent review of the postwar period, see B. G. Hickman, *Growth and Stability of the Postwar Economy* (Washington, D. C.: The Brookings Institution, 1960).

cording to many observers of the contemporary scene in the American economy, this has been the sort of situation that typifies our economic performance since around the early part of 1951. Moreover, it is in this type of economic climate that the controversy over the efficacy of monetary policy seems to thrive.

A. The "Bothersomeness" of Velocity

Recall, from the discussion of the preceding chapter, that the monetary authorities have in recent years developed far better control over cyclical variations in the money supply. However, as better control over the money supply has been developed and maintained, the velocity of circulation has developed more cyclical variation.[13] In fact, in the last two decades cyclical variation in velocity has been more intense than cyclical variation in the volume of money. This, of course, creates problems for the Federal Reserve, for while the authorities can virtually stabilize the volume of money in the latter part of the expansion, they have no direct control over velocity. Thus, even though the supply of money is stabilized (that is, only minimal, if any, increases are allowed), the Federal Reserve officials know full well that, at this stage of the business cycle, velocity will rise, offsetting, at least in part, the stabilization of the money supply.

But why will velocity rise at this stage of the business cycle, even though the volume of money has been stabilized by the authorities? The three motivations for the demand for money—the transactions, precautionary, and speculative motives—were discussed in Chapter 11. Recall that the demand for money for transactions balances (L_t) and the demand for money for precautionary balances (L_p) are primarily a function of the level of income—that is, $L_t + L_p = f(Y)$. For present purposes the two notations $(L_t + L_p)$ are combined into one, L_1, and thus the demand for transactions and precautionary balances may be restated as $L_1 = f(Y)$. Recall also from Chapter 11 that the demand for money for speculative purposes was written as $L_s = f(i)$. This is now rewritten as $L_2 = f(i)$. Thus the expression $M = L_1(Y) + L_2(i)$ states the equilibrium condition for cash balances and the supply of money.

There is, however, on both theoretical and empirical grounds, sub-

---

[13]For a good review of the discussion revolving around the postwar "bothersomeness" of velocity, see Ahearn, *Federal Reserve Policy Reappraised, 1951-1959,* Chapter XI. For a discussion of the recent rise in velocity, see R. T. Selden, *The Postwar Rise in the Velocity of Money: A Sectoral Analysis* (New York: National Bureau of Economic Research, Occasional Paper 78, 1962).

stantial reason to question the presumption that the demand for transactions and precautionary balances is simply a function of the level of
income alone.[14] According to some recent studies, it appears sounder to
say that the demand for L_1 balances is a function of both the level of
income and the level of interest rates. That is, $L_1 = f(Y, i)$, and the
total expression becomes $M = L_1(Y,i) + L_2(i)$. The importance of this
is that the combined liquidity preference function (L_1+L_2) is perfectly interest elastic.

In the later stages of the expansion, recall, the Federal Reserve stabilizes the money supply (M), and in doing so, of course, it causes interest rates to rise. At the same time, there are many investment projects
that hold out the promise of a high marginal efficiency of investment.
But, and this is an important point, the policy actions of the Federal Reserve have restricted the creation of new funds to finance these investment projects. Thus, there are additional pressures on the level of interest rates as the business community seeks out funds that are already in
existence. In other words, interest rates rise in order to attract funds
from the community's L_1 balances to finance investment projects. At the
higher rates of interest, those individuals and businesses who would
have simply held their L_1 balances now find means of "economizing" on
their transactions and precautionary balances in order to lend some of
them out at the higher interest rates. What would have been "idle" balances now become "activated," and this is simply an increase in velocity
(with M constant). In this way, then, velocity rises just as the Federal
Reserve authorities stabilize the money supply in the latter stages of
the expansion, and of course the rise in V counteracts the stabilization
of M.

While this condition might be somewhat disturbing to those who
prefer to view policy in terms of the rather mechanical application of
simplified models, it has certain advantages in the real world in which
we live. With varying degrees of imperfections in all types of markets
(product, resource, and money), there would certainly be a multitude
of shocks throughout the economy if M is stabilized rather abruptly
and V is perfectly inflexible. On the other hand, if V rises as M is stabilized, it then serves somewhat as a "shock absorber" for the effects of
the tight money policy. As one economist has put it:

> . . . one of the main criticisms directed against orthodox anti-inflationary
> monetary policy has been that it is a very dangerous tool which cannot

---

[14]See the essays by W. J. Baumol, "The Transactions Demand for Cash: An Inventory Theoretic Approach," *Quarterly Journal of Economics*, November 1952;
and J. Tobin, "The Interest-Elasticity of Transactions Demand for Cash," *Review
of Economics and Statistics*, August 1956.

be used in moderation—that if effective at all, it is likely to be too drastically effective, precipitating an economic collapse through a shattering of confidence in the money and capital markets. Changes in velocity, however, provide the needed safety valve, tempering and graduating the impact of monetary policy and thereby enabling the central bank to apply more restraint than it might otherwise risk. The role of velocity is thus similar to that of the discount window during a period of limited reserve availability; they both moderate the buildup of undue tightness, and the crises that might otherwise ensue, by distributing pressures and providing outlets through which strains on the payments mechanism can be partially alleviated at the initiative of the market itself.[15]

In this respect then, the rise in velocity when the money supply is stabilized might provide very beneficial results.

B.   Can M Be Decreased?

As the expansionary stage continues, the Federal Reserve first slows up "permissible" increases in the money supply and then virtually stabilizes M as the price level continues to rise, even though full employment may not yet have been reached.[16] Presumably price-level stability becomes the dominant goal in the policy program of the Federal Reserve. But, as was pointed out in the preceding discussion, at this stage of the cycle, velocity will rise, "offsetting" to some extent the effects of a stabilization of M. Thus, the following question may be posed: If the Federal Reserve desires to stabilize the price level, and if it knows that velocity will increase, why do they not decrease the volume of money, rather than simply holding it constant? In this way, the Federal Reserve could control the total amount of spending, that is, MV.

In dealing with this question it is necessary to make an important observation. There is an important difference between (a) banks and other financial institutions not making new loans and refusing larger

---

[15]L. S. Ritter, "Income Velocity and Anti-Inflationary Monetary Policy," *American Economic Review*, March 1959, p. 127, reprinted as Selection 48 in *Money and Economic Activity: Readings in Money and Banking*, ed. L. S. Ritter (Boston: Houghton Mifflin Company, 1961). Some critics have gone so far as to assert that rises in velocity when the Federal Reserve institutes a tight money policy have virtually eliminated the effectiveness of monetary policy. See, for example, H. P. Minsky, "Central Banking and Money Market Changes," *Quarterly Journal of Economics*, May 1957. See Ahearn, *Federal Reserve Policy Reappraised, 1951-1959,* for a careful evaluation of the various views.

[16]There is still the possibility, of course, of the Federal Reserve's permitting some small increases in the money supply that are more or less associated with the initial operation of new plant and equipment that has been under construction in the preceding months.

loans to old customers, and (b) the same institutions actually reducing the amount of loans permitted to individuals and businesses. In the former case (a), further expansion of business activity financed by bank and nonbank loans is, to be sure, constrained and limited. But note that this policy does not entail a reduction in the level of employment of real resources. The other case (b), however, involves a reduction in the level of employment of real resources when commercial banks and other financial intermediaries are forced to reduce the availability of their financial resources. Even though V may rise enough to offset the decline in M, there is no reason to believe that enough resource mobility exists to prevent a decline in aggregate employment. Thus, rather than force a decline in the level of employment of resources upon the economy, the Federal Reserve will tend to avoid reducing the money supply.

But again there is the problem of velocity. Under the tight money conditions imposed by the Federal Reserve, may not commercial banks as a whole simply sell investment securities in order to acquire the reserves necessary to increase their loans to businesses? If they were able to do this, the commercial banks would be in a position to avoid the stringencies imposed upon them by the monetary authorities. Of course, they may do exactly this in order to raise the level of their loans.

Note, however, that these investment securities must be sold to non-banking institutions or to individuals, and in either case the funds used to purchase the securities from the commercial banks would have to come from "idle" balances. In other words, no new funds are made available to finance increased business activity; rather, existing funds are used more actively. This, of course, is simply a rise in velocity that once again tends to soften the impact of the tight monetary policy of the Federal Reserve.

All this discussion of a rise in velocity's offsetting or nullifying the Federal Reserve's policy of stabilizing the money supply, however, overlooks one important point with respect to the behavior of commercial bank managers. For a variety of reasons, as of the 1960's, bank managements on the whole desire to hold a certain minimum amount of investment securities, including short-term government securities.[17] In recent tight money markets it seems that commercial banks have just about reached the limit of what they feel is the desirable distribution between cash, loans, and investments in their portfolios. Thus although there may be, on the part of bank managements, a gradual exchange of

---

[17]See Ritter, "Income Velocity and Anti-Inflation Monetary Policy," p. 128, and Ahearn, *Federal Reserve Policy Reappraised, 1951-1959*, pp. 294-96.

investment securities for loans as the expansion continues, in the latter months of the expansionary stage they consider themselves to be pretty well "loaned up." That is, they could conceivably continue to sell investment securities in order to acquire additional reserves, but they feel that they have about reached the limit of investment securities that they are willing to sell. This limit is, of course, set by convention and managerial decisions, and thus it is not rigid and inflexible over the long run. But insofar as it is effective in the short run, it reduces the motivation of commercial bank managers to exchange investment securities for additional reserves which, in turn, would come from private savings. This therefore means that there is some upper limit to the rises in velocity that offset the Federal Reserve's policy of stabilizing the money supply.[18]

One final important generalization appears to be in order. If perfect or pure competition existed in all types of markets, then a decrease in the money supply could be expected to reduce the price level at this stage of the business cycle; and this could be done without a significant or lasting decrease in output. In other words, the Pigou effect would be fully operable, and the downward wage-price adjustments would take place quickly. But as was indicated earlier, there is a good deal of cost-price inflexibility in the economy, and therefore a reduction in the money supply means that there would be a decrease in output and employment rather than in wage-price levels. To be sure, if enough people could or did go without employment and food for a long enough time, the wage-price level would eventually fall. The basic question is not whether the wage-price level adjustment would take place; rather it is *how long* it would take for the adjustment to occur.

C.   Effects of a Stabilized Money Supply

The discussion thus far has established that the Federal Reserve authorities will attempt to stabilize the money supply as the upper-turning point is neared, and that though velocity will rise as a partial offset to this policy of restraint, there are upper limits to increases in velocity. Moreover, interest rates rise as free reserves become negative and as velocity increases. Let us now consider some of the effects of this policy.

Once again the important question arises—what effect will the in-

---

[18]Ahearn, *Federal Reserve Policy Reappraised, 1951-1959*, concludes that perhaps velocity is approaching an asymptote, and that certainly velocity has become less sensitive to changes in interest rate. This latter trend, he concludes, ". . . suggests an increased effectiveness of monetary policy in the future" (p. 296).

crease in interest rates have on investment activity? Obviously, the interest elasticity of the investment demand curve is significant here. The prevailing opinion, as noted earlier, seems to be that the investment demand curve is very interest inelastic over the relevant range. If this is the case, then the rise in the interest rate will not choke off very much investment. At the same time, so long as income continues to rise, the expectations of business firms (especially those responsible for making investment decisions) may also be high and rising, thus shifting the investment demand curve to the right. Therefore, even though interest rates may rise as a result of Federal Reserve action, the current rate of investment activity may not decline. In other words, Federal Reserve action does not seem to be very effective under these circumstances.

There is one view in Federal Reserve circles, however, that considers the preceding discussion of the impact of changing interest rates on investment as largely irrelevant and beside the point. This view—which is a part of the so-called *"availability thesis"*—holds that under conditions of a constant or nearly constant money supply, the price rationing that results from changing interest rates is largely superseded by a kind of *physical* rationing of credit by the commercial banks and other financial institutions.[19] According to the availability thesis, interest rates rise because credit is physically rationed by the commercial banks, and it is this lack of credit, not the rising interest rates, that is important. The impact of monetary policy, in short, is on the supply side of the loanable funds market, not on the demand side. Thus the degree of interest elasticity of the investment demand curve matters little, for it is the declining *availability* of credit that is important.[20]

However, even if the availability doctrine is valid, there are still fur-

---

[19]See the references to Roosa and Ellis in footnote 1, as well as J. H. Williams, "The Implications of Fiscal Policy for Monetary Policy and the Banking System," *American Economic Review*, March 1942. For a critical evaluation of the "availability doctrine," see Lindbeck, *The "New" Theory of Credit Control in the United States*, and especially Ahearn, *Federal Reserve Policy Reappraised, 1951-1959*.

[20]One aspect of the availability thesis that seems to have received an exaggerated amount of attention concerns whether commercial banks are willing to sell government securities at a loss in order to acquire additional funds to make loans. This is the so-called "locking-in effect," which concludes that asset holders (including commercial banks) will prefer to hold on to assets when prices are falling rather than sell and take a book loss. For a discussion of the "locking-in effect," see C. R. Whittlesey, "Monetary Policy and Economic Change," *Review of Economics and Statistics*, February 1957; W. L. Smith, "On the Effectiveness of Monetary Policy," *American Economic Review*, September 1956; H. S. Ellis, "Limitations of Monetary Policy," Chapter 6 in *United States Monetary Policy*, ed. N. H. Jacoby (New York: Columbia University Press, American Assembly, 1958), pp. 151-54; and Lindbeck, *The "New" Theory of Credit Control in the United States*, pp. 22-25.

ther doubts as to the effectiveness of monetary policy at this point in the cycle. Consider once again the imperfect markets theme. Under conditions of rising money income, large firms appear to have every incentive to raise prices, and organized labor has every incentive to press for higher money wages. Under these conditions a wage-price spiral may very easily set in, with administered prices and wages pushing and pulling each other up farther and farther.

Now if this sort of inflationary pressure is experienced before full employment has been reached, the monetary authorities appear to be in a predicament. If they allow continued increases in the money supply in order to eliminate the unemployment, the inflationary pressures will continue, and both money wages and prices will continue to creep up. On the other hand, a very restrictive monetary policy—one in which the money supply would actually be decreased—would hold the price level in check, but output and employment would probably decline. Even if the Federal Reserve follows the policy of maintaining the money supply at some constant level, "creeping inflation" would continue. It is in this sense that the Federal Reserve finds itself in a real dilemma. (The significance of administered wages and prices in the inflationary process are examined in more detail in the next chapter.)

In summary then, whatever the reasons, experience with monetary policy in periods of credit restriction (at least since the statement of "Accord" in 1951), suggests that even when monetary policy was tight enough to "bite," inflationary pressures have continued and the price level has continued to rise. The strong advocates of monetary policy have suggested that this has resulted from the unwillingness of the monetary authorities to pursue a really tight monetary policy. On the other hand, some economists have suggested that, on balance, monetary policy has been quite effective as an anti-inflationary weapon, and that there has actually been too much concern over the relatively "mild" inflation experienced since 1951. One definite conclusion that can be reached is that we have not, since 1951, been able to achieve successfully high levels of output and employment along with stable price levels, even toward the upper-turning point of the business cycle.

D. The "Discriminatory" Effects of a Tight Monetary Policy

Another area of controversy surrounding the use of a tight monetary policy as an anti-inflationary device concerns the "discriminatory effects" of the policy. Many of the points in this controversy are difficult to evaluate, not only because of the purely economic matters involved, but also because they involve difficult matters of equity.[21]

In the first place, monetary policy is obviously discriminatory. In fact, if it is to be effective at all it must be discriminatory against some persons or firms who apply for loans but either cannot receive them or have to take a smaller amount than desired. The basic question then is not whether monetary policy is discriminatory, but whether its discriminatory effects make a functional contribution to certain economic goals.

One dominant, though intuitive, opinion is that probably a tight monetary policy is unduly discriminatory against smaller firms, for the larger firms are less concerned about the cost impact of rising interest rates.[22] Indeed they rely heavily on their own internal sources of financial funds, and though the interest cost (as an opportunity cost) might be rising for them, they still have access to these internal sources. Further, the larger firms have better access in general to the money markets than do the smaller firms. Small firms, on the other hand, must perforce turn to the commercial banks as a major source of financial funds, and thus they bear directly the brunt of higher interest costs and the declining availability of funds.[23]

On balance, the studies conducted by the Federal Reserve itself on this topic are (as might be expected) somewhat inconclusive. The most ambitious empirical study that has been made concludes that within the commercial banking system, the small firm has not been unduly discriminated against during conditions of tight money.[24] Of course, in order to answer the question satisfactorily, the scope of the inquiry would have to be enlarged to include not only the commercial banking system, but also the entire capital market system; and thus far no definitive study of this sort has been conducted.

Most of the empirical and quasi-empirical studies of this problem

---

[21]See, for one point of view, J. K. Galbraith, "Market Structure and Stabilization Policy," *Review of Economics and Statistics,* May 1957. For the alternative point of view, see G. L. Bach and C. Huizenga, "The Differential Effects of Tight Money," *American Economic Review,* March 1961, and their replies to D. Carson (*American Economic Review,* December, 1961) and A. D. Tussing (*American Economic Review,* September 1963). The most recent and elaborate statement of the Bach-Huizenga position that a tight money policy results in few discriminatory effects, as between different sizes of business borrowers, is found in Bach, "How Discriminatory is Tight Money?" Chapter 14 in *Banking and Monetary Studies,* ed. Carson.

[22]See, for example, Galbraith, "Market Structure and Stabilization Policy."

[23]On this, see W. J. Baumol, *Business Behavior, Value, and Growth* (New York: The Macmillan Company, 1959), Chapter 3.

[24]See the references to the Bach-Huizenga study in footnote 21.

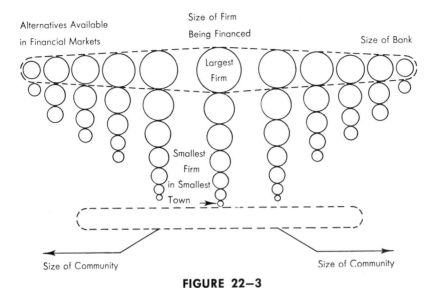

Alternatives Available
in Financial Markets

Size of Firm
Being Financed

Size of Bank

Largest
Firm

Smallest
Firm
in Smallest
Town

Size of Community

Size of Community

FIGURE 22–3

Illustration of Hypothetical Relationship between
Size of Business Firm, Size of Banks, and Range
of Alternatives in Financial Markets

have tended to center simply on the differential effects according to the size of the borrowing firm. Let us refer to Figure 22–3 as a basis for further discussion of the discrimination issue. This illustration is merely a means of putting into perspective a suggested relationship between the size of the borrowing firm, on the one hand, and the size of the banks with which it is likely to deal (as well as the number of financial alternatives available to it), on the other. At the top of the figure are the largest corporations, which tend to have their financial and corporate headquarters in the larger cities and thus have close contact with the larger commercial banks. These corporations also have the largest number of other financial arrangements available to them. Note that these alternatives include not only many different types of financial institutions, but also direct access to the security markets.

On the other hand, as suggested at the bottom of the figure, the smallest borrowing firm in the smallest community is, for all practical purposes, likely to have only one bank from which it can borrow. Moreover, it has only a few other financial alternatives available to it, being limited perhaps to the local "loan shark." In fact, in these smallest communities interest rates on loans experience very little fluctuation, no matter the degree of tightness or looseness in the money market. This of course suggests anything but a competitive market, at least so far as the small firms located in these communities are concerned.[25]

There are several possible situations other than the two extremes pictured in the illustration. For example, small firms, by virtue of being located in a larger community, may have access to a large number of banks of varying sizes, as well as a large number of financial alternatives. Nevertheless, as the size of the borrowing firm grows, its bargaining position with respect to any kind of financial institution improves, and therefore interest rates would be both lower and more competitive as a result of the economies of larger scale lending, perhaps lower financial risk, and more important, simply a greater degree of perfection in the capital markets. All these factors indicate that the burden of proof would appear to rest with those who maintain that tight money markets are not unduly discriminatory toward the smaller firm.[26]

E. Some Concluding Remarks

The experiences of the last decade suggest that, for a number of reasons, monetary policy by itself has been insufficient to control completely the upward movement of the price level, even in the face of less than full employment. The impasse between these two apparently conflicting goals of monetary policy will presumably continue until the upper-turning point sets in. However, the conclusion that monetary policy is not totally effective in reconciling these two goals does not mean it should be abandoned. Since money is a man-made device, it must be managed, and this in turn means that there must be some sort of monetary policy. The tentative conclusion at this point simply is that, given present American institutions and attitudes, monetary policy by itself is not sufficient to reconcile the strictly stated goals of price-level stability and continuing full employment.

6. The Upper-Turning Point

Let us now assume that the monetary authorities predict that the upper-turning point is about to be reached—that is, they have observed

---

[25]One is reminded of the local banker in Texas (or Georgia, or upstate New York) who had been in the banking business for fifty years and never knew that there was an interest rate other than 10 per cent.

[26]One is reminded of Keynes' statement to the effect that if you owe your banker $1,000 you are in his power, but if you owe him $1,000,000 he is in yours.

that some, but not all, of the traditional business cycle indicators have turned downward. What can be expected of monetary policy at this stage of the cycle?

One fundamental proposition may be suggested. If monetary policy is to be effective in postponing, or even ameliorating, the upper-turning point, the easing action on the part of the policy makers must be quick and decisive. Of course, a prerequisite of any easing policy is the decision by the Federal Reserve authorities that the upper-turning point is upon them. But recall the discussion in Chapter 4 in which it was pointed out that the upper-turning point is not really a point at all, but rather an "area" or "zone." And recall also the discussion in Chapter 2 that the so-called leading indicators give no clue as to the exact timing of the upper-turning point. Thus the Federal Reserve authorities face a difficult task in making this decision.

But why must monetary policy be quick and decisive if it is to be effective at this stage of the business cycle? Essentially, the Federal Reserve must act to ease monetary conditions and allow an increase in free reserves or member bank reserves while a buoyant loan demand on the part of the private business community still exists. Presumably the Federal Reserve, in the latter part of the expansionary stage, has limited the availability of funds to such an extent that there is, even at the high interest rates, some unsatisfied loan demand. So long as this is the case—that is, so long as the investment demand curve does not shift to the left—the increasing availability of funds would actually allow the financing of some additional investment activity.

But business expectations about the future are also sensitive to the behavior of some of the same leading indicators that the Federal Reserve authorities use. The investment demand curve thus cannot be expected to remain stable under these circumstances for any substantial period of time. Accordingly, if the existing, unsatisfied investment demand is to be unleashed, the reversal of Federal Reserve policy from tightness to ease must come quickly and decisively. Otherwise, general pessimism will set in, the investment demand curve will shift to the left, and the contraction will follow.

Commercial bankers have traditionally been expected to "pull in their horns" in anticipation of the upper-turning point. What is being suggested here, however, is that commercial bankers as a group will be willing actually to increase their loans, even though the Federal Reserve expects business activity to decline. This does not mean, of course, that any and every commercial bank loan officer will approve any and every loan. It does mean, however, that at the upper-turning point there are some loans which appear to be basically sound, but which were not made in prior months simply because of the lack of available funds. Although bank loan officers may well make some adjustment of credit standards, if they anticipate a significant decline in business activity, there is no reason why they should be unduly concerned about "pulling in their horns" (unless, of course, they anticipate a liquidity crisis).

Thus we return to an important point made in the preceding chapter—namely, the confidence of commercial bankers in the "liquidity giving powers of the Fed." Confidence in the basic liquidity of bank assets on the part of commercial bankers is a necessary condition in order for them to satisfy any remaining loan demand that exists at the upper-turning point of the business cycle when the Federal Reserve has reversed itself from a tight to a loose policy. Therefore, the confidence that commercial bankers have in the liquidity giving powers of the Federal Reserve is a vital prerequisite for any ameliorating effects that a loosening of monetary policy may have at the upper-turning point of the cycle.

A.   The Special Case of Residential Construction

At this point particular attention should be given to the unique case of residential construction financing. Virtually everyone is aware that most buyers of new homes require mortgage credit in order to negotiate successfully a real estate purchase. In recent years, however, downpayments have tended to decline percentage-wise, and the duration or length of years of the mortgage loan instrument has tended to increase. Thus interest payments make up a very sizable proportion of the total periodic loan payments of the typical home buyer. In other words, here is an area of economic activity in which the interest cost is a very substantial proportion of the total cost, and in this respect the domestic housing industry is almost unique among other major industries in the American economy.[27]

There are other important characteristics of this industry that merit discussion. In the post-accord period there has been ample capacity for increased residential construction, even at the upper-turning point of the cycle.[28] Also, a large percentage of actual construction is conducted by a large number of small independent builders scattered all over the country. These builders are traditionally under-financed and are, there-

---

[27]See any good textbook on industry studies and/or financial institutions for a discussion of this industry.

[28]See Hickman, *Growth and Stability of the Postwar Economy*, especially pp. 117-19, 358-59.

fore, responsive to changes in the availability of both construction loan funds and mortgage loan funds, at least as long as the demand for residential housing remains reasonably high. Finally, there are virtually two types of mortgage loan markets—the conventional market and the so-called "FHA market." In the FHA market the interest rate is administered, and it is a financial fact of life that mortgage rates in the conventional loan market fluctuate more intensively throughout the business cycle than the administered FHA rates. Moreover, conventional mortgage financing arrangements frequently bear higher interest rates, usually require higher downpayments, and typically carry a shorter total mortgage loan life than do FHA loans. Therefore, at virtually any stage of the business cycle the demand by householders for FHA financed construction is somewhat more buoyant than it is for conventionally financed construction.

Consider now some of the possible repercussions of a change in Federal Reserve policy at the upper-turning point, when monetary conditions become appreciably looser. As additional loans become potentially available in the loanable funds market, interest rates decline, and expectations may develop that rates will decline further in the future. Under these conditions, mortgage loan rates in general, and FHA rates in particular, begin to look relatively more attractive to those financial institutions engaged in a broad range of activities, including real estate financing. One reason for this is that market rates of interest, especially on outstanding corporate and government securities, begin to react very quickly to the change in monetary policy. On the other hand, mortgage loan rates in general, and FHA rates in particular, are somewhat stickier and react more slowly to changing monetary conditions. And we might note in passing that the typical house buyer is probably not nearly as interest rate conscious as is the financial institution's mortgage loan buyer, who is equipped with a sharp pencil and a yield table.

What is being suggested here is that, given all of the above circumstances and given the characteristics of the mortgage loan and residential construction markets, a change in Federal Reserve policy is apt to bring a surge of additional potential funds to the mortgage loan markets. Further, if national income has not fallen but is subject rather to a decreasing rate of increase, householder demand for new residential construction can be expected to hold up, despite the Federal Reserve's presumed prediction of the upper-turning point in the business cycle. Thus the additional availability of mortgage loan funds, particularly via the FHA route, will result in a clearing up of inventories of new but previously unsold construction owned by the small builders. Also the small builder, under these circumstances, is very likely to be able to secure from the financial institutions (or their agents) a forward commitment for mortgage loan financing of new construction that he is ready and willing to undertake. The forward commitment on permanent financing means that it is a relatively simple matter for the builder to secure in turn a temporary construction loan in order to make the actual residential construction possible.

The above chain of events can take place in a very short period of time—literally in a matter of days.[29] Thus, here is an area in which a change in Federal Reserve policy may very well result in a surge of new funds coming into a market to finance additional construction. It is therefore a case in which a change in Federal Reserve policy can result in an increase in residential construction activity which is, of course, a significant segment of *total* gross private domestic investment. (In one respect, this is really a description of one facet of the "availability thesis." If the above analysis is at all correct, it really means that here is an area in which market imperfections are a contributing factor to increases in income and employment when monetary policy is loosened.)

B.   The Significance of the "Bills Only" Doctrine

Toward the end of the 1950's, an apparently vital controversy existed both in and out of Federal Reserve circles over the proper "raw materials" for Federal Reserve open market operations.[30] Important and influential Federal Reserve officials, particularly in the Washington (or Board of Governors) group, maintained that the proper item for open market purchase and sale was the shortest term government security, namely United States Treasury Bills. There was, on the other hand, an articulate group, apparently a minority within the Federal Reserve, which maintained that there is no reason for the Open Market Committee to limit its open market operations to "bills only."

Philosophically, the rationale of the "bills only" doctrine apparently was that in controlling the volume of member bank reserves, and in turn the money supply, the operations of the Federal Reserve would be least disruptive to the private market system if purchases and sales were

---

[29]For a good illustration of this during the contraction of 1953-1954, see Hickman, *Growth and Stability of the Postwar Economy*, pp. 117-19.

[30]See Ahearn, *Federal Reserve Policy Reappraised, 1951-1959*, Chapters IV-VI, for a review of the debate; see also O. Eckstein and J. Karaken, "The 'Bills Only' Policy: A Summary of the Issues," Selection 36 in *Money and Economic Activity: Readings in Money and Banking*, ed. Ritter.

confined to an item on the liquidity scale that is the closest to money itself. (Note that if this attitude were carried to the extreme, there would be no open market operations at all, and regulation of the money supply would have to take place almost entirely through changes in the legally required reserve ratio.)

The purpose here is not to present the pros and cons of the "bills only" controversy. In one sense, the entire controversy was rather fictitious anyhow, since usually most of the Federal Reserve's operation would actually be in bills. It is appropriate to note, however, that the upper-turning point in the business cycle is one situation in which the "bills only" doctrine would appear to be a very unnecessary constraint on Federal Reserve action. If the objective of the Federal Reserve is to loosen fast once they have committed themselves to a change in policy towards ease, there would appear to be no valid reason for the Federal Reserve to confine its operations to the purchase of bills only and let the effect in turn diffuse over the yield curve from left to right. To the contrary, the change in the interest rate structure may be quicker and more dramatic if the Open Market Committee were to move out into intermediate-term maturities, and even into long-term maturities, as it makes its purchases. Further, under these conditions the expectations effect may well be stronger, better harnessed, and better controlled.

C. Some Concluding Remarks

Few people would suggest that monetary policy could ever eliminate the upper-turning point and push business activity on upward. But if a change in monetary policy is quick enough and decisive enough, there is reason for cautious optimism in the sense that it may soften the blows which traditionally have followed the upper-turning point. As will be seen in Chaper 24, monetary policy, especially in conjunction with the "automatic stabilizers," may "buy a little time" in which the more discretionary aspects of fiscal policy can be organized and applied.

7. Contraction

Once the upper-turning point has occurred and the contraction has set in, then of what use is monetary policy? If the contraction is simply a part of a minor cycle—one in which inventory adjustments seem to be causal—monetary ease may be helpful in that it can aid in financing inventory reaccumulation once the over-extension of inventories has been worked down. But even here monetary policy can be considered only as permissive and not causal in initiating a recovery or expansion.

If, on the other hand, the contraction is the result of a decline in private investment in plant and equipment, there are reasons to be even less optimistic over the effects of monetary policy. A policy of monetary ease, in conjunction with the decreasing demand for loanable funds, would of course be expected to bring about a significant decline in the level of interest rates. But at the same time the investment demand curve is falling, and thus few positive results can be expected to follow from the decreasing level of interest rates. Accordingly, with respect to the private sector of the economy, the Federal Reserve authorities, along with the general public, would simply have to wait for some increase in private investment activity.

In fact, if the decline is long enough and deep enough, so that a liquidity trap is finally reached, additional monetary ease and increases in the money supply would not even be effective in lowering the rate of interest any further. There is a bare possibility that in the liquidity trap area a further increase in bank reserves and the money supply *may* make some financial institutions more willing to lend. But if the rise in investment demand is not forthcoming from the private sector, little may be expected from monetary policy.

This is a situation which most observers consider to have characterized the Great Depression of the 1930's. And it was this situation which gave rise to such old barbs as "you can lead a horse to water but you can't make him drink" and "you can't push anything with a string." It was in fact this period that produced deep skepticism about the effectiveness of monetary policy in a severe contraction—a skepticism which still holds today.

8. A Note on the Domestic versus the International Implications of Monetary Policy

Thus far the analysis has been limited to an economy rich in resources and developed industrial capacity. Further, it has considered only the domestic aspects of monetary policy. But if the American economy were at a lower stage of development, or if it had to rely very heavily on international trade in order to provide for a higher level of development, then we would have to pay more attention to the international aspects of monetary policy.

Although in recent years the American economy has not had an import-export problem, it is considered to have had a so-called "balance of payments" problem.[31] The nature and significance of that problem will not be evaluated here, but a brief review of it will serve one important purpose—namely, to show that domestic monetary policy may at times be influenced by international financial, economic, and political events. Hence, in response to the "balance of payments" problem, the Federal Reserve authorities early in the 1960's attempted (either implicitly or overtly) to "rotate the yield curve in a clockwise direction."

The objective of this manipulation was ostensibly quite straight forward. If the left end (the short-term end) of the yield curve could be raised, this would presumably make short-term funds less likely to move from the New York money market to other leading money markets around the world where short-term rates were relatively higher. Thus raising the short end of the yield curve would, *ceteris paribus*, lessen the differential between New York money rates and money rates in other international financial centers. Presumably the lesser outflow of funds would, in turn, mean a reduction in the outflow of gold; and it was the outflow of gold that led to the objective of raising the short end of the yield curve.

At the same time, the level of private investment activity and gross national product within the United States itself was not considered to be at a satisfactory height. There was still unemployment of the magnitude of 5 to 7 per cent of the labor force. Hence, simultaneously with the attempt to raise the short end of the yield curve, the authorities attempted to lower the long end of the curve. The objective here was to lower the long-term rates of interest and stimulate net, new investment spending.

In short, the Federal Reserve authorities rotated the yield curve in a clockwise manner, raising the short end and lowering the long end. The basic mechanism by which the rotation was accomplished was essenti-

---

[31]In the latter part of the 1950's and early part of the 1960's, the American economy experienced a net gold outflow. As a result, in 1960 the Federal Reserve acted to stem the outflow, but in so doing it had to depart from the "bills only" policy. Finally in early 1961 the Federal Reserve made a public pronouncement on this matter:

> The System Open Market Account is purchasing in the open market U. S. Government notes and bonds of varying maturities, some of which will exceed five years. Authority for transactions in securities of longer maturity has been granted by the Open Market Committee of the Federal Reserve System in the light of conditions that have developed in the domestic economy and in the U. S. balance of payments with other countries.

Federal Reserve Bulletin, February 1961. See Ahearn, *Federal Reserve Policy Reappraised, 1951-1959,* pp. 109-11.

ally simple: a simultaneous set of open market operations was put into effect in which the Federal Reserve sold short term securities and purchased long terms. Note that if the amounts of the purchases and sales were identical, the volume of member bank reserves would be unchanged, and hence the total money supply would be unaffected.

We shall not attempt here a full evaluation of the action of rotating the yield curve. Suffice it to say that a modicum of success was probably achieved, though it is difficult to separate out the international and domestic factors at play in this particular situation. Note also that if the attempt to maintain a rotated yield curve is to be pursued for any substantial length of time, the cooperation of the Treasury in changing the "maturity mix" of the national debt would be required.

9.   Summary

In this chapter we have concentrated upon the Federal Reserve's traditional objective of controlling the volume of money by controlling the volume of member bank reserves. The major exception to this was the discussion in sections 1-B and 8, in which the impact of monetary policy upon the yield curve was considered.

The main conclusion is that traditional monetary policy, implemented by traditional means, is generally permissive rather than causative with respect to maintaining economic stability. The ability of monetary policy alone to maintain price-level stability under the inflationary pressures that emerge at the top of the cycle is open to serious question, especially in view of the cost-price rigidities and other institutions in the contemporary economy. At the upper-turning point, on the other hand, the Federal Reserve can reverse its earlier tight money policy quickly and decisively and thus ameliorate or soften the blows that follow the upper-turning point. And recall that this reversal of policy may lead to an increase in residential construction. Once the contraction is under way, there is little that the Federal Reserve can do to reverse it, though again they can adjust their policy to accommodate to the declining levels of business activity.

All in all, standing by itself, traditional monetary policy appears to be inadequate to accomplish the goals of economic stability. This does not mean, of course, that it is to be rejected. To the contrary, it has a definite role to play in achieving the twin goals of stability and growth, but only in conjunction with other types of public policy.

One final comment. A number of economists in recent years have suggested broadening the concepts and definitions of monetary policy, and this in turn means granting the Federal Reserve powers and methods that it does not now possess or use.[32] Regardless of what anyone may think of the merit of these individual proposals, or even what their authors may actually think of them, they all stem from a dissatisfaction with traditional monetary policy.

---

[32]See the several references cited in footnote 1.

QUESTIONS

22-1. Distinguish between the "direct" and "intermediate" effects of monetary policy.

22-2. Using the concept of the "yield curve," show the effects on the structure of interest rates when the Federal Reserve authorities raise the long-term rates of interest and lower the short-term rates. How can they accomplish this result?

22-3. Under what circumstances would you expect the Federal Reserve authorities to pursue the policy described in question 22–2?

22-4. Under what circumstances would you expect the monetary authorities to follow a course the opposite of that described in question 22–2?

22-5. Trace through what you expect that the Federal Reserve authorities will do during *each* stage of the business cycle. Be sure to differentiate between the early, middle, and late phases of each stage.

22-6. How is it that "velocity" creates problems for the monetary authorities? Give some historical evidence of the "bothersomeness" of velocity.

22-7. Discuss the unique position that residential construction can hold in monetary policy at the upper-turning point of the cycle.

22-8. What are your views on the discriminatory effects of monetary policy? Be sure to evaluate the various sides before you arrive at any conclusion.

Bibliography

Ahearn, B. S., *Federal Reserve Policy Reappraised, 1951-1959.* New York: Columbia University Press, 1963.

Anderson, C. J., *A Half-Century of Federal Reserve Policy Making, 1941-1964.* Philadelphia: Federal Reserve Bank of Philadelphia, 1965.

Carson, D., ed., *Banking and Monetary Studies.* Homewood, Ill.: Richard D. Irwin, Inc., 1963, Chapters 9-10, 13-14, 22-23.

Eastburn, D. P., ed., *The Federal Reserve on Record: Readings on Current Issues from Statements by Federal Reserve Officials.* Philadelphia: Federal Reserve Bank of Philadelphia, 1965.

Galbraith, J. K., "Market Structure and Stabilization Policy," *Review of Economics and Statistics,* May 1957.

Hickman, B. G., *Growth and Stability of the Postwar Economy.* Washington, D. C.: The Brookings Institution, 1960.

Jacoby, N. H., ed., *United States Monetary Policy.* New York: Columbia University Press, The American Assembly, 1958, Chapters 4, 6-7.

Lindbeck, A., *The "New" Theory of Credit Control in the United States.* Stockholm: Almqvist & Wiksell, 1959.

Ritter, L. S., ed., *Money and Economic Activity: Readings in Money and Banking.* Boston: Houghton Mifflin Company, 1961, Chapters 6-13.

Samuelson, P. A., "Reflections on Central Banking," *National Banking Review,* September 1963.

Smith, W. L., "The Instruments of General Monetary Control," *National Banking Review,* September 1963.

23

Long-Run Monetary Policy and Wage-Price Adjustments

If there are doubts and debate over the effectiveness of monetary policy's contributions to the goal of economic stability, there is even greater uncertainty with respect to the role it has to play in the process of economic growth. To be sure, the stock of money must rise proportionately to long-run increases in real output if there is to be reasonable long-run stability in the price level. But there have been some economists who argue that the price level should decline secularly,[1] just as there have been others who conclude that some secular inflation is an important stimulant to economic growth.[2] About all that can be done here, therefore, is to review some of the more important positions on long-run monetary policy. In doing this, however, some of the theories of "administered" wages and prices (as compared to "competitive" wages and prices) and thus some theories of "cost-push" and "administered-price" inflation will also have to be reviewed.

---

[1]H. G. Moulton, *Industrial Price Policies and Economic Progress,* (Washington, D. C.: The Brookings Institution, 1938); and E. G. Nourse, *Price Making in a Democracy* (Washington, D. C.: The Brookings Institution, 1944).

[2]See, for example, S. S. Slichter, "On the Side of Inflation," *Harvard Business Review,* September and October, 1957.

1.   Secular Increases in the Money Supply: Two Views

Recall (from Chapter 16) that an important corollary of continued, uninterrupted economic growth is relative stability of the price level. If, for example, significant inflation occurs, the full-employment, moving equilibrium is disturbed and cyclical repercussions follow. Similarly, a serious deflation will lead to the same result.[3] Thus, there must be relative price-level stability.

This condition of smooth growth may be stated in terms of the Quantity Equation:

$$M = kPO,$$

where M stands for the stock of money, P for some weighted index of output prices, O the current output of the economy, and k the fraction of income that the community desires to hold in the form of money.

Thus if P is to be held reasonably constant over time, M must rise proportionately with kO. Moreover, so long as there is economic growth (that is, O is rising), and so long as k is *relatively constant over time*, M must increase at the same rate at which output is rising. This approach, therefore, indicates the necessity of a monetary policy that permits a secular rise in the quantity of money. As Fellner puts it: "Continuous growth requires . . . that [aggregate] demand should be rising at the proper rate, provided that the supply of money is being increased at a rate which keeps the general price level reasonably stable. This is essentially a joint condition or double requirement."[4]

There are, however, conflicting views over how the stock of money is to be increased over the long run. First, there are those who contend that the secular increase in the money supply should be *irregular*, primarily because of the cyclical disturbances that accompany the growth process. In their view, the money supply should be increased during a contraction and reduced (or at least stabilized) during an inflationary expansion, though over the long run the supply of money is to rise. The major argument here is that reasonable price-level stability in the short run makes a positive contribution to long-run growth. This will be referred to as the *irregular-secular increase program*.

On the other hand, there are some economists who argue that the stock of money should be increased secularly at the same average annual rate of growth of output—say, 3 to 4 per cent per year—*regardless*

---

[3]See Chapter 16 for the analysis underlying these conclusions.

[4]W. J. Fellner, *Trends and Cycles in Economic Activity* (New York: Holt, Rinehart, & Winston, Inc., 1956), p. 182.

of what is happening in the short run. In other words, this school of thought argues that monetary policy should be geared solely to the long run and should not be used in the short run as a contracyclical weapon. This is referred to as the *steady-secular increase program.* Thus while both schools of thought call for a secular increase in the money supply, they differ significantly as to how this objective is to be achieved. Let us examine each of these programs in a bit more detail.

A.   Irregular Long-Run Increases in the Money Supply

So far as the irregular-secular increase program is concerned, little needs to be added to the discussion of the two preceding chapters. The advocates of this approach contend that traditional monetary pol- icy alone usually is sufficient in controlling the cycle, although in a severe contraction fiscal policy may also be necessary.[5] But there are certain complicating factors that need to be considered.

Monetary and fiscal policy employed in the United States have cre- ated large amounts of liquid assets held by commercial banks, other financial intermediaries, nonfinancial corporations, and individuals. These assets take the form of near moneys. Now once the lower-turning point occurs and the expansion gets underway, there is a tendency for cash balances to be spent and for near moneys to be converted into cash balances that also can be spent. Thus as the expansion continues and inflationary pressures build up, some restrictive monetary policies will usually be put into effect. The logical, traditional procedures of the Federal Reserve are to stabilize the volume of member bank re- serves and hence the money supply by engaging in open market sales and raising the discount rate.

However, so long as there is a large national debt, the effectiveness of the Federal Reserve's policy is somewhat reduced. The open market sales, if carried far enough, could depress the prices of government securities much below par, and this in turn could seriously interfere with the Treasury's "refinancing" operations.[6] This possibility arises primarily from the psychology of the securities market or, perhaps better, from the Federal Reserve and Treasury's interpretations of the psychology of the securities market. If security prices are allowed to fluctuate wildly, financial investors are apt to become discouraged and

---

[5]*Ibid.,* pp. 369-70.

[6] See Chapter 25 for a fuller discussion of Treasury refunding operations.

refuse to purchase the new government securities that the Treasury offers to refinance maturing obligations. Under these circumstances, the Federal Reserve may not use its open market operations as fully as necessary to control the inflationary forces. That is, at some price they will stop selling, and perhaps even begin to buy, in order to support the prices of government securities. Thus:

> . . . given a large public debt, central banks and treasuries may be expected to follow a line of compromise in meeting periodic inflationary pressures. The unloading of government securities on the central bank will not be made literally impossible in all circumstances. Instead, the central bank is likely to start supporting the market only if and when bond prices have fallen to some "abnormally" low level.[7]

This behavior by the Federal Reserve, however, helps to set the stage for some secular inflation.

Recall from the preceding chapter[8] that the Federal Reserve is not likely to exercise its powers fully in the latter stage of the expansion. Rather the monetary authorities elect to pursue a mildly anti-inflationary policy than run the risk of correcting the inflation by bringing on a major contraction. This predilection of the Federal Reserve, along with its tendency to support government security prices before the inflation is completely controlled, certainly implies that there will be some secular upward drift in the price level. However, as long as the secular inflation is "mild enough," it need not interfere with the growth process.[9]

The irregular-secular increase thesis thus concludes that there must be a secular increase in the quantity of money as growth proceeds. This is essential. At the same time the increase is to take place irregularly as the money supply is adjusted in the short run to changing cyclical conditions. Nevertheless, because of certain psychological and institutional arrangements, there is a strong likelihood that the stock of money will rise faster than output, and therefore some secular inflation is in store for the future. But as long as the rise in the price levels remains within the "limits of tolerance," growth will continue without major disturbance (provided, of course, that the other necessary conditions are met), although it is virtually impossible to designate precisely what these "limits of tolerance" actually are.

---

[7]Fellner, *Trends and Cycles in Economic Activity*, p. 371.

[8]Especially sections 4-5.

[9]Fellner, *Trends and Cycles in Economic Activity*, pp. 168-71.

B.   Automatic Increases in the Money Supply

The *steady-secular increase theorists,* on the other hand, are opposed
to the monetary authorities' carrying out anticyclical monetary policies
in the short run. As one advocate of this thesis has put it:

> . . . there would be an improvement in its performance if the monetary
> system were put on automatic pilot. This suggestion is not a new one.
> The Reserve Board had to contend thirty years ago with proposals for
> automatized monetary control and turned them down in favor of "judg-
> ment in matters of credit administration."

What instructions are to be fed into an automatic monetary pilot?
From the long list of alternatives that have been proposed in the history
of monetary thought, one of the simplest appears most feasible. It is
that, year in and year out, the nominal supply of money should be increased by the *average* rate of growth of demand for money at a stable
level of commodity prices. According to usual estimates, which should
be refined, the appropriate annual growth rate would be on the order of
3-4 per cent.[10]

The *modus operandi* of this program calls for some significant re-
forms in the monetary and banking system. For one thing, the advocates of this proposal contend that the Federal Reserve authorities have
not acted very wisely and judiciously in the past, often putting into
effect the wrong policies, or perhaps the right policies at the wrong
time. And they see no reason why the Federal Reserve will necessarily
improve in this respect. Indeed, one of the major themes of this school
of monetary policy is that "discretionary" policy decisions and actions
should be eliminated and replaced by "rules" to which the monetary
authorities must adhere. The major emphasis is upon "automaticity" in
contrast to "discretion" in monetary policy.[11] As Friedman has put it:

> Relying so largely on the discretion of authorities in so important an
> area of policy is highly objectionable on political grounds in a free soci-
> ety. Experience has demonstrated that it has also had unfortunate mone-
> tary consequences. It has meant continual and unpredictable shifts in the
> immediate guides to policy and in the content of policy as the persons
> and attitudes dominating the authorities have changed. . . . It has meant

---

[10]E. S. Shaw, "Money Supply and Stable Economic Growth," Chapter 2 in
United States Monetary Policy, ed. N. H. Jacoby (New York: Columbia University
Press, The American Assembly, 1958), pp. 59-60.

[11]The controversy over "rules" versus "authority" in monetary policy stems back
at least to H. C. Simons, "Rules versus Authority in Monetary Policy," *Journal of
Political Economy,* February 1936, reprinted as Chapter VII in his *Economic
Policy for a Free Society* (Chicago: University of Chicago Press, 1948). See also
L. W. Mints, *Monetary Policy for a Competitive Society* (New York: McGraw-Hill
Book Company, 1957).

continual exposure of the authorities to political and economic pressures and to the deceptive effects of short-lived tides of events and opinions. This is the justification for their alleged "independence." Yet the vagueness of their responsibilities and the wide range of their discretion has left them no other means than "wisdom" and personal perspective of withstanding contemporaneous pressures and has denied them the bulwark that clearly assigned responsibilities and definite rules would have provided. Reliance on discretion in pursuing general goals has meant also the absence of any satisfactory criteria for judging performance.[12]

Thus, in order to eliminate the discretionary area of monetary policy action, this school of thought recommends that the monetary officials act according to some rule—in this case, a steady increase in the money supply of 3 to 4 per cent per year, *regardless of what is happening in the economy in any particular year*. These economists are quite emphatic on this last point, and E. S. Shaw has stated their position quite forcefully:

> Some may ask: In a serious economic recession, should not the monetary authorities be required to augment the money supply even *more* than this rule would call for? The answer is "no." When the *nominal* supply of money is growing at a stable rate, a serious recession would itself generate a very large increase in *real* money. If the door is opened even slightly to discretionary monetary management, there is no point at which it can be closed.[13]

We shall, of course, have to return to this point later on.

The *modus operandi* of this monetary program calls for still other changes and proposals. One of these deals with the 100 per cent reserve system, in which commercial banks would be required to operate with 100 per cent reserves behind their time and demand deposits. The major purpose of this proposal is obviously to remove from the commercial banking system any control it has over the money supply. One hundred per cent reserves, of course, eliminates the "lending function" of the commercial banks, leaving them to serve only as "depositories" for the cash balances of the community. The required 100 per cent reserves may be held in the form of government securities, giving the commercial banks an interest income; and the banks will continue to receive income from the service charges they levy on their customers. Further, the 100 per cent reserve system does not completely preclude commercial banks from lending, for they can still make loans from

---

[12]M. Friedman, *A Program for Monetary Stability* (New York: Fordham University Press, 1960), p. 85.

[13]Shaw, "Money Supply and Stable Economic Growth," p. 62.

their capital surplus. However, this proposal, if put into effect, would virtually eliminate commercial bank influence on the money supply.[14]

The steady-secular increase theorists also recommend that debt management be taken away from the Treasury and placed in the hands of the Federal Reserve. This would achieve the objective of concentrating debt management and monetary policy in one single agency and thus reduce the likelihood of two separate agencies working at cross-purposes. Further, discount rate policy is to be discontinued, as is the gold reserve requirement. Finally, the Federal Reserve is to be given the power to issue its own securities, since the task of debt management is to be transferred to it.[15]

How is the program to operate, once all of these changes have been made? First, the Federal Reserve is to be instructed to increase the money supply at the rate of 4 per cent per year. The Federal Reserve could voluntarily adopt this rule, or, alternatively, Congress could instruct the Federal Reserve to follow it. The figure of 4 per cent per year is selected because ". . . on the average it would be expected to correspond with a roughly stable long-run level of final product prices."[16] Actually, as Friedman has observed, there is nothing magical about the figure of 4 per cent; but the rule of a roughly stable price level

> . . . would have required a rate of growth of slightly over 4 per cent per year on the average of the past 90 years—something over 3 per cent to allow for growth of output and 1 per cent to allow for a secular decrease in velocity, which is to say for the increase in the stock of money per unit of output that the public has wished to hold as its real per capita income rose. To judge from this evidence, a rate of increase of 3 to 5 per cent per year might be expected to correspond with a roughly stable price level. . . .[17]

---

[14]The 100 per cent reserve proposal is by no means new; it dates back at least to Irving Fisher's *100% Money* (New Haven: The City Printing Company, 1945), although the first edition was published in 1935. See also Simons, "Rules versus Authority in Monetary Policy," Friedman, *A Program for Monetary Stability,* and Mints, *Monetary Policy for a Competitive Society.* For two critical discussions of this position, see R. S. Sayers, *Central Banking after Bagehot* (Oxford: The Clarendon Press, 1957), and A. G. Hart, *Money, Debt, and Economic Activity* (New York: Prentice-Hall, Inc., 1953), pp. 437-39.

[15]See Friedman, *A Program for Monetary Stability,* for a fuller discussion of this and other points.

[16]*Ibid.,* p. 91.

[17]*Ibid.* For his discussion of the empirical basis of this, see M. Friedman and A. J. Schwartz, *A Monetary History of the United States, 1867-1960* (Princeton: Princeton University Press, 1963). This is a study of the National Bureau of Economic Research. For a critical review of the Friedman-Schwartz analysis, see J. M. Culbertson, "United States Monetary History: Its Implications for Monetary Theory," *The National Banking Review,* March 1964.

The major purpose of the policy is to eliminate "rapid and sizable fluctuations in prices" that are so seriously disturbing to economic stability. When the stock of money and the price level fluctuate widely and unpredictably, economic decisions are indeed difficult to make; and economic instability, no matter what the basic cause, would certainly be aggravated. However, while the advocates of this long-run monetary policy do not contend that its adoption and implementation will eliminate the business cycle completely, they do argue that it would significantly mitigate economic disturbances and thus facilitate planning for continued and smoother economic growth. As Friedman puts it: "A fixed rate of increase in the stock of money would almost certainly rule out . . . rapid and sizable fluctuations, . . . and it would give a firm basis for long range planning on the part of the public"[18]

Let us return to the question of how the policy is to operate and thus achieve its objectives. To begin with, assume a full-employment situation that is, for some reason or other, disturbed by a slump in aggregate demand. According to this analysis, there would be a restriction in output and an increase in unemployment. Further, it is argued that the levels of money wages and prices would fall, raising the real value of money. At the same time that these events are taking place, the money supply is increased by 4 per cent. Individuals and businesses are thus able to satisfy their desire to hold real cash balances with fewer nominal dollars since the real value of money has risen. Also there are more nominal dollars in existence. Thus the public is in the position of increasing its demand for goods and services. In other words, with the stock of money rising and the price level falling, the rising real value of money will permit aggregate demand to rise until full employment is restored.

This is, of course, nothing more than the *Pigou effect* once again, but with a slight twist. Now the stock of money is increased as the price level falls, and thus there is a two-edged effect upon the real value of money. On the other hand, in an inflationary period, the Federal Reserve continues to increase the money supply by 4 per cent per year. But so long as prices are rising, the real value of money is declining, and accordingly the public can satisfy its demand to hold real cash balances only by holding more nominal dollars. Thus the inflationary demand for goods and services is reduced, slowing down the rise in the price level. Again the two-edged Pigou effect is at work.

What are the major benefits to be derived from this policy if it is

---

[18]Friedman, *A Program for Monetary Stability*, p. 92.

adopted and implemented? We had best allow one of its major advocates to speak in its behalf.

> The major gains would be, first, effective insurance against major monetary disturbances; second, a notable reduction in short-term monetary uncertainty and instability; third, a wider scope for private initiative and enterprise in the allocation of capital. The first would contribute to, if not effectively guarantee, the avoidance of those major economic disturbances that from time to time have threatened to tear our social fabric assunder. The second would promote a greater degree of stability in short-run movements in economic activity and thus contribute to what has become one of the major aims of national economic policy. The third would expand the area of economic freedom and promote a more efficient utilization of our resources, whether for current consumption or to increase our rate of growth.[19]

These are indeed important gains; but, as has been done with other theories and policies, this particular program must now be examined in more detail.

2. Price-Level Stability and Chronic Unemployment

It is rather obvious that the steady-secular increase monetary program is based on the assumption that money wages and prices are highly flexible. Otherwise, if prices and wages are rigid downwards, the unemployment that results from a slump in aggregate demand would not be quickly eliminated, but rather would persist for some time.

Friedman, however, has taken a strong position that the American economy is characterized by highly competitive conditions in nearly all markets.[20] In fact, in his view even trade unions have little monopoly power, serving primarily as thermostats through which changes in the basic forces of supply and demand are registered. Though some unions may, because of special circumstances, possess monopoly power, Fried-

---

[19]*Ibid.*, p. 99. See also Shaw, "Money Supply and Stable Economic Growth," pp. 66-71, for his statement of expected benefits.

[20]For references to Friedman's position on the extent of competition in the American economy see L. A. Dow and L. M. Abernathy, "The Chicago School on Economic Methodology and Monopolistic Competition," *American Journal of Economics and Sociology,* April 1963.

man believes that the great majority of them have little direct impact on either the general wage level or the structure of relative wage rates.[21] For this reason Friedman has ridiculed the distinction between "demand-pull" and "cost-push" theories of inflation, arguing that there is no need to have one type of theory to explain inflation from 1775 to 1955 and another type to explain inflation since 1955.

As has been pointed out earlier, however, there are good reasons to believe that the American economy is not as competitive as the steady-secular theorists assume. Rather it seems to be characterized to an increasing extent by administered prices and wages, as well as by structural and legal impediments to resource mobility. Under these circumstances the Pigou effect—two-edged or otherwise—cannot be expected to operate so as to provide for continuing full employment *and* price-level stability. Recall the earlier discussion of the "Phillips curve,"[22] in which it was pointed out that in order to have price-level stability there will be 5 to 7 per cent of the labor force unemployed. If there were greater flexibility of wages and prices, the Phillips curve would not register a "cut-off point" on the horizontal axis at 5-7 per cent unemployment, but rather at a point closer to 3-4 per cent. However, if conditions actually are as indicated by the Phillips curve, and if unemployment falls below 5 to 7 per cent of the labor force, demand pressures in certain sectors of the economy build up, creating cost pressures that are in turn transmitted to the rest of the economy. The rise in the level of input prices will be reflected in a rise in the general price level, and so long as aggregate demand conditions permit it, a cost-price spiral may follow.

Thus, so long as the conditions indicated by the Phillips curve exist, and if we want to adopt the steady-secular increase program but at the same time avoid inflation, aggregate demand must remain at the level over time that permits only 94 per cent employment of the labor force.[23] Otherwise, if the money supply increases at a constant rate, and if unemployment is less than 6 per cent of the labor force—that is, if wages and prices are rising—the real stock of money (M/P) will de-

---

[21]See his essay, "Some Comments on the Significance of Labor Unions for Economic Policy," Chapter X in *The Impact of the Union*, ed. D. Mc. Wright (New York: Harcourt, Brace & World, Inc., 1951).

[22]See Chapter 13 for a review of the Phillips curve.

[23]The rest of this section relies heavily on A. P. Lerner, "A Program for Monetary Stability," Part II, in *Conference on Savings and Residential Financing*, eds. M. D. Ketchum and L. T. Kendall (Chicago: The United States Savings and Loan League, 1962). The figure of 6 per cent is arbitrarily selected because it is the midpoint.

cline. As long as the price level rises relative to the increase in M, the community will cut back its demand for goods and services as they reallocate nominal dollars to their cash balances in the effort to satisfy their desired cash holdings. The resulting decline in real aggregate demand will of course slow down the rise in the price level and may even reduce the price level to its former position—but it will also re-store unemployment to the 6 per cent rate.

On the other hand, if unemployment is greater than 6 per cent, then the price level is relatively low when the annual increase in M takes place. Thus the ratio M/P will rise, that is, the real value of money and hence real demand will rise as the community discovers it needs fewer nominal dollars to satisfy its real savings desires. As a result unemploy-ment will decline until it reaches the 6 per cent rate and "equilibrium" will once again be established. But note that if aggregate demand con-tinues to rise, so that unemployment falls below the 6 per cent rate, then a wage-price spiral will set in, reducing the real value of M. In this case, M/P will fall, and the community will cut back on its aggre-gate demand. Presumably the fall in aggregate demand will continue until the price level adjusts to the new money supply and the demands for real savings are satisfied. Once more, however, the 6 per cent unem-ployment rate is reestablished.

Therefore under the circumstances indicated by the Phillips curve, adoption and implementation of the steady-secular increase program implies a continuing, chronic unemployment rate of 6 per cent of the labor force, although the program will provide price-level stability. We shall refer to this as the "zero-inflation standard," in contrast to the "labor standard" discussed in the next section. That is, the economy will experience "zero inflation," but at the same time it will experience an unemployment rate of about 6 per cent of the labor force.

Of course, the "zero-inflation standard" may be accepted and imple-mented without adopting the steady-secular increase monetary pro-gram. If they desire to do so, the monetary authorities can accomplish the same end results by means of discretionary policy actions. But the point still remains: under the circumstances indicated by the Phillips curve, we can accomplish price-level stability only with 5 to 7 per cent of the labor force unemployed; and adoption and implementation of the steady-secular increase program would, under these circumstances, assure us of zero inflation with chronic unemployment. If inflexibility of wages and prices is so important, then the wage-price structure of the economy must be examined. This leads us to a consideration of further theories of inflation.

3. Cost-Push and the Labor Standard[24]

At the very beginning it is important to note that there is no generally accepted version of the so-called cost-push theory of inflation. In
its crudest form the argument runs like this: suppose that the economy
is at full employment and there is no excess demand in either labor or
commodity markets.[25] Assume also that productivity is increasing at an
annual rate of 3 per cent. Now consider the effects that may occur
when the unions bargain for and receive wage increases greater than
the productivity gains. The crude version of the theory concludes, with
very little analysis, that the end result must be that average costs per
unit of output rise and that employers respond to this by passing the
higher average costs on in the form of higher prices. Ergo, increases in
the general wage level in excess of increases in productivity result in a
rise in the general price level.

This sort of analysis and conclusion is too crude to warrant much
discussion. As is well known, productivity gains are unequally distributed among industries and even among firms in the same industry;
some industries and firms are advancing faster than the average, and
others are lagging. Also, not all industries are organized, nor are all
firms and industries in a position always to pass on the higher costs per
unit in the form of higher prices. All in all, there are enough complications present that the crude version of the cost-push (that is, wage-
push) theory falls far short of providing a satisfactory explanation of
inflation.

However, most economists who may be classified as advocates (in
some sense or other) of the wage-push theory of inflation reject the
crude version of the theory.[26] In fact they do not even offer it as a
substitute for excess-demand theory; rather they develop more sophisticated versions of the theory and then advance these as supplements to
the excess-demand theory. These more sophisticated versions are used
to explain why and how the price level rises faster than the excess-

---

[24]In this section the terms "excess-demand" and "demand-pull" inflation are
used to designate a rise in the price level attributable to aggregate money demand
being greater than aggregate supply.

[25]For an excellent critical discussion of this version (and others) of the theory,
see W. G. Bowen, *The Wage-Price Issue: A Theoretical Analysis* (Princeton: Princeton University Press, 1960).

[26]For example: J. M. Clark, *The Wage-Price Problem* (New York: The American
Bankers Association, 1960); G. Haberler, *Inflation: Its Causes and Cures* (Washington, D. C.: American Enterprise Association, 1960); W. Röpke, *Welfare, Freedom and Inflation* (University, Alabama: University of Alabama Press, 1964).

demand theory tells us, and, moreover, why and how the price level
rises in certain periods when the excess-demand theory tells us it
should remain constant or even fall. As one advocate has put it:

> There can be no inflation without an expansion in aggregate demand
> and there can be no large and sustained expansion in aggregate demand
> without an increase in the supply of money. This also holds in the case
> of wage-push.
>
>   It follows that demand pull and expanding money supply are more
> basic than wage push. However, wage push by labor unions can be a
> potent factor in the double sense that (a) it tends to speed up demand
> pull inflation (though it may also shorten the inflationary period by
> bringing things more quickly to a head) and (b) in case monetary de-
> mand does not expand any more, wages may still be forced up faster
> than output per man-hour rises so that prices continue to creep up; the
> resulting unemployment and loss of output and income provide a strong
> inducement to expand monetary demand and inflate prices.[27]

Actually, there is need to distinguish between two variants of the
more sophisticated wage-push theory. The only major difference between them is that the one assumes monetary-fiscal policy is neutral,
while the other assumes that monetary-fiscal policy is carried out according to the Employment Act of 1946.

Consider first the case in which monetary-fiscal policy is neutral. If,
under these circumstances, unions push up wages faster than productivity rises, there will be unemployment. Recall that in a discussion of
this sort, the term "productivity" is taken to mean the *average* rise for
all firms and industries in the economy. As noted above, some firms
and industries will experience greater than average increases, while
others will lag behind the average. But if the increase in the *general*
level of *money* wages exceeds the average rise in productivity, certain
consequences will result.

First, consider the very unrealistic situation in which all workers
share equally in the general wage rise. In this instance, since average
and marginal costs of all firms have risen, prices will be increased, and
if aggregate demand remains constant, the higher prices will lead to a
reduction in the aggregate quantity demanded. The result then will be
that some firms will shut down, and therefore there will be some unemployment along with the higher price level. In short, aggregate supply
has fallen relative to aggregate demand.

There are two major points to make about this conclusion. In the
first place, it is important only if aggregate demand remains constant
(or at least does not rise much). But the assumption of a neutral mone-

[27]Haberler, *Inflation: Its Causes and Cures,* pp. 35-36.

tary-fiscal policy does not insure this, for it is conceivable that income velocity (V) could rise, and the monetary-fiscal authorities have no direct control over V. Thus, if consumers were voluntarily to increase V enough to prevent the unemployment, there would be continuing full employment, though the price level will still be higher. There is, however, no good reason to expect that this will automatically happen.

The second major point revolves around an assumption common to nearly all variants of the wage-push theory—namely, that under unionism, wages are flexible upwards but rigid downwards. Thus, the unemployed workers are unable to acquire employment by offering their services at lower wages, for if they could do this, the analysis does not hold. That is, if the unemployed could move into other jobs at lower wages, their new employers could offer lower prices. Whether this would force a general competitive reduction in prices, or whether it would at least compensate for the rise in prices of some products, is conjectural, depending upon the particular situation.

There are still other assumptions that the advocates of this version of the wage-push theory must make. One of these—and a rather critical one at that—is that the unions are little concerned over the employment status of their membership. Thus, as wages are pushed up faster than productivity rises, presumably the unions care little about the resulting unemployment of members. There is, however, a good deal of doubt about the validity of this assumption. Although some labor economists agree with it,[28] others have questioned it.[29] There may well be some upper limit to which wages and unemployment can be pushed by trade-union action before the unemployed members become so disgruntled as to leave the union. The assumption, in short, calls for a good deal of critical examination.

Consider now the second version of the sophisticated wage-push theory, the one in which monetary-fiscal policy is carried out according to the full-employment commitment found in the Employment Act. In this case, when wage costs per unit of output are pushed up and prices rise accordingly, unemployment results. But now the monetary and fiscal authorities will take positive action to increase aggregate demand so that the unemployed workers will have job opportunities available to them. Thus there will be continuing full employment, but at higher wage and price levels. This is what Professor J. R. Hicks has referred

[28]For instance, A. M. Ross, *Trade Union Wage Policy* (Berkeley and Los Angeles: University of California Press, 1948).

[29]For instance, G. P. Schultz and C. A. Myers, "Union Wage Decisions and Employment," *American Economic Review*, January 1950.

to as the "Labour Standard," under which the final outcome is a stair-stepped rise in the general levels of wages and prices at full employment.[30]

In an important sense, this second version of the wage-push theory is simply a variant of the excess-demand theory, with wage increases serving as the stimulant for increases in aggregate demand. In other words, there are localized pressures, which in turn become generalized via the response of the monetary-fiscal authorities. But this, of course, is nothing new—every situation of excess money demand is a generalized response to particularized pressures, whether they occur in the housing market, in agriculture, private business investment, or what have you. The response is the same—the locus of the particular pressures is different.

Of course, the monetary-fiscal authorities can and will react to the pressures as they see fit or as they are instructed. Presumably, according to the wage-push theorists, the pressures emanating from the union movement and the Employment Act are so overwhelming that we will (at least for a time) adhere to the "Labour Standard." This, however, is a matter that carries us into the areas of politics, psychology, and ethics. For instance, Professor Haberler has stated:

> . . . unions have acquired over the years *de jure* or *de facto* numerous immunities and exceptions which go far beyond anything accorded to business and other private associations. It is difficult to believe that legal reforms restoring a more balanced power equilibrium between the parties in wage bargains, and eliminating violence and other abuses, would not have some effect in relieving inflationary wage pressure.
>
> . . . probably more basic and important than legal reform, is a change in the attitude of public opinion and of all branches of government. It should be possible to arouse public opinion to the dangers of wage inflation and to bring its weight to bear on unions which by force of crippling strike and intimidation impose inflationary wage increases on the economy. Then the aroused public opinion could force the government, in its executive as well as in its legislative branch, to pick up some courage, instead of maintaining a studious neutrality in wage bargaining and issuing platidudinous appeals to everybody to behave, or outrightly capitulating to striking unions and bringing pressure on employers to capitulate. If instead of that unions were told in no uncertain words that their wage demands are inflationary and intolerable, one could expect to observe quickly a marked tendency for moderation in wage bargains.[31]

---

[30]J. R. Hicks, "Economic Foundations of Wage Policy," *Economic Journal*, September 1955.

[31]Haberler, *Inflation: Its Causes and Cures*, pp. 77-78. For a critical comment on this work, see E. E. Liebhafsky's review in the *Southern Economic Journal*, April 1961.

But let us return to the economics of the problem. Thus far some of the assumptions underlying the wage-push theory have been examined. Let us now follow a different approach and inquire into the measurement of wage-push increases in the price level.

4. Measurement of Wage-Push Inflation

If there is a rise in the general price level, how much of it can be attributed to pressures emanating from the wage-push side? As will be seen, this question is quite difficult to answer and in fact may be impossible to answer until we acquire better analysis and data.

A fundamental point in the wage-push theory is that wages rise faster than productivity, thus forcing price level increases. Does this mean, therefore, that every time that wage increases outstrip productivity gains that we have wage-push inflation? Hardly! Even in a period of *obvious* excess demand inflation, such as 1946-47, wages rise faster than productivity simply because businessmen bid for more and more labor.[32] If the economy is at or near full employment, then businessmen can acquire the necessary labor only by bidding against each other, and this of course pushes wages up, usually faster than productivity rises.[33]

Thus, in the later stages of nearly every expansion the general wage level rises faster than productivity advances. In fact some economists argue that in a period of excess-demand inflation labor unions operate to slow down the advances in the wage level because of the time lag built into many collective bargaining contracts. Aside from this, the important point is that a situation in which the money-wage level increases faster than productivity does nothing at all to indicate whether the inflation is of the excess-demand or the wage-push type, let alone any combination of the two.

If the statistical data are so inadequate, then how can wage-push inflation be recognized? Professor Haberler has offered the following suggestion:

> Only under certain circumstances is the conclusion [that there is wage-push inflation] valid . . . [1] if wages outrun productivity, or in fact if they rise at all, during a period of depression and unemployment when

---

[32]P. A. Samuelson and R. M. Solow, "Analytical Aspects of Anti-Inflation Policy," *American Economic Review,* May 1960.

[33]See T. Hultgren, *Changes in Labor Costs During Business Cycles in Production and Business,* Occasional Paper 74 (New York: National Bureau of Economic Research, 1960).

aggregate demand stagnates or contracts. Thus, when wages and prices rose during the recession of 1957-58, we had a clear case of wage-push inflation. Moreover, during a period which cannot be regarded as a depression period, because output and employment are rising—[2] if wages in any particular industry where there is still much unemployment, we would have to speak of wage push, surely under these circumstances a wage rise could not happen in a competitive labor market. Thus the labor contracts in the automobile industry in 1958 and in steel in 1960 would seem to be cases of wage push.[34]

Now it is important to note that the rise in wages and prices during the 1957-1958 contraction was the result of a number of forces.[35] In the first place, the wage increases that went into effect in 1957 and 1958 were the lagged consequence of earlier agreements under long-term contracts. Second, wages rose because of a combination of escalator clauses and an increase in the consumer price index. The consumer price index rose primarily because of autonomous increases in food prices. Third, the fact that wages rise in a contraction is not a sign that prices automatically must rise. And finally, consider the possibility that the rising price and wage levels may have contributed significantly to the shortness of the 1957-1958 contraction. As Hickman has put it:

> It should be reiterated that wage stability during business contractions has a positive as well as a negative aspect. Wage stability inhibits the formation of adverse price expectations which could amplify deflationary pressures and reduce production and employment along with prices. Moreover, wage increases which occur after a contraction has been underway for some months and product demands are already depressed, may augment real income and contribute to a business upturn. Under those circumstances, oligopolistic firms may temporarily absorb wage increases without raising prices or reducing production and employment. If so, the resulting stimulus to consumption demand might outweigh the adverse effects, if any, of the wage increase on investment.[36]

In short, to attribute a rise in the general price level in a contractionary period to one single variable overlooks the complexity of the economy, a complexity that has been emphasized throughout this volume. Again, what is needed is more concrete analysis, as well as better measurement and careful interpretation of particular historical episodes, before wage-push inflation can be discussed in any meaningful quantitative sense.

---

[34]Haberler, *Inflation: Its Causes and Cures*, p. 24.

[35]See B. G. Hickman, *Growth and Stability of the Postwar Economy* (Washington, D. C.: The Brookings Institution, 1960), pp. 404-407, for a fuller discussion of these points.

[36]*Ibid.*, p. 406.

This is not to deny the existence or importance of wage-push inflation. Obviously rises in the general level of wages have an impact on the level of prices. Our only point is that there are numerous other forces that influence prices, and that therefore wage increases must be fitted into their proper perspective in the overall picture. If nothing more, there is always the proverbial "Which came first, the hen or the egg" question, though in this case of course the question is "Which came first, the price increase or the wage increase?" In other words, there is an interaction in the inflationary process between wages and prices, and we turn to this in the next section.

5. Interactions in Demand-Cost Inflation

Discussion in earlier chapters has clearly revealed that the inflationary spurts in 1946-47 and 1950-51 and 1955-56 were due to excess demand. In all three cases the pressures on the price level originated in increases in the stock of money or income velocity (or both). However, even though these episodes may be labeled as excess-demand inflation, surely wage-push pressures also figured in. Once the consumer price index begins to rise, increased pressures for higher wages begin to emerge. Recall, however, that the wage level will rise even in the absence of unions. And once money wages creep up, there is the additional possibility that the price level will rise further, if monetary-fiscal conditions permit. This, in turn, stimulates additional price-level increases, and thus there develops the so-called "wage-price spiral."

In this interactive process it is difficult, if not impossible, to determine how much of the inflation is wage induced and how much is induced by excess demand. There is indeed an interactive process, although there cannot be wage-push inflation at full employment unless demand conditions permit it. Here again is the so-called "Labour Standard," under which the monetary-fiscal authorities are more concerned with continuing full employment than with price-level stability.

But there are other types of interaction of wage-push and demand-pull pressures. Consider the case in which collective bargaining contracts contain an escalator clause and in which autonomous changes in agriculture raise food prices. The cost-of-living index will, of course, rise (*ceteris paribus*) and thus so will the money-wage level. This seems to be one of the major reasons for the wage increases during the 1957-58 contraction. Alternatively, consider the case in which, because of changes in the housing market, rents rise. Again both the cost-of-living index and the wage level will rise. Indeed, anything that raises the cost-of-living index, even in a period of slumping aggregate demand, will result in rises in the money-wage level. Is this, however, a case of wage-push inflation? Or is it, on the other hand, a case of *autonomous* changes pushing up the price level and then these changes being transmitted to higher wages via collective bargaining? Surely both situations are conceivable.

Another type of interaction occurs when there are shifts in the composition of aggregate demand.[37] Assume that total aggregate demand remains constant, but that consumers shift their preferences between commodities. Assume also that the products for which their demand falls are produced in oligopolistic industries which display a downward rigidity in prices. Thus the prices of the commodities for which demand has risen will increase, while the prices of those for which demand has fallen will not decline. The net result is a rise in the general price level. This is the so-called "demand-shift" theory of inflation.

Still another possibility relates to a situation in which wage increases result in an increase in aggregate demand and employment. This might be called the "bargaining theory of employment."[38] Assume a case in which the demand for the aggregate product has a price elasticity of less than one, and assume that in the short run there is poor substitution of capital for labor. Thus the demand for labor also has a wage elasticity of less than one. Assume finally that the propensity to consume of the workers is relatively high. Now under these conditions a rise in wages will increase the total wage bill of the workers, who in turn will spend most of their newly acquired income. Thus, even though the price level rises, money expenditures may rise proportionately. Trade unionists, however, are prone to assert that the increase in money expenditures is apt to be more than proportional to the price-level rise resulting from the initial wage increase, and thus total demand rises and increases the level of employment.

In short, the interrelationships of wages and prices are quite complicated, and accordingly it is presently impossible to arrive at any clear-cut, hard and fast conclusions. There are a number of possible situations, both theoretical and historical, and each needs to be exam-

---

[37]C. Schultze, *Recent Inflation in the United States*, Study Paper No. 1, Joint Economic Committee, September 1959. For an empirical study that lends support to the "demand-shift" theory, see W. G. Bowen and S. H. Masters, "Shifts in the Composition of Demand and the Inflation Problem," *American Economic Review*, December 1964.

[38]See K. W. Rothschild, *The Theory of Wages* (New York: The Macmillan Company, 1954), Chapter IX, for further discussion.

ined on its own grounds. Thus we can only repeat our earlier conclusion—until more analysis and research are done, only conjectures about the presence, extent, and significance of wage-push inflation can be proposed.

One interesting study in this respect has reached the tentative conclusion that the timing evidence on changes in per unit labor costs and changes in the wholesale price index indicate that the demand side is more relevant.[39] Figure 23–1 shows the two relevant indexes—unit costs

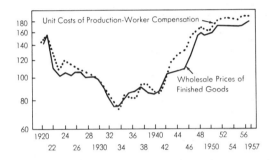

Source: A. Rees, "Patterns of Wages, Prices, and Productivity," p. 25.

FIGURE 23–1

Indexes of Unit Costs of Production-Worker Compensation
and Wholesale Prices of Finished Goods,
1919-57 (1929 = 100)

of production-worker compensation and whole prices of finished goods —from 1920 to 1957. Note that following 1920 the wholesale price index fell more rapidly than the unit-cost index, though by 1929 they had both fallen by the same amount. From 1929 to 1933 both indexes again fell, with the price index again leading the unit-cost index, though the latter index continued to fall until 1934 while the price index began to rise. From then up to 1938 the two indexes moved up, with the price index leading the way; and from 1938 to 1940 both fell until they were equal in 1941. During the war period (up to 1946) both indexes rose, but the unit-cost index rose far more from 1942 to 1946, indicating that

---

[39]A. Rees, "Patterns of Wages, Prices, and Productivity," Chapter I in *Wages, Prices, Profits and Productivity*, ed. C. A. Myers, (New York: The American Assembly, 1959).

price controls were more effective than wage controls. Since 1946 the two indexes have moved more or less parallel to each other.

What do the data in Figure 23–1 reveal? For one thing, there is the obvious point that movements in wholesale prices and unit labor costs are closely related. But this does not imply any cause-effect relationship. On the other hand, does the timing of the two indexes imply anything? The data in Figure 23–1 are presented in tabular form in Table 23–1 in which the peaks and troughs can be identified more easily. Presumably, if the price index at the trough leads the unit-cost index, then demand forces are at play; on the other hand, if the unit-cost index rises first, this implies that wage-push inflation is at work.

TABLE 23–1

Indexes of Unit Cost of Production-Worker Labor and
Wholesale Prices of Finished Goods,
Manufacturing, 1919-1957
(1929 = 100)

Year	Unit Labor Cost*	Wholesale Prices of Finished Goods†	Year	Unit Labor Cost*	Wholesale Prices of Finished Goods†
1957	193	184	1937	94	92P
1956	193	178	1936	81	87
1955	187	173	1935	81	87
1954	186T	173	1934	84	83
1953	190P	172T	1933	72T	75
1952	186	174	1932	79	74T
1951	183	175P	1931	85	81
1950	167T	160	1930	94	93
1949	168	157T	1929	100	100
1948	170P	162	1928	103	101
1947	163	150	1927	106	100
1946	150	123	1926	109	106P
1945	133	108	1925	111	106
1944	131	107	1924	117	102T
1943	123	106	1923	120P	105
1942	108	104	1922	107T	102
1941	93	94	1921	127	109
1940	86T	86	1920	159P	158P
1939	88	85T	1919	145	138
1938	94P	87			

* Based on the BLS index of production-worker payrolls, wage supplements from Rees, pp. 15-16, and Kendrick's index of manufacturing, extended to 1957 by the Federal Reserve Board index. The letter P identifies a peak in the series, and the letter T identifies a trough.

† BLS index of wholesale prices of finished goods converted into a 1929 base.

Source: A. Rees, "Patterns of Wages, Prices, and Production," p. 27.

Five cycles can be rather easily identified in each series. In 1922 the rise in the unit-cost index preceded the rise in the price index by two years, indicating a wage-push inflation. In all other cases, however—that is, in 1932, 1939, 1949, and 1953—the price index led the unit-cost index at the troughs. This then indicates that for this period demand inflation was much more dominant than wage inflation. As Rees points out: "The timing evidence thus suggests that the common element in the two series . . . arises from the demand," though he hastens to point out that such ". . . annual data are extremely crude tools for such an analysis, and this result must be taken with great caution."[40]

What can be concluded? Again, not very much. According to whoever is writing, there is or there is not wage-push inflation; or there is wage-push inflation to a greater or lesser degree; or the evidence shows that there may be or may not be wage-push inflation, though the evidence is not very clear on this point. And, after having reached such an ambiguous state of affairs, the student is left with two questions—is there wage-push inflation, and if so, how significant is it? If you throw your hands up in despair and reply, "How can I be expected to answer such a question?" we can only reply, "Well, at least try. If nothing else, you will learn some economics."

6. Administered-Price Inflation

In recent years a number of economists have considered the role of "administered" pricing in the inflationary process, although it is not quite correct to say that a *theory* of administered-price inflation has been developed. Galbraith,[41] Ackley,[42] Lerner,[43] Means,[44] and others

---

[40]*Ibid.*, p. 26.

[41]J. K. Galbraith, "Market Structure and Stabilization Policy," *Review of Economics and Statistics*, May 1957.

[42]G. Ackley, "A Third Approach to the Analysis and Control of Inflation," in *The Relationship of Prices to Economic Stability and Growth*, Compendium of Papers submitted before the Joint Economic Committee, Congress of the United States, March 31, 1958: this work will be referred to as *Compendium.*
See also Ackley, "Administered Prices and the Inflationary Process," *American Economic Review*, May 1959; J. Duesenberry, "The Mechanics of Inflation," *Review of Economics and Statistics*, May 1950; F. Holzman, "Income Determination in Open Inflation," *Review of Economics and Statistics*, May 1950.

[43]A. P. Lerner, "Inflationary Depression and the Regulation of Administered Prices," in *Compendium*. See also his *Everybody's Business* (East Lansing: Michigan State University Press, 1961).

[44]G. C. Means, *Pricing Power and the Public Interest: A Study Based on Steel* (New York: Harper & Row, Publishers, 1962). See also his *The Corporate Revolution in America: Economic Reality vs. Economic Theory* (New York: Crowell Collier & Macmillan, Inc., 1962), especially Chapters 4-7.

have constructed various hypotheses that attempt to explain administered-price inflation, but none of these is complete. Also important is
the fact that none of these hypotheses is really capable of being tested
empirically, though some studies[45] have been made. All in all, the concept of administered-price inflation is as vague and incomplete as the
cost-push theory. Some of the hypotheses of administered-price inflation are considered in this section.

First, it must be noted that the term "administered price" is not very
useful for analytical purposes. In a sense, all prices are administered
since they are set rather arbitrarily by management. But obviously the
range of managerial discretion in administering prices varies considerably between firms. In the more or less competitive sector of the economy, management will administer price according to conditions largely
beyond its control. Impersonal market forces will determine whether
price will be changed, and insofar as the firm must maximize profits in
order to survive, the price adjustments will take place quickly and
frequently.

On the other hand, there are cases in which management has a
rather wide range of discretion in its decision making function. In firms
of this type, which are usually monopolistic or oligopolistic, management may select from a number of alternatives when dealing with a
particular situation and still have a reasonable expectation of surviving.
For example, a reduction in demand for the firm's product will not
necessarily result in a drop in price; instead, management may hold

---

[45]Empirical studies on administered pricing flourished during the late thirties
and early forties. Some of the important early studies are G. C. Means, *The Struc-
ture of the American Economy*, Part II (Washington, D. C.: U. S. National Plan-
ning Board, 1940); A. C. Neal, *Industrial Concentration and Price Inflexibility*
(Washington, D. C.: American Council of Public Affairs, 1942); J. T. Dunlop,
"Price Flexibility and the Degree of Monopoly," *Quarterly Journal of Economics*,
August 1939; E. S. Mason, "Price Inflexibility," *Review of Economics and Statistics*,
May 1938.

More recent studies are J. W. Markham, "Administered Prices and the Recent
Inflation," Research Study Two in *Inflation, Growth, and Employment*, a series of
studies prepared for the Commission on Money and Credit (Englewood Cliffs, N. J.:
Prentice-Hall, Inc., 1964); R. T. Selden, "Cost-Push versus Demand-Pull Inflation,"
Journal of Political Economy, February 1959; H. J. DePodwin and R. T. Selden,
"Business Pricing Policies and Inflation," *Journal of Political Economy*, April 1963;
M. J. Bailey, "Administered Prices in the American Economy," in *Compendium*;
O. Eckstein and G. Fromm, "Steel and the Postwar Inflation," Study Paper No. 2,
prepared for *Study of Employment, Growth, and Price Levels* for the Joint Eco-
nomic Committee, 86th Cong., 1st sess., November 1959; see also the reports pre-
pared by the Subcommittee on Antitrust and Monopoly of the Committee on the
Judiciary, U. S. Senate, pursuant to S. Res. 231, 85th Cong., 2nd sess., especially
Administered Prices: Steel (March 13, 1958) and *Administered Prices: Automobiles*
(November 1958).

price constant and make adjustments in output and inventories. In such firms, price flexibility, especially downwards, is not apt to be as great as in the more competitive firms.[46]

Administered-price inflation accordingly is related to firms that exercise a fairly significant range of discretion in setting prices. These firms may adjust prices to changing conditions in any of a variety of ways, even to the extent of raising prices during a contractionary period. One interesting thing to observe is that administered prices are generally less inflationary than competitive prices during expansions, but that over a period of several cycles they increase more than competitive prices.[47] The major reason for this appears to be a ratchet effect built into administered prices; during the periods of expansion, they rise (though less than competitive prices), but during periods of contraction they do not fall, and indeed may continue to rise even more.[48] Competitive prices, on the other hand, tend to rise sharply during expansions and to fall during contractions. On net balance, therefore, administered prices have risen more over time than have competitive prices.

Let us examine a version of administered-price inflation.[49] Consider the case in which the firms in question price by some markup formula —that is, they apply a stipulated percentage markup to average total costs. Assume also that a large number of wage bargains made by these firms contain an escalator clause. Now, if for some reason the cost-of-living index rises, wages will also rise, pushing up the average *total* costs of these firms. (Productivity is assumed to be unchanging.) This, of course, means *ceteris paribus* a rise in the general price level as the percentage markup is applied to the higher average total costs. But as the price level rises, the escalator clause will force wages higher, and clearly an inflationary spiral will develop.

The administered-price inflation may get underway for other reasons. Most businesses are, in some way or another, suppliers of inputs to other businesses. Thus if a few firms raise their markup in the at-

---

[46]This argument, of course, relates to the theory of oligopoly and the kinky demand curve. Oligopolists are reluctant to cut prices for fear of setting off a price war. On the other hand, under conditions of rising demand and costs, price increases are initiated on the assumption that the rivals in the industry, experiencing similar conditions, will follow the price leader.

[47]Markham, "Administered Prices and the Recent Inflation," pp. 148-49.

[48]Galbraith, "Market Structure and Stabilization Policy."

[49]G. C. Ackley has done the most to develop the hypothesis discussed here. He refers to it as "mark-up inflation"; see the references in footnote 42. A. P. Lerner has developed a similar thesis, though he refers to it as "sellers' inflation"; see the references in footnote 43.

tempt to acquire larger profits, the costs of the firms they supply will rise, these higher costs will then be passed on in the form of higher prices, and again the inflation gets underway. As Lerner has put it:

> But a sellers' inflation could just as well be started by an increase not in wages but in the markup. Prices would rise and wages would then be raised by workers in attempts to maintain (or restore) their original buying power. Business would then "innocently" raise their prices again only in proportion to the increase in their costs, and we would have the inflation upon us as well as the endless dispute about who started it first—the famous chicken and egg.[50]

However, managements in the administered-price sector of the economy need not raise prices to the full extent indicated by the markup. During an expansionary period, these firms may not take full advantage of their pricing power and thus raise prices less than they could. Then during the contractionary stage, they continue to raise prices rather than lower them, taking advantage of the "unliquidated monopoly gains" built up during the preceding expansion.[51] This particular hypothesis explains why, during the expansionary stage of the cycle, administered prices are less inflationary than competitive prices, and why they are more inflationary than competitive prices over several cycles.

On the other hand, Ackley maintains that markups vary directly with the business cycle—that is, they are increased during the expansionary stage and reduced, though not by much, during the contraction.[52] This, of course, would tend to aggravate the rising price level during expansion but not allow the prices to fall during the contraction. Subsequent price increases during the contraction, however, would be less than the price rises during the expansion. Further empirical evidence on this matter is needed before any conclusion can be reached.

What are the implications of administered-price inflation for economic policy? Obviously general stabilization controls will be ineffective. If the economic system is made up of both administered-price and competitive-price sectors, the administered-price inflation can spill over into the competitive sector. Assume that some firms in the administered sector raise their markups and the inflationary process gets underway. As the administered prices rise, customers may well shift their demand over to the commodities produced in the competitive

---

[50]Lerner, *Compendium*, p. 259.

[51]Galbraith, "Market Structure and Stabilization Policy."

[52]Ackley, *Compendium*, p. 630; "Administered Prices and the Inflationary Process," pp. 425-28.

sector, where prices have not yet risen. If this is carried far enough, there could be a shortage of demand in the administered-price sector and an excess of demand in the competitive sector. Further, some unemployment would occur in the administered-price sector.

Under these circumstances, the competitive prices would tend to rise, but the administered prices, being sticky downwards, would not necessarily fall. The result then would be a general rise in the price level, which *appears* to be the consequence of general excess demand.[53]

Obviously, however, if the inflation occurs for the reasons stipulated above, general monetary and fiscal policies will not be useful. Already there will be some unemployment in the administered-price sector (as a result of the shift in demand), and restrictive monetary-fiscal policies designed to reduce aggregate demand will only increase the unemployment in this sector. On the other hand, if the unemployment becomes great enough to induce the use of expansionary monetary-fiscal policies, the price level will continue to rise. Certainly, general monetary and fiscal policies are inadequate to cope with administered-price inflation; other techniques must be used.

What can be done to control administered-price inflation? One suggestion that has been made is to establish a centralized regulatory commission which will be charged with approving changes in administered prices and wages.[54] Lerner's proposal is based on the notion that the regulatory commission would prevent only *restrictive prices* and *restrictive wages* from being set. "A restrictive price is one that results in the demand for a product falling below capacity output. A restrictive wage is one that results in less than full employment in the specific labor market to which it applies."[55]

In its prevention of restrictive prices and wages, the commission would do several things.[56] First, it would permit an increase in an administered price only when production and sales are at capacity, even though profits are already high. Second, it would enforce price reductions when sales and production are substantially below capacity. The commission should enforce a price decrease even though profits are low—perhaps negative—so long as the price more than covers short-run marginal costs. Third, wages in general should be allowed to rise at a rate equal to the average *trend* of increase in productivity for the

---

[53]This is a version of the "demand-shift" theory of inflation mentioned in section 5 of this chapter.

[54]Lerner, Compendium, pp. 267-68; Ackley, *Compendium,* pp. 632-36.

[55]Lerner, *Compendium,* p. 267.

[56]*Ibid.*

economy as a whole. Fourth, the commission may permit wage increases in excess of the average trend in productivity *only* where the labor market is substantially higher than the average. Finally, the commission may permit smaller increases in *administered* wages or allow no increases at all wherever the labor market is significantly slacker than on the average.

Lerner is among the first to realize that this proposal will result in the charge of *price* and *wage control*. His answer to this is as follows:

> But price regulation is not price control—it is almost the exact opposite. Price control consists of an attempt by authority to *interfere* with the price mechanism by establishing a price below that which clears the market. . . . Price regulation on the other hand *restores* the price mechanism. It interferes only with interferences, preventing the monopolist or cartel or trade union or whatever else determines an administered price or wage, from setting it above the "correct" level. . . . The cry of "price control" would be entirely without justification.[57]

It is very difficult to evaluate this position. Lerner is simply asking that the price be set so that it equals or slightly exceeds marginal cost, even if this entails losses as well as profits. "A defender of the free market or profit or loss system should not be appalled at the emergence either of profits or of losses."[58] But this, of course, is a value judgment as to what is the most proper mechanism of setting prices and wages.

On the other hand, those who would object to Lerner's proposal must, somehow or another, justify the existing markups. The administered-price inflation analysis reveals that rises in labor costs are not always the cause of inflation; rather, increases in markups may set off the wage-price spiral. Labor always contends that it must (should) receive its "fair" share; and management, by maintaining its markup, is making the same claim. Administered-price inflation hypotheses reveal fairly clearly that, in an important sense, the quite old concepts of "just price" and "just wage" have not been clarified, nor have the disputes over them been resolved.

7. Another View of Long-Run Monetary Policy

The preceding five sections have shown that the structure of the economy has a great deal of bearing on the effectiveness of monetary policy, both for the short run and the long run. Inflexibility of wages and prices clearly interferes with the steady-secular increase program

[57]Lerner, *Everybody's Business*, p. 90.
[58]*Ibid.*, p. 91.

for achieving, as best as possible, continued growth *and* full employment. Similar conclusions apply to the irregular-secular increase program. Administered prices and wages create problems that require alternatives to monetary policy, as well as general fiscal policy. But does this mean that monetary policy has no contribution to make to long-run growth? Hardly, for the long-run rate of interest and the general availability of credit do have some influence on long-run investment decisions.[59]

Consider a long-run monetary policy that reduces the long-run interest rate (and perhaps lowers it even further) and creates more general availability of credit. This could well have a positive impact upon capital formation. Some econometric studies have concluded, very tentatively of course, that lower rates of interest do tend to stimulate capital formation.[60] However, these studies have been quite fragmentary and their major conclusions have been advanced very cautiously. Note that this policy entails (on net balance) continuous open-market purchases by the Federal Reserve System, and unless the national debt rises *pari passu* the Federal Reserve will end up being the single, certainly the largest, holder of outstanding government securities. If the debt does not rise enough, so that the Federal Reserve is the sole owner of the outstanding debt, presumably then it would have to start purchasing other assets from the public and the commercial banking system.

Obviously this long-run monetary policy will result in a secular increase in the stock of money, since the Federal Reserve is continually buying in the open-market. During periods of inflation, therefore, this particular policy could aggravate significantly the rising price level.

The second part of this program is designed to deal with such a condition; it recommends the aggressive use of an austere fiscal policy to control the inflationary pressures. If tax rates are raised and kept high and/or government expenditures reduced enough, the inflation can be controlled.

Finally, the short-term rate of interest must be handled by unorthodox means in order to prevent its falling so low that short-term funds will flow out of the economy. If this is not done, the international balance of payments position will worsen, creating further difficulties

---

[59]The following discussion relies heavily on P. A. Samuelson, "Fiscal and Financial Policies for Growth" in *Proceedings of a Symposium on Economic Growth* (New York: The American Bankers Association, 1963).

[60]These and other studies are critically reviewed in R. Eisner and R. H. Strotz, "Determinants of Business Investment," Research Study Two in *Impacts of Monetary Policy,* a series of research studies prepared for the Commission on Money and Credit (Englewood Cliffs, N. J.: Prentice-Hall, Inc., 1963).

The effectiveness of this policy depends upon the effectiveness of fiscal policy as a means of counteracting short-run cyclical disturbances. This is the subject matter of the next two chapters.

8. Summary

In this chapter we have examined some alternative proposals for long-run monetary policy. One of these, the steady-secular increase program, would result in chronic unemployment of about 6 per cent of the labor force *if* the conditions implied by the Phillips curve actually prevail. It also would not make use of monetary policy for achieving the goal of short-run stability. Another proposal, the irregular-secular increase program, also calls for a rise in the stock of money over time, but accompanied by short-run changes of a contracyclical nature. The implementation of this program would, given existing institutions and psychological attitudes in the securities market, probably result in some secular rise in the price level.

The discussion of these programs, particularly the secular-increase argument, led to an examination of the role of administered prices and wages. Several variants of the "cost-push" and "administered-price" theories of inflation were examined, with the major conclusion that they are not very well developed and are difficult to test empirically. This does not mean, however, that they are without significance. To the contrary, they appear to be forthright efforts to explain the impact of administered prices and wages on the inflationary process. Although much more work needs to be done in this area, these efforts do recognize the importance of "noncompetitive" sectors of the economy and the way in which these sectors have an influence upon aggregate economic behavior and the effectiveness of aggregate economic policy.

Finally we examined another program of long-run monetary stability which also relies upon a secular increase in the stock of money. This, however, is the result of implementing a policy of getting the long-term rate of interest low and keeping it low as a means of stimulating capital formation. Short-run cyclical disturbances are to be dealt with by contracyclical fiscal policy. This then leads us to the next two chapters.

QUESTIONS

23-1. Discuss the economic rationale of the "irregular-secular increase program." What does this imply about the size of the national debt?

23-2. Discuss the economic rationale of the "steady-secular increase program." What alterations in the commercial banking system and in monetary control does this program require?

23-3. Demonstrate the significance of the Pigou effect for the "steady-secular increase program."

23-4. Write a summary statement of section 2 of this chapter. Be sure to refer to the major sources cited in the footnotes.

23-5. What is meant by the "Labour Standard"? Which cost-push theory of inflation best supports the so-called labor standard?

23-6. "Whenever the average wage level rises faster than productivity increases, then obviously there is cost-push inflation." Do you agree?

23-7. Evaluate the long-run monetary policy discussed in the last section of this chapter. Do you think that it is feasible? Elaborate.

23-8. Discuss some of the interactions between demand-pull and cost-push inflation.

23-9. Discuss what is meant by "sellers' inflation" and "mark-up inflation." Are these two views inconsistent or are they compatible? Explain.

Bibliography

Ackley, G. "Administered Prices and the Inflationary Process," *American Economic Review*, May 1959.

Brown, W. G., *The Wage-Price Issue: A Theoretical Analysis*. Princeton: Princeton University Press, 1960.

Clark, J. M., *The Wage-Price Problem*. New York: The American Bankers Association, 1960.

Friedman, M., *A Program for Monetary Stability*. New York: Fordham University Press, 1960.

Haberler, G., *Inflation: Its Causes and Cures*. Washington, D. C.: American Enterprise Association, 1960.

Jacoby, N. H., ed., *United States Monetary Policy*. New York: The American Assembly, 1958.

Means, G. C., *Pricing Power and the Public Interest: A Study Based on Steel.* New York: Harper & Row, Publishers, 1962.

Meyers, C. A., ed., *Wages, Prices, Profits, and Productivity.* New York: The American Assembly, 1959.

The Relationship of Prices to Economic Stability and Growth. A compendium of papers submitted to the Joint Economic Committee, Congress of the United States, March 31, 1958.

Selden, R. T., "Business Pricing Policies and Inflation," *Journal of Political Economy,* April 1963.

24

Fiscal Policy: The Framework for Fiscal Control

One of the major conclusions of the three preceding chapters was that although monetary policy is necessary, it alone cannot provide for continuing high levels of income and output, relative price-level stability, and economic growth. Obviously, therefore, other areas of public policy must be explored and utilized if government is to make any material contribution to the important goals of economic stability and growth.

There are several major types of economic policy other than monetary policy that can be used by government. These include: (1) anti-monopoly policy, primarily with respect to business organizations, though it may also apply to labor unions; (2) government loan and guarantee programs; (3) "socialization of income" via the governmental budget, which is the mainstream of fiscal policy; (4) direct controls, such as wage, price, and rationing controls; and (5) outright ownership of the means of production—that is, classic socialism.

These five areas of public policy have been listed more or less in increasing order of their divergence from the policy prescriptions implicit in traditional western economic thought. The list also represents the approximate order of their introduction and length of use in American economic history. In this and the following chapter the primary concern is with the area entitled "socialization of income."

1. Some Preliminary Remarks on Fiscal Policy

As noted in Chapter 21, several theoretical and actual developments occurred during and immediately after World War II that sent monetary policy into the wings and made fiscal policy the leading star. This does not mean, however, that fiscal policy was unanimously accepted. To the contrary, a good deal of debate over its effectiveness characterized the growth and use of fiscal policy, and the controversy has not yet abated. This debate, however, cannot be examined in detail until a firm foundation of the scope and instruments of fiscal policy has been established.

A. Socialization of Income

The term "socialization of income" refers simply to the deliberate actions taken by government in directing the flow of money income through the public budget. More specifically, it refers to the use of fiscal powers by government to channel through the public sector of the economy money income that would otherwise have flowed through the strictly private sector. Government, of course, in socializing income makes use of its powers of taxing and spending—that is, whenever it taxes, money income is channeled away from the private sector of the economy and into government; and when government spends, the funds are channeled back into the private sector.

Note that the term "socialization of income" is used here in a forthright descriptive manner, and as such it does not imply any particular value judgments. Thus, socialization of income is not to be confused with government ownership of the means of production. In fact, historically in the United States, despite any prevailing myths to the contrary, there has been very little increase in the outright ownership by government of productive means. On the other hand, one of the most significant historical changes in the structure of the economy in the last-half century has been the movement towards increasing socialization of income. In short, as noted above, fiscal policy has acquired an increasingly important role.

For example, in 1929 government purchases of goods and services constituted only about 8 per cent of the estimated gross national product. In recent years, however, this figure has increased substantially and is now running in the vicinity of 20 per cent. The greatest portion of the increase has been for both direct and indirect defense expenditures. (Of course, government purchases of goods and services do not reveal the whole story, for government transfer payments must be taken into account. Once this is done, the total level of government expenditures exceeds 25 per cent of the gross national product.)

B.   Allocational and Distributional Impacts

Although the primary concern of the remaining chapters is with government taxing and spending as they influence the aggregate levels of economic activity, there are other consequences of these programs that must be considered. It takes but a moment's reflection to realize that governmental taxing and spending programs have strong resource allocative effects, as well as significant income distributional impacts.[1] And since taxing and spending by government are, in the American economy, primarily a product of purely discretionary decisions by legislative and executive officials, the allocational and distributional effects will usually be the result of a hodgepodge of nonmarket forces. Certainly political factors figure strongly in determining the type and extent of fiscal policy that will be used at any particular time.[2]

Here the contrast between monetary and fiscal policy is striking. For the most part, monetary policy is administered on the assumption that allocational and distributional decisions are still made in the private market sector of the economy. Fiscal policy, on the other hand, is administered with the full knowledge that it will supplement, or perhaps even counteract, the decisions made in the private market place. This, at one and the same time, points to the potentiality and the danger of fiscal policy. The potentiality relates to the fact that fiscal policy may be used to make adjustments where the "body politic" is either dissatisfied with the decisions resulting in the market or distrusts the decisions that it anticipates will be made. The danger, at least as seen by some, is twofold: first, there is the fact that the decisions resulting from the political process, as opposed to those from the economic market place, will not be subject to objective tests of efficiency and appropriateness; second, there is the possibility that if too many decisions are made outside of the market place, the market system will not function in anything like the idealized manner. In a sense, the first danger is associated with the

---

[1] See any good text on public finance for a discussion of these impacts.

[2] See the questions raised in section 4 about the problems of spending, taxation, balance-imbalance, and debt management.

qualitative factors in fiscal policy, and the second is associated with the quantitative factors.

2.   The Instruments of Fiscal Policy

Fiscal policy is defined as the use of taxation, government spending, and other fiscal devices in the attempt to achieve the goals of economic stability and growth. These goals, of course, are equally relevant for both monetary and fiscal policy, but the instruments used in reaching them, as well as the motivation underlying the use of the instruments, may be quite different. The instruments of fiscal policy may be listed quite simply:

1. Government expenditures;
2. Taxation;
3. A combination of expenditures and taxation so that the budget is either balanced or unbalanced, and if unbalanced, has either a surplus or a deficit;
4. Government debt management, which, though closely related to monetary policy, is a segment of fiscal policy.

Technically, all four of these instruments can be used at every level of government—national, state, and local. However, the subsequent discussion is limited to fiscal policy at the national level for three important reasons. First, the volume of tax revenues and expenditures is greatest at the federal level, far outstripping state and local spending and taxing.[3] Second, both political and economic power is by far the greatest at this level of government. Third, this is the only level of government where there is something like a central "control point," from which a single unified view can be maintained with respect to objectives, operations, and implementation of policy decisions. Furthermore, fiscal policy at the national level can, through such devices as grants-in-aid, tax substitution remission, and so on, affect the fiscal activity at state and local levels quite significantly.

One other important point needs to be considered. This is to make a distinction between two types of fiscal policy—really, two different methods of determining the timing of expenditure and tax revenue decisions. These are discretionary and automatic fiscal policy.

---

[3]In the post-World War II period, however, there has been a tremendous increase in state and local receipts and expenditures. In fact, state and local fiscal activity is increasing at a far more rapid rate than that at the federal level. From $12.3 billion in 1946, state and local revenues rose to $68.4 in 1963-64. Expenditures over the same time period rose from $11.0 billion to $69.3 billion.

Discretionary fiscal policy refers to the situation in which the Congress and the chief executive make deliberate, discretionary decisions as to the amount and timing of spending and taxing. For example, if there is a slump in the levels of output and employment, the federal government *must* decide whether to increase its spending in order to counteract the contraction. And if the decision is made in favor of greater spending, the government must further arbitrarily determine how much is to be spent, and for what. In this branch of fiscal policy, therefore, the emphasis is upon deliberate, arbitrary, discretionary decision making.

Automatic fiscal policy, on the other hand, refers to the fact that some changes in taxing and spending are *functionally related* to the levels of output and employment—that is, changes in income will induce changes in government spending and tax revenues. Consider the case of unemployment benefits. A slump in income and employment will induce a rise in government spending as more unemployment compensation benefits are paid out, while at the same time the lower personal incomes lead to a reduction in tax revenues. Discretionary fiscal policies are discussed in more detail in the next chapter. The automatic stabilizers are considered in the next section.

3. The Automatic Stabilizers

In recent years a great deal of attention has been devoted to the so-called automatic or built-in stabilizers. The chief merit of the automatic stabilizers is that they affect the level of income contracyclically, but without any discretionary action by Congress or the executive branch of the government. Consider, for example, unemployment insurance. When the economy enters the contractionary stage of the cycle, government spending automatically rises as more and more unemployed workers draw their unemployment compensation, while at the same time governmental revenues dwindle because of the declining income tax base. Thus, this particular stabilizer prevents the incomes of the covered workers from falling to zero, and concurrently it tends towards a deficit in the governmental budget. It is to be noted and emphasized that these results occur without any arbitrary action being taken by the public officials—that is, they are automatic, or built in the tax expenditure structure of the government.

Interestingly enough, the automatic stabilizers that are embodied in fiscal legislation were not enacted with their contracyclical effects in mind. Indeed, it is safe to say that the more important stabilizers—the personal and corporate income taxes, excise taxes, Old Age Survivors Insurance, and unemployment insurance—were put into effect for quite different reasons, and at the time they were enacted little, if anything, was known about the "automatic stabilizers."[4] In a sense this is rather important, for it means that the laws will not be tampered with arbitrarily as a means of combating the cycle, and thus their effectiveness as automatic stabilizers will not be reduced or impaired.[5]

Let us consider some of the important built-in stabilizers. The anti-contractionary impact of unemployment insurance has already been examined. By the same token, when the economy begins its expansionary march, this particular stabilizer tends to put on the brakes and thus to reduce inflationary pressures. That is, as unemployment falls, so do governmental payments in the form of unemployment compensation; and at the same time tax revenues begin to rise as workers experience rising personal incomes. Thus, during the expansion there is a tendency towards a surplus in the governmental budget.

Another automatic stabilizer is the personal progressive income tax. As personal incomes rise during the expansion, the tax rate rises progressively, thus taking successively larger bites out of personal income. In other words, disposable income does not rise as rapidly as personal income, and insofar as consumption is a function of disposable income, the brakes may be applied to inflationary consumer expenditures. But note that, *given* the government's expenditure program, this particular stabilizer tends to create a surplus in the budget as the expansion continues, and accordingly it tends to be anti-inflationary.

On the other hand, it serves as an anti-contractionary control as incomes and employment drop. Because of the progressivity of the tax rate, disposable income falls less rapidly than personal income. Put otherwise, governmental tax revenues fall more rapidly than personal incomes, and as a result there is a tendency towards a deficit in the budget.

The two stabilizers discussed thus far have been very effective in the post-World War II economy, primarily because they are closely and directly linked to changes in important economic variables—em-

---

[4]See N. F. Keiser, "The Development of the Concept of 'Automatic Stabilizers'," *Journal of Finance*, December 1956.

[5]This point is stressed by M. O. Clement, "The Concept of Automatic Stabilizers," *Southern Economic Journal*, January 1959. Parts of this section rely heavily on Clement's article, which should be referred to by anyone interested in the automatic stabilizers.

ployment and income—and hence they display a high cyclical sensitivity. So far as the personal income tax is concerned, its effectiveness is attributable to (1) the cyclical volatility of the tax base, (2) the progressivity of the tax rate and (3) the fact that much of the tax revenue is collected currently via the withholding procedure. The other important taxes—the corporate income tax and excise taxes—have also served well as automatic stabilizers, not because of any progressivity features, but because of the cyclical volatility of the base. Moreover, inasmuch as corporations tend to operate on the basis of accruing tax liabilities, current collection tends to add to the significance of the corporate income tax as an automatic stabilizer.[6]

Along with the automatic stabilizers already discussed, there are certain other forces that act in the same manner, although they do not take the form of legislation. For example, many large corporations tend to follow a "steady-dividend" policy—that is, they tend to pay approximately the same dividend period after period, regardless of their earnings. Thus, even though profits may be running very high in a period of expansion, the same dividend is paid, and this tends to stabilize the dividend income of the stockholders. On the other hand, in a period of contraction, when personal incomes are falling, this dividend policy also tends to stabilize the incomes of the stockholders.

Perhaps one of the most important built-in stabilizers is aggregate consumer behavior. Insofar as current consumption is a function of the highest income recently received, consumers strive to maintain their consumption as income declines. Thus, during a period of contraction the average propensity to consume rises, and during the expansion the average propensity to consume falls as income approaches its former highest level. We have already discussed this aspect of the consumption function in several of the preceding chapters, and its significance as an automatic stabilizer should not be minimized.

Two or three final points about the stabilizers. First, their economic significance can be shown in Figure 24–1, in which the TT curve reflects government tax revenue and the GG curve represents government expenditures. Each curve is drawn on the assumption that there is a *given* tax structure and spending program; that is, tax rates and expenditures are not *arbitrarily* altered as GNP changes. Please note that as GNP rises the TT curve also rises, indicating increased revenues. This, of course, is to be expected. But note also that the TT curve begins to rise more rapidly as GNP grows. This is the result of the progressivity in the personal and corporate income tax rates. The GG curve, on the other hand, has a negative slope, illustrating the fact that as GNP rises, government spending will automatically fall. Thus,

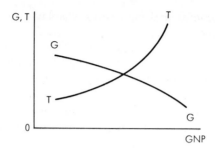

FIGURE 24-1

the stabilizers tend towards a surplus as the expansion continues and towards a deficit as the contraction goes on. We shall return to this in the next chapter.

Second, it is important to note that the automatic stabilizers cannot prevent a turning point in the cycle; nor, once the expansion or contraction is underway, can they reverse the economy. They do, however, prevent the expansion and contraction from becoming worse once they are underway, and in this respect they reduce the amplitude of the business cycle. The really important thing about this aspect of the automatic stabilizers is that they provide more "breathing room" for the policymakers to decide upon and implement discretionary fiscal policies.

Finally, some economists have become concerned over the effectiveness of the stabilizers, arguing, in fact, that they are so effective that they prevent the economy from reaching full employment.[7] That is, as the expansion continues, the built-in stabilizers "take hold" and not only slow down the expansion, but also prevent it from reaching the full-employment ceiling. How substantial this argument is remains to be seen, but it should not be overlooked. At any rate, it is quite safe to conclude that the automatic stabilizers have been very effective in the American economy in reducing the amplitude of the business cycle in the post-World War II period.[8]

---

[6]*Ibid.* See also E. Cary Brown, "Pay-As-You-Go Corporate Taxes," *American Economic Review*, September 1947.

[7]D. Hamburg, "Fiscal Policy and Stagnation Since 1957," *Southern Economic Journal*, January 1963.

[8]See especially W. Lewis, Jr., *Federal Fiscal Policy in the Postwar Recessions* (Washington, D. C.: The Brookings Institution, 1962), for a good discussion of the effectiveness of the automatic stabilizers.

4.   Types of Decisions in Fiscal Policy

The issues and problems in the area of fiscal policy are numerous, difficult, and diverse. This is true whether the focus of attention is upon expenditures, taxation, budgetary balance or imbalance, or debt management. Consider just some of the problems associated with government expenditures. Should the government purchase goods and services, or should it limit itself simply to making transfer payments? If and when transfer payments are made, should they be made to elderly people, or should they be made to younger persons? If, on the other hand, goods are purchased, ought they be investment goods for projects such as T.V.A. and the Hoover Dam, or should they be primarily for consumer services, such as police protection and regulation of communication? If expenditures are for investment goods, then it must be decided whether they will be for tangible things, such as public housing, or intangible things, such as education and care for the mentally ill. And finally, the most important question—what will be the induced effects of any of these types of expenditures?

With respect to taxation, again serious questions arise. Who is to pay the taxes? Should new taxes or changes in existing taxes apply only to corporations or to individuals or to both? Are tax rates to be based on income, sales, assets, or what have you? And are the rates to be proportional, progressive, or regressive? Should they be ad valorum or ad hoc? And what kind of presumptions should Congress make about whether the burden of a particular tax may be shifted to some other group? Will the yield from the tax be cyclically sensitive or insensitive? And again, what are the overall economic effects of a tax change.

There are also important questions under the heading of budget balance and imbalance. For instance, if there is to be an imbalance, should it be on the deficit side or on the surplus side? And how large should the surplus or deficit be at any given time? Why are changes in the budget balance-imbalance to take place? And when are they to occur, particularly with respect to the stage of the business cycle? Should the decisions be fixed by legislative action, or should some discretionary authority be left with the chief executive? Finally, once the decisions have been made, how are they to be carried out in practice?

With respect to debt management such questions as follows are relevant: Are new issues of debt to be long term or short term? Should income tax concessions on interest income derived from holdings of the national debt be made? What sort of efforts should be made to sell new debt or to refund debt to individuals, nonfinancial corporations, or financial institutions?

All of these questions, along with many others, must of course be resolved in the political arena. To be sure, the economist may be able to offer a great deal of advice on each, but the final decisions rest with the governmental process. One thing that must be kept in mind is that, difficult though these questions may be, *they are indeed settled* one way or another, whether implicitly or explicitly, by acts of Congress and by executive action. The important task is to examine the economic repercussions once the decisions have been made.

5. Fiscal Policy and the Level of Income

Consider first the effects of government expenditures on aggregate demand, using a rather traditional approach. In nearly all of the theories reviewed in Parts 2–4 government did not figure in as an important variable. That is, it was assumed that $Y = C + I$. Now, however, since the economic significance of fiscal policy is under review, the income formula must be modified to read as $Y = C + I + G$, where G stands for governmental expenditures for goods and services. Further, the magnitude of consumption (C) can be influenced by the changes in disposable income that result from changes in tax collections. In other words, the assumption that government is minimal and neutral must be dropped, and the economic impact of changes in taxation and governmental expenditures must be considered.

The rest of this section assumes that changes in the levels of expenditures and tax revenues are *institutionally determined*. Thus changes in income do not induce changes in G (governmental spending) and T (tax revenues), although a change in G or T will cause the level of income to rise or fall via the multiplier effect. In short, the automatic stabilizers are being abstracted from. This is indeed an unrealistic assumption (and it is relaxed in part in the next section), but it permits us to isolate the multiplier effects of changes in government spending and tax revenues. Also, private investment is assumed to remain constant (that is, induced investment is ignored). Finally some unemployed resources are assumed to exist.

A. Government Expenditures Multiplier

First consider the case of a substantial increase in governmental spending. Let us begin the analysis by assuming a budgetary balance $(G = T)$ which is turned into an imbalance by a rise in government spending of $10 billion. This rise in G is financed by borrowing, *not by a rise in tax revenues*.[9] Obviously there is going to be a rise in the level of income, for now G is included in the formula $Y = C+I+G$. The question is, by how much will Y rise.[10]

Once again it is necessary to fall back upon the familiar multiplier analysis. Recall that the formula for the multiplier effect is k times the increase in spending, where $k = 1/[1-(\triangle C/\triangle Y)]$. Thus the multiplier effect is written as

$$Y = k \cdot \triangle G,$$

where $\triangle G$ stands for the rise in government spending.

Assume that the marginal propensity to consume (b) is .5. In this case income will rise by $50 billion. That is:

$$\triangle Y = k \cdot \triangle G$$
$$\triangle Y = \frac{1}{1-b} \cdot \triangle G$$
$$\triangle Y = \frac{1}{1-.8} \cdot \$10 \text{ billion}$$
$$\triangle Y = \frac{1}{.2} \cdot \$10 \text{ billion}$$
$$\triangle Y = 5 \cdot \$10 \text{ billion}$$
$$\triangle Y = \$50 \text{ billion}.$$

In short, an increase in G (with T constant) will give rise to a multiplier effect in exactly the same way as an increase in private invest-

---

[9]There are several sources of borrowing, but only three are really important. If the Treasury finances the deficit by borrowing from the Federal Reserve System or from the commercial banking system, the money supply and/or excess reserves in the commercial banking system will rise. On the other hand, if the Treasury borrows from the "public" (that is, private individuals and businesses other than commercial banks), there will be no increase in reserves and the money supply. The lenders will simply be providing "idle balances" to the Treasury who will, in turn, put them back into circulation. Thus the money supply is not affected, though velocity of the money supply is increased.

[10]It must be cautioned that the discussion in this section is quite incomplete. As noted above, it is presented only as an introduction to the more detailed analysis given in the next chapter.

ment. Conversely, a reduction in G will, *ceteris paribus*, result in a negative multiplier effect. The only difference is that we have substituted changes in G for changes in I.[11]

B.   The Tax Multiplier

What will happen to the level of income if there is a change in tax revenues (T)? Note at the outset that the tax multiplier, and hence the tax multiplier effect, will be less than the expenditures multiplier effect. The reason for this is that a change in tax revenues first influences disposable income, then consumption, and then income. Consider the case of a $10 billion reduction in tax revenues.[12] Once again begin with a budgetary balance, where G = T, but now T is reduced while G remains constant. Thus a deficit in the budget will materialize.

The $10 billion reduction simultaneously increases disposable income by the same amount. If the marginal propensity to consume (b) is .8, then aggregate consumption will rise by $8 billion, and the remaining $2 billion of the increased disposable income will go into personal savings. Now the usual multiplier ($1/1—b$) may be applied

---

[11]All this can be stated in a different way. The formula for gross national product is

$$Y = C + I + G.$$

Recall that consumption is a function of disposible income, that is,

$$C = a + bY_d.$$

The difference between GNP and Y_d can be written as

$$Y_d = Y—D—T + P + G + I,$$

where D stands for total capital consumption allowances, T for total tax collections, and P for aggregate transfer payments.

By substituting, we obtain

$$Y = a + bY_d + I + G$$
$$Y = a + bY—bD—bT + bP + I + G$$
$$Y = \frac{1}{1—b}(a—bD—bT + bP + I + G).$$

Of course, $1/1—b$ is the usual multiplier effect. Thus any change in the items in the parentheses will cause Y to change via the multiplier effect. But note that if the multiplier effect is to work out in the manner indicated above, the items in the parentheses must be independent of each other. This, of course, is patently impossible. For example, a rise in G that increases Y will also lead to a rise in T, perhaps induce additional I, affect transfer payments, and so on.

[12]We deal here only with personal income taxes and hence ignore corporate taxes. Also we assume that the change in T does not significantly alter the distribution of income.

to the *additional consumption spending* in order to determine how much Y will rise.

$$\triangle Y = k \cdot \triangle C$$
$$\triangle Y = \frac{1}{1-.8} \cdot \$8 \text{ billion}$$
$$\triangle Y = 5 \cdot \$8 \text{ billion}$$
$$\triangle Y = \$40 \text{ billion.}$$

Thus, in the case of a reduction of tax revenues, *ceteris paribus*, spending will rise by $b \cdot \triangle T = .8 \cdot \$10$ billion $= \$8$ billion, to which the usual multiplier is then applied.

The reason the tax multiplier is less than the expenditures multiplier is simply that the rise in government spending increases total spending immediately by $10 billion, while the tax reduction increases total spending immediately by only $8 billion. Therefore, the expenditures multiplier effect is greater than the tax multiplier effect for equal changes in G and T.

A *rise* in tax revenues will, *ceteris paribus*, result in a negative multiplier effect. An increase in T by $10 billion will, of course, reduce disposable income by the same amount. Thus, if the marginal propensity to consume is .8, aggregate consumption will fall by $8 billion. The negative multiplier effect, then, will be $k \cdot \triangle C = 5 \cdot -\$8$ billion $= -\$40$ billion.

C.   Balanced Budget Multiplier

What will happen to the level of income if government spending and tax revenues rise by the same amount? That is, what will occur if a $10 billion increase in government spending is financed by a simultaneous increase of $10 billion in tax revenues? At first glance it would seem that there would be no positive multiplier effect, for the rise in income due to the expenditures multiplier would be nullified by the negative multiplier on the tax side.

Closer examination, however, shows that is not the case. Assume that the rise in G and T is $10 billion and that the marginal propensity to consume is .8. Now the expenditures multiplier will be:

$$\triangle Y = k \cdot \triangle G$$
$$\triangle Y = \frac{1}{1-.8} \cdot \$10 \text{ billion}$$
$$\triangle Y = 5 \cdot \$10 \text{ billion}$$
$$\triangle Y = \$50 \text{ billion.}$$

On the other hand, the tax multiplier effect would be:

$$\triangle Y = k \cdot \triangle C$$
$$\triangle Y = \frac{1}{1-.8} \cdot -\$8 \text{ billion}$$
$$\triangle Y = 5 \cdot -\$8 \text{ billion}$$
$$\triangle Y = -\$40 \text{ billion.}$$

Thus the positive expenditures multiplier outweighs the negative tax multiplier effect by $10 billion. The reason for this is simply that government has increased aggregate spending by the amount of $10 billion. So long as the expenditures rise by at least the amount that revenues rise, there will be a positive multiplier effect.

More important, however, is the fact that if expenditures rise relative to revenues, *so that there is a deficit in the budget* (or a reduction in the surplus), the positive expenditures multiplier effect will be greater than the negative tax multiplier effect. Conversely, if revenues rise relative to expenditures, *so that a surplus develops* (or a deficit is reduced), the negative tax multiplier effect will be greater than the positive expenditures multiplier effect. Thus the net effects must be examined in evaluating the economic impact of fiscal policy. Whether there is a net expenditures multiplier or a net tax multiplier is of great importance.

6.   Changes in G, T, and Y

So far the discussion has assumed that T remains constant as G and Y change. This, of course, is highly unlikely, for as Y changes, T will also change. As G rises, so that there is a positive expenditures multiplier, Y and therefore T also rise. The reason for this is that the bulk of tax revenues are a function of Y. This can be written as

$$T = f(Y),$$

though this does not tell very much. It is also necessary to specify as precisely as possible what the functional relationship is. As a first approximation assume that the tax rate is proportional. In this case, then,

$$T = tY,$$

where t is the tax rate. Since the tax is proportional (say, at 20 per cent), no matter what taxable bracket a family is in, or how it spends its income, the same tax rate applies. This can be shown graphically (Figure 24–2), in which the slope of the curve OT is the tax rate. This

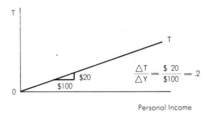

FIGURE 24–2

is referred to as the government's *marginal propensity to tax* (t).

Now if G rises by $10 billion, what will happen to the level of income? In the preceding section we concluded that, with the marginal propensity to consume at .8, Y would rise by $50 billion. However, now the marginal propensity to tax must be included in the analysis, and this reduces both the multiplier and the multiplier effect.

As G rises by $10 billion, income will also rise immediately by the same amount. This does not mean, however, that C will rise by $8 billion (recall that the marginal propensity to consume, b, is .8), for now the government's marginal propensity to tax (t) must be taken into account. If $t = .2$ (as assumed above), then $2 billion of the $10 billion increase in income will be taxed away, leaving the income recipients with additional *disposable* income of only $8 billion. Since consumption is a *function of disposable income*, and since the marginal propensity to consume is .8, C will rise by .8 ($8 billion) = $6.4 billion. In the next round of spending, 20 per cent of this will be taxed away, leaving only $5 billion (approximately) of additional disposable income, of which .8 ($5 billion) = $4 billion will go into extra consumption. And so on for each successive round of spending.

Obviously, then, the government's expenditures multiplier effect is less than what was calculated in the preceding section, for now there are *two leakages*—savings and taxes. The extent to which income will increase is given by

$$\triangle Y = k' \cdot \triangle G,$$

where k' stands for the multiplier that takes into account increases in T as Y rises.

The procedure for deriving k' is as follows: recall that $Y = C + I + G$, and that $C = f(Y_d)$, more specifically, $C = a + bY_d$. The difference between Y and Y_d is, in this case, T; that is, income less total tax revenues equals disposable income.[13] Recall also that $T = tY$, where t is the tax rate. Thus the consumption function can be written as $C = a+b(Y—T)$, or $C = a+b(Y—tY)$. Substituting this into the income formula,

$$Y = a+b(Y—T)+I+G$$
$$Y = a+b(Y—tY)+I+G$$
$$Y = a+bY—btY+I+G.$$

Then

$$Y—bY+btY = a+I+G$$

and

$$Y(1—b+bt) = a+I+G.$$

Dividing both sides by $(1—b+bt)$,

$$Y = \frac{a+I+G}{1—b+bt}$$

or

$$Y = \frac{1}{1—b(1—t)}(a+I+G).$$

Thus, the multiplier k′ is

$$\frac{1}{1—b(1—t)}.$$

In this example, then, the multiplier effect of a $10 billion rise in G, when $b = .8$ and $t = .2$, is

$$\triangle Y = k' \cdot \triangle G$$
$$\triangle Y = \frac{1}{1—b(1—t)} \cdot \triangle G$$
$$\triangle Y = \frac{1}{1—.8(1—.2)} \cdot \$10 \text{ billion}$$
$$\triangle Y = \frac{1}{1—.8(.8)} \cdot \$10 \text{ billion}$$
$$\triangle Y = \frac{1}{1—.64} \cdot \$10 \text{ billion}$$
$$\triangle Y = .36 \cdot \$10 \text{ billion} = \$3.6 \text{ billion (approximately)}.$$

---

[13]This illustration abstracts from transfer payments and capital consumption allowances. See footnote 11.

The reason why the multiplier is smaller in this case than it was in the preceding section (in which it was five) is because of the additional leakage due to the tax.

7. A Brief Look Ahead

The analysis of the two preceding sections is highly arbitrary and unrealistic. Although it is logically correct, given the underlying assumptions, it ignores numerous aspects of the real world. In actuality, the multiplier effect never works out as indicated by the formulas. Several impediments are present in the legislative and executive processes of the government. For instance, lags exist between making the decision to change G and/or T and the time at which the multiplier begins to materialize. As Y rises, due to the multiplier effect, the automatic stabilizers not only tend to increase T, but also to reduce G. More important, during the period in which the multiplier is operating the economy may have moved into another stage of the business cycle, necessitating a reversal in fiscal policy. Also autonomous shifts in the consumption function and investment demand schedule may occur. And certainly changes in G and/or T may induce changes in private investment expenditures, as well as in each other. All told, the government expenditures and tax multipliers never work out as assumed in theory. Many complicating factors are at play in an economy as complex as ours. Some of these are considered at length in the next chapter in which fiscal policy is discussed in greater detail. The formal analysis in this chapter is designed merely to serve as a point of departure for the subsequent discussion.

8. Summary

This chapter is simply a brief introductory statement to fiscal policy. Though we shall be concerned with fiscal policy as a means of affecting the levels of output, employment, and prices, it is quite necessary to realize that it has substantial allocational and income distributional impacts. For purposes of what follows, the major instruments of fiscal policy are government spending, taxing, budgetary balance and imbalance, and debt management. Sometimes these instruments come into play automatically when some variable (such as income) changes—that is, they are automatic stabilizers. At other times they come into play by deliberate, discretionary decisions by the Congress and/or chief executive, in which case they are discretionary fiscal policy.

In sections 5-6, a highly oversimplified analysis of the consequences of changes in the levels of tax revenues and government spending was presented. The tentative conclusion drawn there was that the net effect on the levels of output and income depends upon the relative magnitude of the positive expenditures multiplier and the negative tax multiplier effects. One special case is the balanced budget, which concludes that when expenditures and revenues rise by the same amount there will be a positive multiplier effect equal to the amount of additional government spending. In the next chapter we shall examine the economic implications of fiscal policy in much more detail.

QUESTIONS

24-1. What are the major differences between discretionary and automatic fiscal policy?

24-2. Comment on the political and economic origins of the automatic stabilizers.

24-3. Illustrate how each of the following may operate as an automatic stabilizer, and comment on the effectiveness of each:

(a) the progressive personal income tax;
(b) the progressive corporate income tax;
(c) the unemployment compensation program;
(d) the farm-price support program.

24-4. How do the personal and corporate income taxes differ as automatic stabilizers?

24-5. Using your own assumed data, show the different impacts on the level of income resulting from a:

(a) government expenditures multiplier;
(b) tax multiplier;
(c) balanced budget multiplier.

24-6. Explain how the government's marginal propensity to tax tends to reduce the multiplier effect of a given increase in private investment spending. Be sure to answer in terms of a multiplier (k') that takes into account the government's tax program.

Bibliography

Allen, C. M., "Fiscal Marksmanship," *Oxford Economic Papers*, March 1965.

Keiser, N. F., "The Development of the Concept of the 'Automatic Stabilizers'," *Journal of Finance*, December 1956.

Lewis, W., Jr., *Federal Fiscal Policy in the Postwar Recessions*. Washington, D. C.: The Brookings Institution, 1962.

Ott, D. J., and A. F. Ott, "Budget Balance and Equilibrium Income," *Journal of Finance*, March 1955.

Scherer, L., "On Measuring Fiscal Policy," *Journal of Finance*, December 1965.

25

Fiscal Policy: Economic Stability and Growth

How can fiscal policy be used to contribute to the important goals of economic stability and economic growth? In answering such a question it is necessary to keep in mind many of the difficulties involved in implementing fiscal decisions. It is one thing, of course, to say that a tax reduction will (*ceteris paribus*) yield a positive multiplier effect or that more liberal depreciation allowances may stimulate net, new investment that will lead to a multiplier-accelerator effect; but it is quite a different thing to assume blithely that things will work out in reality as the theory implies. Institutional factors play an important and fundamental role in the area of fiscal policy.[1]

1. Some Institutional Considerations

Obviously the source of revenues for the federal government will have a decided impact upon aggregate economic activity. If, for exam-

---

[1]A. E. Holmans, *United States Fiscal Policy, 1945-1949* (Oxford: The Clarendon Press, 1961), especially Chapter 1. See also the various *Economic Reports of the President.*

ple, the government elected to raise most of its revenues from a general sales tax, as opposed to the personal income tax, consumption behavior would be substantially influenced. By the same token, if the government decided to increase the share of total tax revenue derived from the corporate income tax, the investment decisions of many large corporations would definitely be affected. Governmental decisions, in short, as to the sources of tax revenues must be carefully evaluated and analyzed. The same conclusion holds true for decisions pertaining to the types and amounts of government expenditures.

The problem is complicated, however, by institutional reality. If there is any one statement that can be made with confidence about today's tax structure, and thus about today's sources of tax revenues, it is this—the current structure is very much the same as it was last year. While this may not be of much help to either the policymaker or the student of fiscal policy, it does have a good deal of empirical relevance. To be sure, there have been changes in the tax structure over the years, but there is no doubt that the tax system as a whole has, somewhat like Topsie, "just growed." There seem to have been little forethought and long-run planning involved, and the changes that have been introduced have usually come about on a piecemeal basis.[2]

Most of the major changes in the tax structure have been bred in wartime and war-related periods, when Congress believed that it had to provide additional revenues quickly, although this is hardly the type of situation that induces consistent, goal-oriented planning. But the important thing to note is that once a change in the tax structure has been introduced, it tends to become institutionalized as a more or less permanent part of the overall structure.

This process of institutionalization, which is as relevant for broad changes in taxes as it is for specific changes, has a significant bearing on the influence of fiscal policy. For example, when the personal income tax was first introduced, it became a permanent part of the tax system, as did the corporate income tax. And sales taxes at the state level have become a permanent part of consumer expenditures. Similarly, the rather specialized taxes that call for some sort of preferential treatment for vested interests also tend to become institutionalized.

Consider, for instance, the matter of the "27½ per cent depletion allowance" that is applicable to the oil and gas producing industries. Even if an open-ended depletion allowance is justified on some combination of economic, political, and military grounds, there still is no systematic or scientific means of determining exactly what the allowance

---

[2]See any good treatment of the fiscal history of the United States.

should be. The current figure of 27½ per cent, in fact, resulted from a compromise in Congress, when one house approved a 25 per cent rate and the other a 30 per cent rate. But since there have been years of experience with the 27½ per cent figure, and since any proposal to reduce or to increase it immediately creates extremely vocal reactions on the part of the various vested interest groups involved, it appears that the figure must be regarded virtually as a given datum. In short, the institutionalization of the tax structure makes it extremely difficult to alter taxes in order to use them to achieve certain goals and objectives, although some experimentation has taken place in recent years.

So much for the institutional aspects, but they must be kept in mind, for they will crop up again in later discussion in this chapter.

2.   Tax Changes and the Investment Demand Curve

In the United States there apparently has been a great deal more willingness to experiment with business taxation than with personal income taxation. That is, Congress seems to have been more willing to use the carrot instead of the stick by extending special tax concessions or de facto tax reductions that are designed to encourage corporations to do particular things. Consider a few examples.

Congress has been willing to "liberalize" the tax treatment of depreciation, as well as to tolerate administrative decisions within the Internal Revenue Service designed to accomplish the same result, in the hope that additional private investment expenditure will materialize.[3] For the business firm, liberalization of depreciation means either (a) shortening the total time period in which a depreciable asset may be written off the business' books for tax purposes, or (b) allowing a larger proportion of the total costs of a depreciable asset to be taken as a deductible business expense in the earlier years of its useful life. The result of either approach is to increase the amount of depreciation expense and hence, *ceteris paribus,* to reduce the amount of the current annual income tax liability in the early years of the useful life of the asset. The consequence, therefore, is at least a temporary increase in after-tax corporate profits.[4]

---

[3]This legislation was enacted in 1954 and 1962.

[4]R. Eisner, "Effects of Depreciation Allowances for Tax Purposes," *Tax Revision Compendium* (Washington, D. C.: Government Printing Office, 1959), Vol. 2, Committee on Ways and Means, House of Representatives, Congress of the United States. See also Eisner's "An Appraisal of Proposals for Tax Differentials Affecting Investment," *Income Tax Differentials* (Princeton: Tax Institute, 1958).

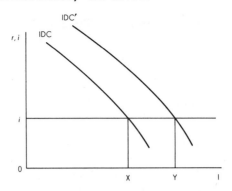

FIGURE 25–1

The important question now is this: What effect will these changes in depreciation rules for tax purposes have on private business investment? Quite often the reasoning lurking behind proposals to liberalize depreciation rules runs as follows: assume that business investment decisions are made according to the concept of an investment demand schedule, on which various investment proposals are ranked in descending order of their internal rates of return (that is, their marginal efficiencies). Recall that the present values of the cash flows resulting from a planned investment project are equated with the price of the capital goods. Since the cash flows are calculated after taxes, the effect of liberalizing the tax treatment of depreciation is to raise the entire investment demand schedule of the firm. Thus, given the marginal cost of capital, the major result is a shift of the curve to the right, as shown in Figure 25–1. In other words, a higher level of investment will take place, and as a result, all other things equal, there would be a positive multiplier effect.

But remember that what knowledge we have of the ways in which business investment decisions are made is rather inadequate. To the extent that business firms rely on some sort of before-tax payback method of making their investment decisions, or, for that matter, to the extent that they rely on just plain "hunch," much of the preceding analysis does not apply. Also recall that the height and shape of the investment demand curve, both at the firm level and the aggregate level, are largely determined by the status of expectations of the future, and accordingly the curve may be wildly unstable, subject to drastic, abrupt, and frequent shifts. At times these changes in the investment demand curve may be so great that they virtually nullify any changes in investment activity that might take place as a result of changes in the tax treatment of depreciation.

3.   Budgetary Balance and Imbalance

One of the major points in the earlier discussion of monetary policy was that the policy makers must make the "big decision" of determining the total amount of the money supply. A similar decision must be made in the area of fiscal policy—namely, determination at any given time of the budgetary balance or imbalance. That is, should expenditures be equal to revenues, or does the overall economic situation indicate the need for a surplus or a deficit? Moreover, just as the monetary policy makers have a very important, but not absolute, control over the money supply, so also do the fiscal policy makers have an important degree of control over the amount of the surplus or deficit. Again, however, just as in the case of monetary policy, their control is not absolute.

Reduced to its simplest form, fiscal policy may be put in these terms to the policy maker—fight depressions with deficits and fight inflations with surpluses. Given the general reluctance to act in the last twenty-five years on the part of both the congressional and executive branches of the government, this oversimplification has much to recommend it.[5] There is still a quantitatively important segment of thought in the United States that calls for annually balanced budgets, except perhaps in times of war, regardless of the level of aggregate output and employment; and many American newspaper editors, even in times of acknowledged underemployment, have called for a program of annual debt reduction and hence continuous annual budgetary surpluses.

However, to return to the simple rule given above (that is, deficits in depressions and surpluses in inflations), consider Figure 25–2, which presents a graphic illustration of the relationship of *expected* levels of government revenues and government expenditures (in current dollars), *given the tax program and the expenditures program*. The TT curve portrays the tax revenue schedule, associating different amounts of revenue with different levels of GNP. The positive slope of TT is attributable to the automatic stabilizers on the revenue side, while the upward curvature of TT at higher levels of GNP is largely the result of the cyclical sensitivity of the personal and corporate income taxes.

[5]G. Colm and M. Young, *The Federal Budget and the National Economy* (Washington, D. C.: National Planning Association, 1955), Planning Pamphlet No. 80.

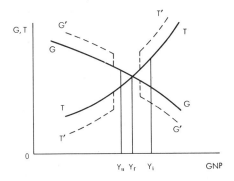

FIGURE 25–2

The total expenditures curve GG shows the various levels of expenditures at different levels of GNP, given the government spending program. The height of the curve is determined by the total continuing expenditures by the government for "housekeeping" details and the more or less continuous expenditures for the automatic stabilizers. The negative slope of GG is attributable to the operation of the automatic stabilizers on the spending side, reflecting the fact that the total dollar amount of spending for these programs declines as GNP rises. Further, there is some downward curvature in the GG curve since some of the spending on the automatic stabilizers will, at high levels of employment, decline more rapidly than GNP rises.

At any given level of GNP, therefore, the vertical distance between the GG and TT curves measures the amount of the surplus or deficit. Now, in its simplest form, fiscal policy concludes that deficits constitute a boosting effect upon aggregate demand, while surpluses impose a depressing effect. Remember, however, that GNP in Figure 25–2 is measured in terms of current dollars, and thus it cannot be said definitely whether the boosting effect of a deficit will result wholly in a rise in output, a rise in the price level, or some combination of the two. By the same token, it cannot be said categorically whether the dragging effect of a surplus will result in a decline in output, a decline in the price level, or a combination of both.

It is also important to recall that the GG and TT curves are the consequence of *given* expenditures and revenue programs. Congress may, of course, add anticyclical discretionary measures to both of these programs. This is shown by the dotted lines in Figure 25–2, which indicate the possibility of Congressional discretionary changes in expenditures and revenues. The curve G'G' thus shows that Congress may increase expenditures above what would otherwise take place at low levels of GNP and reduce spending below what would otherwise occur at high levels of GNP. Similarly, T'T' illustrates that Congress may make adjustments in tax rates and thus revenues in order to combat unemployment or inflation. Thus, the surplus or deficit can be made larger or smaller by discretionary action.

Now the thorny problem of the intersection of the GG and TT curves —that is, the balanced budget—must be examined. Ideally this intersection should occur at the full-employment level of GNP; and presumably if there were perfect cost-price flexibility in the economy, this is where the intersection would occur. Assume for the moment that the intersection is at Y_f, where the subscript f signifies a full-employment level of GNP. Under these conditions, any rise in GNP would be purely in nominal terms; that is, it would be measured by a rise in the price level with no increase in the output of real goods and services. The resulting surplus then would presumably exert an anti-inflationary force, since revenues would rise and expenditures would decline. Whether the anti-inflationary impact would be sufficient without discretionary cuts in spending and/or increases in tax rates is a matter for debate.

On the other hand, if the level of income is to the left of the intersection, so that there is less than full employment, the resulting deficit would presumably give a boost to the economy. Revenues would fall and expenditures would rise automatically, although discretionary actions will yield a more positive result.

There is no reason, however, to assume that the intersection of the GG and TT curves would, or even could, occur at Y_f with a stable price level. Recall the earlier discussions on the conflict between the full-employment objective and the price-level stability goal. The analysis of the modified Phillips curve (Chapters 13 and 23) indicated that if the economy is to experience price-level stability, it must pay the price of an unemployment rate of from 5 to 7 per cent. Conversely, if the goal of full employment is reached and maintained, the price level will tend to rise by approximately 3 per cent per year. Thus, to say that the intersection of the GG and TT schedules can occur at Y_f with a stable price level is rather idealistic, for presumably under current conditions this dual objective cannot be attained.

There is still another problem that must be considered, namely, where the intersection should be. Is it to occur at full employment, with some inflation (Y_f); or at less than full employment, with relative price-level stability (Y_u); or at greater than full employment, with substantial inflation (Y_i)? Even though this is a difficult question, it is one that the national legislature must resolve in one way or another. The GG and TT schedules do, of course, represent real economic phenomena in the real world, and the point at which they intersect is quite important. The Council of Economic Advisers has, in recent years, grappled with this problem at great length, and as a result it has introduced the analytical concept of the "full-employment surplus." This concept, while by no means new, has important policy implications; at least the Council has relied heavily on it for policy purposes.[6]

4. The Full-Employment Surplus

The full-employment surplus may be defined very simply as the budgetary surplus that would exist *if* there were full employment, *given the present schedules of tax revenues* (TT) *and expenditures* (GG). In other words, if the economy moves to full employment, then the existing tax and spending programs would yield a surplus in the budget. This is shown in Figure 25–3 in which AB measures the surplus at full employment Y_f. On the other hand, if the budget is balanced at C, then there will be underemployment Y_u. Of course, and this is the point made ear-

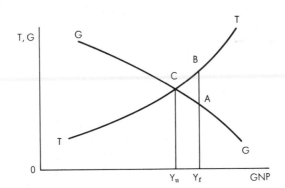

FIGURE 25–3

[6]The Council first presented the concept in the 1962 *Economic Report of the President,* pp. 78-81. However, in its 1966 report to the President the Council did not even refer to the full-employment surplus. Nevertheless, the concept is important for our purposes.

lier in discussing the automatic stabilizers, tax and spending programs that will yield a full-employment surplus are restrictive—that is, they operate to prevent full employment from being achieved. The reason for this is that as income rises, tax revenues tend to rise and government spending tends to fall. This of course tends to retard the expansion in income.

One of the important points made by the Council is that over the past decade the full-employment surplus has been positive, ranging from a little less than $5 billion (in 1958) to about $12.5 billion (in 1960).[7] Why has this been the case? Recall the earlier discussion about the tendency of Congress to balance the budget as nearly as possible. Recall also that Congress has a tendency to adjust revenues to the "housekeeping details" and the automatic stabilizers, that is, to what it considers to be the "necessary" expenditures. Now if these expenditures happen to be at the level indicated by C (in Figure 25-3), and if total revenues are adjusted as closely as possible to C, there will be less than full employment, *ceteris paribus.* In other words, the revenue and spending programs are serving as a constraint to the full-employment performance of the economy. The Council has preferred to put the same point somewhat differently: given the existing tax and spending programs, a surplus of AB would occur if the economy were to move to full employment. However, the budget that yields a full-employment surplus unfortunately prevents the economy from achieving full employment.

What, therefore, can be done? The Council's answer is clear enough. One alternative is to adjust the tax program, leaving the expenditures program unchanged, so that the TT schedule will shift downwards to T'T', as shown in Figure 25-4. The T'T' schedule will intersect the GG curve at point B, that is, at full employment. Thus the full-employment surplus will be wiped out and we will have a balanced budget at Y_f. The full-employment surplus, then, is really a fiscal measurement of how much the economy is falling short of its full-employment performance; and it also gives strong hints as to what sort of fiscal policy is to be put into effect. In this case, the Council has recommended a tax reduction.

The second alternative, of course, would be to hold the tax program constant and increase spending. This would result, *ceteris paribus*, in the GG schedule's shifting up and intersecting the TT schedule at point A. Again the full-employment surplus is wiped out, and the economy

---

[7]See the *Economic Report of the President,* 1962 (pp. 77-81), 1963 (pp. 67-69), 1964 (pp. 41-42), and 1965 (pp. 62-65).

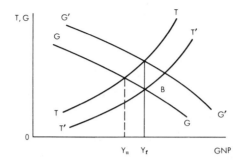

FIGURE 25–4

will be at full employment with a balanced budget. In this instance, however, the budget will be balanced at a higher level of government spending than in the preceding case.

The final alternative, of course, is some combination of the two preceding possibilities—that is, cutting tax revenues and increasing government spending so that the surplus will be eliminated and the budget balanced a full employment.

One major result of the full-employment surplus analysis is that once the budget is balanced at full employment, the heavy emphasis in the growth process is placed on the private sector of the economy. Once more the roles played by private saving and private investment move to the front, and the process of smooth, uninterrupted full-employment growth is determined by planned investment's being equal to actual private savings from one period to the next. And so long as the federal budget remains balanced at full employment, government spending and taxing play a neutral role.

The actual performance is shown in Figure 25–5. In every year from 1956 to 1963, the estimated full-employment surplus has been restrictive—that is, the governmental taxing and spending programs tend to retard the expansion of gross national product necessary to provide for and maintain full employment. Thus the Council has concluded:

> . . . the experience of the past 10 years has illustrated the tendency of the full-employment surplus to build up to expansion-retarding levels as the economy grows. The tax reductions of 1964 will be a giant step to remove a burdensome fiscal restraint *before* the economy levels off or

goes into a recession, and to provide a framework for continued vigorous growth.[8]

Elimination of the full-employment surplus can be very important in
stimulating economic growth. Adjustments in the tax schedule may entail altering tax provisions in order to stimulate net private business investment; and certainly personal income tax reductions will tend to

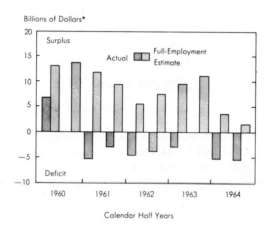

* Seasonally adjusted annual rates.

Sources: Department of Commerce, Bureau of the Budget, and Council
of Economic Advisers.

FIGURE 25-5

Federal Surplus or Deficit: Actual and Full-Employment Estimates
National Income Accounts Basis

---

[8]*Economic Report of the President,* January 1964, p. 42. Contrast this optimistic
statement with the following, which is taken from the January 1965 *Economic
Report of the President:*

> The Council's 1964 Annual Report estimated that a personal tax cut of nearly
> $9 billion would result in a direct increase of more than $8 billion in con-
> sumption. Subsequent rounds of spending and respending would add another
> $10 billion to consumption—producing a tax cut "multiplier" of about two.
> Thus, through increased consumption alone, GNP would ultimately be raised
> by more than $18 billion above what it would have been in the absence of
> the tax cut.
>   The evidence to date indicates that this expectation is being borne out. . . .
> The Council estimates that the total increase in consumer spending alone re-
> sulting from the tax cut's impact was $9 billion in 1964, and had reached an
> annual rate of $13 billion by the end of the year (p. 65).

stimulate private consumption expenditures. On the other hand, increases in governmental spending may be directed towards such things as expanded and improved highway systems, water control, and investment in housing, education, mental health facilities, and research of various sorts, all of which may be quite important in providing· new knowledge and the social overhead investment essential to long-run economic growth. However, as already noted on several occasions, the effectiveness of using fiscal policy in this manner depends upon Congress' willingness to experiment.[9]

5. Budgetary Imbalance: The Use of Deficits

Although the discussion of the preceding section concluded that the budget should be balanced at full employment (so long as inflationary pressures are not too great), this does not mean that there should never be budgetary imbalance. To the contrary, whenever the economic system deviates from the full-employment growth path, fiscal policy may be used as a strong policy control. In this and the next section fiscal policy in its contracyclical role is examined in detail.

Consider first the case in which there is enough involuntary unemployment to cause some concern, and an additional $5 billion federal deficit seems desirable. (Let us assume further that Congress is acquiescent to this recommendation.) Now from a resource allocational standpoint, it might be preferred that the additional deficit come about through an increase in expenditures, particularly if the expenditures would facilitate long-run growth. Finally, remember that the multiplier effect of an increase in government expenditures will be greater than the multiplier effect of a $5 billion decrease in government revenues. Assume also that Congress is as much disposed toward an expenditure increase as it is towards a tax decrease, a rather unlikely situation.

It should be noted, however, that historically tax decreases can become effective immediately upon the signature of the tax bill by the President (or can even be made retroactive), while some substantial delays are inevitably involved in implementing the expenditure program and actually making the payments. Because of these circumstances, and so long as the major concern at the moment is with cyclical factors, most policymakers would probably press for a tax reduction rather than for

---

[9] For a quantitative and critical appraisal of the full-employment surplus concept, see M. E. Levy, *Fiscal Policy, Cycles, and Growth* (New York: National Industrial Conference Board, 1963).

an increase in expenditures, simply because the effect of the additional deficit would occur much more quickly.

There are still other factors that must be considered. Congress has historically been reluctant to raise tax rates. The importance of this is that, politically speaking, a reduction in rates is, given present Congressional attitudes, unlikely to be easily reversible a few years later in time of inflation. Tax rates may be cut easily, but they are extremely difficult to raise at a later date. There is also the question of whether the tax decrease might have a greater or lesser impact on consumer expectations and private incentives to invest than an expenditure increase of the same amount might have.

There is still one other effect to be considered in arriving at a final decision—namely, the monetary effect of the deficit. The Treasury must in some way or other finance the $5 billion deficit, and the means by which it does this cannot be ignored. Basically, the Treasury may borrow the funds from the public, the commercial banks, or the Federal Reserve System. If the $5 billion are borrowed from the public, there will be no direct impact upon the money supply, for the persons and institutions purchasing the government securities will pay for them from idle balances. Note, however, there will be a redistribution of money income in this case, for if government spending rises, the idle balances are transferred from those who are unwilling to spend them to persons and institutions with a higher propensity to spend. Thus, while the stock of money is unaffected, velocity will rise, and this could give a boosting impact to the economy.

On the other hand, if the Treasury borrows the $5 billion from the commercial banks, and the banks pay for the securities from excess reserves, the money supply will be increased. The reason for this is that when the Treasury spends out the $5 billion to private individuals and businesses, it becomes a part of the money supply. This procedure entails nothing more than a monetization of $5 billion of excess reserves that presumably the commercial banks were unwilling to lend to private borrowers. The net result then is a rise in the money supply and the provision of excess reserves in the commercial banking system that can serve as the basis for a further expansion of the stock of money. Note also that there will be some interest rate effects, for if the commercial banks are reluctant to extend loans to the federal government for some reason or other, the Treasury may have to offer the issue at a lower price. Thus the interest rate will tend to rise, a consequence that is not particularly desirable in time of unemployment. The Federal Reserve, however, can offset this by providing excess reserves to the commercial banks, at least to an extent to overcome the banks' reluctance to make loans to the Treasury.

Finally, the Treasury may borrow the $5 billion from the Federal Reserve. In this case the Federal Reserve pays for the government securities simply by setting up a demand deposit for the Treasury. Then, as the Treasury spends, both the money supply and excess reserves in the commercial banking system are increased. There is, however, little or no need for the interest rate to be affected by this method of financing the deficit. In any event, the policy maker must examine what will happen to the money supply, excess reserves, and the interest rate in making his recommendation.

It should be obvious that no two policy makers will consider all of the preceding factors in the same way. And for that matter there is no reason to believe that the same policy maker would view the factors in the same way during the same stage of two succeeding cycles. But we can probably be assured of one thing: whether the policy maker resolves his recommendation in favor of the expenditure increase or the tax decrease, he would not place a great deal of faith in the precise simple arithmetic of the multiplier. Many factors are hidden in *ceteris paribus*, and these may operate to reduce the multiplier's magnitude and to increase the length of time necessary for it to work out.

6. Budgetary Imbalance: The Use of Surpluses

In a period of inflation, the logical fiscal policy to pursue is surplus financing—that is, the federal government collects more in tax revenues than it is spending. This can be accomplished either by raising taxes, cutting spending, or some combination of the two. The major goal, of course, is to bring about a negative multiplier effect, thus reducing the inflationary pressures.

The first thing to note is that the surplus reduces the money supply, and hence aggregate money demand, by the amount of the surplus itself. If, for example, the Treasury collects $5 billion more in revenues than it is spending out, that amount is transferred from the demand deposits of the public to a Treasury deposit at the Federal Reserve. Thus the money supply and money demand are reduced by $5 billion. Whether this negative result is lasting depends, *ceteris paribus*, upon what the federal government does with the surplus. If it decides to spend it, the negative impact is completely nullified. On the other hand, if it decides to retire debt held by the public, again the effect is nullified, although there will probably be some reduction in velocity. If debt held by the commercial banks is retired, the surplus then takes the form of excess reserves in the banking system which can be loaned out, offsetting the negative effect. Finally, if the Treasury is instructed to retire debt held by the Federal Reserve, the negative effect is retained. And, of course, if the Treasury just simply holds its deposit at the Federal Reserve, the negative effect is retained. Thus surplus financing is anti-inflationary only if the surplus is not spent and not used to retire part of the national debt, or if only the debt held by the Federal Reserve is retired.

In what follows the tax surplus is assumed to be held on deposit by the Treasury in the Federal Reserve, and thus there is a negative multiplier effect. However, the multiplier effect will not work out in the simple manner indicated by the formula. In the first place, as noted on several occasions, the product and factor markets in the United States economy are far from being perfectly competitive. Indeed, rigidity of wages and prices characterizes many particular markets. Hence, a reduction in aggregate monetary demand will not necessarily result in a decline in the price level, unless the surplus is carried to such an extent as to create general widespread involuntary unemployment.

Second, it is necessary to take into account the structure of aggregate demand. Not all markets (product and factor) are likely to be equally saturated with inflationary excess demand, and hence inflationary pressures are apt to be unevenly distributed between the various sectors of the economy. Thus, a reduction in aggregate monetary demand through a budgetary surplus could conceivably lead to a decline in demand for the products and factors in markets where the inflationary pressures are the least; and if the policy is pursued too far, there could be substantial unemployment in these markets before the inflationary sectors begin to respond to the budgetary surplus.

Perhaps the major difference between the use of fiscal policy and monetary policy to combat inflationary pressures is that if the political and institutional arrangements permit, a greater segmentation of attack is possible under fiscal policy. By the same token, less dependence is placed on the private market structure as the medium through which the impact of the policy actions will work out.

Consider taxes, for example. Their structure, as well as the rates, could theoretically be adjusted to depress demand in either the investment or consumer goods markets, according to the diagnosis of the inflationary situation. From the expenditures side of the budget, the least desirable government expenditures can be reduced first in combating inflation—that is, the least desirable from the standpoint of accomplishing other goals. To put it bluntly, while monetary policy must work completely through the market system, fiscal policy allows at least some possibility of bypassing the private market system.

A specific note on the growth objective is in order at this point. It is conceivable that a tight monetary policy might actually cause certain private investment projects to be held off, although these projects could make a substantial contribution to the future growth of the economy. By way of conrast, any investment projects financed in the public sector of the economy that the policy makers want maintained under a tight fiscal policy can actually be kept in the budget.

While there are some conceptual problems in the application of fiscal policy to combat inflation that have not been discussed, it appears that the really basic problems are more administrative than conceptual. These include such problems as timing, recognition lags, the policy-forming lags, and the implementation lags involved in increasing tax revenues or in decreasing expenditures. Short of a real emergency, the automatic stabilizers may, as a practical matter, constitute the largest source of strength in anti-inflationary fiscal policy.

7. Debt Management

It was stated much earlier that national debt management policy is an integral part of fiscal policy, although it also has strong monetary implications. Debt management, however, must not be confused with the matter of budgetary balance-imbalance. The amount of the surplus or deficit in the traditional federal budget each year will determine the change (decrease or increase) in the total amount of debt outstanding. Debt management decisions, on the other hand, have to do with changes in the composition or "make-up" of the outstanding debt. Thus it deals with such problems as what form newly issued national debt items will take and the determination of the type or types of investors to whom the new items will be sold. One very important problem relates to "refunding". Except for some currency items (such as United States notes), all of the national debt items previously issued, that is, the cumulative result of previous deficits and surpluses, carry specific maturity dates. And as time passes, these national debt items mature and must be refunded. Refunding simply means that new debt items are sold and the proceeds of the sale are used to pay off the maturing items, or that new debt items are physically exchanged for the maturing debt items at the invitation of the Treasury, if the bondholder is willing to make the exchange. Thus, with the national debt approaching a third of a trillion dollars, the Treasury has some tremendous problems that it must deal with.

On the surface, there do not appear to be any insurmountable problems of debt management. Typical elementary textbook treatment usually points to the relative significance of how different classes of investors who acquire national debt items can monetize debt aggregates. Debt can be said to be monetized when the debt items are acquired by financial institutions whose liabilities include an item that is a constituent part of the money supply.

The acquisition of new debt items by non-bank investors does not affect the supply of money proper, while acquisition of new national debt items by commercial banks will increase the volume of demand deposits, *ceteris paribus;* and the increase in holding of new national debt items by the Federal Reserve banks, *ceteris paribus,* will result in an increase in both member bank reserves and demand deposits in the commercial banks. Similarly, when the national debt is decreasing, retirement of national debt held by non-bank investors would leave the volume of both demand deposits and member bank reserves unchanged; retirement of national debt held by commercial banks would, *ceteris paribus,* result in a decrease in demand deposits; and retirement of national debt items held by Federal Reserve banks would result in a decrease in both member bank reserves and demand deposits.

Let us now examine debt management policy in a period of less than full employment, when both monetary and fiscal policy are "easy." In this case, fiscal policy would call for the presence of deficits in the federal budget, and thus the Treasury would have new securities to place in the hands of investors. At the same time, the easy monetary policy would be directed towards supplying additional member bank reserves so that free reserves would be positive perhaps by several hundred millions of dollars. Federal Reserve action, in other words, would permit commercial banks to possess the necessary reserves for easy acquisition of the new Treasury securities.

The maturity dates of the securities range over the entire spectrum from short-term Treasury bills to longer-term bonds due several decades in the future. Presumably neither the monetary nor fiscal authorities would be much disturbed if the commercial banks were to acquire substantial holdings of any of these maturities, even including the short-term Treasury bills. In fact, given the greater boosting effect emanating from the increased money supply, they would probably prefer an increase in bank held debt, regardless of the maturities involved.

By way of contrast, if the economy were functioning at a level of activity approximating full employment, the concern of the Federal Reserve authorities would be over combating inflationary pressures.

Under these circumstances, both monetary and fiscal policy would presumably be "tight." The Treasury might even be generating surpluses and thus could use the net tax revenues to "buy back" securities and retire them. The securities being retired could be current maturities (which would, of course, reduce the aggregate volume of short-term securities outstanding), or the Treasury might exercise its "call privilege" on certain issues and even acquire intermediate securities from the market for retirement.

Note that under these circumstances, it would be possible for the Federal Reserve authorities to maintain a tight money policy to the extent that the full deflationary impact of the Treasury surpluses would be felt in the money and capital markets. That is, it is possible for the Treasury to retire part of the national debt held by the Federal Reserve banks. This would result in a decrease in both member bank reserves and demand deposits, and the Federal Reserve authorities would not engage in any monetary actions to counteract these anti-inflationary results. As a practical matter, judging from the Federal Reserve's behavior in monetary policy over the past thirty years, the combined tight money and fiscal policy probably would *not* result in a decrease in the money supply, but rather would prevent an increase in the stock of money.

Another point about periods of tight money is that they provide an opportunity to lengthen the average maturity of the national debt, a result that is necessary from time to time. Otherwise, a mere passage of time would lead to a gradual shortening of the average maturity of the debt. If the old issues are replaced with a more than proportionate share of new short-term issues, the shortening process of the average maturity of debt would take place even more rapidly.

The concern of the Treasury and the Federal Reserve with the average maturity of the debt stems from the possibility that if too much of the national debt matures in any short period of time, then a certain degree of monetary-fiscal control may pass from the hands of the policy makers to the hands of those who own the maturing debt. Those who own the maturing items have the perfectly legal right to demand cash payment at maturity, rather than accepting the option of taking new debt items. If substantial numbers of maturity debt holders demand cash, the national debt managers are faced with the necessity of going into the market with large quantities of new issues. These large additional quantities may be difficult to place without resorting to the age-old merchandising technique of price concessions; and this will, among other things, raise the cost of the national debt substantially. Moreover, insofar as the entire interest rate structure in the private market is tied to the yield curve on U. S. government securities, the entire interest rate structure in the private sector of debt will also rise. Such a massive forced sale of new federal debt items will entail other complicating factors not mentioned here; but the results are all the same—a substantial rise in interest rates, perhaps beyond the level considered desirable by either the monetary or fiscal authorities.

The only other solution is to sell the additional securities to the Federal Reserve Banks. That is, open market operations of the Federal Reserve would be used, not as a principal device of monetary policy *per se,* but rather as an instrument of expediency to get the national debt managers out of an embarassing situation. In this case, monetary policy would likely be much "easier" than the monetary authorities would consider desirable, and just at the wrong time. The result of either of these two possibilities means that Federal Reserve personnel would have lost effective control over monetary policy. Perhaps a combination of the two methods might have to be resorted to. In either case, however, additional impediments are put in the way of smoothly functioning monetary and fiscal policy.

So far, so good. That is, the preceding discussion seems to be consistent with historical fact and with sophisticated guesses about what the monetary and/or fiscal authorities will be likely to accomplish in the future. However, we have dealt only with those situations that are rather clear-cut—that is, obvious involuntary unemployment and obvious inflation. Actually, in the most of the post-World War II period, we have not experienced either of these situations for any prolonged stretch of time. Rather, the economy has usually hovered between these two extremes, and it is here that certain very real problems exist in national debt management, at least from the viewpoint of the Treasury officials who are charged with the responsibility for making debt management decisions. Employment has been sustained at levels below full employment, and at the same time there have been inflationary pressures. Very early in this volume we referred to this situation as "high level stagnation." Under these circumstances, the problems of debt management are not quite so simple.

In the first place, with unemployment as high as it is, the Treasury officials fear to sell the longer-term issues since this would have a tendency to raise the long-term rate of interest. Insofar as private investment demand is influenced by changes in the long-term rate of interest, one of the chief channels of reaching full employment is blocked off. Furthermore, the Treasury officials may feel that the demand for capital goods is unstable and that a rise in the long-term rate of interest would result in a downward shift of the entire investment demand schedule. And there may be the fear that, if business expectations are none too high, the sale of additional Treasury long-terms may compete much too effectively with the supply of high-grade mortgage loan instruments and with the supply of high-grade corporate bond instruments. In either case, investment may be stifled.

It is difficult to evaluate these fears of the Treasury debt managers. If the market for capital instruments is fluid and competitive (that is, if the various short-term and long-term debt items, both public and private, are good substitutes for each other), then the fears probably have some basis in reality. On the other hand, if the market for capital instruments is sufficiently segmented, so that a rise in the rate on long-term Treasury issues is not easily transmitted to other securities, then the Treasury fears are less realistic or at least exaggerated. Any detailed and systematic treatment of the complex subject of national debt management, however, is beyond the scope of this volume. Suffice it to say that national debt management is a prime example of an area in which it is extremely difficult for theory to be applied.

The theorist who deals with rather simplified models is likely to ignore the complexities of the capital market organization and its mores, procedures, and legal and cultural constraints upon the operations of financial institutions in the market. On the other hand, those who are closely associated with these institutional and other arrangements in the financial markets are apt to stand aghast at times when they consider the complete dismissal of the significance of these factors. This is indeed a challenging area of economic analysis and policy action in which there is a need for much more fruitful work.

8. International Constraints on Domestic Monetary-Fiscal Policy

Thus far the discussion of policy formation (both monetary and fiscal) has ignored the impact of changing international economic conditions. Obviously we do not live in a closed economy, and policy makers must be cognizant of what is going on in other parts of the world as they set forth domestic policy.

Over the last several years, for example, we have seen the "dollar gap" give way to the "dollar glut." We have seen the scramble for international liquidity held in the form of American dollars change to virtually a world-wide nonchalance towards American exchange in comparison to the exchange of certain other productive economies. Rel-

ative to the price and export structure of other countries, particularly
in western Europe, Japan, and Canada, we have seen something of a
saturation in the relative demand for American dollar exchange. Accompanying these conditions, partially as a cause and partially as a result, there was a substantial outflow of gold from the United States in
the late 1950's and early 1960's. Of course, this outflow has been viewed
with alarm by many laymen and by some economists.

It is not our purpose here to provide an analysis of the international
conditions that have given rise to the so-called gold problem; nor do
we intend to proceed with an item-by-item consideration of the constituent parts of balance-of-payments accounting, pointing out what the
gold outflow does and does not mean. Rather, our purpose is to observe
in general that the outflow of gold is symbolic of a set of conditions of
change in the world that are, from the standpoint of the American
economy, neither necessarily good nor bad. And more important, these
world conditions have, as a factual matter, added another set of constraints to the formulation of both monetary and fiscal policy. Constraints, as interpreted here, means complications.

As an example, during the closing years of the Eisenhower administration, and in the early years of the Kennedy-Johnson administration,
there was an attempt on the part of the monetary and fiscal policy makers to cause a clockwise rotation in the yield curve. By clockwise rotation is meant a reduction in long-term rates of interest (in accord with
an easy monetary policy at home designed to stimulate additional domestic investment), coupled with an increase of short-term interest
rates (ostensibly designed to minimize the interest-rate differentials between the money market in New York and the money markets in the
financial centers of western Europe). The purpose of the increase in
short-term rates was to decrease the likelihood of internationally "yield
conscious money" (that is, short-term investible funds) flowing out of
the United States to other nations to take advantage of higher interest
rates there. This action presumably was prompted by the gold outflow,
since the flow of funds out of New York would ultimately be followed
in some proportion or other by an additional gold outflow.

The rotation of the yield curve was, therefore, an attempt by the policymakers in the United States to "play both ends against the middle"
in achieving simultaneously a satisfactory domestic policy and a satisfactory international policy. However, with the developments that occurred in western Europe at about the same time, it is difficult to ap-
praise the success of these actions.

Another example of an international constraint occurred in late 1964.
Press coverage of statements by Federal Reserve officials, Treasury

officials, and even by the White House indicated significant differences in opinion over the appropriate course that monetary policy should take in the ensuing months, particularly with respect to the degree of tightening that was to take place in money markets. However, when the bank rate in London was raised from 5 to 7 per cent, the Federal Reserve authorities immediately raised the discount and advance rate here at home. It is difficult to determine the reasoning of the Federal Reserve underlying this particular action. On the one hand, we are told that international factors were responsible for raising the discount and advance rate. On the other hand, we were assured by the Chairman of the Board of Governors that the action would have virtually no effect on domestic interest rates and that the Open Market Committee would maintain, under the then prevailing conditions, an adequate supply of free reserves. It is indeed a strong temptation to conclude that the Federal Reserve authorities have devised a new use for moral suasion with respect to the international scene. How effective this will be waits to be seen. However, this still serves as an example of how the international scene must be considered when domestic monetary policy is laid down.

Just a brief note on the mechanical devices employed in attempting to change the slope of the yield curve at its various points. So far as the Federal Reserve is concerned, the major tool is open market operations. Consider the case in which the Open Market Committee buys long-term securities and simultaneously sells short-terms. The purchase of long-terms would drive their price up and the yield (and hence interest rates) down. The sale of short-terms, on the other hand, would depress their price and simultaneously raise the yield. (The reverse of these, of course, would tend to cause the yield curve to rotate in a counterclockwise direction.) In addition, the simultaneous purchase and sale may create an expectations effect of unknown intensity and duration.

Meanwhile, the Treasury could collaborate in these efforts, and as a matter of fact, did so in the early 1960's, by issuing relatively more new short-term securities and relatively fewer long-term securities. This would affect the aggregate supplies of each category of security, though it might also create certain other problems with which the Treasury would have to cope.

These are the most important means by which the monetary and fiscal authorities may affect the shape of the yield curve as opposed to its height. Note that if long-term securities are perfect substitutes for short-terms in the minds of most participants in the government securities market, it would be extremely difficult for the policy makers to exert any significant or lasting influence on the yield curve by these methods. Any change in the relationship between short-term and long-term rates would be quickly eliminated as holders shift from one to the other.

If, on the other hand, the various maturities in the federal debt structure tend to be quite imperfect substitutes for each other, and if the market for government securities is quite segmented, then these results will be more lasting. By segmentation is meant that, for example, on the demand side of the market, there are institutions who want short-terms *only,* almost irrespective of the price and yield present in the long-term segments of the market.

To return to the main theme of this section, and indeed of this book, it is obvious that there are several constraints on domestic policy; and it must be conceded that these constraints are often quite important in determining the shape and structure of domestic monetary-fiscal policy. But then, as theory and policy make so abundantly clear, the road to economic Nirvana is twisted and tortuous and it may be blocked at almost any turn that we take in the future.

QUESTIONS

25-1. Explain in detail what is meant by the "full-employment surplus" concept, and show how a full-employment surplus retards aggregate economic activity.

25-2. Discuss several ways in which monetary policy and debt management policy may be in conflict with one another.

25-3. "A budgetary deficit is always expansionary because it increases the money supply." Comment.

25-4. "Although a tax surplus raised by the federal government is always contractionary, the end result depends upon what is done with the surplus." Comment.

25-5. Do you believe that liberalized depreciation allowances (or similar tax benefits to business) will by themselves increase private investment spending? Elaborate.

Bibliography

Colm, G., and M. Young, *The Federal Budget and the National Economy*. Washington, D. C.: National Planning Association, 1955.

Commission on Money and Credit, *Fiscal and Debt Management Policies*. Englewood Cliffs, N. J.: Prentice-Hall, Inc., 1963.

Holmans, A. E., *United States Fiscal Policy, 1945-1949*. Oxford: The Clarendon Press, 1961.

Levy, M. E., *Fiscal Policy, Cycles, and Growth*. New York: National Industrial Conference Board, 1963.

Economic Report of the President. Various annual reports.

Author Index

647

Subject Index

653

Harrod's theories (*cont.*)
 major implication, 432-437
 savings and capital output assumptions, 422-423
 warranted rate of growth, 424-
  429
Hawtrey's theory:
 critical evaluation, 147-153
 policy implications, 146-147
 purely monetary, 136-146
Hicks' purely endogenous model,
  437
Historical consumption function,
  250-252
Historical cost, 88
Homeowner, 68
Home ownership, determinant of
  consumption, 260
Hoover Dam, 87
Households, 76
Housing market, governmental activity, 106
Human capital, 87, 88, 286
Hybrid cycle, 99, 100, 101, 107,
  129
Hyperinflation, 143

Ideal employment, 488, 491
Identity and behavioral equations,
  230-232
Identity equation of multiplier, 301-
  303
Idle balances, 552, 554
Imperfect markets theme, 557
Implicit price deflator, 40
Improvement factor, 469
Income:
 determinant of short-run consumption, 252
 disposable, 311
 multiplier-accelerator concepts,
  300-332
 optimum distribution, 489, 497
 per capita, 170
 socialization, 604-605
Income-employment equilibria, 227
Income measurement, Keynes, 232-
  233
Income-product statements, 68-76
Income tax, 608

Income velocity, 137
Incremental capital-output ratios,
  314, 395-396, 421-422
Incremental income-consumption
  relationship, 243, 247
Index of industrial production, 50-
  52
Index of production, lag, 55
Indirect business taxes, 44
Indirect taxes, 48
"In Dispraise of Economics", 484
Individual proprietorships, 58
Induced investment:
 defined, 168- 169
 multiplier-accelerator interaction,
  313-314
 Hicks' model, 324-325
 Hicks' model criticized, 327-328
 equilibrium, 365
 Hansen's analysis, 450-451
Induced net disinvestment, 326-327
Industrial revolution, 366, 367
Inflated recession, 5
Inflation:
 administered-price, 593-598
 cost-push theory, 583-587
 creeping, 4, 495, 496, 550, 557
 defined, 493-494
 degrees, 494
 demand-cost, 589-595
 demand shift, 597
 growth theory, 365
 Keynesian system theory, 346-
  352
 mark-up, 595
 price level stability, 493
 wage-push measurement, 587-
  589
Inflation-conscious, 4
Innovation:
 clustering, 180
 distinguished from invention,
  172-173
 major cycle, 97
 new or young firms, 464
 types, 173
Innovational investment, 168, 169
Innovational theorists, 168-196
Innovator, 174
Input-output ratio, 491